Correctional Assessment, Casework & Counseling,

5th Edition

Anthony Walsh, Ph.D. and Mary K. Stohr, Ph.D.
Boise State University

Mission of the American Correctional Association
The American Correctional Association provides a professional organization for all individuals and groups, both public and private, that share a common goal of improving the justice system.

American Correctional Association Staff
Harold W. Clarke, President
James A. Gondles, Jr., CAE, Executive Director
Gabriella M. Klatt, Director, Communications and Publications
Alice Heiserman, Manager Publications and Research
Jeannelle Ferreira, Associate Editor
Ryan Bounds, Intern, George Washington University
Leigh Ann Bright, Graphics and Production Associate
Cover by Leigh Ann Bright

Printed in the United States of America by Victor Graphics, Inc., Baltimore, MD.

You may order this publication from:
American Correctional Association
206 N. Washington St., Suite 200
Alexandria, VA 22314
1-800-222-5646 ext 0129
Information on publications and videos available from ACA: www.aca.org/store

Library of Congress Cataloging-in-Publication Data

Walsh, Anthony, 1941-
 Correctional assessment, casework and counseling / Anthony Walsh and Mary K. Stohr. – 5th ed.
 p. cm.
 Includes bibliographical references and index.
 ISBN 978-1-56991-307-9
 1. Social work with criminals. 2. Criminals–Counseling of. 3. Criminals–Rehabilitation. 4. Parole officers. 5. Probation officers. I. Stohr, Mary K. II. Title.
 HV7428.W35 2010
 365'.661–dc22
  2009039447

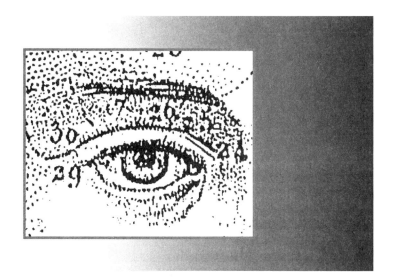

Contents

Continued on the next page

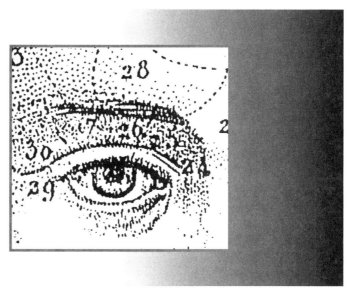

Foreword

This best-selling textbook provides sound guidance to those who will work in probation, parole, and other areas of corrections. It offers a framework of biological explanations for behavior along with traditional sociological and psychological descriptions and is an exhaustive resource that both novice and veteran professionals will find useful.

Anthony Walsh and his new co-author, Mary Stohr, have experience in the field so when they describe how those involved with the criminal justice behave, they are relying on firsthand knowledge buttressed by multidisciplinary scholarship. The chapters on interviewing and interrogating offer students an opportunity to try out their skills in the classroom before they use them in the field with clients. Other chapters offer descriptions of methods of counseling and for writing pre-sentence investigative reports. Additional chapters describe the methods needed to evaluate a variety of types of offenders—substance abusers, sex offenders, the mentally ill and mentally deficient, juvenile delinquents, females, and elderly offenders. The appendices provide samples of actual assessment instruments.

All the chapters enable the student to go out into the field with an understanding of how to assess and counsel offenders. We hope that all those using this book will find a career in corrections and social work rewarding and decide to become members of the American Correctional Association (ACA). We offer both student and professional memberships. Details about ACA membership, programs and publications can be found on our website at www.aca.org.

James A. Gondles, Jr., CAE
Executive Director
American Correctional Association

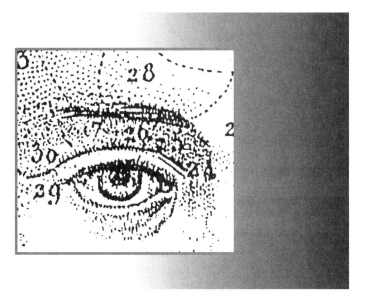

Introduction

In the introduction to the first edition of this book, Walsh wrote:

> Most social work and psychology texts to which many of us have had to turn for guidance in interviewing and counseling do not respond to the special needs of criminal justice clients. These works proceed on the assumption that counseling clients are largely self-selected and are motivated to explore the problems that brought them to the counselor's office. Criminal justice clients, on the other hand, are usually extremely reluctant to be in any counseling situation, are often impervious to the problems that led to such a situation, and typically have a congenital dislike for anyone who works for the system. This book assesses the special problems of interviewing and counseling under these conditions.

These words continue to be true in this fifth edition because nothing has changed about offenders since then (they still do not like us very much). A number of publishers have discovered the need for interviewing and counseling texts specific to corrections since the first edition of this book, however. Good! Competition keeps us all on our toes and constantly improving; hence, the fifth edition of this book. Although the first edition was widely recognized as the most complete and comprehensive book of its kind, we have continued to make improvements over the various editions. This edition has improved on the earlier editions in a number of ways:

1. We extensively updated and revised it using the latest research and data. Many exciting new ideas and new research have emerged over the past few years in corrections and in the behaviors (criminal, substance abuse, and so forth) that bring people to involvement in it.

2. It contains a new chapter on therapeutic communities (TCs). Therapeutic communities are playing an ever more important role in the rehabilitation of drug addicts and alcoholics.

3. We rewrote the legal chapter to cover legal issues in corrections that have emerged since the publication of the last edition. In our increasingly litigation-happy society, it has become imperative that correctional workers become aware of the rights of offenders and of situations in which they might be liable for negligent treatment.

4. It contains more "Perspectives from the Field," pieces written by practicing professionals in corrections. These perspectives have been popular with students looking for that "practical" view from the trenches.

5. It pays more attention to case management techniques than previous editions.

6. We have used more figures and tables than in previous editions.

7. We have included the increasingly popular method of Motivational Interviewing.

The most important change is the addition of a co-author, Dr. Mary K. Stohr, whom I hope will continue to take this book into ever more new editions after this old dude has laid down his pen. Dr. Stohr has been a friend and colleague for more than fifteen years. She has published extensively on various corrections issues both in books and in journal articles. In addition to being a respected academic, she has field experience as a correctional officer and counselor in the Washington State correctional system. In short, I can think of no one better able to continue this work than she can.

The fifth edition, like the previous editions, has benefited greatly from reviews and criticisms of the first edition that both the editorial staff of the American Correctional Association and I solicited. We have accommodated most of the suggestions made by these reviewers and critics, both academics and practitioners.

We continue to explore theories of criminal behavior, which more and more "hard-headed" practitioners are realizing are important. We begin with an exploration of criminal behavior from sociological, psychological, and biosocial perspectives. Our belief is that adequate assessment and counseling of any type of client, criminal or otherwise, must proceed from an adequate understanding of the presenting problem. As a former police officer and probation officer, I (Walsh) am aware that many practitioners distrust theory, but as an academic with practical experience, I also am aware of the links between theory and practice. Practice without theory is like a cart without a horse–it will not go anywhere, and we might get hernias trying to push it ourselves. In writing these theory chapters, we constantly kept before us the question: "How does this theoretical discussion enhance the practitioner's understanding of criminal behavior as he or she will experience it in practice?"

We geared the chapters on interviewing and counseling exclusively to the correctional client. The chapter on interviewing contains a section on interrogation, and the counseling chapters address individual and group counseling in both community and institutional settings.

Unlike most counseling works, this one recognizes that proper assessment is a necessity before any type of counseling or other intervention is attempted. Thus, we have included two chapters on assessment and classification, which include numerous examples of the various instruments now used in corrections for this purpose. The professional assessment of clients has been a central part of the counseling course I teach, and I have always found it useful to use case studies. The instructor's manual contains a variety of cases in presentence investigation report format. I use these cases to role-play and to provide students with practice in using the various assessment and classification tools. We also include a "Perspective from the Filed" written by Dr. Carl Clements, perhaps the foremost authority on correctional assessment and classification in the United States today.

We recognize that correctional clients need more than counseling to turn their lives around. The correctional worker is as much a broker of community resources as a counselor or supervising agent. Consistent with that view, we include a chapter outlining how correctional workers can use community resources, including volunteers. Recognizing and including the community in the goals of contemporary corrections work is at the heart of the philosophy of restorative justice.

This book encompasses a tremendous amount of material, all of which is available in more detail elsewhere. As we point out in the chapter on presentence report writing, the secret of professional report writing is the ability to glean from voluminous and diverse sources all that is necessary—not merely nice—to know. We hope that we have done that in this book.

We acknowledge the input of the academics and correctional practitioners who reviewed previous editions of this book, their thoughts and suggestions have proved very valuable. We also thank professors and students who have informally discussed with us the strengths and weaknesses of previous editions, and the professionals who have shared their field experiences with us in their Perspectives from the Field. Thanks also to our editor, Alice Heiserman, whose good-natured encouragement and advice helped get us through this extensive revision. All these people have contributed to making this edition a better one than it otherwise would have been.

Mary Stohr said, "I would like to acknowledge my husband, Craig Hemmens and our daughter Emily Rose Stohr-Gilmore, for their love and support. I could do nothing without them."

Anthony Walsh said, "Special thanks to my wife, Grace Jean (a.k.a. "Grace the face"). She is the center of my world, the core of my existence, the light of my life. People sometimes ask me why I go around whistling and singing all the time like the village idiot. Grace's love has adorned me across the years and has made my heart sing and my mind dance, so if I'm a fool, I'm a fool for love. Thank you, Gracie, mia bella donna. (I wrote the preceding thank you to Gracie more than ten years ago. Does it still apply? You bet, even more so and with bells on!)."

— Anthony Walsh

CHAPTER 1

Understanding the Need for Theory

There is nothing so practical as a good theory.

—Kurt Lewin

The purpose of this book is to introduce students to the process of "correcting" the antisocial behavior of criminally convicted offenders. Correcting offenders' antisocial behavior means that some correctional agency or institution is charged with attempting to change undesirable (criminal) behavior to desirable or appropriate behavior while offenders are in custody (jail or prison) or under supervision (probation or parole).

Figure 1.1 on page 3 shows the number of people under the various types of correctional supervision from 1990 to 2005 (note that probation supervision is the backbone of corrections in the United States). The figure points out that there are a lot of people on probation, parole, or in prison. It also shows many folks out there who our society expects its correctional workers to change for the better. Consequently, the first lesson in this book is that the correctional worker is in the behavior-change business and in the community-protection business. These amount to the same thing because whatever helps offenders to jettison their criminal ways is at the same time a blessing for the community at large.

1

A great deal of skepticism and cynicism surround the corrective process exemplified by the frequently heard lament that "nothing works." This sentiment has some basis in reality, but in many ways, it is not warranted. If we believe that "nothing works," then we will tend to operate consistently with this belief, and the outcomes will justify our beliefs. If we believe that people can change, and that many of them do so every day, then we will act in accordance with that belief. Prophecies tend to be self-fulfilling.

Of course, you will run into some people for whom nothing works. Realize also that nothing works for everybody. Nevertheless, some things work for some people some of the time, and other things work for other people at other times. The failure rate in probation and parole (in other words, those sent to or returned to prison) is a disheartening 65 percent, but on the bright side–the success rate is 35 percent (Champion 2005). Furthermore, ample evidence proves that we could improve this success rate by implementing programs that research consistently shows to reduce recidivism substantially (Lipsey and Cullen 2007). Let us focus on the positive, while never losing sight of the negative.

Casework, Assessment, Counseling, and Criminal Justice

Casework, or case management, in corrections is simply the management of cases on a caseload. A "case" is the records and details of a particular offender's offenses, supervision history, and progress toward the goal of rehabilitation, or habilitation, since many offenders have never experienced anything approaching satisfactory social adjustment in the first place (Crow 1998). Like everything else, individuals can accomplish casework well or poorly, depending on their personality, knowledge, and motivation. They can work the case by assuming a reactive posture by supervising and conducting surveillance of offenders until they do something wrong and then pounce on them. Some may consider this better than nothing ("At least it gets another scumbag off the streets") while others see it as counterproductive in that it engenders resistance to probation/parole officers' directives (Taxman 2008). Whatever the case may be, it is not nearly as productive as proactive casework in which the aim is to prevent that "something wrong" from ever happening in the first place. The motivating idea behind proactive correctional casework is not "bleeding heartism." It recognizes that the best protection for the community is through strategies that aid offenders to live up to community standards. The community is safe to the extent that those who prey on it cease to do so.

Proactive case management involves the design and implementation of monitored programs of activity with the goal of assisting offenders to lead productive and law-abiding lives. Everything in this book is about proactive case management. Good (effective) case management involves the responsivity principle (Litt and Mallon 2003). This principle essentially means that whatever you do for and with offenders must be responsive to their needs and abilities. Integral components of good proactive casework are assessment and counseling. Working within the responsivity principle, Marshall and Serran (2004: 311) state: "The only way to understand the client's abilities and learning style is to conduct a comprehensive assessment prior to treatment."

Figure 1.1   Number of Persons under Correctional Supervision 1990-2005 by Type of Supervision

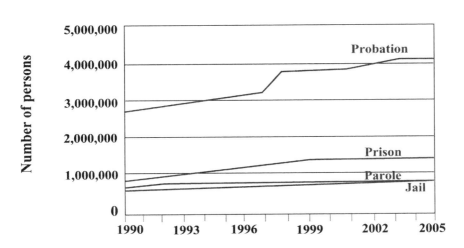

Source: L. Glaze and S. Bonczar, 2006. Probation and Parole in the United States, 2005. *Bureau of Justice Statistics Bulletin.*

Assessment is the process of subjecting offenders to a formal evaluation and analysis of their deficiencies and needs, and the risks they pose to the community so that the counselor can develop realistic counseling plans and strategies. To accomplish this assessment, the counselor uses well researched and tested instruments, some of which are included or referenced in this book. Attempting to supervise, counsel, and otherwise help an offender without a thorough assessment is rather like a physician performing surgery without first conducting a thorough diagnostic work-up of a patient.

Counseling is a process in which the counselor leads offenders to explore their feelings and concerns; in the case of offenders, many of those feelings and concerns have led them to behave irresponsibly. We hope that the counseling process will lead offenders to an increased awareness of the self-destructive nature of their behavior and alternative behavior choices. It aims at removing barriers to self-direction and personal growth and uncovering resources that offenders can use to forge a prosocial lifestyle.

Correctional counseling is different from general counseling in three important ways:

1. Offenders, generally, do not seek counseling voluntarily. Therefore, you are more likely to encounter reluctance and resistance to the counseling process than you would be in other counseling settings.

2. Offenders, in general, have fewer coping resources on which to draw than do clients in other counseling settings.

3. Offenders often have a psychological and economic investment in retaining their current lifestyle. These differences led to the writing of this book. Few general counseling texts address the special problems of dealing with offenders with their special needs.

Correctional counselors also enjoy an advantage in corrections that counselors in other areas do not have. This advantage is that we often possess a wealth of verified information about offenders' backgrounds and past behavior from a variety of sources such as juvenile files, police reports, and social and psychological evaluations. This information allows us to assess offenders more readily than counselors can in many other settings.

However, before physicians conduct a diagnostic work up, they must have a grounding in the disease or condition that could account for the patient's complaint. Similarly, you should have grounding in the causes of the type of behavior that you are trying to correct. With this analogy in mind, the authors have structured this book around understanding criminal behavior and its correlates, assessing the individual problems and needs of offenders, and using that understanding and knowledge to counsel offenders effectively.

Criminology is the study of the causes of crime. It is, or should be, an interdisciplinary study, encompassing genetics, neurology, physiology, psychology, economics, and sociology (Walsh and Ellis 2007). Yet, much of criminology is limited to sociological analysis. Sociologists often ignore individual differences. One gets the impression from sociological criminology that everything is responsible for crime except the people who commit it. While sociological insights are important in understanding crime, they do not exhaust the causal possibilities.

This is not a textbook on criminological theory. We made no effort to be comprehensive in this area. We briefly present the theories of criminology. This should help you to understand more fully the theories of counseling addressed later. It should enhance the quality of your application of them in practice. In other words, we are interested in criminological theories here only as they provide a foundation upon which you can ground counseling techniques. We begin with a discussion of the usefulness of theory in general, and then examine theories of the etiology (cause) of crime.

The Usefulness of Theory

Workers in any field must understand the nature of the phenomena with which they work. As a correctional practitioner, or as a student aspiring to be a practitioner, you must understand the phenomenon of crime and its causation so that you may deal more effectively with offenders under your supervision. As Goff and Owens (1999: 25) put it: "Public policy and agency practice in the field of probation and parole must be guided by a theory of why people commit crime. To intervene [to prevent further offending] there must be an understanding of the causative factors of the original offense." Cullen and Gendreau (2000: 145) augment this view: "[C]orrectional treatments must be based on criminological knowledge." Theories of crime seek to offer plausible explanations of how to link together the correlates of crime. Empirically generated facts are silent, in themselves. Only theories of their interrelationships give voice to what would otherwise be a babble of unintelligible static; facts rarely speak for themselves.

A **theory** is an intellectual scaffold around which the practitioner constructs an edifice of useful knowledge. Empirical facts are the bricks of the edifice, each one slotted into its proper place to form a coherent whole. People wonder, given the numerous competing theories of crime, which one is "true."

Physicians do not ask which theory of disease is the true one, because there are many different kinds of diseases with many different causes. No physicians ever treat a person for "illness." Rather, they treat a specific disease syndrome. Like disease, crime is not a unitary phenomenon explicable in terms of a single cause or set of causes, but we tend to think and act as if it were when we treat all offenders for "criminality." Even treatment for specific disease syndromes often varies according to such things as age and gender, and is differentially successful according to how cooperative patients are, their personality type, and the level of psychosocial support they enjoy. Why should it be any different when dealing with criminals in all their diversity?

Theories about crime and criminality must be context-specific, but even then, one cannot consider any theory true in any absolute sense. Truth for the scientist is tentative, relative, and open to qualification and falsification. If a theory generates useful empirical research and provides order and consistency within the domain of interest, we are more faithful to the spirit of science to call it *adequate* than to call it *true*. A good theory conforms to the pragmatic, correspondence, and coherence theories of truth as outlined by philosophers of science. That is, a theory is useful to the extent that it

1. Provides useful guidance for the further exploration of the phenomena of interest

2. Corresponds with the factual data already known about the phenomena of interest

3. Fits those data into propositions to form a logically connected and coherent whole

The usefulness of a given theory is context specific. This means it must address the specific kinds of questions asked. It would be of little help to a sociologist seeking to explain fluctuations in the crime rate over the past fifty years, for instance, to learn that neurophysiologists have discovered that a certain category of criminal shows a higher than expected frequency of dysfunction involving certain regions of the brain. Likewise, the neurophysiologist is little interested in the sociocultural variables alleged by the sociologists to account for differentials in the crime rate.

The sociologist and the neurophysiologist are simply dealing with different units of analysis: societies and brains, respectively. Criminal justice practitioners seeking to understand offenders, however, must be sensitive to the macro- (large scale) analyses of the sociologist and the micro- (small scale) analyses of the physiologist, and to all the disciplines in between that attempt to understand the phenomena of crime and criminality at their particular level of analysis.

Becoming sensitive to these perspectives does not mean that you have to become expert in them all, which is impossible. It does mean that you should become acquainted with them and understand their language. Much of the heat generated by theorists of different macro/micro persuasions results from failing to distinguish between crime and criminality.

Crime refers to socially disapproved behavior. Rates of crime fluctuate with various social, political, and economic conditions over time. Anyone can fall afoul of the law and commit an out-of-character crime given a chance permutation of factors conducive to it. Criminality, on the other hand, refers to "stable differences across individuals in the propensity to commit criminal (or equivalent) acts" (Wilson and Herrnstein 1985: 23). Crime is thus a fluctuating property of sociopolitical systems, but criminality is fairly stable in individuals. It is fair to say that sociologists are more interested in crime, and other types of scientists are more interested in criminality.

As a correctional worker dealing with individuals, quite naturally, you will find theories dealing with individuals' behavior and their immediate environment to be the most suitable for your purposes. After all, these are the areas most accessible to perception and most amenable to change within the context of the correctional worker/offender relationship. Nevertheless, when you are engaged in interviewing, assessing, and counseling criminal offenders, you will be able to perform the task more professionally if you have an adequate understanding of crime causation at all levels of analysis. Therefore, we shall briefly examine five theories of criminality dealing with different levels of analysis ranging from the macro-sociological to the biosocial.

Figure 1.2   Criminal "Causal" Funnel and Explanatory Theories

Figure 1.2 is a schematic diagram representing the route or routes that may have led offenders to you. Some consider the forces in the larger sociocultural environment as criminogenic (crime generating). Although a number of contending theories exist, we will consider only the best known at each level.

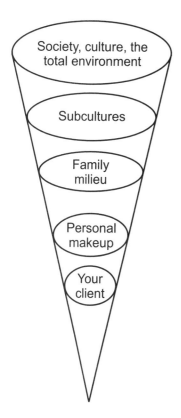

ANOMIE
Cultural values, norms, social structure, lead to a lack of legitimate opportunities

DIFFERENTIAL ASSOCIATION
Gangs, peer pressure to conform to subcultural values and beliefs opposed to lawful behavior

CONTROL
Unique personal experiences leading to lack of attachment and to criminal beliefs

PSYCHOPATHY
Criminals have specific patterns of thinking and acting

LIFESTYLE THEORY/BIOSOCIAL FACTORS
Inherited and acquired characteristics, such as differential autonomic nervous system functioning, possibly resulting from severe love deprivation in childhood

CHARACTERISTIC WAYS OF THINKING
Alcoholism, drug addiction, personal problems, yield a "bad attitude"

Anomie/strain theory illustrates criminological theory at its most comprehensive or macro-level. Differential association theory provides a less inclusive analysis. The subcultural branch of this theory holds that all Americans share the larger sociocultural environment of the United States, but only a rather small portion of us share in subcultures declared criminogenic by differential association theory. Even individuals within a criminogenic subculture experience different socialization within the context of their family environment. These experiences are the subject matter of control theory, which focuses on the family. Taking the analysis one-step further, experts recognize that similar environmental experiences can have vastly different affects on different people. Biosocial theories examine how individual biological differences interact with environmental factors to produce criminal behavior.

Lifestyle theory, although concentrating on thinking patterns, incorporates concepts from many other theories to attempt to explain why criminals think the way that they do. We examine lifestyle theory in Chapter 11 when we discuss cognitive-behavioral treatment programs for offenders.

Please note that the diagram implies intimate connections among all levels of analysis. This does not mean that each of the theories cannot stand alone as a plausible explanation of crime at its respective level of analysis. Neither does it mean that a person who commits a crime because he or she lacks legitimate opportunity (as anomie theory sets forth) necessarily belongs to a gang (as differential association theory describes), or lacks family attachments (as control theory proposes). It simply means that we cannot view the development of individuals in isolation from the micro- or macro-environments, which constitute their reality, nor can we separate the effects of those environments from the effects of the personal attributes and unique experiences individuals bring to them.

Correctional Philosophy and Restorative Justice

This book is about correctional casework, assessment, counseling theory and practice, without a great deal of attention to the broader topic of correctional theory and practice. However, the area of correctional theory with broad applicability to our purposes is the ideology or philosophy of punishment and justice that is in vogue within the criminal justice system. The prevailing correctional philosophy influences correctional workers' day-to-day practices and decisions relating to offenders whether they are aware of it or not (Lauen 1997).

Two guiding philosophies have jockeyed for preeminence throughout the present century: the retributive and the rehabilitative (sometimes referred to as the just deserts and treatment models, respectively). Both philosophies are offender driven (that is, what do we do with the offender?). Both have been severely criticized as ineffectual because they have conflicting goals—retribution versus rehabilitation.

Partly in response to these criticisms, a new philosophical model has arisen, which, according to its supporters, has taken workable aspects from both older models, thrown out the unworkable, and added some concepts of its own. This new philosophy or guiding framework is restorative justice. Restorative justice is based on the premis that every action that is primarily oriented toward justice repairs the harm that has been caused by the crime and this "usually means a face-to-face confrontation between victim and perpetrator, where a mutually agreeable restorative solution is proposed and agreed upon" (Champion, 2005: 154). Restorative justice is particularly popular in Canada, having received the seal of approval from the Canadian

Supreme Court, which views it as one part of a sentencing dichotomy (restorative versus punitive) that can better serve justice (Roach 2000).

The American Correctional Association (ACA) also endorsed the philosophy of restorative justice in its policy on sentencing January 14, 2004. The ACA policy statement avers that sentencing should have as a major purpose restorative justice–righting the harm done to the victim and the community. The restorative focus should be both process and substantively oriented, with victims or their representative included in the justice process. The sentencing procedure should address the needs of the victims, including their need to be heard and as much as possible to be and feel restored to wholeness again

As we see from the ACA policy statement, restorative justice should be as much victim- as offender-driven. The primary defining difference between restorative justice and previous models is its belief in the effectiveness of active community participation in the corrections endeavor. Correctional theorists long have contended that corrections cannot reintegrate the offender successfully back into the community without the community's active help and support (Bazemore 2000). This philosophy humanizes justice by bringing the victim and the offender together to negotiate a mutually satisfying way to correct the wrong done. Although developed for juveniles, and primarily confined to them, practitioners fruitfully use restorative justice with nonviolent adult offenders (Perry 2002). Correctional departments across the country are implementing restorative-justice principles. The Minnesota Department of Corrections has incorporated restorative justice principles into its mission statement, its training academy, and into its promotion requirements for all institutional and community corrections agents and officers (Pranis 1996).

Just as the retributive model emerged (or more accurately, reemerged) after the alleged failure of the treatment or medical model, the restorative justice model has emerged with the apparent failure of such punishment oriented efforts as "Scared Straight" programs, shock probation, and boot camps (Welch 1996). Strong victims' rights/advocacy movements also have played a leading role in the emergence of the model (Shapiro 1990). However, the restorative model may not suit all victims because it blurs the distinction between civil and criminal law and many victims understandably feel that things cannot be "put right" so easily and want the offender punished by the criminal justice system. Restorative justice systems have a tendency to ignore the role of professional criminal justice workers (prosecutors, judges, and probation officers) in favor of informal arbitration facilitated by professionals outside the criminal justice system (Olson and Dzur 2004).

Restorative justice differs from the other models in several important ways. Perhaps, most fundamentally, it "personalizes" crime by defining it as a harmful act committed by one person against another rather than an act committed against an abstraction called "the state." This recognition of concrete victims provides an entree for the offender to be actively involved in repairing the harm done and restoring the situation to its pre crime status. Under the older models, the "debt" the offender owed to "society," and arguments about the extent of that debt took place (and still do, of course) between professionals standing in for the real victim and the victimizer.

The restorative justice model seeks to replace this method of obtaining justice with more direct involvement of victims to the extent that it is feasible and desirable. Make no mistake, this is not a new age "touchy feely" approach to corrections. It holds offenders fully accountable for their actions by applying appropriate punishment and adds the additional dimensions by requiring offenders to accept responsibility for taking action to require them to repair the harm done (Bazemore 2000).

Within the wide philosophical umbrella of restorative justice are a number of specific programs. The so called balanced approach has the broadest scope. The balanced approach (to justice) gives approximately equal weight to three important objectives in corrections work:

1. Community protection

2. Offender accountability

3. Offender competency

It views the community, the victim, and the offender as equal clients of the criminal justice system. Restorative justice presumes all receive tangible benefits from the restorative process (Bazemore and Maloney 1994). The desired initial results of this process are that victims' losses are restored and that victims and offenders become reconciled. The belief is that to the extent that both victim and victimizer come to see that basic fairness and justice is attained when a violation of one person by another is made right by the violator, the violator will have taken a step to reformation and the community will be a safer place in which to live (Coates 1990).

This is an idealized description, and this approach no more "works" in every case than more traditional punitive or treatment approaches. Some people are skeptical that such an approach, best applied in close-knit homogeneous communities, can work in our loosely knit heterogeneous urban society (Walker 2001). A meta-analysis (a study of a large number of other studies of the same topic to assess the common findings and conclusions) found that overall restorative justice programs had a weak- to-moderate positive effect on victim satisfaction, a weak-positive effect on offender satisfaction and nonrecidivism, and a moderate effect on restitution compliance (Latimer, Dowden, and Muise 2005). Evaluate these findings in light of the fact that both victims and offenders self-select to be part of restorative justice programs, however. While much of the promise of restorative justice has yet to be proven, it does have many unique properties that recommend it over the old models. Thus, correctional casework and counseling will take note of the aims of restorative justice. We make frequent references to restorative justice throughout the book. Dr. Kay Carter, a pioneer in this approach, provides in her Perspective from the Field an excellent summary of the restorative justice and the balanced approach.

Perspective from the Field
Restorative Justice and the Balanced Approach

By Kay Carter, Ph.D.

Dr. Carter is the director of Ada County (Idaho) Juvenile Court Services. She has been a pioneer in the development and teaching of the balanced approach in juvenile corrections. In addition to her work at the juvenile court, Dr. Carter is an adjunct faculty member of the criminal justice, social work, and dispute resolution departments at Boise State University.

● ●

Probation officers can apply the balanced approach, originally developed as a model for juvenile probation, to work with adults. The application of this model has accomplished a great deal in juvenile justice, especially the reconciliation of historically opposing views. As an intern coordinator, it has always struck this author that social work students tend to see juvenile justice issues in shades of gray, while criminal justice students tend to see juvenile justice issues only in black and white. As criminal justice students move into the profession, it is necessary to provide them with training, which will allow them to develop a more empathetic and understanding approach to working with delinquent youth, and to help social work professionals to develop a better understanding and appreciation of the necessity for holding delinquent youth accountable.

Applying the balanced approach to juvenile probation has clarified and simplified the training for new probation officers. It also has reduced philosophical tensions within the agency, as everyone, regardless of their personal views, must endorse the values and goals of the balanced approach. Balanced-approach training is so important that it is an upper division course elective for both criminal justice and social work majors.

The balanced-approach model requires probation officers to assess youth, develop case plans, and consider community protection/public safety, youth accountability, and competency development. By doing so, probation officers and agencies no longer struggle with the age-old philosophical dichotomy of punishment versus rehabilitation, because each youth must be assessed individually within the context of the balanced approach, ultimately accomplishing punishment (accountability), rehabilitation (competency development), and community protection (detention, probation).

After the development of the balanced-approach model, others built upon this model and overlaid or encircled it with the concept of restorative justice. The restorative justice concept is holistic, in that, it views crime as harmful to victims, communities, and offenders and sees the primary mission of corrections as ensuring that harm is repaired, in other words restoring victims and communities, and making amends. Offenders who are individually assessed using the balanced approach might have a case plan, which requires them to give back to the victim in some way (through reparation, restitution, mediation, and so on). They must participate in competency development designed to provide them new skills, and to assist in restoring them to a more productive lifestyle. The,n they are expected to give back to the community through community service.

The following case is an example of how a probation officer might apply the balanced approach with restorative justice to a youth who has committed a crime:

A.G., age fifteen, admitted to the court that he and two friends had committed petty theft and burglary at a local store. This was his first offense. His parents, though divorced, were supportive of A.G. and the court judged him not to be at high risk to reoffend. His probation plan required the following:

1. Community protection:
   A. Sixty days detention, suspended
   B. Serve one year of probation
2. Competency development:
   A. Complete a decision-making class
   B. Pay for and complete a petty theft class
   C. Obtain a drug/alcohol assessment and complete the recommendations contained therein
   D. Abstain from any use of drugs/alcohol while on probation
   E. Complete a law-related education class
3. Accountability:
   A. Pay all petition fees
   B. Perform forty hours of community service
   C. Have no avoidable contact with the codefendants
4. Restorative justice:
   A. Write a letter of apology to the store (victim)
   B. Attend a victim's panel
   C. Participate in victim/offender mediation, if desired by the victim

Many juvenile justice professionals believe that community involvement is essential for justice truly to occur. The community is both a part of the problem and a part of the solution. If many delinquency issues grow out of problems in the community, school, or family, then it is clearly one-sided to focus the solution on the individual involved. Restorative justice, in the purest sense, requires institutions and individuals to change, to be accountable, and to participate in promoting strategies for safer communities.

This is an exciting time in juvenile justice because the system is shifting from its singular focus on offenders to a dual focus on offenders and victims. New victims' rights legislation has been instrumental in causing many of the changes the system is making, and heightened awareness of victims' needs has been the impetus for additional changes.

Ada County Juvenile Court Services has implemented a victims' program, in which trained volunteers visit the home of all victims of juvenile crime to inform them about the court, its operations, its language, victims' rights, and programs for victims that the court operates. The victim-impact program uses students and volunteers to provide many of these services, with one full-time paid coordinator. Victims now have a voice in how an offender should make

Continued on the next page

Perspective from the Field, *continued*

amends, be held accountable, provide community protection, and competency development.

To ensure that probation staff use the balanced approach fully, every court report must address the three areas of the balanced approach. Additionally, probation officers receive intensive training in facilitating groups and must facilitate or co-facilitate competency-development groups. This accomplishes many goals, such as allowing the probation officer to count the group session as a probation "contact," seeing youths in a group environment with their peers, assessing competency-development needs firsthand, and helping to prevent burnout by providing job variety and enhanced skill development for probation officers.

Probation officers within our juvenile court now have significant resources available to them as they use the balanced approach. Among the programs available at our court are the victims' program, community service program, weekend detention, an alternative school, and an employment program, and a variety of competency-building groups such as anger management, decision making, and thinking errors. Additionally, the court now is focusing more attention on the parents of youthful offenders and involving them in competency-building groups. The court offers the parent project and parent-adolescent groups on a regular basis at the court, with some parents court-ordered to attend.

Grants fund many of our programs such as the parent project, community service, and the victim-impact program, with grant funds used to pay trained mediators and facilitators. One of the unforeseen benefits of the balanced approach is that it also provides a funding roadmap for agencies. Resources must be allocated in a balanced way, with all three objectives (community protection, accountability, and competency development) considered of equal importance.

Retributive justice has gained much public attention recently. Politicians and the public alike are concerned about crime, particularly juvenile crime, and demand a "just-get-tough" policy. However, public vengeance and provision of punishment through our traditional adversarial processes have not been particularly effective, and the cost–in terms of both human beings and dollars–is prohibitive. It seems more appropriate to approach corrections from a restorative framework, focusing on repairing the damage or harm done to victims and communities, while holding offenders accountable and helping them to develop more competencies.

Juvenile probation officers (care workers in other jurisdictions) in our department are required to assess the strengths and weaknesses of the family and to formulate a case plan to address them. The balanced approach takes an eclectic approach to probation practices and explanations of delinquency. The practice and application of the balanced approach seem to be acceptable to the public, politicians, and practitioners—a rare achievement. Finally, the balanced approach and restorative justice model provide a logical framework for making funding decisions and allocating resources.

Summary

This author obviously believes that rehabilitation is possible with a thoroughly professional approach to the business of correcting the offender's behavior through proactive casework. Many negatives are associated with counseling offenders, foremost of which is the non-voluntary nature of the offender/counselor relationship. However, there are also certain advantages not found in other types of client/counselor relationships such as the availability of a great deal of information about the offender, well tested assessment tools, and the amount of control you can exercise over offenders' activities.

We must emphasize the usefulness of theory. Practitioners of any profession should be fully grounded in the knowledge available to that profession. Remember, theory is the jumping-off point for adequate practice. Without some theoretical understanding of the phenomena with which you are working, you will be floundering in the dark, making mistakes, and possibly thwarting offenders' chances of becoming useful citizens.

The philosophy of restorative justice recognizes both the need to involve victims (and their need for justice) and the offenders' need for reformation. This process strives to instill in both victims and victimizers the belief that they have attained fairness and justice, and thus, there is a rehabilitative effect on the offender.

References and Suggested Readings

American Correctional Association. Policy on Sentencing. Passed by the Delegate Assembly, January 14, 2004 at www.aca.org/government/policies.asp

Bazemore, G. 2000. "What's 'New' about the Balanced Approach?" In P. Kratkoski, ed., *Correctional Counseling and Treatment*. Prospect Heights, Illinois: Waveland Press.

Bazemore, G. and D. Maloney, 1994. Rehabilitative community service: Toward restorative service sanctions in a balanced justice system. *Federal Probation* 58: 24 35.

Champion, D. 2005. *Probation, Parole, and Community Corrections*, 5th Ed. Upper Saddle River, New Jersey: Prentice Hall.

Coates, R. 1990.Victim Offender Reconciliation Programs in North America. In B. Galaway and J. Hudson, eds., *Criminal Justice, Restitution, and Reconciliation*. Monsey, New York: Criminal Justice Press.

Crowe, A.1998. Restorative justice and offender rehabilitation: A meeting of the minds. *Perspectives* 22: 28-40.

Cullen, F. and P. Gendreau. 2000. Assessing correctional rehabilitation: policy, practice, and prospects. In *Criminal Justice 2000*. Washington, D.C.: National Institute of Justice.

Glaze, L. and T. Bonczar. 2006. Probation and parole in the United States, 2005. *Bureau of Justice Statistics Bulletin*. U.S. Department of Justice.

Goff, D. and B. Owens. 1999. Results driven supervision. *Perspectives* 23: 24-27.

Latimer, J., G. Dowden, and D. Muise. 2005. The effectiveness of restorative justice practices: a meta-analysis. *The Prison Journal* 85: 127-144.

Lauen, Roger. 1997. *Positive Approaches to Corrections: Research, Policy, and Practice*. Lanham, Maryland: American Correctional Association.

Lipsey, M. and F. Cullen. 2007. The effectiveness of correctional rehabilitation: A review of systematic reviews. *Annual Review of Law and Social Science* 3: 297-320.

Litt M. and S. Mallon. 2003. The design of social support networks for offenders in outpatient drug treatment. *Federal Probation* 67: 15-22.

Marshall, W. and G. Serran. 2004. The role of the therapist in offender treatment. *Psychology, Crime, and Law*, 10: 309-320.

Olson, S. and A. Dzur. 2004. Revisiting informal justice: restorative justice and democratic professionalism. *Law and Society Review* 38: 139-176.

Perry, John. 2002. *Repairing Communities through Restorative Justice*. Lanham, Maryland: American Correctional Association.

Pranis, K. 1996. Restorative justice catching on in Minnesota corrections. *Overcrowded Times* 7: 1-9.

Roach, K. 2000. Changing punishment at the turn of the century: Restorative justice on the rise. *Canadian Journal of Criminology* July: 249-280.

Roberts, John. 1997. *Reform and Retribution: An Illustrated History of American Prisons*. Alexandria, Virginia: American Correctional Association.

Shapiro, R. 1990."Is Restitution Legislation the Chameleon of the Victims' Movement?" In B. Galaway and J. Hudson, eds., *Criminal Justice, Restitution, and Reconciliation*. Monsey, New York: Criminal Justice Press.

Taxman, F. 2008. No illusions: Offender and organizational change in Maryland's proactive community supervision efforts. *Criminology and Public Policy* 7: 275-302.

Walker, S. 2001. *Sense and Nonsense about Crime and Drugs: Policy Guide*. Belmont, California: Wadsworth.

Walsh, A. and L. Ellis. 2007. *Criminology: An Interdisciplinary Approach*. Thousand Oaks, California: Sage.

Welch, M. 1996. *Corrections: A Critical Approach*. New York: McGraw Hill.

Wilson, J. and R. Herrnstein. 1985. *Crime and Human Nature*. New York: Simon and Schuster.

CHAPTER 2

Sociological and Psychological Theories

Criminological theories are often not so much proven wrong as simply pushed to one side in favor of newer interpretations. The hope of the social sciences, of course, is to achieve an elegant simplicity, and perhaps, in time, the explanation of crime will form a coherent whole.

—Gresham Sykes

Anomie/Strain Theory

The term *anomie* is French and means "lacking in rules" or "normless." Anomie is a relative term, for no society is completely lacking in rules for the regulation of social life. French sociologist Emile Durkheim first used this term in his book *The Division of Labor in Society* (1951). His basic idea was that as societies become increasingly complex, the problem of maintaining social cohesion becomes more problematic. Crime (and other forms of deviance) grows in proportion to the loss of social cohesion. A loss of social cohesion results in considerable ambiguity and contradictions of the rules and standards of moral behavior.

Durkheim, however, did not view crime as abnormal. He argued that because all societies at all times have crime, it is a normal and inevitable phenomenon. What we need to examine, according to Durkheim, are the social-structural conditions and contradictions that result in different levels of criminal activity in different nations and at different times (Durkheim 1950). The 300 percent increase in Hungarian crime since the demise of communism (Gonczol 1993) and the roughly similar figures reported from the former Soviet Union (Dashkov 1992) attest dramatically to the criminogenic effects of rapid social change.

American sociologist Robert Merton (1957) expanded Durkheim's concept of anomie and developed a popular sociocultural explanation of crime, known as *strain theory*. Like all other macrosociological theories of crime, Merton's anomie/strain theory involves three major elements: social structure, social values, and social norms. This theory views crime not as a symptom of personal inadequacies but rather as a "normal" response to the various ways that these sociocultural elements impinge on and limit the responses of certain groups of individuals.

According to anomie theory, the basic cause of crime is not located within individuals. Rather, the structural contradictions within society place strain on individuals, which may lead them to commit crimes. Merton identifies the structural contradiction or the disjunction or contradiction between the cultural value of material success and the lack of equal access to legitimate means of accomplishing it as the most important factor in generating criminal behavior. As Merton (1957: 146) states:

> It is only when a system of cultural values extols, virtually above all else, certain common success goals for the population at large while the social structure rigorously restricts or completely closes access to approved modes of reaching these goals for a considerable part of the same population, that deviant behavior ensues on a large scale.

Although researchers formulated these theories in an American context, they also apply to other societies that share to one degree or another similar values and social arrangements. American society has taken what traditional morality considered as base and evil—acquisitiveness and usury—and elevated them to the status of prescriptive (required or recommended) goals. Material things (a Coach handbag, a Lexus in the driveway, an I-Pad) equal happiness, prestige, and self-worth in the American equation. If you do not possess at least a modicum of these visible trappings of self-worth, it is obvious to all that something is remiss in your character—you are not a participant in the "American Dream." Pause and reflect a moment: is this not the constant message you receive from all quarters on a daily basis? The most popular heroes of the movies and television are rich and powerful men and women playing with a lot of expensive toys. To maintain a sense of self-worth, then, advertisers exhort individuals to strive to achieve culturally approved goals.

According to this theory, however, society systematically denies certain groups of individuals access to the competition because of various structural impediments such as race and class. In other words, we are all encouraged to develop champagne tastes, even if we only have beer budgets. It is not the beer budget per se that generates the sort of dissatisfaction that may lead to crime, it is the size of one's budget relative to the size of one's culturally defined wants and needs. It is difficult to be happy, as Eastern philosophers have long maintained, if expectations exceed accomplishments or if wants and needs are not proportionate to means. As Durkheim himself dramatically put it (1951a: 246): "No living being can be happy or even exist unless his needs are sufficiently proportioned to his means." We can view happiness as an equation:

$$\text{Happiness} = \frac{\text{Accomplishments}}{\text{Expectations}}$$

To bring this equation into balance, individuals either have to increase their accomplishments or decrease their expectations. In other words, people have to adapt.

Modes of Adaptation

Merton identifies five modes or methods of adaptation to a social structure that exhorts us to strive for accomplishments but which denies some persons legitimate access to the means by which they can be realized. This is due to the processes of conformity, ritualism, retreatism, rebellion, and innovation.

Conformity. Most of us are conformists in this Mertonian sense. If we were not, our current society would be in a lot of trouble. *Conformists* are individuals who accept the validity of the cultural goals and of the socially approved methods of achieving them. Such people quietly live out their lives and probably never will get themselves into any serious trouble with the law.

Ritualism. The *ritualist* is the nine-to-five slugger who has long given up on ever achieving the prescribed cultural goals but who, nevertheless, continues to work ritually within the boundaries set forth as legitimate. Although Merton considered the ritualist adaptation as deviant because of the rejection of the cultural goals, it is not a criminal adaptation. The ritualist satisfied with the security his or her job provides, is rarely in trouble with the law.

Retreatism. The *retreatist* rejects both the cultural goals and the institutionalized means of attaining them. People in this category drop out of society and often take refuge in drugs, alcohol, and transiency. They are frequently in trouble with the law because of crimes committed to support a drug and/or alcohol habit. This type of individual often presents the greatest challenge to the criminal justice worker.

Rebellion. *Rebels* reject both the goals and the means of capitalist American society, but, unlike retreatists, they wish to substitute alternative goals and alternative means. They are committed to some form of sociopolitical ideal, such as socialism, which they believe will provide a more just and equitable society. You rarely will have to deal with rebels unless they become radicalized to the point of putting ideology into actions that break the law.

Innovation. Finally, we have the *innovator*. This individual fully accepts the validity of the cultural goals of monetary success but rejects (possibly because of having been denied access to them) the legitimate means of attaining them. The innovator best exemplifies Taylor, Walton, and Young's (1973: 93) image of American society: "The desire to make money without regard to the means in which one sets about doing it is symptomatic of the malintegration at the heart of American society." Innovators do not work and stash a few dollars in the bank, and then watch it slowly gather interest; that is for suckers. It is a lot faster, takes a lot less effort, and is far more exciting to rob a bank. In other words, crime is an innovative avenue to success—a method by which deprived people get what their culture teaches them to want.

General Strain Theory [*Personality characteristics*]

Criminologist Robert Agnew extended Merton's concept of strain, which he considered too limiting, in a series of papers in the 1980s-1990s leading to what he calls general strain theory. Agnew's extension broadens the concept of strain to include many other strains besides being prevented from achieving goals. Agnew (1992: 50) adds strain resulting from efforts by others to remove or threaten to remove things we value (such as the termination of a job or valued relationship), and strain resulting from others who present us with negative or noxious stimuli (such as being a victim of child abuse or sexual harassment). More importantly, Agnew includes the variety of ways people respond to those strains, and the characteristics of individuals that might lead them to adopt one response rather than another.

Identifying those who perceive a situation as a criminal opportunity and those who do not is obviously important. According to Agnew, the personal traits which may help us to differentiate between those who choose one option over the other include ". . . temperament, intelligence, creativity, problem-solving skills, interpersonal skills, self-efficacy, and self-esteem" (1992: 71). Simply put, strain is likely to lead to crime or delinquency when the individual cannot effectively manage it.

In 1997, Agnew went further to move strain theory from its original macrosocial context to include attention deficit hyperactivity disorder (ADHD), impulsivity, and insensitivity to his list of individual differences that contribute to criminality. More recently, Walsh (2000) has attempted to place strain theory in a behavioral-genetic context by pointing out that all the individual differences Agnew describes are moderately to highly heritable (the degree to which a trait is attributable to genetic factors). If the traits contributing to criminality are heritable, and if these traits are negatively associated with the achievement of occupational success, we cannot ignore them. Agnew (2005) appears to agree with this position in his book in which he posits that the "super traits" of low self-control and irritability (the tendency to respond to many kinds of stimuli in an ill-tempered manner) interact negatively with all other life domains (family, school, work, marriages) over the life course to produce negative outcomes.

Agnew (2005) further narrowed his search for traits conducive to criminal behavior in his general theory of crime. In this theory, he identifies five life domains that we all share, but which also contain possible crime-generating factors: personality, family, school, peers, and work. Agnew asserts that personality traits "condition" the effect of social variables on crime because they set individuals on a developmental trajectory that influences how other people in the family, school, peer group, and work domains react to them. He identifies the traits of low self-control and irritability as "super traits" that encompass many other traits associated with criminal offending such as sensation seeking, impulsivity, poor problem-solving skills, inattentiveness, and low empathy. People with low self-control and irritable temperaments are likely to evoke negative responses from family members, schoolteachers, peers, and workmates that feed back and exacerbate those tendencies over the life course. Agnew notes, "biological factors have a direct affect on irritability/low self-control and an indirect affect on the other life domains through irritability/low self-control" (2005: 213). He also integrates genetics, evolutionary psychology, and the neurosciences into his theory, and shows how the various components (domains) influence each other developmentally across the lifespan. Figure 2.1 summarizes Agnew's theory.

Figure 2.1 Agnew's General or "Super Traits" Theory

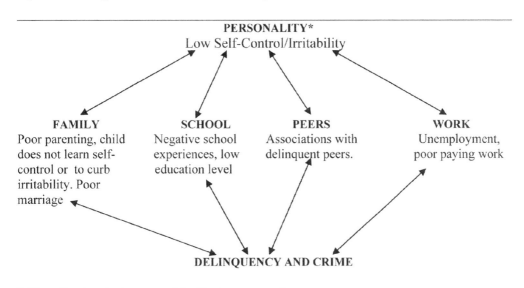

PERSONALITY*
Low Self-Control/Irritability

FAMILY	SCHOOL	PEERS	WORK
Poor parenting, child does not learn self-control or to curb irritability. Poor marriage	Negative school experiences, low education level	Associations with delinquent peers.	Unemployment, poor paying work

DELINQUENCY AND CRIME

* These five domains interact and feed back on one another

Source: Walsh and Ellis, 2007. *Criminology: An Interdisciplinary Approach.* Sage/Pine Forge Press. Reprinted with permission.

Lessons and Concerns

As useful as this theory may be to the macrosociologist, it has little practical utility for the correctional worker dealing with individual "retreatists" or "innovators." The correctional worker could derive few, if any, implementable policy recommendations from it. In part, this is the reason why those in positions of power within the criminal justice system reject this, and many other sociological theories (Gilsinan 1990: 103). The "cure" for crime logically derived from anomie theory is the expansion of legitimate opportunities and equal access to them.

However, every correctional worker can recount numerous instances in which he or she has labored to obtain employment for offenders only to see them "blow it" for one reason or another in short order. It is not enough simply to provide jobs for some offenders who may have come to prefer taking advantage of illegitimate opportunities.

As a criminal justice worker, you must convince such people of the ultimate futility of their short-run hedonism and the necessity of their becoming responsible human beings. Offenders have to be convinced to make a realistic assessment of their situations and to adjust their aspirations accordingly. Further, you must not be seduced into accepting the propositions of anomie theory as excuses for criminal behavior. Being a criminal does not necessarily mean that legitimate opportunities have not been made available, the assertions of Merton notwithstanding. In fact, one of the flaws in anomie theory is that it is tautologous (it argues circuitously). That is, it poses a cause of crime (lack of legitimate opportunity) and then uses the alleged effects of that cause (crime) as a measure of the opportunities one has not had.

Agnew's extension of anomie/strain theory is more useful, although he expanded his concept of strain to include anything and everything that might frustrate a person. Is he really adding anything to the classical notion that humans are animals fundamentally motivated by the desire to maximize pleasure and minimize pain? The more useful part of his theory lies in pulling us back to the understanding that people are very different, and those differences determine whether strain (which we all experience in one way or another in Agnew's conceptualization) leads to criminal behavior. For instance, Merton makes much of strain generated by the lack of occupational success, but he views this lack as entirely the result of social discrimination. Agnew's inclusion of intelligence and temperament provides us with an alternate explanation of why some people do not achieve occupational success, for nothing predicts occupational success in an open society better than IQ and conscientiousness (reviewed in Walsh 2000).

However, we find Agnew's extension of anomie theory into the interdisciplinary realm a most welcome addition to the literature. It illustrates how personality differences among people, while initially they may be minor, may be magnified over the life course as individuals evoke different responses from other individuals. In other words, people with low self-control and with a tendency to be irritable will tend to evoke negative responses from others. This may exacerbate low self-control and irritability. Conversely, people respond to pleasant individuals positively, which will tend to reinforce pleasantness—the rich get rich and the poor get poorer.

A lesson of anomie theory that is worth the attention of correctional workers is the notion that criminal behavior can be a rational response to social conditions, as the offender perceives them. Rational means that there is a logical fit between a desired goal and the means used to attain it. Rational action in pursuit of a goal does not imply that the action is "right" or "moral." It merely means that those engaging in such action have sought a goal at a price they feel that they can afford.

A criminal who risks life and limb in the illegitimate pursuit of legitimate cultural goals certainly is not behaving irrationally from the point of view of a middle-class observer. However, we must define rationality in terms of the actor, not the observer. The innovator simply has more to gain and less to lose through criminal activity than does the middle-class observer. Of course, middle-class people themselves can be "innovators" if the price is right. Perhaps realization of this will lead you to develop a deficiency rather than a pathological definition of criminal behavior. Therefore, it is important to view criminals as deficient in the attributes that produce lawful-behavior—not psychologically defective (unless proven otherwise).

Differential Association Theory

Differential association theory, first formulated by sociologist Edwin Sutherland (Sutherland and Cressey 1978), focuses on subcultural elements (as opposed to personal characteristics) that may predispose an individual to one or another of Merton's adaptations. This theory stresses the potency of group pressures. It asserts that, like chameleons, we all take on the hues and colors of our environments. We blend in; we conform. We tend to like football, hot dogs, and apple pie, rather than soccer, bratwurst, and strudel, not because the former are demonstrably superior to the latter but because we are born Americans and not Germans. We view the world differentially according to the attitudes, beliefs, and expectations of the groups around which our lives revolve.

The Assumptions

We can compress the nine propositions or components of differential association theory, into four general principles:

1. Individuals learn criminal behavior in interaction with other people. Criminals do not biologically inherit their behavior, nor is it the result of psychological abnormalities, or invented anew by each criminal.

2. For the most part, the learning of criminal behavior occurs within intimate personal groups. This learning includes specific techniques, motives, rationalizations, justifications, and attitudes.

3. Individuals derive the direction of the cognitive components of learned criminal behavior from definitions of the legal code (the law) as favorable or unfavorable to violations of the law. Thus, people become criminals because they hold an excess of definitions favorable to the violation of the law over definitions unfavorable to violations of the law.

4. Associations with others holding definitions favorable to violation of the law vary in frequency, duration, priority, and intensity. That is, the earlier in life one is exposed to criminal norms of conduct, the more often one is exposed to them, the longer those exposures last, and the more strongly one is attached to one's mentors, the more likely one is to become a criminal.

A number of empirical studies support the general validity of this line of thinking (see Matsueda 1982, for a review). The correlations between association with delinquent peers and delinquency are some of the strongest links in social science. According to critics of this theory, however, various reviews of friendship patterns (Rodkin et al. 2000) have shown that the propensity for a given pattern of activity (including antisocial activity) precedes association with like-minded individuals. "Birds of a feather flock together," and become more alike based on their association. According to critics, association with delinquent peers acts more as a "releaser" of delinquent behavior than as a stimulator for otherwise prosocial individuals to engage in criminal activity. This is not to say that associations do not increase the propensity, however.

The theory also has been criticized as both "true and trivial" because it reduces to the commonsense idea that people are apt to behave criminally when they do not respect the law (Nettler 1978: 265). We can apply it as a causal explanation to all sorts of values, attitudes, tastes, and behaviors as a general theory of socialization within subcultures. "Culture" explains everything in a global sense, and, therefore, explains nothing in a specific sense. The commission of crime is a specific behavior engaged in by a few individuals within cultural settings with varying degrees of tolerance for antisocial behavior, and in no sense is it a normative cultural expectation.

Differential association theory is a variation on the social pathology theme. Criminal behavior is cooked up in the simmering caldron of pathological neighborhoods, stirred by morally bankrupt companions, spiced by trouble, toughness, and excitement, and dished up with an urban philosophy of "do onto others as they would do onto you—but do it first!" It is from this conflict with middle-class attitudes and values that individuals devise "definitions favorable" to law violation and translate them into criminal behavior.

Figure 2.2 Differential Association Theory

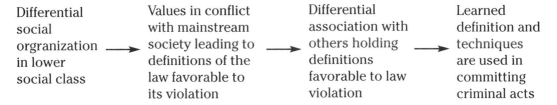

| Differential social orgranization in lower social class | → | Values in conflict with mainstream society leading to definitions of the law favorable to its violation | → | Differential association with others holding definitions favorable to law violation | → | Learned definition and techniques are used in committing criminal acts |

Lessons and Concerns

Although we cannot deny the cogency of the line of thought differential association theory presents us, it contains little practical leavening to lighten the dense dough of theory. As a correctional worker, you will be able to do nothing to mitigate the pernicious effects of poor neighborhoods. You merely can help offenders to act responsibly within them. Nonetheless, you must be sensitive to the burden of peer pressures felt by criminal justice offenders. An awareness of those pressures will enable you to formulate realistic goals for treatment rather than moralize with offenders about the company they keep.

However, be aware that probation and parole conditions have regulations regarding offenders' associations with other criminal types. Differential association theory dictates that this is a plausible prohibition, and that introducing offenders to activities that lead them to associate with prosocial others is a reasonable treatment plan. However, life in the ghettoes and barrios of the United States often necessitates belonging to a gang and participating in its attitudes and activities. A young man, and sometimes a young woman, living in a ghetto who does not take advantage of the comradeship and protection of the local gang may not be acting in his or her best interests.

Nonparticipation in such groups leaves one naked to the preying designs of those more in tune with the reality of their existence. Thus, supporters of this theory (in answer to the criticism that people choose their associations based on personal predilections) insist that the area in which people grow up adequately accounts for the associations they have. It is only when delinquent and nondelinquent associations equally are available that we should evoke individual propensities to explain association patterns (Stark 1987). You can take some comfort that quite often the simple acts of getting married and/or obtaining legitimate employment may distance many less criminally involved offenders from their former companions and place them in the company of others with a more prosocial set of values.

Other critics take issue with the basic assumption of differential association theory that antisocial behavior is learned, stating that it comes naturally to the unsocialized individual: "What is there to be learned about simple lying, taking things that belong to another, fighting and sex play" asks an early critic (Glueck 1956: 94). Assuredly, individuals learn to get better at doing these things because of their associations with other like-minded individuals, but they do not have to be taught such natural acts. What they have to be taught is how to curb them, what constitutes moral behavior, and how to consider the rights and feelings of others. We now consider a theory that recognizes this.

Social Control Theory

Whereas anomie and differential association theories focus on causes said to propel individuals into crime, control theory focuses on the conditions of the environment that restrain them from it. According to control theorists, criminologists need not so much to explain why some of us behave badly but why most of us behave well most of the time. Control theory insists that self-interest is innate, that we are born asocial, and that we must learn painful lessons. We must learn that civilization occurs at the cost of the repression of natural urges and that our wants and needs are inextricably linked to the wants and needs of others. If we do not learn these lessons, we are heading for trouble.

Identifying the "Typical" Criminal

The version of control theory examined here—that of Travis Hirschi (1977)—is compelling. It is consistent with what we are reasonably certain we know about the personal and demographic characteristics of those who commit crimes, and with the perceptions of crime causation held by most workers in the criminal justice field. Hirschi starts with the correlates of the "typical" criminal and finds him to be a young male who grew up in a fatherless home in an urban slum, who has a history of difficulty in school, and who is unemployed. Of course, there are also female criminals, but the following discussion uses the masculine pronoun to emphasize that we are talking about Hirschi's typical criminal.

Having defined the typical criminal, Hirschi makes a series of logical deductions flowing from the nature of crime. His first observation is that criminal activity is contrary to the wishes and expectations of others. From this, he deduces that those most likely to commit crimes are least likely to be concerned with the wishes and expectations of others. Criminal activity is contrary to the law and involves the risk of punishment. Therefore, those who commit crimes are least likely to accept the moral beliefs underlying the law, and are least likely to concern themselves with the risk of punishment. Finally, criminal acts take time and are engaged in by those who have the time that such acts require (they are unemployed).

What demands explanation are the conditions of the typical criminal's life that lead him to run roughshod over the wishes and expectations of others, his lack of belief in the moral order, his relative lack of concern for punishment, and his possession of the excess time that criminal activity requires. Hirschi answers this by saying that the typical criminal lacks a bond to society. There are four elements of the social bond existing in the environments of noncriminals, which restrain them from criminal activity that are absent in the environments of criminals. These restraining elements of the bond are attachment, commitment, involvement, and belief.

The Four Elements of the Social Bond

Attachment refers to one's psychological and emotional closeness to others. It implies a reciprocal relationship in which persons feel valued, respected, and loved, and in which they value the favorable judgments of others to whom they are attached.

Sociologists use the concept of significant others and reference groups to refer to the people we consider important to us and whose good opinions we value. Significant others are close family members and friends, and reference groups are those groups of people who we admire and seek to emulate. We look for guidance in our behavior, values, and attitudes to these people. Much of our behavior can be seen as attempts to gain favorable judgments from our reference groups and significant others.

For many years, parents are the most important behavior-orienting significant others. It follows that those who do not care about parental reactions are those who are most likely to behave in ways contrary to their wishes. Risking the good opinion of another is of minor concern when that good opinion is not valued. Why that good opinion is not valued is a question that need not concern us at this point. In general, however, such a state results from the absence of a relationship between parent and child in which love, respect, value, and concern are constantly demonstrated.

Lack of attachment to parents and the attending lack of respect for their wishes easily spill over into a lack of attachment and respect for the broader social groupings of which the child is a part. Much of the controlling power of others outside the immediate family lies in the threat of reporting juvenile misbehavior to parents. If the child has little fear of parental sanctions, the control exercised by others has limited effect simply because parental control has limited effect.

The family is the nursery of human nature. If the family is in disarray, if there is little love, concern, or attachment within it, then the product will be defective. Children of such families will fail to form a conscience. They will lack the ability to sympathize and empathize with others. They will learn that the world is a cold and heartless place and will act toward it, accordingly. However, it is naive to posit that all life's ills have their origins in the lack of early childhood attachment. After all, numerous other life events intervene and have an impact on the probability of one becoming criminal.

Commitment refers to a lifestyle in which one has invested considerable time and energy in the pursuit of a lawful career. We assume the pursuit of such a lifestyle to be rewarding to the individuals, who, therefore, have a valuable stake in conforming to the moral standards of their society. People, who make this considerable investment, or who aspire to it, are not likely to risk it by engaging in criminal activity. The benefit/cost ratio (what individuals stand to benefit from crime contrasted with what they stand to lose if caught) renders the cost of crime prohibitive for such a person.

However, the lower the stake with which one enters the criminal game, the more appealing are the possible prizes. The poor student, the truant, the dropout, and the unemployed risk less in the benefit/cost comparison. For example, although the bank president and the casual laborer equally may desire to engage the services of an underage prostitute, the bank president probably is more likely to restrain the urge because he stands to lose far more than the laborer if he is caught and exposed. The successful acquisition of a stake in prosocial conformity, of course, requires success in school. Success in school requires disciplined application to tasks that children do not particularly relish but which they nevertheless complete to gain the valued approval of significant others, especially parents. Again, if approval is not forthcoming or is not valued, children will busy themselves in tasks more congenial to their natural inclinations, inclinations that almost certainly do not include algebra or the principles of grammar. Attachment, then, would appear to be an essential prerequisite to any genuine commitment to a prosocial lifestyle.

Involvement is a direct consequence of commitment. It is a part of a conventional pattern of existence. Essentially, involvement is a matter of time and energy constrictions placed upon us by the demands of our commitments. Involvement in lawful activities reduces exposure to illegal activities. Conversely, the lack of involvement in lawful activities increases the possibility of exposure to illegal activities: "The devil finds work for idle hands," moral considerations aside, is a cogent statement.

Belief refers to the ready acceptance of the social prescriptions and proscriptions regulating conduct. Individuals free of the constraints on their behavior imposed by attachment, commitment, and involvement evolve a belief system shorn of conventional morality. It is a system of belief containing narrowly focused images of self-interest. Unlike differential association theory, control theory does not view the criminal belief system as causative in the sense that it generates criminal behavior. Rather, criminals act according to their urges and then justify or rationalize their behavior with a set of instrumental statements such as "Suckers deserve what they get," "Everybody does it—why not me?" and "Do onto others as they would do onto you—only do it first." These are the statements of alienated individuals—Merton's innovators, who are reflecting and rationalizing the lifestyle of the unattached. For control theorists, the behavior gives birth to the belief rather than vice versa.

Control theorists agree with differential association theorists that like-minded individuals reinforce criminals in their beliefs. However, they strongly disagrees with the proposition that such peer groups are intimately connected, loyal to one another, and bound by a prescriptive code of conduct. The criminality of group members reflects their weak bonds with conventional society more than their attachment to one another. Any worker in the criminal justice field will attest to the fact that when in a legal bind, criminals will trip over one another in the race to be the first to "cut a deal" favorable to themselves to the detriment of their "friends."

Figure 2.3 Hirchi's Control Theory

The lack of attachment, commitment, involvement and belief constitutes the lack of social contraols ⟶ Lack of social control releases natural inclinations to satisfy wants and needs expendiently ⟶ **Crime**

A point of central importance to understanding control theory is that the lack of attachment, commitment, and involvement to and with conventional others, does not constitute a motive for crime as an "excess of definitions favorable to the violation of the law" is alleged to provide in differential association theory. The lack of these controls represents social deficiencies (the lack of social bonds) that have the result of reducing the potential costs of engaging in criminal activity. Nor is a criminal belief system a motive for crime; it is merely an after-the-fact justification for antisocial behavior. The correctional worker, of course, should consider both the behavior and the alleged justification for it very unacceptable. Figure 2.3 presents a diagrammatic representation of Hirschi's social bond theory.

From Social Control to Self-Control

With colleague Michael Gottfredson, Hirschi has moved from a focus on social controls in explaining crime to a focus on self-control; that is the "extent to which (different people) are vulnerable to the temptations of the moment" (1990: 87). Gottfredson and Hirschi accept the classical idea that crimes result from natural human impulses to enhance pleasure and avoid pain. We all have these impulses, but most of us learn to express them in socially appropriate ways. Consistent with the shift from social- to self-control, instead of beginning with the social location of the typical criminal as their foundational facts ("young, fatherless male," and so forth), Gottfredson and Hirschi begin with what we know about the typical crime as their foundational fact. In other words, the typical crime is an impulsive act designed to provide the offender with immediate short-term gratification.

If this is the defining characteristic of the typical criminal act, it follows that the defining trait of the typical criminal is low self-control. According to the theory, people with low self-control possess the following cognitive and temperamental traits that make offending more probable for them than for others (Gottfredson and Hirschi 1990: 89-90):

- They are oriented to the present rather than to the future, and crime affords them immediate rather than delayed gratification.

- They are risk-taking and physical as opposed to cautious and cognitive, and crime provides them with exciting and risky adventures.

- They lack patience, persistence, diligence, and crime provides them with quick and easy ways to obtain money, sex, revenge, and so forth.

- They are self-centered and insensitive, so they can commit crimes without experiencing pangs of guilt for causing the suffering of others.

Crime affords such people with quick and easy ways to satisfy their needs immediately, and their personal characteristics enable them to enjoy the satisfaction of their needs without experiencing the pangs of guilt or empathy.

Gottfredson and Hirschi trace the origin of low self-control, which they consider a stable component of a criminal personality, to poor parenting practices. Children do not learn low self-control. On the contrary, the defining traits of low self-control are the "default" options that occur naturally in the absence of adequate parenting. In other words, low self-control is not "caused;" high self-control is. Parents must teach children self-control through their warmth, nurturance, discipline, and vigilance. Thus, any set of family circumstances that make this type of parenting difficult to achieve negatively effects the development of self-control. Gottfredson and Hirschi list parental criminality, large families, and single-parent families as some of the major family circumstances that reduce parental supervision (Gottfredson and Hirschi 1990: 100-105).

Low self-control is a necessary but not sufficient cause of criminal offending, for it must be paired with an opportunity to commit it. A criminal opportunity is a situation that presents itself in which an individual lacking in self-control can satisfy his or her needs with minimal mental or physical effort (Gottfredson and Hirschi 1990). These criminal opportunities include an open window, a young woman walking alone in a dark alley, a car with keys in the ignition, and a distracted shopkeeper. A person with self-control would not construe the same situations as criminal opportunities.

Case Study
Control Theory and Rehabilitation

By Robert M. Freeman, Ph.D.

Dr. Freeman earned his bachelor's and master's degrees in psychology from Indiana University of Pennsylvania. His doctorate is in criminal justice and criminology from the University of Maryland. Dr. Freeman is an assistant professor in the Department of Criminal Justice at Shippensburg University in Shippensburg, Pennsylvania. From 1970 to 1990, he served as superintendent of two Pennsylvania Department of Corrections adult men's facilities, including the 2,600-bed Camp Hill Prison, where he served during the riots. He has extensive experience in every phase of correctional management.

● ● ● ● ● ● ● ● ● ● ● ● ● ● ● ● ● ● ●

During my first five years in corrections, I was a psychologist involved in developing treatment plans for adult male offenders. The last fifteen years of my corrections career consisted of administrative duties, some of which involved initiating and monitoring a variety of specialized treatment programs. The foundation for both individual treatment planning and program development was the medical model of rehabilitation.

The medical model of rehabilitation, which was so influential in corrections from the late 1950s to the mid-1970s and still forms the basis for most treatment planning for incarcerated offenders, has four basic tenets:

1. Criminal behavior is a symptom of a personal deficiency.

2. These personal deficiencies can be identified through appropriate classification techniques.

3. Deficiencies can be corrected by application of specific treatment programs and techniques.

4. Once deficiencies have been corrected, the symptoms no longer will occur.

My colleagues and I were taught that criminals should be viewed as people whose behavior was created by the inability to gain legal employment because of deficiencies in education and training. These deficiencies were to be corrected by enrollment in academic and job-skill development classes. Alcohol and/or drug dependency were symptoms resulting from a deficiency in self-esteem

Continued on the next page

Case Study, *continued*

and coping skills and could be corrected by individual counseling and/or group therapy or placement in a therapeutic drug community. Assaultive crimes were symptoms of low-impulse control and/or self-esteem to be corrected by participation in counseling programs focused on anger management and impulse control.

Academic and job-training programs were a generic prescription based on the belief that success in these activities would bolster self-esteem and teach self-discipline, as well as create employment opportunities. Counseling designed to bolster the offender's self-image was frequently added to the treatment plans under the assumption that all offenders, regardless of presenting symptoms, had a poor self-image. If the offender did well with in-house programming, then a variety of pre-release programs (work release, college, furloughs) could be made available for both reward and societal reintegration purposes.

Underlying the medical model is a belief in the propositions of control theory. Control theory postulates that people do not commit crimes when they are firmly attached to a conventional lifestyle because they have a "stake in conformity," which they cannot afford to lose. Those individuals attached to conventional individuals at an early age learn conventional behavior, spend their time in conventional activities, believe in conventional values, and function as law-abiding citizens. Criminals, not attached to a conventional lifestyle, have no stake in conformity, and are free to break the law because they have nothing to lose. The goal of the medical model is to provide offenders with a stake in conformity. This occurs through attachment to conventional activities learned through participation in treatment programs provided by conventional members of society.

Control theory sounds plausible and we can use it to help explain why many individuals drop out of crime when they get married, obtain a full-time job, or enter military service. Logically, a treatment approach based on control theory should produce impressive results. However, one of the hardest lessons a beginning practitioner has to learn is that all theories have limitations. No matter how plausible the theory, failures will occur when they are applied in practice. An example follows:

During my third year as a psychologist, this author developed a treatment plan for an inmate named George, a twenty-two-year-old white, unmarried male from a broken family, who had been in trouble as a juvenile, and was serving his first adult sentence for burglary. He had dropped out of school in the ninth grade, had no vocational skills, and sporadically had held a number of marginal jobs. Psychological testing with the Minnesota Multiphasic Inventory (MMPI) showed a personality profile within normal limits. George was articulate, polite, very personable, had an I.Q. of 137, and had no history of alcohol or drug dependency. He expressed a sincere desire to improve his life and talked convincingly of his revulsion at the burglaries, which had sent him to prison.

This author put George in his therapy group, which focused on building self-esteem and gaining insight into the relationship between experiences and current behavior, enrolled him in the General Equivalency Degree (GED) program, and carefully monitored his performance in the kitchen and on the cellblock. Six months later George had earned his GED, was tutoring other students, receiving exemplary reports from kitchen supervisors, and showing an extraordinary level of insight in the group. Block officers were unanimous that George should be an accelerated candidate for pre-release programming. This author was delighted. The next step was to enroll George in a community college program. He had expressed a desire to receive an associate degree in computer programming, and the college admissions personnel agreed that he had the necessary aptitude. George did so well in the program that the college offered him a part-time job in their student records office. He met a conventional young woman while on weekend furlough, fell in love, and married her in the prison chapel shortly before he was granted parole. George left prison with three months left in his college program and the offer of a full-time job after graduation. On the day of George's graduation, this author knew he had a success story.

A year after graduation, George walked into my office dressed in the blue clothing given to all new receptions. He had been convicted of stealing used car tires from a warehouse. This author was stunned. According to control theory, George should have been a success. He had received his "stake in conformity:" a wife, a college degree, a good job, and the approval and acceptance of conventional members of society. What could possibly have gone wrong? "Why did you return to crime when you had so much going for you? His answer, given after a minute of thoughtful reflection: "I got bored."

I got bored! The reality is that we cannot use a single theory to explain or change all human behavior. Would another approach, possibly one based on reality therapy, have worked with George? We will never know. The superintendent of the facility operated under the principle of "One and you're done." George had had his "one." Two weeks later, he was transferred to a maximum-security prison where he became just another number.

Lessons and Concerns

The utility of control theory (both versions presented here) for the correctional worker is that it provides a certain amount of meaningful guidance in working with offenders. Obviously, you can do nothing about your offenders' levels of attachment to their families. You cannot visit the past and interfere with pathological family dynamics, unfortunate though that may be. You can take steps in your role as a counselor and a broker of community resources to involve offenders in a conventional lifestyle. Correctional workers have considerable power over the activities of offenders. That is to say, you can lead the horses to water, and, with a little judicious use of authority, persuade them to sip a little. Perhaps they even may acquire a taste for it.

Contrary to the nihilistic "nothing works" philosophy, this author has witnessed many remarkable turnarounds by offenders who have had the guidance of caring criminal justice professionals. Many reviews of the rehabilitation literature substantiate this view. Although control theory offers practical guidance to commend it over the other two theories examined, it is certainly not the final word in the understanding of criminal behavior. It does not account for those who simply appear to prefer a criminal lifestyle despite receiving numerous opportunities to forge a conventional one (*see* Dr. Freeman's case study).

Control theorists view criminal activity as a poor second choice made by unhappy individuals whose socialization has rendered them largely unfit to pursue conventional avenues to success. In the majority of cases, this is an accurate assessment. Most individuals caught up in criminal activity might well prefer acceptance into the "moral community," $90,000 a year from a straight job, a house with a white picket fence, and membership at the country club. Unfortunately, their experiences during their formative years have not prepared them psychologically, emotionally, or intellectually to accept the possibility that such a lifestyle could be a reality for them. They have a tremendous burden of inertia preventing them from taking that first step on the long journey to social respectability, and a stifling orientation to the here and now.

Control theory does not address that small percentage of criminals who have genuine contempt for the "straight life," those who, by their natures, find it extremely difficult to function in a conventionally acceptable way. There are individuals who, despite the best efforts of parents to teach them self-control, never learn it. Some children bring with them to the socialization process a temperament so difficult as to test the patience of saints.

Self-control theory neglects children's effects on parenting, just as it neglects the fact that low self-control (impulsiveness) is related to levels of the neurotransmitter serotonin, which are primarily—though not entirely—under genetic control (Wright and Beaver 2005). These people enjoy hurting others; they crave the danger, excitement, and adventure provided by a life of crime. Life without the opportunity to hurt and dominate others, without drugs and alcohol, without violence and predation, without fast cars and faster women, would be unbearable to them. We call such people psychopaths, sociopaths, or "antisocial personalities." Although they constitute a small minority of the criminal population with which you will have contact, it is important to have an understanding of them because they are engaged in a level of criminal activity out of all proportion to their numbers.

Summary

Anomie and differential association theories locate the causes of crime in the criminal's environment, and both theories agree with the proposition that societies get the type of criminals they deserve. Anomie theorists believe that American socioeconomic conditions, which emphasize monetary success but at the same time deny access to legitimate avenues to this goal to a significant number of people, manufacture criminals. The retreatist and innovator modes of adaptation to this cultural disjunction are the modes that generate criminal behavior. The conformist and the ritualist modes of adaptation produce individuals who, in the main, are law abiding. Only under certain circumstances does the rebellious mode generate illegal behavior.

Differential association theory concentrates on specific subcultural environments that predispose individuals to adopt specific modes of adaptation. This theory emphasizes that criminals learn criminal behavior within subcultures where criminal behavior is more or less "normal" behavior. Differing levels of criminal behavior depend on the frequency, duration, priority, and intensity of association with criminals and criminal values and attitudes. Thus, differential association theory agrees with anomie theory that criminal behavior can be a rational adaptation to the conditions in which people find themselves. In short, theorists in both of these camps tend to give the impression that everyone is guilty of crime—except the criminal. Although these theories offer no policy recommendations that the criminal justice worker, could put into practice, they do illuminate the relationship between criminality and the social arrangements in which it exists. Their main value to you should be that they lead you to a deficiency rather than a pathological interpretation of criminal behavior.

Control theory differs from the other two theories in that rather than looking at conditions that may lead people to commit crimes, it looks at conditions that isolate people from it. Those conditions, or controls, are attachment, commitment, involvement, and belief. The presence of the latter three controls depends largely on the initial presence of attachment. Criminal beliefs do not "cause" one to commit crimes, they merely serve as rationalizations for those who do. Control theory fits well with the perceptions of crime causation held by most criminal justice practitioners. Its later emphasis on self-control also fits well the perceptions of criminal justice personnel.

The important point to remember about self-control is that low self-control emerges in the absence of adequate parenting. Control theory recognizes that individuals' lack of controls (either social or self-control) is not entirely their own fault, but it does not attempt to justify irresponsible behavior by pointing to this lack as a cause. Control theory offers some useful practical guidance for correctional workers, both for understanding criminal behavior and for pointing to conditions that possibly may be rectified in the counseling and supervision process.

References and Suggested Readings

Agnew, R. 1992. Foundation for a General Strain Theory of Crime and Delinquency. *Criminology* 30: 47-87.

———. 1997. Stability and Change over the Lifecourse: A Strain Interpretation. In T. Thornberry, ed. *Developmental Theories of Crime and Delinquency*. New Brunswick, New Jersey: Transaction Publishers.

———. 2005. *Why do Criminals Offend?: A General Theory of Crime and Delinquency*. Los Angeles: Roxbury.

Agnew, R., T. Brezina, J. Wright, and F. Cullen. 2002. Strain, Personality Traits, and Delinquency: Extending General Strain Theory. *Criminology* 40: 43-73.

Dashkov, G. 1992. Quantitative and Qualitative Changes in Crime in the USSR. *British Journal of Criminology* 32: 160-165.

Durkheim, E. 1950. *The Rules of the Sociological Method*. Glencoe, Illinois: Free Press.

———. 1951a. *The Division of Labor in Society*. Glencoe, Illinois: Free Press.

Gilsinan, J. 1990. *Criminology and Public Policy: An Introduction*. Englewood Cliffs, New Jersey: Prentice Hall.

Glueck, Sheldon. 1956. Theory and Fact in Criminology: A Criticism of Differential Association Theory. *British Journal of Criminology* 7: 92-109.

Gonczol, K. 1993. Anxiety over Crime. *Hungarian Quarterly* 129: 87-99.

Gottfredson, M. and T. Hirschi. 1990. *A General Theory of Crime*. Palo Alto, California: Stanford University Press.

Hirschi, T. 1977. Causes and Prevention of Juvenile Delinquency. *Sociological Inquiry* 47: 322-341.

Matsueda, R. 1982. Testing Control Theory and Differential Association: A Causal Modeling Approach. *American Sociological Review* 47: 489-504.

Merton, R. 1957. *Social Theory and Social Structure*. New York: Free Press.

Nettler, G. 1978. *Explaining Crime*. New York: McGraw Hill.

Rodkin, P., T. Farmer, R. Pearl, and R. Van Acker. 2000. Heterogeneity of Popular Boys: Antisocial and Prosocial Configurations. *Developmental Psychology* 36: 14-24.

Stark, R. 1987. Deviant Places: A Theory of the Etiology of Crime. *Criminology* 25: 893-909.

Sutherland, E. and D. Cressey. 1978. *Principles of Criminology*. Philadelphia, Pennsylvania: Lippincott.

Taylor, I., P. Walton, and J. Young. 1973. *The New Criminology*. New York: Harper and Row.

Thornberry, T. P. ed., *Developmental Theories of Crime and Delinquency*. New Brunswick, New Jersey: Transaction Publishers.

———. 2005. *Why do Criminals Offend? A General Theory of Crime and Delinquency.* Los Angeles, Roxbury.

Walsh, A. 2000. Behavior Genetics and Anomie/Strain Theory. *Criminology* 38: 1075-1107.

Wright, J. and K. Beaver. 2005. Do Parents Matter in Creating Self-Control in their Children? A Genetically Informed Test of Gottfredson and Hirschi's Theory of Low Self-Control. *Criminology* 43: 1169-1202.

CHAPTER 3

Biosocial Theories

From the fact that crime is a phenomenon of normal sociology, it does not follow that the criminal is an individual normally constituted from the biological and psychological points of view.

—Emile Durkheim

Many sociologists interpret Durkheim's dictum that the causes of social facts "should be sought among the social facts preceding it" (1982: 110) to mean that there are no other sources of human social behavior. The epigraph to this chapter, also written by Durkheim, reminds sociologists that his dictum is simply a definition of their discipline's boundaries, not an assertion of biological and psychological irrelevance (Udry 1995). As indicated in Chapter 1, crime is a social fact, and its definition, spread, concentration, and prevalence are rightly within the domain or boundaries of sociology. However, criminality is a characteristic of persons possessing brains, genes, hormones, and personalities, which are the domains of psychology and biology. This chapter provides a brief overview of some of the contributions of these sciences that should be part of correctional workers' repertoire of knowledge.

No researcher in these traditions posits the existence of "crime genes." However, some genes through a variety of neurohormonal routes lead to particular traits and characteristics that increase the probability of criminal behavior. As one group of researchers put it: "The question in no longer whether but how genes influence behavior" (McGue, Bacon, and Lykken 1993: 107). This is not to say that genes influence behavior independently of the environment, or that one is more important than the other is. To ask whether genes or the environment is more important to behavior is like asking whether the violin or the violinist is more important to the music. We can analyze both the qualities of the player and the instrument separately, but the music is the result of the interaction of both. The time is long past due to put the sterile nature versus nurture debate out to pasture, and to acknowledge the reality of nature via nurture.

Psychopathy

Psychopaths have been with us since the dawn of time, and many early writers recognized many of the same characteristics that we do today. For instance, in the *Nicomachean Ethics*, Aristotle speaks of "brutish nature," which arises from three sources: (a) "by reason of injuries to the system, (b) by reason of acquired habits, and (c) by reason of originally bad nature" (1947: 453).

French psychiatrist Phillipe Pinel introduced the term psychopath in the eighteenth century, and it has had a checkered career ever since. Conceptual and ideological arguments associated with the psychopathic syndrome moved Gibbons (1973: 171) to state: "We regard any attempt to proceed further with the psychopathy/criminality line of inquiry a futile business." Numerous studies prior and subsequent to Gibbons' cavalier dismissal of the usefulness of the concept of psychopathy strongly suggest that his opinion was ill considered. Such studies have shown rather convincingly that psychopaths can be distinguished from nonpsychopaths biologically, psychologically, and sociologically (Mealey 1995, Hare 1996, Pitchford 2001, Walsh and Wu 2008). Although the behavior of psychopaths and sociopaths is essentially identical, most researchers in this area reserve the term *psychopath* for those whose antisocial behavior they consider primarily genetic in origin, and *sociopath* for those whose antisocial behavior is mostly environmental in origin.

It is well known that a small number of recidivists account for the lion's share of serious crime. The classic study of a birth cohort of 10,000 males in Philadelphia found that 35 percent of the boys were arrested one or more times before reaching adulthood (Wolfgang, Figlio, and Sellin 1972). However, a mere 18 percent of those arrested (6.3 percent of the total cohort) accounted for 52 percent of all offenses and 66 percent of all violent offenses committed by members of the cohort. Other cohort studies in various countries have shown essentially the same results; that is, a relatively small number of offenders are responsible for roughly two-thirds of all serious crimes (Tracy, Wolfgang, and Figlio 1990, Farrington 2001).

Although the studies were interested in identifying recidivists and not psychopaths per se, it is reasonable to assume that many of those chronic and violent recidivists possessed many of the descriptive features of psychopaths. Note that not all criminals are psychopaths, and not all psychopaths are criminals. While estimates of the number of psychopaths in society range between 3 to 4 percent (Walsh and Wu 2008), they make up 15 to 20 percent of our prison population (Hare 1996). Psychopaths are also overrepresented in occupations that require ruthlessness and callous exploitation such as the highly competitive corporate world and elite military forces. Of course, the great majority of people in these occupations are not psychopaths.

However, how do we determine who is and who is not a psychopath? Some estimate that between 1 and 3 percent of the male population and less than 1 percent of the female population are psychopaths (Pitchford 2001). Currently, the most widely used measure of psychopathy is the Psychopathy Checklist-Revised (PCL-R) devised by Robert Hare, arguably the leading expert in psychopathy (Bartol 2002). Clinicians rate patients as either having or not having each of twenty behavior/personality traits presented in the PCL-R, such as those listed below and receive an overall score. Diagnoses require interviews of about two hours, augmented by pertinent file data from probation/parole and prison sources. Persons who receive a total score of thirty or higher receive a diagnosis of psychopathy (Hare 1996). Correctional workers cannot validly use the PCC-R unless they are registered doctoral level clinicians trained in the method. Hare's website (http://www.hare.org/pclr/) provides full information on the skills and background required to administer the PCL-R.

Theories of Psychopathy

Researchers from a variety of sources (Hare 1993, Lykken 1995, Mealey 1995) describe the most common features of psychopaths:

- Unable to profit from experience
- Lack a sense of responsibility
- Unable to form meaningful relationships
- Lack impulse control
- Lack moral sense
- Consistently antisocial
- Punishment has no effect in changing their behavior
- Emotionally immature
- Glib and superficial
- Unable to experience feelings of guilt
- Extremely self-centered

The majority of researchers in this area tend to agree that psychopathy is the result of interplay of genetic and environmental influences. Genes and the environments are positively correlated; that is, they are not random with respect to one another. This idea enables us to conceptualize the indirect way (there is no direct way) that genes help to determine what aspects of the environment will be important and rewarding to us. Offenders, like the rest of us, take an active part in forging their own environment and are not merely the pawns of it. Behavior geneticists speak of three kinds of gene/environment correlation: passive, reactive, and active (Rutter 2007).

The basic idea behind passive gene/environment correlation is that parents provide children with genes for particular traits and an environment conducive to their development. For instance, athletic parents pass on genes related to athletic ability (strength, speed, coordination, and competitiveness) to their offspring and provide them with an environment (equipment, training, and the modeling and encouragement) that facilitates the expression of the genes underlying athleticism. The term *passive* does not imply that children do not actively engage their environment, it simply means that they have merely been exposed to it and have not been active in forming it. That is, the trait(s) in question develop independently of anything the child has done. The role of passive gene/environment correlation is limited to infancy and toddlerhood, after which the child's interactions with others outside the family begin to exert their influence.

Reactive gene/environment correlation picks up the developmental trajectory started by passive gene/environment correlation, and refers to the reactions of others evoked by the child's expression of his or her traits. A pleasant, outgoing, cooperative, and well-mannered child will evoke positive responses from parents, teachers, and peers, whereas a child exhibiting the opposite traits will evoke negative responses. The typical social science explanation of children's behavior is that it is shaped by the way others treat them, ignoring the fact that the treatment of children by others is as much a function of children's evocative behavior as it is of the interaction style of those who respond to them. The traits children bring with them to their interactions increase or decrease the probability of evoking certain kinds of responses from others.

Some children may be so resistant to parental control that parents either resort to extreme forms of punishment or give up on the child altogether. Social scientists have a tendency to attribute the behavioral problems of such children to their parent's "harsh" or "permissive" parental style, ignoring completely that "parental styles" evolved, in large part, in response to the children's behavior. An extreme punitive or permissive parental response will tend to make such a child's antisocial traits worse and drive him or her to seek environments in which such behavior is accepted. Individuals similarly disposed usually populate these environments: "Birds of a feather flock together."

Active gene/environment correlation refers to the seeking of environments compatible with our genetic dispositions. Our genes, within the range of cultural possibilities and constraints, help to determine what features of the environment will be rewarding to us, and what features will not. Active gene/environment correlation gains momentum as individuals mature and acquire the ability to take greater control of their lives and to construct their environments consistent with their innate dispositions. Daring and adventurous people are not likely to seek careers as accountants or bankers, and fearful and introverted people are not likely to become police officers or firefighters. The affects of genes on forming these environments can be gauged by studies showing that the intelligence, personalities, and attitudes of monozygotic (identical) twins are essentially unaffected by whether they were reared together. That is, identical twins reared apart construct their environments about as similarly as they would have if they had been reared together and considerably more similarly than dizygotic (fraternal) twins and no twin siblings reared together (Wong, Gottesman, and Petronis 2005).

The second behavioral genetic concept is that of gene/environment interaction, which is different from, but related to, gene/environment correlation. It involves the reasonable assumption that, largely because of genetic differences, different people will interact with and respond to their environments in different ways. For instance, relatively fearless and impulsive children are genetically more vulnerable to opportunities for antisocial behavior in their environment than are more fearful and less impulsive children, and the effects of parental scolding in response to poor behavior may have a positive effect on future behavior for some children, no effect on others, and even a negative effect on others. In other words, identical environments may have radically different meanings for different individuals and thus result in quite different behaviors.

Reward Dominance Theory

Reward dominance, or BIS/BAS theory, is a neurological theory of psychopathy and criminal behavior based on the proposition two opposing mechanisms; the behavioral activating (or approach) system (BAS) and the behavioral inhibition system (BIS), which regulate our behavior. The BAS motivates us to pursue things that are rewarding to us, and the BIS prevents us from going too far in that pursuit (Kruesi et al. 1994). The BAS acts like an accelerator rushing us toward the fulfillment of some desire (food, drink, cognitive, physical, emotional and sexual pleasures), and the BIS acts like a brake, which, in response to punishment cues from the environment, stops us from overdoing it. A normal BAS combined with a faulty BIS or vice versa may lead to a "craving brain." This can get us into all sorts of physical, social, moral, and legal difficulties, such as obesity, alcoholism, drugs, gambling, and sexual addictions (Ruden 1997).

The BAS is primarily associated with dopamine (one of a class of chemicals known as neurotransmitters) operating on an area of the brain known as the nucleus accumbens, a structure particularly rich in neurons (brain cells) that produce and respond to dopamine. The nucleus accumbens is a major "pleasure center" in the brain. The BIS is primarily associated with serotonin, another kind of neurotransmitter that often serves as a neuromodulator. Regardless of where it operates, dopamine facilitates goal-directed behavior, and serotonin generally modulates that behavior (Depue and Collins 1999).

The BAS and BIS are balanced (in a state of dopamine/serotonin equilibrium) in most people most of the time. In other words, we are more or less equally sensitive to both reward and punishment (Ruden 1997). For others, one system might dominate the other most or all of the time. Reward-dominance theory asserts that criminals, especially chronic criminals and psychopaths, have a dominant BAS. This means that they tend to be overly sensitive to reward contingencies and relatively insensitive to punishment cues (Yacubian et al. 2007, Lykken 1995). Persons with a relatively strong BIS and/or a relatively weak BAS, are likely to suffer from obsessive-compulsive disorder. Such persons are polar opposites of psychopaths–wracked with unreasonable guilt and self-doubt (Yacubian et al. 2007).

Experts add a third system of behavior control, the fight/flight system to the BAS/BIS model. The fight/flight system is a subsystem of the autonomic nervous system (ANS) specializing in responding to threats. The ANS has two complementary branches, the sympathetic and the parasympathetic. The sympathetic branch mobilizes the body's endocrine system to pump out epinephrine (adrenaline) in response to environmental threats. The sympathetic branch of the ANS (specifically, the fight/flight system) responds to fear and mobilizes an organism to do something about it by changing numerous aspects of its physiology from its normal balanced state. Unlike the BAS, which activates us to seek rewarding experiences, the fight/flight system activates us to escape from actual and potential treats to our well-being. The parasympathetic branch restores the body to equilibrium after the threat is over.

Just as individuals differ in terms of BAS/BIS functioning, they differ in terms of arousal, most having a fight/flight system that is neither too active nor too sluggish.

However, a small number of people have a hyperactive fight/flight system. These people are very fearful and condition very easily because fight/flight-system arousal produces punishing visceral feelings associated with anxiety, guilt, and fear. They are very law-abiding because even the contemplation of nonconforming behavior arouses uncomfortable feelings. Erasing or dismissing these antisocial thoughts provides the person with a visceral reward in the form of restoring the fight/flight system to equilibrium. The reduction of fear and anxiety is one of the most powerful rewards known to psychology.

A hyperactive fight/flight system is thus a protective factor against criminal behavior, even among people at high environmental risk for crime. Brennan and her colleagues (1997) found that males in high-crime environments who had highly reactive fight/flight systems were significantly less likely to exhibit antisocial behavior than males in the same environment who had a normal or a hyporesponsive fight/flight system (an example of gene/environment interaction). In fact, they even committed fewer antisocial acts than males in low-crime environments with normal or hyporeactive systems.

Individuals with a hypo-arousable fight/flight systems are relatively fearless and difficult to condition. They do not receive visceral reinforcement for conforming behavior because they are not viscerally aroused to fear, anxiety, and guilt in the first place, and thus cannot receive positive reinforcement in the form of a return to an unaroused state (Raine 1997). Individuals with a relatively unresponsive fight/flight system are low in the neurotransmitter norepinephrine, and are by definition, relatively fearless, an attribute that can be quite useful when engaging in criminal activity (as well as a number of prosocial activities such as acting as a police officer or firefighter). A review of forty studies of ANS arousal and criminal and antisocial behavior found that thirty-eight (95 percent) supported the link and only two had nonsignificant results (Ellis and Walsh 2000: 282).

Figure 3.1 presents a model of reward-dominance theory. According to the theory, psychopaths or chronic criminals are high on novelty seeking (strong BAS), low on inhibition (weak BIS), and relatively fearless (hypoarousable fight/flight system). The acquisition of rewards is the dominant concern for them rather than the avoidance of punishment. Obsessive-compulsive disordered individuals occupy the polar opposite in the figure because whereas psychopaths are very self-confident and relatively guilt free, obsessive compulsives are plagued with self-doubts and unreasonable guilt (Kruesi et al. 1994).

Figure 3.1   BAS, BIS, and FFS with Locations of Psychopaths and Obsessive Compulsives

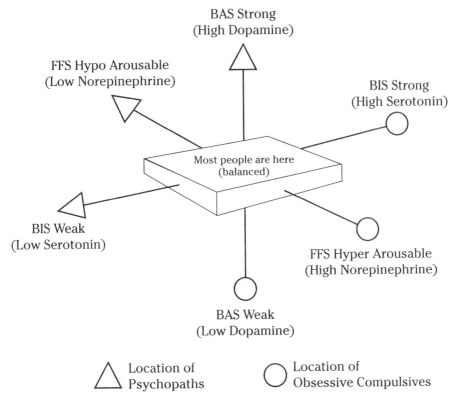

Suboptimal Arousal Theory

As the name implies, suboptimal arousal theory also concentrates on differential arousal levels, but focuses on a more primitive brain structure called the *reticular activating system* (RAS). The RAS is a finger-sized bundle of neurons extending from the spinal column into other brain areas and is a vital regulator of neurological arousal. Suboptimal arousal theory is based on the well-established finding that different levels of neurological arousal correlate with different personality and behavioral patterns (Ellis 1996). The theory states that in the range of everyday environmental situations, the level of stimulation most people find optimal some find boring, and others find uncomfortably overstimulating. To be "optimally aroused" means that the environment is neither too constant nor too varied for you. What is an optimal level of environmental stimulation for most of us will be stressful for some and boring for others.

Some individuals are augmenters of environmental stimulation; that is, they possess a RAS that is highly sensitive to incoming stimuli (more information is taken in and processed). Others are reducers possessing a RAS that is unusually insensitive (less information is taken in and processed). Augmentation or reduction is solely a function of the differential physiology of the RAS; no conscious attempt to augment or reduce incoming stimuli is implied. Males tend to be reducers and females tend to be augmenters, although there is a great deal of overlap (Walsh and Ellis 2007).

Augmenters tend to prefer more constancy than variety in their world and seek to tone down the level of environmental stimuli that most of us find to be "just right." We rarely find such people in criminal populations. Reducers, on the other hand, tend to become easily bored with "just right" levels of stimulation, and continually seek to boost stimuli to more comfortable levels (van Goozen et al. 2007).

Relative to the general population, criminals, especially serious criminals, are chronically underaroused as determined by EEG brain wave patterns, resting heart rate, and skin conductance measures (van Goozen et al. 2007). Individuals who are chronically bored and continually seeking intense stimulation are not likely to apply themselves to school or work (much too boring!), and tend to find the level of stimulation they require in drug usage, risk-taking, sexual promiscuity, and criminal behavior. Antisocial behavior relieves miscreants of their suboptimally aroused (bored) state (see Dr. Freeman's "Case Study" in Chapter 2). Many criminals report that the primary reward that they receive from their activities is the "buzz," or the "high" they get from it rather than any monetary rewards, which are often far too meager to serve as motivators (Gove and Wilmoth 2003, Young 2003).

Cheater Theory

Cheater theory (Mealey 1995) is based on evolution by natural selection. Genes underlying any trait that somehow conferred an advantage in terms of survival and reproduction were selected for retention in future generations. Reproductive success refers to the number of offspring an animal produces that survive and reproduce. They can achieve reproductive success by fair means or foul. A small percentage of males in many nonhuman species follow what biologists call a cheater reproductive strategy (Mealey 1995). Males following this strategy do not abide by the normal courtship rules of the species, but rather achieve sexual intercourse by coercive and/or sneaky tactics (Alcock 1998).

Although the traits conducive to cheating behavior are normally distributed in the population, a small but stable percentage of individuals are at one extreme of the distribution and for them cheating is a genetically obligatory strategy. An obligate cheater strategy is likely to evolve alongside the more typical rule-based strategy (in which cheating behavior is environmentally dependent rather than genetic) when its reproductive gains are frequency-dependent. Frequency-dependent selection occurs when an alternative mating strategy, in other words, high reproductive success when few practice it, but low success when it becomes more common. That is, when there are few cheats, each one employs numerous exploitation opportunities, but when many follow the strategy, there are fewer potential victims per cheat, and there is also a greater awareness of the strategy, and thus a lowered probability of its success (Machalek 1995). Cheaters in ancestral environments enjoyed enough reproductive success that they passed on genes underlying the traits for the strategy.

What does all this talk about sex and reproductive success have to do with criminals? Quite a lot. Cheater theory avers that psychopaths are the human analogs of cheater males in other species. That is, a small but stable number of human males exist and for them noncheating behavior (rule-based) behavior is almost impossible. This applies to any sort of behavior, not just sexual behavior, because the traits useful for pursuing a cheater reproductive strategy (manipulation; deceitfulness; aggression, lack of empathy, shame, and altruism, and so forth) are also useful in following a criminal strategy.

A large amount of evidence supports the relationship between criminal and promiscuous sexual behavior. Both male and female criminals have significantly more sex partners and begin having sex at an earlier age than do people in general. A review of fifty-two studies from seven different countries found that fifty-one reported a significant positive relationship between the number of sex partners and a variety of criminal/antisocial behaviors, but only one found a nonsignificant relationship. Regarding age of onset of sexual behavior, all thirty-one reviewed studies found that the earlier the onset of sexual activity, the greater the involvement in criminal behavior (Ellis and Walsh 2000: 227). A British cohort study found that the most antisocial 10 percent of males in the cohort fathered 27 percent of the children (Jaffe et al. 2003), and a molecular genetic study found the same genetic polymorphisms that were significantly related to number of sexual partners were also significantly related to antisocial behavior (Beaver, Wright, and Walsh 2008).

The probable adaptation aiding psychopaths in the pursuit of their goals is the muting of the neurohormonal mechanisms regulating the social emotions so that they have little real understanding of what it is like to feel guilt, shame, anxiety, and empathy (Mealey 1995, Weibe 2004). Social emotions have evolved as integral parts of our social intelligence that serve to provide clues about the kinds of relationships (cooperative versus uncooperative) that we are likely to have with others (Walsh 2006). Emotions animate, focus, and modify neural activity in ways that lead us to choose certain responses over other possible responses from the streams of information we constantly receive. They cause positive and negative feelings when we survey the consequences of our behavior.

For instance, cooperation evokes rewarding emotions such as a deepened sense of friendship and a heightened sense of obligation and gratitude that enhances future cooperation. Mutual cheating evokes negative emotions, as both parties feel rejected and angry. When one party cooperates and the other cheats, the cooperator feels angry and betrayed, and the cheater feels anxiety and guilt. The more intensely we feel these emotions, the less likely we are to cheat, and the less we feel them, the more likely we are to cheat. In short, emotions move us to behave in ways that enhanced our distant ancestor's reproductive success by overriding decisions suggesting alternatives to cooperation (in other words, cheating), which may have been more rational in the short term, but which were ultimately maladaptive.

The defining neurophysiological characteristic of psychopaths (the quintessential cheats) is their inability to "tie" the brain's cognitive and emotional networks together (Mealey 1995, Patrick 1994). Because psychopaths operate "below the emotional poverty line" (Hare 1993: 134), they do not reveal clues that would allow others to judge their intentions, thus making it easier for them to manipulate and deceive others. Lacking emotional self-regulation, they also tend to make social decisions exclusively based on rational calculations of immediate costs or benefits. Thus, it is important not to attribute the psychopath's inability to learn from experience and for the inability of punishment to alter his or her behavior to low intelligence, but rather to defective emotional controls.

Prefrontal Dysfunction (PFD) Theory

The prefrontal cortex (PFC) is a particularly prominent and important feature of the human brain. The prefrontal cortex is responsible for a number of uniquely human attributes such as making moral judgments, planning, analyzing, synthesizing, and modulating emotions. These are collectively referred to as executive functions. Given this important function, any dysfunction of the prefrontal cortex can result in antisocial behavior. Studies have found that individuals with lesions to the prefrontal cortex have reduced anxiety and fear and are less reactive to stressors of all kinds (reviewed in Raine 1997). Prefrontal cortex damage need not be anatomically discernible to affect behavior negatively; damage could be at the cellular level and be the result of genetic factors that affect neurons during the earliest stages of frontal lobe growth and development, or maternal substance abuse during pregnancy (Pihl and Bruce 1995). Experts have linked even slight damage to the prefrontal cortex, particularly to the left hemisphere, to a number of cognitive deficits (Reiss et al. 1996).

Adrian Raine (1997) claims that prefrontal dysfunction theory can account for some of the physiological arousal factors observed in antisocial individuals by relating physiological functioning with psychological processes. For instance, reduced physiological arousal is associated with reduced arousal in certain areas of the prefrontal cortex. Evidence is most sound for criminals convicted of impulsive crimes, as we might expect, given the executive function of the prefrontal cortex. A number of brain-imaging studies find impulsive offenders to show less prefrontal cortex arousal, and those diagnosed with antisocial personality disorder (APD) to have less prefrontal gray matter, and to evidence reduced ANS activity (Raine et al. 2000).

Arousal Theories and Child Abuse/Neglect

Human beings have powerful neurological and hormonal structures that demand the formation of bonds of affection (Fisher 1998). Lacking the physical manifestations of love during infancy often produces people who are themselves unable to love (Kraemer, 1992, Walsh 1995). People who lack the ability to love, that is, to care, respect, nurture, give, and empathize, find it easy to victimize others. Glasser (1976: 187), for instance, estimates are that about 85 percent of those in constant and violent conflict with the law have not had these needs met. Abuse and neglect is a palpable indicator of unmet love needs, and these experiences are stamped on the brain (Glaser 2000, Shore 1997).

The brain is a marvelously plastic organ whose functioning, and even some aspects of its structure, is very sensitive to early environmental input (Pine 2000). Plasticity essentially refers to the physiological calibration of the brain in response to environmental experience, especially early experience (Teicher et al.1997). The experiences that cultivate our beings are perceived, processed, and acted upon through intricate electrochemical interactions among some conservatively estimated 100 billion neurons. Our neurons are connected to each other through a maze of axons and dendrites, with the general structural pattern contained in our genetic blueprints. However, there are not enough DNA molecules in the blueprint to provide specific information about how two neurons are to be connected. The specific patterning and organization of the brain cells are a function of synaptic connections that have become "habitual" through having made frequent connections (a synapse is the interface between neighboring neurons).

Interneuronal connections occur when neurons send axons snaking out to seek other neurons,which are the sources of certain chemicals needed to make the synaptic connection. Interneuronal communication happens with greater facility the more often electrochemical synapses have been made. Organisms, including humans, raised in stimulus-enriched environments develop greater cortical density and greater quantities of essential neurotransmitter chemicals than organisms raised under less stimulating conditions (reviewed in Shore 1997). The young brain makes many more connections than will survive.

Synaptic connections and neuronal pathways are selected for retention or elimination in use-dependent fashion in a process Edelman (1998) refers to as *neural Darwinism*. This is why early experience is neurologically so much more important than later experience. As Perry and Pollard (1998: 36) point out: "Experience in adults alters the organized brain, but in infants and children it organizes the developing brain" (emphasis added). The stimuli associated with affection (touching, kissing, and cuddling) are tactile assurances for the infant that it is loved and secure, and are very important for neural development.

Lack of tactile stimulation and general neglect during the early development of the brain have adverse effects (Gunnar and Quevedo 2007). For instance, the brain's emotional center, the limbic system, contains areas (the hippocampus and the amygdala) that appear quite vulnerable to damage by abuse and neglect. The possible affects of abuse and neglect on these limbic system structures have particular relevance to the operation of the BIS. The hippocampus is a crucial component of the BIS, and protracted abuse and neglect may alter the BIS' threshold setting so that it may often fail to perform its appropriate inhibitory role. The damage is probably the result of the excessive production of stress hormones called *corticosteroids* in response to abuse (Teicher et al. 1997).

Similarly, frequent excitation of the amygdala in response to abuse and neglect may eventually lead to subconvulsive (as opposed to convulsive or epileptic) seizures (van der Kolk and Greenberg 1987). Subconvulsive seizures in the amygdala (the most seizure prone area of the brain) often do not have any immediate environmental derivation. We use the term episodic dyscontrol to describe behavior resulting from subconvulsive seizures (Suchy, Blint, and Osman 1997). Such seizures are related to impulsively violent and acting-out behaviors, but not to any kind of planned criminal behavior (Ellis and Walsh 2000).

Perry (1997) suggests that children who spend a great deal of time in a low-level state of fear tend to focus consistently on nonverbal cues of imminent danger because the brain has been habituated to do so. Perry further remarks that a cognitive profile in which performance IQ is significantly greater than verbal IQ (P>V) is a marker of this tendency. David Wechsler (1958: 176) noted long ago: "The most outstanding feature of the sociopath's test profile is the systematic high score on the performance as compared with the verbal part of the scale." One reviewer of the P>V/crime relationship writes: "This [PIQ > VIQ] relationship was found across studies, despite variations in age, sex, race, setting, and form of Wechsler scale administered, as well as differences in criteria for delinquency" (Miller 1987: 120).

A significant P>V discrepancy at the .01 probability level requires an approximate twelve-point difference between the two IQ subscales. While the P>V profile has been consistently linked with psychopathy and chronic criminal offending (reviewed in Walsh 2003), a significant V>P profile is often found to be a marker of prosocial behavior (Cornel and Wilson 1992). One study of more than 1,800 prison inmates found that V>P males were twenty-nine times less likely to be found in prison populations than P>V males (Barnett, Zimmer, and McCormack 1989). The possible affects of abuse and neglect on cognitive profiles were further evidenced in a study of 513 male delinquents. The study found that illegitimate boys raised by a single mother had higher abuse/neglect scores, higher delinquency scores, and both the highest mean PIQ and lowest mean VIQ scores (and hence the greatest P>V discrepancy) than boys born and reared under other circumstances (Walsh 1990).

It is important to realize that a superior PIQ relative to one's VIQ is indicative of superior right hemisphere brain functioning relative to its left hemisphere functioning. Abused and neglected children may preferentially store their memories in the right hemisphere because abuse and neglect may be "associated with greater left-hemisphere dysfunction, which may lead to greater dependence on the right hemisphere. Increased right frontal function, in turn, may lead to enhanced perception and reaction to negative affect" (Teicher et al. 1997:197).

Physiological arousal patterns may also be affected by childhood abuse and neglect. If a child experiences chronic stress during the organizational phase of brain development, the upshot may be the development of a hyporesponsive ANS as an "inoculation" to stress (Raine 1997). It certainly appears reasonable that children who experience unusual levels of stress and emotional disturbance are likely to develop a mechanism for handling future stress. Experiments have shown that repeated aversive stimuli (for example, electric shock) administered to laboratory animals has a steadily decreasing effect on ANS arousal until they become almost completely unreactive to stimuli that initially produced extreme symptoms of fear and anxiety, such as shaking, urinating, and defecating (Lykken 1995).

Of course, child abuse and neglect does not invariably lead to later antisocial behavior. A team of researchers examined the relationship between child abuse/neglect and an enzyme in the brain that removes excess neurotransmitters called MAOA after they have performed their task. Subjects were a New Zealand male birth cohort followed from birth to age twenty-six (Caspi et al. 2002). Records were available indicating which subjects had suffered childhood forms of maltreatment that included rejection by the child's mother, frequent changes of primary caregiver, physical abuse resulting in injury, and sexual abuse. The combination of maltreatment and low MAOA predicted four antisocial outcomes:

- The psychiatric diagnosis of adolescent conduct disorder (persistent fighting, bullying, lying, stealing, behaving cruelly to people or animals, vandalizing, and disobeying rules)

- Official court records of conviction for violent offenses (assault, robbery, rape, domestic violence, homicide).

- Aggressive personality traits (willingness to harm others for own advantage, interest in and enjoyment of violent material)

- Symptoms of adult antisocial personality disorder (a long-term history of repeated law violations, deceitfulness, conning, impulsivity, physical aggression, and irresponsibility with respect to jobs, spouse, or children, plus lack of remorse).

The most dramatic of the findings in this study was that the odds of subjects with a combination of maltreatment and low MAOA were 9.8 times more than the odds of similarly low MAOA subjects who were not maltreated to be convicted of a violent crime. These subjects also self-reported a significantly greater disposition for violence than low MAOA/nonmaltreated subjects did, and although they constituted only 12 percent of the male cohort, they accounted for 44 percent of its violent convictions. Maltreatment did not result in a significantly elevated risk for violent conviction nor for a greater propensity to self-reported violent disposition among high MAOA subjects. This study provides evidence that genes moderate children's sensitivity to environmental adversities and partly explains why not all abused and neglected children grow up to victimize others.

Good Guys Start Last and Finish First

Self-report studies long have told us that far more teens (especially males) commit delinquent acts than are actually caught and convicted. Some consider boys who do not commit such acts as "statistically deviant" (Farrington, Ohlin, and Wilson 1986: 40). However, after reaching a peak at around sixteen years of age, offending drops sharply, and by the age of twenty-eight about 85 percent of offenders desist from further offending (Moffitt 1993: 675). The vast majority who do not desist in early adulthood are offenders who commenced offending at an earlier age than those who do desist. Moffitt suggests that these two offender groups (early starters/late finishers and late starters/early finishers) represent two different etiological pathways to criminality. However, what is it about adolescence that produces such a surge of antisocial behavior in many teenagers, particularly males?

First, males experience a ten to a fifteen-fold increase in aggression-facilitating (not "causing") testosterone at puberty, which provides them with a lot of gas but nowhere to go. Females also get a slight increase, but males have about twenty times the activating testosterone of females.

Second, MRI studies of brain development confirm what parents have always known, the adolescent brain, particularly the prefrontal cortex, is immature (Giedd et al. 1999, Sowell et al.1999). As noted earlier, the prefrontal cortex serves various executive functions, such as modulating emotions from the limbic system and making reasoned judgments and plans. Most teenagers are not very good at these things. Other MRI studies show that the link between the prefrontal cortex and the limbic system (the seat of our emotions) is not as well connected in adolescent brains as in adult brains (Monk et al. 2008). Adolescence appears to be a period in which the fine-tuning of the brain occurs. This may indicate that the adolescent brain, superimposed on an unfamiliar and diffuse state of physiological arousal, may facilitate a tendency of the young to assign faulty and often negative attributions to the actions of others, which may result in antisocial responses.

Of course, all teenagers undergo this physiological maturation process, but only a few continue to commit serious antisocial acts after adolescence. Terrie Moffitt calls these *life-course persistent offenders*. Moffitt proposes that life-course persistent offenders have temperamental and neuropsychological problems that are evident in early childhood and initiate a number of cumulative negative interactions between them and their environment placing them on a developmental trajectory toward antisocial personality and behavior. As Moffitt describes this trajectory: "biting and hitting at age four, shoplifting and truancy at age ten, selling drugs and stealing cars at age sixteen, robbery and rape at age twenty-two, fraud and child abuse at age thirty; the underlying disposition remains the same, but its expression changes form as new social opportunities arise at different points of time" (1993: 679).

A large number of studies have shown that life-course persistent offenders tend to be hyperactive, inattentive, negatively emotional, and have low-impulse control, and low IQ (Moffitt 1993: 680-681). All these traits are at least partially under genetic control through the operation of the various neurotransmitter and hormonal substances they produce. Hyperactivity and inattentiveness are related to sluggish RAS arousal and negative emotionality (Ellis and Coontz 1990), and low-impulse control to low serotonin, a major mood-modulating neurotransmitter (Spoont 1992).

We will also see later that IQ is substantially inheritable. We can be quite confident, then, that the most serious and persistent of criminals have biological disabilities that put them at risk for offending. This observation does not mean that the social environment is not important to the understanding of life-course persistent offenders' behavior also. Negative emotionality and low-impulse control also have been related to rearing in abusive and discordant families (Caspi et al. 1994), as have ANS hypoarousal and low IQ (reviewed in Walsh 1995). However, behavior is the result of complex interactions between biological and environmental factors.

Moffitt (1993) calls juveniles who discontinue their offending in early adulthood *adolescent-limited offenders*. These offenders begin their offending at puberty, a biological event that suffuses them with boundless energy, strength, fragile confidence, and a strong desire to cut apron strings. Two or three generations ago, boys would have experienced puberty one or two years later, and probably would have obtained socially responsible roles, such as a relatively well paid full-time jobs, fairly shortly afterwards. Given the education required to participate responsibly in today's complex society, modern youth are trapped in a gap of about ten years duration between biological and social maturity rather than the one- or two-year gap experienced two or three generations ago. This gap is tailor-made to be filled with antisocial behavior.

According to Moffitt (1993), many adolescent-limited boys gravitate to the excitement of antisocial peer groups led by "cool" life-course persistent males. Once in these groups, adolescent-limited offenders learn the techniques of offending by mimicking life-course persistent offenders. They receive reinforcement for doing so by receiving material and psychological rewards. With neurological and social maturity (marriage, a job, parenthood, and so on), the vast majority of adolescent-onset offenders recognize the foolishness of their behavior and desist from further offending.

Note how Moffitt's theory differs from differential association, which posits a single causal route to criminality: association with delinquent peers. Moffitt asserts that for the great majority of offenders, association with delinquent peers leads only to temporary antisocial characteristics and offending, and is driven by a biosocial maturity gap. For life-course persistent offenders, association with delinquent peers is driven by their antisocial characteristics, which are the result of temperamental and neurological deficiencies combined with poor parenting. In other words, life-course persistent offenders possess stable antisocial characteristics, which precede and drive antisocial associations, while association with delinquent peers precedes the development of temporary antisocial characteristics for adolescent-limited offenders.

Despite its relatively recent origin, Moffitt's theory has developed a considerable following among criminologists of conservative, moderate, liberal, and even radical views (Walsh 2002). More importantly, and like no other existing theory, Moffitt's theory has been strongly supported over the past decade by researchers working from sociological, psychological, genetic, evolutionary, and neurohormonal perspectives (Moffitt and Walsh 2003).

From Theory to Practice

Correctional worker may use information from these biosocial theories to increase understanding and assessment of their charges. For instance, IQ information is often readily available from schools and/or clinical workups of offenders, and we can calculate P>V discrepancy scores. If psychologists discover a significant P>V, they often will point out that the P>V discrepancy is a marker of psychopathy in their clinical reports. However, you should not conclude that if a person has a significant discrepancy score (twelve or more points), he of she is a psychopath; the P>V test is only a marker, not a definitive test. People who have superior visual/spatial skills, such as mathematicians and engineers, undoubtedly score significantly higher on PIQ than on VIQ. However, both sets of scores for such professionals would be in the superior range, whereas criminals with a P>V profile tend to have an average PIQ (around 100) coupled with a low (below 90) VIQ.

Another marker of violent behavior, favored more by psychiatrists than psychologists, is a history of enuresis (bedwetting), fire setting, and cruelty to animals, all of which are related to suboptimal arousal levels. The response to the necessity to void our bladders during sleep usually results in waking up and doing so. Parents of many violent and psychopathic individuals often report that their children wet the bed well into late childhood or adolescence. Not awakening in response to the urge to void (in the absence of any organic pathology, of course) may be seen as a function of a hyporeactive ANS failing to arouse the child and a general difficulty in the voluntary control of impulses. Ellis and Walsh (2000: 242) found twenty-one studies supportive of the link between enuresis and antisocial behavior and three studies with no significant results.

Setting fires and watching them burn is an exciting activity. Most of us limit this kind of activity to burning leaves and garbage, but some find setting fires to buildings to be intensely stimulating. Since psychopaths lack that attribute, we call a conscience, they may have few qualms about sacrificing someone's home in the pursuit of the visceral excitement they crave. Recall that this need for excessive excitement is a function of sluggish reticular and autonomic systems, which inclines some to consider what many of us find exciting to be eminently boring.

The third behavior of the triad, cruelty to animals, is indicative of the lack of love and sympathy psychopaths have for other living things and their lack of empathy for the suffering of others. The budding psychopath finds cats and hamsters suitable targets for his cruelty until he gets big enough to take on humans.

Any one of these three behaviors taken alone requires a variety of interpretations that do not concern us. Taken together, they constitute an excellent diagnostic tool. Of course, many other variables are predictive of violent behavior. This one, unlike many other predictors, is included almost routinely in the psychiatric reports that you will be reading as correctional workers.

To the extent that Moffitt's two-pathway model of offending is accurate, and studies from around the world support the belief that it is, offenders' rap sheets should tell you a lot about them. All other things being equal, the earlier they began offending, the less likely they are to discontinue, and the less likely they are to respond positively to correctional treatment.

Lessons and Concerns

What are the implications of biosocial theories for the correctional worker beyond an increased understanding of the problem of criminal behavior? Certainly, you can do nothing about the early developmental history of offenders. If abuse and neglect is reflected in the actual structure and functioning of the brain, the answer to the problem, if there is one, lies in social engineering related to child-rearing practices on a massive scale. We thus have returned to sociology and to the same sort of practical difficulties we encountered when examining sociological theories. Bryan Vila (1997) offers abundant evidence that money spent on what he calls nurturant strategies (good quality pre-and post-natal and childcare, paid maternity leave, prevention of unwanted pregnancies, support for families, monitoring of infant development, home health care visits, and so forth) would be money well invested (see also Walsh 1991 and Walsh and Ellis 1997). As corrections practitioners, we can only say is that it would be nice, but we have to adapt ourselves to conditions as they exist. We have the difficult job of trying to correct the damage done, allegedly by the failure to implement such strategies.

The psychopath (who may be synonymous with Moffitt's life-course persistent offenders) is a poor candidate for rehabilitation. Robert Hare (1993: 198-200) states that psychopaths are apparently incapable of the empathy, warmth, and sincerity needed to develop the type of emotional relationship required for effective therapy, and that treatment often makes them worse (they learn how to better push others' buttons). Not only do psychopaths lack these attributes, they lack the anxiety that prods change, and see nothing wrong with themselves, anyway.

Andrews and Bonta (1998) are less pessimistic, insisting that early identification and family interventions such as those recommended by Vila (1997) may work. A correctional worker who is to achieve any success with such individuals must be prepared to set strict limits on their behavior and stand doggedly by them. He or she must be to some extent an authority figure, albeit a warm "parental" authority figure, with offenders assumed to possess this character disorder. Reality therapy (discussed later) may prove to be the most effective method of dealing with the psychopath in a correctional setting.

Criminology for the Twenty-First Century

By Ilhong Yun, Ph.D.

Ilhong Yun is an assistant professor teaching criminology and policing courses at Boise State University. He acquired his master's degree in criminal justice from Michigan State University and doctoral degree in the same area from Sam Houston State University. Before he pursued his graduate degrees, he was a police captain in South Korea for ten years. His research interests include comparative criminal justice issues, fear of crime, and victim services.

● ●

As a recent Ph.D. recipient in the discipline of criminal justice, I have gone through my share of rigor by taking numerous criminology classes throughout graduate school. These classes equipped me with a range of varying theories on causation of crime, which imparted a degree of confidence as I began the academic journey as a researcher and teacher. However, a recent exposure to biosocial approaches to criminology began to cast serious doubt on the confidence that I had. In short, this encounter made me clearly aware that my training in criminology was quite askew—a predominant emphasis on sociological theories of crime while almost ignoring biological explanations.

Sociological paradigms dominated criminological theories during the better part of the twentieth century. In comparison, early biology-based explanations of criminal behavior saw a dramatic decline in the discourses on the causes of crime. Such downturn stemmed in large part from the deliberate or unintentional perversion of "scientific" policies born out of early deterministic biological theories. For example, in the early 1900s more than thirty American states passed laws allowing sterilization of individuals with supposedly criminogenic traits deemed genetically determined. More than 64,000 individuals between 1911 and 1930 were sterilized. For similar reasons, numerous individuals were also lobotomized: a disturbing procedure that entailed massive destruction of the prefrontal cortex. According to sociologists, deterministic biological theories were employed to reinforce racism, rank people, and prevent the spread of "inferior" genes.

Early biological theories were clearly unscientific and soon fell into disfavor, and the aforementioned policies were discontinued outright. Yet, it seems many contemporary criminologists still associate any mention of biology with past unscientific and unjust policies and practices. Therefore, any attempt in the discipline to include biological elements to explain criminal behavior frequently invites hostile derision. Contemporary criminologists, most of whom were trained sociologically, explicitly distance themselves from biosocial criminology theories so much so that theories that incorporate learning, culture, bonding, socialization, and poverty must de-emphasize genes, neurotransmitters, hormones, and evolutionary psychology. For them, any theory that emphasizes individual differences is inherently sexist, racist, or classist. This

Continued on the next page

Criminology for the Twenty-First Century, *continued*

sentiment culminated in 1992 when a plan for an academic conference on genetics and crime faced severe criticism from academics and withdrawal of funding from the National Institute of Health, finally resulting in cancellation of the conference.

The current practice of training new Ph.D.s in criminology and criminal justice attests that biology has taken a conspicuous backseat to sociology. One should realize, however, that this continuing disregard of biology jeopardizes the discipline and does serious disservice to all concerned. Most of all, the current tradition does not take into account the very important fact that biological sciences have accomplished remarkable progress in recent decades in unraveling causes of human behavior, including criminal behavior. The progress is so remarkable that one observer pointed out: "The biological sciences have made more progress in advancing our understanding about behavior in the last ten years than sociology has made in the past fifty years" (Robinson 2004: 72). For instance, brain-imaging techniques and electroencephalographic (EEG) research allow us to peer literally into the minds of murderers and other criminals, revolutionizing our understanding the causes of crime. Exciting and liberating knowledge on brains, hormones, and genes is being poured out everyday. This knowledge was unknown just a few decades ago. What this piling cutting-edge knowledge is pointing at is unequivocally clear and consistent: criminal behavior is a product of the interplay between nature and nurture, genes and the environment.

Take the study recently conducted by Caspi and his colleagues on monoamine oxidase A (MAOA). This enzyme metabolizes brain neurotransmitters including serotonin. Despite decades of sociological research that has consistently demonstrated that abuse of children is a significant predictor of later criminality, children with high MAOA in Caspi et al.'s study were not likely to take the path to delinquency and crime. Those who took the criminal path were children who experienced both a bad environment (abuse and maltreatment) and "bad" genes (low MAOA). In this seminal study, biology provided criminologists a much sought-after answer to the question: why do only some, not all, of the abused and maltreated children grow up to become law violators?

Contrary to sociological "wisdom" asserting that crime is a social phenomenon and can thus only be understood through searching for sociological antecedents, the biosocial approach is an integrative one. It acknowledges that society prepares the stage for crime, but it also emphasizes human beings with brains, genes, and hormones commit crime. Such an integrative approach is essential in criminology because any theory attempting to explain criminal behavior must include both nature and nurture, because any trait, characteristic, or behavior of any living thing is always the result of biological factors interacting with environmental factors (Cartwright 2000, Carey 2003).

The biosocial approach counters the typical argument that any criminology theory that incorporates biology is deterministic is that such argument stems from uninformed and misguided notions of biology. In contrast, the biosocial approach argues that genes and brains are in fact active, constantly responding to the environment, thus shaping and reshaping innumerable neural pathways in the brain. Genes are not puppet masters pulling the strings of our attitudes and behaviors; they dismantle and rebuild in response to their experiences. Take the recent study of cab drivers in London. Structural MRI scans of cab drivers by scientists at University College London showed that the drivers developed a larger posterior hippocampus—a brain structure associated with memory and navigation in animals—than a control group. The longer the cab driver has been on the job, the larger the posterior hippocampus was. This means that the brain is able to change physically according to the way it is used. The result of this study is an ever-apparent testimony to the obvious interplay of environment and biology surrounding humans and their behaviors.

Fortunately, serious scientists are increasingly recognizing that biological processes are at play in the development of criminal behavior. Public interests in this perspective are also increasing. Nevertheless, the discipline of criminology is still reluctant to embrace this emerging body of knowledge seriously. Many reasons might underlie this lingering reluctance other than the historical and moral suspicions of the earlier deterministic approach to crime causation. It might be interdisciplinary rivalries or fear of having to learn an ocean of new vocabulary and knowledge.

In any case, criminology must not remain stagnantly caged in ideological wrangling. It is high time to look for truth grounded on newly emerging scientific facts. Ignoring this compelling scientific evidence is to set criminology aimlessly wandering into sociological badlands. It will do more damage to the discipline than good. As the Asian sage, Confucius, said, true knowledge begins from acknowledging what one does not know yet. Criminologists must know that they do not know what they do not know. There lies true wisdom. Only from there will criminology as a disciple move forward, embracing both biology and sociology.

SUMMARY

The perspective presented in this chapter shows the tendency toward crime is located in the individual. This does not mean that some people are born criminals or that crime is "in the genes." The first concepts we discussed were gene/environment correlation and interaction, noting that genes are constantly in a complex dance with their environments: neither genes nor environments "cause" behavior independently.

We next explored the BIS/BAS concept and noted that inveterate criminals tend to have a dominant BAS. In other words, they tend to be far more sensitive to rewards than to punishment. We looked at psychopathy in terms of suboptimal arousal levels of ANS (specifically, the fight/flight system) and RAS operation and the functioning of the prefrontal cortex. A person with a hyporeactive fight/flight system does not feel the same level of fear and anxiety that those people with a more normally functioning one does. Not being overly concerned with the punitive consequences of criminal activity, lacking a sense of guilt, and lacking sympathy for their victims, psychopaths tend to engage in crime with alarming frequency. Psychopaths and career criminals tend to have high dopamine and low serotonin and norepinepherine levels.

A person with a sluggish RAS is prone to boredom. He or she seeks higher levels of excitement than do most of us, a search that often ends in trouble. A person who is quickly bored is also not very likely to spend much time in academic pursuits that lead to a rewarding legitimate career. Such a person is also quite likely to seek artificial stimulation with drugs and "thrill-seeking" crimes.

We then looked at the possible influence of child abuse and neglect on the structure and functioning of the brain. The experiences that we undergo during the phases of rapid brain cell growth influence the structure and function of our brains. Positive experiences in the form of plentiful stimuli, especially tactile stimuli, have the effect of wiring the brain to experience pleasure in the company of others. Negative early experiences have the opposite effect. Extremely negative experiences during infancy and childhood may lead to future violent behavior of psychopathic proportions.

We then examined Terrie Moffitt's dual-pathway model of the etiology of criminal offending. This model emphasizes that biological factors may be more important than environmental factors in explaining the small percentage of recidivistic offenders she calls "life-course persistent offenders." On the other hand, environmental factors are probably more important for explaining the offending behavior of the majority of offenders who desist with social maturity (adolescent-limited offenders). Moffitt does not neglect environmental factors in the etiology of life-course persistent offenders, however. She emphasizes that inept parenting may interact with temperamental and neurological factors to produce antisocial characteristics.

References and Suggested Readings

Alcock, J. 1998. *Animal Behavior: An Evolutionary Approach*, 6th ed. Sunderland, Massachusetts: Sinauer Associates.

Andrews, D. and J. Bonta. 1998. *The Psychology of Criminal Conduct*. Cincinnati, Ohio: Anderson Publishing.

Aristotle 1947. *Introduction to Aristotle*, Richard McKeon, Ed. New York: The Modern Library.

Baird, A., S. Gruber, D. Fein, L. Maas, R. Steingard, P. Renshaw, B. Cohen, and D. Yurgelun-Todd. 1999. Functional magnetic resonance imaging of facial affect recognition in children and adolescents. *Journal of the Academy of Child and Adolescent Psychiatry* 38: 195-199.

Barnett, R., L. Zimmer, and J. McCormack. 1989. P>V Sign and Personality Profiles. *Journal of Correctional and Social Psychiatry and Offender Treatment and Therapy* 35: 18-20.

Bartol, C. 2002. *Criminal Behavior: A Psychosocial Approach*, 6th ed. Upper Saddle River, New Jersey: Prentice Hall.

Bouchard, T., D. Lykken, M. McGue, N. Segal, and A. Tellegen. 1990. Sources of human psychological differences: The Minnesota study of twins reared apart. *Science* 250: 223-228.

Beaver, K., J. Wright, and A. Walsh. 2008. A gene-based evolutionary explanation for the association between criminal involvement and number of sex partners. *Biodemography and Social Biology* 54: 47-55.

Brennan, P., A. Raine, F. Schulsinger, L. Kirkegaard-Sorenen, J. Knop, B. Hutchings, R. Rosenberg, and S. Mednick 1997. Psychophysiological protective factors for male subjects at high risk for criminal behavior. *American Journal of Psychiatry* 154: 853-855.

Carey, G. 2003. *Human Genetics for the Social Sciences*. Thousand Oaks, California: Sage

Cartwright, J. 2000. *Evolution and Human Behavior*. Cambridge, Massachusetts: MIT Press.

Caspi, A., J. McClay, T. Moffitt, J. Mill, J. Martin, I. Craig, A. Taylor, and R. Poulton. 2002. Evidence that the cycle of violence in maltreated children depends on genotype. *Science* 297: 851-854.

Caspi, A., T. Moffitt, P. Silva, M. Stouthamer-Loeber, R. Krueger, and P. Schmutte. 1994. Are Some People Crime Prone? Replications of the Personality-Crime Relationship Across Countries, Genders, Races, and Methods. *Criminolgy* 32: 163-195.

Cornell, D. and L. Wilson 1992. The PIQ>VIQ discrepancy in violent and nonviolent delinquents. *Journal of Clinical Psychology* 48: 256-261.

Depue, R. and P. Collins.1999. Neurobiology of the structure of personality: Dopamine, facilitation of incentive motivation, and extraversion. *Behavioral and Brain Sciences* 22: 491-569.

Durkheim, E. 1982. *Rules of Sociological Method*. S. Lukes, trans. New York: Free Press.

Edelman, G. 1999. Building a Picture of the Brain. *Daedalus* 127: 37-69.

Ellis, L. 1990. Universal Behavioral and Demographic Correlates of Criminal Behavior: Toward Common Ground in the Assessment of Criminological Theories. In L. Ellis and H. Hoffman, eds. *Crime in Biological, Social, and Moral Contexts*. Westport, Connecticut: Praeger.

———.1996. Arousal theory and the religiosity-criminality relationship. In P. Cordella and L. Siegel, eds., *Readings in Contemporary Criminological Theory*. Boston: Northeastern University Press.

Ellis, L. and P. Coontz. 1990. Androgens, Brain Functioning, and Criminality: The Neurohormonal Foundation of Antisociality. In L. Ellis and H. Hoffman, eds. *Crime in Biological, Social, and Moral Contexts*. Westport, Connecticut: Praeger.

Ellis, L. and A. Walsh. 2000. *Criminology: A Global Perspective*. Boston: Allyn and Bacon.

Farrington, D. 2001. Cross-National Comparative Studies in Criminology. In H. Pontell and D. Shichor, eds. *Contemporary Issues in Crime and Criminal Justice*. Upper Saddle River, New Jersey: Prentice Hall.

Farrington, D., L. Ohlin, and J. Wilson. 1986. *Understanding and Controlling Crime: Toward a New Research Strategy*. New York: Springer-Verlag.

Fisher, H. 1998. Lust, attraction, and attachment in mammalian reproduction. *Human Nature* 9: 23-52.

Gibbons, D. 1973. *Society, Crime, and Criminal Careers*. Englewood Cliffs, New Jersey: Prentice Hall.

Giedd, J., J. Blumenthal, N. Jeffries, F. Castellanos, H. Liu, A. Zijenbos, T. Paus, A. Evans, and J. Rapoport 1999. Brain development during childhood and adolescence: A longitudinal MRI study. *Nature Neuroscience* 2: 861-863.

Glaser, D. 2000. Child abuse and neglect and the brain—A review. *Journal of Child Psychology and Psychiatry* 41: 97-116.

Glasser, W. 1976. *The Identity Society*. New York: Harper and Row.

Gove, W. and C. Wilmoth. 2003. The neurophysiology of motivation and habitual criminal behavior. In A. Walsh and L. Ellis, eds., *Biosocial Criminology: Challenging Environmentalism's Supremacy,*. Hauppauge, New York: Nova Science. pp. 225-245.

Gunnar, M. and K. Quevedo. 2007. The neurobiology of stress and development. *Annual Review of Psychology* 58: 145-173.

Hare, R. 1993. *Without Conscience: The Disturbing World of the Psychopaths among Us*. New York: Pocket Books.

———. 1996. Psychopathy: A Clinical Construct Whose Time Has Come. *Criminal Justice and Behavior* 23: 25-54.

Jaffe, S., T. Moffitt, A. Caspi, and A. Taylor. 2003. Life with (or without) father: The benefits of living with two biological parents depend on the father's antisocial behavior. *Child Development* 74: 109-126.

Kalil, R. 1989. Synapse Formation in the Developing Brain. *Scientific American* 76: 85.

Kraemer, G. 1992. A Psychobiological Theory of Attachment. *Behavioral and Brain Sciences* 15: 493-541.

Kruesi, M., H. Leonard, S. Swedo, S. Nadi, S. Hamburger, J. Lui, and J. Rapoport 1994. Endogenous opioids, childhood psychopathology, and Quay's interpretation of Jeffrey Gray. In D. Routh, ed., *Disruptive Behavior Disorders in Childhood*. New York: Plenum.

Lykken, D. 1995. T*he Antisocial Personalities*. Hillsdale, New Jersey: Lawrence Erlbaum.

Machalek, R. 1995. Basic dimensions and forms of social exploitation: A comparative analysis. *Advances in Human Ecology* 4: 35-68.

McGue, M., S. Bacon, and D. Lykken. 1993. Personality Stability and Change in Early Adulthood: A Behavioral Genetic Analysis. *Developmental Psychology* 29: 96-109.

Mealey, L. 1995. The Sociobiology of Sociopathy: An Integrated Evolutionary Model. *Behavioral and Brain Sciences* 18: 523-599.

Miller, L. 1987. Neuropsychology of the Aggressive Psychopath: An Integrative Review. *Aggressive Behavior* 13: 119-140.

Moffitt, T. 1993. Adolescent-limited and Life-course Persistent Antisocial Behavior: A Developmental Taxonomy. *Psychological Review* 100: 674-701.

Moffitt, T. and A. Walsh. 2003. The Adolescent-Limited/Life-Course Persistent Theory of Antisocial Behavior: What have we Learned? In A. Walsh and L. Ellis, eds., *Biosocial Criminology: Challenging Environmentalism's Supremacy*, Hauppauge, NY: Nova Science. pp. 123-144.

Monk, C., R. Klein, E. Telzer, E. Schroth, S. Mannuzza, J. Moulton, M. Guardino, C. Masten, E. McClure-Tone, S. Fromm, R. Blair, D. Pine, and M. Ernst. 2008. Amygdala and nucleus accumbens activation to emotional facial expressions in children and adolescents at risk for major depression. *American Journal of Psychiatry* 165: 90-98.

Patrick, C. 1994. Emotion and Psychopathy: Startling New Insights. *Psychophysiology* 31: 319-330.

Perry, B. 1997. Incubated in Terror: Neurodevelopmental Factors in the "Cycle of Violence." In J. Osofsky, ed., *Children in a Violent Society*. New York: Guilford Press.

Perry, B. and R. Pollard 1998. Homeostasis, Stress, Trauma, and Adaptation: A Neurodevelopmental View of Childhood Trauma. *Child and Adolescent Psychiatric Clinics of America,* 733-51.

Pihl, R. and K. Bruce. 1995. Cognitive Impairments in Children of Alcoholics. *Alcohol, Health, and Research World* 19: 142-147.

Pinel, J. 2000. *Biopsychology*, 4th ed. Boston: Allyn and Bacon.

Pitchford, I. 2001. The origins of violence: Is psychopathy an adaptation? *The Human Nature Review* 1: 28-38.

Raine, A. 1997. Antisocial behavior and psychophysiology: A biosocial perspective and a prefrontal dysfunction hypothesis. In D. Stoff, J. Breiling, and J. Maser, eds., *Handbook of Antisocial Behavior*. New York: John Wiley.

Raine, A., T. Lencz, S. Buhrle, L. LaCasse, and P. Colletti. 2000. Reduced prefrontal gray matter volume and reduced autonomic activity in antisocial personality disorder. *Archives of General Psychiatry* 57: 119-127.

Reiss, A., M. Abrams, H. Singer, J. Ross and M. Bencla. 1996. Brain development, gender and IQ in children: A volumetric imaging study. *Brain* 119: 1763-1774.

Robinson, M. 2004. *Why Crime? An Integrated Systems Theory of Antisocial Behavior*. Upper Saddle River, New Jersey: Prentice Hall.

Ruden, R. 1997. *The Craving Brain: The Biobalance Approach to Controlling Addictions*. New York: Harper Collins.

Rutter, M. 2007. Gene-environment interdependence. *Developmental Science* 10: 12-18.

Shore, R. 1997. *Rethinking the Brain: New Insights into Early Development*. New York: Families and Work Institute.

Sowell, E., P. Thompson, C. Holmes, T. Jernigan, and A. Toga. 1999. In vivo evidence for post-adolescent brain maturation in frontal and striatal regions. *Nature Neuroscience* 2: 859-861.

Spoont, M. 1992. Modulatory Role of Serotonin in Neural Information Processing: Implications for Human Psychopathology. *Psychological Bulletin* 112: 330-350.

Suchy, Y., A. Blint, and D. Osman. 1997. Behavioral Dyscontrol Scale: Criterion and Predictive Validity in an Inpatient Rehabilitation Unit Population. *Clinical Neuropsychologist* 11: 258-265.

Teicher, M., Y. Ito, C. Glod, F. Schiffer, and H. Gelbard. 1997. Early Abuse, Limbic System Dysfunction, and Borderline Personality Disorder. In J. Osofsky, ed., *Children in a Violent Society*. New York: Guilford Press.

Tracy, P., M. Wolfgang, and R. Figlio. 1990. *Delinquency Careers in Two Birth Cohorts*. New York: Plenum.

Trivers, R. 1991. Deceit and Self-Deception: The Relationship Between Communication and Consciousness. In M. Robinson and L. Tiger, eds., *Man and Beast Revisited*. Washington, D.C.: Smithsonian Institution Press.

Udry, J. R. 1995. Sociology and Biology: What Biology Do Sociologists Need to Know? *Social Forces* 73: 1267-1278.

van der Kolk, B. Greenberg, and M. Greenberg. 1987. The physiology of the trauma response: hyperarousal, constriction, and addiction to traumatic reexposure. In B. van der Kolk, ed., *Psychological Trauma*. Washington, D.C.: American Psychiatric Press.

van Goozen, S., G. Fairchild, H. Snoek, and G. Harold. 2007. The evidence for a neurobiological model of childhood antisocial behavior. *Psychological Bulletin* 133: 149-82.

Vila, B. 1997. Human Nature and Crime Control: Improving the Feasibility of Nurturant Strategies. *Politics and the Life Sciences* 16: 3-21.

Walsh, A. 1987. Distinguishing Features of Diagnosed Psychopaths among Convicted Sex Criminals. *Free Inquiry in Creative Sociology* 15: 40-42.

———. 1990. Illegitimacy, Child Abuse, and Neglect, and Cognitive Development. *Journal of Genetic Psychology* 151: 279-285.

———. 1991. *Intellectual Imbalance, Love Deprivation and Violent Delinquency: A Biosocial Perspective*. Charles C Thomas.

———. 1995. *Biosociology: An Emerging Paradigm*. Westport, Connecticut: Praeger.

———. 2000. Evolutionary Psychology and the Origins of Justice. *Justice Quarterly* 17: 841-864.

———. 2002. *Biosocial Criminology: Introduction and Integration*. Cincinnati, Ohio: Anderson Publishing.

———. 2003. Intelligence and Antisocial Behavior. In A. Walsh and L. Ellis, eds., *Biosocial Criminology: Challenging Environmentalism's Supremacy*, Hauppauge, New York: Nova Science. pp. 105-124.

Walsh, A. and L. Ellis. 1997. The Neurobiology of Nurturance, Evolutionary Expectations, and Crime Control. *Politics and the Life Sciences* 16: 42-44.

———. 2007. *Criminology: An Interdisciplinary Approach*. Thousand Oaks, California: Sage.

Walsh, A., J. Beyer, and T. Petee 1987. Violent Delinquency: An Examination of Psychopathic Typologies. *Journal of Genetic Psychology* 148: 385-392.

Walsh, A. and T. Petee. 1987. Love Deprivation and Violent Delinquency. *Journal of Crime and Justice* 10: 45-61.

Walsh, A. and H-H. Wu. 2008. Differentiating antisocial personality disorder, psychopathy, and sociopathy: Evolutionary, genetic, neurological, and sociological considerations. *Criminal Justice Studies* 21: 135-152.

Wechsler, D. 1958. *The Measurement and Appraisal of Adult Intelligence*. Baltimore, Maryland: Williams and Wilkins.

Weibe, R. 2004. Expanding the model of human nature underlying self-control theory: Implications of the constructs of self-control and opportunity. *The Australian and New Zealand Journal of Criminology* 37: 64-84.

Wolfgang, M., R. Figlio, and T. Sellin. 1972. *Delinquency in a Birth Cohort*. Chicago, Illinois: University of Chicago Press.

Wong, A., I. Gottesman, and A. Petronis. 2005. Phenotypic differences in genetically identical organisms: The epigenetic perspective. *Human Molecular Genetics* 14: 11-18.

Yacubian, J. T. Sommer, K. Schroeder, J. Glascher, R. Kalisch, B. Leuenberger, D.F. Braus, and C. Buchel. 2007. Gene-gene interaction associated with neural reward sensitivity. *Proceedings of the National Academy of Sciences* 104: 8125-8130.

Young, J. 2003. Merton with energy, Katz with structure: The sociology of vindictiveness and the criminology of transgression. *Theoretical Criminology* 7: 389-414.

CHAPTER 4

The Self: Principal Tool of the Correctional Helper

The most important factor effecting behavior is the self-concept... The self is the star of every performance, the central figure in every act. Persons engaging in the helping professions, therefore, need the broadest possible understanding of the nature, origins, and functions of the self-concept.

—Arthur Combs, Donald Avilla, and William Purkey

As Garrett (1982) points out, it is important that professional interviewers (and counselors) have more than a casual knowledge of human behavior and motivation, and that, "They should apply this knowledge, not only to an understanding of their clients' personalities, needs, prejudices, and emotions, but also to an understanding of their own. The wise maxim of the ancient Greeks, 'Know thyself,' applies especially to interviewers." Knowing yourself implies an honest self-appraisal of all your strengths and weaknesses with the intention of honing your strengths and working diligently to eliminate, or at least acknowledge and deal with, your weaknesses.

The goal of this chapter is to get you to examine what you really think about yourself–to examine your self-concept. The theme of this chapters is summed up in Claudia Dewane's (2006: 543) statement that: "Melding the professional self of what one knows (training, knowledge, and techniques) with the personal self of who one is (personality traits, belief systems, and life experience) is the goal of skilled practice."

The Self-Concept

Many tools are available to you to modify the behavior of offenders, but your own self-concept is the most important. Correctional personnel may decline the use of other tools, but corrections work demands the use of the self. Effective helping behavior involves interaction between two selves. The offender's self, almost by definition, is deficient in some important aspects. His or her involvement in the criminal justice system demonstrates some degree of difficulty in behaving in a responsible manner. To compensate for the deficiencies of one-half of the interacting dyad (the offender), the other half (the correctional worker) must possess some extraordinary qualities if the relationship is to be an effective one.

Before we discuss the interviewing process, it is a good idea to examine briefly the primary tool used in that process. The importance of self-concept in understanding your behavior and that of the offenders is of the utmost importance. Your self-concept is who and what you believe that unique individual you refer to as "me" is all about. It is the central core of your existence, your focus of reality from which you experience and evaluate the world around you. The self-concept is not the "real self" (whatever that is). It is rather the picture we have of ourselves about the kind of persons we are. Your self-concept is both the product and producer of your experiences. If you are capable of giving and receiving love, if you consider yourself a worthwhile person, if you are confident in yourself, and if you behave responsibly, you will be able to bring positive feelings about yourself to the helping relationship.

You have developed these ideas about yourself through a lifetime of interacting with others and incorporating both their attitudes and feelings about you and their evaluations and expectations of you. Thus, your self-concept is largely the product of your experience. Since you do have a positive self-concept derived from the positive beliefs about you held by significant others, your behavior will tend to confirm their beliefs and yours in a kind of psychological version of the "rich get richer" spiral.

A pundit said, "What a man [or woman] thinks of him [or her] self contains his [or her] destiny." In this way, your self-concept produces your behavior. Now, consider individuals whose experiences have resulted in poor self-evaluations, a negative self-concept. Their behavior also will tend to confirm their perceptions of themselves derived from those unhappy experiences. If their experiences are such that they develop negative self-concepts, they are likely to view the world as an unfriendly place and to engage in behavior not likely to endear them to others.

Such people may feel trapped in a way of life without much hope of improvement, being victims of their own self-perceptions, or "stinkin' thinkin'," as many counselors refer to it. The psychological spiral now swirls in the opposite direction: "the poor get poorer." "I'm no good. I can't be–nobody loves me, wants me, or cares for me." "Who cares anyway? Not me; they can all go to hell!" "I can't get a job because I'm not very smart—everyone says so." "I'll just get what I need by taking it from all those suckers out there, and just let them try to stop me." This is the mindset of many offenders caught up in the criminal justice system, and this is the mindset that the criminal justice-helper must wrestle with and help the offender to overcome.

However, to accomplish this task, and it is an arduous and lengthy one, your own self-concept must be up to it. As Combs, Avila, and Purkey (1971: 56-57) so well put it:

Since new concepts of self are learned as a consequence of interactions with the helper, effective helpers must be significant people. They cannot be nonentities. One cannot interact with a shadow. The helping relationship is an active one, and a passive helper is unlikely to teach his [or her] client anything but his [or her] own futility. The personality of the helper must play a vital part in any helping relationship. It is the helper's use of his [or her] self which makes the interaction whatever it is to become.

Self-Esteem

Although commonly considered so, the terms self-concept and self-esteem are not synonyms. The self-concept involves two separate motives: the motive to think well of the self–self-esteem, and the motive to protect the self from change–the self-consistency motive (Rosenberg 1979: 53). You can view all counseling as efforts to enhance offenders' self-esteem and efforts to get them to examine the self-consistency motive to get them to change the image of the self in positive directions

It is easy to recognize low self-esteem in people. People with low self-esteem are either "accepters" or "deniers." Accepters recognize the low regard that they have for themselves and constantly put themselves down, sometimes publicly, often privately. Deniers fight against their low opinions of themselves by constantly putting other people down so that they may feel superior by comparison. Accepters take little pride in their appearance or personal hygiene; deniers dress flashily and often outrageously. Both types are psychological traps that will lead to miserable unfulfilled lives. People should not have to face the complexities of modern living carrying around a picture of themselves as worthless failures.

However, because people have had plenty of experience with themselves, we have a built-in bias against changing our self-image, even if we do not like the image. People need a sense of order and consistency in their lives, so what they have become used to doing and thinking becomes habitual and comfortable. This is as true of what they think of themselves as it is of what they think of baseball, chocolate pudding, or Madonna. To maintain this comfortable consistency we often engage in selective perception, which is seeing only what we want to see.

We also may perpetuate our self-images by distorting reality, meaning that we find it difficult to really hear or understand the meaning of any message about ourselves, positive or negative, that does not fit the pictures we have about ourselves in our heads. Dowd (2004: 412) points out that we surround ourselves with a cognitive-protective belt around our self-images because "Rapid change can threaten the very sense of self upon which our identity is built, a deeply frightening experience for all of us." Yet, people with low self-esteem must have their self-consistency motive challenged (albeit, one small step at a time) if they are to build their self-esteem.

The desire for self-approval (to think of oneself as worthy) is perhaps the dominant force in a person's motivational system (Reasoner 2004). Many theorists firmly place the taproots of self-esteem in the ability to give and receive love, an assertion that has received much empirical support (Walsh and Balazs 1990). According to many authorities, criminals do not usually feel worthy, and this lack of self-esteem gets them into trouble with the law. They take drugs and alcohol in vain attempts to feel better, and seek out other deviant ways to bolster their damaged self-esteem (Vermeiren et al. 2004). Yablonsky (1990: 449) writes that violent youths (adults too) are "because of their low self-esteem, acting out self-destructive behavior; they have limited concern about whether they live or die." Part of your job as a correctional worker is to help offenders recognize their self-destructive behavior, to challenge their self-consistency motives, and to change their patterns of self-talk that contribute to their negative self-esteem. This is a tall order, but a challenging and exciting one for the dedicated and effective correctional worker.

Robert Vermeiren and his colleagues (2004) point out that there are subtypes of self-esteem based on its source, and that its affects on behavior depend on the type being examined. In other words, people do not always have the same evaluations of themselves across all situations. There are social situations in which you feel good about yourself, and those in which you do not. In this study of juveniles in Belgium, self-esteem gained from academic competence was negatively related to offending (the higher the academic competence, the lower the offending), but self-esteem based on perceived peer popularity was positively related (the higher the self-esteem gained from this source, the greater the offending). David and Kistner (2000) report similar findings and ask if positive self-perceptions have a "dark side?"

Indeed, there is a shady side to the conventional wisdom that high self-esteem is conducive to prosocial behavior and that low self-esteem is conducive to antisocial behavior. Many highly antisocial individuals, especially psychopaths, have greatly exaggerated opinions of their self-worth (Walsh and Wu 2008), and many even have a god-like attitude believing that they are the center of the universe (Sharp 2006). On the other hand, shy, insecure, and self-deprecating individuals (those who we have termed "accepters") are underrepresented in criminal populations (Baumeister, Smart, and Boden 1996).

Research finds that most male/male assaults and homicides arise from trivial incidents that threaten bloated opinions of the perpetrator's self-worth rather than low self-esteem (Anderson 1999, Baumeister, Smart, and Boden 1996). Of course, we can always claim that such bloated self-esteem is really egotism, narcissism, conceit, and arrogance (typical of those we have called "deniers"), rather than "true" self-esteem, and that someone with "true" self-esteem would be immune to minor assaults on his or her self-worth. The kind of self-esteem earned on the streets ("juice") does not tolerate being "dissed," and is therefore dangerous self-esteem (Barash and Lipton 2001). This kind of self-esteem, called "discrepant self-esteem," is fragile, unstable, and unrealistic. It is not anchored in any kind of worthwhile accomplishments (Zeigler-Hill 2005). Zeigler-Hill (2005) found that people with the highest levels of discrepant self-esteem had the highest levels of narcissism.

However, people earn even discrepant self-esteem in a way that is valued and respected on the streets of our urban slums. It will prove difficult to convince those who have it that it is worthless and damaging to them. Earning status and respect in a more prosocial manner makes little sense to those embedded in a criminal subculture. They think their "bad ass" reputations entitle them to do as they please. You will find yourself up against this kind of self-esteem, and this unhealthy self-esteem must change.

Qualities of Effective Correctional Workers

This chapter is about the correctional worker—you, or the potential you—not about assessment, casework, and counseling, the criminal personality, and so forth. However, you must become comfortable with all those things, as well as with yourself in correctional situations so that you may effectively use them. As Jeffrey Schrink (2000: 58) puts it: "Counseling in a correctional setting with clients who may have long histories of failure demands a level of physical and psychological intensity that is unusual in the helping professions."

Corrections is a fascinating but emotionally demanding line of work, and not everybody can do it. Probation and parole officers, for instance, have dual roles, which are often difficult to navigate successfully. They help and advocate for those under their supervision, but they also dispense sanctions when offenders fail to follow through, and demand honesty from offenders and then may violate them because of what they tell us (Clark 2007). We designed the rest of this chapter to give you some feeling about whether you can become comfortable and effective in this line of work—to see if you have "the right stuff."

Much research has gone into determining what constitutes effective correctional supervision. And guess what? Most of it emphasizes the primary importance of the correctional worker's self. Andrews and Bonta (1998) summarize this research and provide five dimensions of effective correctional supervision and counseling. We briefly summarize these dimensions here:

1. Relationship factors: Correctional workers should relate to inmates/offenders in an open, enthusiastic, and caring way

2. Authority factors: Be firm but fair. Distinguish between rules and requests. Reinforce behavioral compliance; do not use dominance and abuse to force it

3. Anti-criminal modeling and reinforcement: Demonstrate and reinforce noncriminal styles of thinking, feeling, and behaving

4. Concrete problem solving: Help offenders to build skills and remove obstacles to prosocial behavior in home, school, and in a work setting

5. Advocacy and brokerage: Help offenders to help themselves by brokering services offered in the community that will help them with the prior dimension

Meditate on those five dimensions for a while. Realize that the type of person you are means more to the success or failure of the endeavor than anything else except the kind of person the offender is. All this points to the conclusion that correctional workers must possess some extraordinary qualities if they are to have a meaningful part in helping offenders change their lives. In addition to a positive self-concept, a genuine liking for people, a good sense of humor (boy, does that help in this line of work!), and intellectual maturity, there are other qualities that are desirable for the effective correctional worker. We now will briefly look at what those qualities are, and at some potential problems associated with unidentified areas of the correctional worker's self that may detract from the helping process.

The Correctional Worker Must Possess a Thorough Knowledge of Criminal Behavior and its Correlates.

You should develop the interest and the patience to conduct an ongoing study of the forces and events affecting the lives of offenders. Knowledge of criminological theories and theories about substance abuse and abnormal psychology enable you to view more objectively offenders' frame of reference; they lessen the impulse toward moralizing about their behavior, and they improve your chances of success with your offenders. As Van Wormer aptly phrased it: "Much of casework failure ... results not from poor practice but from poor theory" (1999: 55). The subject matter of your field is people with problems that cause them to act irresponsibly. Individuals who aspire to be professionals must know their subject matter. No one expects you to be a specialist in all areas pertaining to criminal behavior. Think of your role as analogous to that of a physician in general practice. That is, you should know something about a wide range of crime-related subjects, but you should be wise enough to know your limitations and to refer to someone more knowledgeable—a specialist—when those limits are reached.

The Correctional Worker Must Be Realistic, Neither a Pollyanna nor a Cassandra.

A Pollyanna is a person whose excessive and irrepressible optimism finds good in everything; the glass is always half full, and the grass is always greener wherever you are. Criminals are not villains; they are victims of an unfair society and need hugging not slugging. While all this is nice, such people often fail to see danger signals or discount them. They avoid or discourage negative feedback and are extremely reluctant to confront resisting or reluctant offenders. Pollyannas are gullible. They take what offenders say at face value, and allow them to get away with too many minor infractions. They believe that this leniency marks them as nonauthoritarian and nondirective counselors. What they really are, however, are individuals who provide no meaningful guidance or supervision to offenders whose personal and legal needs require it. While it is great to be optimistic, life sometimes really is lousy, and some people really are nasty.

Cassandras are the opposites of the Pollyannas. They are the prophets of gloom and doom who see negativism in everything; their glass is always half empty, and the grass is always greener elsewhere. Criminals are villains, plain and simple, and definitely need slugging rather than hugging. People in this category also lack a sense of competence and feed such lack by discounting positive feedback. Cassandras are cynical. They do not trust offenders at all, and attempt to avoid positive interactions with them. They also tend to set their goals and expectations impossibly high, thus ensuring offender failure.

Whereas Pollyannas tend to provide unwarranted positive feedback when confrontation is required, Cassandras give feedback only when the offender has not lived up to expectations, but they will not reinforce positive behavior with positive feedback. Both of these working styles are unrealistic and reflect attitudes about the self as well as toward offenders. The Pollyanna sees corrections work solely as social work and wants to "help." The Cassandra views it as police work and wants to control. One study of probation/parole officers assessing the consequences to offenders of officers adopting a law enforcement or social work approach found that law enforcement types issued technical violation almost eight times (42.5 percent of their caseloads) as often as social worker types (5.4 percent of their caseloads) (Taxman 2008).

Realistic corrections workers view their task as both and have sufficient self-understanding and self-confidence to know when the use of either role is appropriate. Lauen (1997: 169) sums up this balance well "Effective rehabilitative efforts involve workers who are interpersonally warm, tolerant, and flexible, yet sensitive to conventional rules and procedures."

Miller and Rollnick (2002: 173-174) provide us with an excellent example of the "middle-ground" between the Pollyanna social worker and the Cassandra cop in a scenario of a first meeting between a probation officer and probationer in which the officers says:

> I have two different roles here, and it is sometimes tricky for me to put them together. One of them is as a representative of the court, to ensure that you keep the conditions of probation that the judge set for you, and I have to honor this role. The other is to be your counselor, to help you make changes in your life that we agree would be beneficial. There are also likely to be some areas we will discover, where I am hoping to see a change that you're not sure you want to make. What I hope is that by talking together here (when you report), we can resolve some of those differences and are able to find areas of change we can agree on. I'm sure I'll be asking you to consider some changes that right now don't sound very good to you, and that's normal. We'll keep exploring those issues during our time together, and see if we can come to some agreement. How does that sound to you?

Note how the officer admits the difficulties inherent in wearing two hats, but makes clear that he or she will wear the appropriate hat when needed. The officer also clarifies what the goals of probation are (behavior change and compliance with court orders) and recognizes that the probationer will not be entirely happy with either, but also states the goals to be met in terms of an alliance with the probationer, not something that he or she will make happen "or else!"

Correctional Workers Do Not Use Offenders to Satisfy Their Needs.

If the correctional worker has unresolved needs, the counselor/offender relationship is not the place to attempt to satisfy them. As Van Wormer warns: "Correctional counselors, such as probation officers, find themselves in a position of extreme power imbalance that, if handled incorrectly, can be the death knell of a therapeutic treatment relationship (1999: 56). The insecure worker who needs to feel powerful, for instance, will overcontrol interactions. He or she will dominate the direction of counseling sessions, pose as an expert, and will try to convert offenders by preaching at them. Power-hungry counselors feel safe in pursuing their needs in this way with a captive clientele, but it is counterproductive and a misuse of authority.

Other correctional workers may attempt to satisfy their needs for warmth and acceptance through the offenders. They design their interactions with the offenders to elicit cues that they are liked and accepted. Like Pollyannas, they will blind themselves to negative cues because they fear rejection, and they are opening themselves to manipulation. It is quite all right to be friendly with offenders, but not friends (of course, not enemies either).

In contrast, there are unresourceful counselors who are fearful of control or fearful of closeness. Whereas the power-hungry and the acceptance-needers suffocate the offenders with attention, the weak and the distance-needers avoid contact as much as possible. Those who fear control will neglect to offer offenders advice and direction when needed and generally will be passive onlookers. Those counselors who fear closeness will act distant with the offenders, will avoid addressing offenders' positive feelings, and will not develop the involvement necessary for the helping process. To put it another way, correctional workers must like people and enjoy frequent contact with them. They must like to solve different problems presented, and must take pride in doing a job that many people cannot do.

The Correctional Worker Inspires Trust, Confidence, and Credibility

Effective helping requires that offenders feel confident that they can share themselves with the helper. If they are to share their feelings, hopes, fears, and concerns openly, they first must sense a nonjudgmental acceptance on your part. They must come to view you as a credible professional, have confidence in your abilities and motives, and trust you to accept their feelings and concerns without criticizing, shaming, or ridiculing them. To be perceived this way, you must be this way. You cannot long feign openness, honesty, concern, and acceptance. You must cultivate these self-attributes. This does not mean that you should naively accept at face value everything offenders say anymore than you should always distrust them; but do have reality-based expectations of them.

The Correctional Worker Reaches Inward as Well as Outward

You should develop a commitment to nondefensive self-examination and awareness: "Who am I? What am I like as a person?" "Am I almost always honest, trustworthy, likable, and accepting?" "Am I the type of person who inspires confidence and trust?" "Do I really make an effort to understand offenders and their environments?" "Am I a competent person?" "Do I find myself using people to satisfy my needs for power or for acceptance?" "Do I have the courage to change those aspects of myself that I do not like?"

As a correctional worker, you often will have offenders who are different from you. What are your attitudes about people who are different? Do you harbor racist or sexist attitudes and stereotypes? Can you accept and interact with individuals of a different race, sex, sexual preference, or socioeconomic background as easily as with individuals with whom you have these things in common? Do you value, or are you fearful of, diversity of attitudes and values? Do you accept different religions, political ideologies, and sexual lifestyles as being alternatives rather than regarding them as deviant? The more you learn about the various types of people with whom you will come into contact, and the more you explore your attitudes toward them and toward yourself with an open mind, the more you will become the sort of person who is an effective helper.

Perspective from the Field
Pollyanna and Cassandra: Two Sides of a Bad Coin

Robert M. Freeman, Ph.D.

Dr. Freeman is an assistant professor of criminal justice at Shippensburg University, Pennsylvania. His BA and MA degrees are in psychology and his Ph.D. is in criminology and criminal justice. For twenty years, he held a number of positions in the Pennsylvania Department of Corrections, including psychologist and deputy superintendent for treatment at the State Regional Correctional Facility at Greensburg, superintendent of the State Regional Correctional Facility at Mercer and the State Correctional Institution at Camp Hill. He is the author of Strategic Planning for Correctional Emergencies *and* Correctional Organization and Management, *published by the American Correctional Association.*

● ●

During my more than twenty years as a corrections practitioner, I observed time and again the powerful impact of staff attitudes toward offenders and the quality of interaction between staff and offender and effective decision making. If we view attitude toward offenders on a positive-to-negative continuum, most correctional staff will be located somewhere in the middle. They understand the nature of the offender and the systems within which they and the offender are interacting, have a balanced attitude toward offenders, and can be counted on to be realistic in their interactions and decisions. However, a minority of staff are located at both extremes of the continuum: on the left is the Pollyanna who sees the offender through rose-colored glasses; on the right is the Cassandra whose offender-perception is one of darkness and threat. Pollyannas and Cassandras are distinguished from each other by differences in their language and behavior. What they have in common is an inability to interact objectively and realistically with offenders. This invariably leads to flawed decision-making.

The Pollyanna operates with a deterministic philosophy, which stipulates that offenders are not bad people, and that the crime does not reflect the offender's true nature. Instead, criminal behavior represents an understandable response to societal victimization by a basically good person. Society makes criminals of good people by being racist, discriminatory, class-oriented, and unfair in the distribution of wealth and opportunity. As a food services instructor once told me: "There are no bad people. The people we call criminals are just the most vulnerable victims of this lousy society." The Pollyanna assumes that all offenders want to change their attitudes, behavior, and lifestyle and eagerly will do so, if society is only willing to give them the opportunity. Offenders, regardless of crime, will respond to the willingness of staff to accept their basic humanity: "Extend the hand of trust and you will never be sorry," was the common expression of a social worker I once knew. If opportunity is not provided, the offender has no choice except to remain a criminal.

Continued on the next page

Perspective from the Field, *continued*

Pollyannas often come into conflict with other staff and administrators because of their willingness to ignore objective data and make high-risk decisions based on their belief that there is good in everybody. A typical supervisor-Pollyanna discussion might be as follows:

Supervisor: You've been recommending a disproportionately high number of inmates for pre-release programming very early in their sentence. I'm particularly concerned with one case: a twenty-four year-old heroin addict with a history of rape beginning at the age of twelve who has received misconducts for poor kitchen work performance and disrespect to block officers.

Counselor: You mean John?

Supervisor: Yes, John has served nine months of the current sentence, so he met the sentencing criteria, but his criminal history bothers me.

Counselor: I guess I understand your concerns, if you just go by the paperwork. But I go by the feelings John has been showing me. There's no reason to worry. John understands where he went wrong. He won't make the same mistakes again. He has enormous potential and is motivated to succeed.

Supervisor: How do you know John isn't just blowing smoke?

Counselor: Because we talk once a week and he gets very emotional when he talks about the harm he's done to his family by doing drugs. In one session, he actually cried.

Supervisor: What about the rapes?

Counselor: John says those happened when he was off heroin and drinking heavily. He lost control because of the alcohol, but says that won't be a problem on work release because he doesn't need to drink when he's working.

Supervisor: John has been in trouble since he was twelve. Why do you think nine months in this prison have changed him?

Counselor: Because he's finally found someone he can trust. He says he's never had a counselor so willing to help a man straighten himself out. When he looks me in the eye and promises he's a changed man, I know he's not lying.

Supervisor: What about four misconducts for poor work performance and disrespect?

Counselor: John is doing his best. If the supervisors and guards would let up on him, they'd find out just how good a man he can be. He just gets irritable when he's nagged.

Supervisor: What about the psych evaluation? It describes John as a "stainless steel psychopath."

Counselor: I don't trust tests. My gut-level feeling is better than any test. Besides, those tests were administered the week after reception and don't take into consideration the adjustment shock John was probably experiencing.

By refusing to confront the inmate with the reality of his past behavior, and uncritically accepting his platitudes that all is well because he had now found someone to trust, the Pollyanna is not helping the offender. The Pollyanna actually sets the stage for future acting-out.

The Cassandra operates in accordance with a free-will philosophy that stipulates that all offenders are social parasites who are criminals because of a conscious decision to become criminals. Offenders have no hope of redemption because they derive far too much satisfaction from criminal activity and will actively manipulate those staff foolish enough to try and help them. As a counselor once confided to me: "Staff who trust inmates are the same people who trust lawyers and politicians. They deserve to get burned." The Cassandra has an almost paranoid fear of being "burned" by manipulative offenders and this fear results in a refusal to trust or take chances.

The supervisor of a counselor who is a Cassandra will tend to receive numerous complaints from inmates concerning the counselor's negative attitude, abruptness when they try to stop him or her in the hallway to ask questions, and reluctance to recommend inmates for pre-release status. A typical supervisor-Cassandra discussion will be the following:

Supervisor: I receive more inmate complaints about you than any other counselor. Why is that?

Counselor: They all know I have their number. They figure if they complain to you, you'll get me off their backs, tell me to get with the program. They figure you'll push me into getting conned by them. But, I don't let anybody con me.

Supervisor: Is that why you haven't recommended anybody on your caseload for pre-release placement in four months?

Counselor: You got it. I have a bunch of trailer trash on my caseload. No way I'm letting any of them out of here before they've done their full minimum.

Supervisor: Why aren't you running groups (counseling)?

Counselor: The Superintendent said group work was voluntary. I have no time to waste listening to a bunch of crybabies whine about how tough they got it. What these guys need is to serve hard time. That's better than any counseling. I've been here longer than you. I know these guys better than you. Give an inch, they take a mile.

Supervisor: The inmates are also complaining that you never see them in person. Do you see them when they request a meeting?

Continued on the next page

Perspective from the Field, *continued*

Counselor: You know how busy we all are. If an inmate puts in a request slip, then I respond in writing. That's all I have time for. Besides, that way no inmate can accuse me of saying something I never said. What I say is always in writing. I always protect my back.

Supervisor: With that attitude, why remain a counselor?

Counselor: Because somebody has got to make these guys toe the line. I'm the only counselor you've got who isn't afraid to say "no" and mean it. I leave and these guys will take over the place. I've been here nine years, and all inmates ever do is screw up every opportunity handed to them and then whine that their failure is somebody else's fault when the real reason they fail is because no one is willing to hold them accountable for not even trying. Well, I hold them all accountable. Nothing you say is going to change that.

Neither of these counselors is effective. Both have attitudes that interfere with objectivity and limit their ability to focus on the real issues the offenders are facing. Pollyannas and Cassandras are not just topics of theoretical interest to academicians. The decisions they make can have dramatic effects, especially if they are in a position of authority over other staff.

Early in this author's corrections career, he attended a counseling seminar designed to sharpen the diagnostic and treatment skills of a selected group of psychologists and counselors. The group was a mixture of novices, including himself, and veterans of many years of institutional work. On the afternoon of the second day, the instructor presented a case study of a nineteen-year-old inmate in a maximum-security institution who had been gang raped a month after reception. After three weeks in the prison infirmary, he was placed in protective custody in the Behavioral Adjustment Unit where his behavior deteriorated, and he began to receive misconducts for various forms of acting-out. After discussion, the group decided that the motivation for the acting-out was the anger and humiliation created by the rape. The instructor agreed and told us to develop a counseling plan of action. A variety of therapeutic interventions were suggested, with the general consensus being that the job of the counselor would be to help the young inmate understand how anger and humiliation were motivating his behavior and assist him in learning to substitute positive coping skills for the current self-destructive behavior.

Noting that one member of the group, a twenty-year veteran who was the chief psychologist of a maximum-security institution, had contributed nothing to the discussion, the instructor asked how he would respond to the situation. The response was: "What that punk needs is a good kick in the butt. That'll straighten him out better than all this talking." Clearly, this was the response of a Cassandra. One can imagine the damage that type of attitude was doing to vulnerable inmates under the jurisdiction of this psychologist's staff.

But Pollyannas in positions of administrative authority also can cause damage. An administrator at a facility with a highly successful work-release program made the decision to place an inmate recently received from a maximum-security institution on work release status. The inmate's history was extremely negative: drug addiction and a high frequency of assaultive crimes. There were numerous contraindications to work-release placement, but the administrator, operating on the basic Pollyanna principle that "Everybody deserves a second chance," approved the inmate for work release. Weekend furloughs followed shortly thereafter. During one of these furloughs, the inmate murdered a young woman. The murder generated extensive publicity and calls for action.

The result? A work-release program that had successfully provided opportunity to hundreds of inmates was abolished overnight. Future inmates at that facility would have to pay the price of denied opportunity for one Pollyanna's mistake.

The Pollyanna and Cassandra are not limited to the ranks of treatment staff. They can be found in every category of correctional staff, from the block officer to the laundry supervisor to the clerk-typist. Regardless of their title and job, the Pollyanna and Cassandra represent a major challenge to supervisors, colleagues, and offenders.

The Benefits of Self-Disclosure

One of the most important qualities that correctional workers should possess is the willingness to share themselves with others, including offenders, through self-disclosure. Self-disclosure means to communicate personal information to another who normally would not have that information. One may reasonably inquire what use it is for the correctional worker to communicate personal information to an offender: isn't the offender's self the focus of the offender/helper relationship—indeed, the reason for its existence? Yes, it is, and it was not until the advent of humanistic psychology that self-disclosure was considered appropriate and beneficial (Okun 1987: 261). However, the willingness of the correctional helpers to share themselves serves some very useful functions.

First, it is a form of modeling behavior that encourages reluctant offenders to reveal intimate facts about themselves. The difficulty that offenders experience in revealing their most intimate feelings, thoughts, and valuations may be lessened by the helper's example. Remember, reciprocal self-disclosure is the basis of the success of various self-help groups such as Alcoholics Anonymous. Confession is good for the soul, and it yields an abundance of needed information for the assessment of the offender. Jose Arcaya puts the self-disclosure process in a criminal justice context when he writes: "For the ex-offender forced to present himself [or herself] before a probation officer, rehabilitation counselor, or psychologist, no meaningful dialogue will occur unless the client can identify a glimmer of his [or her] own humanity in the individual with whom he [or she] deals" (1978: 231).

Second, self-disclosure gives the offender a new perspective on things derived from your personal experiences. Again, the sharing of personal experiences, the implanting of possibilities for alternative frames of reference in the minds of others, is part of the modus operandi of self-help groups in which offenders come to see reflections of themselves in others. This process of self-disclosure, of course, should be free of value judgments, moral exhortations, and self-serving and boastful exhibitionism. Besides being bad practice, it is not considered good taste to advertise what a great person you are. If the contrast between the offender's experience and yours is too great, he or she will not view your revealed frame of reference as being realistic. If you moralize and pass judgment, the offender is not likely to reveal any further personal information to you that could invite further denigration.

You always must be aware of the feelings and humanity of the offenders. If, for example, Bob reveals that he has experienced great difficulty obtaining employment because of his lack of a high school diploma and the vagaries of his lower-class upbringing, you may reply with sensitivity, revealing your own class origins, the possibility of obtaining a general education diploma (GED), and describe how you managed to acquire an education despite acknowledged early deficiencies.

Rendered in this nonthreatening manner, your experience may strike a responsive chord of the possible within the offender. If you couch it in terms designed to emphasize your moral superiority ("I did it, why can't you?" "It takes guts, buddy." "You can get a job if you get off your lazy ass and start looking."), Bob is very likely to react negatively to such an assault on his self-concept, either by becoming hostile or by clamming up. Either way, you have lost the opportunity to further the meaningful interaction necessary for an adequate assessment of the offender. You also have reinforced Bob's sense of hopelessness and his feeling that "nobody cares" and revealed your own inadequacies as a helper. If such an exchange takes place during the initial interview, and if Bob is subsequently placed under you supervision as a probationer, parolee, or inmate, efforts to counsel him will meet with resistance because you have communicated to him that he is not worth much and that you are not really interested in him or his problems.

Some caveats about self-disclosure to an offender are in order at this point. First, Boyd Sharp (2006) rightfully points out that while self-help groups such as AA are peer-to-peer relationships in which self-disclosure is beneficial; the correctional worker-offender relationship is not.

Second, the offender's problems must be the focus of any interview or counseling session. Therefore, the worker's self-disclosure should be infrequent, relevant, and focused and should not give the offender the impression that you are working out your own problems with him or her. Chatty and unstructured conversations are inappropriate during a session designed to gather information about the offender, although they may have use in later counseling sessions if your motives are consistent with establishing a genuine atmosphere of informality. Gerard Egan's (1998: 179-180) advice, which I paraphrase, is instructive here: Make sure your disclosures are appropriate, keep them selected and focused, and don't burden your client with too much of it. In short, you should be willing and able to disclose yourself in reasonable ways, but should do so only if it is clear that it will contribute to the client's progress.

Third, when in doubt about self-disclosure—don't disclose. Some authorities strongly discourage self-disclosure with criminal populations, asserting that offenders use this information to sidetrack the counselor, and even use tidbits of information to manipulate him or her (Sharp 2006). This is very true in institutional settings in which counselors may have daily contact with inmates, and inmates have nothing better to do than play their games. Perhaps guarded self-disclosure is best only practiced in community settings where probationers or parolees may be able to put the disclosed information to some immediate use.

Improving Your Self-Concept through Self-Disclosure

Training exercises in self-disclosure, such as those given at the end of this chapter, should be an integral part of the correctional worker's training. They are necessary for two reasons. First, they provide the helper with a gut-level understanding of the feelings of the offenders as they are asked to reveal intimate information. Disclosing intimate information can be highly embarrassing and intimidating to the offender. Imagine the embarrassment of a sixty-year old minister who has been found guilty of molesting a child as he is being asked to reveal details of his sex life to a probation officer or other correctional counselor young enough to be his grandson or granddaughter! The investigating or counseling officer must be highly sensitive to this embarrassment if he or she is to conduct a successful interview and make an adequate assessment. One of the best ways to learn this sensitivity is to experience the same sort of discomfort by self-disclosure in a classroom setting.

Of course, the classroom setting will not be as threatening to the student as the real-life setting is for the offender. Students can easily role-play rather than deal with real concerns. That is, they can manufacture fictitious problems that do not threaten them rather than exploring real problems that they may have. Only by realistically exploring problems can you gain insight into what it is like to be an offender. Remember, all prospective psychoanalysts have to undergo intensive psychoanalysis before they are allowed to practice their skills on others.

The second reason for engaging in realistic self-disclosure is to improve your greatest asset—your self-concept. As Franken (1994: 443) opines: "Self-change is not something that people can will, but rather depends on self-reflection. Through self-reflection, people often come to view themselves in a new, more powerful, way, and it is through this new, more powerful way of viewing the self that people can develop possible selves."

As previously stated, people have a strong desire to preserve the picture they have of themselves—the self-consistency motive. If we protect the self from change, by definition, we cannot, grow psychologically. As paradoxical as it may seem, to preserve self-consistency, some people may retain low self-esteem to protect the self-esteem they do have. People who expect little of themselves cannot fail. If expectations are low, a weak performance easily meets the meager expectations they have of themselves Psychological growth implies that we have the courage to test ourselves to our limits and to acknowledge the possibility of failure.

It is important for us to assess ourselves, to know what kind of people we are, to know our strengths, weaknesses, potential, and problem areas so that we can effectively operate in our environment. Some authorities consider wholesome self-disclosure to be as necessary for mental health as proper exercise and nutrition are for physical health. South (2007) wrote that to reduce our alienation from ourselves and from others we must open ourselves to ourselves by disclosing ourselves to others. The more we know about ourselves, the better able we will be to understand others. Self-knowledge is desirable for all people, but it is vital for those in the helping professions because understanding others is a prerequisite to helping them. How can you help offenders come to terms with feelings that are hindering their functioning if you have not confronted and dealt with similar feelings in yourself?

We must not harbor static images of ourselves. If we do, we will have unrealistic pictures of the world and our relationship to it. A static self-concept cuts us off from the fullness of the experiences that the world offers us, thus stunting our emotional and intellectual growth. Rather than building walls and defenses against life's fullness, we should accept all experiences and fit them into our self-concepts. We must adapt positively to the environment as it changes. To accomplish this successfully, we must receive information about ourselves from concerned others and use it for positive change. To receive information about ourselves from others, however, we must be strong enough to be willing to share ourselves with others. Both the receiving of information about ourselves and the sharing of ourselves is accomplished by meaningful self-disclosure. You will be asking the offenders to do all these things: adapt positively to their environments, experience lifestyles different from the one they have grown accustomed to, share themselves through disclosure, and receive information from you that you will expect them to employ fruitfully. If this is not a part of your personal operating philosophy, you will not be successful in imparting it to the offenders.

The Johari Window: An Aid to Self-Understanding

A useful framework for viewing self-concept and understanding how self-disclosure is valuable in improving it is the Johari Window (Luft 1963), shown in Figure 4.1. This device divides the self into four components or "cells," representing aspects of the self, ranging from those known to almost everyone to aspects of which you yourself are not aware. Positive self-disclosure should have the effect of enlarging Cell I (the public-self) while shrinking the other three cells correspondingly. The following is a general discussion of the principles of self-disclosure, which should not be viewed within the context of the counselor/offender relationship. You certainly will not be asking offenders to help you to explore your intimate concerns.

Figure 4.1   The Johari Window (adapted from Luft, 1963)

	Known to self	Unknown to self
Known to others	I Public self	II Blind self
Unknown to others	III Private self	IV Unknown self

The public-self is the self that habitually is shared with others. It is an area of self-knowledge which you have no qualms about revealing. The private-self obviously has relevance to self-disclosure. You need not, or even should not, burden others with excessive and exhibitionist disclosure of the private self: "If only you knew what I've accomplished in my life, and against what odds, you too would realize what a great person I really am." The idea is to disclose only those aspects of the private self that can help others with the exploration of those aspects that are of concern to you, such as values, weaknesses, and social and sexual identities.

The blind self is that part of the self that others see but we do not. It is involved in self-disclosure only if others bring their images of you to your attention and if you are willing to acknowledge the validity of the transmitted information. The transmitted information may not be an accurate assessment of you, but it may be beneficial to at least to recognize the possibility that it is. If the revealed information is negative, do not throw up fences and retreat from it. Instead, work with that aspect of the self to see how it can be improved. Never ignore traits or characteristics that others perceive and that may be negatively affecting your effectiveness as a helper or as a person.

The unknown self is the area of latent, inchoate, subconscious, and preconscious facets of the self. It is an area of shadowy fears and weaknesses, but also a reservoir of great untapped potential and talents that we all, including offenders, have. An unwillingness to explore unknown areas of the self is indicative of a frozen self-concept. In the process of exploring the blind self, it is possible that aspects of the unknown self will become accessible to you so that you may confront them and develop those that are desirable or deal constructively with those that are not.

Whereas it is generally agreed that self-disclosure (moving information contained in cells II, III, and IV into cell I) facilitates personal growth, it may result in growth-inhibiting outcomes. Whether self-disclosure is beneficial or harmful depends on the state of the receiver and the quality of the relationship shared by the receiver and the transmitter. Inevitably, self-disclosure involves a certain amount of risk-taking. A turtle never moves forward until it sticks its neck out.

Self-disclosure demands trusting and making an investment in the other person. As a professional criminal justice worker, you will be asking offenders to trust you and invest in you. If you are to perform your task in an effective and efficient manner, you must prove worthy of that trust and investment by responding to offenders in a sensitive, empathetic, and fully involved way. Furthermore, you also must be secure enough in yourself to be completely honest with the offender. Your honesty, openness, and acceptance do not guarantee that the offender will act likewise, but these characteristics certainly make it more probable.

Application to the Offender

Although the Johari Window was conceived of as a strategy for self-exploration, it can be fruitfully adapted to serve as a model for the officer/offender relationship. For instance, the situation representing the immediate state of your "knowledge" of the offenders in your first meeting with them is presented in Figure 4.2. The major difference between exercises in voluntary self-disclosure for self-growth and the officer-offender encounter is that the public-self in this case is the self that the offender chooses to present to you, not the public self that he or she habitually shares with family, friends, and acquaintances.

Figure 4.2 The Johari Window (Applied to the Client)

	Known to officer	Unknown to officer
Known to client	I Public client / Official client	II Blind client
Unknown to client	III Private client	IV Unknown client

Your knowledge of the offender's public-self, for the moment, is limited to information written down in various official documents. Therefore, even getting to know the offenders as others know them may prove to be an exacting assignment, for at this point you know only the official offenders. Your initial task is the melding of the two subsections of cell 1 to form a unified picture of offenders as they normally present themselves to others. Offenders may have a number of aspects of the public-self that they are unwilling to share with you. Consequently, they will erect barriers to protect those areas. The barriers can be scaled by an effectively conducted interview with the offenders and by collateral interviews with others acquainted with them.

The private offender is that part of the offender's self that he or she wishes to keep unscrutinized by others, especially by the correctional worker. It represents the behaviors, feelings, and motivations that the offender habitually hides but that may be revealed when he or she chooses. These behaviors, feelings, and motivations, since the offender is aware of them, most probably will be the first target areas for mutual exploration. They are not necessarily problem areas. They just as well may be growth-promoting areas that, with a little support and encouragement, the offender could actualize. If aspects of the private offender are of this kind, he or she possibly may be more disposed to relating them to a relative stranger who is perceived as caring and accepting than to more familiar others from whom he or she may fear ridicule.

The blind offender represents those aspects of the self of which the offender is unaware but that the officer perceives and to which the officer is sensitive. Just as the corrections worker is able to enhance the self by feedback in an atmosphere of openness and trust, so may the offender. The correctional worker should place initial emphasis on the positive aspects of the offender's self of which the officer is aware, such as positive statements by others. If, for instance, an officer has access to school records indicating that the offender scored well on IQ tests, the officer may discuss the nature of IQ and the potential and possibilities open to the offender with such scores. This type of information, needless to say, is most welcome and tends to spill over into congenial discussions of other aspects of the offender's blind self, which he or she might not be so readily willing to accept.

The unknown offender represents those aspects of the offender's self that are unknown to the officer and the offender alike. Realistically, we know that many facets of the offender's unknown self will remain unknown. The initial interview, for whatever reason it is conducted, is not the place to attempt to probe into this area. Under supervision, however, the offender should be encouraged to explore it to discover the unknown potential that we all possess. You must have faith in this proposition if you are to be an effective correctional worker.

The Johari Window is a useful framework for conceptualizing the process and purpose of interviewing. However, we never should forget that offenders come to the interviewing process with vastly different biographies, motives, and attitudes. Each interview is a unique process between human beings who are far too individualized to be reduced to precise formulas. Interviewing is an art rather than a science. However, certain basic principles exist that enable the helper to conduct a successful interview. We discuss these in the next chapter.

The Mask

The following essay by an anonymous writer is an anguished cry for understanding and acceptance. It illustrates our discussion of self-disclosure, as well as the discussion of listening still to come. Notice how the writer has built a false self-image and barriers to protect it, and how painful the writer finds his or her inauthenticity. We all want to be accepted and loved, but many of us fight against what we so desperately need. The writer wants to be authentic by disclosing his or her true self and true feeling, but is so terribly afraid of rejection. This could have been written by any offender, perhaps even by some of your classmates (or even you). Remember it when you do your exercises in self-disclosure. Above all, remember it when you are working with real offenders.

Please Hear What I'm Not Saying

Author unknown

Don't be fooled by me. Don't be fooled by the face I wear. For I wear a mask. I wear a thousand masks, masks that I'm afraid to take off, and none of them is me. Pretending is an art that's second nature to me, but don't be fooled, for God's sake don't be fooled. I give you the impression that I'm secure, that all is sunny and unruffled with me, within as well as without. That confidence is my name and coolness is my game, and that I need no one.

But don't believe me. My surface is my mask. Beneath dwells the real me in confusion, in fear, in aloneness. But I hide this. I don't want anybody to know it. I panic at the thought of my weakness and fear being exposed. That's why I frantically create a mask to hide behind, to shield me from the glance that knows. But such a glance is precisely my salvation—that is, if it's followed by acceptance, by love. It's the only thing that can liberate me from my own self-built prison walls. It is the only thing that will assure me of what I can't assure myself–that I'm really worth something. But I'm afraid to tell you this; I'm afraid that your glance will not be followed by acceptance and love. I'm afraid you'll laugh, and that laugh will kill me. I idly chatter to you in the suave tones of surface talk. I tell you everything that's really nothing, and nothing of what's everything, of what's crying within me.

Please listen carefully and try to hear what I'm not saying, what I'd like to be able to say, what for survival I need to say. I'd really like to be genuine and spontaneous, and me, but you've got to help me. You alone can release me from my shadow-world of panic and uncertainty, from my lonely prison. It will not be easy for you. A long conviction of worthlessness builds strong walls. The nearer you approach me, the blinder I may strike back. I am irrational–I fight against the very thing that I cry out for. But I am told that love is stronger than strong walls. Please try to beat down those walls with firm hands, but with gentle hands–for I am very sensitive. Who am I, you may wonder. I am someone you "know" very well, I am every man you meet and I am every woman you meet.

Summary

This chapter emphasizes the primacy of the self in the helping process. Nothing is more important to the success or failure of a counseling relationship than the quality of the helper's self. The self-concept is the product and producer of experience. Positive experiences lead to a positive self-concept, and a positive self-concept leads to further positive experiences. The opposite progression, often found in offenders, is also true.

We looked at the various attributes that characterize the professional criminal justice worker. You should examine these attributes closely to determine how you measure up. You can explore deficiencies and weaknesses in any of the areas in the process of self-disclosure.

To improve the self-concept, a person must accept a wide variety of experiences and integrate them into his or her self-concept. One way of doing this is through meaningful self-disclosure. Self-disclosure helps us to gain knowledge about ourselves by receiving feedback about ourselves from others. Every prospective counselor should experience self-disclosure in a number of sessions before actually practicing counseling, not only to gain valuable self-insight but also to experience the process in which he or she will be asking offenders to engage. The Johari Window is an excellent device for guiding self-disclosure of this type. Few bits of advice are more useful than the ancient injunction to "know thyself."

Exercises in Self-Exploration through Disclosure

The purpose of this activity is twofold: (1) to improve self-exploration by disclosing to a partner various aspects of yourself and (2) to give you some experience of what it is like to reveal yourself to a relative stranger. During the initial session, you may, out of fear, anxiety, or embarrassment, decide upon some relatively nonthreatening topic. Or, you may possess the self-assurance to pick a topic that is of real concern to you. It is preferable, of course, to choose aspects of the private self, especially those of an interpersonal nature, for exploration. The section asking you to explore values and attitudes toward various types of individuals should prove to be valuable in developing an empathetic understanding of them if both your disclosure and feedback are open and honest.

Exercises should be done in pairs, with frequent changes of partners. If your instructor chooses not to assign partners, it is preferable that you do not sit with the same person too often. Make an effort to sit with someone of a different race, sex, or ethnic background. You will find this to be a good learning experience and very rewarding. Each student should take turns in disclosing the chosen issue to the other. Remember, you are not engaging in a conventional conversation. The disclosing person should have control of the communication. The listener should listen, and pay attention to the techniques of active listening as outlined in the next chapter. The listener should speak only for the purposes of clarification and of prompting further disclosure by the use of probes. Each of the following suggested topics is suitable for a discussion of about five-to-ten minutes.

Topic One: Generalities

The kind of people I like best are___

The kind of people I like least are___

I try to avoid thinking about___

I think that the most important thing in life is___

I feel most competent when I___

I feel least competent when I___

My career goals are___

I would really like to be able to___

Topic Two: Values and Attitudes

My values are important to me because___

Here's how I REALLY feel that the relationship between the sexes should be___

Here's how I REALLY feel about blacks/whites___

Here's how I feel about alcoholics___

Here's how I feel about drug abusers___

Here's how I REALLY feel about homosexuals___

Here's how I REALLY feel about criminals___

An open mind is desirable because___

Topic Three: Feelings

I am happiest when___

I get the most depressed when___

I get embarrassed when___

I get very angry when___

I feel guilty when___

I am sometimes ashamed of___

I feel very hurt when___

I feel anxious when___

Topic Four: Identity

Who are you, what kind of person are you? Odds are that you have never really thought too much about your identity. Try writing out ten separate answers to the question "WHO AM I?" Next, eliminate those answers that simply signify your various ascribed and achieved statuses, such as "American," "student," "male," or "nineteen-years old." With your partners, explore those aspects of the self that you have left on your lists. You may have written, for example, "I am a shy person." Explore this aspect with your partner. Why do you think you are shy? What does your shyness do to your social life? How much more successful do you think you would be in life if you were not shy? How do you feel about your shyness? What do you think you can do about it?

Topic Five: Strengths and Weaknesses

Make a list of your five greatest strengths and five greatest weaknesses and discuss each one with your partner. These strengths and weaknesses should be developmental "feeling" topics rather than statements such as "I'm a good/poor tennis player." For instance, how do you relate to other people, especially those close to you? Are you secure in your sexual identity? Are you a leader or a follower? Do you respect the feelings of others? Are you an autonomous person? Can you take constructive criticism?

Topic Six: Effectiveness as a Correctional Helper

Go back to the description of an effective criminal justice helper and rate yourself according to those attributes. Where are you weak, and where are you strong? What personal attribute do you possess that will aid you in becoming a more effective helper, and what personal attribute do you think will most detract from your ability to become an effective helper? Discuss these strengths and weaknesses with a partner.

References and Suggested Readings

Anderson, E. 1999. *Code of the Street: Decency, Violence, and the Moral Life of the Inner City*. New York: W.W. Norton.

Andrews, D. and J. Bonta. 1998. *The Psychology of Criminal Conduct*. Cincinnati, Ohio: Anderson Publishing.

Arcaya, J. 1978. Coercive Counseling and Self-Disclosure. *International Journal of Offender Therapy and Comparative Criminology* 22: 231-237.

Barash, D. and J. Lipton. 2001. Making Sense of Sex. In D. Barash, ed., *Understanding Violence*. Boston: Allyn and Bacon. pp. 20-30.

Baumeister, R., L. Smart, and J. Boden. 1996. Relation of Threatened Egotism to Violence and Aggression: The Dark Side of Self-Esteem. *Psychological Review* 103 :5-33.

Clark, M. 2007. Motivational interviewing for probation officers: Tipping the balance toward change. *Federal Probation* 70: 38:44.

Combs, A., D. Avila, and W. Purkey. 1971. *Helping Relationships: Basic Concepts for the Helping Professions*. Boston, Massachusetts: Allyn and Bacon.

David, C. and J. Kistner. 2000. Do Positive Self-Perceptions Have a 'Dark Side'? Examination of the Link between Perceptual Bias and Aggression. *Journal of Abnormal Child Psychology* 28: 227-337.

Dewane, C. 2006. Use of Self: A Primer Revisited. *Clinical Social Work Journal* 34: 543-558.

Dowd, E. 2004. Cognition and the Cognitive Revolution in Psychotherapy: Promises and Advances. *Journal of Clinical Psychology* 60: 415-428.

Egan, G. 1998. *The Skilled Helper*. Monterey, California: Brooks/Cole.

Franken, R. 1994. *Human Motivation*, 3rd ed. Pacific Grove, California: Brooks/Cole.

Garrett, A. 1982. *Interviewing: Its Principles and Methods*. New York: Family Services Association of America.

Hare, R. 1993. *Without Conscience: The Disturbing World of the Psychopaths among Us*. New York: Pocket Books.

Hartman, H. 1978. *Basic Psychiatry for Corrections Workers*. Springfield, Illinois: Charles C. Thomas.

Ivey, A. 1983. *Intentional Interviewing and Counseling*. Monterey, California: Brooks/Cole.

Lauen, R. 1997. *Positive Approaches to Corrections: Research, Policy, and Practice*. Lanham, Maryland: American Correctional Association.

Luft, J. 1963. *Group Process: An Introduction to Group Dynamics*. Palo Alto, California: Henry Holt and Company.

Miller, W. and S. Rollnick. 2002. *Motivational Interviewing: Preparing People for Change*. New York: Guildford Press.

Okun, B. 1982. *Effective Helping*. Monterey, California: Brooks/Cole.

Reaoner, R. 2004. *The True Meaning of Self-Esteem*. National Association for Self-Esteem. http//www.self-esteem-nase.org/whatisselfesteem.shtml

Rosenberg, M. 1979. *Conceiving the Self*. New York: Basic Books.

Schrink, J. 2000. Understanding the Correctional Counselor. In P. Van Vooris, M. Brasswell, and D. Lester, eds., *Correctional Counseling and Rehabilitation*. Cincinnati: Anderson.

Sharp, B. 2005. *Changing Criminal Thinking: A Treatment Program*, 2nd ed. Alexandria, Virginia: American Correctional Association.

South, B. 2007. Combining Mandala and the Johari Window: An Exercise in Self-Awareness. *Teaching and Learning in Nursing* 2: 8-11.

Taxman, F. 2008. No illusions: Offender and organizational change in Maryland's proactive community supervision efforts. *Criminology and Public Policy* 7 :275-302.

Van Wormer, K. 1999. The Strengths Perspective: A Paradigm for Correctional Counseling. *Federal Probation* 63: 51-59.

Vermeiren, R., J. Bogaerts, V. Ruchkin, D. Deboutte, and M. Schwab-Stone. 2004. Subtypes of Self-Esteem and Self-Concept in Adolescent Violent and Property Offenders. *Journal of Child Psychology* 45: 405-411.

Walsh, A. and G. Balazs. 1990. Love, Sex, and Self-Esteem. *Free Inquiry in Creative Sociology* 18: 37-42.

Walsh, A. and H-H. Wu. 2008. Differentiating antisocial personality disorder, psychopathy, and sociopathy: Evolutionary, genetic, neurological, and sociological considerations. *Criminal Justice Studies* 21: 135-152.

Yablonsky. L. 1990. *Criminology: Crime and Criminality*. New York: Harper and Row.

Zeigler-Hill, V. 2005. Discrepancies between Implicit and Explicit Self-Esteem: Implications for Narcissism and Self-Esteem Instability. *Journal of Personality* 74 :119-140.

CHAPTER 5

Interviewing and Interrogating

It is not easy to achieve the ideal balance between relieving a client (offender) of the unbearable burden of what seem to be insurmountable difficulties and leaving him with essential responsibility for working out his own destiny. . . . One of the most important skills of the interviewer is a knowledge of his [her] own limitations.

—Annette Garrett

The interview is a focused process of communication by which you gather information to assess the interviewee. It is a structured and purposeful method of getting to know another person. Any interview, regardless of the context in which it takes place, is designed to help the interviewer make decisions, usually about the interviewee (Is he or she suitable for the job, eligible for benefits, serious about this task, a good candidate for treatment?). Correctional workers spend the major portion of their time conducting interviews with offenders, victims, police officers, and many other people involved in some way with offenders' activities. Surveys of probation departments in Canada and the United Kingdom revealed that despite variations in political and structural contexts, interviewing and interpersonal skills were the most important skills for community corrections work (Braken 2003). Thus, it is necessary that you become informed about the basic principles of effective interviewing.

Interrogation is also part of the correctional worker's task. Like interviewing, interrogating involves information gathering, but the focus is more sharply delimited. As Vessel (1998: 1) puts it: "Obtaining information that an individual does not want to provide constitutes the sole purpose of interrogation." You conduct an interrogation either to get an admission of guilt from a person or to eliminate that person from suspicion. The ability to conduct an effective interrogation is also a necessary part of your professional development.

Purpose of the Criminal Justice Interview

The Offender

Interviewing offenders is a diagnostic tool that will enable you to arrive at a preliminary understanding of them and their problems and to recommend and implement effective treatment modalities. A well-conducted interview also is the first step in the counseling process if it creates an arena in which offenders can formulate an honest picture of their problems, and if they gain an understanding of the motives and resources of the helping person.

As criminologist and prominent correctional administrator Paul Keve put it: "The most important step in the investigation process is the first interview with the defendant, and if you handle it skillfully, you not only have the basis for a truly competent report, but you also have gone a long way toward launching the treatment job that must develop later" (quoted in Hartman 1978: 309). The implication is that the interview can be the beginning of the rehabilitative process, or it can be merely a ritual in which uninterpreted demographic data is gathered and reported. The principles of interviewing are the same regardless of the specific purpose of the interview: preparing a presentence investigation report (PSI), meeting a newly assigned probationer or parolee, or conducting an intake interview for a new arrival at an institution.

To explain the interview process from beginning to end it is useful to introduce an investigative interview model recommended for use to the British police and designed by psychologist Gisli Gudjonsson (1994). This model uses the mnemonic PEACE, which stands for:

- *P*=Prepare and plan
- *E*=Engage and explain
- *A*=Account
- *C*=Closure
- *E*=Evaluate

We will now elaborate on each of these stages of the model.

Prepare and Plan

The Physical Setting: The results of your interview probably will have a significant impact on the offender's future. Due to the importance of this process, give the offender your undivided attention during the time you are together. Although the physical facilities in many criminal justice agencies may not be ideal, it is important that the interview setting be as private and free of distractions as possible. Instruct the receptionist to hold all nonemergency telephone calls, and display a "Do not disturb" sign on your office door. Some interruptions may be inevitable, but they must never be of the personal or frivolous kind. You must convey to offenders that this time belongs to them and that they are the only topic of importance to you during this period.

Familiarity with the Case: Before interviewing the offender, thoroughly familiarize yourself with the case materials obtained from police and prosecutor's files. Based on these materials, formulate the questions that you plan to ask. See a comprehensive semi-structured interview schedule used in probation and parole agencies nationwide in Chapter 7. This is an excellent tool for the beginning interviewer because it covers everything of importance for interviewing of the typical offender.

While the schedule begins by asking questions regarding offenders' attitudes toward the offense and offense patterns, questions pertinent to the crime and to the offenders' criminal history are best left until last because these are the questions most likely to threaten the offenders, and may require the use of interrogation rather than interviewing techniques (Navarro 2003). Offenders will answer questions about the offense and about any prior offenses more easily after you establish a friendly rapport and they feel less threatened by the situation in which they find themselves.

Most probation departments use an intake form, which the offender fills out prior to meeting the probation officer. This form should request basic demographic data such as name, place and date of birth, current address and telephone number, names and addresses of family members and places of work, schools attended, and the offender's financial situation. It also should ask offenders for pertinent medical information and a recitation of prior involvement with the law and should include a section that asks them to write out their version of the offense.

The use of such a form serves a number of functions:

1. It gives structure to the interview.

2. It sensitizes the offender to the type of questions you will be asking in more detail.

3. It provides the offender with an opportunity to decide in private if he or she is going to be honest with you.

4. It gives you the opportunity to decide if the offender indeed has been honest with you by checking the written statement against "the record."

5. It gives you some insight into the offender's level of communication skills.

6. It minimizes the recording of factual information (age, phone numbers, addresses, and so on) during the interview, which would detract from its smooth flow. A discussion of a typical social history questionnaire is included in Chapter 7, and an example is included in the appendix.

Engage and Explain

Initiating the Interview. A criminal justice offender's first contact with a community corrections agency is usually the result of a referral to a probation department for a presentence investigation report (PSI) after being found guilty of a crime or having pled guilty to one. Because the PSI interview is perhaps the most important interview the offender will experience, we will assume in the following discussion that we are conducting such an interview. Given the circumstances of the PSI referral, it is necessary to realize that the offender probably will view it as punitive rather than as an opportunity to receive help and guidance. In light of the involuntary nature of the offender's presence, and in light of the offender's possible ingrained mistrust and disregard for authority, it is particularly important that the interview get off to a good start.

Meeting the Offender: Respect and Rapport. The first contact with the offender is crucial. The offender may be anxious and nervous, and you should convey your respect and concern. First impressions certainly will color much of what will follow between you and the offender. It is essential, then, that you establish positive rapport at this time. Greet the offender by looking him or her straight in the eyes and offering a smile and a firm handshake. First names should not be used at the first meeting, especially with older offenders.

Traditionally, the superordinate individual addressed the subordinate individual by first name, whereas the person in the inferior position was expected to use the presumed superior's full title and last name. This convention, designed to emphasize social distance, is something you definitely wish to avoid. However, you should establish a more informal first-name relationship as soon as you perceive that the offender is amenable to it. Your initial statement should be something like, "Good morning Mr. Smith. My name is Joyce Williams. I will be your probation officer." If you don't put the offender at ease, the nonverbal behavior he or she demonstrates (fidgeting, feet jiggling, sitting tensely, and so forth) may lead you to view it as signs of deception when, in fact, it may be simple nervousness (Navarro 2003).

You now have introduced yourself and your role. Although your offenders are troubled individuals whom you are seeing because they have committed some crime for which they may be deeply ashamed, there must not be any hint of a patronizing, condescending, or judgmental attitude in either your voice or your nonverbal behavior. You may have extremely negative feelings about the type of behavior that has brought the offender to you. Any attempts to deny to yourself that your offender's behavior elicits those feelings in you will result in an artificial, stilted, and unproductive interview. Acknowledge to yourself that these feelings exist and that they are normal and expected. However, also recognize that their expression in a professional goal-oriented setting is inappropriate. If you reveal your anger or embarrassment, even subtly or unconsciously, the offender will pick up on your cues and perhaps respond with his or her own anger and/or embarrassment.

Negative emotions, either yours or the offender's, are not conducive to an effective interview. Professional recognition and control of personal feelings rather than denial and repression of them is a goal for which you should strive.

Early in the probation career of one of your authors (Walsh), he had a female offender whose appearance and crime had a very negative effect on him. She had paid a number of neighborhood boys to have sex with her over a period of several months. Although he struggled to rid himself of the sexist attitudes acquired through socialization, he could not free himself of the notion that women simply "were not supposed to act that way." Consequently, he perceived her crime as much more odious than he would have if she had been a man convicted of similar behavior. Furthermore, when he met her, her physical appearance made matters worse. She was an extremely obese woman with multiple chins thickly folded upon an expansive bosom, and she had a body odor too strong to ignore.

He tried hard to respond positively to her, but, on later reflection, he realized how completely artificial he must have seemed to her. He ran through the interview and approached the embarrassing (both to her and to himself) question of her offense with insensitivity. In other words, he let his attitudes and feelings about the offender obscure her basic humanity. The interview was a simple ritual. She was placed on probation to him, but their relationship never did manage to overcome that disastrous first encounter. First impressions are indeed vital! He learned a lot about himself and his attitudes through that encounter and tried hard to not to make the same mistake again.

His experience with this woman underscores the desirability of examining your attitudes and prejudices relating to various kinds of people and their behavior before ever dealing with them in a field situation. Treat each person as a unique individual, not as a member of some larger group from whom you expect or do not expect certain ways of behaving. A colleague has a saying on her office wall, which she said she read at the beginning of every day: "There is so much good in the worst of us, and so much bad in the best of us, that it ill behooves any one of us to find any fault with the rest of us."

Explaining the Purpose of the Interview. The actual interview should begin by asking the offender if he or she knows the purpose of the interview. If an offender does not know—and many do not—then, you should fully explain the purpose. You should inform the offender of the type of information you wish to obtain, its use, and who will have access to it. Although an explanation of the uses to which a PSI report will be put (to aid in sentencing decisions, and, if the offender is incarcerated, in prison classification and parole hearings) can raise the anxiety level of an offender, the offender will appreciate the honesty.

It is a good idea at this point to ask offenders if they understand what they have been told so far and if they have any questions. It is very important, however, not to respond with any opinion to such questions as "What do you think I'll get?" or "What are my chances?" Remember, you do not make the final sentencing decision, and you do not wish to raise false hopes or to generate needless anxiety. If you tell an offender that you are "sure" that he or she will receive probation, and the offender is incarcerated instead, that person surely will feel bitter and betrayed. One such incident may have a lasting negative affect on any subsequent dealings that offender may have with you or with any other correctional worker. Conversely, if you tell an offender that he or she is as good as on the bus to prison, but the offender actually is placed on probation, his or her attitude toward you could be one of smug contempt: "The judge didn't buy your recommendation. Just goes to show how valuable your opinion is, doesn't it?"

Some authorities disagree on this point, feeling that if incarceration seems probable, it is a humanitarian gesture to prepare the offender for it. This is rather like the physician's dilemma when asked, "How long have I got?" An honest appraisal in either case, so the argument goes, gives the individual the opportunity to prepare for it by saying goodbyes and putting personal affairs in order. However, in the case of an offender told that he or she will probably be sent to prison, the goodbyes may well be out of the jurisdiction of your state. If you do offer the offender an opinion that turns out to be wrong, or if it leads the offender to abscond, you have only yourself to blame for the consequences. Instead, politely reply that you do not engage in second-guessing judges and that it is not your place to speculate. You now are ready to begin the interview proper.

Account

The Interviewer's Language and Demeanor. The account stage begins the actual interview with the offenders in which he or she responds to your questions. If you are using an offender-intake form, the interview is to clarify and elaborate on the information the offender has written down. When questioning an offender, you are making contact with another human being. Gear your questions both to the offender's vocabulary and to his or her pace. Avoid legalistic or sociological jargon, street talk, and ten-dollar words. The use of fancy phraseology will embarrass the offender whose vocabulary is limited and will not impress a person who is as articulate as you are. Either way, it will distance the offender from you. Similarly, the use of street slang is unprofessional. It will give the offender the idea that you are either patronizing or playing buddy-buddy. Use conventional and easily understandable English. Just as importantly, do not adopt street mannerisms such as an artificially laid-back posture or the latest fad in handshakes. Do not say or do anything that is artificial to you; it will be blatantly visible to those used to being treated dishonestly.

The Use of Authority. A final concern is the officer's proper use of authority. Experts in the counseling field disagree on the issue of whether the use, or even the possession, of authority is detrimental to the helping process. Authority and helping can be incompatible, however, if you use and abuse it to emphasize the moral distance between you and your offender and to puff yourself up with your own importance. The bombastic "big stick" approach only will alienate offenders. They immediately will type you as "just another cop in social workers' threads," and will scoff at your insistence that you only want to "help" them.

Yet, authority comes with the job and you cannot deny it. Offenders will view your failure to use your authority, when appropriate, as weakness. Many offenders value strength and are adept at manipulating perceived weakness. Like feelings, officers' authority must be recognized and accepted, but used with professional restraint. The accouterments of force, such as guns or handcuffs, should not be on display at the first meeting with the offender.

Dealing with Awkward Offenders. Some offenders will be fearful or angry and thus will act hostilely or refuse to answer certain questions. They may be trying to maintain a sense of dignity and control in the only way they know. When such an attitude becomes apparent, do not continue with the interview as if you hoped that ignoring it would make it go away. Say something such as:

"Mr. Jones, I know that this is unpleasant for you and that you must be feeling a little uptight. It's quite natural for you to feel that way. Lots of people do. Why don't we agree to be civil to one another? What do you say?"

This lets Mr. Jones know that you are aware of his feelings, that others have felt that way, that you accept his feelings as natural, and that you are willing to start over again on a new footing.

In those rare instances when offenders continue to refuse to answer questions, or when they continue to respond in a sarcastic, rude, or an abrupt manner, let them know in no uncertain terms that this type of attitude is simply unacceptable. Inform them that if they continue in such a way, then you will terminate the interview and that it will be necessary for them to return to the department to try again after they have rethought their approach. You also may indicate that you will convey such an attitude to the sentencing judge if it continues. If this tactic does not work, try a phone call to the offender's attorney outlining the problem. This never fails to bring about a change in the offender's demeanor.

Most often, however, offenders are anxious to be cooperative and to convey a positive impression during the initial interview. They are feeling you out just as surely as you are feeling them out. Most offenders are aware that their attitudes will be reported to the judge and that they may influence your recommendation. Reluctance and uncooperativeness are much more common among offenders under actual supervision than they are prior to formal supervision. The presentence investigator and the parole board usually see offenders at their best. It is the supervising probation and parole officers who are most frequently confronted with uncooperative offenders. For this reason, it is of the utmost importance that you lay the groundwork for the development of a trusting relationship at the initial interview, a period in which the offender's frame of mind is most conducive to it. (The problem of the reluctant offender is addressed in more detail in Chapter 10).

Regardless of the offenders' level of cooperation, their overall demeanor will provide valuable clues for your assessment. Someone who comes to the interview smelling of alcohol or under the influence of drugs is not taking the process very seriously and obviously will be difficult to supervise if placed on probation. A servile or arrogant manner also will provide clues to character assessment and possible supervision strategies.

These initial observations will assist you in designing a preliminary plan of treatment and will help you to decide if a referral to specialized treatment is in order. When you decide a referral is advisable, discuss the matter with the offender and explain your reasoning. Do not antagonize offenders or put them on the defensive by flatly stating that they have a problem. Try to steer offenders toward that conclusion themselves by asking them how the problem you perceive them as having affects their relationships with others, and how they would feel if they could find support in controlling the problem. You then may discuss the services provided by the agency in question and the benefits they may derive from talking with a counselor there. Remember, the initial interview is positively your best opportunity to get your foot in the door to obtain offenders' cooperation and compliance.

Closure

The interview should be terminated in a planned way so that the offender can anticipate it rather than ending it in an abrupt way. At the end of the interview, summarize with the offender what has gone on during it. Your summary provides the opportunity to determine if anything important has been overlooked and gives the offender the chance to change, clarify, or add to the information he or she has provided. Ask offenders if they have anything to add or anything else to ask. If not, you may conclude the interview, shake the offenders' hand, inform them what will happen next in the sentencing process, state that you will be in touch in the near future, and then walk them to the door.

Evaluate

Back in your office again, immediately go over your notes and write down additional impressions while they are fresh in your mind. Review what went on in the interview within the context of the legal case against the defendant, and determine what, if any collateral interviews will be necessary.

Techniques of Interviewing

The goal of interviewing is to gather information given voluntarily. It is not as difficult as you may think to obtain voluntary information from offenders. Most people like nothing better than to talk about themselves. Even reluctant, angry, or embarrassed offenders probably will succumb to the temptation to talk if they perceive that you are genuinely interested in them. For this reason, the development of genuineness, caring, and empathy are essential. Too much emphasis on technique detracts from the humanness of the interviewing process, and can be painfully transparent if not developed properly in a training situation.

Active Listening |9

This does not mean that techniques are not valuable; they are extremely valuable. The most valuable of these techniques is active listening. Active listening (the opposite of passive listening) is the key to effective communication. Active listening is different from hearing (or passive listening), which is simply the physiological registering of sound not requiring any intellectual effort on the part of the receiver (Gorden 1992: 82). Listening means paying complete attention (intellectually focusing on the sounds) to the information being offered by the offender, and conveying your attention to the offender in verbal and nonverbal ways.

In other words, you must make a conscious decision to attend to the speaker. People want to be listened to and always have. Note the plea from the Biblical Job: "Listen to me, but do listen, and let that be the comfort you offer me; bear with me while I have my say." Note also that Job is saying that simply to be listened to is to be offered comfort.

To communicate to the offender that you are actively listening, maintain eye contact. In addition to conveying interest, eye contact enables you to observe the offender's nonverbal responses to uncomfortable questions. When does the offender avert his or her eyes, when does he or she flush, smile, or sneer? You cannot determine this if you are not watching. There are, however, certain subcultural differences attached to the meaning of eye contact. Middle-class people tend to view frequent eye contact as a sign of honesty and the averting of the eyes as indicative of furtiveness. Inner-city residents, especially blacks, feel that too much eye contact is a nonverbal challenge, so it may provoke hostility. Be very careful that your efforts to maintain eye contact do not inadvertently turn into an attempt to stare the offender down. Additionally, in some American Indian cultures, individuals are taught that it is impolite to gaze directly at someone else.

When you are listening to the offender, you should be sitting about two-arm lengths apart (do not have a desk or other physical objects between you). Maintain a slightly forward-leaning posture. Leaning forward at certain points during the interview conveys an intensification of interest. Do not get so close to offenders as to make them feel uncomfortable–that is, so that you are invading their personal space. This is particularly important if the offender is of the opposite sex.

It is all too easy to convey unintended messages of a sexual nature this way. This author once had a female offender who started to cry during the PSI interview. He offered her a tissue and placed a comforting hand on hers. She took immediate advantage of this gesture of sympathy to grasp his hand and say: "I'll do anything to get out of this." This obvious sexual invitation was disquieting. Offenders who make such offers expect something in return (a favorable sentencing recommendation, easy supervision conditions, a blind-eye to certain violations, and so forth). Had he succumbed to her invitation, he may well have found himself paying the $700 in restitution she owed, violated his professional code of ethics, and, not the least, opened himself to a criminal charge. You must be very careful that your behavior is not open to this kind of misinterpretation.

Questioning and Probing

Although the purpose of the interview is to listen to what the offender has to say, your job is to guide the communication toward relevant topics. You are interested in gathering information about offenders' backgrounds and lifestyles, about their attitudes about the offense, and about concerns and problems that may have led to it. To get this information, you have to ask questions. As Colwell, Hiscock, and Memon (2002: 289) advise as to the progress of the interview: The steps of the interview begin with the most open, least leading forms of questioning, and then progress to more specific questioning as circumstances require. The initial goal is to provide every opportunity to give a free narrative account before more specific questions are used. After the free narrative is provided, the participant [the interviewee] is prompted to elaborate on details mentioned in the narrative through the introduction of open-ended questions.

We will discuss two types of questions here: OPEN and CLOSED. According to Ivey (1983: 41):

> Open questions are those that can't be answered in a few short words. They encourage others to talk and provide you with maximum information. Closed questions can be answered in a few short words or sentences. They have the advantage of focusing the interview and obtaining information, but the burden of talk remains with the interviewer.

Offenders often will be unwilling to explore their personal lives and feelings with you. It is rare, however, that they outright will refuse to answer your questions. With reluctant offenders, it is necessary to encourage sharing through the use of probes. *Probes* are indirect open-ended questions that encourage the offender to explore some point to which he or she has alluded. Probes are verbal tactics for prompting offenders to talk about themselves and to share their thoughts, feelings, and concerns with you in a specific and concrete way.

For example, if Debbie indicates to you that her marriage is an unhappy one and that she "wants out," do not be content with that raw datum. Explore. Say something such as "So you feel terrible about your marriage and feel trapped. About what do you feel worst?" You are encouraging Debbie to clarify her general statement by relating specific and concrete instances that give rise to her generalized feelings of dissatisfaction. Your probing may give Debbie the first real opportunity she has ever had to really explore and vent her feelings with regard to her marriage. Furthermore, Debbie's trouble with the law may be a direct or indirect consequence of her poor marital relationship. If this turns out to be the case, you will have discovered a starting point for your later counseling sessions with her if she is placed on probation.

Probing questions should be open-ended, meaning that they cannot be answered by a simple yes or no. Questions should be of the type: "Now that you know what the problem is between you and your husband, what do you plan to do about it?" They should not be of the type: "Now that you know what the problem is between you and your husband, do you plan to do anything about it?" A response of yes or no to this question will lead to further questions, giving Debbie the impression that she is being grilled. Using open-ended questions reduces the number of questions you ask and give the offender some sense of control.

It obviously is desirable in some cases to use closed questions, which require simple answers, such as "What was the last school you attended?" Closed questions probably will be used most often in your follow-up to offender responses to open questions and in dealing with factual information such as whether an offender is married. Closed questions sometimes have to be used when open-ended questions would be preferable, such as when working with adolescents and with mildly retarded offenders who verbalize poorly. Sometimes you will run into streetwise offenders who make it a practice of not volunteering any information that is not specifically requested, which means that to get the information you want, you will have to rephrase your open question as a closed one. You never should stop trying, however, to get the offender to speak freely about himself or herself by the use of open questions.

Regardless of the type of question used, you should not rush offenders by throwing questions at them in staccato fashion. Your tone of voice and rate of speech indicate clearly how you feel about another person and whether you really have been listening to previous replies. Think of the many ways that you can say "I'm really interested in you." Give offenders ample time to think through their answers to your questions. Do not be embarrassed by silence or attempt to fill it in with small talk. The offenders may be groping for ideas during such breaks in the conversation, and small talk will interrupt the flow of thought. If the silence becomes overly long, continue the interview by asking the offenders to tell you more about the last point you covered. Do not attempt to break the silence by putting words into their mouths. They may grasp at your idea and agree with it in an effort to please you or to avoid saying what was really on their mind. Either way, you will be recording and evaluating offenders' response as theirs when they are actually your own. "A good criminal justice interview," writes Alexander (2000: 103), "permits silence."

Listening

Evaluating responses to questions requires active listening. Active listening requires a lot of practice. Some people are easy to listen to, and some are difficult. Prejudices and biases on the part of the officer will interfere with active listening to the offender, as will poor communication skills on the part of the offender. When either of these conditions is present, it is especially important to make an extra effort to listen to what the offender is saying. Active listening requires much alertness and flexibility. Be especially alert to any recurring thoughts or concepts that the offender presents and mentally flag them so that you can raise them later for further and deeper discussion. Be flexible enough to deal with issues as the offender presents them. If you insist only on dealing with topics when you are ready for them, you may miss some vital information because offenders may no longer feel as disposed to discuss these issues as they were at the time they first broached them. In short, active listening implies what psychologist Theodore Reik (1956) calls "listening with the third ear." This does not require the mere auditory recording of the offender's actual words so much as listening to what he or she is trying to tell you.

Offenders may be telling you things that they have no conscious intention of revealing. Does the offender reveal self-centeredness by the overuse of personal pronouns? Does the offender reveal overdependence or a lack of responsibility by constantly blaming others for every little misfortune? Does the offender bemoan his or her sins as vigorously as they are committed, thus perhaps revealing false remorse? What do the adjectives the offender uses to describe significant others reveal about the state of his or her interpersonal relationships? What type of defense mechanisms (to be discussed later), such as rationalization, projection, and displacement, does the offender use to distort reality?

This third-ear listening will tell you a lot more about the offender than face-value responses of the "what he did to me and what I said to her type." However, you must restrain the urge to play Dr. Freud by reading too much into nonspecific responses at this stage. You simply do not yet have sufficient knowledge of the offender to make unsupported speculations in a report that has so much importance to his or her future. Third-ear insights should be noted for your future use, but they should not be relayed to the sentencing judge as facts. When you begin to develop an empathetic understanding of the offender, and when a positive relationship has formed between you, then you may broach such issues. Of course, if you perceive something about an offender's responses that has direct applicability to the present offense (such as rationalizing or intellectualizing about the crime) and that has implications for sentencing and supervision, such responses should be explored with the offender then and there.

Resist the Temptation to Interrupt

Have you ever noticed while conversing with someone that instead of truly attending to what the other person is saying, you were thinking of the next thing you wanted to say or that you interrupted that person in midsentence? Have you ever noticed how annoying this can be when others do it to you and how it causes you to lose your train of thought? When you are interviewing an offender, you are not engaged in a debate in which your objective is to score points.

It is all too easy to interrupt offenders when you perceive their verbal responses to your inquiries to be off the track. Do not let yourself become irritated and impatient with offenders' digressions. They may be approaching the topic you brought up in the most direct way they know how. There are limits, of course, to the amount of digression that you may tolerate, but an interruption made too soon may prevent the emergence of significant information. Some people simply need more time to arrive at their destination. Although side excursions can be time-consuming, a little extra time allowed during the initial interview actually can conserve time when you are attempting to establish a working relationship with an offender.

Keeping the Offender in the Foreground

Give the offender the lion's share of the "air time" during the interview. Unfortunately, in probation interviews, probation officers out-talk offenders in terms of word count by about three to one (Clark 2007). This is exactly the opposite of how it should be. Goyer, Redding, and Rickey (1968: 14) have suggested that if you find yourself talking uninterruptedly for as little as two minutes during an interview, you are failing to get through to the offender. It follows that it is a good idea to reduce interviewer talk time as much as possible. After all, we have agreed that the time is theirs. You must resist the temptation to thrust your opinions and advice onto offenders and talk them into a coma. Many offenders will be only too happy to allow the interviewer to babble on as a tactic to avoid exploring their own problems. Talk only when necessary to elicit information or to refocus or channel the interview in fruitful directions.

Some Further Impediments to Active Listening

You should guard against certain other impediments to active listening. These are daydreaming, detouring, arguing, and rehearsing. We all are guilty of each of these errors at one time or another. It is important in your chosen field to be aware of them and to take steps to reorient yourself to the content of offenders' communication when you perceive yourself to be drifting away from it.

Daydreaming occurs when you are bored with what you are hearing or when you have pressing needs unrelated to the present concerns. You may veer off on your own personal track and leave the offender behind, forgetting that the interview time belongs to the offender. You must never daydream during offender interviews. It soon becomes apparent to the offender that you are not interested in his or her problems, and you will experience failure in your efforts to establish a firm relationship. Frequent daydreamers are out of touch with their present reality. They fail in many tasks because they focus more on a future "could be" than on what is actually going on now.

Detouring occurs when some piece of communicated information reminds you of something not immediately relevant. You then may tend to let your thoughts wander off on tangents, coming back now and again to touch the actual line of communication. By the time your thoughts again make contact with the offender's, you never can be sure that the track you are on accurately corresponds to the offender's track. More often than not, it will not. Whether on the highway or in an interview, detours can get you lost. Frequent detourers are inclined to be scatterbrained; they have difficulty focusing on the problem at hand.

Arguing occurs when an offender makes a statement that rankles you in some fashion and you cut off the offender's line of communication to present your opinions. You are forgetting that it is the offender's opinion and not yours that is the present concern. Allow offenders to express and explore their feelings fully without debating them. Do not argue with offenders, either by actually voicing your opinions or just by debating the offender in your mind. Arguers tend to be either self-righteous or contentious individuals who are overly concerned with their own viewpoints.

Rehearsing occurs when, instead of continuing to attend to the offender, you pause to consider how you will respond to an earlier statement. Rehearsers tend to be either unsure of themselves or perfectionists. They feel that responses are never adequate if they are not well formulated before delivery. They seek just the right word or example to make a point. The trouble is that, while you are thinking of that "perfect" response, you will have missed what else the offender says, including things that might make your response irrelevant.

Regardless of counseling orientation or the purposes of an interview, the most crucial skill of all is listening. Listening is the prerequisite for all other skills. After all, if you have not really listened to what the offender has been saying, you cannot formulate meaningful follow-up questions; you cannot develop rapport; you cannot even begin to understand the offender, and your assessment will be sloppy at best. Poor listening will frustrate and alienate offenders, and you may become part of their problem rather than part of the solution.

Responding: Guiding the Offender's Disclosure

No matter how hard you have been listening, it often is necessary to verify an offender's message so that you do not jump to wrong conclusions. When you perceive a response to be somewhat ambiguous, you should ask for clarification. Clarification involves a question of the type "Are you saying that. . . . ?" or "Do you mean that. . . . ?" Your request for clarification gives the offender the opportunity to confirm your understanding. Paraphrasing, a simple restatement of the offender's message in the interviewer's words, is similar to clarification. Paraphrasing is used to restate a message with factual content, such as a description of a person, place, event, or situation, to clarify the message, to let offenders know that you have been attending, and to encourage them to focus on the content more deeply.

In contrast, reflection is a rephrasing of the emotional content of the offender's message. Reflection is useful when you want to identify the offender's feelings about the factual message presented to you. People do not always express feelings verbally but may be identified by nonverbal cues such as rigid body posture, reddening of the face, pursed lips, tone of voice, and so forth. The purpose of reflection is to help offenders to become fully aware of their feelings and to encourage them to explore them.

A hypothetical dialog illustrates these techniques. A thirty-year-old single mother of three children, Betty, has been found guilty of child endangering. Her oldest son, Jason, age nine, was hospitalized with a broken arm. A physical examination revealed that he frequently had been physically abused. You ask her to explain why she abuses Jason. Some possible interviewer responses follow her reply. Try to think of some of your own replies by imagining what it would be like in Betty's shoes.

> **OFFENDER:** I don't really know why I do these things to Jason. I do love him. I'd do anything to change things. I'm not proud of what I did. He's a beautiful boy. I guess I just get so frustrated having to bring three children up on what the child support pays you. You know, it's no easy task trying to raise three kids. I can't get work because the kids are all so young. I just sit at home thinking about the future. I find myself drinking more heavily as time goes on. All that sitting and drinking hasn't done much for my figure. I weigh about 210 right now. Who would want to hire a slob like me? If only I could get a job I know things would be better for us all.

> **INTERVIEWER** [Clarification]: Are you saying that one of the hardest things facing you right now is your inability to get work,

which would enable you to make a better life for yourself and your children? Do you mean that your situation leads you to do these things to Jason?

INTERVIEWER [Paraphrase]: You love Jason, but your responsibility for raising your family by yourself is very difficult for you. You are having a tough time of it.

INTERVIEWER [Reflection]: You feel frustrated and angry about your inability to take care of your children as you would like. You feel terribly guilty about doing what you did to Jason. You feel embarrassed about your weight.

The Victim

A growing, but long-overdue, awareness of the victim as the "forgotten party" in the criminal justice system has prompted a number of states to require that victims have a more active part in the sentencing process. For instance, most states require that a "victim-impact statement" be included in each PSI, and that the judge must consider statements contained in the victim-impact statement when making the sentencing decision. This requirement demands something more than the perfunctory telephone call to ascertain financial losses that used to be the norm. A telephone call will suffice, however, when the victim in a case of theft, burglary, or forgery is a business establishment (where no one individual has been personally victimized) and you merely wish to determine restitution figures.

In the case of personal victimization, however, victims should be given the courtesy of a face-to-face meeting with you. Both you and the victim can benefit from such an interview. You gather information that will help you to evaluate the offender; the victim can receive assurances of safety and a feeling that he or she has not been forgotten or ignored by the criminal justice system.

Interviewing the Victim: Preparation

With the ascent of the restorative-justice philosophy in criminal justice, a concern for victims' needs and feelings finally has emerged. Victims' input in plea bargain negotiations and sentencing and parole hearings may restore some of the confidence they may have lost in the criminal justice system, and also may restore some sense of control over their lives. Remember, under the philosophy of restorative justice, the victim is also your client, and you should do everything you can to make this component of the philosophy as meaningful and successful as possible.

Your first approach to the victim should be a phone call to make an appointment. Explain the reason for your wish to meet personally with the victim and set up a time at his or her convenience. To relieve victims of any further inconvenience, and as a courtesy, the meeting should take place in the victim's home unless he or she wishes otherwise. When you meet with the victim, identify yourself as an officer of the court by presenting your credentials. You then may go over the purpose of the interview again. Some victims welcome the opportunity to speak about the crime again in the informal and familiar setting of their own homes, but for others it is a nuisance that they rather would avoid. Let the victim know that your presence indicates the concerns the legal system has about his or her experience and that it is an opportunity to have some input into the sentencing process. This assurance tends to ease some of the pain and anger of all except the most cynical, and it returns a sense of control to those victims who feel that they have lost much of it by their victimization.

Personal criminal victimization is an intensely negative experience. Even if the crime is a nonviolent one in which the victim never had to confront the offender, the experience can leave a person with feelings of complete helplessness and violation. These feelings quite naturally tend to generate anger and a certain measure of self-blame, especially among victims of sexual assault. The typical experience of the victim as the case progresses through the courts sometimes involves interminable delays and postponements, which does nothing to mitigate these feelings.

The victim may displace some of that anger and self-blame onto the pre-sentence investigator. Be prepared to encounter such a natural reaction and deal with it in a sensitive manner. Your most trying experiences in the field may be to conduct interviews with parents who have lost a child to a drunken driver or with relatives of loved ones who have been brutally raped or murdered. Extreme sensitivity and understanding are absolute musts in such instances. In no case should you imply sympathy for the offender or make any suggestion that the victim may have contributed to his or her own victimization even if you think it, and never argue with a victim or the victim's survivors. Investigators should possess a self-concept strong enough to allow victims or their survivors to vent their anger on them without retaliation.

When Not to Interview

The matter of interviewing child victims of sexual abuse is entirely different. Avoid any contact with such victims. It is not merely uncomfortable for a child to recount the episode; it may add to the psychological damage the child suffers. Henry Hartman, a criminal psychiatrist of many years experience, puts it this way (1978: 217): "Intense emotional reactions on the part of the parents, repeated questioning by police, unpleasant appearances and cross-examination in courtrooms may all be as traumatic or even more traumatic than the offense itself."

There is no point in risking further trauma for the sake of a little additional insight into the offense. There are children who, even after long-term sexual victimization by adults, have suffered no ill effects until the relationships were discovered and the children subjected to responses like those Hartman names. Such social reactions lead children to believe that much or all of the blame for what transpired belongs to them. Certainly it does not, and the investigating officer should not call up the child's residual feelings of guilt and shame in the pursuit of a "complete" PSI. You should interview parents of the children, and allow them to discuss the effects of the offense on their children.

Conducting the Interview: Asking for Details of the Offense

It is not advisable to request the details of the offense from victims in all cases. They have already recounted them numerous times to other officials, and the retelling may be quite painful for them. However, offer them the opportunity to speak about the offense if they desire to do so. Say something like "I know this has been an awful experience for you and you would probably like to forget it, but is there anything at all that you would like to add that you didn't tell the police or the prosecutor?" In posing the question this way, you have conveyed to the victim your recognition of his or her ordeal, and you have given the victim the option of elaborating. The decision must be entirely the victim's, and the officer should not press the issue in the face of obvious reluctance.

Reassuring the Victim

One of the things that crime victims need most is reassurance of their safety. Many victims fear retaliation or worry that a burglar will come back. In this author's experience as a police officer and as a probation officer, he has never known perpetrators to retaliate against the victim after the case had been adjudicated, or a burglar to hit the same house twice. This is not to say that such things do not happen, but they are extremely rare. Make a clear statement to this effect to frightened victims. In the event that the victim and offender are known to each other, you even may indicate that in the event that the perpetrator is placed on probation, you will make it a condition of probation that he or she is to have no contact of any sort with the victim. Victims need to hear such reassurances.

Promises to the Victim

It is important that you not make any promises to the victim that you cannot keep or make statements regarding the defendant's probable sentence. Some states have made provisions for victims to have input into the sentencing of those who have offended against them. If your state has a statutory provision for a victim's recommendation for sentencing, you, of course, should request one. Whether these recommendations actually have an impact on sentencing decisions is a question awaiting a body of research.

Research indicates a statistically significant relationship between victim's recommendations and sentences imposed in sexual assault cases, but the relationship disappeared when the researcher controlled for the effects of seriousness of crime and the offender's prior record (Walsh 1986). Future research may show different results. Whatever the case may be, do not lead the victim into the belief that his or her recommendation necessarily will be heeded. Be as honest with victims as you are with offenders. Do not risk victim's future anger and disrespect for the sake of their momentary peace of mind and satisfaction. Specific questions that you should ask the victim are listed in Chapter 6 on the PSI report.

Terminating the Interview

Terminate the interview with victims by reiterating your assurances and thanking them for their cooperation. Give victims your card and tell them that they are welcome to call you with further concerns at any time in the future. The victims may view this invitation as a further indication that they are not the forgotten party in the criminal justice process. Finally, if it is not the practice of the prosecutor's office in your jurisdiction to apprise victims of sentencing dates, tell victims that you will notify them personally. At the very least, inform the victim of the final disposition of the case.

Interrogating the Offender

Reasons for Interrogation

Many jurisdictions legally define their probation and parole officers as law enforcement officers. As a law enforcement officer, you are responsible for monitoring the behavior of offenders. When offenders break the law or some condition of their supervision, or are suspected of doing so, it is your duty to question them.

As you will see, your questioning under such circumstances will require a different strategy. This type of questioning is interrogation.

To those who enter the community corrections field with the notion that their only role is that of a helper, this definition is sometimes distasteful, probably because they associate interrogation with the third-degree tactics of yesteryear. Do not lose sight of the fact that you are functioning both as a law enforcement officer and as a counselor, but those two roles do not necessarily conflict. As a law enforcement officer, you sometimes may have to use the techniques of interrogation. For instance, you may need to learn the truth about acts committed by offenders that place them in violation of their probation or parole. Offenders do not readily admit to violations. You are not doing justice to your role, or ultimately to offenders, if you do not learn and deal with details of their violations.

You also may need to interrogate offenders during a presentence investigation interview if they flatly deny having committed the crimes of which they have been convicted. This is not unusual. An unpublished study at the author's department found that 18 percent of a sample of 416 offenders denied their crimes during the PSI interview. Since denial has implications for decisions about sentencing and treatment, it behooves the investigating officer not to report simply that the offender denies the crime and leave it at that. Many offenders will tell you that they are innocent and that they pled guilty on their lawyer's advice, or that they did so to obtain a plea bargain agreement.

Although it is not unknown for innocent offenders to plead guilty because their lawyers have considered the case against them to be too strong, the fact that the case is now before you makes the possibility rather remote. Given the legal restraints on police questioning (restraints that you do not have in the presentence investigation situation), and the defendant's privilege of silence in court, your interrogation may be the first opportunity to get to the truth of the matter. Probably about one out of every four offenders who initially denies their guilt finally admits it under questioning and at least two of the others make statements that are sufficient to dispel doubts of guilt.

Distinguishing between Interviewing and Interrogation

You conduct a thorough investigation of a specific allegation brought against a suspect through systematic and formal questioning. There are two basic differences between interviewing and interrogation. The first concerns your relationship with the offender. You have temporarily discarded the helping attitude of the counselor and adopted the skeptical manner of the law enforcement officer. The second concerns purpose. Interviewing has the broad goal of gathering general information, whereas interrogation involves the drawing out of quite specific information which the offender may be highly motivated to keep hidden—namely, whether the offender did or did not commit the act that you, the police, or some other party accuse him or her of committing (Vessel 1998).

The interrogation is also different from the interviewing process in that it requires that the interrogator, not the offender, control the flow of activity. You must control the timing, content, and wording of your questioning with your singular purpose in mind. Suspect offenders must be given only enough initiative and control to allow them to relate their stories. They must come to understand that you mean business and that for the moment you are not interested in anything else but the question at hand (Navarro 2003).

On a legal note, if the matter for which you are conducting the interview involves a new offense, and if what you learn from the offender is to be used in a court of law for evidentiary purposes, you must inform the offender of his or her Fifth Amendment rights as required by *Miranda*. In *United States v. Deaton* (1972), the Court ruled that a probationer or parolee is under more pressure to respond to his or her probation/parole officer than to a police officer, and therefore the *Miranda* warnings must be given.

Being Confident by Being Prepared

Preparing yourself for an interrogation is both different from and similar to preparing for an interview. The major difference is that an interrogation is often a battle of wits and the atmosphere can be quite charged because the offender is aware of that fact. If you are to conduct an effective interrogation, one that will lead you to the truth regarding the matter at hand, you have to approach the task with confidence. Convey an impression of confidence to the offender. To achieve this level of confidence, be fully prepared. This means that you must be completely familiar with all of the evidence supporting the offender's guilt, as well as any evidence that might indicate otherwise. Depending on the situation, such evidence might include police reports, victim statements, or information from an informant. Not having all the information that is available to you will put you at a serious disadvantage once the interrogation begins.

Conducting the Interrogation

The interrogation may take place in your office or it may take place in a cell at the county jail. In any case, as the offender's supervising officer, unlike a police officer, you will have had an ongoing relationship with him or her. Consequently, you are able to dispense with the usual police lead-ins to interrogation such as requests for demographic information including name, address, and place of employment. You should greet offenders in a friendly but businesslike manner and inform them of your purpose by saying something like, "Jim, I've asked you to come to see me (or, I've come to see you) to get to the bottom of this matter that has come to my attention." You, then, may begin your questioning.

As indicated, confidence in your professionalism and in your preparation is of the utmost importance. A lack of confidence is reflected by frequently referring back to reports, hemming and hawing around, squirming in your chair, acting impatiently. This will convey the impression to the offender that perhaps the evidence against him or her is not all that strong. Demonstrate to offenders that the evidence that is in your possession leads you to the firm conviction that they are guilty. This conviction should be stated in a nonemotional and clinical manner. The credibility of the interrogator depends on these two points: his or her thorough knowledge of the matter under discussion, and the offender's perceptions of him or her as a competent professional. Do not "blow" the positive relationship with offenders that you have worked so hard to gain by becoming frustrated and angry because you feel that you cannot break down their defenses.

Style

Differences exist between interviewing and interrogation, but much that was said about interviewing also applies to interrogating. First and foremost, you must approach the task in a completely professional manner. Any attempts to borrow the techniques of the movie detective will prove disastrous. Do not put up a "tough guy" front. The typical criminal will see through this and match you verbal blow for verbal blow, a competition that could well end up being decided in favor of offenders who rely on such tactics to survive every day of their lives. If this happens, you reveal yourself as a phony, and you can forget about any respect that your offender may have had for you.

Clifford Unwin, an experienced British police inspector, indicates that although the interrogator must control the psychological situation, it is not wise to adopt a role of complete psychological domination. He writes: "The problem is that if the interrogator limits himself [or herself] to displays of power he [or she] may find in certain situations that he [or she] is running the risk of doing exactly the opposite. It may cause the suspect to confirm his [or her] beliefs that the interrogator is the enemy and is someone to be defied, particularly with a hardened or seasoned criminal" (1978: 1875).

As implied by Unwin, never adopt the attitude of "NIGYSOB" ("Now I've got you, you son-of-a-bitch") described by Eric Berne (1964) in his book *Games People Play*. If you project such an obviously self-satisfied attitude to offenders undergoing interrogation, in effect you are issuing a challenge and inviting resistance. You also imply that your objective all along has been "to get" offenders rather than to help them.

There is quite a bit of experimental evidence to suggest that alternating questioning styles produces better results than a single style (Vrij 2006, Vrij, Mann, and Fisher 2006). Using this strategy, the officer begin an interrogation with interview-like information gathering using open-ended questions ("What did you do that particular evening"), then switches to an accusatory interrogation style ("Hey, I know you're hiding something from me"), and then back again to information gathering ("Tell me again what happened on that evening"). Of course, only long experience will inform you of the optimum times to switch back and forth and ultimately with what type of style works best with what type of offender.

Ask Leading Questions

Questioning within an interrogation context often will be of the leading type. A leading question is one in which the wording strongly encourages a specific answer (this kind of question should never be used in an interview). For example: you receive a complaint from Jim's estranged wife that he was drinking last night, and that he went over to her home and slapped her around. Jim's parole conditions include maintaining sobriety and staying away from his wife. You may confront Jim with: "You were in the Western Bar drinking last night weren't you? Isn't it also true that you became drunk and went over to your wife's home and beat her up?" Such questions, asked in a businesslike tone, have the psychological effect of making it more difficult to deny than a simple "Were you drinking last night?"

Reveal a Little Information

Reinforce both your confidence and the offender's anxiety by revealing some of the evidence you have indicative of guilt, or in a PSI situation, some of the evidence gathered by police agencies, taking careful note of how the offender deals with this information. However, do not reveal all evidence in one giant salvo. If the offenders successfully weather the initial attack, the officer has nothing left in reserve with which to surprise them. Always keep offenders on the defensive by letting them guess at the extent of the evidence in your possession. Point out inconsistencies in their stories and ask them to account for them (this cannot be done if you have not thoroughly assimilated the "official" version and paid complete attention to the offender's version).

Some offenders will respond to a straightforward statement from you indicating that alibis or protestations of innocence are "bullshit." On more than one occasion, this author has been confronted with a knowing smile, followed by the real story, after such a remark. This usually works with an offender who has been through the system before, and who tends to look upon what is going on between you as some sort of "game." This, of course, depends on the seriousness of the consequences to the offender of making such an admission. Other offenders will react defensively to a direct statement such as the above. With such offenders, it is preferable to state: "You haven't told me the whole truth," than to say: "You've been lying to me." The difference is a subtle one, but a real one, nevertheless. Only experience will tell you when either approach is preferable. Usually, however, the latter method works best with the more "respectable" and less "streetwise" offenders.

Letting Offenders Damn Themselves

John E. Reid and Associates, a respected trainer of law enforcement personnel in the art of interviewing and interrogating, claims that interrogators can achieve their goal (arriving at the truth of the matter) with 85 percent accuracy by watching carefully for various verbal and behavioral cues (Kassin et al. 2007). Every month this company offers Web Tips to members. Some of these tips are free to all and often come with interesting illustrative cases. These tips can be viewed by going to www.reid.com/educational_info/r_tips.html.

It is often a good ploy to allow the offender to make statements that you know are lies and for you to give the impression that you are accepting them at face value. The awkward thing about a lie is that it requires additional lies to support it. Eventually, this compounding of falsehoods should paint offenders into a very uncomfortable corner from which only truth will remove them. If the interrogator allows offenders to get themselves into such a psychologically uncomfortable position and then points out a series of inconsistencies, he or she has created a strong motive (the removal of psychological discomfort) for them to "come clean."

Taking Advantage of Offender Discomfort

If this does not provide the desired admission, signs of guilt, such as confusion, stammering, nervous sweating, an active Adam's apple, the refusing to maintain eye contact, and other emotional reactions, point out to the offender that you take these signs as indicative of guilt. Take advantage of such signs of physiological discomfort by looking squarely into the offender's eyes and repeating some of your most threatening questions. You also may ask the offender to repeat his or her story three or four times at different points in the interrogation. It is easy to be consistent if the story is true, but it is very difficult to remember little details used to support a falsehood. That is, you can tell the truth in a dozen different ways, but it is hard to do the same with a lie. Knowing that you are aware of their discomfort often prompts offenders to unburden themselves by making a confession.

Often, the use of morally neutral words rather than negatively or emotionally loaded ones will help guilty offenders unburden (Inbau and Reid 1985). Think of the emotional differences between the statements given below:

Neutral	Emotionally Loaded
"John, I want you to *tell me the truth*."	"John, I want you to *confess*"
"Alice, did you *take* those items?"	"Alice, did you *steal* those items?"
"Did you *shoot* Mr. Brooks?"	"Did you *kill* Mr. Brooks?"

You will not be as far along in the interrogation as you may want to be if you ask "Did you have sex with Kathy?" as opposed to "Did you rape Kathy?" But, the greater likelihood that the offender will answer affirmatively to the more emotionally neutral question gives you a further advantage.

Bluffing

Bluffing is a weak form of interrogation. Bluffing means conveying to offenders the impression that you have access to information which is damaging to them when, in fact, you do not. For instance, you may be interrogating Jack on the basis of police information that he has been trafficking in drugs. You may indicate to him that you have "accurate" information from "confidential informants" that he has been selling drugs. Bluffs such as this may pay off large dividends, but they are more likely to be "called." If Jack calls your bluff, all you can do is withdraw as gracefully as possible. What if he really is not guilty of trafficking? Your crude "poker" tactics will offend him sorely and perhaps do irreparable damage to the supportive relationship you have been seeking to develop with him. The cost/benefit ratio of such tactics do not recommend their use. Be honest with offenders. It is always the best policy.

The "Back Door" Approach

Some authorities on police interrogation advocate a "back door" approach to interrogation (Napier and Adams 1998, Unwin 1978). That is, prompt a confession from a suspect by downplaying the seriousness of the offense the individual is suspected of committing, conveying sympathy and "understanding" of why such a crime would be committed under the circumstances, placing the burden of blame on victims or accomplices, or intimating that the act was perhaps accidental. Although such an approach may be used successfully by police interrogators, it is not advocated for the corrections worker. Confessions using this psychological ploy are obtained by lessening the guilt felt by the suspects by conveying to them that their actions were not really that bad that others would do the same thing in their shoes, and by blame-sharing. While this suits police purposes by "clearing" crimes, it is counterproductive to the correctional goal. Rehabilitation is not accomplished by providing offenders with easy rationales for their actions. Correctional workers always must be aware of their dual role, and should not compromise one aspect of it to satisfy the immediate requirements of the other.

Terminating the Interrogation

The way that you terminate the interrogation will depend on the circumstances. If the interrogation was necessitated by a technical violation of supervision conditions, such as associating with known criminals, continuing substance abuse, failing to report to you, or any other violation of this kind, the action you take may be discretionary. You may feel it necessary to initiate formal proceedings for the revocation of probation or parole, or you may decide to resume your helping relationship.

If the interrogation resulted from an arrest for a new crime, any further action on your part has to await formal adjudication. In any case, the offender should be informed of your next step as soon as you have decided what it is to be. You may be able to inform the offender of your decision then and there, or you may feel it necessary to investigate further and think the matter over before declaring your intentions. In any case, explain your decision to the offender and give your reasons for making it. Regardless of what that decision might be, make every effort to reestablish your working relationship with the offender. Even if you have decided to initiate revocation proceedings, most offenders realize that you are only doing your job and will not permanently alienate themselves from you if you have dealt fairly, honestly, and professionally with them.

Summary

This chapter has introduced the techniques of interviewing and interrogation. Prepare for both tasks by thoroughly familiarizing yourself with all the pertinent information available. An effective interview must begin by establishing rapport. This is particularly important in criminal justice where offenders are not exactly enthusiastic about being in your office. Offenders are convicted criminals, but they are also human beings who are deserving of consideration and respect. Make them as comfortable as possible, and show that you are concerned and are willing to listen to them.

Listening, really listening, is the most important aspect of an effective interview. Give the offender the "air time," and resist interruptions and debates–the interview time belongs to the offender. Offenders must be encouraged to explore themselves and their behavior. Encourage this exploration through the frequent use of probes and open-ended questions. Make sure that you understand what offenders are trying to tell you by using paraphrasing, clarification, and reflective techniques. Even the most awkward offenders will settle down and provide you lots of valuable assessment information if you treat them with patience and respect, but also with firmness, when it is required.

Interviewing victims requires a special sensitivity to their victimization. Any reluctance on their part to be interviewed or to approach certain subjects should be respected absolutely. Do not dig for details of sexual offenses (they are in the official record, anyway). It is extremely unadvisable to interview child victims of sexual assault. Never argue with victims about anything, and do not upset yourself if they sometimes use you as a convenient target for their verbal anger. Finally, reassure victims as much as possible, but, as with offenders, do not make any promises that are not within your power to keep.

Sometimes interrogation techniques are required. Any interrogation should be approached in a calm, clinical, and professional manner. Unlike the interview in which the purpose is to gather large amounts of general information, the interrogation is geared to one specific aim–"did you do it?" Also, unlike the interview, you—rather than the offender–will control the content and pace of the interrogation. Know the evidence supportive of your offender's guilt, but do not jeopardize your relationship with the offender by coming on like the movie detective. Useful interrogation techniques such as letting offenders damn themselves and taking advantage of offender discomfort are included. Use these recommended techniques when it is necessary for you to interrogate, but above all, be honest and fair with the offender and be yourself.

Exercise in Listening and Interviewing

This is an exercise in listening using the Client Management Classification (CMC) semi-structured interview schedule reproduced in Chapter 7. Although this exercise will familiarize you with the type of questions asked in a typical PSI interview, its main purpose is to provide experience in listening. Divide students into groups of two, with one student taking the part of the interviewer and the other the interviewee. Rather than role playing, the interviewee should relate to the interviewer actual aspects of his or her life. For instance, when asked "How do (did) you get along with your father?" the interviewee should respond accurately with reference to his or her own father.

The main purpose of this interview exercise is to develop your ability to listen actively. Did you ever buy a lottery ticket or bet on a ball game and then listen for the results on the radio? Think back to that time and how you listened to the results. You sat close to the radio and faced it with intense interest. You leaned toward it, and you were impervious to all other stimuli surrounding you. That is how you should proceed with this exercise–with intensity and interest. Ask the questions provided in the schedule, but you should use, when appropriate, probes, open-ended questions, ask for clarification, paraphrase responses, and reflect feelings.

On the basis of the interview, you should write a brief social history of your partner (a PSI without offense, criminal history, and evaluation and recommendation material) based on the information obtained. After writing this history, give it to the interviewee for evaluation. The interviewee should evaluate the history and your interviewing performance according to the following criteria:

1. Eye contact was maintained without gazing or staring.   Yes__ No__

2. Body posture was appropriate (relaxed, slight forward lean).   Yes__ No__

3. He/she made me feel comfortable and relaxed.   Yes__ No__

4. He/she made me really think about things which I have not thought about for some time by the use of probes.   Yes__ No__

5. He/she seemed to be genuinely interested in me.   Yes__ No__

6. He/she delivered questions without hesitations.   Yes__ No__

7. He/she often asked for clarification and paraphrased often.   Yes__ No__

8. I felt that I could tell him/her just about anything he/she asked about my personal life.   Yes__ No__

9. He/she accurately reflected my feelings.   Yes__ No__

10. On a scale of 1 (low) to 10 (high), I would rate his/her reported accuracy of my social history as

    1 2 3 4 5 6 7 8 9 10 (circle one).

After each student has taken a turn at being both the interviewer and interviewee, share these ratings with one another. Ratings should be the honest evaluations of the rater, and not designed to ignore poor technique in the name of "smooth sailing." Constructive feedback should be viewed by the interviewer as just that. Think of it as another exercise in self-disclosure in which your partner has revealed something of your "blind self," in this case, your ability to conduct an effective interview. The benefits of these exercises will be enhanced greatly if you have access to a video recorder so that you will receive visual and audio feedback of your interview behavior. Lastly, do not forget that it is your first attempt. Learn from it.

Perspective from the Field
On Rules and Crisis Intervention

By Charles L. Miller

Chuck Miller spent six years as a police officer before entering the corrections field. His corrections experience includes supervision of maximum-security and death-row sections and command of the SWAT team at the Idaho State Penitentiary. He is a certified self-defense instructor. He holds an MS degree in human relations from Abilene Christian University in Texas.

● ●

The supervision of a high-security prison unit will provide numerous opportunities to practice and experiment with different aspects of crisis intervention. A crisis may occur at any time and for any reason. The key to good crisis intervention in an institutional setting begins long before a crisis ever occurs. The counselor involved with the crisis intervention must have developed a great deal of credibility with the inmates. He or she must demonstrate a willingness to enforce the rules of the institution consistently, equally, and fairly, and at the same time demonstrate a genuine concern for the welfare of the inmates.

My experience leads me to the belief that inmates have an unrecognized desire to be controlled. While they try all sorts of devious things to circumvent the rules, and even may riot when rules become too oppressive, they desire some sort of structure. A great many of them desire rules to make up for the self-control that they personally lack. Lack of self-control probably got them into prison in the first place. They do not have the controls necessary to live within the boundaries established by society and its laws. Many come to see the prison rules as a sign of caring on the part of those who enforce them.

I remember a young man I dealt with when I was a street cop. "Ted" had served time in a juvenile facility and had been released to live with his sister. His sister lacked the ability or desire to enforce any rules. Ted soon found himself in all kinds of trouble with the law again. The funny thing is that it seemed as though he wanted to be caught. He either turned himself in or made it extremely easy for us to catch him. The upshot was that he was returned to the juvenile facility.

About nine months later, I was sitting in a coffee shop on a break when Ted walked in with a friend who had been incarcerated with him. They sat down with me and we talked about a number of things. I asked Ted if he hadn't been trying to get caught for his crimes in order to be returned to the institution nine months before. He proudly explained that he was. I asked him why—wasn't it a prison? I'll never forget his answer: "I liked it there because the people there cared enough about me to tell me what I could and couldn't do." His friend chipped in "Yeah, that's right." It appeared that Ted had become institutionalized at an early age—unable to function in open and free society as a result of his juvenile incarcerations.

Ted proved me wrong for a while. He had married an older woman who kept him in line. But she left him, tired of playing mother as well as wife, after he came home stoned one day.

I next saw Ted as an inmate in prison. He was a model prisoner who never caused any trouble. Ted is on parole now and seems to be doing well. What will happen when he is no longer supervised will be interesting.

Another way that a person demonstrates genuine caring is through the art of listening. Far too often we see counselors acting before they really have listened. When a crisis threatens, we often see them taking strong security actions or opening their big mouths to make matters worse. We all could be more effective and demonstrate more caring if only we would listen. Listening is a skill that we must work on. It is more than simply hearing what a person says. The listener must demonstrate that he or she understands the implications of what is being said. I have always tried to be a listening supervisor. I have found that at those times when I have not taken the time to really listen, the level of tension on the tier increases. I have never been an inmate, but I can understand

Continued on the next page

Perspective from the Field, *continued*

how their frustrations and impotence to change their environments can lead to violence. Many potentially dangerous crisis situations can be averted by empathetic listening.

Crises in prisons occur with disquieting frequency. They occur when inmates are thrown off emotional balance by the various frustrations of inmate life. The best way to deal with crises is to anticipate them by being sensitive to precipitating conditions and by listening empathetically to complaints. When they do occur, remain calm and project self-confidence. Listen to the complaint, and with the inmate(s), examine what can be done about it. However, never promise anything you cannot produce, and produce what you have promised. Through conscious efforts to show a caring attitude, a great number of potentially major incidents can be defused.

References and Suggested Readings

Alexander, R. 2000. *Counseling, Treatment, and Intervention Methods with Juvenile and Adult Offenders*. Belmont, California: Brooks/Cole.

American Correctional Association. 1993. *Understanding Cultural Diversity*. Lanham, Maryland: American Correctional Association.

Berne, E. 1964. *Games People Play*. New York: Grove Press.

Braken, D. 2003. Skills and Knowledge for Contemporary Probation Practice. *Probation Journal* 50: 101-114.

Clark, M. 2007. Motivational interviewing for probation officers: Tipping the balance toward change. *Federal Probation* 70: 38-44.

Colwell, K., C. Hiscock, and A. Memon. 2002. Interviewing Techniques and the Assessment of Statement Credibility. *Applied Cognitive Psychology* 16: 287-300.

Cumming, G. and M. Buell. 1997. *Supervision of the Sex Offender*. Safer Society Press. Available from the American Correctional Association, Lanham, Maryland.

Garrett, A. 1982. *Interviewing: Its Principles and Methods*. New York: Family Services Association of America.

Gorden, R. 1992. *Basic Interviewing Techniques*. Itasca, Illinois: F.E. Peacock.

Goyer, R., C. Redding, and J. Rickey. 1968. *Interviewing Principles and Techniques*. Dubuque, Iowa: Wm. C. Brown.

Gudjonsson, G. 1994. Investigative Interviewing: Recent Developments and Some Fundamental Issues. *International Journal of Psychiatry* 6: 237-246.

Hartman, H. 1978. *Basic Psychiatry for Corrections Workers*. Springfield, Illinois: Charles C. Thomas.

Inbau, F. and J. Reid. 1985. *Criminal Interrogations and Confessions*. Baltimore, Maryland: Williams and Wilkins.

Ivey, A. 1983. *Intentional Interviewing and Counseling*. Monterey, California: Brooks/Cole.

Kassin, S., R. Leo, C. Meissner, K. Richman, L. Colwell, A. Leach, and D. La Fon. 2007. Police Interviewing and Interrogation: A Self-Report Survey of Police Practices and Beliefs. *Law and Human Behavior* 31: 381-400.

Napier, M. and S. Adams. 1998. Magic Words to Obtain Confessions. *Law Enforcement Bulletin* 67: 11-15.

Navarro, J. 2003. A Four-Domain Model of Detecting Deception: An Alternative Paradigm for Interviewing. *Law Enforcement Bulletin* 72: 19-24.

Reik, T. 1956. *Listening with the Third Ear*. New York: Grove Press.

United States v. Deaton, 468 F.2d 541, 544 (5th Cir. 1972).

Unwin, C. 1978. Interrogation Techniques. *Police Review* 85 :1874-1877.

Vessel, D. 1998. Conducting Successful Interrogations. *Law Enforcement Bulletin* 67: 1-6.

Vrij, A. 2006. Challenging Interviewees during Interviews: The Potential Effects on Lie Detection. *Psychology, Crime, and Law* 12: 193-206.

Vrij, A., S. Mann, and R. Fisher. 2006. Information Gathering vs Accusatory Interview Style: Individual Differences in Respondent's Experiences. *Psychology, Crime, and Law* 12: 193-206.

Walsh, A. 1986. Placebo Justice: Victim Recommendations and Offender Sentences in Sexual Assault Cases. *Journal of Criminal Law and Criminology* 77: 1126-1141.

CHAPTER 6

The Presentence Investigation Report (PSI)

The presentence investigation is the first step in the attempt to correct the offender's behavior. . . . It requires great skill in the study, evaluation, and supervision of offenders; familiarity with community resources; and an understanding of their subculture.

—**Harvey Treger**

The presentence investigation report (PSI) is the end product of the interviews you have completed with the offender, the victim, arresting police officers, and other interested parties. Some estimate that more than 1.5 million PSIs are written annually in the United States (Pastore and Maguire 2003). Probation officers spend a large proportion of their time writing PSI reports; thus, it is very important that those aspiring to a career in community corrections have a thorough grounding in what they are, what they contain, and the uses to which they are put. Dean Champion (1999: 74) provides a comprehensive definition of the PSI:

> [a] document, usually prepared by a probation agent or officer, which provides background information on the offender including name, address, occupation (if any), potential for employment, the crime(s) involved, relevant circumstances associated with the crime, family data, evidence of prior record (if any), marital status, and other relevant data such as the results of psychological examinations.

The quality and usefulness of the report depend on how well you have conducted your interviews and how well you can summarize and communicate a voluminous amount of material, and make a reasoned selection of pertinent information from the mass available to you. You must learn to discriminate between information that is necessary to know and information that is merely nice to know. Too much unnecessary material will clutter the report and confuse the reader. Some reports are padded liberally with trivia that add nothing to the understanding of the offender and cloud the issue of sentencing decisions.

Studies exploring the decision-making process have shown an inverse relationship between the sheer weight of data and appropriate or useful decisions (Norman and Wadman 2000). In the Norman and Wadman study, 45 percent of readers (judges, prosecutors, defense attorney's prison and parole officials) of PSI's indicated that they did not read the entire report (although 90 percent of responding judges claimed they did so). The main reason respondents gave for not reading the entire report is that PSIs often inundate the reader with more information than can be absorbed. Would you, if you were the sentencing judge, want to read a fifteen-page report full of irrelevancies when you had to read perhaps ten other reports?

Commonsense should guide you in deciding what demographic information to include in the PSI and when to, or not to, elaborate on that information. If a fifty-five-year-old offender dropped out of high school in the ninth grade, do we really need to know why? Just report that he or she dropped out and leave it at that. If this offender has been unemployed for a number of years or has had multiple jobs over a short period of time, it is worth knowing why. The opposite would be true of an eighteen-year-old offender. In neither case do we need to know that he or she loves dogs and drives a used Ford.

Good report writing is an art that flows from practice and feedback from classroom instructors, coworkers, supervisors, and judges. There is no easy substitute for the twin processes of practice and feedback. However, a discussion of specific content areas of the PSI should lay the groundwork for the writing of thorough, factual, concise, readable, and useful PSIs.

Uses of the Presentence Investigation Report

A brief review of the uses to which a PSI investigation report is put will underline the importance of making sure that your reports will exhibit these attributes. Functions they fulfill fall within the general areas of decision-making aids and treatment aids.

Judicial Sentencing Decisions. Presentence investigations aid judge in the selection of appropriate case dispositions and serve the positivist philosophy of individualized justice. Probation officers are charged with the task of putting this philosophy into practice by presenting to the courts their assessments of "individualized" offenders and making sentencing recommendations consistent with those assessments. Numerous studies show that probation officers are very successful in gaining judicial compliance with their recommendations (Abadinsky 1997, Norman and Wadman 2000, Walsh 1984, 1985a), although the advent of sentencing guidelines that indicate mandatory sentences based on crime seriousness and prior record have diminished the importance of extralegal factors such as those outlined by Champion in the first paragraph of this chapter (Conaboy 1997). Nevertheless, Champion points out the "Probation officers exercise considerable discretion to influence the favorableness or unfavorableness of these reports for offenders" (2005: 91). Thus, given that officers' recommendations, which should flow naturally from the information contained in the PSI, can have a profound effect on an offender's life, it is imperative that they accurately and fairly reflect the facts.

Departmental and Institutional Classification. Probation departments use the diagnostic information contained in the PSI to determine the supervision level of offenders placed on probation. Information such as prior supervisions, arrest record, attitude, needs and risk assessments, and the nature of the crime are quantified on a scale (such as the risk and needs scales to be examined later) to determine the type and frequency of supervision. If the offender is incarcerated, the institution uses his or her medical, psychological, and criminal history, as well as vocational and educational information as an aid in determining security level, work assignments, and vocational, educational, and counseling needs.

Parole Decisions. The PSI accompanies the offender to the institution and, in addition to classification, is used as an aid to parole-release decision. The parole officer to whom the offender is released also uses information contained in the report in formulating initial treatment and supervision plans. In the case of parole-revocation decisions, presentence investigation information is used as a baseline to gauge the offender's progress (or lack of it) since his or her initial assessment.

Counseling Plans and Community Agency Referrals. The probation officer who is supervising the offender (who may or may not be the officer who wrote the report) uses the treatment plans outlined in the presentence investigation report for guidance. These reports also aid the officer in making appropriate referrals to agencies that deal with any specific problems of the offender beyond the officer's purview or expertise. The receiving agency uses the report as a planning guide, relieving the agency of the necessity of gathering duplicate information. Do not provide such information to the agency, however, without the written consent of the offender.

Sample Presentence Investigation Report

An actual PSI investigation report is presented here to illustrate its areas of content. As you examine it, bear its uses in mind. We altered names, locations, and circumstances sufficiently to protect anonymity. This particular report was selected because of its excellent quality and because it illustrates some interesting applications of the criminological and/or counseling theories that we have examined or will examine. This report is only one of several PSI formats, which can range from two to fifteen pages in length–the variability largely a function of agency requirements and case complexity.

THE ADRIAN COUNTY ADULT PROBATION DEPARTMENT
LOWMAN, IDAHO
PRESENTENCE REPORT

NAME: William (Bill) Bloggs   JUDGE: Joseph B. Lynch
ADDRESS: Currently in Adrian County Jail
     Formerly: 780 N 30th, Lowman, ID.   INDICTMENT # 06-3457
AGE: 26; DOB 7-25-84
SEX: male   ATTORNEY: S. Bonnetti
RACE: white
PENDING CASES/DETAINERS: none   MARITAL STATUS: married
OFFENSE: DEPENDENTS: none
Aggravated Robbery
IRC # 2911.01   DATE: October 19, 2010
Attempted Murder   PROBATION
IRC # 2923.02   OFFICER: Paul Corrick

CIRCUMSTANCES OF OFFENSE

On 6-13-2010, at approximately 1:30 A.M., the defendant entered the Big Man Restaurant, located at 1324 Main St., through an open rear door and announced his intention of robbing said establishment. Armed with a .38 caliber pistol, the defendant ordered the manager to fill a bag embossed with the Lowman College seal, which he had brought with him, with the day's takings. The manager, Barry Harbourne, complied with the demand and filled the bag with cash totaling $1,203.32. The defendant then picked up the bag and exited through the back door. As soon as he left the restaurant, Mr. Harbourne called the police to the scene. Upon leaving the scene, the defendant stopped to remove his sweater, gloves, and the face mask he was wearing. The police arrived as he was doing this and spotted him. At this point, the defendant saw them and started to run. The police ordered him to stop. He did not heed this warning and kept on running. The police were firing at him as he ran. The defendant returned the fire with two rounds, one shot hitting Patrolman Williams in the leg. The defendant was able to elude the pursuing officers at this time. However, the police found a 1996 Buick Special parked three buildings east of the Big Man registered to the defendant. In making good his escape, the defendant dropped the bag containing the money and a number of personal artifacts. The bag was the aforementioned Lowman College bag containing a man's wallet with the defendant's driver's license and other identification inside. The gun was found in the grass in a storm ditch across from Ray's Auto Supply Store, located at 1200 Main.

The defendant, accompanied by his attorney, turned himself into the Lowman police the next morning and made a full confession. He confessed to the present offense, as well as to two previous robberies of the same establishment, and one at the Big Man Restaurant at State and Glover on 4-12-06.

STATEMENT OF THE DEFENDANT

The defendant wrote out his statement for this officer. It is reproduced verbatim to preserve its flavor.

"On the morning of June 13, 2006, I robbed the Big Man Restaurant. In order to understand why I needed the money, first we should examine my childhood in order to find some underlying reason(s) for my behavior. Our family had a farm and a dog food processing business. The family hobby was hunting and trapping, totally our father's idea. The family businesses left very little time for our parents to be parents, they were most always in the position of boss.

"During the years previous to meeting the woman who became my wife (she was not my first girlfriend), I did not see myself in any real one-to-one loving relationships. Even the pets I had would be taken from me, eventually I learned not to become attached to anything for fear it would be taken away. Death of something which I had compassion for never received mourning–the family was conditioned against it. The dog food processing experience also made me cold in the need for caring relationships with anything. The horses I saw were many times slaughtered, shot before my very eyes, then we as a family would skin, bone, grind up and package the meat. We even killed and trapped animals for "sport." The business would have been great if adults did all the work.

"I never became close friends with any girls until after I graduated from high school. Never really finding anyone who cared as much for me as I cared for them until I met Susan, it became an obsession for me to please her, at times I probably ran her life. I hated her to work so she quit a good job as a secretary. I don't think she ever asked for anything that she didn't get. Now we both admit that our direction was wrong, and we have done something about it. We have sold many of our possessions and she has a job. She still does not want to work and I don't like the idea but it's part of reality–Bill cannot make enough money! Never again will I work third shift and regular weekends, I was so busy working I did not know what was happening to my brain. The more money I made the more I spent and the more I felt the need for money, which was not real but imagined.

" Since my imprisonment, we have sadly learned the need for Susan to lose Bill, if not through imprisonment then through death. Shortly after I was arrested, Susan had a life reading, and one of the results has been this realization that she would lose Bill. In a past life she lost me through death very early, and has past Karma to overcome. I am sure of the need for Bill's punishment to correct the Karma he has for his crimes. I also know that Bill had the choice to do what he did or not to do it. What Bill does not know is this, how would Susan correct her Karma if I were not imprisoned. Would I die? This is a good question. What I have done is not easily forgivable, but I know that when I'm free, Bill will grow and hopefully will still have Susan to grow with him. I have been saved from a terrible future, no one was killed but many were hurt and hurt seriously and it will take a lot of hard work to correct the mistakes, I hope I have the chance to correct them–in this life."

We can glean from this statement that the defendant is interested in mysticism and paranormal phenomena. The "life reading" to which he refers is retrogressive hypnosis. This technique supposedly takes the offender back into his or her past to elicit memories buried in the subconscious. The true initiate apparently believes that this even extends to prior existences in other times and places.

The defendant believes that he lived before in what he calls the "horse and buggy" days. In that life, he and his wife reversed sex roles; in other words, the defendant was the female and his wife was the male. The defendant stated that he died of a brain tumor at the age of thirty-five on his last sojourn on earth. He/"she" was also a robber in that life. The combination of his early death and his antisocial career drove his wife/"husband" to alcoholism (Is he projecting his perceptions of his wife's possible reactions to his current predicament into this story?). He feels that the "bad Karma" built up by their actions in the former life has to be worked out in this one.

Karma is an ethereal "something," which automatically adheres to the perpetrator of an evil act (something akin to sin). It must be canceled or "worked off" by a positive act which has a measure of good proportionate to the evil of the negative act. If this is not accomplished, the self is caught up in an endless cycle of birth and death. This belief, so the defendant states, enables him to tie everything he has done in this life to past lives of himself and his wife. He says that prison is necessary for him to equilibrate his "bad Karma." He wants to do volunteer work in the prison and upon his release to build up his reserve of "good Karma."

Although the defendant has a teleological view of life, he does not claim that he was "fated" to commit his crimes. He stated that "Bill has the free will that he was blessed with" (it is interesting to note that he often referred to himself in the third person. It is as though he disassociates himself and views himself as an object apart from himself). He did occasionally lapse into fatalistic explanations. For instance, when asked how he was able to elude capture and avoid getting hit by police fire, his eyes turned heavenward, and he replied with a cryptic "them." Who "them" are was not made clear. Notwithstanding the interesting story he tells, at bottom, the reason he committed the robberies was simply that he "needed" more money than he was making to indulge his wife's expensive tastes.

PRIOR RECORD   BIR # 234569   FBI # 356 953 V1

Juvenile:
Adrian County juvenile authorities report no juvenile record.
Adult:
6-14-06 LPD a) Attempted Murder b) Aggravated Robbery
Two other counts of Aggravated Robbery nolled (dismissed) in CR06-4357.

One count of Aggravated Robbery nolled (dismissed) in CR06-4358
LCPD, BCI, FBI, and Juvenile record checks made and received.

STATEMENT OF VICTIM (Patrolman Fredrick Williams)

Patrolman Williams stated that he and his partner responded to a robbery call at the Big Man Restaurant at about 1:30 A.M. on the morning of 6-13-10. As they came upon the scene, he noticed the defendant in a field taking off his sweater. The defendant fled as he and his partner approached, and he refused to stop when ordered to do so. Williams was chasing the defendant on foot when the defendant turned and fired two shots, one of which struck Williams in the leg. Patrolman Williams stated that his wound required six weeks off work and two weeks light duty. When asked his opinion of the defendant, and what he thought should happen to him, Williams replied: "The guy's sick; he needs help. As far as I'm concerned, you can put him away for eighty years."

FAMILY AND MARITAL HISTORY

The defendant is the youngest of four children born to James and Mary Bloggs. The defendant, up until his marriage, lived his entire life on the family farm located at Box 3123, Rural Route 10, Elko, ID. Information received from the defendant's wife and certain of his siblings revealed that his childhood was characterized by excessive work demands, physical abuse, and forced incestuous relationships with his sisters. Details of the above are contained elsewhere in this report. It is quite clear that the entire Bloggs family was under the strict and uncompromising figure of Mr. Bloggs. The defendant had very little time to pursue any personal interests that he may have had, always having to acquiesce to the wishes of his father. His whole life evidently revolved around the family business, which he despised.

The defendant's older sister related that her father was "absolutely livid" when he found out that her mother was pregnant with the defendant He did not even visit his wife in hospital during her confinement. She further stated that the defendant would often get blamed for things he did not do, and was made to feel unwanted. She went on to relate how both the defendant and his older brother were bed-wetters up to a relatively late age, and that her father would "hog-tie" them and keep them lying in bed in their urine all day. Interestingly, the defendant denied a history of enuresis to court psychologists as if to block out all memory of these extremely unpleasant occurrences.

The defendant left home at the age of twenty-two to take up residence with his girlfriend, now his wife, Susan Overton. This marriage took place on 9-15-2000 in the Adrian County Jail. In an interview with Susan at this office, she described herself as an "old fashioned" type who did not wish to go out to work. She described the defendant as being "jealous and possessive," adding that he is prone to "snap in and out of an explosive temper." She stated that he felt like he owned her, and that he once hung and killed a kitten of hers when he suspected that she was seeing another man. When I inquired, in light of the above negative statements, and in light of the prison sentence that the defendant is facing, that she would marry him, she replied that they are "fated" to be together. She said that she could not cope with his death in their previous existence, and that she must now learn to cope with his absence in this one.

When asked why she thought that the defendant committed his crimes, she indicated the aberrant family situation previously mentioned. She stated that Mr. Bloggs slept with both of his daughters and had on numerous occasions forced them to instruct the defendant and his brother in sexual matters while he watched. On a second interview with the defendant I questioned him about this. He felt that this was no "big deal," and stated that he was about ten when these incestuous encounters began.

While Susan believes that this sexual deviance may have been a distinct influence, she felt that the more proximate cause for the defendant's criminal behavior was his desire to satisfy her request for a big wedding, which he could not afford. It is ironic that their desire for a conspicuous and grandiose wedding may have led them to nuptials in a barren jail cell with a corrections officer as a witness. Her final statement to me was "Don't send him to prison, he won't come back." The defendant's father and mother were interviewed at their family farm. Mr. Bloggs is fifty-four years old, has two years of college, and is a self-employed farmer. He is an impressive professorial-looking person who is obviously accustomed to being in control of any situation. He spoke slowly and deliberately, and appeared to take great pains to use just the right word. He stated that he is at a loss to explain his son's behavior, that he loved him, and will continue to support him. He denied any mistreatment of the defendant beyond what he called "normal chastisement." I did not feel it appropriate to raise the issue of the alleged incest with him in front of his wife.

The defendant's mother is fifty-three years old, has one year of college, and describes her occupation as "housewife." She is a timid-looking soul who complements her husband's personality with a passivity which approaches sycophantic proportions. She was never able to complete two successive sentences without her husband finishing them for her. She profusely praised her husband as a father and a provider, and also denied that he was excessively punitive. One wonders if she has any knowledge of her husband's sexual abuse of their children. A computer record check revealed no criminal history for either parent.

The defendant's oldest sister, Patricia Knowles, is a high school graduate who currently drives a cab for Black and White. Pat has been married and divorced twice, and has a ten-year old daughter and a nine-year old son. Pat has a criminal history of child endangering and drug abuse. Pat does not presently associate with her father, stating that "He f—ed all of us kids up. He's the one that should be in jail."

Ann, the defendant's second sister, has similar feelings about her father. She is a high school graduate. She stated that she ran away from home right after graduation, and openly admits that she went to Los Angeles to become a call girl. She eventually quit that occupation after becoming pregnant (she kept her child). She is currently on welfare in Los Angeles. A check with LAPD revealed numerous soliciting arrests for Ann.

Fredrick Bloggs, the defendant's older brother, could not be reached. However, Pat indicated that Fred dropped out of high school at the age of sixteen, has been married and divorced, and is now an "alcoholic bum" in Omaha, Nebraska. It would appear that the defendant is not the only victim of Mr. Bloggs' highly distasteful personality.

EMPLOYMENT HISTORY (Social Security # 902-42-9986)

At the time of his arrest, the defendant was working for Lowman Cascade as a press operator. He has been employed there since 4-14-09. He works all the overtime that he can get, and frequently brings home in excess of $400 per week. The defendant's immediate supervisor characterized him as "a good and dependable worker who gave us no trouble."

The defendant had taken the entrance examination to become a Lowman City police officer. Lt. Murdock of LCPD indicated that the defendant was to be called to the next class at the academy.

The defendant relates no other employment except at his family business.

PHYSICAL HEALTH

The defendant is a white male, 26 years of age, 5' 7" tall, and weighs 155 lbs. He has dark blonde hair, blue eyes, and a fair complexion. He describes his current physical health as "excellent." He has suffered no hospitalizations or serious diseases, and relates no defects of hearing, speech, or vision. There is a family history of hypertension, and he feels that he is disposed to it himself. He is an infrequent consumer of alcohol, stating that the last time that he was drunk was over two years ago. He smoked marijuana rather heavily while in college, and stated that he frequently uses amphetamines while working the night shift at Lowman Cascade to stay awake. He did not feel that he was addicted to them, however.

MENTAL HEALTH

The defendant graduated from Capital High School in 2002. He graduated 31st out of a class of 63, with a GPA of 2.27 on a 4.0 scale. School IQ testing saw the defendant obtain a full-scale IQ of 113, placing him in the 85th percentile of the U.S. population IQ scores. Were his educational attainments commensurate with his IQ percentile ranking, the defendant would have placed ninth in his class. The defendant stated that he was too busy working on the farm to do justice to his studies.

Upon graduation from high school, the defendant entered Boise State University. He majored in, of all things, criminal justice. He was still attending BSU at the time of his arrest. He has obtained a cumulative GPA at BSU of 2.49. His criminal justice advisor stated that he was a "quiet student who participated very little in class, but his written work showed evidence of real independent thinking."

The Court Diagnostic and Treatment Center report indicates that their testing saw the defendant obtain a full-scale IQ score of 114, indicating a certain consistency in mental ability. It is noted that he scored significantly above average in tasks requiring nonverbal and short-term memory skills. It is too easy to ascribe some form of mental abnormality to one who subscribes to the worldview described by the defendant. It should be remembered, however, that his views are a valid discourse for millions of people in the world. I am more inclined to view his neurotic materialism as indicative of mental instability than his new-found religious eclecticism. He himself views his seemingly insatiable acquisitiveness as being responsible for his criminal actions. He was socialized in a family seemingly obsessed with making money. Neither can we discount the incestuous behavior he was forced into as a generating factor. It is clear that love was not a prevalent quality in this man's life. This deficiency may explain his clinging, jealous, and paranoid attraction to the one person (Susan) who showed a loving interest in him.

Although the CD and TC report states that he is experiencing high levels of anxiety and depression, he now states to me that he is "more at peace" with himself. He spends much of his time in his cell these days reading the Bible and esoteric literature. He describes himself as "driven to achieve," and feels that he is very aggressive in a nonviolent way. Given his crime, the hanging of the kitten, and Susan's statement about his "explosive temper," one might well dispute this description. The CD and TC report also describes him as being "in the early stages of a schizophrenic reaction, specifically of a paranoid type." His frequent reference to himself in the third person perhaps augments the impression of disassociation. Overall, this officer gained the impression that the defendant is a very bright, knowledgeable, and articulate person. He has been completely cooperative, and was a pleasure to talk with.

EVALUATIVE SUMMARY

Before the Court is a 26-year-old married male facing his first criminal conviction. He is an extremely bright, articulate, and personable young man. He evidently had a childhood in which he wanted for nothing materially, but which was characterized by excessive labor, harsh punitive treatment, and forced incestuous episodes. It is evident from the defendant's own statements, and from information uncovered in the course of this investigation, that he was severely deprived of close and loving interpersonal relationships. His father was viewed by family members as the great patriarch, or as the defendant put it: "as a boss, not a father." His father bestowed praise and approval only when the defendant met his excessive demands. Love, if there indeed was any, was withdrawn on the slightest pretext. His mother was viewed as a good person, but also as a pusillanimous alter-ego to the father.

The defendant's lack of experience of loving relationships rendered him ill-equipped to function well within one when Susan came into his life. He was obviously obsessed with making good this deficit. His relationship with Susan, now his wife, appears to have been a clinging obsession with him. He was paranoid about the possibility of losing her, and hypersensitive to her "needs," which everyone concerned agree were considerable. He wanted only the best for her, and often worked seven days a week, even while attending college, to get it for her. Even his considerable income was not sufficient to purchase all of the things he felt were necessary to ingratiate himself.

Nonetheless, we cannot overlook a string of armed robberies and the shooting of a police officer. It is evident that the robberies were well-planned and executed. In any objective sense, he was not in any desperate need of money, as he was earning a wage well in excess of average. He needed love, and his materialistic background told him that love was just another expensive commodity to be purchased with cash.

His intelligence, desire to learn, and intensity of purpose will stand him in good stead upon his release from the institution. His new-found spirituality, coupled with psychological counseling, will, I believe, function to prevent any further criminality in the future. He is well aware of the terrible crimes he has committed, and stands ready to accept the consequences. The extreme seriousness of his crimes point to the necessity of imposing consecutive sentences.

STATUTORY PENALTY OF

IRC #2911.01 Aggravated Robbery	"...shall be imprisoned for a period of 4, 5, 6, or 7 to 25 years and/or fined up to $10,000."
IRC #2923.02 Attempted Aggravated Murder	"...shall be imprisoned for a period of 4, 5, 6, or 7 to 25 years and/or fined up to $10,000

RECOMMENDATION

Regarding 06-1234, Aggravated Robbery, it is respectfully recommended that the defendant be sentenced to 4 to 25 years at the Idaho State Penitentiary and ordered to pay the costs of prosecution.

Regarding 06-3456, Attempted Aggravated Murder, it is respectfully recommended that the defendant be sentenced to 5 to 25 years at the Idaho State Penitentiary, and that he be first conveyed to the Idaho Medical and Reception Center for evaluation and classification. It is further recommended that said sentences be served consecutively, and that the defendant be ordered to pay the costs of prosecution.

Respectfully submitted, Paul E. Corrick, Probation and Parole Officer

Discussion of Sample Report

We will explain, section-by-section, the type of information required in each section of the presentence investigation report. Then, we will comment on each content area using examples from the Bloggs PSI.

Circumstances of Offense

Approximately 90 percent of all felony cases are disposed of through plea negotiations rather than by trial (Champion 2005). Consequently, the sentencing judge often is quite unaware of the circumstances that brought the offender before the bench for sentencing until he or she has read the PSI. This section, then, should lay out the official (police) version of all pertinent details of the offense. It should contain basic information such as the place and time of the offense, the names of any co-defendants, whether any weapons were involved, and the names and address of the victim, and it should report injuries or financial loss suffered by the victim. Additionally, you should report the circumstances surrounding the defendant's arrest: How was the defendant discovered? What was the defendant's condition at the time of arrest (drunk, high)? Did he or she resist arrest, or did the person voluntarily surrender to the police? Be concise but thorough.

Statement of the Defendant

A recitation of the offender's version of the offense assists you in filling in gaps in the official version. It is quite likely that the presentence investigation interview is the offender's first occasion to tell his or her side of the story. The police usually are concerned only with the question of commission and often do not care about the whys and wherefores of the case. As for defense attorneys, offenders often seem to think that their only interest is to "sell" them the plea agreement.

Nevertheless, you must never allow an offender's sob story to distract you from the facts contained in the official version. Your job is not to retry the case in your PSI. Judges do not take too kindly to such efforts. Some interrogation techniques may be necessary, however, to attempt to reconcile any major discrepancies between the offender's story and the official version. Interrogation should not be carried out until you have listened objectively to the entirety of the offender's story. You must note discrepancies and go over them one at a time with the offender until you are satisfied that they are resolved.

Do not let your humanitarian impulses get in the way if you believe that the offender is trying to snow you. Note how the story is told. Is it just too slick and obviously memorized? Are there claims of memory loss (a favorite ploy with child molesters)? Are there major inconsistencies within the offender's own version of the offense? If you think that the story is untrue, come right out and say so. This may be all that is needed to get the real story. You can be burned badly if you succumb to the natural impulse to put your unconditional faith in the poor troubled human being sitting beside you. Not only will you be putting your credibility with the judge and your colleagues in jeopardy, but you also will be compromising it with the offender. Worse yet, you could be opening yourself up for a lawsuit if, as a result of your report, a dangerous offender is released on probation and subsequently harms someone else. (Actually, the PSI investigator has quasi-judicial immunity from lawsuits, but you could still get burned in other ways.) Dig hard and dig deep. If you cannot reconcile the different versions, simply note them in your report. If you believe that unresolved discrepancies are the result of deliberate attempts at deception, report this in the PSI and fully support your reasoning behind the belief.

An important variable to assess is the offender's attitude about the offense. Is there remorse? Is the remorse apparently genuine, or is it just sorrow for getting caught? Experience will sensitize you to signs of genuine remorse. Shame, as an indication of remorse, is signaled by blushing and sighing when the crime is discussed, attempting to avoid discussing embarrassing details of the offense, stuttering, stammering, showing apparent confusion, and avoiding eye contact previously established.

Similarly, guilty feelings are good indicators of genuine remorse. Behaviors consistent with a sense of guilt include voluntary confessions and the acceptance of complete blame, surrender to the police, a tendency to dwell on details of the offense, and the expression of a willingness to make amends in any way necessary. Offenders who display some or all of these indicators of shame and guilt are usually individuals who normally conduct themselves according to conventional moral standards. The interviewer should be sensitive to the inclination toward depressive states, and even suicidal ideation, among offenders of this type. Such offenders are rare, however. Most will try to claim some sort of mitigation such as bad company, victim precipitation, or alcohol. In Walsh's (1983) unpublished study of 416 probation offenders, 52.7 percent of them tried to shift the blame for the offense in directions other than themselves.

"Victim precipitation" is a favorite excuse in assaultive crimes, alcohol or drug abuse in property crimes. In those cases involving multiple defendants, fully 92 percent placed the blame on bad company, neglecting to realize that each was the whipping boy of the other. This is not to assert that all claims of mitigation lack any substance. Your good judgment will help you decide what degree of credence you will give to such claims.

You also should discuss victims' losses with offenders and inquire about their attitudes for making restitution and their ability to do so. Restitution may include victims' medical bills, time lost from work, or replacement costs for property lost or damaged. The court may order payment of restitution either directly to the victim or to his or her insurance company. The offender's willingness and realistic ability to pay restitution probably will be an important factor in both your recommended disposition of the case and in its actual disposition. Restitution cannot legally be ordered in many states; however, if the offender's plea was "no contest" rather than "guilty." This limitation displays a disregard for victim's rights and is one of the major injustices of the criminal justice system.

Application to Sample Presentence Investigation Report

Bill's version of the offense exactly mirrors the official one, and he does not attempt to deny any aspects of it. His statement written: "in order to understand why I needed the money," however, is most instructive and interesting. His story is a psychiatric delight that illustrates many of the ego-defense mechanisms that we discuss later. Constant themes throughout his statement are his severe deprivation of love and the pressures of life with an authoritarian father. His love for Susan was a clinging, cloying, jealous one. He was willing to go to any lengths to buy from her the love he so desperately needed. He was painfully aware that he had grown up in a loveless environment, so much so that he "learned not to become attached to anything for fear it would be taken away." Susan was inadequately filling his desperate need for love, his deeply felt deficiency. His jealousy, and indeed his crimes, can be viewed as stemming from his unrealistic attempts to cling to someone toward whom he had finally developed a form of attachment.

He had convinced himself (apparently genuinely) that this attachment extended back to a prior existence. We note that the processing probation officer did not disparage Bill's bizarre story but, instead, tried to understand it and fit it into the offender's frame of reference for the readers of the report. However, he correctly did not let this sway him from consideration of the extremely serious nature of Bill's crimes. To understand is not to excuse. The probation officer also perceptively picked up on Bill's use of the third person when discussing himself and nicely tied it in with evidence from the examining psychiatrist, who indicated that Bill may have been in the "early stages of a schizophrenic reaction."

Was Bill remorseful, and if so, was his remorse genuine? He did turn himself in to the police, and he did make a full confession. However, given that he left behind so much identifying evidence at the scene of the crime, we can hardly assume that his cooperation was indicative of remorse. Further damaging to any interpretation of genuine remorse is the fact that the present offense was his fourth such robbery within a short time. But, he did accept full responsibility for his crimes ("Bill has the free will that he was blessed with"), and he did accept the legitimacy of his impending punishment. The overall impression one gains is that Bill would have continued his crime spree had he not been caught. His apparently genuine remorse was late in coming, was related to the situation he was in at the time of the interview, and could not be viewed as a mitigating factor when considering sentencing.

Statement of Victim. As already noted, under the influence of the philosophy of restorative justice, an increasing number of jurisdictions are requiring that a victim-impact statement be included in the PSI. Such a statement is worth including even in the absence of a legal requirement. The statement should include the victim's version of the offense and the physical, psychological, and financial impact of the crime on him or her. You also should obtain an itemized statement of any financial losses from the victim or the victim's insurance company. It is not unusual, although it is understandable, for victims to inflate the extent of their losses. This author always solicits a statement of the victim's feelings and a recommendation on the disposition of the case.

Application to Sample Presentence Investigation Report. Given the seriousness of this offender's crimes, it was obvious from the onset that incarceration had to be the recommended disposition. Therefore, no attempt was made to ascertain financial losses to Patrolman Williams or the police department (notwithstanding the defendant's inability to pay restitution if incarcerated, the courts cannot monitor payments if the defendant is under the jurisdiction of the department of corrections). Since Officer Williams' version of the offense was an integral part of the official version, his additional statement throws no more light on it. His understandably negative response in his opinion of the defendant, and what he thought should happen to him, was of no value in the formulation of a sentencing recommendation.

Prior Record. Judges consider the offender's criminal history to be the most important information in the PSI (Norman and Wadman 2000), so you must make every effort to get the most accurate picture available. Before you interview the offender, a complete criminal history should be available to you. This should include juvenile, local police, state bureau of criminal investigation, and Federal Bureau of Investigation (FBI) arrest sheets ("rap sheets"). Most of these records should be included in the prosecutor's case file. Immediately upon receiving the case, however, you should run your own computer check for an updated history. A computer check also will reveal any outstanding warrants for the offender.

If you discover that the offender is wanted, you should make inquiries with the issuing clerk of courts concerning the particulars of the warrant. It is your duty to place the offender under arrest if the warrant indicates a serious crime. For obvious reasons, do not reveal your knowledge of the warrant until you conduct the interview. Telling an offender that he or she will be arrested at the conclusion of the interview will not make for a very productive interview. If the warrant was issued for something as innocuous as nonpayment of traffic fines, it is probably a better idea to tell the offender to take care of them before you see him or her again rather than making an arrest.

At this point, avoid confrontation about relatively unimportant matters. Having gathered arrest records as well as any previous presentence investigation reports and records, review this history of criminal activity with the offender. Ask the offender to explain any particularly serious prior arrests and convictions, and try to discern any pattern among the arrests. For instance, are the crimes all of a similar type (property, sex, violent), or is the record one of a polymorphous deviant? Do they reveal a pattern of increasing seriousness? At what point in life did the offender start acquiring a criminal record? Are any or most of the crimes related to alcohol and/or drug abuse? Is the pattern one of planned criminality, or do the crimes seem mostly those of opportunistic spontaneity? Finally, does the offender readily admit all crimes to you, or does the offender attempt to rationalize away the majority of them?

Application to Sample Presentence Investigation Report. The lessons to be learned from a perusal of the offender's criminal history are many and valuable. In Bill's case, it is very instructive that he had no previous arrests, either as a juvenile or as an adult. Yet, his offenses were extremely serious. In the normal progress of a criminal career, one graduates over a period of years from committing far less serious crimes to the types of crimes Bill committed. It is so extremely rare to find an offender who, at the age of twenty-six, begins a criminal career with armed robbery that you immediately should be alerted to the fact that there are some very special circumstances involved.

Family and Marital History. Although not necessarily reported in the PSI, a family history should contain the names and addresses of parents, siblings, children, spouse, and any former spouses and indicate the current status of each family member (deceased, divorced, retired, imprisoned, whereabouts unknown). These data will yield important information about the offender's family dynamics. Inquire into the offender's relationship with his or her parents during the formative years. Were they divorced early? With whom did the offender live? Did either or both of the parents remarry, and what type of relationship did the offender have with his or her stepparents? What are the offender's current relationships with his or her parents and significant others–supportive or rejecting? Exploration of parental reactions to the present predicament will provide access to the type of moral environment in which the offender was raised. You can use collateral interviews with parents, if time allows and the seriousness of the case warrants, to validate and expand on the offender's perceptions.

It may be instructive to inquire into the offenders' friendship networks. Do they associate with known criminals? If so, ask why. How do they spend their leisure time with friends–in productive or nonproductive ways?

Then, obtain the offender's marital history, if any. How many times has the offender been married? Frequent marriages, common-law or otherwise, indicate an inability to form lasting relationships and a certain lack of responsibility. If the offender has been divorced, what was the reason for the divorce? Placing the blame on the spouse may reflect an overall pattern of blaming others for negative outcomes. Find out if the offender has any children from former relationships and, if the offender is living up to his or her financial support obligations.

Next, examine the quality of the relationship with the current spouse. If there are any major difficulties, explore their nature and extent. Is the offender responsibly supporting dependents, or does his or her lifestyle demonstrate neglect? Again, a collateral interview with the spouse may prove useful. You many conduct a collateral interview by telephone, although you lose much of the flavor if you do. You certainly would want to find out the spouse's attitudes about his or her criminal activity and how he or she would cope if the offender were imprisoned.

Application to Sample Presentence Investigation Report. Officer Corrick's collateral interviews with Bill's wife, his parents, and selected siblings certainly paid off in terms of insight into the origins of Bill's criminal behavior. Although Bill's family was comfortably middle class and demonstrated commitment to, involvement in, and belief in typical American success values, beneath the veneer of respectability lay an abominable family situation. Attachment, genuine reciprocal love, was obviously absent. Bill appeared to have tried very hard to gain his father's love and approval. His father, however, seems to have been a patriarchal, sadistic, sexually perverted, and over-demanding individual. His absolute control over the family is quite in evidence in the report. His mother "complements her husband's personality with a passivity, which approaches sycophantic proportions." Note that she never mentioned anything to Corrick regarding the incestuous behavior that went on for so many years. It is not at all unusual for wives to deny, even to themselves, that such behavior occurs. This behavior first came to light during the collateral interview with Susan. It was then incumbent on Officer Corrick to verify the information, which he did with Bill himself and with two of his siblings. Such potentially damaging information should never be included in a report based on one individual's statement.

The effects of growing up under the conditions that existed in the Bloggs family have resulted in many negative outcomes for Bill's siblings as well. Pat has had two broken marriages in four years and has a record of child abuse and drug abuse. Ann has one illegitimate child and was a prostitute for a time with numerous soliciting arrests. Fred, a high school dropout, was divorced after one year of marriage, and is an admitted alcoholic. All this occurred, in spite of having access to all the "objective" advantages of a white, middle-class status, which supports Officer Corrick's analysis of the origin of Bill's behavior as presented in the evaluation section of the PSI.

Susan's statements indicate that she shared Bill's unusual interpretation of their relationship ("they are 'fated' to be together"). She quit her job when she and Bill started living together, and she was evidently quite happy to allow Bill to work all hours of the day and night to satisfy her considerable material wants. Her comments about Bill's "explosive temper" and his hanging of her kitten provide all those who will use the PSI in the future with valuable insight not gleaned from either Corrick's or the diagnostic center's interviews with Bill.

Very few collateral interviews will ever be as valuable to you as the ones presented here. Further, for less serious cases, time constraints usually will prohibit going to the extraordinary length which Corrick went here. Nor would it be especially productive if the offender fit the profile of the typical armed robber. The typical armed robber would fit a certain profile that, by definition, is associated with most others who commit such crimes (lower-class, poorly educated, broken home, unemployed, and so on). The atypicality of Bill's criminal profile led Corrick to dig as deeply into Bill's past as he did.

Employment History. The section covering employment history explores the offender's employment or other sources of income such as welfare, social security, or disability income. A complete and verified employment history is a vital part of any offender assessment. As the theories we have examined have informed us, a steady work history, evidence of prosocial commitment, involvement, and access to a legitimate avenue of success are incompatible with serious criminal involvement. Of the 416 offenders in this author's unpublished (1983) study, only 55.8 percent were working at the time of the presentence investigation interview. Of those working, 86.6 percent were in unskilled dead-end occupations. Only 2.8 percent were in managerial, technical, or professional occupations, and all of those were first-time sex offenders.

The name, address, and telephone number of the offender's current place of employment is the first item on the agenda. To avoid putting the offender's jobs in jeopardy, verify their employment by having them bring in their most recent paycheck stubs. Verify length of employment through the offenders' tax records. Ask offenders what type of work they do and if they enjoy it. Are there opportunities to move up in the company? Do they feel that their present income is sufficient to meet their basic needs? Do they criticize the company excessively? Why?

Verify former employment directly. Send a standard form should to former employers asking them to indicate type of work, length of service, reason for leaving, and an evaluation of an offender's work performance and of his or her general character. What is the offender's pattern of movement in the workforce? Does the offender work steadily and quit employment only to obtain a better position, or does the offender quit on any pretext after minimal periods? This information will give you a general picture of the offender's level of responsibility, his or her ability to get along with others, and his or her general persistence. You should fully explore all gaps in employment history. You also should ask the military for a copy of the offender's service record, if any, although you may not receive it until long after sentencing.

Application to Sample Presentence Investigation Report. Bill's employment history is an atypically good one. At the time of his arrest, he had been working for more than two years for the same company. He worked hard and earned a good income. Management at his place of employment was very positive toward him, even to the extent of planning to promote him to supervisor. He also worked part time on the family farm and had passed the examination to become a police officer. Bill's exemplary work history obviously impressed Officer Corrick and further alerted him to dig beyond surface demographics to explain Bill's behavior.

Physical Health. An assessment of offenders' physical health (self-reported, or, if necessary, verified by a physician), noting how their social and vocational functioning could be affected by it, should be included. Note recent hospitalizations and diseases, use of medications or prosthetic devices, and drinking habits and drug abuse in this section. Substance abuse should be the central concern of this section because of its association with many criminal acts. Drugs and alcohol are chemical substitutes for the lack of love and meaning in many offenders' lives–a method of temporarily shutting out the cruelties and responsibilities of life. Inquire into the extent and frequency of offenders' drinking, noting if they have any alcohol-related offenses, such as drunk driving, on the rap sheet.

Next, address extent, frequency, and type of drug abuse. Not all offenders will be willing to admit abuse, but with careful observation you will know when to probe. We examine physical indicators of drug abuse in Chapter 16. A word of warning here: some offenders will exaggerate the extent of their substance abuse in the hope that blame will be shifted from them to the substance and that they will touch a sympathetic cord in the officer. This author's (1983) study found that 13.5 percent blamed substance abuse for their crimes. If offenders claim drug dependency, or if you suspect it, immediately refer them to a drug dependency clinic for a complete workup and evaluation.

Application to Sample Presentence Investigation Report. Nothing unusual was uncovered in Bill's physical health history that is pertinent to decisions on his sentence, classification, or treatment. He did report heavy use of marijuana while in college and current use of amphetamines. However, given the ubiquity of marijuana use among the young and his stated reason for taking amphetamines, there is no cause for undue alarm. We do note that those seeking intensified stimulation favor the use of amphetamines.

Mental Health. The first item for consideration under the heading of mental health is the offender's education. You should list names and locations of all schools attended, including dates of attendance, and request records from the offender's last high school or college. From school records you should note grade point average, class standing, IQ, vocational testing, and attendance and behavioral history. If the offender dropped out of high school, inquire about the reason. If you feel that your sentencing recommendation will be probation, explore the possibility of the offender attending General Equivalency Degree (GED) classes. Offenders' responses to this and similar ideas will give you some idea of their motivation to better themselves. IQ and vocational testing results will provide you with an offender's range of possibilities, but do not be misled by low scores and dismiss an offender as a hopeless case.

One study showed that probationers attending General Equivalency Degree classes at a probation department had significantly fewer arrests, and committed significantly fewer serious crimes, than a matched group of dropout probationers not attending classes (Walsh 1985b). Discuss any psychiatric or psychological workups done on offenders with them and integrate it into your own assessment. Discuss any discrepancies that may exist between the stories they have told you and those they have related to mental health professionals. Lies told have an awkward tendency to be soon forgotten.

Do not be afraid to disagree with or add your own opinions to those of the mental health professionals—you are a professional in your own right. Studies have shown that when the recommendations of probation officers conflict with those of mental health professionals, judges are somewhat more apt to agree with the officers (Walsh 1990). Remember, the training and role expectations of mental health workers lead them to see mental pathology in nearly all cases they review. Although real mental illness does exist, a deficiency view rather than a pathological view of criminal behavior is both more productive and less stigmatizing. Never contend with mental health professionals, however, if they advise psychiatric hospitalization. Such recommendations are not rendered lightly, and you must respect boundaries of expertise.

When discussing aspects of their mental functioning with offenders, concentrate on how they feel about themselves, their aspirations, their goals, and their usual ways of coping with stress and adversity. If you feel that a particular offender has some special problems that require the assistance of mental health professionals, refer him or her for a workup, indicating the areas you wish the diagnostic center to explore.

Application to Sample Presentence Investigation Report. We already have addressed many of the possible underlying reasons for Bill's criminal behavior. It is interesting to see how Officer Corrick added and integrated his own findings into those of the Court Diagnostic and Treatment Center. However, he did not step beyond the boundaries of his professional expertise to contest the findings and opinions of the center's personnel. He merely added to their insights and provided additional light. His collateral interviews with family members made him privy to information unavailable to the court diagnostic personnel.

We know that enuresis and cruelty to animals are two of the childhood and adolescent behaviors predictive of violent behavior and that Bill exhibited two of them. We do not know if Bill was also into fire setting, so perhaps we should not make too much of this since it is the three behaviors taken together that are considered predictive. Nevertheless, Corrick was aware of Bill's late enuresis (we note that Bill denied it to the examining psychiatrist) and his hanging of Susan's pet kitten; court diagnostic personnel were not. Would they have labeled Bill passive aggressive (shooting a policeman and hanging a kitten is certainly aggressive, but hardly passive) had they known? Nor were they aware of the sexual perversities into which Bill's father forced him and his siblings. This is an excellent example of the use of collateral interviewing when appropriate. The court diagnostic center's other diagnosis of Bill as being "in the early stages of a schizophrenic reaction" was supported by Officer Corrick's observation that Bill often spoke about himself in the third person.

Other revealing pieces of information contained in this section help us gain a clearer picture of Bill. Whereas Bill's high school GPA of 2.27 is respectable, it, as well as his class standing, is considerably below what one would expect from someone with an IQ in the bright-normal range. Is this indicative of an underachiever or of someone kept too busy working for his father to do justice to his studies, as Bill claimed? The consistency of IQ test scores taken seven years apart reveals that regardless of what other mental problems Bill may have had, he suffered no deterioration of intellectual functioning.

Alert students will have noted an important piece of information that Officer Corrick reported but on which he did not comment: Bill "scored significantly above average in tasks requiring nonverbal and short-term memory skills." We noted in the section on psychopathy that the performance IQ is determined by performance on such tasks, and that many authorities consider performance IQ clearly in excess of verbal IQ as a clear marker of psychopathy. Unfortunately, Corrick did not report the performance and verbal IQ subscales but only the full-scale score. We do not know, therefore, if Bill's performance IQ was "clearly in excess" of his verbal IQ. However, this piece of information in conjunction with Bill's enuresis, cruelty to animals, apparent inability to form close loving relationships, and history of deprivation of love renders the application of the psychopathic label plausible. Had Corrick picked up on this (assuming that he was aware of the theory behind it), he may have been led to investigate further along those lines.

This observation again underscores the necessity for criminal justice workers to be conversant with criminological theory. Finally, it is clear that Officer Corrick was very much impressed with Bill, but he did not let that reaction cloud his judgment when he made his sentencing recommendation.

Evaluative Summary. The evaluative summary is the most challenging section of the PSI to write. In Norman and Wadman's (2000) study of the professional consumers of the PSI, they found that none of them skipped the evaluative summary and recommendation sections. You are summarizing the facts contained in your report and drawing reasoned conclusions from them. This section represents the distilled wisdom of the investigator and separates the true professional from the data gatherer. It is the product of a disciplined effort to organize, synthesize, and analyze your collected data. No new data should be included in this section; your sole task here is to draw meaning from what you already have reported.

Since this section requires the inclusion of value judgments, make every effort to minimize any feelings you may have for or against offenders and/or their behavior. Fully appraise your subjective feelings by asking yourself: "Why do I feel this way?" The tone of your report can convey impressions of the offender to the reader that may have a major impact on the offender's future. Emotion-laden terms, such as "morally bankrupt" or "a picture of womanly virtue," reveal more about the investigator's attitudes than about the offenders and should not be a part of a professional report. If you find that your offender evokes this kind of heavy emotional response, it is a good idea to consult with your supervisor or your colleagues before writing this section to clarify and objectify your thoughts.

This does not mean that you should not take a firm and positive stand. Indeed, as a professional this is your duty. Ambiguous, "wishy-washy" hedging statements are indicative of investigators who are uncomfortable in their role and uncertain of their expertise. Such beating around the bush undermines the authority of the entire report, and causes the reader to have doubts about the advised plan of action.

Of course, you should firmly ground all strong statements in the information uncovered and set these down in other sections of the report. Of the utmost importance is your evaluation of the offenders' strengths and weaknesses, their patterns of criminal behavior, their potential for reform, and their amenability to various kinds of treatment and training. This evaluation requires a thorough knowledge of available community resources as well as of the offender. This knowledge serves as the basis for a treatment plan, which is the logical conclusion of the evaluative summary.

The treatment plan should be realistic and rendered with full knowledge of the possibilities. The recommendation of a treatment plan that cannot be implemented is frustrating to the person who must act on your recommendations. One offender with a string of armed robberies to his name was released on parole after serving ten years and was in jail for a parole violation for yet another robbery. He received a recommendation from his officer that he be allowed to go to another state under the care of a Christian youth camp. The officer had been convinced by the offender and by the offender's spiritual counselor that he was a "born-again Christian." The officer skillfully sold his recommendation to the sentencing judge, who allowed the offender to go. After this fifty-three-year-old man found himself surrounded only by youths and discovered that they expected him to work for his daily bread, he left the camp and committed further crimes before police apprehended him. Needless to say, that officer found his credibility seriously compromised.

In formulating a treatment plan, give the threat that the offender poses to the community equal consideration with the offender's rehabilitative needs. The nature of the present offense and the length and seriousness of the person's criminal record provide clues to this threat. Weigh various alternative plans in terms of their advantages and disadvantages for the offender and the community. Give reasons for plans that you decide to reject, and show complete justification for the accepted plan in terms of both offender and community concerns. Formulate treatment plans that involve other agencies in concert with them. Their special expertise may uncover deficiencies in an offender's character or motivation that in their opinion renders him or her unsuitable for the plan you have in mind. If this is the case, respect their professional evaluation and concentrate on an alternative plan.

Application to Sample Presentence Investigation Report. Officer Corrick begins his evaluative summary by reiterating the fact that the present offense is Bill's first conviction, and he rendered his positive feelings about the offender based on objective criteria and on his dealings with him. He then launched into a thoughtful examination of the possible origins of Bill's behavior. He emphasized the lack of love, the punitive and incestuous milieu in which Bill grew up, and the excessive acquisitiveness of both Bill and Susan. After you read this evaluation, you feel that you "know" Bill fairly well without ever having seen him. You should strive for this ideal.

Officer Corrick did not outline a treatment plan for Bill because he felt that the seriousness of Bill's crimes warranted incarceration in spite of Bill's "first-offender" status. He seemed to feel that the experience of being caught, incarcerated, and having the opportunity to examine his behavior would deter Bill from future criminality.

Recommendation. Like the denouement of a mystery novel, the recommendation should flow logically from all the information preceding it. It also should be consistent with the legal requirement of the state. Certain crimes, such as murder, rape, and aggravated robbery, are not probationable, and certain crimes outside that category may contain elements that render them non-probationable. Officers must be aware of the penal codes of their jurisdictions.

The recommendation should state concisely the number of years the offender is to spend in prison or on probation (some jurisdictions, however, require that the investigator only recommend probation or prison without specifying a time to be served). If you recommend probation, state special conditions of probation, such as amount of restitution and the name and address of payee, attendance at alcohol or drug centers, fines to be paid, amount of time that you feel that the defendant should serve locally in jail or a work release program, and so forth.

Application to Sample Presentence Investigation Report. Corrick's estimation of community feelings, the possible threat Bill posed to the community, and the extreme seriousness of the offense led him to recommend that Bill serve two consecutive prison sentences of four to twenty-five years and five to twenty-five years. The judge imposed those sentences. What would you have recommended?

Presentence Investigation Checklist. The most useful summary of this chapter takes the form of a checklist of factors that you should consider in any presentence investigation. Styles and formats of PSIs vary from department to department, and some areas we have discussed such as the victim's statement and the officer's recommendation may be optional inclusions at your department. Remember one thing above all: the presentence investigation will have a significant impact on the offender's future. Accuracy is of the utmost importance.

1. Circumstances of present offense(s). Present a concise summary of all the relevant details of the offense(s) for which the offender is to be sentenced.

2. Offender's version. How does the offender's version differ from the official version? What is the offender's attitude about the offense, and what type of attitude does he or she have overall? The officer should evaluate and make judgments about these questions.

3. Prior record. Provide a complete and verified criminal history of the offender. Note patterns of criminality.

4. Family history. Include family demographics, characteristics, conflicts, migrations, child-rearing practices, marital history, and so on.

5. Employment history. Present a complete and verified history of the offender's employment and financial situation.

6. Physical and mental health. List recent hospitalizations and diseases. Include drug and/or alcohol abuse. Describe the level of intellectual functioning (school grade completed, GPA, IQ). Include vocational training and psychological information.

7. Evaluative summary. This is a capsulated version of the entire report, evaluating its overall meaning. It includes the officer's professional assessment of what is to be done to amend the offender's behavior.

Perspective from the Field
A Few Words about Presentence Investigations

By Mike Moser and Kim Brown

Mike Moser is a Section Supervisor for the Idaho Department of Corrections. He supervises the presentence investigators that provide presentence reports for Ada, Boise, and Elmore County judges in the Fourth Judicial District Court, in Idaho. He received his undergraduate degree at Lewis Clark State College. Mr. Moser has twenty-nine years in the criminal justice field. He has worked as a police officer, detective, juvenile probation officer, and felony probation/parole officer.

Kim Brown is a senior presentence investigator with the Idaho Department of Correction. She has ten years experience writing presentence investigations in the Fourth Judicial District (Idaho). She received her undergraduate degree from California State University-Fresno.

● ● ● ● ● ● ● ● ● ● ● ● ● ● ● ● ● ● ● ●

Offenders' involvement in the criminal justice system starts with their planning and/or committing a crime, and ends with them satisfying the sentencing court's judgment. The midpoint on that spectrum is the sentencing hearing. We trust our judges to make wise and informed sentencing decisions, and their ability to do so is greatly effected by the quality of the presentence investigation

Continued on the next page

Perspective from the Field, *continued*

(PSI). An offender pleads guilty or is found guilty at trial and, unless the court and counsel agree to sentence the offender without the benefit of a PSI, the court orders one and schedules a sentencing hearing some weeks later, typically four or five. This applies to Idaho specifically and may not be the case in other states (in many states the PSI is mandatory).

In a nutshell, the PSI aims to provide the court with an offender's criminal background and social history, though there are other key features, as listed below. In Idaho, an offender and his or her attorney may decide that the less the judge knows about the offender, the better, and chose to waive the offender's right to the investigation. The judge, however, can veto that waiver and order the report over the offender's objections. This brings up a key point about the PSI process. To a large degree, the quality and quantity of information a PSI can provide the judge is dependent on the offender's level of participation and honesty in that process.

The typical PSI contains:

- **Official information about the crime**, in the form of police reports, along with a subjective version of the crime from the viewpoint of both the offender and any identifiable victim. In crimes such as drug possession, the state is considered the "victim." Thus, no victim statement is gathered. Victims have an opportunity, through the PSI, to communicate directly to the judge and have their input become part of the written record. This portion of the PSI also provides the court a window into the offender's criminal thinking, beliefs, and values.

- **The offender's self-disclosed social history**, from birth to the time of sentencing, includes input gathered by the investigator from the offender's family and friends. Some offenders want no one to know about their crime, while others have support, sometimes overwhelming support, from people who submit character reference letters. Additionally, the court often orders professional evaluations such as mental health, domestic violence, sexual offender, and substance abuse, depending on the crime, for inclusion in the PSI.

- **A recommendation that the offender be supervised** in either an institutional or community setting. Base this recommendation on offenders' perceived risk to themselves and/or the community, as determined by the presentence investigator or professional evaluator.

An investigator can be working on up to twenty PSIs at any given time, concerning crimes ranging from homicide to forgery. Investigators' clear understanding of the criminal justice system is vital, as is their ability to ask probing questions and communicate clearly and concisely in written form. Because presentence investigators make sentencing recommendations, we have to make sure that our information is factual and our conclusions are well grounded. This involves interviewing large numbers of people who know the defendant, including friends, relatives, and professional contacts. Presentence investigation reports are also a conduit for defendants and victims to express their feelings to the court.

The investigator also must keep up with changes in rehabilitation services and service providers, and maintain an effective network with other criminal justice professionals. Effective and empathetic interviewing skills are crucial in the gathering of information for a balanced report. Obviously, time management is an essential skill for the presentence investigator.

Writing the PSI is a difficult juggling act, gathering bits of information from different sources, from all the people involved in any given criminal case, and weaving that information into a timely, accurate, and well-written report. You cannot simply "ask questions" and expect to get meaningful answers in criminal justice settings. You always will get answers to your questions regardless of how you ask them, but they will not necessarily be helpful or truthful. You must establish a relationship in which the defendant can feel comfortable in revealing intimate information to you. That is quite a challenge.

A presentence investigator's job is, at times, exhilarating, emotionally draining, and exhausting, all in the span of one day, but it is a rewarding profession and a critically important part of the criminal justice system. In many ways, you can view it as the beginning of the rehabilitative process.

References and Suggested Readings

Abadinsky, H. 1997. *Probation and Parole: Theory and Practice*. Upper Saddle River, New Jersey: Prentice Hall.

Champion, D. 2005. *Probation, Parole, and Community Corrections*, 5th ed. Upper Saddle River, New Jersey: Prentice Hall.

Clear, T., V. Clear, and W. Burrell. 1989. *Offender Assessment and Evaluation: The Presentence Investigation Report*. Cincinnati: Anderson.

Conaboy, R. 1997. The United States Sentencing Commission: A New Component in the Federal Justice System. *Federal Probation* 61: 58-63.

Norman, M. and R. Wadman. 2000. Utah Presentence Investigation Reports: User Group Perceptions of Quality and Effectiveness. *Federal Probation* 64: 7-13.

Pastore, A. and K. Maguire, eds. 2003. *Sourcebook of Criminal Justice Statistics*, 2002. Albany, New York: Hindelang Criminal Justice Research Center.

Robin, G. 1987. *Introduction to the Criminal Justice System*. New York: Harper and Row.

Walsh, A. 1983. *Differential Sentencing Patterns among Felony Sex Offenders and Non-Sex Offenders*. Ann Arbor, Michigan: Michigan University Microfilms International.

———. 1984. Gender-Based Differences: A Study of Probation Officers' Attitudes about, and Recommendations for, Felony Sexual Assault Cases. *Criminology* 22: 371-387.

———. 1985a. The Role of the Probation Officer in the Sentencing Process: Independent Professional or Judicial Hack? *Criminal Justice and Behavior* 12: 289-303.

———. 1985b. An Evaluation of the Effects of Adult Basic Education on Rearrest Rates among Probationers. *Journal of Offender Counseling, Services and Rehabilitation* 9: 69-76.

———. 1990. Twice Labeled: The Effects of Psychiatric Labeling on the Sentencing of Sex Offenders. *Social Problems* 37: 375-389.

CHAPTER 7

Assessment Tools and Guidelines in Community Corrections

Justice consists of treating equals equally and unequals unequally according to relevant differences.

—**Aristotle**

Aristotle's epigraph signifies the philosophy of individualized justice. You can achieve individualized justice by responding to specific offenders with respect to their needs and to the risk, they pose to the community, and with respect to the nature of the crimes they have committed. To do this we rely on actuarial models that make statistical predictions based on the observed outcomes of similarly situated offenders in the past. Corrections workers thus attempt to operationalize (define a concept in terms of the operations used to measure it) justice by assigning numeric scores on assessment scales according to observations they make relevant to offenders, their behaviors, and their needs. These tools attempt to determine Aristotle's "relevant differences" so that justice can be done as equitably as possible (Walsh and Hemmens 2008). Everyone benefits from the more structured and reasoned approach to decision-making made possible by research-grounded tools such as those presented in this chapter (See also Lauen, 1997). The assessment tools presented in this chapter apply mainly to presentence evaluations and to community corrections. (See the discussion of assessment and classification of prison inmates in Chapter 8.)

Offenders benefit by more just and consistent treatment than was previously the case, and the community is better served by a more accurate assessment of the risks offenders pose to it. Many jurisdictions use the assessment and guideline approach to set bail, and in prosecutors' offices to screen cases for dismissal or prosecution. It also guides plea bargain arrangements. Some argue that we could save hundreds of millions of tax dollars with little additional risk to the community, if adequate numerical guidelines were developed to stem this nation's burgeoning jail and prison crowding problem (Pollock 1997, Carlson, Hess, and Orthmann 1999).

This chapter provides instruction on the various assessment tools used in many probation and parole agencies. The processing officers fill out these forms and scales based on their evaluation of the offender. If your instructor assigns practice presentence investigation interviews, he or she will provide you with actual cases for practice interviews and assessments. If you are role-playing the offender, you will have access to information supplied by the offender. It is the "officer's" task to elicit this information from the "offender" using the interviewing techniques described in Chapter 5.

If you are role-playing the interviewing officer, you will receive only case materials that are normally provided from sources other than the offender. These include circumstances of the offense, the criminal record, the victims' statements, and school records. Drawing on the information provided by the offender and other sources, perform an evaluation of the offender, make a realistic recommendation, and formulate a treatment plan. There are no "correct answers." There are only good or poor evaluations, realistic or unrealistic recommendations, and workable or unworkable treatment plans.

When considering each section in the practice presentence investigation reports, reread the appropriate section in Chapter 6 to determine if you have considered everything pertinent before deciding on an evaluation and recommendation. Do not hesitate to recommend imprisonment if you feel that the case warrants such a disposition. However, for the purposes of formulating a treatment program, assume probation placement even if you recommended imprisonment. All the assessment tools covered in the following discussion appear in the Appendix.

The forms and scales in this chapter are presented in the order that officers in the field encounter them. That is, offenders fill out the social history questionnaire before meeting the officer assigned to the case, the officer then may make use of the structured interview schedule, after which he or she will complete the sentencing guideline. The risk and needs scales are completed after the offender is sentenced to probation or granted parole, as are the treatment plans.

Social History Questionnaire

The first tool you should become familiar with is the social history questionnaire (SHQ). There are perhaps as many social history questionnaires as there are state or county probation departments in the United States; this is just one of them. The social history questionnaire asks for relevant demographic information such as the offender's address, educational level, family, work history, and so forth. An intake officer or the agency receptionist hands this questionnaire to the offender referred for a presentence investigation. Offenders are requested to fill it out completely before they meet with the presentence investigator. For conducting presentence exercises, students role-playing offenders should complete copies of the form using the data provided by their "offender" PSI. Each item is self-explanatory.

Felony Sentencing Worksheet

The first instrument typically used by the presentence investigator is some sort of sentencing guideline used to assist him or her to make a sentencing recommendation. The Felony Sentencing Worksheet is one of several sentencing guidelines used throughout the nation. (See the Appendix.) This Felony Sentencing Worksheet is a sentencing guideline used by the courts in Ohio. It is a discretional guideline (meaning that it is not binding on the sentencing judge) rather than a mandatory one. Sentencing guidelines were developed as a compromise between factions in criminal justice who believe either that the punishment received by an offender should "fit the crime" or that punishment should fit the offender and be appropriate to rehabilitation. The guidelines address both of these positions, with the seriousness of the offense weighted more than the character of the offender.

American Correctional Association Policy on Sentencing

Introduction:

Changes in U.S. sentencing policies have been a major cause of an unprecedented increase in the prison population. The sentencing process should attempt to control crime as much as possible, at the lowest cost to taxpayers and in the least restrictive environment consistent with public safety. There should be a balanced consideration of all sentencing objectives.

Sentencing policy today takes many forms. In some venues, legislatures have taken authority over that policy, leaving little discretion in the sentencing of individual offenders to the judiciary. Under these circumstances, "sentencing" discretion is shifted to the prosecutors and takes the form of plea bargaining and charge selection. In others, judges and parole boards retain wide discretion on a case-by-case basis. In still others, sentencing commissions have been given responsibility for defining how offenders are punished. Regardless of the form, sentencing policy directly affects what the correctional practitioner does on a daily basis, and to the extent that this policy fails in fairness and rationality, then correctional practice is adversely affected.

As implementers of sentencing policies, corrections professionals have a unique vantage point from which to provide input on their effectiveness and consequences. If corrections does not voice its collective experience on this matter, then sentencing practices nationwide will fail to be as soundly based as they should be in this important public policy area.

Policy Statement:

The American Correctional Association actively promotes the development of sentencing policies that should:

Continued on the next page

American Correctional Association Policy on Sentencing, *continued*

A. Be based on the principle of proportionality. The sentence imposed should be commensurate with the seriousness of the crime and the harm done;

B. Be impartial with regard to race, ethnicity and economic status as to the discretion exercised in sentencing;

C. Include a broad range of options for custody, supervision and rehabilitation of offenders;

D. Be purpose-driven. Policies must be based on clearly articulated purposes. They should be grounded in knowledge of the relative effectiveness of the various sanctions imposed in attempts to achieve these purposes;

E. Encourage the evaluation of sentencing policy on an ongoing basis. The various sanctions should be monitored to determine their relative effectiveness based on the purpose(s) they are intended to have. Likewise, monitoring should take place to ensure that the sanctions are not applied based on race, ethnicity or economic status;

F. Recognize that the criminal sentence must be based on multiple criteria, including the harm done to the victim, past criminal history, the need to protect the public and the opportunity to provide programs for offenders as a means of reducing the risk for future crime;

G. Provide the framework to guide and control discretion according to established criteria and within appropriate limits and allow for recognition of individual needs;

H. Have as a major purpose restorative justice—righting the harm done to the victim and the community. The restorative focus should be both process and substantively oriented. The victim or his or her representative should be included in the "justice" process. The sentencing procedure should address the needs of the victim, including his or her need to be heard and, as much as possible, to be and feel restored to whole again;

I. Promote the use of community-based programs whenever consistent with public safety; and

J. Be linked to the resources needed to implement the policy. The consequential cost of various sanctions should be assessed. Sentencing policy should not be enacted without the benefit of a fiscal-impact analysis. Resource allocations should be linked to sentencing policy so as to ensure adequate funding of all sanctions, including total confinement and the broad range of intermediate

> sanction and community-based programs needed to implement those policies.
>
> *This Public Correctional Policy was unanimously ratified by the American Correctional Association Delegate Assembly in 1994 and reviewed and amended January. 14, 2009.*

Professionals developed guidelines to attempt to minimize wide sentencing disparities for similar crimes and similarly situated individuals. They aim to structure judicial discretion in sentencing and to promote consistency by providing judges with sentencing norms based on the past practices of their peers. Implicit in the idea of guidelines is the notion that disparity flowing from legitimate variation (relevant differences) among different crimes and different offenders is acceptable, but disparity shorn of just or coherent reason is not (Walsh and Hemmens 2008). Consider sentencing guidelines as an application of Aristotle's definition of justice as relying on relevant differences.

The processing probation officer scores the Felony Sentencing Worksheet by assigning the indicated numerical scores based on the legal and social factors addressed in each subsection. Some sections simply require the recording of factual data, such as the degree of the offense, multiple offenses, prior convictions, and repeat offenses. Other sections, covering culpability, mitigation, and credits, require a great deal of interpretation. If you receive a case to assess for sentencing, do not be confused if you and your classmates arrive at different Felony Sentencing Worksheet scores.

Since judgments are called for, the Felony Sentencing Worksheet allows for the intrusion of ideology in its scoring. One study showed that practicing probation officers differentially score the Felony Sentencing Worksheet according to their ideological convictions, with conservative officers assigning significantly higher scores than liberal officers (Walsh 1985). Thus, while sentencing by arithmetic is not impervious to ideological intrusion, it does constitute an improvement over unstructured sentencing. An earlier study of the effects of the guideline on sentencing found a predictive accuracy of 85 percent; that is, judges imposed the suggested sentence in 85 percent of the cases, with 8 percent being harsher than indicated and 7 percent being more lenient than indicated (Swisher 1978). This study occurred a year after implementation of the guidelines. Judges may have been more willing to abide by sentencing guidelines initially because of the novelty effect. We believe that it is of utmost importance to develop value-free guidelines and to make it mandatory that sentences they suggest be heeded except under special circumstances that are fully justified in writing.

After the officer assigns scores and adds for both the offense and the offender categories, the officer applies them to a grid on the reverse side of the Felony Sentencing Worksheet at the point at which they intersect. The grids indicate a suitable sentence for offenders whose crimes and whose criminal histories fall into it. These are suggested sentences only. Do not be hesitant to recommend sentences that are not consistent with the grid if you feel there should be alternatives and you can justify them. In fact, it is probably a good idea for practice purposes to ignore the scoring of the Felony Sentencing Worksheet until after you have decided on a recommendation. You then may score the Felony Sentencing Worksheet and see how closely your decision comes to the suggested sentence.

As a quick exercise, score Bill Bloggs on the Felony Sentencing Worksheet. He was a first offender and thus is scored zero on the "offender rating" section of the sheet. In the "degree of offense" subsection, Bill would receive the maximum points (four) because both of his crimes were first-degree felonies. In the "multiple offenses" category, he would receive two points because he was convicted of aggravated robbery and attempted aggravated murder. In the "actual or potential harm" category, he would receive two points for his wounding of the police officer. His eight points thus far already put him beyond the Felony Sentencing Worksheet's range for probation. You might also assess two points against Bill in the "culpability" section for "shocking and deliberate cruelty," but could you justify deducting any points in the "mitigation" category? If not, Bill would get ten offense-rating points assessed against him, a score that places him in the upper-left hand square of the grid.

Sentencing guidelines can be a major tool in more just and sensible sentencing, or they can serve as "scientific" rationales for more draconian penalties. For instance, while federal sentencing guidelines have reduced disparities within the federal system, they have done so by incarcerating an increasing number of more nonviolent criminals (particularly drug users) at tremendous expense to taxpayers (Champion 2005: 85).

The number of inmates in federal prisons increased by 164 percent from 1985 to 1995 (Bureau of Justice Statistics 1995), and there has been an average annual growth of 6.4 percent each year since (Bureau of Justice Statistics 2000). The guidelines per se are not responsible for this increase, but they do provide a type of justification (Schmalleger 2001). This author remains convinced of the utility of sentencing guidelines, and agrees with Roger Lauen, former state director of community corrections in Colorado, who wrote:

> The passage of sentencing guidelines legislation has been an effective tool in reducing prison use for selected offenders. However, without widespread public support, sentencing guidelines, sentencing grids, and sentencing commissions are unable to maintain their organizational independence and stay removed from the 'get tough' political rhetoric (1997: 113).

Assessment and Classification Instruments

Just as there are guidelines that quantify the seriousness of an offense and of the offender's criminal history to assist judges in making sentencing decisions, there are instruments that assist probation and parole officers to assess the risks posed by probationers and parolees and to assess their treatment/supervision needs. Officials also use them during the presentence process to determine offenders' amenability to community supervision. Assessment of offenders was mostly based on the clinical judgment of correctional workers and other professionals such as psychiatrists and psychologists. Researchers classify this form of assessment as "first generation" assessment. In the 1970s a shift to actuarial assessment occurred; in other words, the use of objective statistical data based on known risk factors to predict the probability of an outcome (in the case of corrections, reoffending). Actuarial methods became known as "second generation" assessment, and constituted a big improvement over clinical judgment. As Gottfredson and Moriarty (2006: 180) state: "In virtually all decision-making situations....actuarially developed predictions outperform human judgments."

Because actuarial assessment by definition uses historical data (offenders' criminal record, history of drug abuse), all risk factors were static, and thus no way of gauging diminished or increased risk This limitation led to the "third-generation" of assessment tools in the 1980s. Third generation tools are more evidence-based and dynamic. In other words, they take into account offenders' constantly changing situations (family dynamics, criminal friends, treatment progress, and so forth). They are thus sensitive to an individual offender's risks and needs.

We are now in the era of "fourth-generation" assessment. Fourth generation assessment tools (like third-generation tools) are based on the risk-need-responsivity principle. Recall that this principle maintains that if offenders are to respond to treatment in meaningful and lasting ways, correctional workers must be aware of offenders' different development stages, learning styles, and need to be treated with respect and dignity (Andrews and Dowden 2007). Fourth-generation instruments are more theory-driven. They fine-tune older instruments and address additional risk and needs factors. An example of such an instrument is the Level of Service/Case Management Inventory (LS/CMI) developed by Canadian researchers.

Very few American agencies are using the LS/CMI at present because it is relatively expensive in comparison to other instruments. Keiser (2003) lists a blizzard of such instruments in use in the United States, some of which are commercially marketed and therefore expensive, and some of which were developed cheaply "in house." According to a National Institute of Justice survey (Hubbard, Travis, and Latessa 2001), the most widely used instrument is the Case Management Classification System (CMC), used by 36.1 percent of responding agencies. The next most popular instruments are the risk and needs assessments, which are part of the CMC system, but used alone by 26.3 percent of agencies. The Level of Service Inventory-Revised (LSI-R), used by 15 percent of agencies, is next, followed by many other lesser-known instruments.

The LSI-R is a computer-based system that provides ratings of offenders' risks and needs based on the information investigators feed into the system. It addresses fifty-four variables related to reoffending and generates a total LSI-R score for the offender (Dal Pra 2004). The LSR-I is gaining in popularity. British probation officers accept it readily (Maung and Hammond 2001). However, its proprietary nature (it costs) prevents a number of financially strapped agencies from adopting it. Anyway, the CMC functions much the same way (although to our knowledge it is not yet computerized) and has been around for at least twenty years. It is tried and true, and last but not least, it is in the public domain (it is free!). We now turn to a discussion of this popular instrument.

Client Management Classification Assessment Instrument

The Wisconsin Bureau of Community Corrections developed The Client Management Classification Assessment instrument (CMC) after much study and research (Crooks 2000). Whereas the social history questionnaire deals primarily with factual demographic data, the CMC offers guidance for exploration of offenders' attitudes and feelings and is useful for supervision and treatment planning. When using this schedule, do not feel bound to repeat the questions exactly as they are printed on the page. There is sufficient leeway to incorporate your own style into the questions and to allow for unusual situations. However, preserve the meaning of each question even when you translate it into your own words. Also, leave the issues addressing the crime and criminal history until the end of the schedule, at which time you should have developed sufficient rapport to make these questions less threatening to offenders. This semi-structured interview schedule is reproduced in its entirety in the Appendix.

In actual practice, the CMC is scored so that probation and parole officers can assign offenders to one of four treatment modalities (selective intervention, environmental structure, casework control, and limit setting). This scoring, a rather complicated procedure for the uninitiated, uses eight templates (cardboard sheets with holes punched in them that fit over a scoring guide). Probation and parole officers attend three-day workshops and receive extensive follow-up training before they are able to use this system to its fullest. Explaining the system in its entirety is well beyond the scope of this book. In fact, the training material used in these training sessions constitutes a book in itself. Thus, consider the interview schedule included here simply as a guide to the type of questions you should be asking your offenders and as an introduction to the CMC system of offender classification. The classifications obtained from scoring the CMC are highly correlated with the classification scheme obtained from the far more succinct risk and needs scales, which we now discuss.

Risk and Needs Assessment Scales

The risk and needs assessment scales to be discussed are part of the Client Management Classification System, and are designed to be used in conjunction with the CMC interview schedule. The system consists of two separate scales that assess the offender's "risk" and "needs." Offender risk refers to the probability of reoffending and/or the threat the offender poses to the community. Assessment occurs by assigning numerical scores to the offender on variables known to correlate with recidivism. The earlier one begins a criminal career, the more involved one is in it, the more one turns to chemical substances, the less one is legitimately employed, and the more negative one's attitude is, the more likely one is to reoffend. The more likely offenders are to reoffend, the greater their risk to the community, the more closely they must be supervised. In many jurisdictions, offenders are moved up one level of supervision if they have a history of assaultive offenses. The appendix contains risk and needs scales, and a complete scoring guide.

Risk factors are of two types: static and dynamic. Static risk factors are those that cannot change (gender, ethnicity, and other background variables, including criminal history). Dynamic risk factors (substance abuse, attitudes, values, behavior patterns) are factors that can change. You can divide the dynamic risk factors into stable and acute dynamic risk factors. Stable dynamic risk factors include substance abuse and self-esteem/self-consistency issues that take a long time to change. Acute dynamic risk factors include such things as being under the influence of alcohol or drugs, anger, and deviant sexual arousal, "all things that can change in relatively short order" (Bartol 2002: 417). This does not mean that anger, substance abuse, and deviant sexuality issues are easy to change, quite the contrary—only that any single manifestation of them lasts a short time.

Offender needs refers to deficiencies in offenders' personal repertoires and lifestyles that may prevent them from making any commitment to a conventional moral pattern of behavior. Scores on the risks and on the needs sections of the scale tend to be highly correlated. That is, an offender who is high risk tends to have high needs, and offenders with few needs are not high risk. The needs section constitutes the area in which the probation and parole officer's counseling skills and knowledge of community resources are of great value so that he or she can target needs that will assist offenders to adjust to a prosocial lifestyle. Whenever completing such scales, you always should be mindful of the need for complete accuracy. The safety of the people of the community and the rehabilitative needs of the offender depend on your accurate assessment. Read the instructions carefully before making any assessment.

Let us see how Bill Bloggs would do on the risks and needs scales. Going over the risks scale, we would assess Bill only three points (he was between the ages of eighteen and twenty-nine at the time of the current offense). However, the "assault factor" automatically would place him up one level of supervision in most departments.

In the "emotional stability" section of the needs scale, we would assign Bill two points. On the one hand, given some of his weird behavior and statements, he should be assessed more than two. On the other hand, his symptoms do not prohibit adequate functioning, so we also would assess three points against him in the "living arrangements" category. The only other assessment against him is one point for "situational or minor difficulties" under "financial status," but we would assess five points under "officer's impressions," for a total of eleven points.

If we turn to the supervision-level matrix (Figure 7.1), we discover that Bill's level of supervision without the assault override, would have been minimum. Such a supervision level is clearly untenable for someone who committed the type of crimes that Bill did (this level might be fine if he were being classified for parole rather than probation and if information from prison authorities justified it). Such a possible classification problem underscores two points: (1) that Bill was clearly an atypical case and (2) that the suggestions of these scales, based as they are on the "typical" criminal, are not cast in stone. In the extremely unlikely event that Bill had been placed on probation, you would have been seriously remiss if you had followed these guidelines unquestioningly.

Figure 7.1   Risk and Needs Supervision Level Matrix

0–10	5 → 13	14 → 28	29 → 61
	Minimum	Medium	Maximum
11–20	Medium	Medium	Maximum
21–37	Maximum	Maximum	Maximum

The risk and needs scale we are discussing is one of a number of other "third-generation" scales based on empirical research that incorporate more (and more sophisticated) indices of risk, as well as treatable needs. As Lauen explains:

Third generation-risk instruments allow practitioners to measure dynamic-risk factors and better illuminate where and how the change process might be enhanced for a particular offender. Offender assessment data derived from well-integrated risk/need tools organizes and profiles populations according to various 'criminogenic' needs areas, as well as risk levels. Multiple scales are used so that the assessment can differentiate which need areas are the most urgent and, in so doing, establish case-management priorities, which, in turn, are most likely to result in real reductions in criminal behavior (1997: 126).

A perusal of the risk/needs scales contained in the Appendix will reveal that they address the major non-biological risk factors for offending identified by multiple researchers and summarized by Weibush, Baird, Krisberg, and Onek (1994). These major factors are as follows:

1. Age at first adjudication or conviction

2. Criminal history (number and type of arrests, incarcerations, probation/parole periods prior to current offense)

3. History of extent of drug and alcohol use

4. Education and vocational skills

5. Employment history and potential

6. Family stability

7. Emotional stability

8. Intellectual ability

If used in conjunction with the CMC, the correctional worker also will be able to identify offenders' friends and social network, as well as their attitudes and beliefs regarding crime and life in general. It remains to be seen if fourth-generation instruments will outperform these third-generation instruments.

Supervision-Level Matrix

Based on scores obtained in both sections of the assessment scale, offenders are placed under minimum, medium, or maximum supervision. These levels of supervision closely correlate with the case management classification system derived from the CMC. Correct assessment of offenders contributes greatly to the efficient use of officers' time. Caseworkers can spend the time not wasted in "over-servicing" low-risk and low-needs offenders with those who require more attention.

Five cells of the supervision-level matrix represent maximum-supervision, three represent medium, and only one cell represents minimum supervision. Only offenders with ten or fewer risk points and thirteen or fewer needs points fall into this minimum category. Do not be alarmed by the number of cells calling for maximum supervision. It has been empirically determined that only about 15 percent of probation and parole offenders fall into these five cells. About 50 percent of the offenders will fall into the medium-level of supervision, and the remaining 35 percent will require only minimal supervision (Idaho Department of Corrections n.d.: 19). These figures will vary according to the probation/parole granting practices of a given jurisdiction. If, for whatever reasons, a jurisdiction relies heavily on community-based corrections, the number of offenders requiring maximum and medium supervision will be a lot greater than in jurisdictions that only reluctantly grant probation/parole. In the latter type of jurisdiction, the number of offenders requiring minimum supervision may be perhaps 60-70 percent.

Case Management

Effective case management is an integral part of corrections work. The techniques of case management are borrowed from social work. Social workers have long experience in trying to connect (or reconnect) their clients to their communities by securing services for them from a variety of sources, coordinating the efforts of the various agencies providing those services, and monitoring their clients' use of them. According to Healey (1999: 2), you can distill case management into five sequential activities:

1. Assessing a client's needs

2. Developing a service/treatment plan

3. Linking the client to services

4. Monitoring his or her progress

5. Acting as an advocate for the client

This chapter focuses on activity numbers 1, 2, and 4. We address the remaining two activities elsewhere in this book.

Healey (1999) also identifies general models for implementing these activities: the strength-based and assertive models. The strength-based model delivers services and makes expectations about results based on the clients' strengths. Caseworkers first identify clients' strengths (with the help of the clients) and then formulate a management plan so that the clients can build on those strengths. Andrews and Bonta (1998: 245) refer to this as the responsivity principle of treatment delivery, and define it as providing treatment "in a style and mode that is consistent with the ability and learning style of the offender." The assertive model requires that the worker delivers the needed services to clients assertively (even aggressively) rather than simply offering those services to them. Applied to correctional "clients," case management must be both strength-based and assertive.

Brun and Rapp (2001: 279) offer a definition of case management that includes both of Healey's models: "Strength based case management is specific implementation of the overall strengths perspective, combining a focus on client's strengths and self-direction with three other principles:

1. Promoting the use of informal helping networks

2. Offering assertive community involvement, and

3. Emphasizing the relationship between client and case manager.

Some commentators view this emphasis on case management as a radical departure from previous models of probation and parole practice. Some suggest that the Probation Service in the United Kingdom be renamed the Offender Risk Management Service (Robinson 1999: 420). Nellis (1995: 27) appears to decry the trend, arguing that the rehabilitative ideal of earlier models focusing on offender needs have been replaced by a soulless quest for "accurate prediction and effective management of offender risk." Effective management of offenders must be, of course, the first and foremost concern of correctional personnel, with offender needs being of secondary importance. After all, rehabilitation is desirable primarily because it reduces risk to the community, and only secondarily because the offender will benefit from it personally. There is no real antithesis between the rehabilitative ideal and re-inscribing it in a risk-management model. After all, an accurate assessment can help determine "who warrants the investment of probation resources (according to the logic of risk) and what needs to be changed in order to reduce the risk of reoffending" (Robinson 1999: 429, emphasis in original).

When the offender is placed in the appropriate supervision level, case management proper now begins. Based on all the information you have gathered, you now have to formulate a plan aimed at his or her rehabilitation. It is of the utmost importance that treatment plans represent a balance between the offender's treatment needs and the offender's present coping resources. This is an example of strength-based case management. We will return to this issue in Chapter 10. You have identified the offender's needs, so the next task is to prioritize them according to their importance relative to his or her legal difficulties. The supervision planning form will aid you in this endeavor. It asks you to list the offender's strengths/resources and problems/weaknesses. In rank-ordering problem areas, give extra weight to the problems most amenable to speedy change so that the offender can begin to develop an orientation of success.

The officer should be particularly alert to what may be a primary or "master" problem, a particularly debilitating one that may be the source of most of the offender's other problems. For instance, lack of education and employment, poor financial status, and poor spousal relationships are highly interdependent areas that possibly may be mitigated by meaningful vocational training and subsequent employment. Perhaps all these areas, as well as others such as the influence of criminal companions, themselves, are dependent on some form of substance abuse. If an evaluation of the offender's problems leads the officer to believe that most of them are secondary to substance abuse, then the obvious plan is to rank substance abuse as the top priority for change.

With the offender's rehabilitative needs, identified and prioritized, draw up a tentative supervision plan according to the form reproduced in the Appendix. The tentative supervision plan includes a problem statement, a long-range goal, short-range objectives, a probationer/parolee action plan, and an officer/referral plan. For instance, the officer may identify alcoholism/problem drinking and vocational training as the problems needing immediate attention. A second problem, which the system may identify, is an offender's lack of marketable skills, which keeps him or her from obtaining worthwhile full-time employment.

The long-range goals, therefore, would be to maintain sobriety and complete vocational training. As we will see in Chapter 9, a good case management plan should be simple, specific, and something the offender must do as soon as possible rather than something he or she should stop doing. The officer may state the short-range goal to be two days of sobriety and attendance at the next AA meeting for alcoholism. Then, the officer will formulate a probationer action plan and request that the offender indicate commitment to it by signing it. The officer/referral action plan may state the officer's commitment to the plan by indicating that he or she will attend the first AA meeting with the offender, and that the offender is to be referred to an alcohol treatment facility for further evaluation of the extent of his or her drinking problem and for treatment recommendations. The procedure for the second problem area is, likewise, simple and focused.

Implement the reassessment plan after the outcomes of the tentative plans have been determined. For instance, the information received from the alcohol treatment facility may have advised more intensive treatment, or concluded that the officer perhaps had overemphasized the offender's drinking problem. In either case, the officer will plan the next supervision phase accordingly. Assuming that the caseworker referred the offender for vocational training, and that this training was successfully completed, the long-range plan now may be to secure and maintain full-time employment, and the short-range plan may be for the offender to file a designated number of applications for employment every day until he or she has secured a job. Caseworkers must reassess and change supervision plans frequently as circumstances dictate.

After six months, and semiannually thereafter, there should be a reassessment of the offender's risk and needs. Reassessment may result in a higher or lower supervision category based on the offender's progress or lack of progress in the preceding six months. We next see some of the characteristics of the offenders who fall into each of four classifications the CMC describes (paraphrased from the CMC training manuals).

Selective Intervention

Offenders in the selective-intervention category require the least time and present the fewest supervision problems. As the term implies, the supervising officer will intervene in the offender's life only on an "as needed" basis. Offenders in this category usually fall into the low-risk category as determined by the risk and needs scales. Generally, they have relatively stable, prosocial lifestyles, and their current offense is frequently their first involvement with the law. Their offenses may be a temporary lapse or suspension of an otherwise normal value system. They often show strong indications of guilt and embarrassment. Avoid increasing guilt and criminal identification in these offenders without allowing them to intellectualize or minimize their criminal acts.

These offenders respond best to a warm, supportive relationship with their officers and to the use of rational problem-solving approaches to counseling. Avoid giving the impression to such offenders that you are trying to run their lives for them or that you lack trust in them. Research evidence shows that low-risk offenders actually may become worse if they are overly restricted and "treated" by well-meaning correctional workers. Lowenkamp and Latessa's (2004) review of the literature found opposite treatment effects for low- and high-risk offenders placed in the same treatment programs; recidivism is reduced for high-risk offenders but is increased for low-risk offenders. Why would low-risk offenders be harmed by treatment? One reason is that you are exposing them to high-risk offenders, and you know the old sayings about bad company and rotten apples spoiling the whole barrel. Another is that placing low-risk offenders in the types of restrictive programs that high-risk offenders need may disrupt the very factors (family, employment, and other prosocial contacts) that made them low risk in the first place (Lowenkamp and Latessa 2004).

The message is "leave low-risk offenders alone as much as possible." If your agency uses a system of minimal contact, such as allowing low-risk offenders to report into the agency by mail or by telephone, make sure that offenders know that you are available to help them through temporary crises or emotional problems that may prompt further criminal activity. Caseworkers should not put these offenders on minimal supervision or write-in status until they deal with any of their treatment needs satisfactorily. Remember, less intrusive supervision strategies tend to work best for these offenders.

Environmental Structure. Offenders who need environmental structure generally fall into the low end of the medium-risk category and require regular supervision. Intellectual, vocational, and social deficits contribute considerably to their criminal activities. They tend to lack foresight, to have difficulty learning from past mistakes, and to be overly dependent on like-minded individuals for acceptance and approval. Usually, they are not committed to a criminal career, and malice as a motivation for criminal activity is rare.

The typical goals to seek with these offenders are to develop and/or improve intellectual, social, and work skills, to find alternatives to associations with criminal peers, and to increase control of impulses. Be more directive and concrete with these individuals than with your selective-intervention offenders. Move slowly to build a success identity for the offenders by balancing your expectations of them with their present coping resources (the subject of Chapter 10). Initially, you often may have to do things with and/or for them (such as taking them job hunting), but take care that you do not foster overdependence. Many of the offenders in this category can become productive citizens with a warm and accepting officer who knows the available community resources.

Casework/Control. Casework/control means that offenders placed in this category require more intensive casework and that their activities should be more tightly controlled. Offenders in this category are at the high end of the medium-risk and needs scale. They evidence a generalized instability in their lifestyles. They lack goals in their lives and have difficulty with interpersonal relationships and in finding and keeping employment. They tend to have had chaotic and abusive childhoods, which they repeat with their own families. You frequently will find alcohol and drug abuse among these offenders, and many of their criminal convictions reflect this abuse.

The basic goals for this group are much the same as those outlined for the environmental structure offenders, but they are more difficult to achieve because of their substance abuse and greater emotional problems. These offenders require a great deal of your time and considerable coordination of auxiliary programs. You must monitor attendance and involvement with outside programs strictly, and you should allow them to suffer the consequences of their noncompliance, such as short periods in the county jail. Consequently, use all your leverage to promote offender compliance. These offenders will try your patience and professional competence, but a knowledgeable, caring, and no-nonsense officer can turn them around.

Limit Setting. Offenders who need strict limits set for them by their officers are high risk on the risk and needs scale. They are quite comfortable in their criminal lifestyles and demonstrate a pattern of long-term involvement with criminal activities. They delight in their ability to beat the system and tend to minimize or deny any personal problems. They see themselves as normal individuals who simply have chosen a criminal lifestyle for themselves. Indeed, in comparison to the structured-environment and casework/control offenders, they often show quite superior ability to function normally (if not morally) in society.

This ability, of course, is the hallmark of psychopathy. A special intensive supervision officer generally receives offenders in the limit-setting category. Intensive supervision officers usually enjoy small caseloads, enabling them to devote the time necessary to supervise high-risk offenders. Protection of the community through surveillance and strict control (often with the aid and cooperation of the police) of the offenders is of primary concern. Such offenders are extremely manipulative and frequently will test your resolve. They will interpret any failure on your part to act assertively as weakness. Thus, you always must be prepared to confront them with even minor infractions of the rules. If you do not, they will not respect you, and you can be sure that they will escalate their violations.

These offenders respond best to the techniques of reality therapy described in Chapter 10 and to rational discussion because their criminal behavior is often more a function of choice than of emotional or intellectual deficiencies. Figuring the cost/benefit ratio of crime as explained in Chapter 12 may be beneficial to these offenders. Since they also tend to be quite energetic and to possess adequate native intelligence, they have capabilities that you can channel into profitable and legal endeavors. Attempt to develop challenging and innovative opportunities to provide them with satisfying alternatives to a criminal lifestyle.

For offenders who have defeated all your best efforts, who have repeatedly sabotaged treatment plans and exhausted existing programs, and who plainly lack any sort of motivation to change, it may be appropriate to discontinue major efforts to restructure their lives. When all else has failed, but you have not initiated formal legal action against them, expect nothing more than legal conformity from them. Make it clear, however, that any legal violation, no matter how minor, will result in official action.

A Final Word about the CMC System

It is important that neither the seasoned officer nor the student see the CMC system as just bureaucratic paper-pushing. It may seem like a lot of extra work to the officer used to supervising offenders in accordance with his or her "intuition" or "experience." The CMC system is actually an efficiency-enhancing device that ultimately will save time. A study (Lerner, Arling, and Baird 1986) found that high-risk offenders on CMC supervision experienced 8 percent fewer parole revocations than regularly supervised ("seat of the pants") high-risk offenders. Medium-risk CMC offenders experienced 6 percent fewer revocations than non-CMC medium-risk offenders. Both these differences were statistically significant. The substantive difference represented by these percentages was ninety-five fewer parole violation reports—a lot of time spared. More importantly, it meant that ninety-five offenders were saved from the futility of the revolving prison door because their needs had been identified and efficiently serviced. CMC supervision of low-risk offenders resulted in only 1 percent fewer (6 percent versus 7 percent) revocations than that of the regularly supervised low-risk offenders. This seemingly insignificant difference is more a function of the generally good performance of low-risk offenders than the inapplicability of the CMC system to them. Michael Schumacher, Ph.D., Chief Probation Officer of Orange County, California, is an enthusiastic supporter of CMC.

Probation programs. . . . can no longer rely upon the assertions of "doing good" for people based upon a subjective model of human behavior. The risk/needs approach provides an objective look at offenders based on characteristics shown to have some predictive value for the success or failure of other probationers. It supports a healthy balance between the peace officer role [and the] social work role. It is a tool that has been a long time coming and shows promise for probation supervision as a major factor in the resocialization of offenders. Longitudinal research conducted in jurisdictions where this system has been fully implemented has shown encouraging results in the reduction of criminal behavior by probationers. If this system is properly implemented, I am convinced reductions in recidivism rates will result (1985: 454-455).

Perspective from the Field
Objective Approaches to Offender Assessment

By Carl B. Clements, Ph.D.

Carl Clements is a clinical psychologist and has been on the faculty of The University of Alabama since 1971. His work in the field of corrections includes consultation and testimony in several landmark prison crowding cases, development and evaluation of objective offender-classification methods, and training of psychologists for work in the justice system. He has written several articles and chapters on offender classification and is the author of Offender Needs Assessment *(1986) published by the American Correctional Association.*

● ●

Those in the criminal justice system are asked to collect what seems to be an enormous amount of information about offenders. This information presumably shapes our decisions and recommendations–pretrial, presentence, prerelease and post-incarceration. No doubt, each piece of information is potentially useful (or was once thought to be); the data range from nuts and bolts demographics (age, race, employment, and crime history) to educational, medical and psychological profiles. Our purpose spans the dimensions of risk assessment, needs identification, supervisory placements, and treatment assignment. Although the assessment-decision sequence rarely has operated smoothly or in a systematic fashion, recent advances have improved the link between these two processes.

The fundamental goal of assessment in the criminal justice system is the identification of relevant offender characteristics from which to formulate differential responses. Except for basic identification and tracking purposes, there is no need to conduct assessments unless they lead to improved decision-making. This rationale, then, forces us to examine both the accuracy (reliability) and the value (validity) of the information being collected. Does this or that psychological test really predict who will respond to drug treatment? Does an offender's risk scale score accurately reflect the level of supervision needed?

Increasingly, the answers are likely to be, "yes." In recent years, improved instruments and processes have been developed to assess salient offender characteristics, background, current adjustment, and the like. In turn, these tools increase our ability to match offenders to the best available options. The reality of scarce resources demands that we use them wisely. Of course, we cannot conduct all the necessary experiments to test the validity of an instrument (nor should we expect error-proof assessments). For example, we cannot randomly assign a group of presumably high-risk offenders to the community just to see if they really will reoffend. More often, such tests have occurred through "natural experiments." For example, a selected group of offenders may be released to the community through judicial order or in response to prison crowding. These "low-risk" offenders (as assessed by objective instruments) typically prove to recidivate at a predictably low rate.

At the other end of the spectrum, in a classic study involving mentally disordered offenders, a federal court found unconstitutional the commitment law under which "dangerous, mentally ill" patients were being held. After release, this group evidenced quite low crime and violence rates despite their previous diagnoses. We can predict reoffense in such groups more accurately by past crime and violence history than by mental illness status. In this case, the prediction of dire consequences was off the mark.

Both in the field of clinical psychology and within the workplace, broadly defined, we have clung to the questionable belief that intuition, "clinical judgment," experience, and clever interviews provide the best predictors of success. Alternatively is the belief, that all we need to know is something about the traits of an individual, giving no thought to environmental factors that promote or inhibit the behaviors we hope to predict and manage. To address the first of these concerns, techniques of risk and needs assessment have moved out of the purely subjective, highly discretionary realm into a more objective, empirically based approach. This trend has proven to be an improvement for at least five reasons:

- Diverse staff consistently can identify important offender characteristics.

- Those features can be evaluated against outcomes.

- If done correctly, the information necessarily points to a preferred response or package of services across a range of offender-management issues.

- Assessment results can be assembled for large groups of offenders, allowing an agency or system to better know its offender base and the correlated demand or need for particular correctional resources.

To some, the use of structured interviews, point systems, and checklists (such as those noted in this chapter as well as in Chapter 8 on assessment and

Continued on the next page

Perspective from the Field, *continued*

classification) may unnecessarily inhibit or minimize the case manager's personal feel for the offender. What becomes of the rapport believed to enhance candor and positive influence? In fact, no such conflict exists. Conducting structured assessments is not automatically a coldly impersonal process. While a major benefit is to remove subjectivity, the offender typically can participate in reviewing findings and learning about the rationale for recommended interventions. Indeed, well-developed assessment packages may confer more credibility and fairness to the process and the resulting dispositions.

However, it is also the case that a few "points," one way or the other, can make a difference in an offender's institutional custody rating, for example, or in the stringency of recommended parole supervision. Thus, expect offenders often to debate or challenge certain facts that lie behind these calculations.

At the same time, research shows the accuracy of formulations based on objective systems are superior to clinical intuition or individual "experience." (Interestingly, the experience factor often shows up in objective or data-driven approaches; yet, some of the variables included in most models were derived from accumulated wisdom.) In several correctional systems in which this author has consulted or served as part of a technical assistance team, the move to objectifying assessments and decision-making was directly tested against existing classification methods.

With respect to security and supervision in prison settings, for example, somewhat less restrictive alternatives typically were recommended for a sizable group of offenders. In virtually every instance, neither increased risk to the community (such as escapes) nor disruptions of facility routines were observed. In some cases, sweeping recalculations of offender custody ratings sometimes underscored the statewide need for more minimum-security and community-based alternatives.

To be sure, this "correction" in course often has taken place in the context of acknowledged crowding of facilities and a general reliance on highly secure housing for most offenders. Objective classification systems, however, are policy neutral and just as easily can result in recommendations for more stringent supervision if criteria are met. Nevertheless, the negative repercussion of further crime by an offender who was prematurely released or inadequately constrained tends to make the risk assessment and decision-making process quite conservative.

Assessments must be connected firmly to decision making. As an example, consider the question, "Should we give a particular personality test to all offenders?" The answer should be based on a series of conditions:

- Will specific decisions, dispositions, assignments, or intervention strategies be determined or influenced by the results of this test (or structured interview, or risk scale)?

- Does this test validly measure the traits or behaviors that are relevant to this (or these) choice(s)?

- Are those offenders "selected" or identified by this test significantly more likely to benefit from X (respond to Y, commit less violence, and so forth) than those with different scores?

"No" answers to any of the questions suggests that the instrument or scale is irrelevant, invalid, or both.

On the other hand, an instrument may be valid for one purpose but not another. Do not expect a treatment-oriented assessment to predict an offender's inclination to escape from custody. Few multipurpose instruments exist, although the recently developed Levels of Supervision Inventory (LSI-Revised) used in the Canadian system addresses several elements of both risk and needs (see Lauen 1997, Latessa 1999).

The most deficient aspect of the assessment-planning-intervention link is the storehouse of available intervention regimens and validated treatments. As exemplified by the Client Management Classification (CMC) system described in this chapter, a "diagnosis" should be directly linked to a differential response or tailored package of interventions. Not only are such connections likely to promote community supervision success, for example, but more expensive resources also can be concentrated on those offenders who need and are most likely to benefit from intensive or highly structured (and typically more costly) interventions.

Similarly, within correctional settings, the classification process should go well beyond basic assignments to the traditional "minimum," "medium," and "maximum" custody designations. Research clearly supports the value of additional layers of differentiation. This will promote more homogeneous groupings of offenders. Caseworkers can match them with compatible and effective supervision strategies. However, developing differential approaches for different offender subgroups remains a challenge.

A final benefit of objective assessment systems is the potential to communicate the rationale and elements of the process. Justice personnel, whether in probation or institutional corrections, are more likely to trust the assessments, understand the derived profiles, and participate in (or support) the prescribed interventions when they see the connections across these steps. Involvement in such a proactive process also should reduce professional burnout and cynicism.

Chapter Summary

The proper assessment of correctional offenders has become increasingly important in criminal justice. The various scales, forms, and questionnaires found in this chapter constitute efforts to classify and treat offenders in a more rational and equitable way.

The Social History Questionnaire and the Client Management Classification Interview Schedule are interviewing and assessment aids. They are used prior to sentencing. The Felony Sentencing Worksheet assists you in making sentencing recommendations by providing you with sentencing "norms" based on experience.

The risk and needs assessment scales are supervision aids. These scales provide you with information relating to the risk offenders pose to the community, and the needs they have in order to lead a more productive life. They also provide you with the information you need to develop treatment plans for offenders. Treatment plans begin by identifying major problem areas and devising a "tentative treatment plan" based on the need to alleviate these problems. You should reassess these plans as frequently as necessary, or at least every six months. The use of the tools contained in this chapter has resulted in a remarkable improvement in corrections supervision over the old "seat of the pants" methods of supervision.

References and Suggested Readings

Allen, H. and C. Simonsen. 2001. *Corrections in America*. New York: Macmillan.

American Correctional Association. 2009. *Policy on Sentencing*. Alexandria, Virginia: American Correctional Association.

———. 2006. Resolution on American Bar Association's Blueprint for Cost-Effective Pretrial Detention, Sentencing and Corrections Systems. Alexandria, Virginia: American Correctional Association.

Andrews, D. and J. Bonta. 1998. *The Psychology of Criminal Conduct*. Cincinnati, Ohio: Anderson.

Andrews, D. and C. Dowden. 2007. The Risk-Need-Responsivity Model of Assessment and Human Service in Prevention and Corrections: Crime-Prevention Jurisprudence. *Canadian Journal of Criminology and Criminal Justice* October: 440-459.

Bartol, C. 2002. *Criminal Behavior: A Psychosocial Approach*. Upper Saddle River, New Jersey: Prentice Hall.

Bonta, J. 1991. Correctional Halfway Houses: The Evidence on Effectiveness. *Second Annual Corrections Research Forum Proceedings*. Ottawa: Correctional Service of Canada.

Brun, C. and R. Rapp 2001. Strength-Based Case Management: Individuals' Perspectives on Strengths and Case Manager Relationship. *Social Work* 46: 278-288.

Bureau of Justice Statistics. 1995. *Prisoners in 1994*. Washington, D.C.: U.S. Department of Justice.

———. 2000. Prisoner Statistics. www.usdoj.gov/bjs/prisons.htm

Carlson, N., K. Hess, and C. Orthmann. 1999. *Corrections in the 21st Century*. Belmont, California: West/Wadsworth.

Champion, D. 2005. *Probation, Parole, and Community Corrections*, Fifth ed. Upper Saddle River, New Jersey: Prentice Hall.

Crooks, C. H. 2000. The Case Management System in Ohio. In *Correctional Counseling and Treatment*, P. Kratkoski, ed., Prospect Height, Illinois: Waveland Press. pp. 269-275.

Dal Pra, Z. 2004. In Search of a Risk Instrument. In *Assessment Issues for Managers*, D. Faust, ed. National Institute of Corrections, Washington, D.C.: U.S. Department of Justice. pp. 9-12. http://www.nicic.org

Gottfredson, S. and L. Moriarty. 2006. Statistical Risk Assessment: Old Problems and New Applications. *Crime and Delinquency* 52: 178-200.

Healey, K. 1999. *Case Management in the Criminal Justice System*. National Institute of Justice Research in Action. Washington, D.C.: U.S. Department of Justice.

Hubbard, D., L. Travis, and E. Latessa. 2001. *Case Classification in Community Corrections: A National Survey of the State of the Art*. National Institute of Justice. Washington, D.C.: U.S. Department of Justice.

Idaho Department of Corrections (n.d.). *Supervision Levels*. Internal mimeograph.

Keiser, G. 2003. *Offender Assessment*. U.S. Department of Justice. National Institute of Corrections. http://www.nicic.org

Latessa, E., ed. 1999. *Strategic Solutions: the International Community Corrections Association Examines Substance Abuse*. Alexandria, Virginia: American Correctional Association.

Lauen, R. 1997. *Positive Approaches to Corrections: Research, Policy and Practice*. Lanham, Maryland: American Correctional Association.

Lerner, K., G. Arling, and C. Baird. 1986. Client Management Classification: Strategies for Case Supervision. *Crime and Delinquency* 32: 254-271.

Lowenkamp, C. and E. Latessa. 2004. Understanding the Risk Principle: How and Why Correctional Interventions Can Harm Low Risk Offenders. In *Assessment Issues for Managers*, D. Faust, ed. U.S. Department of Justice, Washington, D.C.: National Institute of Corrections, U.S. Department of Justice. pp. 3-7. http://www.nicic.org

Maung, N. and N. Hammond. 2001. *Probation Officers' Views on Two Assessment Instruments Used to Assess Risk of Offending and Offenders' Needs*. Home Office Research Report. London.

Nellis, M. 1995. Probation Values for the 1990s. *The Howard Journal* 34: 19-44.

Pollock, J. 1997. *Prisons Today and Tomorrow*. Gaithersburg, Maryland: Aspen.

Robinson, G. 1999. Risk Management and Rehabilitation in the Probation Service: Collision and Collusion. *The Howard Journal* 38: 421-433.

Schmalleger, F. 2001. *Criminal Justice Today*, Sixth ed. Englewood Cliffs, New Jersey: Prentice-Hall.

Schumacher, M. 1985. Implementation of a Client Classification and Case Management System: A Practitioner's View. *Crime and Delinquency* 31: 445-455.

Swisher, T. 1978. *Sentencing in Ohio*. Columbus, Ohio: Ohio State Bar Research Foundation.

Walsh, A. 1985. Ideology and Arithmetic: The Hidden Agenda of Sentencing Guidelines. *Journal of Crime and Justice* 8: 41-63.

Walsh, A. and C. Hemmens. 2008. *Law, Justice, and Society: A Sociolegal Introduction*. New York: Oxford University Press.

Weibush, R., C. Baird, B. Krisberg, and D. Onek. 1994. *Risk Assessment and Classification for Serious, Violent, and Chronic Juvenile Offenders*. San Francisco, California: National Council on Crime and Delinquency.

CHAPTER 8

Assessment and Classification in Institutional Corrections

Through its diagnostic and coordinating functions, classification not only contributes to the objective of rehabilitation, but also to custody, discipline, work assignments, officer and inmate morale, and the effective use of training opportunities

—Presiding judge in *Morris v. Travisono* (1970)

This chapter builds on the previous one in which we discussed at length offender assessment in the context of community corrections. It concerns assessment in the context of institutional corrections; thus, many of the points and issues addressed in Chapter 7 apply here. With about two-million inmates in American jails and prisons, it appears that America is "addicted to prisons" (Marquart 2008: 153). If this is so, we must be mindful of former U.S. Supreme Court Chief Justice Warren Burger's famous lines: "To put people behind walls and bars and do little or nothing to change them is to win a battle but lose a war. It is wrong. It is expensive. It is stupid" (cited in Schmalleger 2001: 439).

The first stage in Burger's war-winning strategy must be (to remain with his metaphor) to gain usable "intelligence" about the "enemy's" strengths and weaknesses through classification. Institutional assessment is obviously more concerned with security issues when classifying inmates than are probation and parole officers. Classification is simply a method of ordering the way we relate to or deal with objects, situations, or people.

Historical Overview of Inmate Classification

Early attempts at classification consisted simply of separating men from women and children within prisons. In the late 1700s, the Walnut Street Jail in Philadelphia inaugurated a classification process to separate serious offenders from less serious offenders. Those classified as serious offenders were placed in isolation and were not allowed to work or interact with other prisoners.

Some fifteen years later, in 1804, the Charleston Prison in Massachusetts established a tri-level system of classification based on prior convictions of offenders. Distinctive uniforms identified each of the three groups classified by this system, and groups were segregated from one another. Based on this classification, offenders were assigned quarters, prison work, and differential access to various amenities. First-time offenders received the best quarters, job assignments, and food. Second-time offenders were allowed only two meals per day and performed the less desirable work. Third-time, or habitual offenders, did the most menial tasks and received the worst food and accommodation.

In the early 1800s, prison administrators experimented with a variety of new custodial and classification systems. One such system, which was to provide the model for most prison construction for the next 150 years, was the Auburn Prison, opened in New York in 1819 (Roberts 1997). Prisons based on this model were invariably maximum-security with harsh conditions of confinement. Administrators expended little effort to establish inmate classification as an integral part of prison administration.

The intervention of the courts, as much as anything else, provided the impetus toward better classification systems. As late as 1966, the courts generally avoided interfering in specific classification decisions, recognizing "that discipline and the general management of such open institutions are executive functions with which the judicial branch will not interfere" (*Cohen v. U.S.*, 25 F. Supp. 679, at 688 [1966]). However, as a result of a court action in Rhode Island in 1970, the Federal District Court issued the first order that a meaningful, nonarbitrary classification system be designed and implemented. The court further recognized that inmate classification is a management tool that enables the prison administrator to allocate scarce resources to areas where the greatest good may be achieved. As stated by the court (*Morris v. Travisono*, 310 F. Supp. 857 at 965 [1970]):

> Classification is essential to the operation of an orderly and safe prison. It is a prerequisite for the rational allocation of whatever program opportunities exist within the institution. It enables the institution to gauge the proper custody level of an inmate, to identify the inmate's educational, vocational, and psychological needs, and to separate nonviolent inmates from the more predatory.

Those of a more radical persuasion want to give inmates a voice in determining their various classifications (Richards and Ross 2003), but for others, this is pure folly: "Power sharing and asking the confined for their permission to change course [is] not an option" (Marquart 2008: 155). Marquart's (2008) two decades of studying prisons leads him to assert that the prison staff must run 100 percent of the prison, and no less. We agree with Marquart and add that controlling the prisons and their unwilling guests requires proper classification using the latest tools administered by correctional staff who know what they are doing.

Thus, the courts have charged correctional administrators with the task of minimizing the risk of injury to the public, to inmates, and to the correctional staff. This is to be accomplished while placing each offender in the least-restrictive setting consistent with the safety and security goals of the institution and with the needs of the offender. Before 1980, however, only the federal and California prison systems used objective classification methods, but now all U.S. prison systems do (Austin 2003). As you may well imagine, inmate classification is perhaps the most involved and all-encompassing aspect of inmate supervision because it addresses issues of security, treatment, and the safe and smooth operation of the prison. As Clemens Bartollas remarks in his book on *Becoming a Model Warden*: "The classification of inmates is important in a humane prison. Proper classification can do much to provide a safe and secure facility" (2004: 156).

Classification Today

Professional practitioners within their respective disciplines have developed elaborate systems of classification relating to the phenomena with which their disciplines deal. These practitioners have gone beyond subjective methods to embrace more objective methods. For instance, psychologists and psychiatrists classify various systems of behavior in a manual called the *Diagnostic and Statistical Manual of Mental Disorders* (DSM-IV-TR) that allows for the classification of individuals' characteristics in terms of clinically important factors. It provides a common bond of understanding within the family of mental health professionals. This facilitates management of caseloads and the implementation of treatment modalities.

Unfortunately, the classification of institutionalized offenders is not yet quite as neat and tidy as that provided by the DSM-IV-TR. Although the causes and treatment of criminal behavior have been important items in the criminal justice agenda since it was first suggested that there just might be alternatives to flogging, mutilating, and torturing, several reasons exist for the lack of consistency in inmate classification. It is a major imperative that we come as close as possible to making inmate classification reliable, valid, and standardized for the sake of the institution and its staff, the inmates, and ultimately for the sake of society.

To ease and standardize inmate classification on a national level and to address court mandates, the American Correctional Association (ACA) has established a set of standards for classification. The *Principles of Classification* (in the Appendix) are excerpted verbatim from *Prison Classification: A Model Systems Approach*, 1981, pp. 20-26, reprinted with permission from the National Institute of Corrections (NIC) (1984). The National Institute of Corrections developed them based on research of professional practitioners. The National Institute of Corrections has several publications on classification that have been developed since then as well.

Classification, first and foremost, is about making predictions, and involves three types of procedures: (1) anamnestic (an unnecessarily fancy word related to memory) which is based solely on an individual's past behavior, (2) clinical, which is based on expert diagnosis and evaluation, such as the DSM-IV, the Minnesota Multiphasic Personality Inventory (MMPI), and other tools to be reviewed in this chapter; and (3) statistical or actuarial, which are based on individual behavior patterns in comparison with similar behavior patterns of others (Austin and McGinnis 2004).

Problems exist in the classification process because predictions about human behavior are always far from perfect. We have two types of prediction problems: false positive and false negative. A false positive prediction is one in which we predict offender risk when there is not any risk, and a false negative is predicting no offender risk when there is some risk.

The false-positive situation can be illustrated by the assessment of an excessively long prison sentence based on the offender's past behavior (anamnestic) without regard to other factors such as age, type of crime, and actuarial information. Subsequently, we continue this error when we predict that the offender will continue to pose a risk when the risk is no longer present. Classification errors tend more often to be false positive than false negative, indicating the tendency of classification instruments to err on the side of caution (Bench and Allen 2003)

An interesting randomized experiment conducted by Bench and Allen (2003) suggested that many inmates classified as maximum-security risks can be safely housed in medium custody, which would result in the savings of considerable sums of money. They randomly assigned inmates classified as maximum security either into maximum or medium security. Neither the inmates nor correctional staff (except the prison's warden) were aware of the study inmates' "true" classification. The researchers found no significant difference in the discipline records of the inmates treated as medium security but whose "true" classification was maximum and other inmates living in medium-security conditions. Bench and Allen concluded that the classification label may be more a determinant of inmate behavior ("I'm a medium-security risk and will act like one") than offender characteristics.

However, legal and ethical issues arise from the question of false positive and false negative predictions. If offenders who pose a real and present risk to the prison population are not classified in a manner that affords protection to others (false negative), institution security and order are threatened. The experimental group (classified maximum-security inmates assigned to medium security) in the Bench and Allen study did have a higher weighted mean number of disciplinary write-ups even if the mean difference was not statistically significant.

On the other hand, if we err and deprive offenders of rights and privileges (false positive) afforded under the U.S. Constitution and correctional agency policy, we become excessively punitive at a greater fiscal cost to society. In either circumstance, violations of the Eighth (cruel and unusual punishment) and Fourteenth Amendments (due process) to the U.S. Constitution often are alleged. Correctional agencies then may become involved in lengthy and costly litigation, which ultimately must be borne by the public.

Another, and closely related problem, deals with predicting individual behavior. As indicated earlier, the complexity of the human organism precludes 100 percent accuracy in predicting individual behavior. We can classify an individual as belonging to a particular group whose members have the same characteristics. For example, we know that young males have a greater propensity to commit crime than other groups, and we know that the early onset of criminal behavior, the seriousness of the first offense, and the frequency of offending predict future criminality. Thus, the group, as an entity, may present a significant risk to a society; however, the individual offender as a separate sub-entity may not. Consequently, it is very risky, regardless of the classification tool, to predict that a given individual will behave in a particular manner in any given instance.

Unlike classifications within the free world, predictions within the criminal justice system tend to deprive individuals of their liberty and access to goods and services. We have suggested that the decision process for the assignment of individuals to various classification levels is far from perfect. Because of the possibility of diminution or loss of freedom, it is necessary to develop and use classification procedures that remove as much subjectivity as possible so as to be less capricious and arbitrary. Standardized procedures encourage uniformity and fairness for the offender, for the institution, and for the public.

The problem is one of objective classification versus subjective classification. Traditionally, the validity of the various methods used by administrators to assess levels of security or custody to which inmates were assigned has relied on the more subjective evaluation of the *Diagnostic Statistical Manual* (DSM) criterion, interpretation of the MMPI and other diagnostic tools used by trained professionals. However, the interpretation of the offender characteristics depicted by the criteria presented and the interpretation made by the evaluator can vary among evaluators. Even minimal differences can result in classification to custody and security levels, which dramatically limit inmate choices and liberty.

The objective classification of inmates using models that attempt to evaluate inmate characteristics through use of a standardized criterion and variables enhances the validity of inmate classification. The reliability (the consistency of the assessments across different assessors) and validity (how well the instrument reflects reality—it predicts what it was designed to predict) of actuarial assessment is significantly higher than that achieved by professional judgment alone (Austin and McGinnis 2004). By developing objective actuarial models, we are able to reduce the incidence of error and avoid legal challenges under 42 USC § 1983.

---

42 USC § 1983, Civil Rights Act of 1871

Every person who under color of any statute, ordinance, regulation, custom, or usage of any state or territory, subjects or causes to be subject, any citizen of the United States or other person within the jurisdiction thereof to the deprivation of any rights, privileges, or immunities secured by the Constitution and laws, shall be liable to the party injured in an action at law, suit in equity, or other proper proceedings for redress.

42 USC § 1983. Violation of this statute by a public official can result in a civil action against those officials and their supervisors when acting under the color of state law if they deprive an individual of his or her constitutional rights. Two conditions must be met to make a valid claim under 42 USC § 1983: (1) the public official acted under the color of law that is in the capacity of his or her assigned duties, and (2) the person who was wronged was deprived of some right or immunity guaranteed by the Constitution or laws of the United States.

Classification to specific levels of security and custody determines to a great extent the amenities that an offender will be afforded. In *Rhodes v. Chapman* (452 U.S. 337 [1981]), the court held that the constitution "does not mandate comfortable prisons" but neither does it permit inhumane ones. Court cases have determined that "the treatment a prisoner receives in prison and the conditions under which he is confined are subject to scrutiny under the Eighth Amendment" (*Rhodes v. Chapman*, 349).

Figure 8.1 Physical Security Levels

SECURITY ELEMENTS	SECURITY LEVELS		
	I (MINIMUM)	II (MEDIUM)	III (MAXIMUM)
Housing	Dormitories, cubicles, or rooms	Rooms and/or multiple cells	Single cells, very secure, with heavy duty hardware
Perimeter Security	None, or single fence; occasional patrol	Double fence; electronic alarm system; patrol of perimeter or towers	A combination of double fence; wall; towers; constant armed perimeter surveillance; and electronic alarm system
Internal Security Measures	Inmate census taken at least 3 times daily	Inmate movement controlled by pass system; formal census at least 4 times daily, plus frequent informal census	Frequent informal census; capability to quickly separate the inmates into groups of 50 or less; directly supervised and/or escorted when outside cellhouse or living area; formal census taken at least 6 times daily

Figure 8.2 Custodial Levels

ACTIVITY	CUSTODY LEVELS		
	MINIMUM	MEDIUM	MAXIMUM
Observation by staff	Occasional; appropriate to situation	Frequent and direct	Always supervised when outside cell
Day movement inside facility	Unrestricted	Observed periodically by staff	Restricted; directly observed or escorted when outside cell
Movement after dark	Intermittent observation	Restricted, with direct supervision	Out of cell only for emergencies; in restraints when outside cellhouse, or as approved by watch commander
After evening lockdown	Intermittent observation	Escorted and only on order of watch commander	
Meal periods	Intermittent observation	Supervised	Directly supervised or in cell
Access to jobs	Eligible for all, both inside and outside perimeter	Inside perimeter only	Only selected day jobs inside perimeter, or directly supervised within the housing unit
Access to programs	Unrestricted, including community-based activities	Work and recreation, inside perimeter; outside perimeter only as approved by CEO	Selected programs/activities inside the facility perimeter, as approved by CEO
Visits	Contact; periodic supervision, indoor and/or outdoor	Contact, supervised	Noncontact or closely supervised (1-1)
Leave the institution	Unescorted/escorted	Direct staff escort; handcuffs, with chains and leg irons (optional); armed escort (optional)	Minimum of two escorts with one armed, full restraints; strip search prior to departure and upon return
Furlough	Eligible for unescorted day pass and furlough*	Eligible for staff-escorted day pass or furlough*	Not eligible

*Definition: Day Pass-Permits inmate to be away from institution only during daylight hours. A furlough authorizes overnight absence from the facility.

This custody classification system is used as a guideline to determine the following:
1. Assignment is made to an institution that provides the level of security consistent with the inmate's custody requirement.
2. Assignments are made to institutional programs that are consistent with custody needs. These assignments include housing, work, and other programs such as education, visiting, and any activity that involves risk to staff, other inmates, or the community.

In its prohibition of "cruel and unusual punishments," the Eighth Amendment places restraints on prison officials, who must provide humane conditions of confinement; prison officials must ensure that inmates receive adequate food, clothing, shelter and medical care and just "take reasonable measures to guarantee the safety of the inmates," *Hudson v. Palmer* (468 U.S. 517 [1984]); *Washington v. Harper* (494 U.S. 210 [1990]); and Estelle (429 U.S. at 103). Indeed, a prison official's "deliberate indifference" to a substantial risk of serious harm to an inmate violates the Eighth Amendment (*Helling v. McKinney*, 509 U.S. 25 [1993]) and thus raises a 1983 action. One of the purposes of classification is to assign the inmate to the appropriate security and custody level consistent with the risk presented to the institution, staff, and other inmates, as well as to respond to the needs of the inmate.

Security and Custody

As you will note from Figure 8.1, security levels are of a physical nature. They refer to the environmental factors of perimeter security and use of towers, patrol, and other detection devices. Custodial levels (Figure 8.2) refer to the degree of supervision the inmate/offender receives. Programs are the activities that are provided, such as educational and vocational opportunities, counseling services, and recreational and hobby activities. Figure 8.2 makes it clear that access to jobs and programs is an inherent function of custodial classification.

Classification Data

Standards and Principles of Classification

Classification of behavior in the *DSM-IV-TR* provides an organized, systematic, and established procedure for assessing offender characteristics. This classification, in turn, allows for differential treatment modalities. In institutional corrections, not all criminals exhibit the same behavior or present the same risk to security. For example, the criteria for diagnosis of the Antisocial Personality (*DSM-IV-TR* 1994: 360) is specific, yet provides diagnostic discretion for the trained professional to evaluate the individual offender's risk to society.

In the past, we have not normally observed differential approaches to offenders; rather, we have tended to treat all inmates in a similar manner. Now, we have the tools to make distinctions and the rationale of cost savings to do so (Lauen 1997).

Reception and Diagnostic Unit

Following a sentence of imprisonment, offenders are transported to the designated facility. For offenders being sentenced to prison for the first time, this is very likely the most frightening experience of their lives. Consider for a moment the confusion and fear that the offender must be experiencing as he or she tries to come to grips with the consecutive ordeals of trial, conviction, sentencing, and arrival at the "big house." According to Handyman, Austin, and Peyton (2004), all institutions conduct a standard "core" of prison-intake functions, and the standard stay at an intake or reception facility is forty days for males and thirty-one days for females. The identified intake functions include:

1. Identifying the prisoner (photographing, fingerprinting, and so forth)

2. Developing the prisoner's record

3. Performing medical and mental health assessments

4. Determining the prisoner's threat to safety and his/her security requirements

5. Identifying security threat groups

6. Identifying sex offenders, sexual predators, and vulnerable inmates

Upon arrival at the institution, all offenders are considered close-custody inmates pending initial classification. The function of the security staff at this point is to instill the reality of prison security in the newly committed inmate. Armed guards are present, orders are given, and immediate compliance is demanded. Inmates are stripped naked, all their property is seized, and a strip search is conducted. Based on who conducts the search, the policy of the institution, and security considerations, this search may include a body cavity search.

The strip search is very likely the greatest intrusion of one's privacy known. Inmates are then ordered to shower, with instructions to apply a delousing agent to all areas of body hair. At no time during these initial orientation processes is an inmate allowed out of sight of a member of the correctional staff. Following the shower, inmates are issued a drab prison uniform and a number. All vestiges of individuality are removed. The inmate has effectively become a nonentity, totally vulnerable and dependent upon his or her keepers. This process is demeaning, but it is unfortunately necessary as both a security and a sanitation precaution. During inmates' stay at the reception and diagnostic unit, security and programming staff closely observe them. Their observations of adjustment and behavior are forwarded to the classification committee for inclusion in their assessments and evaluations.

Tests

During the reception and diagnostic period, inmates are examined by medical staff and are tested in accordance with the policies of the particular state or institution. These tests may include the Nelson Reading Skills Test, the General Aptitude Test Battery (GATB), the Wechsler Adult Intelligence Scale (see Chapter 3), the Minnesota Multiphasic Personality Inventory (MMPI), the Human Synergistics Lifestyle Inventory, and the Myers-Briggs Type Indicator (MBTI). We will take a brief look at each of these tests.

Nelson Reading Skills Test. The simplest of these tests in terms of inmate understanding is the Nelson Reading Skills Test. It is designed to evaluate the offender's reading grade level and vocabulary level. This test tends to establish offender eligibility for participation in subsequent testing. If the offender does not read and understand written communications at least at the sixth-to-eighth grade level, the results of subsequent testing are invalid.

General Aptitude Test Battery. The General Aptitude Test Battery, developed in 1947, is often administered by governmental employment services and is designed to measure aptitudes that have been found to be significant in many occupations.

The GATB is not normally administered to anyone who does not read at least at the sixth grade level. Although it was designed to test adults and high school seniors, conversion tables have been devised for converting scores obtained by those reading at less than twelfth grade level.

Areas for which scores are obtained are presented below. Combining specified scores provides a composite score, which is then cross referenced with specific occupational areas, indicating a general aptitude for that field.

1. *General learning ability* (G). The ability to understand instructions and underlying principles; the ability to reason and make judgments.

2. *Verbal aptitude* (V). The ability to understand the meanings of words, the ideas associated with them, and the ability to use them effectively. The ability to comprehend language, to understand relationships among words, and to understand meanings of whole sentences and paragraphs.

3. *Numerical ability* (N). The ability to perform arithmetic operations quickly and accurately.

4. *Spatial ability* (S). The ability to comprehend forms in space. Frequently described as the ability to visualize objects of two and three dimensions.

5. *Form perception* (P). The ability to perceive pertinent details in objects or in pictorial or graphic material.

6. *Clerical perception* (Q). The ability to perceive pertinent details in verbal or tabular material.

7. *Motor coordination* (K). The ability to coordinate eyes, hands, and fingers rapidly and accurately in making precise movements with speed.

8. *Finger dexterity* (F). The ability to move the fingers and manipulate small objects with them rapidly and accurately.

9. *Manual dexterity* (M). The ability to move the hands easily and skillfully.

Combining the G, V, and N scores provides a score related to cognitive abilities. A functional "performance" score is obtained by combining the S, P, Q, K, F, and M scores. Although comparing results from instruments designed for different purposes is a risky business, it is interesting to note the similarity of criminal profiles obtained by the GATB and Wechsler IQ (WAIS) tests. As indicated in Chapter 3, criminals tend to score significantly higher on the performance test of the (WAIS) than on the verbal test. Likewise, inmates tend to score significantly higher on the functional areas than on the cognitive sections of the GATB. These significant differences are not reported when either the GATB or the WAIS is administered to noncriminal samples. GATB scores correlate with full-scale IQ at about 0.86 (Frey and Detterman 2004).

The importance of educational and vocational training while incarcerated highlights the importance of tests such as these. A meta-analysis of ninety studies linking prison educational and vocational training indicate overall lower rates of disciplinary activities while in prison and lower recidivism rates after release for offenders receiving such education and training (Adams et al. 2004). Adams and his colleagues found that inmates with the lowest levels of education benefited most from participation in academic programs, and suggest that this participation and success raises their self-images.

Minnesota Multiphasic Personality Inventory. The MMPI, developed in the 1930s, is one of the most widely used personality inventories in corrections. It consists of 550 affirmative statements to which the test taker responds with "true," "false," or "cannot say." A MMPI-based typology of criminal offenders is one of five psychological classification systems used by the Federal Bureau of Prisons (Van Voorhis 1988).

The MMPI has ten scales relating to ten different clinical disorders:

- Hypochondriasis (Hs) (morbid concern over one's health)
- Paranoia (Pa)
- Depression (D)
- Psychasthenia (Pt) (neurotic state with irrational phobias, obsessions and compulsions)
- Hysteria (Hy)
- Schizophrenia (Sc)
- Psychopathic deviate (Pd)
- Hypomania (Ma)
- Masculinity-femininity (Mf)
- Social introversion (Si)

Three additional control scales are built into the inventory. The Lie (L) scale is designed to assess a person's tendency to try to "look good." The Validity (F) scale is intended to reveal confusion and carelessness. The Correction (K) scale is more subtle than the L or F scales. A high K score tends to indicate that the respondent either is highly defensive or is attempting to "fake good." A low K score is indicative of either an attempt to "fake bad" or a tendency to be overly self-critical.

In 1979, Edward Megargee constructed a classification system for youthful and adult offenders based on the MMPI profiles. The scales that he developed allow administrators to obtain computer-generated classifications of offenders arranged in hierarchical models from least to greatest risk. Rather than using the scales of the MMPI, the Megargee model constructs an aggregate composite based on the analysis of scale. Since the University of Minnesota released a new version of the MMPI, Megargee and his team have adapted his model to the new (MMPI-2) version (Van Voorhis 1994). Some studies have found the Megaree/MMPI-2 to predict prison assault and misconduct, but in terms of post-release behavior, it has found weak or no support (reviewed in Andrews and Bonta 1998).

Human Synergistics Lifestyles Inventory. The Human Synergistics Lifestyles Inventory (HSLI), developed by Dr. C. Lafferty, is another self-report test. People taking the HSLI test are asked to select which statement of two is more descriptive of them. The respondent receives a series of paired statements. Each statement is repeated often, with alternative pairings. A profile is developed of individual lifestyle preferences from the responses. Here are brief descriptions of those preferences.

1. *Humanistic.* Enjoys helping, developing, and teaching others. Regards people as inherently good and accepts them unconditionally. Likes people and understands them. Needs to establish and maintain open, warm, and supportive relationships.

2. *Affiliative.* Cooperative, friendly, and open with others. High need for relationships with many friends. Wants to like and be liked.

3. *Approval.* Overly concerned with being liked. Bases own opinion of self and things on what others think.

4. *Conventional.* A conformist, takes few risks, covers mistakes, and follows rules.

5. *Dependent.* Does what is expected without question. Compliant and eager to please. Highly influenced by others.

6. *Avoidance.* Tendency to stay away from any situation that may pose a threat. Needs to protect self-worth rather than experience life and growth.

7. *Oppositional.* Needs to question things, including resisting authority. Critical tendencies may be a reaction against the need to be close to others. Behavior can be antagonistic, causing defensiveness in others.

8. *Power.* Tends to be hard, tough, bossy, and aggressive. Needs to gain influence and control over others to maintain personal security. Authoritarian and dictatorial as a leader.

9. *Competitive.* Self-worth is based on winning. Turns many situations into contests. Strong need for commendation and praise. Can be self-defeating because failure is unacceptable.

10. *Competence.* Driven, needs to appear independent and confident. Selects high expectation for self to the point that they are unreasonable. Failure to meet perfectionist standards results in self-blame.

11. *Achievement.* Feels that personal effort makes the difference in the outcome. Needs to set own standards of excellence and pursue set goals. Willing to take some risks if they may produce positive results.

12. *Self-actualizing.* Concerned with personal growth and development. Responsible, confident, relaxed, and unique. Motivated

by internal need to accomplish set goals. Perceptive and understanding of others, and accepts life in all its fullness.

High scores in a specific series can provide a composite of specific traits. Individuals scoring high in areas 1, 2, 11, and 12 tend to have a realistic view of themselves. Such people are extremely rare within prison walls. Individuals scoring high
in areas 3, 4, 5, and 6 are insecure, but mask it to gain approval. They avoid risks and
are easily influenced. High scorers in areas 7, 8, 9, and 10 tend to keep people at a distance and show an inability to deal with their feelings and emotions. They have a
strong distrust of others. This group is heavily represented in institutional settings.

The Lifestyles inventory not only is designed to generate personality profiles but
also is useful in identifying oppositional aspects of respondents' personalities. If an individual scores high on opposing lifestyle areas for example, Humanistic/Opposi-
tional, Affiliative/Power, or Approval/Competitive, he or she is attempting to meet
competing and incongruent needs. Such attempts will probably result in debilitating
intrapersonal conflicts and stress.

Myers-Briggs Type Indicator (MBTI)

Developed in 1962, the Myers-Briggs Type Indicator (MBTI) is based on psychoanalyst Carl Jung's theories of judgment and perception. Jungian theory proceeds
from the premise that, from an early age, people are predisposed to react to the world
in different ways. These preferences of interaction will tend to direct the use of judgment and perception and will influence both what people direct their attention to and
the conclusions they draw from their interactions. Employment counseling and testing uses the MBTI extensively (Kennedy and Kennedy 2004).

The MBTI identifies four separate preference categories. The interaction of the
preference categories provides sixteen separate groupings or "types" of individuals.
These are the four categories.

1. ***Extroversion-Introversion (EI).*** This category reflects the individual's basic attitudes or orientation. An extrovert is oriented to
   the outer world and tends to focus perceptions and judgments on
   people and things. An introvert is oriented inwardly and tends to
   focus judgments and perceptions on concepts and ideas.

   Extrovert (E): The extrovert's interests tend to flow to the outer
   world of actions, objects, and persons. Extroverts have a breadth
   of interests. Thus, they like variety and action and often are impatient with long, slow tasks, preferring to get the task accomplished so that they may see the results of their efforts. They tend
   to work fast, often acting quickly, sometimes without thinking; because of the spontaneity, there is a dislike for complicated procedures. Since they are people oriented, they are interested in
   how other people would accomplish a task; they enjoy the company of others, are good at greeting people, and communicate
   well.

   Introvert (I): Introverts have interests that mainly are directed
   to the inner world of concepts and ideas. They like to know the

idea behind their job and dislike sweeping statements. Where the extrovert has a breadth of interest, the introvert has a depth of concentration, which lends itself to detailed work, and long periods of uninterrupted work on a single project. They prefer quiet environments where they may work contentedly alone; they like to mull things over before they act and sometimes fail to act. Being introspective, and preferring their own company, there is a tendency to have trouble remembering names and faces and they experience some problems in communicating.

2. ***Sensing-Intuiting (SN).*** The SN category indicates the individual's perception functions. The sensing process is dependent on observable objects and occurrences, which are processed through the senses. Intuition is based on "gut feelings" about relationships, things, and occurrences and is beyond the scope of the conscious mind.

   Sensing (S): The sensing preference places a great deal of reliance on facts, and persons with this orientation seldom make errors of fact and are good at precise work. The person who is a sensing type prefers to deal with the immediate, real, practical facts of experience and life. There is a dislike for problems unless a standard and routine solution exists; they are seldom inspired and rarely trust inspiration. They prefer established routines using skills that they already have learned, in preference to learning new skills. There is a tendency to work steadily through a task to reach a conclusion, and there is a realistic idea of the time involved to finish the task. Although patient with routine details, when the details of a task become complicated, sensing types become frustrated and impatient.

   Intuitive (N): The intuitive individual likes solving problems and prefers to perceive the possibilities, relationships, and meanings of experiences. There is a strong dislike for routine details and repetitive tasks especially if the routine or repetitive task requires the expenditure of time to accomplish precision undertakings; however, they are challenged and patient with complicated nonroutine situations. The intuitive type enjoys learning new skills, but not necessarily the use of a new skill. There is a tendency to pursue a task for a short period with a high level of enthusiasm and energy followed by a slack period of low production. The intuitive type follows inspiration, good or bad, often makes errors of fact, and frequently jumps to conclusions.

3. ***Thinking-Feeling (TF).*** The TF category is the judgmental index. Thinking allows the individual to reflect on the probable consequences of choices made. Feeling, in contrast, will provide the basis of personal or social values.

   Thinking (T): The thinking type relies on logic and analysis to make objective and impersonal judgments and decisions while considering both the causes of events and where decisions may lead. The thinking preference types are relatively unemotional and uninterested in the feelings of others. Thus, they make decisions on an impersonal basis, sometimes ignoring the wishes and hurting the feeling of others without knowing it. They are able to reprimand people and fire them, when necessary; thus, they seem to be hard-hearted. Although the thinking type relates well only to other thinking types, they do have a need to be treated fairly.

Feeling (F): A feeling person subjectively and personally weighs the values of choices and how the choices matter to others when making judgments and decisions. The decisions, therefore, may be influenced by their own or other people's likes and wishes. They tend to be very aware of other people and their feelings, and enjoy pleasing others if even in small unimportant ways; thus, they relate well to most people. Feeling-oriented people are sympathetic and dislike telling people unpleasant things; they also require occasional praise. They have a strong preference for harmony, and their efficiency can be badly disturbed by discord.

4. **Judgment-Perception (JP).** This category relates directly to the extroverted function of a person's life—how he or she deals with the outer world. A person who prefers to use judgment in these dealings will assign either the thinking or the feeling process to situations. However, if the individual reports a perception preference, the perceptive functions of sensing and intuition will dominate in relating to outer-world activities.

Judgment (J): A judging type tends to rigid organization and prefers to live in a decisive, planned, and orderly manner, aiming to regulate and control events. Judging persons work best when they can plan their work and follow the plan. Once they have reached a judgment on a thing, person, or situation, they tend to be satisfied. They want only the minimum essentials needed to accomplish a task so that things may be settled and wrapped up; however, they may decide things too quickly, may not notice new things that need to be done, and may dislike interrupting a current project for one with a higher priority.

Perception (P): Perceptive people are ones who live their life in a spontaneous, flexible manner, attempting to understand life and adapt to the changing situations of life. They may have problems making decisions and may postpone unpleasant tasks. They do not mind leaving things open for alterations. They tend to be curious and welcome new perspectives on things, situations, or people; however, the curiosity causes them to start many new projects which they have difficulty finishing. When beginning a new task, they want to know all about it.

Each of the sixteen possible groups, referred to as "types," is derived from factor analyses of the category scores. Each type has particular characteristics associated with it depending on which of the bimodal attributes are dominant, auxiliary, tertiary (meaning "third most important"), or inferior functions.

The purpose of the JP index is to identify the visible, and extroverted function, and by doing so allows us to identify the dominant, auxiliary, tertiary, and inferior functions of the type indicator. Each letter indicates preferences in a fixed order; the first letter indicates the E-I preference; the second refers to the preference for the perceptive function (S-N), the third for the judgment function (T-F), and the fourth letter, the JP index points to the function that is typically extroverted; thus, the other preferred function will be introverted. By identifying each function, we are more readily able to understand the dynamics of behavior.

The dominant function is the function that is most used, most developed, and most allowed the freedom to shape the life of an individual. The individual may use auxiliary functions as the need arises and, on occasion, will resort to tertiary and inferior functions.

For example, an ENTJ is an extrovert whose dominant method of relating to the external world is as a thinking type. The J points to the third letter, which is the judgment function, thinking and feeling, in this case T. The N, on the other hand, points to the second letter which is the perception function, sensing and intuition. Thus, an ENFP would take an intuitive (N) approach as the dominant method of relating to the external world.

In the case of the first example, ENTJ, since the dominant function is extroverted T, the auxiliary function would be introverted intuitive (N). The third function is the opposite of the second and thus would be sensing (S); the inferior function is therefore the opposite of the dominant function, and is feeling, F. By using the same logic, the ESFP functions would be S (dominant), F (auxiliary), T (tertiary), N (inferior).

This may be translated into an offender profile that depicts the offender as decisive, ingenious, and good at many things. The ENTJ offenders are usually good at whatever they attempt, tend to be well organized, and rely on reasoning, logic, and analysis to control their world. Sometimes they are more positive and confident than their experience in an area warrants. They tend to use their intuitive function to look at the possibilities and relationships beyond what is known. The intuitive function hones the thinking function, but tends to negate the sensing function. It is often necessary for the ENTJ to rely on a sensing type to provide the relevant facts and details. Feeling is the least developed process, and the ENTJ may consciously use and manipulate others without regard for their feelings.

The introspective dynamics differ in identifying the dominant and auxiliary functions. Recall from above, that the JP index points to the visible and extroverted function. Thus, if the attitude (E-I) preference is introverted, and the JP index points to the extroverted function, the other preferred function will be introverted. Thus, an ISFP would have a dominant preference of feeling. P points to the perception functions S-N. Since the JP index points to the extroverted, that is, the visible outer-world function, S in this case, the other preferred function, F, must be introverted. Insofar as the E-I attitude is introverted, the dominant preference also must be introverted. The dominant function then is F. Using the same formula and logic described for the extrovert, we can determine that the auxiliary preference is S, the tertiary N, and the inferior is T.

Any further explanation of the MBTI is beyond the scope of this book. Yet, it is very helpful in identifying and understanding offenders' personalities. Once this is achieved, the counselor can assist the offender to develop the tertiary and inferior functions of his or her personality in a wholesome direction. In the case of an ENTP offender, for example, by assisting the offender to deal with routine assignments until completed and by helping to identify flaws in his or her logic which justify aberrant behavior, offender personality development may be enhanced. For further information, please refer to the references and suggested readings at the end of this chapter, specifically, Myers and McCaulley (1985), and for an abbreviated version, Keirsey and Bates (1984).

The results of all of this testing, in conjunction with information extracted from the presentence investigation report, reports submitted by custodial and other staff, and the offender's criminal history, are consolidated by the classification committee to provide a comprehensive profile of the inmate.

Risk and Needs Assessment

Figure 8.3   Custody Classification Decision Tree

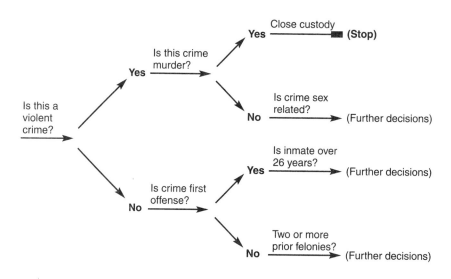

Once all the data has been gathered and consolidated, a classification interview is arranged for the new inmates. The factors that establish the inmates' risk and custody level are explained to them. The psychological, educational, and vocational needs that have been identified during the assessment period also are explained. Inmates are told about available programs and how to get into them.

The final step is the establishment of any override considerations. An override means that unusual factors not addressed in the classification instruments are considered important enough to overrule the determined custody level in favor of another custody option. Areas of concern related to security and maintenance of order include any gang or organized crime affiliations. Areas of concern related to the custodial safety include consideration of any suicidal gestures, the protection of any inmates known to be informants, or the protection of those inmates whose crimes make them targets for abuse, such as child molesters.

The override option provides for both objective and subjective considerations not addressed in the classification instruments. Use care in the exercise of overrides. The committee chairperson should be required to justify in writing the reason for the override action. If the classification instrument is overridden with some frequency, either the classification committee is not properly using the instrument, or the instrument itself is defective and thus invalid. Either condition may result in judicial action to correct the problem.

In the years following the *Morris* decision, referenced earlier in this chapter, several classification models have appeared. The actuarial prediction model summarizes statistical data to predict future behavior. Consensual classification is an incremental process conducted by prison administrators that weighs classification criteria for implementation with individual inmates. Clinically based systems employ psychological test data as predictors of behavior and adjustment. Decision-tree models are sequential. Each decision is based on the evaluation immediately preceding the current choice. Figure 8.3 illustrates the decision flow. It is not to show the ultimate decision, but it displays the beginnings of the decision flow and its progression. "Further decisions" are based on the criteria being met at each level and will lead the decision makers to the custody level appropriate for the individual inmate. The additive model combines both actuarial and statistical data to provide cutoff scores along a continuum.

A common feature among models is the relative simplicity of the instruments used to deal with a complex problem. The issues they address are of the utmost importance, first and foremost being the risk that an inmate presents to society and the institution, as well as the needs of the inmate, which should be met, to minimize that risk. The risk and needs models discussed below offer a closer look at the classification process. They are the *National Institute of Corrections' Model for Custody and Need* and the *Adult Internal Management System* (AIM). Both items are in the Appendix.

The National Institute of Corrections' Model

Custody Classification. The instrument identifies eight areas of assessment that, when properly scored, provide for objective custodial placement. To accurately assess the new inmate, the classification committee needs to refer to the detailed classification manual that accompanies the instrument. After becoming thoroughly familiar with the manual and instrument, committee members need to refer to the manual only to verify adherence to and use of appropriate criteria (Handyman et al. 2002). As we go through the custody classification sections, we will apply them to Bill Bloggs using the information contained in his PSI report in Chapter 6.

1. *History of Institutional Violence. Assault and battery* is any overt act toward another person, including another inmate, in which contact was made and injury attempted. If a weapon were used or serious injury occurred, this section is scored 7. In the event of two similar offenses, only the more serious is scored. Bill Bloggs had no previous institutional history. Therefore, unless he assaulted someone at the reception center, he would have a score of 0.

2. *Severity of Current Offense.* A severity of offense scale is provided on the reverse side of the instrument. Although an inmate may be

committed for several offenses, only the most severe is scored, for a maximum of 6 points. Bill would get 6 points assessed against him because he committed armed robbery.

3. *Prior Assaultive Offense History.* This section reflects offenders' propensity for frequent violent behavior. Attempts to commit battery (simple assault) are scored regardless of the degree of contact or injury. The maximum score is 6. Bill's assaultive history is minimal in terms of frequency. However, shooting a police officer to avoid capture is extremely serious and indicates that Bill can be dangerous when cornered. An assessment of 6 or 4 points is rather discretionary. In light of the seriousness of his assault, this author would assess Bill 6 points.

4. *Escape History.* Any documented escape or attempt within the time framework provided is scored. Any adjudication by an institutional disciplinary hearing committee is sufficient for assessment regardless of any court prosecution. The maximum score is 7. Bill has no escape history. Assess him 0 points.

The first four areas are the primary indicators of the risk that an inmate presents to the security of the institution and the welfare of other inmates and staff. A maximum score of 26 may be obtained. A score of 10 or more requires that the inmate initially be classified to close-custody supervision. A score of 9 or less on the first four classification criteria requires that the last four areas be scored. Bill has had 12 points assessed against him. Thus, he will be placed initially in maximum custody. Assume for the purposes of the exercise that he had 9 or fewer points and score him on the following items.

5. *Alcohol/Drug Abuse.* Abuse causing occasional legal and social adjustment problems is defined as any abuse that has resulted in five or fewer misdemeanor convictions, or interruption of employment within the last three years. Six or more alcohol or drug convictions during an offender's lifetime, or commitment to jail or treatment facilities within the last three years for substance abuse is considered serious abuse. The maximum score is 3. Bill has no history of drug or alcohol abuse causing him legal and social adjustment problems. He gets 0 points here.

6. *Current Detainer.* A detainer is a legal hold that another jurisdiction has placed on an inmate. Prior to releasing the inmate on parole or at the expiration of a sentence, the institution notifies the jurisdiction that holds the detainer so that the agency, which issued the detainer, can make arrangements to transfer the inmate to their jurisdiction. Maximum score is 6. Bill has no current detainers. He gets 0 points here.

7. *Prior Felony Convictions.* This is a simple summation of prior felony convictions. Do not include the current offense. Maximum score is 4. Again, Bill is not assessed any points since the current offense is his first.   ◌

8. *Stability Factors.* Each item should be verified prior to scoring. This is the only area in which the scores are cumulative, thus resulting in a possible score of "minus" 4. Bill would receive the maximum points for stability factors. He was at least twenty-six at the time of his offense ("minus" 2); he is a high school graduate ("minus" 1); and he had been employed for more than six months at the time of his arrest ("minus" 1). If this section were scored regardless of the custody score, Bill would have a total of 12 "minus" 4 = 8 points. This would place him in medium rather than maximum custody. The classification committee well might decide to override the custody classification score and place him in medium custody.

After sections one through eight of the instrument have been completed, sum the scores to provide a score that is used to determine custody level. Recall that a score of 10 or more points in sections 1 through 4 results in close-custody classification. If the score in sections 1 through 4 is 9 or less, the score is totaled with the scores in sections 5 through 8. If the final score is 7 or more, the inmate will be assigned to medium custody. If the score is 6 or less, the assignment will be to minimum custody.

Needs Classification. Identification of inmate needs is based on all gathered data, and the inmate's own perceptions of his or her programming needs. During initial assessment interviews and testing, staff should elicit from inmates their ideas of what they need to become productive citizens. Areas of primary concern are educational, vocational, and medical needs, mental abilities, psychological problems, and substance abuse problems. The instrument reflects the fact that an individual's perceptions of his or her needs are somewhat subjective. For this reason, it is imperative that a high-quality classification interview is conducted by personnel thoroughly trained in the process (see "Initial Inmate Classification Assessment of Needs" in the Appendix).

Following the risk and needs classifications, the classification committee will summarize the findings. Included in the summary will be the custody level and score, any override considerations and justifications for them, a final custody level assignment, and program and job assignment recommendations (see "Initial Classification Summary" in the Appendix, and Austin and McGinnis [2004] for a more thorough discussion of this system).

Adult Internal Management System (AIMS)

According to Seiter (2005), the most widely used internal classification system is the Adult Internal Classification System (AIMS) developed by Herbert C. Quay. This instrument differs substantially from the National Institute of Corrections' model. Quay's model relies on observable behavior patterns as assessed by correctional staff and integrates the documented behavioral history addressed by the NIC model.

This system of classification was adapted from an earlier model designed by Quay for use in the Florida juvenile correctional system, and the Federal Bureau of Prisons and some states have used it in the form discussed here.

The AIMS model, as shown in Figure 8.4, establishes five groups based on the behavioral characteristics of inmates (see Characteristic Behaviors by Group in the Appendix). These groups are identified as Groups I and II ("heavy"), Group III ("moderate"), and Groups IV and V ("light"). The terms heavy, moderate, and light allude to prison argot that describes a perceived risk, threat, or the propensity to victimize other inmates or to be victimized. The basic idea behind the AIMS model is that classifying inmates according to behavioral characteristics can greatly enhance differential treatment modalities.

Under the risk classification model already examined, all five of the AIMS groups may be represented in each custody level. The unspoken assumption behind custody classification based on type of crime is that those who commit similar crimes are similar in terms of more general behavioral traits. At all custody levels, there are a wide variety of behavioral types. There are those who are victimized and those who victimize. The vast majority of inmates, however, are found between these extremes.

Also, within each custody level, it is necessary to provide programs that are duplicated at other levels. AIMS classification is an attempt to discriminate more meaningfully among prisoners so that mixing victimizers and victims does not occur and so that programs are not unnecessarily duplicated. This should result in a reduction of prison violence and an increase in program effectiveness.

Figure 8.4   Characteristic Behaviors by Group

Heavy		Moderate		Light
I	**II**	**III**	**IV**	**V**
Aggressive	Sly	Not excessively aggressive or dependent	Dependent	Constantly afraid
Confrontational	Not directly confrontational	Reliable, cooperative	Unreliable	Anxious
Easily bored Hostile to authority	Untrustworthy Hostile to authority	Industrious Do not see selves as criminals	Easily upset Clinging	Passive Seek protection
High rate of disciplinary infractions	Moderate-to-high rate of disciplinary infractions	Low rate of disciplinary infractions	Low-to-moderate rate of disciplinary infractions	Moderate rate of disciplinary infractions
Little concern for others	Con artists, manipulative	Concern for others	Self-absorbed	Explosive under stress
Victimizers	Victimizers	Avoid fights	Easily victimized	Easily victimized

Correctional Adjustment Checklist

Dr. Quay has devised two very simple checklists, the Correctional Adjustment Checklist (CACL) and the Checklist for Analysis of Life History (CALH), (both shown in the Appendix). The CALH is "designed to assess inmates on personality dimensions known to relate to their ability to be housed successfully with other types of inmates. Checklist items focus on the inmate's adjustment and stability during time spent in the community (Handyman et al. 2004: 4). Scores on the twenty-seven items are transferred to score sheets (also shown in the Appendix) and provide a raw classification score. The raw score then is converted through the use of conversion tables into what statisticians call T-scores. This is not the place to go into detail about the derivation of T-scores. Suffice it to say that they are raw scores that have been mathematically standardized to achieve comparability of scores from distributions of raw scores that are dissimilarly shaped.

To develop the Correctional Adjustment Checklist (CACL), Quay solicited behavioral descriptions from professional correctional practitioners and from mental health professionals with correctional experience. He also incorporated descriptions developed from his own research with juveniles. The checklist contains forty-one behavior descriptions. The CACL tends to identify behavioral extremes of aggressiveness or submission.

In practice, line correctional personnel—that is, the staff that has the most contact with inmates–complete the CACL. Then, the form is submitted to the classification staff for scoring. The scores place inmates in either the "aggressive-manipulation" group (Groups I and II) or the "passive-inadequate" group (Groups IV and V). Group III inmates are not identified by the CACL instrument inasmuch as their behavior is generally acceptable within the prison environment.

Checklist for the Analysis of Life History. The source of data for the Checklist for the Analysis of Life History (CALH) is the presentence investigation report. Quay asserts that the descriptions that should be readily available from the PSI report and from the casework interview can be used to gauge the degree of institutional adjustment and program participation of the inmate (1984). The classification staff completes the CALH and assigns inmates to groups on the basis of their scores (Handyman et al. 2004).

After completing both the CACL and the CALH raw-score forms, the classification committee transfers the data to the Classification Profile for Adult Offenders and converts the raw scores to T-scores (see these forms in the Appendix). Then the T-scores are combined to provide a final classification of the inmate.

As a correctional practitioner, this author believes that the AIMS classification method provides an excellent management tool for the differential assignment of inmates to programs. Studies have shown that it discriminates very well among the inmate behavioral types. Group I inmates are involved in serious disciplinary problems more often than those in other groups, and Group III inmates generally are not involved in violent disturbances and present fewer management problems overall. However, this author would be loath to substitute it entirely for the risk classification tools provided by the NIC's model.

For example, an inmate convicted of homicide, having no prior contact with the criminal justice system, would be classified as a close-custody inmate under the NIC's model. However, it is conceivable that the same inmate could qualify as a Group III inmate (equated with minimum-custody level) solely on the basis of the AIMS criteria. Given the current public mentality regarding incarceration, it is extremely doubtful that we could justify placing a convicted murderer in minimum custody at initial classification.

Figure 8.4 on page 174, summarizes the process of classification starting with the presentence report and ending with the initial classification of an inmate to custody level, job assignment, and various programs aimed at his or her institutional adjustment and personal improvement.

Summary

In this chapter, we briefly looked at what prison classification is, why we classify prisoners, and how it is accomplished. Classification of prisoners is the differential assignment of people to varying levels of security: maximum, close, medium, and minimum. The risk that the prisoner presents to the safe and orderly operation of an institution is the primary influence on the determination of custody level. Custody classification is related to security classification, and the classification level affects an inmate's access to various counseling, educational, vocational, and recreational programs. A general observation is that program access varies inversely with security and custody levels—as security is increased, program access is decreased.

Professional organizations such as the American Correctional Association and the National Institute of Corrections have been influential in the development of classification standards and of models for implementing those standards.

Modern classification procedures have been influenced by the judiciary and by the various human sciences. These influences have resulted in some classification procedures that go beyond the concern for institutional security. Various testing and assessment tools have been developed, which can be used by correctional administrators to evaluate prisoners in terms of their personalities, needs, and potentialities. We briefly examined the GATB, WAIS, MMPI, HSLI, and MBTI instruments.

Numerous classification methods are in use, most of which are hybrids of the two models (NIC and AIMS) presented here. As new data become available through research, we will see the development of more efficient and effective classification systems, just as evolution occurs in the more advanced fields.

References and Suggested Readings

Adams, K., K. Bennett, T. Flanagan, J. Marquart, S. Cuvelier, E. Frisch, J. Gerber, D. Longmire, and V. Burton, Jr. 2004. A large-scale multidimensional test of the effect of prison education programs on offenders' behavior. In M. Stohr and C. Hemmens, eds., T*he Inmate Prison Experience*. Upper Saddle River, New Jersey: Prentice Hall. pp. 300-315.

Allen, H., C. Simonsen, and E. Latessa. 2003. *Corrections in America*, 10th ed. New York: Macmillan.

American Correctional Association. 1981. *Classification* (monograph, series no. 1). Lanham, Maryland: American Correctional Association.

————. 1982. *Classification as a Management Tool: Theories and Models for Decision Makers*. Lanham, Maryland: American Correctional Association.

————. 2002. *Standards for Adult Correctional Institutions*, 4th ed. Alexandria, Virginia: American Correctional Association.

————. 2010. *Standards Supplement*. Alexandria, Virginia: American Correctional Association.

American Psychiatric Association. 1994. *Diagnostic and Statistical Manual of Mental Disorders*, TR, 4th ed. Washington, D.C.: American Psychiatric Association.

Andrews, D. and J. Bonta. 1998. *The Psychology of Criminal Conduct*. Cincinnati, Ohio: Anderson Publishing.

Austin, J. 2003. *Findings in Prison Classification and Risk Assessment*. National Institute of Corrections. Washington, D.C.: U.S. Department of Justice.

Austin, J. and P. Handyman. 2001. Critical Issues and Developments in Prison Classification. National Institute of Corrections. Washington, D.C.: U.S. Department of Justice.

Austin, J. and K. McGinnis. 2004. *Classification of High Risk and Special Management Prisoners: A National Assessment of Current Practices*. National Institute of Corrections. Washington, D.C.: U.S. Department of Justice.

Bartollas, C. 2004. *Becoming a Model Warden: Striving For Excellence*. Alexandria, Virginia: American Correctional Association.

Bench, L. and T. Allen. 2003. Investigating the Stigma of Prison Classification: An Experimental Design. *The Prison Journal* 83: 367-382.

Cohen v. U.S., 25 F. Supp. 679, at 688 [1966])

Frey, M. and D. Detterman. 2004. Scholastic Assessment or g? The Relationship Between the Scholastic Assessment Test and General Cognitive Ability. *Psychological Science* 15: 373-378.

Handyman, P., J. Austin, J. Alexander, K. Johnson, and O. Tulloch. 2002. *Internal Prison Classification Systems: Case Studies in Their Development and Implementation*. National Institute of Corrections. Washington, D.C.: U.S. Department of Justice.

Handyman, P. J. Austin, and J. Peyton. 2004. *Prisoner Intake Systems: Assessing Needs and Classifying Prisoners*. National Institute of Corrections. Washington, D.C.: U.S. Department of Justice.

Keirsey, D. and M. Bates. 1984. *Please Understand Me: Character and Temperament Types*. Del Mar, California: Prometheus Nemesis.

Kennedy, B. and A. Kennedy. 2004. Using the Myers-Briggs Type Indicator in Career Counseling. *Journal of Employment Counseling* 41: 38-44.

Korn, R. and L. McCorkle. 1959. *Criminology and Penology*. New York: Holt, Rinehart, Winston.

Lauen, R. 1997. *Positive Approaches to Corrections: Research, Policy and Practice*. Lanham, Maryland: American Correctional Association.

Lewis, O. 1967. *The Development of American Prisons and Prison Customs*, 1776-1845. Montclair, New Jersey: Patterson-Smith.

Marquart, J. 2008. Addicted to Prisons and Asking "Why Don't They Riot?" *Criminology and Public Policy* 7: 153-158.

Morris v. Travisono, 310 F. Supp. 857 at 965 [1970])

Myers, I. and M. McCaulley. 1985. *A Guide to the Development and Use of the Myers-Briggs Type Indicator*. Palo Alto, California: Consulting Psychological Press.

National Institute of Corrections. 1984. *Prison Classification: A Model Systems Approach*. Washington, D.C.: U.S. Department of Justice.

Richards, S. and J. Ross. 2003. A Convict Perspective on the Classification of Prisoners. *Criminology and Public Policy* 2: 243-252.

Roberts, John W. 1997. *Reform and Retribution: An Illustrated History of American Prisons*. Alexandria, Virginia: American Correctional Association.

Seiter, R. 2005. *Corrections: An Introduction*. Upper Saddle River, New Jersey: Prentice Hall.

Steel, B. and M. Steger. 1988. Crime: Due Process Liberalism versus Law-and-Order Conservatism. In R. Tatalovich and B. Daynes, eds. *Social Regulatory Policy: Moral Controversies in American Politics*. Boulder, Colorado: Westview Press.

Quay, H. 1984. *Managing Adult Inmates*. Lanham, Maryland: American Correctional Association.

Van Voorhis, P. 1988. A Cross Classification of Five Offender Typologies: Issues of Construct and Predictive Validity. *Criminal Justice and Behavior* 15: 109-124.

———. 1994. *Psychological Classification of the Adult Male Prison Inmate*. New York: SUNY.

CHAPTER 9

Nondirective Counseling: Theory and Practice

Love is the increase of self by means of other.

—**Spinoza**

Robert Martinson's article, "What Works? Questions and Answers about Prison Reform" (1974), provided much grist for the mills of those who subscribe to a "lock 'em up and lose the key" philosophy. Many politicians were so excited about Martinson's alleged findings that they translated the rhetorical "what works?" into the nihilistic "nothing works." Thus, they interpreted the Martinson report as a justification for terminating all efforts to rehabilitate criminals in favor of punishing them, preferably by long periods of incarceration.

Disregarding the fact that Martinson (1979) had the courage to admit that he was wrong in 1974, and disregarding the fact that to incarcerate all convicted criminals is financially prohibitive (see Walker's [2001] analysis of the financial waterfall needed to implement this philosophy), to consign all convicted criminals to prison is both morally inhumane and socially insane. Nearly all incarcerated felons will leave prison someday, and they will emerge harder, crueler, more savage and bitter than they were before they went into prison. While there are clearly people who should be set aside from decent society, we tend to overdo it in the United States where we had an incarceration rate of 738 per 100,000 inhabitants in 2006, which is four times the world average (Hartney 2006). According to a report released by the Pew Center on the States (2009), the American corrections system had more than 7.3 million, or 1 in every 31 U.S. adults, under supervision.

Of course, many correctional programs did not work for a variety of reasons. Addressing this issue of program failure, Gendreau and Ross, two researchers in the forefront of efforts to revive the rehabilitation ideal, write:

> The programs recorded in the literature which have failed (and earned treatment a bad name) did so because they were derived from conceptual models (e.g., psychiatric, nondirective counseling methods, clinical sociology) that made little sense in terms of offender populations or were applied to inappropriate target populations or sought to effect behaviors which were unrelated to crime. They failed because they were badly managed, because they were not sufficiently intensive, and because they employed staff who were inadequately skilled, who exerted insufficient effort or who were not aware or supportive of the program's techniques and goals. (1981: 47).

What Gendreau and Ross are saying is that rehabilitative efforts must be based on empirically based knowledge of criminal risk factors, knowledge of what programs have been shown to change offending behavior, and theories and methods geared to the specific clientele (which does not mean that the methods they mention as ineffective have nothing at all to offer). This knowledge should by applied by caring individuals who fully believe in what they are doing. Rehabilitative and habilitative efforts should never be guided by unsubstantiated fads. In an article about what they call "correctional quackery," Latessa, Cullen, and Gendreau (2002) list a number of such fads that ranged from acupuncture to Zen meditation. They even mention one department (which they mercifully did not identify) that on the basis of the belief that male offenders needed to be in touch with their feminine side actually required them to dress in female clothes! We also know of a department that required its clients (they forbade the use of the term offender as too stigmatizing—P.C. is everywhere!) to partake in "poetry therapy" to "get in touch with their gentler inner feelings." Perhaps the only thing that would change because of such bizarre quackery is the emergence of bank robbers in drag whose stick-up notes rhyme.

However, the issue remains: do habilitative and rehabilitative programs work? A review of studies assessing probation success rates found tremendous variability in success rates ranging from a low of 35 percent to a high of 70 percent (Morgan 1995). Results varied widely, however, depending on the kinds of treatment examined. At least some of that variability is attributable to the different treatment styles of different probation departments, but most was attributable to supervision styles (how tolerant the department was of minor violations, and so on) and to the differing levels of probation eligibility in different jurisdictions. That is, departments that tolerate very few technical violations will tend to have artificially low success rate (and vice versa), and departments that supervise only offenders that the courts deem good probations risks will have artificially high success rates (and vice versa).

Even so, before we can determine that something does or does not work, we first have to define thresholds for defining success (Cohn 2002). A rehabilitation program is not a machine that either works or does not when the switch is pulled. Where human beings are concerned, nothing works for everybody, and nothing will ever work for anybody all the time. If it did, we would not be the kind of beings that we are; we would all be programmed robots. So, when we make statements about programs working or not working, we certainly are not demanding that they work for everybody all of the time.

What rate of success is acceptable before we say a program works then: 90 percent, 80 percent, 50 percent, 10 percent, what? Of the 231 studies that Martinson included in his review, he found that 48 percent reported some degree of success. If your criterion for success is a demanding 100 percent, then, indeed, nothing works. For our part, a 48 percent success rate (however "success" was defined in the original studies) is cause for optimism.

In a later review of rehabilitative programs, Gendreau and Ross (1987) found evidence for a great deal of success. They conclude their review by stating that: "it is downright ridiculous to say that 'Nothing works.' This review attests that much is going on to indicate that offender rehabilitation has been, can be, and will be achieved" (1987: 395). Other commentators have stated the belief that properly run community- based programs could possibly result in a 30- to 50 percent reduction in recidivism (Van Vooris, Braswell, and Lester 2000). These figures are overly optimistic on the basis of major meta-analytic reviews, which tend to suggest reductions more in the 10 percent - to 20 percent range (reviewed in Cullen and Gendreau 2000). Lipsey and Cullen's (2007) meta-analysis of a large number of treatment/recidivism meta-analyses conducted from 1989 to 2006 found that treatment reduced recidivism overall by about 20 percent. Nevertheless, we have enough evidence to dismiss the pessimism of the "Nothing works" crowd and explore counseling theories designed to help those caught up in the criminal justice system to come to grips with their problems.

A Congressionally mandated evaluation of state and local corrections programs entitled *Preventing Crime: What Works, What Doesn't, What's Promising* (Sherman et al. 1997) laid out most of what was known about successful and unsuccessful programs up until then. In terms of the concerns of the present chapter, what does not work is unstructured nondirective counseling. Effective programs that do appear to work use multiple treatment components and are structured and focus on developing social, academic, and employment skills, and use directive cognitive-behavioral counseling methods. Such programs also provided for substantial and meaningful contact between treatment personnel and offenders. The counseling theories presented in this chapter, although nondirective, offer lessons on providing this "substantial and meaningful contact between treatment personnel and offenders."

What Correctional Counseling is Not

To begin with, correctional counseling is definitely not having offenders cross-dress, spout poetry, or meditate on their belly buttons. However, there are a number of other things that it is not. According to John Stratton, an experienced supervising probation officer in his insightful essay on "counseling con men," we have to "Beware of helpers. Helpers are con men who promise you something for nothing. They spoil you and keep you dependent" (1975: 125). It is a statement that all who aspire to a helping profession should consider. We enter the so-called helping professions with noble motives, and it makes us feel good to "help" the troubled and the less fortunate. Yet, the point of helping is not to make us feel good; rather, it is to help offenders to help themselves to feel better in prosocial ways and to become more productive members of society. We should never do for offenders what they are capable of doing for themselves. If we do, we foster offender dependence, an inability to be responsible and to stand on their own two feet, and to use a current buzz word, we "enable" them to persist in their self-destructive and immature behavior. This is not true helping or counseling behavior. Certainly, we can allow offenders to lean on us, but only if they lean on us in order to lift themselves.

However, too many corrections counselors view their role as designed to "straighten out" offenders' behavior and to "adjust" their attitudes. They attempt to do this through a series of directives and well-meaning "advice." Indeed, much about correctional casework is coercive in the sense that we must restrain and constrain offenders. Yet, in exercising such restraint and constraint, we will be far more successful if we treat offenders with respect and enlist their cooperation, just as we would if we were engaged in counseling in a noncoercive setting, say, in marriage counseling where there is no authoritative relationship between counselor and clients.

Advice giving also must be avoided in a counseling situation unless specifically requested. As Meier states: "Friends and family give advice; counselors generally don't, particularly in the initial stages of relationship building" (1989: 19). Even advice from family and friends is usually not too well received or attended to unless it is requested–uninvited advice often irritates and angers. As authority figures, we can force our advice on offenders and even force them to follow through with it, but meaningful and lasting results only can be achieved if offenders are personally convinced of its usefulness. Learning and discovery ultimately can come only from within; that is the real task confronting the counselor.

What Counseling Is

Counseling, at its most fundamental level, is a means of helping people to adapt to life and social institutions in healthy and beneficial ways. Let us first differentiate between the terms counseling and psychotherapy. Some claim that there is no essential difference between the two terms since their definitions and roles are interchangeable. Further, the theories presented in a text in counseling are the same theories contained in a text on psychotherapy. However, in keeping with our earlier advice to respect boundaries of expertise, we stress the differences between the two.

Psychotherapy is the "upmarket" version of the product and is practiced by psychiatrists or clinical psychologists with many years of highly specialized training. True, they employ many of the same techniques used by those engaged in counseling, but they have a deeper theoretical understanding of causality pertaining to the conditions they are treating (McLeod 2003).

The term *treating* delineates another important distinction between psychotherapy and counseling. Psychotherapists operate with a pathology interpretation of their patients' problems; counselors are advised to operate with a deficiency interpretation of offenders' problems. Psychotherapy differs from counseling in the depth and seriousness of the problems dealt with and in the intensity of the treatment. If we laid all the psychiatrists and psychologists in the world out couch to couch, we would not have near enough to treat all our criminals, the vast majority of whom do not require "treating." That is why we need counselors.

Counselors attempt to help offenders with specific life-adjustment problems and to develop the personality that already exists. Psychotherapists attempt to help their patients by a restructuring of the basic personality over a long time. Another way of stating this difference might be to say that psychotherapists deal primarily with intrapersonal conflicts, whereas counselors deal primarily with interpersonal conflicts. When an offender is obviously in need of treatment that exceeds your capability as a counselor (he or she has some obvious mental illness), you should not hesitate to relinquish the further handling of the case to those more qualified to deal with it.

Similarity Between Interviewing and Counseling

Counseling is a series of concerned responses offered to offenders who have concerns and problems that adversely affect their functioning. Counseling is essentially an extension of the interviewing process and uses the same communications skills and techniques. However, "techniques" are secondary to the warmth, acceptance, and understanding the counselor brings to the task. Open, warm, accepting, and empathetic counselors operating with different theoretical perspectives are more similar to each other than are good and poor counselors with the same theoretical perspective (Austin 1999). In other words, all the counseling methods and theories we will examine are only as good as the person putting them into practice. If you work on improving the quality of the self you bring to the counseling process, then the techniques should come easily to you.

Differences Between Interviewing and Counseling

Although counseling is an extension of the interviewing process, certain differences between interviewing and counseling in a criminal justice setting should be emphasized. First, you are more likely to encounter offender resistance during the counseling process than during the interviewing process. During the presentence investigation interview or parole hearing, offenders are fairly anxious to reveal a contrite and cooperative demeanor because they know that you make recommendations. After a case has been disposed of, offenders tend to lose some of their motivation to cooperate along with the anxiety about the disposition of the case. This tendency is a good reason to make the best possible effort to establish a working rapport during the initial interview. If you do not establish such a relationship when the offender is fairly amenable, you will find rapport much more difficult to develop later. Do not be disheartened if you do perceive a change in some offenders' demeanor following case disposition. Accept it as a professional challenge.

Second, assuming that you are successful in establishing a working relationship with offenders, you are ready to communicate with them at a deeper level in successive counseling sessions by carefully developing an empathetic understanding of them. You no longer have to gather large amounts of data from them, so you are free to concentrate on specific problem areas from the strength-based and responsivity principles. Therefore, counseling differs from interviewing in its depth.

So, what is correctional counseling? William Lewis, a psychologist with many years of experience counseling offenders, defines correctional counseling as the "ongoing, positive, interpersonal relationships as the vehicle through which a variety of systematic verbal techniques can be applied to increase the counselee's *feelings* of self-satisfaction, *and* improve his [or her] *actual* social adjustments" (1989: 71, emphasis original). The correctional worker who can follow these requirements has a positive and integrated sense of self and can serve as a model of growth-inducing interpersonal relationships.

Counseling Theories

With this brief introduction to counseling, we turn to five of the most popular theories of counseling, two in this chapter, two in the next, and one with a chapter of its own. Just as it is important to have a grasp of criminological theories to understand criminal behavior in general, it is important to understand counseling theories so that you can understand the behavior of the specific criminals with whom you are dealing. A counselor with thirty years experience writes that: "I would find it impossible to function as a mental health counselor without the structure that a good theory provides me" (Weinrich 2006: 161). While theories are very important in our work, we emphasize once again that it is even more important to realize that "the kind of person the worker is or comes across as being, is more important for the therapeutic success or failure than the theories or methods he or she employs" (Smith 2006: 371).

Counseling theory is something on which to hang your hat. It structures your thoughts and behaviors from the chaos of your offender's lives to identify possible ways that you could deal with it, providing you with "Ah, ah," that's what's going on!" experiences. In other words, theories are frameworks for understanding. Important aspects of counseling will be illustrated in the context of the five theories that most strongly emphasize them. Special attention will be paid to the processes of generating rapport and empathy and to the techniques for dealing with reluctant and resisting offenders.

You may view the large number of theoretical orientations to counseling (and there are certainly far more than the five presented here) in two ways. You may consider it to be so much clutter, indicative of a lack of scientific rigor in the field. Alternatively, you may regard it positively as a rich mine of possibilities in which you can dig for counseling gems. No one theory is applicable to all problems and concerns with which you will deal, and no one theory exhausts the uniqueness of each offender.

A sage once said: "Each person is like all other persons, like some other persons, and like no other person." It follows that certain insights from one counseling theory may be universally applicable, be applicable only some of the time, or not be applicable at all on some occasions. The more theoretical insights you have in your repertoire, the better you will be able to respond successfully to the diverse offenders and problems you will encounter.

Loyalty to any one theory may severely limit your effectiveness by leading you to stretch everything to fit it and/or to ignore whatever will not work. Good counselors develop a unique, flexible, and workable style of their own. Studies of professional counselors find that most (30 to 40 percent) view themselves as eclectic or "integrative" counselors (reviewed in Austin 1999). By developing an eclectic approach, picking and choosing those elements that fit your style, serve your needs, and fit different offenders' styles and needs, you will begin to discern some of the common threads woven into all theories. The agreement of greatest importance among all theories is the vital necessity of all human beings to love and be loved.

John McLeod writes that although there is a strong trend toward integration and unification of counseling theories: "It is widely recognized the three 'core' approaches of psychodynamic, cognitive behavioural, and humanistic represent fundamentally different ways of viewing human beings and their emotional and behavioural problems" (2003: 10). The present chapter focuses on psychoanalysis (a psychodynamic theory) and client-centered therapy (a humanistic theory); subsequent chapters address the cognitive-behavioral approach.

Psychoanalysis and client-centered therapy are nondirective forms of counseling. They put great faith in their patients' or clients' ability to discover their own capabilities and find their own directions. Counselors play a relatively passive role and are reluctant to impose their values on patients/clients and provide them with direction. Psychoanalysis and client-centered therapy rarely are used in a correctional setting (but see the extention of client-centered therapy to Motivational Interviewing later in this chapter), primarily because they are too nondirective, and because the terminology and concepts are too abstruse, and the methods are difficult for the nonspecialist to apply. We include them nonetheless, because of certain unique aspects, which we will outline as we continue.

Psychoanalysis: In the Beginning was Freud

Psychoanalysis is the seminal therapy/counseling theory from which all others evolved. Although psychoanalysis is beyond the boundaries of expertise for those of us who are not psychiatrists or psychologists, it contains some very useful insights into the nature of human beings. Whereas the other four theories focus primarily on the present, psychoanalysis puts great emphasis on the role of the past in shaping current behavior. Since so many emotional and behavioral difficulties stem to a large degree from past experiences, it is important to be aware of and explore offenders' pasts as a vehicle for understanding their presents. However, we reject the notion that the past determines present behavior or that people are "victims" of their past.

According to Fine: "The technical task of psychoanalysis has been to elucidate the nature of love" (1973: 16). Freud himself has stated that happiness exists in "the way of life, which makes love the center of everything, which looks for all satisfaction in loving and being loved" (1961: 29). The psychoanalyst basically explores patients' childhoods to uncover underlying reasons for their inability to love.

The psychoanalytic theory of the tripartite structure of the personality—the id, ego, and superego—is too well known to warrant extensive treatment here. The *id* is the biological source of the organism's energy and the driving force of the personality. Its only goal is to seek gratification of its urges–to seek pleasure and to avoid pain. The *superego* acts as the counterforce to the id by exercising socially derived moral prescriptions and proscriptions. We call individuals who give free reign to the id nasty names such as "psychopath" or "criminal," and we call individuals with powerful superegos slightly less offensive names such as "neurotic" or "conformist." The *ego* is a type of synthesis of the biological and social demands on the organism. Well-balanced people have strong egos and are able to obtain gratification of their id drives within the bounds of moral restrictions placed on them by their superego (their conscience).

The value of Freud's theory of personality lies in the recognition of both the "beast and the angel in man." The bestial side of humanity is the side that most concerns the criminal justice worker. As a criminal justice worker, you are striving to assist offenders in understanding themselves, and to enlist that understanding in the task of strengthening the rational ego "so that it can appropriate fresh portions of the id. Where an id was, there shall ego be" (Freud 1965: 80). This emphasis on the ego's control of impulses emanating from the id is reminiscent of Gottfredson and Hirschi's (1990) emphasis on the importance of self-control.

Psychosexual Stages

Psychoanalysis stresses the great importance of the so-called psychosexual stages involved in early character development. These stages represent a series of conflicts between children and their parents. There are three such stages: oral, anal, and phallic that extend from birth to five or six years of age. Freud identified two later stage, latency and genital, but did not consider then as important as the first three states as he considered personality to be essentially fully developed by the end of the phallic stage. Each of these stages focuses on the erogenous zones of the body, and each stage represents the child's first encounters with external restraints on natural urges coming from the id. These encounters supposedly generate negative feelings in the child, such as hostility, hatred, anger, and destructiveness. Since the display of these feelings invites negative reactions from other people, the child learns to repress them, resulting in a later inability to accept and express his or her real feelings. This barrier to self-knowledge must be breached in any counseling session.

Oral Stage: From Birth to Age One. The oral stage encompasses the first year of life. This is the period of life in which the child learns love and security and in which the template for the child's basic personality is formed. At the mother's breast, the infant satisfies its hunger and needs for tactile stimulation. These are unconditioned needs (needs which do not have to be learned), the satisfaction of which the infant "loves" because they are intrinsically rewarding. When the infant identifies the source of its pleasure, it develops a love for that source that is stronger than the love of the pleasures the source affords. In this sense, love for mother is a sort of conditioned response due to the continual associations made between her and the pleasures she provides.

The conflict the infant experiences at this stage is weaning because it deprives the infant of a very enjoyable sensory pleasure. The infant interprets the weaning experience as deprivation and possibly rejection. If this stage is not successfully traversed (in other words, the infant senses that he or she is really being rejected), the person may grow up to be excessively preoccupied with oral activities (eating, drinking, smoking, and so forth). In other words, he or she will develop an oral fixation. (One wonders if Freud's extensive cigar habit meant that he had such a fixation—but then again, he did remind us that sometimes a cigar is just a cigar).

According to Freud, negative behaviors, such as acquisitiveness and aggression, are substitutes for what the individual really needs–love. Unloved individuals feel unworthy, unwanted, and unaccepted and are mistrusting and rejecting of others. They cannot accept either themselves or others because they have not experienced acceptance. Early love experiences are a safeguard against this type of negativism. This does not mean that all people who exhibit these negative characteristics have experienced an unloving childhood, or that individuals who did experience an unloving childhood necessarily will exhibit them. The theory merely asserts that negative adult behaviors are more likely to characterize those individuals who experienced a childhood marked by a lack of love than to characterize those individuals who did not.

Reread the early life experiences of Bill Bloggs in the presentence investigation report. Can we not see his extreme materialism and bursts of aggressive behavior as stemming from his lack of love during the oral stage of his life? By his own admission, he was quite socially isolated and sought to win Susan's love by purchasing things.

Anal Stage: Ages One Through Three. In the anal stage, the child first encounters discipline. The child has received a series of admonitions prior to this stage, such as "Don't touch that oven!" or "Stop biting the cat!" However, children encounter "real" discipline in the anal stage. They learn disciplined self-mastery by learning control of bodily functions through toilet training. Toilet training is given such importance in psychoanalytic theory because it is the first time that the children have to suppress natural urgings until they can be satisfied in the appropriate way and in the appropriate place, and learn that there are negative consequences for "messing" up.

While the child tends to rebel against the unnaturalness of toilet training, when the training is completed, he or she takes pride in the accomplishment of its mastery. Parents should encourage this sense of mastery by allowing the child to explore and to make mistakes. They should emphasize that it is okay to make mistakes if one learns by them. If parents are constantly critical of mistakes that the child makes, the child will be reluctant to explore and expand. If parents show exaggerated concern and do everything for the child, the child will not develop a sense of independence and autonomy. The children of such parents may be stuck forever in a "no-can-do" mode, lacking the self-confidence to expand their horizons and possessing poor self-concepts.

It is easy to view Bill's parents, especially his father, being hypercritical of him during his formative years, given the description of their personalities provided by Officer Corrick. Bill's whole life seemed to revolve around doing things to please his father. He did not leave home until he met Susan, indicating a strong sense of dependency. His hanging of the kitten, bursts of extreme temper, and, not the least, his shooting of a policeman point vividly to his inability to express his feelings appropriately.

Phallic Stage: Ages Three through Five. The phallic stage is a period of early development of conscience and sex-role identification. During this stage, children become aware of their genitals and those of the opposite sex. Masturbation (not in a sexual sense, of course, but more literally in terms of "playing" with oneself) is commonly begun during this stage, and parental response to the discovery of this activity can have serious consequences. If parents are overly moralistic, defining masturbation as something that "nice boys and girls don't do," they are setting the stage for the domination of the superego. Such a rigid conformity to puritanical morality also may preclude the enjoyment of intimacy with others later in life because of inadequate sex-role identification.

We have no information about Bill's experiences during this stage in his life, but it takes no great flight of imagination to see Bill's father as a real authoritarian moralist where the behavior of others was concerned. Bill did have a great deal of difficulty forming intimate attachments with others, and perhaps his belief that he was a woman in his "previous existence" is indicative of sex-role ambiguity. Bill's later forced incestuous experiences would have conflicted seriously with any early development of a moralistic conscience. Bill did have, to say the least, a quite an unusual view of reality.

Defense Mechanisms

The identification of a patient's defense mechanisms is an important part of the psychotherapeutic process. Defense mechanisms, which operate at an unconscious level (the individual is unaware of them), function to protect the ego from a threatening reality by distorting it. Defense mechanisms are not necessarily pathological. We all use some of them to some extent, and they even can be psychologically adaptive in that they serve the self-consistency motive. Only when they become an integral part of a pattern of life leading one to avoid facing reality do they become matters of great concern. The psychoanalytic literature lists numerous defense mechanisms.

Any comprehensive listing of them is beyond the scope of this book. We will discuss only those most commonly seen in a criminal justice setting.

Denial is the blocking out of a portion of reality that is threatening to the ego. Sexual feelings and activities often are subject to this defense mechanism. Otherwise, quite respectable child molesters often will attempt to deny to themselves that the incident ever occurred. This is not simply "forgetting" (repression), but rather refusing to recognize that it happened. Bill's denial of his enuresis may be seen as an attempt to deal with the residual anxiety felt about being "hog tied" and whipped when he wet his bed, and his statement that his incestuous experiences were "no big deal" can be seen as an attempt to divorce himself from the possibility that he could have welcomed them.

Rationalization is the process of providing oneself with acceptable reasons for one's behavior or one's experiences to soothe a damaged ego. This is a definite favorite of offenders. Bill recited a litany of experiences to make Corrick understand "some underlying reason(s) for my behavior," thus creating the impression that he was more wronged than wrong. Rationalization helps us to maintain an acceptable self-image by downplaying our own badness and/or inadequacies. We parcel out blame or disvalue what we may want but cannot get ("I didn't get the job because this is a racist/sexist/elitist society and I'm black/a woman/not one of them. Who wants that stupid job anyway?").

Fixation is being immobilized at an earlier stage of personality development because the more appropriate stage is fraught with anxiety. Many offenders have a childlike attachment to the present because stepping into the future is stepping into the great unknown. Many have developed a pattern of helplessness through their dependence on the welfare system, which is the only financial "parent" many have ever known. To go out and expand one's capacities and explore one's potential is not one of the lessons imparted by the culture of poverty. As a criminal justice helper, you are charged with helping offenders to develop a realistic orientation to the future by attempting to enlarge their sense of self-worth and their sense of the possible.

Displacement is the transference of feelings about someone or something onto another person or object because the original person or object is either inaccessible or too powerful. The individual often displaces anger or aggression onto the innocent. Wife and child battering frequently is displaced aggression generated by others too powerful to attack directly. All too often one finds that offenders have much pent-up anger, the source of which they find difficult to identify. Further, they have not learned to express their feelings in appropriate ways, so they vent them on "safe" targets. The psychoanalyst would interpret Bill's explosive temper and the hanging of the kitten as an expression of the anger he felt toward his father being displaced on non-threatening targets.

Intellectualization is a process of using arguments to deflect the blame from themselves by pointing out how others should be blamed. Some of the better-educated offenders are quite adept in the use of intellectualization. They often will attempt to assail legal reality by intellectualizing their crimes away. The marijuana dealer who launches into a monolog accusing society of hypocrisy, the petty forger who cites chapter and verse on white-collar crime, and the thief who discourses plausibly on corporate irresponsibility are all examples of people trying to avoid the reality of their own malfeasance. You certainly may accept the legitimacy of their position, but you also must impress on such offenders that the issue is their behavior and not that of others, and that they cannot avoid confronting their behavior by trying to re-focus the discussion elsewhere.

Projection is the mechanism by which people attribute to others the feelings they refuse to see in themselves. Individuals are often most troubled by the behavior of others when it mimics their own repressed urges. The rough treatment of child molesters in prisons may be viewed as an attempt by other inmates to convince themselves that they could not possibly harbor such evil urges themselves. Offenders who feel that no one understands or likes them, who harbor hostility toward others, are projecting onto others their negative feelings about themselves, thereby protecting the ego by confusing self with other. So many expressions of hostility and hatred of the world by criminal justice offenders are really expressions of self-hatred. If you can aid offenders to develop more positive feelings about themselves, you will find that they will develop better attitudes toward the world.

Lessons and Concerns

The primary usefulness of psychoanalytic theory for the criminal justice worker is that it provides insights that lead to a better understanding of offenders' struggles with themselves and with the outside world. An understanding of the defense mechanisms is particularly useful in understanding offender resistance to the helping process.

A little knowledge, it has been said, is dangerous. The correctional worker lacks the depth of training necessary to put the techniques of psychoanalysis into practice. To attempt to do so could result in negative consequences. Besides, it is too time-consuming and involved. It is an approach better suited to folks seeking professional absolution for their sins and peccadilloes, and who enjoy richer vocabularies and fatter wallets than the typical offender does. Many psychiatrists and psychologists themselves have turned to more simplified methods to deal with the problems presented to them by the typical offender–methods that generally are more productive of change because few offenders require total personality restructuring. Sometimes the use of psychoanalysis for relatively minor life-adjustment problems is like swatting flies with a baseball bat. This is not, however, to belittle the often-profound theoretical insights into human nature provided by this theory.

Client-Centered Approach

Carl Rogers developed his client-centered (or person-centered) approach to counseling in response to the deficiencies he perceived in psychoanalysis and behaviorist therapies. According to Austin (1999: 16) Rogers' theory is favored over any other single counseling theory by professional counselors, and has been ranked first as the most influential psychotherapist by these same professionals (Ellis 1996). Being a humanist thinker, Rogers rejected what he saw as the biological determinism of psychoanalysis and the mechanistic nature of behaviorism in favor of self-determination and what he considered the natural goodness in humankind (Hill and Nakayama 2000).

Rather than viewing individuals as driven by irrational biological impulses (which Rogers saw as an intimation that humans were basically antisocial) or as simple mechanistic responders to external stimuli (as in behaviorism), this approach sees human beings as basically good, self-driven, and possessing an innate capacity for self-actualization (the capacity to become all that we are able to become). Self-destructive behavior and attitudes arise from faulty self-concepts (the self-concept is central to this theory) and an inability to grasp the fundamental truth that we are free agents in charge of our own destinies. Although the emphasis on innate goodness and self-actualization is somewhat Pollyannaish in that it refuses to see the beast in man, it is ennobling in its enunciation. The basic goal of client-centered therapy is to improve the self-concept.

Rogers' definition of counseling is as follows: "The process by which the structure of the self is relaxed in the safety of the relationship with the therapist, and the previously denied experiences are perceived and then integrated into an altered self" (1952: 70). Client-centered therapy eschews searching for causes and the teaching of counseling techniques in favor of asserting the absolute primacy of the nature of the offender/counselor relationship (Austin 1999). What counselors bring to the relationship in terms of the quality of the self is far more critical than what they do with it in terms of technique.

The absence of loving human relationships is the basic reason that isolated, alienated, lonely, and self-destructive offenders require the counselor's assistance. It follows that the offender must form such a positive relationship with at least one other person if you are to accomplish anything meaningful. That one other person is the counselor. Although the burden of discovering the true goodness of the self is placed squarely on the shoulders of the offender in this essentially nondirective form of counseling, the burden of establishing the type of relationship in which it may be accomplished is placed on the counselor: "If I can provide a certain type of relationship, the other person will discover within himself the capacity to use that relationship for growth and change, and personal development will occur" (Rogers 1961: 33). The counselor functions as a midwife, wresting out of the offender the goodness that is already present and awaiting birth.

Can the correctional worker provide the "love" that Rogers feels so important? Unfortunately, the English language is such that the term love is either confined to romantic love or used indiscriminately as an intense form of liking ("I love golf," or "I just loved that movie."). William Lewis tells us how we can meet offenders' need for love: "A correctional worker can meet the need for love, for example, at the young adult level through such means as courtesy; showing genuine interest and concern; giving instructions in a friendly, respectful way (as opposed to grumpy or profane barking); giving honest praise for work well done; and asking for opinions and respecting them as worthwhile" (1989: 28). Let us define love in the corrections context as "an active concern for the well-being of another."

The only techniques of client-centered therapy are those we talked about before (Chapter 5): engaging in active listening, clarifying, and reflecting of feelings. Evans et al. (1989: 3) characterize Rogers as the "listening counselor." If you were to watch a client-centered counselor at work, you probably would get the impression that nothing is occurring. The counselor simply listens intensely to the offender while making occasional verbalizations such as, "Yes, please go on," "Uh, huh," "Uhm," and "Once again, please," and with other signs of approval such as smiles and head nods. What is going on here is counselee reinforcement in the form of verbal and visual signs of approval, and such reinforcement is considered vital in the counseling process. Offenders tend to talk about those topics that are reinforced, and not to talk about topics that are not. Experiments demonstrate that people's verbal and nonverbal behavior can be shaped systematically in desired directions by such simple acts of reinforcement as these (Evans et al. 1989: 5-6).

Rogers was much more concerned with the client/counselor relationship and the personal attributes of the counselor than with techniques. The three main attributes that the counselor must bring to the relationship are unconditional positive regard, genuineness, and empathy.

Unconditional Positive Regard

According to Rogers, many negative self-feelings and psychological problems develop because others place conditions on their acceptance of us. They like us or love us if we are or if we do what they would like us to be or do. Since we all want to be liked, loved, and accepted, we tend to conform to these conditions. Our conformity to the expectations of others leads us to an inauthentic self-image. To function as psychologically healthy people, we must set our own standards of behavior and self-acceptance. We have the ability to be fully authentic human beings, but we must first experience this unconditional positive regard from at least one person. For Rogers, the counselor fills that role.

Unconditional positive regard occurs when the counselor communicates to the offender a full and genuine acceptance of his or her personhood, warts and all. Acceptance must be uncontaminated by judgments of the offender's attitudes, feelings, or behavior as being wrong or bad. This does not mean that the counselor approves or accepts illegal or immoral behavior; it means that the offender's essential humanity is accepted and valued in spite of his or her attitudes and behavior. This acceptance allows offenders to be free to examine their own behavior in a nonthreatening setting. Thus, they themselves may arrive at the conclusion that their attitudes and behavior are self-defeating. Officer Corrick appears to have had a positive feeling about Bill Bloggs while at the same time soundly condemning his behavior in the presentence investigation report.

"Unconditional positive regard" is an ideal to be striving for, and it is not an all-or-nothing requirement. It is most unrealistic to think that you can develop this type of relationship with all offenders, or even most of them. Any relationship between two people is a chemical mix that may blend or explode. Some offenders are downright determined to make your life as difficult as possible, and they will read only weakness or patronization into your efforts to establish a positive working relationship. Most, however, will respond to your warmth with warmth of their own. The degree to which you can achieve the kind of positive regard that Rogers talks about is largely the degree of success you will achieve in your efforts to turn around an offender's life. At the very least, you should respect the basic humanity of the offender. Be cautious, however, that the relationship does not become one in which the offender depends on you, or that you do not use the relationship possessively to fulfill your own needs for positive regard.

Genuineness

Counselors must be genuine (be completely themselves) with offenders. Counselors must accept and deal with all feelings, whether positive or negative, generated by their interaction with the offender. In short, counselors must be authentic in the presentation of self to the offender. They must avoid pretensions, game playing, and facades. The displaying of false fronts means that the counselor feels a lack of congruence between the real and the public self, which is, according to this perspective, precisely the vulnerable state of the offender. Since it is the task of the counselor to help the offender become more aware of internal incongruities, is it highly desirable that the counselor present an integrated self to the offender. The ultimate aim of self-disclosure exercises for the neophyte counselor is to develop an authentic and congruent sense of self. The goal is that the counselor's authentic self should permeate freely into the offender.

Human genuineness or authenticity exists only on a continuum and must be developed. It is interesting to note the agreement among the giants of the human sciences on this subject of human authenticity. Freud, Marx, and Maslow, despite radically different ideological and theoretical orientations and concerns, all agree that the ability to love and be loved is the key to human authenticity (Walsh 1986).

Empathy

Empathy is the counselor's capacity for participating in the feelings of the offender. Empathy implies more than an intellectual understanding of the offender's feelings. It goes beyond cognitive knowledge about the offender to fuse with the offender, and causes the counselor to experience the offender's feelings as if they were the counselor's own. This implies the kind of gut-level subjective understanding that is granted only to those who have walked in similar shoes. Mayeroff (1971: 41-42) describes the empathetic ability thus:

> To care for another person, I must be able to understand him and his world as if I were inside it. I must be able to see, as it were, with his eyes what his world is like to him and how he sees himself. Instead of merely looking at him in a detached way from the outside, as if he were a specimen, I must be able to be with him in his world, 'going' into his world in order to sense from the 'inside' what life is for him, what he is striving to be and what he requires to grow.

This definition of empathy is like the definition of unconditional positive regard—beautiful in its conceptualization but probably impossible to attain in any absolute sense. Yet, many books on counseling contain statements such as "Respond to the client with empathy." This gives the beginning counselor the mistaken impression that "getting into" a client's frame of reference is not much more difficult than following instructions such as "Place block A on block B and click into place." This could be dangerously misleading and falsely reassuring.

Developing Accurate Empathy

Is empathy possible between persons of different races, social strata, and educational backgrounds? For example, can a white, middle-class, female, college-educated corrections worker really "participate" in the mindset of a semiliterate street male who is of another race and social class? We believe that it is possible, but only in a limited sense. Such ability does not come naturally or easily. You must work very hard to develop it, both by examining your own values, prejudices, and stereotypes and by assimilating as much knowledge as you possibly can about the causes and reasons why offenders live and behave the way they do.

Your ability to empathize with offenders will increase in direct proportion to the time you spend in these endeavors. Even then, it may be counterproductive to convey to offenders the idea that you "understand" their problems until you have had a number of sessions with them in which you actively have listened to what they have to say. For this reason, we did not stress empathy in the chapter on interviewing, but did stress listening. Active listening is the essential prerequisite to empathy.

Egan (1998) distinguishes between what he calls basic and advanced empathy, both of which he subsumes under the general term "accurate empathy." "Basic empathy involves listening to clients, understanding them and their concerns to the degree that this is possible, and communicating this understanding to them so that they might understand themselves more fully and act on that understanding" (1998: 81, emphasis original). For instance, basic empathy might involve communicating understanding of an offender's anger, depression, and anxiety, since these feelings are common to all people, regardless of their unique experiences.

Advanced-level empathy concerns not only what clients say but also what they imply or leave half-expressed. Skilled counselors "often see clearly what clients only half see and hint at" (Egan 1998: 170). This is what Reich (1956) means by "listening with the third ear." However, we should distinguish between its use in an initial interview setting and in a counseling setting. In an interview setting, your primary task is the assessment of offenders, and your secondary task is to prepare the groundwork for future counseling sessions. You are listening to what offenders are implying or leaving half-expressed to gain the best initial understanding you can of their background.

In the initial interview, it is too early in your relationship to challenge offenders about what you think they are implying or half-expressing. You have very limited knowledge of offenders at that point, trust is not established, and you could be completely wrong in your judgments and interpretations. Even if you are right, offenders may not be ready to verify your insight at this time and may deny it. Once some facet of the offenders' deeply private self has been denied, it becomes more difficult for them to admit it later. It is threatening and frightening to be forced to confront a negative feature of the self that formerly has been repressed. Do not risk erroneous assumptions or provoke the offender's denial by premature attempts at advanced empathy.

Empathy, then, is a series of responses rendered by the counselor with a developed sensitivity to the offender's unique set of feelings about the world and his or her place in it. In effect, you are thinking with offenders rather than about them. We will examine some responses using both forms of empathy in a criminal justice counseling session.

Examples of Empathetic Responses

Remember, your responses are never neutral; they are either constructive or destructive. This is particularly important for offenders since they are stuck with you, for better or worse, during their period of correctional supervision. Constructive responses are those that involve offenders in self-exploration so that they may arrive at solutions to their troubles themselves. Fully involving offenders means accepting the reality of their problems and reflecting them back to them.

For example, suppose that Fred comes to you and states that he finds his job (let us say he is a factory assembler) boring, unsatisfying, and unsuitable for his talents and ambitions. Furthermore, he tells you that he wants to quit. You want him to keep his job, knowing that jobs are difficult to find, that he has financial obligations, and that "the devil finds work for idle hands." You respond by saying: "Fred, you feel that your job makes you feel depressed and less than worthy and productive. I can understand that because I've had jobs that made me feel that way too. What is it in particular about your job that makes you feel depressed, Fred?"

What have you accomplished in these three sentences? First, you have recognized the reality of Fred's problem and the fact that it is a genuine concern for him. Second, you have reflected his feelings about the problem, thereby making him aware that you have correctly understood him. Third, you have shown empathy by self-disclosure of your similar experiences. This reinforces Fred's perception of your acceptance of the reality of the problem and gives him a feeling of commonality with you. This will also make Fred more receptive to the plan of action you will decide upon together, since you have modeled the plan in your own life experience. Fourth, you have probed further by the use of an open-ended question asking Fred to identify specific conditions, circumstances, or situations that arouse his negative feelings. Your response has generated a positive atmosphere, which will allow further discussion and exploration, leading, you hope, to a mutually acceptable plan of action for dealing with the problem. In short, you have made excellent use of accurate primary empathy.

Contrast the positive response to Fred's concern with the following negative response: "Fred, you're always complaining about something. This business about your job is all in your head. It does you no good to dwell on it. How can you expect a better job with your education? Besides, you can't quit without my permission, so relax and forget it, buddy."

What have you accomplished here? First, by responding from your frame of reference rather than Fred's, you have denied the reality of the problem and of his feelings about it. Second, you have denigrated him by calling him a complainer and belittling his education. Third, you have distanced yourself from him by (1) showing a lack of concern and understanding, (2) emphasizing differences in educational levels, and (3) emphasizing the relationship of authority that exists between you. Furthermore, by telling him to "relax and forget it" you have guaranteed that he will not. Instead, you will have exacerbated his negative feelings and left him to deal with them in a possibly destructive manner. You can bet that he will not come to you again with his concerns.

In short, Fred will be influenced by the second response just as he would be influenced by the first. The second response, however, generates feelings in Fred that will be destructive to your relationship with him. Your lack of professional concern will make your job more difficult and demanding, and may cause Fred to quit his job despite your warning that he cannot. This, in turn, may lead to a technical violation or further criminality. The golden rule of counseling is "Treat offenders as you would wish to be treated."

Suppose Fred responds to your primary-level empathy with the following statements and nonverbal behaviors. Fred is sitting with his folded hands resting on his thighs and looking at you (a nondefensive, open, and trusting demeanor). "Well, Terry, I didn't mind the job so much when I was on days. It's this night shift stuff."

Fred now straightens up, looks away, and raises his voice slightly (some defensiveness, embarrassment, and anger creeping in). "My wife complains that I don't spend enough time with her. We used to go out dancing once or twice a week, but now I can't because either I'm working, or I'm too damn tired on the weekend."

Fred sits up straight and grasps the arms of his chair. His face reddens a little, and his speech becomes faster and louder (a strengthening of his defensiveness, embarrassment, and anger). "She goes by herself, though. I don't like that, and I tell her so. We've had quite a few arguments about that crap."

You now come to realize that Fred's job is not the real cause of his depression. His more substantial concern is his wife's dissatisfaction, and his statement contains some significant intimations that he is concerned about the possibility that she may be doing more than just dancing with other men. You might engage in the following dialog with Fred:

> **Counselor** Are you saying that it is not the job itself that you want to quit but, rather, you would like to get off the night shift? (Clarification.)
>
> **Fred** Yes, I think things might be better if I went back on days.
>
> **Counselor** The night shift leaves you without much time or energy to devote to your wife, and this is causing some friction between you. (Paraphrase). You are angry and upset because she goes to the dance by herself. (Reflection.)
>
> **Fred** You bet I am! I've told her that it's not right for a married woman to go dancing by herself.
>
> **Counselor** Fred, I can understand your annoyance with your wife, and I know that the two of you have talked about it. Why do you think she continues to go when you have told her that you dislike it? (Probe.)
>
> **Fred** I don't know. We get so mad at each other when we talk about it that I think she does it out of spite. (Angry arguments do have a way of leading one of the participants to act in uncharacteristic ways to "get back.")
>
> **Counselor** What do you think she would do if you let her know your feelings without getting upset? (Open-ended question designed to get Fred to think about his wife's possible reaction to a rational discussion of the problem rather than an emotional confrontation.)
>
> **Fred** I don't really know. We don't argue that much about other things. I don't mind her having some fun, but dancing? My wife's an attractive woman–I see the way that men look at her. (Fred's reply indicates, that, except for this one issue, quarreling is not a major feature of his marriage. He quickly disposes of your question and gets down to his real concern.)
>
> **Counselor** You like your wife to enjoy herself, but you find it unsettling for her to do it in this way because she is in the company of other men. (Paraphrasing and reflecting.) Am I hearing you say that you are concerned that one of her dance partners may make a play for her? I wonder if she realizes that she is hurting you this

way. (Clarifying your perception of Fred's underlying feeling and using advanced empathy.)

Fred I guess I'm kind of jealous. I really love Carla, and it eats me up inside to think that she might be playing around behind my back. I haven't admitted this to myself before today. I suppose I wasn't too eager to think about it. What do you think I should do, Terry? You've made me realize that I don't really want to quit my job–it pays good money and I have my restitution and fine to finish paying–but I don't want to lose Carla. (Fred is now asking for your advice, which up until now you have resisted giving). He will be more receptive now that he has explored the problem himself and has explicitly requested advice. You also have led him to identify for himself what he was feeling—jealousy. This is much better than simply coming out and asking him, "Do you feel jealous?" He may have denied the embarrassing feeling if you rather than he had approached the issue directly.)

Counselor I do not think it's a question of either quitting your job or losing Carla. I might suggest two courses of action for you to think about. First, you could speak with your boss at work to see if there is any possibility at all of getting back on days, even if it means a different job and less pay. Regardless of whether this is possible, you could discuss your feelings openly with Carla as you have done with me. Do this without any hint of accusation or anger, and you will find that, more than likely, she will respond the same way. Since you seem to enjoy dancing yourself, try to arrange it so that the two of you can go together at least once a week. What do you think about these suggestions, Fred?

This exchange illustrates both basic and advanced level empathy. The counselor went beyond the initial problem that Fred presented and probed for a deeper concern. The counselor skillfully led him to explore feelings that he was reluctant to admit to himself, and she offered him, at his request, some helpful suggestions for dealing with them. It took a great deal more time than it would have taken to tell him to stop complaining, but she may have gone a long way in helping Fred to save his job and his marriage. Also, she probably has saved herself time and trouble in the long run.

What Accurate Empathy Is Not

Now that you have a good idea of what accurate empathy is, it is important to understand what it is not. Empathy does not mean that you should condone wrong behavior. If Fred were to tell you, for example, that he goes out and gets drunk because he can't stand Carla's imagined infidelities, nagging, and denigrating him, and then he asks you what you would do in a similar situation, he has put you in something of a spot. He is asking for your sympathy, understanding, and self-disclosure. It is a poor kind of empathy to reply, "I guess I'd do the same thing," even if, in fact, you think that you might do so. Such a reply would imply that you are condoning his behavior. But if you reply that you certainly would not do so, Fred will perceive you as being critical and judgmental. It would be better for you to say, "I'm sure that your wife's behavior makes you feel terrible. I'm not sure what I would do myself. I think perhaps that I would seek marital counseling. Do you think that's a possibility for you?" This reply relieves you of the appearance of condoning the offender's behavior while at the same time recognizing his feelings and offering a constructive alternative to the bottle.

Motivational Interviewing: Expanding the Client-Centered Approach

Any theory that is of use to anyone must evolve as new information emerges. One of the exciting evolutionary adaptations of Rogers' theory is Motivational Interviewing developed by Miller and Rollnick (2002). According to Burke, Arkowitz, and Menchola (2003: 843): "Motivational interviewing is a relatively new and promising therapeutic approach that integrates the relationship-building principles of humanistic therapy with more active cognitive-behavioral strategies targeted to the client's stage of change." Motivational interviewing is still humanistic in the assumption that the solution to our problems lie within us and all the counselor has to do is to act as a midwife. Yet, it is also confrontational, but with a difference. It is not the counselor that directly confronts clients, yet rather the counselor guides clients to confront themselves. To continue the midwife metaphor, the counselor gently asks the client to breathe a certain way and to continue pushing to bring what is inside into the light of day.

Figure 9.1 The Basics of Motivational Interviewing: Officer's Strategy *above*; Hoped for Offender's Responses *below*

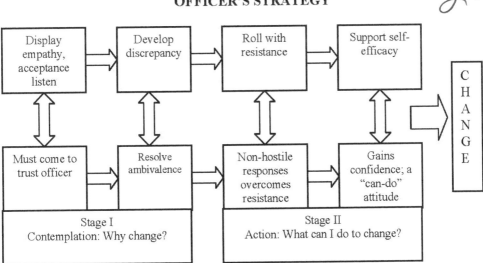

OFFICER'S STRATEGY

HOPED-FOR OFFENDER'S RESPONSE

Figure 9.1, on page 197, presents the basics of Motivational Interviewing in schematic form from the introductory stages to the final goal—behavioral change. While designed around Motivational Interviewing, with slight changes in terminology the figure can serve as a template for any counseling theory. The top part of the figure is the counselor's strategy; the bottom parts are the responses the counselor hopes to elicit from the offender. The first two squares represent the preliminary contemplative stages of the process—developing rapport and creating and increasing motivation for change. The second two squares represent the action stages—consolidating the offender's commitment to change and translating that commitment into actual behavior.

Empathy. The prerequisite for all counseling is the development of a positive and trusting relationship between officer/counselor and offender. If the offender does not develop the necessary trust, the rest of the process will be unworkable for the most part. All that we have previously said about empathy (reflective listening, an attitude of acceptance, educating one's self about the kinds of problems offenders bring with them) applies here. Motivational interviewing also stresses that the counselor must accept that an offender's ambivalence about change is normal (a reflection of the self-consistency motive) and not pathological defensiveness.

Developing Discrepancy. If the offender appears comfortable and trusting, the counselor can move on to the process of developing discrepancy. An assumption of Motivational Interviewing is that offenders are ambivalent about changing their lives; they want to and they do not want to at the same time. Discrepancy development is all about helping the offender identify his or her ambivalent feelings between how he or she is as opposed to how he or she would like to be. In other words, the counselor/officer strives to increase the psychological discomfort of cognitive dissonance so the offender is motivated to reduce it. As Miller and Rollnick (in Clark 2005: 25) put it: "MI [Motivational Interviewing] considers 'confrontation to be the goal, not the counselor's style.' That is, the goal of helping is to create a 'self-confrontation' that prompts offenders to 'see and accept an uncomfortable reality.'" If offenders can be guided to confront a reality that is disquieting to them by themselves rather than having the counselor/officer point it out, they are more likely to accept it and become motivated to do something about it: "People are more persuaded by what they hear themselves say than by what other people tell them" (Miller and Rollnick 2002: 39).

Roll with Resistance. Now we arrive at the action stages; this is where you will likely meet with resistance. The Motivational Interviewing system says that you must "roll with resistance; that is, you must avoid arguments by reflecting feelings back on offenders and by turning problems back on them to work out for themselves. Too much resistance probably means that you have moved into the action phase prematurely and that you should retreat to the contemplative stage and try another strategy. Counseling is an art not a science. People cannot simply throw a switch onto a motivational track; you must know when to move forward and when to move back and this only comes with lots of experience. Dealing with resistance is more fully developed in the next chapter, as are specific plans of action for change.

Support Self-Efficacy. Finally, we arrive at the stage of supporting the offender's self-efficacy. *Self-efficacy* is essentially the confidence persons have in their self to successfully accomplish what they set out to do. You must reinforce any positive statements made by offenders that indicate a "can do" attitude, and your belief in their ability to change for the better may just become a self-fulfilling prophesy.

Lesson and Concerns

The primary reason for including the client-centered approach in this discussion is its emphasis on the offender/counselor relationship. Certainly, we all attend more to the concerns of those whose good graces we value than of those about whose judgments we do not care. Objective understanding and special techniques and stratagems are not necessary to bring about change in the type of relationship Rogers emphasizes.

Although you can apply client-centered counseling fruitfully in some counseling settings, as evidenced by its great popularity among counselors in general, we have to ask ourselves if it is practical in the criminal justice setting. Andrews and Bonta's (1998) review suggests too much focus on the relationship dimension to the exclusion of establishing anticriminal contingencies is ineffectual and may be harmful. Denise Kinsit (2000: 349) also criticizes this aspect of the theory. She writes that although it provides "a wonderful, enriching [counseling] environment... Do we allow sociopathic criminals to spend hours in therapy providing them insight into their morbid and inhumane delights without any form of direction or confrontation?"

The authors believe that unconditional positive regard, genuineness, and empathy as described here are the qualities we manifest only in a very real intimate love relationship with people who are truly special to us. Not being in such a relationship with offenders we counsel, is there a major conflict between being genuine and expressing the idea to offenders that we accept them unconditionally? Is there also a real danger that we will avoid necessary confrontation with an offender so as not to upset the close relationship deemed to be so important? Do we need to set conditions on our acceptance? Consider substituting "active concern for the well being of another" for "unconditional positive regard," when using the client-centered approach with offenders.

As a correctional counselor, positive regard for offenders has to be conditional. This does not mean that you refuse to accept the basic humanity of offenders or that you pass unnecessary judgment on their past behavior. What it does mean is that you must place unambiguous conditions on their future behavior and not be afraid to confront them and let them suffer the consequences when they fail to meet those conditions. Empathy, too, must be guided in responsible directions.

Nevertheless, establishing a positive working relationship with offenders is important. Unconditional positive regard, genuineness, and empathy are continuous variables that you present to offenders in varying degrees. The degree to which you do present them depends on the quality of your concept of self in interaction with the self-concepts possessed by offenders. While you cannot always be your "genuine self," you should not suffer a sense of personal failure if you feel a lack of acceptance of the offenders or an inability to empathize fully with their view of the world.

The addition of the Motivational Interviewing approach to the basic ideas of client-centered therapy has been welcomed with some enthusiasm in criminal justice (Clark 2005). Remember that Motivational Interviewing is an approach to treatment, not a form of treatment, and can be applied to any therapy/counseling theory. It has been welcomed because it is directive rather than nondirective in a subtle way in that the counselor craftily steers (directs) the offenders to confront themselves and direct themselves in positive prosocial directions. A meta-analysis of seventy-two studies using Motivational Interviewing found it highly effective (increasing the rate of change talk and decreasing the resistance to change) over the short term (an effect size of 0.77), which unfortunately decreased to an effect size of 0.30 in one-year follow-ups (Hettema, Steele, and Miller 2005). There are no magic bullets in this business.

A final point about the powerful influence of establishing positive relationships comes not from criminal justice or counseling research but from medical research. William Knaus and his colleagues at the George Washington University School of Medicine set out to discover what variable is most important to survival of patients in intensive care units (ICUs). Using advanced statistical techniques, they looked at such variables as technological sophistication, levels of professional expertise of physicians and nurses, prestige of the hospital, research funding, and patient/caregiver ratio. Their examination of 5,030 intensive care unit patients in a variety of hospitals across the United States over a period of five years found that none of these nominated variables was the crucial one. The crucial variable was the quality of the relationships that existed between doctors and nurses and between nurses and patients. The hospitals that allowed nurses to function semi-autonomously and to interact with patients at an emotional level were the hospitals with the best intensive care unit survival rates (Holzman 1986: 56). The researchers expressed their surprise at this finding; Carl Rogers would have responded with a knowing smile.

Perspective from the Field
Getting Back in the Race

By Lindsey Whitehead

Lindsey Whitehead is the chief probation officer of the Lucas County Probation Department, Toledo, Ohio. He was a probation officer and unit supervisor for seven years before becoming chief. He holds masters' degrees in guidance and counseling and public administration. He is also a Certified Alcoholism Counselor (CAC).

● ● ● ● ● ● ● ● ● ● ● ● ● ● ● ● ● ● ● ●

A few days ago as I was returning from lunch, I saw a young man who looked vaguely familiar to me leaving the probation department. As he approached me, he smiled and asked, "How are you, Mr. Whitehead? You don't remember me, do you?" I wasn't very sure of what the relationship between us had been, but after talking with him for a few moments, the memory was clear.

The last time I had seen him was in 1978, when I was his probation officer. He was eighteen or nineteen years old at the time, and was on probation for his first felony conviction as an adult. He had been convicted of robbing a carry-out store. This young man's social history was very typical of those who are in trouble with the criminal justice system. He was from a broken home, lived in poverty, was inadequately educated, unemployed, and his spirit had been demoralized.

During the time that he was on probation, he obtained his General Equivalency Diploma and enrolled in a vocational school to learn welding. Upon completion of training, he was immediately hired as a welder by a local company. But why is he here at the probation department? I wondered. "Is he in trouble again?" He explained apologetically that he had been caught with some cocaine and was now serving another term of probation. He further explained that this was the first time that he had been in trouble with the law for nine years and that he was still working as a welder with the same company and trying to be productive.

A few years ago, a young mother of beautiful twin girls was placed on probation for forgery. She had little motivation to do anything to try to improve her pathetic situation. But through the persuasion and leverage of the probation department and the court, she enrolled in the department's General Equivalency Diploma program. At first she didn't like it, but in time she became enthusiastic and was a willing participant. At the graduation ceremony, as her daughters looked on, she was extremely proud as she walked across the stage to be recognized for having completed her GED. She had come to realize that her efforts could result in positive changes in her life, and that, at the very least, her probation officer considered her worthwhile and cared for her.

There is nothing unique or unusual about these two cases. Similar experiences are repeated daily in probation and parole departments throughout the country. Pencil and paper no doubt can demonstrate a lack of success in the community corrections function, and perhaps this is so. However, those of us who are in the trenches often have the opportunity to see the human spirit triumphant over what could have been lost lives. A probation or parole officer cannot run the race for those who have dropped out, or for those who never got into the race in the first place. Yet, it is encouraging, if only occasionally, to see people pick themselves up and get into the race of life through the help of caring and professional probation and parole services.

Summary

Counseling differs from psychotherapy primarily in the depth and intensity of treatment. Psychotherapists attempt to restructure the basic personalities of patients with intrapersonal conflicts, whereas counselors deal with interpersonal conflicts and problems of everyday living. You should be alert to those offenders whose problems go beyond your professional ability.

There are similarities and differences between interviewing and counseling. Many of the techniques they use are the same. The quality of the self—your warmth, acceptance, and understanding—is the most important ingredient in both situations. In essence, counseling is an extension of the interviewing process. Counseling requires communication with offenders at a deeper level about more specific issues. You will accomplish this more easily if you have developed a positive relationship with them during the initial interviews.

Freudian psychoanalysis is a theory that offers some profound insights into human nature. It emphasizes the importance of the psychosexual stages of development, especially the importance of love at the earliest stages. The identification of defense mechanisms is useful in criminal justice, particularly denial, rationalization, fixation, displacement, intellectualization, and projection. You will never use the techniques of psychoanalysis in your dealings with offenders in the same way that you will use the techniques derived from other theories. Its usefulness to you as a criminal justice worker lies in its illumination of human nature.

Client-centered therapy shares with psychoanalysis its passive and nondirective approach. This theory asserts the absolute primacy of the offender/counselor relationship. Client-centered counseling rests on three attributes, which the counselor should possess and offer to offenders: unconditional positive regard, genuineness, and empathy. Since many psychological problems are the result of conditions that others attach to their acceptance of a person's self-worth, it is vital that counselors accept those offenders with whom they work, unconditionally as individuals of worth. The counselor also must be genuine (be completely himself or herself); and avoid pretensions, dishonesty, and game playing. The counselor's authenticity will provide a model for the offender to emulate. Counselors always should strive to improve their own authenticity.

The final necessary attribute is empathy. It is very difficult to achieve because it implies the ability to participate actively in the mindset of another, to actually walk in the person's shoes. Primary empathy is the communication to offenders of an initial basic understanding of what they are saying. Advanced empathy implies a deeper understanding, a reading between the lines. Empathy is something that is developed only by experience, by learning all you can about human behavior, and by really caring about what the offender is trying to communicate.

References and Suggested Readings

Andrews, D. and J. Bonta. 1998. *The Psychology of Criminal Conduct*. Cincinnati, Ohio: Anderson.

Austin, L. 1999. *The Counseling Primer*. Philadelphia: Accelerated Development Group.

Burke, B., H. Arkowitz, and M. Menchola. 2003. The efficacy of Motivational Interviewing: A meta-analysis. *Journal of Consulting and Clinical Psychology* 71: 843-861.

Clark, M. 2005. Motivational interviewing for probation staff: Increasing the readiness to change. *Federal Probation* 69: 22-28.

Cohn, A. 2002. Managing the Correctional Enterprise–The Quest for "What Works." *Federal Probation*, 66: 4-10.

Cullen, F. and P. Gendreau. 2000. Assessing Correctional Rehabilitation: Policy, Practice, and Prospects. In *Criminal Justice 2000*. Washington, D.C.: National Institute of Justice.

Egan, G. 1998. *The Skilled Helper*. Pacific Grove, California: Brooks/Cole.

Ellis, A. 1996. *Better, Deeper, and More Enduring Brief Therapy*. New York: Brunner/Mazel.

Evans, D., M. Hearn, M. Uhlemann, and A. Ivey. 1989. *Essential Interviewing: A Programmed Approach to Effective Communication*. Pacific Grove, California: Brooks/Cole.

Fine, R. 1973. Psychoanalysis. In *Current Psychotherapies*, R. Corsini, ed. Itasca, Illinois: Peacock.

Freud, S. 1961. *Civilization and its Discontents*. New York: Norton.

———. 1965. *The New Introductory Lectures on Psychoanalysis*. New York: Norton.

Gendreau, P. and R. R Ross. 1981. Offender Rehabilitation: The Appeal of Success. *Federal Probation* 45: 45-48.

———. 1987. Revivification of Rehabilitation: Evidence from the 1980s. *Justice Quarterly* 4: 349-407.

Gottfredson, M. and T. Hirschi. 1990. *A General Theory of Crime*. Palo Alto, California: Stanford University Press.

Harris, G. 1995. *Overcoming Resistance: Success in Counseling Men*. Lanham, Maryland: American Correctional Association.

Hartney, C. 2006. *U.S. Rates of Incarceration: A Global Perspective*. National Council on Crime and Delinquency, Oakland, California.

Hettema, J., J. Steele, and W. Miller. 2005. Motivational Interviewing. *Annual Review of Clinical Psychology* 1: 91-111.

Hill, C. and E. Nakayama. 2000. Client-Centered Therapy: Where Has It Been and Where Is It Going? A Comment on Hathaway (1948). *Journal of Clinical Psychology* 56: 861-875.

Holzman, D. 1986. Intensive Care Nurses: A Vital Sign. *Insight* 56. December.

Kinsit, D. 2000. Rogerian Theory: A Critique of the Effectiveness of Pure Client-Centered Therapy. *Counseling Psychology Quarterly* 13: 345-351.

Latessa, W., F. Cullen, and P. Gendreau. 2002. Beyond Correctional Quackery—Professionalism and the Possibility of Effective Treatment. *Federal Probation* 66: 43-50.

Lewis, W. 1989. *Helping the Youthful Offender: Individual and Group Therapies that Work*. New York: Haworth.

Lipsey, M. and F. Cullen. 2007. The Effectiveness of Correctional Rehabilitation: A Review of Systematic Reviews. *Annual Review of Law and Social Science* 3: 297-320.

Martinson, Robert. 1974. What Works? Questions and Answers about Prison Reform. *The Public Interest* 35: 22-54.

———. 1979. New Findings, New Views: A Note of Caution Regarding Prison Reform. *Hofstra Law Review* 7: 243-258.

Mayeroff, M. 1971. *On Caring*. New York: Harper and Row.

McLeod, J. 2003. *An Introduction to Counseling*, 3rd ed. Buckingham, England: Open University Press.

Meier, S. 1989. *The Elements of Counseling*. Pacific Grove, California: Brooks/Cole.

Miller, W. and S. Rollnick. 2002. *Motivational Interviewing: Preparing People for Change*. New York: Guilford.

Morgan, K. 1995. Variables Associated with Successful Probation Completion. *Journal of Offender Rehabilitation* 22: 141-153.

Pew Center on the States. 2009. *One in 31: The Long Reach of American Corrections*. Washington, D.C.: The Pew Charitable Trusts.

Reich, T. 1956. *Listening with the Third Ear*. New York: Grove.

Rogers, C. 1952. Client-Centered Psychotherapy. *Scientific American* 187: 66-74.

———. 1961. *On Becoming a Person*. Boston: Houghton Mifflin.

Sherman, L., D. Gottfredson, D. McKenzie, J. Eck, P. Reuter, and S. Bushway. 1997. *Preventing Crime: What Works, What Doesn't, What's Promising*. Washington, D.C.: U.S. Department of Justice.

Smith, D. 2006. Making sense of psychoanalysis in criminological theory and probation practice. *Probation Journal* 53: 361-376.

Stratton, J. 1975. Correctional Workers: Counseling Con Men. In *Correctional Casework and Counseling*. E. Peoples, ed. Pacific Palisades, California: Goodyear.

Van Vooris, P., M. Braswell, and D. Lester. 2000. *Correctional Counseling and Rehabilitation*. Cincinnati, Ohio: Anderson.

Walker, S. 2001. *Sense and Nonsense about Crime and Drugs: A Policy Guide*. Belmont, California: Wadsworth/Thompson.

Walsh, A. 1986. Love and Human Authenticity in the Works of Freud, Marx, and Maslow. *Free Inquiry in Creative Sociology* 14: 21-26.

Weinrich, S. 2006. Selecting a counseling theory while scratching your head: A rational-emotive therapist's personal journey. *Journal of Rational-Emotive & Cognitive-Behavioral Therapy* 24: 155-167.

CHAPTER 10

Directive Counseling: Theory and Practice

To love and to be loved is as necessary as the breathing of air. Insofar as we fail in loving, we fail in living. The most important thing to realize about the nature of human nature is that the most significant ingredient in its structure is love.

—Ashley Montagu

The theories we examined in the last chapter could be described as passive and nondirective: the counselor helps offenders to give birth to their own solutions for what ails them. To be sure, intrinsic motivation is better than extrinsic motivation, but as the hangman once said to the condemned as he placed the loop around his neck: "Good luck." The vast majority of offenders are not capable of arriving at the solutions we want them to arrive at without a great deal of direction. Giving direction is the action phase of the Motivational Interviewing model.

The theories presented in this chapter are very active, directive, and didactic, with equal involvement of the counselor and the offender. These theories—Transactional Analysis and Reality Therapy—were both formulated by traditionally trained psychotherapists who were dissatisfied with the passive methods of traditional psychoanalysis and the extraordinary length of time required for that type of treatment.

Both theories were designed to identify and deal with problem areas quickly, and are oriented toward cognitive rather than emotional approaches. The creators of the theories realized that most offenders must be actively assisted in their endeavors to become rational, responsible, whole individuals. They do however recognize the tremendous importance of the offender/counselor relationship and of the stages of the counseling process as presented in Motivational Interviewing.

The Laws of Thermodynamics and Criminal Offenders

Many learn about the first and second laws of thermodynamics in a physics or chemistry class and remember that they have something to do with energy. The first law is the good news, and basically states that energy cannot be created or destroyed, but it can be shifted around from one type to another. When we eat, we are taking in chemical energy that is used up by work or exercise, or is stored as fat. If we use up that energy in constructive ways, we become healthy and strong; if we store it as fat, we are in danger of falling afoul to all types of health problems. All life is about finding ways to use energy constructively.

The second law is the bad news. It tells us that in any closed system everything tends to disorder, and that this disorder can only increase with time. Your refrigerator, your car, you yourself, and the entire planet, are closed systems that eventually will experience what physicists call entropy (their measure of disorder). If you take an ice cube out of the refrigerator, it becomes disordered as heat flows out. If you want it to become ordered again, you have to apply outside energy to it by putting it back into the refrigerator to refreeze. The refrigerator itself becomes disordered when the electricity goes out; your car will not run without its source of energy, neither will you without your source, and neither will the planet without the ultimate source of all energy, the sun. In other words, if you want to defeat the second law of thermodynamics, you have to put outside energy into closed systems.

However, why are we discussing the laws of thermodynamic in a counseling text? The answer is that the second law has a little brother called Murphy's Law, which is applicable to all our lives. Murphy's Law states that anything that can go wrong eventually will, which is the nonscientist's way of saying that everything tends to disorder. Yet, we have seen that we can thwart the second law in the physical world by putting outside energy into closed systems to make them "go right," even though doing so comes with a price; electricity, gasoline, and food cost, but the price is worth it. The lesson is that to make things "go right" in our lives we have to put energy into them. If we want our health, career, family, and other social relationships, automobile, home, or anything else to "go right," they have to be highly ordered. If we do not put constructive energy into them, they will "go wrong" in so many ways.

Think about it: there are always more possible disordered states than ordered states. If we are complacent and irresponsible about our health, marriages, social relationships, careers, and the upkeep of our possessions, they will deteriorate and dissolve. It is only by assiduous attention to detail that we can halt the natural decent into chaos and enjoy well-ordered lives.

Offenders need to be aware of and understand Murphy's Law. Offenders need to know that they can either move forward to meet the challenges of the world in healthy and constructive ways or they can sit in a run-down trailer park gulping Budweisers and sucking on Marlboros waiting for "a break." They must come to know that the very laws of nature dictate that things just simply cannot get better unless they put energy into them to make them get better and that they have to make their own breaks. They must come to know that they are the "outside energy" that needs to be plugged into the things in their lives that affect them. You as the correctional counselor also serve as a temporary alternative source of outside energy holding the second law at bay until such time as offenders are able to marshal enough of it for themselves. The skills and techniques are directive counseling, which is your source of outside energy.

Jack Powell (2004) offers a five-stage model to get offenders to take control of their lives:

1. Willingness

2. Responsibility

3. Knowledge

4. Application

5. Maintenance

The first stage is the realization that offenders must be willing to change. Willingness opens the door to change; it is a choice to change the direction of the energy in their closed system rather than to continue to use energy concocting fruitless excuses. Willingness will come about more easily when you guide offenders to recognize the discrepancies and ambivalence in their lives.

The second stage is the acceptance of the fact that changing their lives is their responsibility alone. They must overcome any dependence on others and empower themselves. The correctional counselor helps them to make the initial decision, but it is the offender's life that is to blossom or wither. Here it helps to approach offenders from a strength-based perspective to build their sense of self-efficacy so that they become self-reliant. The operating principle is contained in the old saying: "Give a man a fish and you feed him for a day; teach him how to fish and he'll feed himself for life."

The third stage is knowledge (here is where you teach him or her to fish). Offenders are often woefully unaware of the steps that they must take to lead a responsible life, even if they desperately would like to lead such a life. Even if willing to change and to take responsibility for doing so, if offenders lack the requisite skills and knowledge to do so, they will fail. Counseling is a way to provide the needed skills and knowledge. Here begins the action phase of the Motivational Interviewing approach in which you guide offenders to the appropriate programs and classes that will provide them with the specific concrete tools for change.

The fourth stage is applying that skill and knowledge. All the knowledge in the world is useless if it is not applied. We probably all can provide countless examples of people who know that they should not smoke or overeat, but do, or know that they should exercise and get physical checkups, but do not. Knowledge must be applied to keep Murphy's Law at bay. Here you supply some of the extrinsic pressures to augment offenders' intrinsic motivation.

The fifth stage is maintenance. This one is difficult! How many dieters, with all the willingness, knowledge, and application in the world, will relapse after some time? This obviously requires long-term commitment. As they say in Alcoholics Anonymous: "Stick with it one day at a time." Responsible life can be achieved; millions of people have done so, and there is no reason that a fair proportion of your offenders cannot do it also with some guidance from you. Here is where we see how good you the counselor are at rolling with resistance, because relapse is a form of resistance. You will roll with it by acknowledging to the offender the difficulty of staying the course and by getting him or her to revisit all of the arguments for change that he or she hopefully voiced previously. We now turn to transactional theory as one means of helping offenders to achieve that goal.

Transactional Analysis

Transactional analysis (TA) is the brainchild of Eric Berne, a psychiatrist best known for his book, *Games People Play* (1964). TA is generally considered the first counseling theory to emphasize the role of interpersonal (as opposed to intrapersonal) factors in mental health (Nystul 1999). No matter what the origin of a problem disorder may be, it is always expressed interpersonally (Prochaska and Norcross 1994). The shift in emphasis from intrapersonal dynamics to interpersonal dynamics is the major departure of TA from the parent theory, psychoanalysis. TA stresses the cognitive and behavioral aspects of personality and places very little emphasis on emotions.

If a person gains emotional insight from TA, it is through the process of gaining intellectual insight and/or changing behavior patterns. Individuals achieve any type of insight or change by examining transactions between the offender and others. A transaction is simply the act of two or more people interacting together; analysis refers to the process of exploring and explaining those transactions. TA shares with psychoanalysis the assumption that human behavior is influenced rather profoundly by the events of early childhood, particularly events that told the child that he or she was loved or unloved.

Berne feels that the greatest strength of Transactional Analysis lies in its use of colloquial, simple, and direct terms that everyone can easily understand. As Berne stated (1966: 214):

> Transactional analysis because of its clear-cut statements rooted in easily accessible material, because of its operational nature, and because of its specialized vocabulary (consisting of only five words: Parent, Adult, Child, Game, and Script), offers an easily learned framework for clarification.

Offenders using Transactional Analysis soon acquire an easily understood, nonthreatening, and jargon-free vocabulary by which they can interact with the counselor to identify problem transactions. As Jacobs and Spadaro (2003: 106) put it: "Since many inmates are not very self-aware and have conflicts with other inmates, their family, and friends, TA is an excellent model to teach in a correctional setting."

Scripts. Scripts are "memory tapes" that we all carry with us in our heads. The most important scripts are recorded in early childhood because children tend to accept messages unquestioningly, lacking the maturity to do otherwise. The messages communicated by our parents during this critical period contribute strongly to future evaluations of ourselves as worthy ("OK") or unworthy ("not OK") people. By the time we become mature enough to question verbal and nonverbal messages regarding our OKness, any questioning is strongly directed and influenced by the powerful scripting we received in our most impressionable years. If the preponderance of messages told us that we were loved, respected, and appreciated, we will see ourselves as OK. If the preponderance of childhood messages were in the opposite direction, we will see ourselves as not OK. These evaluations of OKness tend to persist throughout our lives– regardless of the messages we receive in later life because of the deeply etched early recordings.

Related to these early recordings is the intense human need for what Berne calls *strokes*. People hunger for strokes, to be touched both physically and emotionally. If they do not receive these strokes, they will not develop into psychologically healthy human beings. According to Berne, we structure much of our time around the pursuit of positive strokes (seeking assurances that we are loved). Positive strokes lead to positive scripting tapes, and negative strokes lead to negative ones. Transactional analysis theorists believe that to change negative scripts into more positive ones, clients require direction from a strong "parent" figure in the form of a counselor.

Four basic life positions result from our scripting and act as backdrops throughout our lives in our interactions with others.

1. **"I'm not OK; you're OK."** This is a position commonly found in children. When they are punished for some transgression, they often feel "not OK." However, their godlike parents, upon whom they depend, are naturally OK in their little minds. You will find this life position in many offenders, especially among substance abusers. They frequently are depressed and will have what Glasser calls in Reality Therapy a failure identity. At least an offender with this life position will consider you OK, so you can concentrate on building up his or her own OKness.

2. **"I'm not OK; you're not OK."** This is the typical scripted life position of an abused child who was led to question the OKness of his or her parents rather early in life. A person like this views the world as a hostile and futile place, for the person is unloved and unloving.

3. **"I'm OK; you're not OK."** This, too, is the position of abused children who have questioned the OKness of their parents. However, they somehow have come to view themselves as OK from their own circumscribed perspective of OKness. They tend to be loners and to project blame for all their problems and actions onto others. The psychopath and chronic criminals operate from this life position in its extreme.

4. **"I'm OK; you're OK."** This is the life position from which correctional workers must operate. To do your job adequately, you must be convinced of your OKness; to do it well, you must strive to generate the offender's OKness. The goal of transactional analysis is

a relationship between counselor and offender with mutual convictions of "I'm OK; you're OK." That is, offenders must divest themselves of the negative scripts left over from childhood and find their own power and OKness.

Games. Games are counterproductive social interactions and are the result of individuals interacting with one another from one of the first three life positions. Transactional Analysis views games as exchanges of unauthentic strokes because ulterior motives are behind the strokes. The ultimate payoff in a game-playing relationship in which one's energy is structured around getting strokes (or giving them to those in positions of authority) is a storehouse of bad feelings that serve only to reinforce negative life scripts. It is only from an authentic "I'm OK; you're OK" position that individuals can engage in a meaningful, game-free, interpersonal relationship.

Games are very much a part of criminal justice supervision and counseling. You quickly must learn to identify and expose them, for they are dishonest and destructive. You might even find yourself playing games with the offenders. We already have mentioned one that officers might play in their law-enforcement role in the section on interrogation: ("Now I've got you, you son-of-a-bitch") when they are using offenders for power strokes. Another one often heard is "I'm only trying to help you," used by those gentler souls seeking acceptance strokes. Both of these games, of course, issue from an "I'm OK; you're not OK" position.

Offenders are very good at playing games–they have had lots of practice. You quickly will find out that they are much better at it than you are (take that as a compliment). A real value of Transactional Analysis for correctional workers is the ability it gives them to expose these games. Games that you will run into with frequency are "Poor me" (reaching for sympathy and "understanding"), "If it wasn't for . . ." and "Ain't it/I awful" (false remorse). Correctional workers who are acceptance seekers or who are ineffectual will easily fall for KIUD ("Keep it up, doc"). Such workers are suckers for offenders who tell them that they are doing a great job while continuing to behave irresponsibly. The payoff for KIUD offenders is that their counselors probably will let them get away with an awful lot of misbehavior in exchange for their dishonest strokes.

Yet another game, often seen in prison settings, is HDIGO ("How do I get out of here?"). Offenders soon learn to tell counselors just what they think they want to hear. They learn the latest social science explanation for their behavior and spew it back while shaking with "self-understanding" and "remorse." Of course, self-understanding and remorse are very much a part of your goals for each offender in your charge. However, it is imperative that they learn to distinguish the real goods from self-serving manipulation of the counseling setting. It is easy, and very human, to accept the game as the real thing because it gives you a feeling of success and a verification of your effectiveness as a counselor. Do not fudge the data for quick and easy self-strokes. If you accept the game as the real thing, the offender will have won the battle but will lose the war against his or her criminality.

Parent, Adult, Child

Parent (P), Adult (A), and Child (C), or PAC, are ego states: three distinct systems of feelings and thinking related to behavior patterns. Each ego state perceives reality differently: the parent judgmentally, the adult comprehensively, and the child pre-rationally. We all slip into and out of these states as we engage in our various transactions, with one usually being dominant over the others.

The *Parent* is critical, controlling, and moralizing, just like Freud's superego. There is a good side to the Parent, though. The good Parent is the Nurturing Parent who reacts to others with care, dignity, and respect, and makes demands that are not overbearing. This is the type of parental figure that the Transactional Analysis counselor is supposed to be. The critical or examining Parent is domineering, self-righteous, and authoritarian. The person who always operates in the parental mode (the constant Parent) excludes the reality of the adult mode and the playfulness of the child. Freud would probably call such a person "neurotic." You probably will not find the constant Parent represented much among offenders. If you do, they almost inevitably will be sex offenders against children.

The *Adult* is logical, realistic, and objective. He or she is much better able to judge the appropriateness of when to allow the less characteristic ego states their expression than is either the Parent or the Child because of a comprehensive and realistic integration of experiences. Like the Parent, though, the constant Adult will enjoy little feeling or spontaneity. Almost by definition, you will not find the Adult among criminal justice clientele. You will find many among your colleagues.

The *Child* is spontaneous, fun-loving, and irresponsible. Many offenders will be of this type. It is perfectly OK to be an Adapted Child, one who enjoys fun and laughter in appropriate ways and in appropriate settings. The problem is the Constant Child, one who consistently excludes the Adult and Parent and refuses to grow up and behave responsibly. The exclusion of these restraining influences means the exclusion of conscience, the total absence of which is psychopathy.

One or another of these ego states predominates in each individual. Berne denies the apparent equivalence of the ego states to the Freudian id (Child), ego (Adult) and superego (Parent) (1966). Berne's ego states are aspects of only the Freudian ego. Further, he states that whereas the id, ego, and superego are "theoretical constructs" (inferred entities not amenable to observation), his ego states are "phenomenological realities" (amenable to direct observation). According to Wood and Petriglieri (2005: 34): "Bernes' model of ego states is alive in a way that Freud's is not: One can see, feel, and recognize the shifts between ego states." Let us see how we can go about making these direct observations.

Structural Analysis

Structural analysis is the process of making these observations. Transactional Analysis counselors use this tool to make offenders aware of the content and functioning of their ego states. A goal of Transactional Analysis is that all offenders become an expert in analyzing their own transactions. If offenders become adept at identifying their characteristic ego states, they can understand better their options for change.

Ideally, the Parent, Adult, and Child should be distinctly separate states with clear-cut boundaries, as they are in part 1 of Figure 10-1 on the next page. Like the Freudian ego, the Adult holds the executive position but admits the Parent and Child, when appropriate. Two types of problem arise in personality structure as viewed in structural analysis: exclusion and contamination.

Exclusion occurs when ego-state boundaries are drawn so rigidly that free movement across them at appropriate times does not occur. The fundamentalist puritan who views all types of sensuous enjoyment as sin, or who lives out his or her

Figure 10.1 Ego States

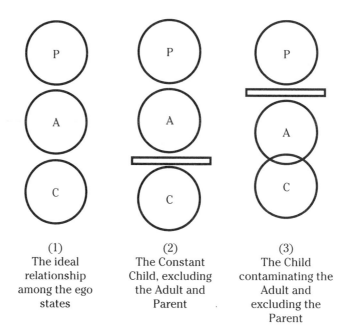

<table>
<tr><td>(1)
The ideal
relationship
among the ego
states</td><td>(2)
The Constant
Child, excluding
the Adult and
Parent</td><td>(3)
The Child
contaminating the
Adult and
excluding the
Parent</td></tr>
</table>

life bound by unexamined rules and strictures, is an example of the Constant Parent excluding the Child and the Adult. However, we do not worry much about puritans in our business. We do have to worry about the Child who excludes the Adult and Parent. This type of individual is the complete opposite of the Constant Parent, doing everything that the Constant Parent would not and doing nothing that the Constant Parent does do. Part 2 of Figure 10-1 illustrates this exclusion.

Contamination occurs when the content of one ego state becomes mixed up with the content of another ego state. We think of contamination in terms of the intrusion of either or both of the Parent or Child states into the rational boundaries defining the Adult state. Contamination of the Adult by the Parent often involves assumptions left over from our early scripting that distort objective thinking. In the chapter on interviewing, this author related how his prejudices regarding proper behavior for women intruded into his Adult when he interviewed the woman charged with sex crimes against children. This contamination ruined the effectiveness of his interview and his subsequent relationship with her. His Child certainly contaminated Bill Blogg's Adult. He wanted success, Susan, a grandiose wedding, and lots of money. Not too much wrong with that, only Bill wanted it "right now!" The childlike nature of his actions hardly needs belaboring. Contamination is illustrated in part 3 of Figure 10-1.

Complementary and Crossed Transactions

Transactions between and among individuals can be either complementary or crossed. The ideal transaction is a complementary one. A *complementary transaction* occurs when a verbal or nonverbal message (the stimulus) sent from a specific ego state is received and reacted to (the response) from the appropriate, or complementary, ego state of the receiver. In TA communication, complementary transactions occur when stimulus and response lines on a PAC diagram are parallel. The lines representing a crossed transaction in a PAC diagram are not parallel.

Figure 10.2 Complementary and Crossed Transactions

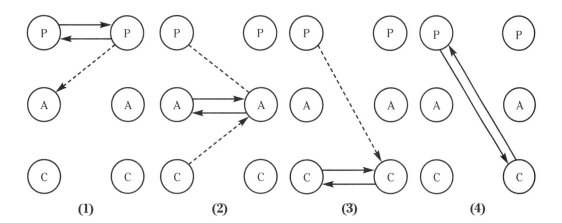

Crossed transactions occur when a stimulus sent from one ego state meets a response from an ego state other than the expected one. Crossed transactions usually cause trouble in our interpersonal relationships. However, crossed transactions sometimes are called for and are beneficial if the unexpected ego-state response leads the stimulus sender to adjust his or her ego state to a more appropriate one.

Figure 10-2 illustrates some complementary and crossed transactions. In part 1 we have Parent-Parent communication. This might be two new probation officers discussing the "ignorance" and "immorality" of "welfare mothers cheating on the system." The Adult may never enter into their conversation to explore the whys of the behavior. If one of the officers suddenly shifts into the Adult mode (indicated by the dotted line), the conversation may not be as congenial as when they were transacting at the same level. However, the shift may bring the conversation to a more appropriate Adult-Adult state, at which point the ego states are again complementary. Do not engage in complementary transactions just for the sake of congeniality when you know that some other ego state is more appropriate. As Rogers would say, "be genuine, be yourself."

Part 2 represents Adult-Adult communication. This could involve a prison counselor and the offender discussing a problem that the offender may be experiencing from a mutual "I'm OK, you're OK" position. The counselor does not contaminate the Adult by talking down to the inmate from the Parent ego state nor make light of the problem by joking about it from the Child ego state. The dotted lines indicate these problematic crossed transactions.

Part 3 illustrates a Child-Child transaction. An example of this would be you and your colleagues planning a Christmas party. Obviously, you should never interact with offenders at this level unless the occasion is something innocuous, such as sharing a joke. A crossed transaction in this context could be something like refusing to take part in the office festivities because they are "frivolous," or responding to the offender's well-meaning attempt at levity with a cold stare. These responses would both reflect a Critical Parent ego state intruding on what should have been an appropriate Child-Child transaction.

Part 4 illustrates a complementary transaction even though the parties are interacting from different ego states (the lines are still parallel). An example of this type of transaction would be a parole officer chastising an offender about some instance of irresponsible behavior. The officer confronts the offender from a parental ego state, and the offender responds as a child might when caught with a hand in the cookie jar: "You're always picking on me." This transaction is complementary because a Parent-Child stimulus has evoked a Child-Parent response. Had the officer confronted the offender from the Adult ego state and asked him or her simply to explain the behavior in question, and had the offender responded from the child state, the transaction would have been crossed.

Remember, any crossed transaction can lead to difficulties in interpersonal relations unless the crossover is purposely designed to shift the transaction to a level that is more appropriate to the immediate situation. In general, crossed transactions usually follow when one party or the other in the transaction operates from one of the first three life positions, which include various combinations of negative "not OK" attributions.

Jacobs and Spadaro (2003) offer many other examples of transactional analyses and suggest that you go the Transactional Analysis website at www.ta-tutor.com for many excellent additional resources relating to the theory

Lessons and Concerns

Transactional Analysis simply and effectively illustrates the consequences of feelings one has about the self or about others in everyday transactions. Berne's genius was his ability to transform complex ideas into colloquial language and easy-to-follow diagrams. Transactional Analysis has been accused of being little more than an over simplification of Freud's theory (Nystul 1999), but unlike Freudian concepts, the ideas of Transactional Analysis can be relayed with relative ease to offenders so that they may analyze their own feelings and behaviors. The emphasis on manipulation and game playing is especially useful for criminal justice workers. Finally, Transactional Analysis nicely describes in a neat linear fashion how early deprivation of love leads to a poor self-concept, how a poor self-concept usually leads to a negative image of others, and how these negative feelings lead to poor interpersonal relationships, a common phenomenon among offenders (Andrews and Bonta 1998).

On the other hand, Transactional Analysis may possess all the vices of its virtues. There is a danger that an inexperienced counselor simply may see counseling as an intellectual exercise consisting of identifying life positions and doing structural analyses. The very simplicity of the theory invites this type of truncated counseling. It is too easy to hide beneath covers stitched from nifty diagrams and cliché phrases such as "strokes" and "games." You have to involve the offenders' emotions and feelings in the counseling process as well as their heads. It is also a theory that makes it easy for manipulative inmates and offenders to con inexperienced (and sometimes even experienced) counselors.

Therefore, use an eclectic approach to counseling. They all have something to offer. Although some offer more than others, none of them offers everything. Used in conjunction with client-centered therapy's emphasis on the nature of the client/counselor relationship and the other theories we will discuss, Transactional Analysis could prove to be a powerful counseling tool for you.

REALITY THERAPY

Reality Therapy, founded by William Glasser (1972, 1975, 1998), has become a favorite counseling approach among those who work in community and institutional corrections. In fact, Glasser developed the basic ideas of Reality Therapy in a correctional setting while he was a staff psychiatrist at the Ventura School for delinquent girls in California (Austin 1999). Thus, and unlike other counseling models, it was developed around the realization that corrections workers have a professional responsibility to hold offenders accountable for their irresponsible behavior. Reality Therapy also shares with Transactional Analysis the happy quality of being relatively easy to understand.

According to (Rachin 1974: 52), the principles of Reality Therapy are common sense interwoven with a firm belief in the dignity of individuals and their ability to improve their lot. Its value is twofold: it is a means by which people can help one another, and it is a treatment technique, applicable regardless of symptomatology. It is simple to learn albeit somewhat difficult for the novice to practice. Experience, not extensive theoretical grooming, is the key to accomplishment.

Reality Therapy takes the outstanding features of the other approaches we have examined and integrates them into a single theory that caseworkers and counselors can apply without modification to offenders. Its basic goal is for clients (to use the vernacular) to "get real," and see themselves in charge of their own lives. In agreement with psychoanalysis, Reality Therapy recognizes that people have basic needs that must be met for healthy functioning. It also agrees that these basic needs are love and a sense of self-worth.

However, Reality Therapy does not dwell excessively on these deficiencies. Rather, like cognitive-behavioral therapy (discussed in the next chapter), it moves the offender away from bemoaning past privations and concentrates on present self-defeating behavior while teaching the offender how to become a more worthwhile person. It is also similar to cognitive-behavior therapy in that it is didactic, concerned with the present, and action oriented. Unlike cognitive behavioral therapy, however, it recognizes the problems inherent in calling antisocial behavior "irrational" and substitutes "irresponsible." This is not just a semantic disagreement. Reality Therapy views rationality in terms of positive or negative consequences of individuals' behavior for themselves. In contrast, Reality Therapy views responsibility in terms of positive or negative consequences of individuals' behavior both for themselves and for others.

As we have seen, one can be rational and engage in criminal activity; but, one cannot be responsible and do so. The reality counselor will not hesitate, however, to point out self-defeating irrational thinking, just as the cognitive-behavioral counselor will not hesitate to point out irresponsible behavior.

It follows that the reality counselor follows a hard-nosed, no-nonsense approach to offenders: behavior is either responsible or irresponsible, period. However, in common with client-centered counseling, reality counseling recognizes the importance of developing a warm, sensitive, and open relationship with the offender as a prelude to effective counseling. The counselor stresses positive regard (not "unconditional"), genuineness, and empathy without the somewhat syrupy and abstruse connotations client-centered therapy attaches to them. Reality Therapy stresses "a friendly, firm, trusting environment and a series of procedures that lead to change" (Wubbolding 1995: 386).

Theoretical Backdrop

William Glasser believes that those who engage in any type of self-defeating behavior, including criminality, suffer from the inability to fulfill basic needs adequately. If these needs are not met, the person will fail to perceive correctly the reality of his or her world and will act irresponsibly (by "reality" Glasser means that individuals realistically perceive not only the immediate consequences of their behavior but also the remote consequences). To act responsibly, offenders have to be helped to face the reality of the world in which they live, and to face reality, they must be helped to fulfill their basic needs. These basic needs are the need to love and to be loved, and the need to feel that we are worthwhile to ourselves and to others.

Glasser goes on to describe how these two needs are interrelated: "Although the two needs are separate, a person who loves and is loved will usually feel that he [or she] is a worthwhile person, and one who is worthwhile is usually someone who is loved and can give love in return" (1975: 11). The person who has these needs met develops a success identity and the person who does not develops a failure identity, which results in the inevitable descent into disorder.

A failure identity is analogous to what Berne calls an "I'm not OK" life position in Transactional Analysis, and a success identity is analogous to an "I'm OK" life position. Glasser feels that a person develops his or her basic identity (success or failure) by the age of four or five. If we are loved, and if we are allowed and encouraged to learn, explore, and experience, we will have a success identity. If we are not loved, if we are neglected and all our positive efforts are stifled, we will have a failure identity. The whole process of Reality Therapy can be seen as an effort to help offenders to develop a success identity, to enhance their self-esteem by guiding them from success (however small) to success.

Glasser's theory nicely ties in at the psychological level with the sociological insights of Hirschi's control theory (1977). The lack of a loving relationship with significant others (attachment) leads to a generalized lack of concern for the expectations and values of the larger society. This unconcern leads to a lack of commitment to a prosocial lifestyle, failure in school and in the job market, and a failure identity. Lacking this commitment, the individual is not involved with enough people with success identities who could model responsible behavior patterns for him or her. Rather, he or she is involved with others with failure identities who justify themselves and their behavior by developing a set of beliefs that are contrary to conventional morality. If early deprivations are severe enough, the individual may develop a psychopathic personality.

Although Reality Therapy refers to causes of behavior, it stresses that the causal understanding of behavior should not be viewed as excuses for that behavior. Glasser agrees with the client-centered perspective that individuals are ultimately responsible for their own identity because in everything we do "We choose what we do or what we do not do" (2004: 340, emphasis original).

Reality therapists fully understand that choices are shaped (limited or expanded) by our genetic endowment and developmental experiences, and by current environmental circumstances, but they insist that only by treating behavior "as if" it were a free choice makes change possible. Wubbolding and his colleagues (2004: 221) believe that if behavior is a choice, this means that it is within each person's ability to change it, and that: "This statement can be both frightening and encouraging. It is frightening because if you accept it, you can not longer blame society for your misery." Accepting responsibility for one's own behavior is encouraging and empowering. It enables us to realize that placing the responsibility for behavior on outside circumstances means that one's being is owned by them, and that the only way one can change is if those circumstances change. Offenders must come to reject that notion completely.

Also in common with client-centered therapy, Reality Therapy asserts that we have a "growth force" within us that strives for a success identity. Reality counseling attempts to activate that force by helping offenders to learn who they are, how to interact with others in a responsible fashion, and how they can be accepted more fully by others. It charges the counselor to be a continuing model of personal responsibility for the offender. This means, once again, that counselors must work on themselves with the objective of becoming the best kind of person they are capable of becoming.

In an interview with Evans (1982), Glasser enumerates seven steps that the counselor must take to effect meaningful changes in an offender's behavior. We can think of the steps (paraphrased below) as the action phase of Motivational Interviewing:

1. Get involved with offenders; develop warm rapport; show respect

2. Understand offenders' personal histories, but deemphasize them in favor of what they are doing now.

3. Assist offenders to evaluate their attitudes and behavior, and help them to discover how they are contributing to their failure identities

4. Explore with them alternative behaviors that may be more useful in developing a success identity

5. After the offender has made his or her decisions regarding alternatives, get a commitment in writing to a plan of change

6. Once the offender makes a commitment, make it clear that excuses for not adhering to it will not be tolerated. Emphasize that it is the offender's responsibility to carry out the plan.

7. Do not be punitive with offenders, but allow them to suffer the natural consequences of their behavior. Attempting to shield offenders from these natural consequences reinforces their irresponsibility and denies the self-directedness of their actions.

THE RELUCTANT/RESISTANT OFFENDER

The attitudes and techniques of Reality Therapy are particularly useful in counseling reluctant and/or resistant offenders. Most counseling theories assume a voluntary client who has actively sought out help with various problems, although studies indicate that most clients, even self-referred ones, exhibit some reluctance or resistance at times (Elliot 2002, Harris 1995). Some authorities even consider voluntary and welcomed interaction with the counselor as an essential prerequisite to the helping process (Slattery 2004). Reality Therapy makes no such assumption. It recognizes that the majority of offenders are inclined to demonstrate resistance to various degrees, and it hardly needs to be said that none of them is in your office by choice and "resistance to counseling by offenders is common" (Shearer and Ogan 2002: 74).

Recognizing Reluctance and Resistance. Offender resistance can range from a sullen silence, through game-playing by their telling you only what they think you want to know, to outright hostility. Most verbal resistance does not take the form of angry name-calling and challenges. It is more often a series of responses such as "I don't know," "maybe," "I suppose," and "you're the boss." In the vocabulary of Transactional Analysis, the offender is acting from a hostile child ego state. Nonverbal resistance can reveal itself in frequent finger and foot tapping, negative nodding, smirky smiles, and arm folding (a gesture of defiance and barrier erection). This type of verbal and nonverbal behavior can be very disconcerting to the beginning counselor who "only wants to help" (Transactional Analysis' nurturing parent) and who is desperately trying to be liked.

Since the counselor's intentions are good, and he or she is doing all the right things learned in Counseling 101 to establish rapport, the counselor finds it very difficult to accept the offender's reluctance and negativism (the transaction is crossed). All of us enjoy positive feelings, and few of us are very good at dealing with negative feelings, either our own or those of others, because it requires confrontation. Rather than acknowledging and dealing with negative feelings (rolling with them), the beginning counselor often tries to deny, downplay, or redirect them (trying to maintain an inappropriate complementary transaction). The negative feelings must be acknowledged and worked through with the offender (temporarily crossing the transaction so that it can be reinitiated at a more appropriate Adult-Adult level). The process requires extra effort on the counselor's part; it is all too easy to coast and avoid uncomfortable issues. A counselor with a strong and integrated self-concept is not afraid to encounter negativism and confrontation, and will "roll with resistance."

Reasons for Resistance

Why do offenders resist well-meaning attempts to help them? For one thing, they do not come into your office asking themselves what you can do for them. They are much more concerned about what you can do to them. You are a symbol of something that many offenders have spent a good proportion of their lives resisting: authority. To cooperate with you may well be an admission of weakness, in their way of thinking, and they are not overly anxious to admit weakness, especially to a representative of "the system."

Resistance is a form of a defense mechanism designed to protect the ego from the disconcerting feeling of the loss of autonomy (Elliott 2002). They also may not want to cooperate because what you want and what they want are two totally different things. You want them to act responsibly and obey the law; they want to get out of your office and out of your life. The very fact that offenders are in your office involuntarily is enough to generate resistance. The principle of psychological reactance tells us that whenever people's sense of autonomy is threatened by forcing them in some way to do something, even if they would otherwise have done it voluntarily, their natural inclination is to resist. Finally, you should ask yourself why offenders should want to surrender themselves to a person who they do not yet trust and to a condition they see as manipulative, for purposes with which they do not, at least for the present, agree.

Dealing with Resistance

As mentioned in Chapter 9, expect resistance. It may be a signal that you have entered an action phase too soon and that you should return to a more contemplative stage. Nevertheless, the expected has arrived, and you must deal with it. The first thing that you must do with resisting offenders is to acknowledge their feelings by reflecting them back and giving offenders the opportunity to vent them. You need not share an offender's views of you or "the system" to acknowledge the offender's right to hold them. Arguing back and forth with offenders at this point only will serve to strengthen their resolve. In fact, Elliot (2002: 43) contends: "that the most important issue in managing offender resistance to treatment is the avoidance of extended debates with offenders." You even may inform them that you do not particularly mind if they feel the way they do as long as they behave responsibly.

Offenders must be reminded that probation or parole (if this is the setting for the relationship) is a conditionally granted privilege and that they cannot be allowed to abuse it. You can inform resistant offenders that you understand their desire to get out of your office and out of your life and that you share this desire with them. That joint objective provides a mutually agreeable starting point. You then can begin to delineate the conditions under which your mutual goal can be successfully achieved. Emphasize that you are responsible for implementing the conditions of probation or parole and that you will not tolerate noncompliance. You also should state that both of you have a vested interest in successful completion of probation or parole, that it, therefore, should be a cooperative endeavor, and that a negative and/or hostile attitude could seriously impede your mutual goal: "Let's help each other out." In the vocabulary of transactional analysis, the laying down of expectations is a Parent-Child transaction, and the treatment contract to be negotiated is an Adult-Adult transaction.

This approach is the one that reality counselors would take. They have not punished the offender by returning hostility for hostility, but have let the offender know that he or she will be allowed to suffer the natural consequences of behavioral noncompliance. The counselor has been strong enough to deal with negative feelings in a constructive way by a judicious use of authority. The counselor has been straight with the offender without being overly authoritarian. The offender has been allowed the dignity of possessing and expressing attitudes contrary to the counselor's but has been told up-front that nonapproved (irresponsible) behavior is not permitted. Most offenders much prefer and respect directness rather than sweet-talking and beating around the bush. The counselor has enlisted the offender's help to accomplish a goal both parties desire. Involving the offender in a shared purpose gives meaning to the relationship. The ability to involve offenders in their own rehabilitation is the major skill of doing Reality Therapy (Powell 2004).

Jacobs and Spadaro (2003: 120) suggest that Reality Therapy provides an excellent tool for correctional counselors for getting to answer four questions:

1. "What do you want?"

2. "What are you currently doing?"

3. "Is what you are doing going to get you what you want?"

4. "What is your plan?"

With these questions answered and some form of general agreement between yourself and your reluctant or resisting offender achieved, you can then channel the discussion to specific areas of concern by the implementation of a concrete plan of action. Initial plans should be microscopic in their breadth to maximize the probability of successful completion. They also should be formalized in writing and signed by the offender and by you in the manner described by the "tentative treatment plan" form contained in the Chapter 7.

This step says to the offender, "Your signature attests to your commitment to achieve this goal, and mine attests to my commitment to support you in your endeavor." Adherence to such a plan begins the process of the development of a "can do" success identity and engenders a sense of responsibility for living up to agreements. Glasser himself has emphasized the importance of commitment: "Commitment is the keystone of Reality Therapy. It is only from the making and following through with plans that we gain a sense of self-worth and maturity" (Glasser and Zunin 1973: 303). Moreover, keeping the expectations of the action plan modest often overcomes an offender's reluctance to comply.

Treatment and Supervision Plans

Figure 10.3 Balancing Treatment Goals

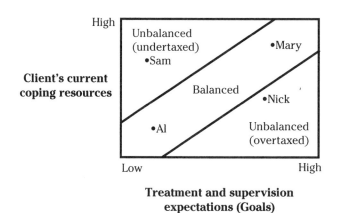

Balance. To minimize reluctance, resistance, and the probability of failure, treatment and supervision plans should be balanced with the offenders' present coping resources. You know these resources—intelligence and educational levels, financial situation, self-concept, strength of interpersonal relationships, and so on—from previous interviews and the needs assessment scale. Similarly, you should be aware of problem areas to be addressed in the treatment and supervision plans. Balanced plans are those whose demands on offenders should neither undertax nor overtax the resources they have available to implement them. Figure 9-3 illustrates the principle of balanced plans.

The diagram has three sections: one balanced and two unbalanced. The upper-left triangle represents an unbalanced condition in which high coping resources are paired with low treatment expectation. The lower-right triangle represents the opposite condition. Sam is in the undertaxed section because he has high coping resources but low demands have been placed on his resources. Sam will be quite happy and content if you allow him to slide right along without having to do anything toward correcting problems that led to his criminal behavior. Of course, Sam may be a first offender who needs no treatment plan and who is best left alone. However, if there are clear problem areas that may lead him to reoffend, you must take advantage of whatever strengths are represented by his relatively high-coping resources for his growth toward responsibility.

Nick's situation is the opposite of Sam's. Heavy treatment demands have been made on his limited coping resources. The dilemma here is that Nick's low level of resources (his intellectual and temperamental capacities) is the very reason that more intense treatment is required. Because his resources are deficient, heavy demands are made on him to correct the deficit. Yet, the lack of resources indicates that he probably will not be able to meet those demands at present. Thus, Nick represents a type of "Catch-22" situation. If you insist on maintaining Nick's present level of treatment, you will be setting him up for resistance and failure, and the consequences that go with this. You must lower present treatment demands on Nick so that they are commensurate with his present capacities to cope with them. As his capacities increase, you then may renegotiate more demanding treatment goals with him.

The treatment goals set for Al and Mary are balanced with their present coping resources. Mary is considered to have coping resources equal to Sam's, but she is being challenged to use them for personal change and growth. Al has extremely low coping resources and thus probably needs a higher level of treatment than Mary. However, his present resources are not sufficiently strong to allow for the same level of treatment. As his resource strength increases (that is, as he slowly builds up a success identity) the demands that you negotiate with him may increase as well. Do not undertax or overtax the offenders' coping resources. Rather, move them slowly toward the ultimate goal one simple step at a time.

Simplicity. To change a failure identity to a success identity, a good plan should be the following:

- Uncomplicated, simple, unambiguous, concrete, to the point: "Attend AA tonight at 6 o'clock."

- Active—something to do, not stop doing: "Attend AA tonight at 6 o'clock," not "Stop drinking alcohol."

- Something that can be done as close to "right now" as possible. "Attend AA tonight at 6 o'clock."

- Entirely dependent on offender's actions for fulfillment, not contingent on the actions of others: not "Attend AA tonight at 6 o'clock if your wife/husband lets you off doing the grocery shopping."

- Something that can be done every day, or as often as possible: "Attend AA tonight at 6 o'clock, and every Tuesday and Thursday at the same time and place for the next month."

- Specific as to what, where, when, how, and with whom it is to be done: "Attend AA tonight at 6 o'clock at St. Anthony Church

> on Pine Street. You (the counselor) will pick me up at my home for the first meeting to introduce me to other members."

The first plan need not be quite so active as this example. It can be something as simple as being on time for the next appointment. Whatever the plan may be, put it in writing and have the offender and you sign it.

Orientation toward Progress

Design subsequent plans to build on the offenders' strengths rather than on their obvious weaknesses (the strength-based approach). Again, the idea is to build a success identity. Too early an emphasis on major weaknesses creates too great a chance of failure, thus reinforcing the offenders' failure identity and generates further reluctance and resistance. For instance, if JoAnn lacks a high school diploma and all indications are that she could successfully complete a General Equivalency Diploma (GED) program, show her that you have confidence in her capabilities and try to secure an agreement from her to enroll in such a program. Do not forget, though, to balance this goal with her capacities. Do not insist that she commit herself if she is overly reluctant. Instead, you must persuade her to at least take a placement test. She may well be more receptive to the entire program if the test shows that she could do well. A study comparing rearrest rates between probationers enrolled in a GED program and a matched group of probationers not enrolled found that those enrolled in the program were significantly less criminally involved over a three-year period (Walsh 1985).

The sense of personal accomplishment, the sense of participating in a socially valued endeavor, the anticipation of legitimate employment, and the idea that the 'system' finds one worthy enough to make an investment in time and resources to provide one with a second chance, may be sufficient to stop an incipient criminal lifestyle (Walsh 1985: 76).

The secret of counseling in criminal justice, then, is to temper your necessary authority to direct your offenders' actions along acceptable avenues while always being aware of, and showing a concern for, their basic humanity. Try to view offender resistance as a normal response to coercion, perhaps even a psychologically healthy one. Examine your own resistance to self-growth and development, and examine your own behavior with offenders to see if you are perhaps doing something to generate resistance.

For instance, you may be a little too directive, too authoritarian, or in too much of a hurry to accomplish your goals. Especially examine the possibility that your goals for the offender are not balanced with the offender's present level of coping resources. As Newman has put it (1961: 38): One of the first major accomplishments of treatment comes about when the offender becomes aware, both intellectually and emotionally, that the officer represents not only authority with the power to enforce certain restraints and restrictions but that he [or she] is also able to offer material, social and psychological aids.

We must not forget that counseling is a very difficult and sometimes draining enterprise. You cannot expect to be an expert at it by simply reading a book, but with experience and caring you will become better and better at it and begin to develop your own style. As Peoples puts it, treatment is often a "maze," but the significant point to emphasize is do something. Shelve the paper work, forget the coffee, get out of the office–and counsel. Risk a little involvement with the human beings on your caseload. Learn, teach and grow with them in experiencing the most vital quicksilver of all, human behavior (1975: 372).

Lessons and Concerns

Reality Therapy is a relatively simple method of counseling that stresses responsible behavior, and professionals can apply it fruitfully. Its "one small step at a time" approach to developing offenders' success identities is particularly useful. Also very useful is its direct and assertive stance that fosters a no-nonsense, but warm and offender-involved relationship. Its assertion is that, at bottom, the origin of many offenders' problems lies in early and protracted deprivation of love.

Finally, a number of studies have concurred with Rachin's (1974: 53) conclusion that "Correctional clients who have proven least amenable to conventional treatment methods respond well to Reality Therapy." For instance, a study from Hong Kong (Chung 1994) showed that Reality Therapy for three-to-six months prior to release significantly increased self-esteem and a sense of responsibility among incarcerated juveniles who received therapy compared with a matched group who did not.

At times it may be necessary to resort to the vocabulary of Transactional Analysis when explaining Reality Therapy. By doing so, you bring the concepts home more strongly. Offenders also will better understand the supervision and counseling process if you introduce them to this simple vocabulary, which is the great strength of Transactional Analysis. The integration of this vocabulary into the reality therapist's repertoire should prove very useful.

EXERCISES IN PRIMARY AND ADVANCED EMPATHY

The exercise in interviewing emphasized practice in listening to what your partner had to say. In these exercises in counseling, you will be taking a more active part. Not only will you be intensely listening to your partner, but you will be communicating to him or her that you understand his or her perspective. You will use all of the techniques outlined in the chapter on interviewing, including the use of paraphrasing, clarifying, and reflecting feelings. Do not be content with vague statements from your partner; make him or her cite specifics.

If you are the student being counseled, choose for discussion a topic of concern to you. Choose one with emotional content, such as the loss of a loved one, the breakup of a romantic relationship, the inability to get along with someone of importance to you, or a perceived personal defect. Such topics make for realistic counseling sessions for both partners. You will gain experience of an offender's feelings when revealing intimate information, and the counselor will gain some experience in attempting to pull out deep feelings that the offender may be reluctant to express. However, please do not feel obligated to choose a topic that is too painful to discuss with an inexperienced counselor. This exercise should be both productive and relatively safe. Therefore, you should be given ample time to decide on a topic.

After you have been through a short counseling session, you and your partner should put your heads together and try to identify strategies for understanding and/or ameliorating the problem discussed. Perhaps you could do some structural analyses on the offender's important relationships. Do you see a pattern of crossed transactions? What is the offender's typical ego state? Does the offender agree? Is his or her usual state consistent with what Berne would predict from the offender's history of strokes? How about irrational ideas that he or she may be harboring? If the counselor did not identify them, maybe you now can do it together as a team. Finally, can you together define a simple plan to work on to eliminate the problematic behavior or feelings the offender experienced. You should find these exercises fun if approached from a mutual "I'm OK; you're OK" position.

Counseling "Real" Offenders

The location of both male and female correctional institutions close to Boise State University affords this author and his students the luxury of going to these institutions to interview and counsel real offenders. However, those not enjoying such proximity also can get the feel of counseling real offenders. If you have written presentence investigations as interviewing and assessment exercises, your instructor may wish to use them as the basis for providing practice in counseling with a criminal justice flavor. The student who initially wrote the PSI again can team up with the same partner to explore more fully the problems and concerns discovered during the PSI process. These problems are many: alcoholism, child molestation, drug abuse, negative self-concept, anger and aggression, and so forth. The student counselor should determine what referrals, if any, might be beneficial for the offender. Explore these problems in turn from each of the three counseling perspectives in this chapter, and then devise some simple "success identity" plans appropriate to the offender.

If you are role-playing the offender, then prior to the counseling session you should think deeply about being in the offender's shoes (empathy) so that you can present a realistic challenge to your partner's developing counseling skills. Much of your partner's success in this exercise will depend upon how well you are able to capture the feelings of the offender. An added bonus for you will be a greater ability to view the world from the offender's perspective.

Perspective from the Field
When Cultures Clash: Resistance and Persistence

By Roman C. Pena

Mr. Pena received his bachelors and his master's degrees in public administration from Idaho State University. He spent four years with the Utah Department of Corrections as a correctional counselor at a halfway house. He is currently a probation and parole officer with an intense supervision caseload.

● ●

I had only been in the intensive supervision program for three weeks when I was notified that I would be getting a new parolee, "Casey Jones." Reviewing Casey's inmate file and conversing with various sources, I became aware of Casey's Aryan Brotherhood affiliation. The Aryan Brotherhood is a white supremacist group that is very active and powerful within prison walls. Well, here's Roman, very much a non-Aryan, going to be this racist's parole

---

officer. Although Casey's involvement in the Brotherhood was minimal, just the fact that he chose to identify with this group and their values was enough for me. Hence, I immediately contrived ways of defending myself in the event of a confrontation.

Sure enough, Casey was seated across the interviewing table the next day. His face and mannerisms displayed hate and anger. I knew that he knew about me from his own sources. As I asked him the required questions and advised him of his responsibilities, he would respond with abrasiveness and sarcasm. It was tempting to retaliate, but I knew that it was necessary to maintain a professional demeanor.

The first two months of continual daily face-to-face visits were uneventful. Casey's attitude did not improve, and I often hoped that he would abscond from supervision. Nevertheless, he was content in doing as little as possible in most areas of concern, and he managed to stay within the "gray zones" of behavior and attitude. His welcoming remarks to me at home visits were, "Ya, what do you want?" and "Not you again!" His acquisition of a guard dog (which once nipped the back of my leg) became an object in our power struggle. Casey enjoyed watching my approach to the front door, as I tended to proceed with some trepidation. His enjoyment was short-lived as the dog befriended me.

Two more months passed until Casey experienced the setback of being laid off from his job. I could not help feeling that his negativism was a factor in his layoff. Casey started showing signs of worry. Christmas was only three weeks away and the job market was stagnant. One day an employer from a local mobile home factory called me up and asked me if I knew of someone who would like a job installing mobile home windows. I quickly went and notified Casey. He got the job. From that point on he began to be more friendly. He would even greet me at the door with a friendly "Hello!" He began to share personal problems. I listened intently and offered guidance when possible. He thought I was "one of a kind." Casey completed his six-month intensive parole period and was transferred to regular parole supervision.

Casey's new parole officer was—are you ready for this?—a Mr. Rodriguez. Mr. Rodriguez was firm yet fair with Casey. He told him that there would not be any sidetracking on cultural issues. Compliance with supervision standards was to be the priority. Casey agreed to cooperate with him the best that he could. One day Casey called Mr. Rodriguez on the telephone. Mr. Rodriguez's face showed concern and empathy as he consoled Casey on the death of his newly born son. This was a major turning point in Casey's life. He became increasingly receptive to assistance and cooperative in matters of supervision.

As I now submit Casey's final recommendation for discharge to the parole board, I remember our first two months in the program together. I have witnessed a miracle in human relations, not only in Casey but also in myself. Casey's departing comments to me were, "You know, you're not so bad after all—for a Mexican. Thanks for everything." For some reason, his Aryan values and my Mexican culture seemed so insignificant.

Summary

The laws of thermodynamics have applicability to everything in the universe, including human affairs. When applied to human affairs, the second law has been called Murphy's Law, which states that if anything can go wrong, it will. The point being made is that everything tends toward disorder unless strong efforts are put forth to prevent it. We presented the five stages of responsible behavior as a guideline for thwarting Murphy's Law.

This chapter has outlined two counseling approaches often used in criminal justice settings. These theories have a place in corrections because they are relatively easy to understand and apply, emphasize the offender's own responsibility for change, and include equal involvement of offender and counselor.

Transactional Analysis is built around five simple words: Parent, Adult, Child (the ego states), game, and script. Much of our behavior is a playback of scripts laid down during infancy and childhood. The type of scripts we have in our heads depends on the quantity and quality of the strokes (love) we received early in our lives. Our scripting leads to the four basic life positions from which we carry out our transactions with others: "I'm not OK; you're OK," "I'm not OK; you're not OK," "I'm OK; you're not OK," "I 'm OK; you're OK." The large majority of offenders will be operating from one of the first three life positions. We must strive to conduct all of our transactions from the "I'm OK; you're OK" life position.

Parent, Adult, and Child are three distinct ego states we slip into and out of during our various transactions. Offenders tend to operate mostly from the Child ego state. Many of them exclude the Parent altogether, and their Adult states frequently are contaminated by the intrusion of the Child. When interacting with offenders, you should be operating from the Adult ego state. You also should strive to get offenders more involved with their Adults.

Reality Therapy views self-defeating behavior as being the result of not having one's basic needs adequately met. These interrelated needs are the need to love and be loved and the need to feel worthwhile. People who do not have these needs met tend to develop a failure identity. Your task is to assist offenders to develop success identities by becoming actively involved with them.

Reality Therapy is especially useful in dealing with resistant and reluctant offenders. You will often run into this type of offender in the criminal justice field. Offenders resist your help because you are a symbol of authority, and they have spent much of their lives resisting authority. They also resist because they are not in voluntary association with you. You must recognize and confront their resistance rather than ignoring or downplaying it. Allow them the dignity of their opinions, but make it clear that you will not tolerate behavioral nonconformity. Indicate that you will allow them to suffer the natural consequences of nonadherence to the conditions of their supervision.

To minimize resistance, and to develop offenders' success identities, treatment plans must be balanced with their present coping resources. Neither overtax nor undertax offenders' coping resources. Overtaxing invites resistance, and undertaxing is not growth producing. Treatment plans should be as simple and as concrete as possible, and they should be in writing and signed by both parties.

References and Suggested Readings

Andrews, D. and J. Bonta. 1998. *The Psychology of Criminal Conduct*. Cincinnati, Ohio: Anderson.

Austin, L. 1999. *The Counseling Primer*. Philadelphia: Accelerated Development Group.

Berne, E. 1964. *Games People Play*. New York: Grove Press.

———. 1966. *Principles of Group Treatment*. New York: Oxford University Press.

Brown, J. and R. Pate, eds. 1983. *Being a Counselor: Directions and Challenges*. Monterey, California: Brooks/Cole.

Chung, M. 1994. Can Reality Therapy Help Juvenile Delinquents in Hong Kong? *Journal of Reality Therapy* 14: 68-80.

Elliott, W. 2002. Managing Offender Resistance to Counseling—the '3R's." *Federal Probation* 66: 43-50.

Evans, D. 1982. What Are You Doing? An Interview with William Glasser. *Personnel and Guidance Journal* 61: 460-462.

Glasser, W. 1972. *The Identity Society*. New York: Harper and Row.

———. 1975. *Reality Therapy: A New Approach to Psychiatry*. New York: Harper and Row.

———. 1998. *Choice Theory*. New York: Harper and Row.

———. 2004. A New Vision for Counseling. *The Family Journal* 12: 339-341.

Glasser, W. and L. Zunin. 1973. Reality Therapy. *In Current Psychotherapies*, R. Corsini, ed. Itasca, Illinois: F. E. Peacock.

Harris, G. A. 1995. *Overcoming Resistance: Success in Counseling Men*. Lanham, Maryland: American Correctional Association.

Hirschi, T. 1977. Causes and Prevention of Juvenile Delinquency. *Sociological Inquiry* 47: 322-41.

Jacobs, E. and N. Spadaro. 2003. *Leading Groups in Corrections: Skills and Techniques*. Alexandria, Virginia: American Correctional Association.

Lytle, M. 1964. The Unpromising Client. *Crime and Delinquency* 10: 130-134.

Newman, C. 1961. Concepts of Treatment in Probation and Parole Supervision. *Federal Probation* 25: 34-40.

Nystul, M. 1999. *Introduction to Counseling: An Art and Science Perspective*. Boston: Allyn and Bacon.

Peoples, E. 1975. Sorting from the Treatment Maze. In *Readings in Correctional Casework and Counseling*. E. Peoples, ed. Pacific Palisades, California: Goodyear Publishing.

Powell, J. 2004. Five Stages to Responsible Human Behavior. *International Journal of Reality Therapy* 23: 27-30.

Prochaska, J. and J. Norcross. 1994. *Systems of Psychotherapy: A Transtheoretical Analysis*. Pacific Grove, California: Brooks/Cole.

Rachin, R. 1974. Reality Therapy: Helping People Help Themselves. *Crime and Delinquency* 20: 45-53.

Shearer, R. and G. Ogan. 2002. Measuring Treatment Resistance in Offender Counseling. *Journal of Addiction Offender Counseling* 22: 72-82.

Slattery, J. 2004. *Counseling Diverse Clients: Bringing Context into Therapy*. Belmont, California: Brooks/Cole.

Walsh, A. 1985. An Evaluation of the Effects of Adult Basic Education on Rearrest Rates among Probationers. *Journal of Offender Counseling Services and Rehabilitation* 9:69-76.

Wood, J. and G. Petriglieri. 2005. Transcending Polarization: Beyond Binary Thinking. *Transactional Analysis Journal* 35: 31-39.

Wubbolding, R. 1995. Reality Therapy Theory. In *Counseling and Psychotherapy: Theories and Interventions*, D. Capuzzi and D. Douglas, eds. Columbus, Ohio: Merrill.

Wubbolding, R., J. Bricknell, L. Imhoff, R. Kim, L. Lojk, and B. Al-Rashidi. 2004. Reality Therapy: A Global Perspective. *International Journal of the Advancement of Counseling* 26: 219-228.

CHAPTER 11

Cognitive-Behavioral Approaches

"Nothing is good or bad, but thinking makes it so."

— Shakespeare's *Hamlet*

This chapter deals with cognitive-behavioral approaches to offender treatment. John McLeod (2003: 123, 139) asserts that: "The cognitive-behavioural approach represents the most overtly 'scientific' of all major therapy orientations"... probably because there is "a strong emphasis on measurement, assessment, and experimentation," ...and because "it stresses that therapists should also be scientists and integrate the ideas of science into their practice." This may be so, but the techniques of cognitive-behavioral counseling have been around a long time.

Albert Ellis (1989: 5) claims that great religious leaders such as Buddha and Jesus were basically cognitive-behavioral therapists, "and their followers were, in a sense, clients." These and other great religious leaders essentially were trying to get people to change their behavior—from short-run hedonism to prudence, from cruelty to compassion, from hate to love, and from immoral behavior to moral behavior—by appealing to their rational self-interest (make these changes and you will go to Heaven/attain Nirvana, and you will feel pretty good about yourself as well).

Changing antisocial and self-destructive behavior into prosocial and adaptive behavior by appealing to offenders' best interests is the nuts and bolts of correctional treatment. If we were able to fuse Freud, Glasser, Berne, and a few other counseling luminaries into one "mega-therapist" with all the warmth and techniques in the world and then set them about counseling offenders, few would change their habitual ways of behaving unless they come to believe that it is in their best interests to do so.

Cognitive-behavioral therapy includes a variety of specialized interventions, the common element among which is: "an emphasis on broad human change, but with a clear emphasis on demonstrable, behavioral outcomes achieved primarily through changes in the way an individual perceives, reflects upon, and, in general, thinks about their life circumstances" (Wilson et al. 2005: 173). Cognitive-behavioral therapy is about the belief that changes in thought processes lead to changes in behavior, and, thus, those thought processes must be changed before behavior can change.

Unlike psychoanalysis, transactional analysis, client-centered therapy, and reality therapy, the cognitive-behavioral approach is difficult to define. It might be said that cognitive-behavioral therapy is a systematized eclectic theory. As Vennard, Sugg, and Hedderman (1997: 5) inform us: "Cognitive behaviourism is not a unified, distinct psychological theory or method but a term given to a range of interventions derived from the following three psychological theories." They then go on to identify behaviorism, cognitive theory, and social learning theory as the component parts of cognitive-behavioral therapy. Let us briefly look at these component parts.

Behaviorism is a theory that asserts that behavior is determined by its consequences. The consequences of any particular behavior are either rewarding or punishing to various degrees. If a behavior is rewarding, it is said to have been reinforced and, therefore, likely to be repeated. If a behavior is punished, it is less likely to be repeated. Future behavior thus is contingent on the ratio of rewards to punishments a person has experienced following a particular behavior in the past. Criminal behavior has many consequences that are both rewarding and punishing, but as we saw in Chapter 3, many criminals are overly sensitive to rewards and relatively insensitive to punishments. It has even been proposed that criminal behavior is intrinsically rewarding to some chronic criminals because the risks involved arouse the same reward/pleasure systems in the brain that drugs and other substances do (Fishbein 2003; Gove and Wilmoth 2003). The behavioral theorist, however, maintains that the level of sensitivity has been shaped by previous experience and thus can be changed by shaping it in the opposite direction.

Many of the techniques of pure behaviorism (classical and operant conditioning) cannot be implemented by correctional workers, particularly by community corrections workers, because they depend primarily on the ability of the counselor to shape behavior by rewarding or punishing such behavior as soon as possible after it is performed. This ability, of course, requires that the therapist have almost complete control of the environment in which the shaping is to take place (such as so-called token economies in institutional settings, therapeutic communities, or halfway houses). Such control is perhaps achievable to some extent inside prisons, but not in community corrections. However, the principal behavior is governed by its consequences. That is, offenders must come to understand the maladaptive consequences of their criminal behavior.

Glasser's (1972) use of contracts, discussed in the previous chapter, is an example of the application of this principle. The feeling of accomplishment, rewarded by the positive response of the corrections worker for fulfilling it, is reinforcing, just as allowing the natural consequences of not fulfilling the contract is punishing. In other words, the offender's behavior is the focus, what he or she has done, not what he or she thinks or believes. The assumption is that changes in thinking will follow behavioral change.

Cognitive theorists agree that ultimately, maladaptive behavior has been shaped by experience. However, they assert that at a more proximal level, self-defeating behaviors are the result of unproductive thought patterns relating to these past experiences (Austin 1999). We can do nothing about past experiences, but we can do something to put the way we think about those things into proper perspective.

After all, thinking, not a series of old experiences, is the most immediate pre-cursor of our behavior. We may be able to trace a straight line from those experi-ences to the way we think about certain situations, but we still can change our behavior in those situations by changing our thinking, for as the Greek philosopher Epictetus (50-130 A.D.) was fond of saying: "Men are not disturbed by things but by the view they take of things." For the cognitive counselor, criminal behavior is the result of faulty views of things and faulty thinking (dwelling on the past, egocentric thinking, and "I can'tism," among numerous other thoughts), or as we like to say in corrections, "stinkin' thinkin'."

Social-learning theory is essentially a sociological view of socialization. Behav-ior is not only learned in stimulus/response/reward/punishment fashion as behav-iorists assert, but also learned by modeling and imitation. That is, people observe the behavior of others and come to deem it appropriate or inappropriate for them-selves. This has more to do with the status of the person or persons we model our-selves on than with rewards or punishments, although the psychological rewards of successful imitation of valued others cannot be overlooked. A major difference be-tween social learning and cognitive theory is that the former consider cognition as only one "link in a behavior-cognition-environmental loop that gives primacy to none of these components..." and that "cognitions are mediators, whereas in cognitive ther-apy they are causes as well" (Arkowitz and Hannah 1989: 152-153). The primary con-tribution of social learning theory to cognitive-behavioral therapy is the teaching of social skills and problem-solving training (Vennard, Sugg, and Hedderman 1997).

Although behaviorist and social learning concepts are incorporated into cog-nitive-behavioral counseling, what actually is practiced is cognitive therapy with some behavioral and modeling techniques applied, when possible. The theories, both directive and nondirective, that we have examined so far can be seen as cognitive-behavioral in some sense, since they all engage in "talk therapy" with the aim of changing the client's thought patterns and behaviors.

What differentiates cognitive-behavior therapies from the others we have en-countered is that uncovering, challenging, and changing maladaptive thought pat-terns takes on a central role in treatment. Cognitive behaviorists acknowledge that we may be driven to some extent by unconscious processes (as claimed by psychoana-lysts), and that our behavior is shaped to some extent by external contingencies (as claimed by behaviorists). However, they assert that most of our behavior is guided by processes of which we can easily be made aware, even though they normally are not a part of our awareness. These processes are the thought processes that define our reality for us. The definitions of reality (our thoughts, attitudes, and opinions about others and about situations) we hold are more important to the way we act than what is objectively real. This concept is captured nicely in sociology's famous

Thomas' Theorem: "If men define situations as real, they are real in their consequences" (cited in Walsh 2002: 121).

Changing Criminal Minds

Criminals think differently than the rest of us–who ever doubted it? The idea of criminals thinking differently from the rest of us, however, was something of a radical idea in the 1970s when blaming criminal behavior on factors entirely external to the offender was in vogue. The idea of criminal thinking patterns originated with psychiatrist Samuel Yochelson and psychologist Stanton Samenow, whose failed treatment methods based on "outside circumstances" models with institutionalized offenders, led them to abandon them and develop their own model. In a series of books (Samenow 1998 and 1999; Yochelson and Samenow, 1976) they developed treatment theories based on the tactics and thinking errors of people who make crime a way of life. Samenow (2000: xii) states that: "Once we understood the world from the criminal's point of view and stopped imposing our own theories and explanations, we were able to understand how they perceive themselves and the world." This approach struck a responsive chord with corrections workers in daily contact with offenders, especially incarcerated offenders.

According to Vanstone (2000: 172), cognitive-behavioral methods in corrections are "used to address issues such as self-control, victim awareness and relapse prevention, and to teach among other things critical reasoning and emotional control." Adding to this, Chavaria (1997) points out that cognitive-behavioral programs must teach offenders to recognize (1) their patterns of thinking, feeling, and perceiving, (2) how these patterns support their criminal/dysfunctional behavior, (3) how to make the decision to change these patterns to change their lives, and (4) how to follow the decision to change with a program aimed at developing social competency. This, of course, is easier said than done given what we know about criminal thinking patterns.

Boyd Sharp (2006: xvi) cites a *Calvin and Hobbes* cartoon to illustrate a typical line of criminal "stinking thinkin'." Calvin is speaking to his father, saying:

> I have concluded that nothing bad I do is my fault . . .being young and irresponsible I'm a helpless victim of countless bad influences. An unwholesome culture panders to my undeveloped values and it pushes me into misbehavior. I take no responsibility for my behavior. I'm an innocent pawn in society.

No doubt this cartoon produced some chuckles from its readers, but such thinking is no laughing matter. If Calvin continues thinking this way, you might see him on your caseload one day. From where does such thinking arise? We might start by noting that we live in a society in which a significant number of people refuse to take responsibility for their own behavior (McDonald's made me fat; Phillip Morris made me smoke), preferring to see themselves as victims.

We might also note that mainstream criminology seems to have made an industry (not intentionally, of course) of making excuses for criminals—"It's society, poverty, racism, capitalism, et cetera and ad nauseam, that is to blame." These nostrums are repeated in the news media for all to read and digest, and criminals and their defenders are certainly happy to make a meal of them. Defense lawyers pick up the remaining slack by coaching their clients in denial and advising them not to admit anything. Of course, it is natural to want to deny something that can have negative consequences, and lawyers are only doing their jobs, but when respected professionals reinforce criminal denial and excuse making by encouraging it, it becomes very difficult to change. This kind of ingrained pattern of denial is primarily responsible, according to Sharp (2006), for making criminal thinking so difficult to change.

Sharp devised a therapeutic community treatment program based on cognitive-behavioral principles within prison walls in Baker City, Oregon. It is a strict, no-nonsense program for mainly alcoholic and drug-abusing offenders based on the premise that offenders are liars, manipulators, sneaks, and egotists. Of course, staff members do not call participating offenders these things directly. However, participants know that staff members perceive them this way because each participant is given a list of thirty-six thinking errors characteristic of the criminal personality, and a list of tactics criminals use to obstruct their own treatment. These lists let participants know that the staff is well aware of their thinking patterns and behavioral characteristics, and, thus, they would not likely be able to pull the wool over the eyes of any staff member.

The program uses many inmate/counselor contracts, standard educational programs, social skills training, and individual and group counseling. Inmates are in the program from between six to fifteen months, and Sharp claims a great deal of success in meeting most of the program's goals. Unfortunately, the only goal not met was a reduction in rearrest rates, which is, of course, the one goal that really matters. Changing criminal behavior is indeed very difficult.

Moral Reconation Therapy and Reasoning and Rehabilitation

Among the variety of cognitive-behavioral therapies, two of the dominant ones are Moral Reconation Therapy and Reasoning and Rehabilitation. Reconation is a rather nebulous word marrying the prefix re, meaning to "go back again" to the noun conation, meaning the act of striving or willing. In Moral Reconation Therapy, conation is viewed as a link between cognition and emotion, and thus re-conation is the act of returning to (or in the case of offenders, gaining) the ability to link thought and affect (Zhu 2003).

Moral Reconation Therapy is based on Lawrence Kohlberg's (1981) theory that moral development progresses through six stages, with only the Mother Theresa's among us reaching stage six. The first two stages are called pre-conventional because they are based purely on "How do I avoid punishment?" and "What's in it for me?" type thinking. The next two stages are the conventional because people in them are concerned with what others think of them and are thus conformity driven. The final two post-conventional stages (beyond behaving well because that is what others expect from us, but rather behaving morally because of one's own abstract ethical principles) involves being able to take the perspective of another (empathy).

A number of studies find overwhelmingly that criminals are stuck primarily in the pre-conventional stages of moral reasoning, primarily because of low abstract reasoning abilities and low levels of empathy (Walsh and Ellis 2007). The developers of Moral Reconation Therapy (Little and Robinson 1988: 135) identify a smorgasbord of other deficits that retard positive change when they write: "clients enter treatment with low levels of moral development, strong narcissism, low ego-identity strength, poor self-concept, low self-esteem, inability to delay gratification, relatively strong defense mechanisms, and relatively strong resistance to change and treatment." Moral Reconation Treatment in prison makes use of a manual of exercises directed at groups of from ten-to-fifteen inmates who meet twice a week for about two hours.

Wilson, Bouffard, and Mackenzie (2005) conducted a meta-analysis of six studies assessing the effectiveness of Moral Reconation Therapy. They found that the five-year recidivism rate for Moral Reconation Therapy graduates was 41 percent compared with 56 percent for matched non-Moral Reconation Therapy offenders, a modest effect size, but not one to be sneezed at. These studies also found that Moral Reconation Therapy participants had lower levels of criminal involvement at all follow-up periods on all indicators of reoffending.

Reasoning and Rehabilitation also begins with the premise that offenders are prevented from behaving prosocially by cognitive and social deficits. Reasoning and Rehabiliation is described by its developers as a program focused on: "modifying the impulsive, egocentric, illogical and rigid thinking of the offenders and teaching them to stop and think before acting, to consider the consequences of their behaviour, to conceptualize alternative ways of responding to interpersonal problems and to consider the impact of their behaviour on other people, particularly their victims" (Ross, Fabiano, and Ewles, 1988: 31).

Unlike Moral Reconation Therapy, Reasoning and Rehabiliation does not focus on improving offenders' moral reasoning but on improving their self-control, critical thinking, and interpersonal problem solving. Wilson, Bouffard, and Mackenzie's (2005) meta-analysis of Reasoning and Rehabilitation programs found them to significantly reduce recidivism, but not as strongly as Moral Reconation Therapy programs. In fact, both programs show only modest effect sizes, but Wilson, Bouffard, and Mackenzie rightly point out that modest effect sizes over large numbers of offenders mean a very large number of crimes not being committed.

Rational-Emotive Behavior Therapy

Because cognitive-behavior therapy is not a unified and distinct theory, the approach will be discussed further by focusing on a well-defined and long-lived theory that identifies itself as cognitive-behavioral: Rational-Emotive Behavioral Therapy. Albert Ellis, who first called it rational therapy, then rational emotive therapy, and finally rational emotive behavioral therapy in 1993, formulated this theory. Ellis is an extremely well-respected person in the counseling field. In 1991, he was ranked as the most influential psychotherapist by Canadian clinical psychologists, and second (behind Carl Rogers) by American clinical psychologists (Ellis 1996: xii). He is considered the most influential figure in the cognitive-behavioral revolution in counseling/therapy (Dowd 2004).

Ellis takes issue with the assumptions and practices of both psychoanalysis and client-centered therapy. Psychoanalysis is concerned with the darkness of the unconscious mind and nonrational biological drives. Client-centered therapy zeroes in on the emotional rapport of the client/counselor relationship. Rational-emotive behavior therapy fully recognizes that we share biological drives and emotional states with other species, but relegates them to minor importance in favor of cognition, a unique quality of humankind. It also downplays the client/counselor relationship while acknowledging that it is important, nevertheless.

According to Rational-Emotive Behavioral Therapy, problem behaviors arise from faulty thinking and irrational beliefs, and they can be corrected by helping offenders to understand and acknowledge that their beliefs are at odds with logic. It follows from this assumption that the Rational-Emotive Behavioral Therapy counselor takes a very active role in the counseling process and considers the quality of the offender/counselor relationship to be secondary to what takes place within that relationship. Rational-Emotive Behavioral Therapy counseling is highly directive, didactic, challenging, and often confrontational and painful for the offender.

The A-B-C Theory of Personality

Rational-Emotive Behavioral Therapy counseling revolves around Ellis' A-B-C theory of personality (actually, this concept is more a proposition about, or model for explaining, people's faulty perceptions than a theory of personality, but we will endure the accepted phraseology). A is the experience of an objective fact, a so-called Activating event; B is the subjective interpretation of or Belief about that fact; and C represents the Consequence, that is, emotional content accompanying the meaning (B) that the experience of the fact (A) has for the individual. Most people view an activating event as causing the emotions they are experiencing ("I'm happy, sad, depressed, suicidal, because he/she asked me for a divorce") in the following way.

Figure 11.1

Activating Event A ⟶ Consequence

A leads directly to C

Figure 11.2

Belief about A
↓

Activating Event A ⟶ B ⟶ C Consequence

A leads to B which leads to C

Ellis says, there is always an interpretive process that goes between A and C as shown in Figure 11.2. Rational Emotive Behavioral Therapy counselors use the ABC diagram as a way of monitoring cognitive reactions (thoughts about an event) similar to the way transactional analysis counselors use the PAC model. The important point for Rational Emotive Behavioral Therapy counselors to impart is that A is not the direct cause of C, but rather that B, the individual's belief about A, causes C. If A caused C, then everyone experiencing the same A would experience the same C, which obviously is not the case. The reason that everyone experiencing the same activating event does not experience the same emotional consequence is that the intervening belief about A is different from person to person.

The Rational Emotive Behavioral Therapy counselor sees problems of living as resulting from illogical and negative thinking about experiences (the interpretive processes) that the offender reiterates in a self-defeating monolog. The offender is reluctant to let go of irrational beliefs because they serve to protect a fragile ego. ("She's to blame for my depression because, after all, she was the one who asked for the divorce."). This process resembles the Freudian defense mechanism of rationalization—a mechanism that serves the self-consistency motive. Empathizing with the offender's definition of reality in the Rogerian manner, according to Ellis, only serves to reinforce faulty thinking and is counterproductive. Passive listening to an offender's monolog, as in psychoanalysis and client-centered counseling, is replaced by an active and assertive dialog between counselor and offender. Counseling is not a warm relationship of relating partners; it is more akin to a teacher/student relationship, complete with lectures and homework assignments, which is the behaviorist aspect of the theory.

Thus, behavioral change per se is not the goal of cognitive-behavioral counseling. Behavior is considered a symptom of the way we think about things, and the ultimate goal is thus to change the causes (faulty thinking) not the symptoms that are the results of that cause. Changing behavior without changing thinking is considered temporary symptom relief (like taking pain medication while waiting for your turn in surgery). As Dowd (2004: 420) describes it: "Behavior change is used in the service of cognitive change, and the ultimate goal is to bring about a profound philosophical change rather than simple symptom relief."

This is not to say that behavioral change is not welcome. Behavior is often the cause of attitudes, and if attitudes and behavior conflict, it leads to that unpleasant state psychologists call cognitive dissonance, which extensive research tells us is more likely to be resolved by changing one's attitudes than one's behavior (Wood and Wood 1996: 602). Thus, if the new behavior suggested by the cognitive-behavioral counselor leads to more pleasant outcomes for offenders, and they should, since the old behavior was, by definition, causing problems, they will change their attitudes and thought processes in conformity with the new behavior. This is what Dowd means by "behavior change is used in the service of cognitive change."

It is the counselor's task to strip away self-damaging ideas and beliefs by attacking them directly and challenging the offender to reinterpret experience in a growth-enhancing fashion. Ellis (1996) added D (Disputing) and E (Effective new philosophy) to his ABC model. Disputing dysfunctional ideas and beliefs and replacing them with a new, healthy philosophy, was always part of Rational-Emotive Behavioral therapy, but by "letterizing" those components, Ellis has placed them on a par with A, B, and C. Thus, after uncovering a dysfunctional idea or belief, the next stage is to dispute it.

The Rational Emotive Behavioral Therapy counselor operates from the assumption that no matter how well offenders come to understand the remote origins of their behavior, they often are unable to make the vital link between those origins and current behavioral problems. Rational-Emotive Behavioral Therapy counselors will rapidly cut short any offender's attempt to "explain" his or her behavior by asking, "But what are you doing to correct it?" Rational Emotive Behavioral Therapy counselors quickly cut through the quagmire of reasons, causes, explanations, and rationalizations, to nail offenders down to one or two basic irrational ideas considered to be the "real" reason for their disturbed behavior. After those ideas are identified, the Rational Emotive Behavioral Therapy counselor challenges the offender to validate those ideas. When the offender cannot validate them, the counselor will point out the lack of a reality basis for those irrational ideas. The focus is on the strength of the offender and on his or her capacity to change rather than extended exploration of the origins of "problems."

This business of tearing into offenders' irrational ideas should not be done in a dogmatic or condescending way–"What a damn stupid idea! How can you be so dumb"? It must be accomplished in a way that does not move the offender to dig in defensively or to completely cut you off: "Alex, do you really believe what you're saying is true"? This is creating a discrepancy for Alex to resolve. As noted in our discussion of Motivational Interviewing, it is better if the counselor can guide clients to dispute the irrational idea themselves by saying something like, "Do you really mean that? Can you think of some other way to interpret what went on that perhaps would not make you feel as if it is a catastrophe?"

If the Rational Emotive Behavioral Therapy counselors need backup, many will suggest bibliotherapy, the practice of having offenders read books that the counselor knows will challenge their views (see the use of bibliotherapy with a sex offender discussed on pages 241-243). Some offenders also will be asked to keep journals of their relevant daily activities and thoughts. The whole idea is that individuals have indoctrinated themselves with false and irrational ideas about themselves that lead to self-devaluation. The task of the Rational Emotive Behavioral Therapy counselor is to re-indoctrinate offenders with more realistic thoughts about themselves, which may include the deflation of a overly inflated image based on their antisocial behavior, through the medium of reality-based logical thinking.

MUSTurbations

Ellis has identified eleven ideas that he considers to be pervasive in our society. These ideas are highly irrational and lead to "widespread neurosis." He calls these ideas MUSTurbations and sums them up thus: "I now see that I have given up any addiction to MUSTurbation many years ago–to thinking that I must do well; that others must treat me considerately or fairly; and that the world must provide me with the things I want easily and quickly" (1982). Most of us are addicted to certain of these MUSTurbations (or absolutist thinking) to some degree or another.

An examination of some of these ideas will help to identify self-defeating "musts," "shoulds," and "oughts" in both your own thinking and that of the offender. Six of these ideas are adapted from Ellis' delightful book *A New Guide to Rational Living* (1975). These six are especially applicable to offenders (and sometimes to correctional workers as well). As you read them, note that they represent dichotomous thinking of the type: "If people don't love me, they must hate me;" "I failed my statistics exam, so I must be real stupid."

1. *It is essential that one be loved or approved by virtually everybody.* We all would like our desires for universal approval to be satisfied, but we do not really need them to be. You would hardly be human if you did not derive intense satisfaction from the positive judgments of others, but preoccupation with your own demands for love and approval may prevent you from seeing the lovable traits in others. Put otherwise, by not concentrating on your demands that you be loved, you free your psychic energies so that you are able to love. Furthermore, if you believe that you are not a worthy person unless you are universally liked, you guarantee that you will be an insecure and self-devalued person because you are chasing an unattainable rainbow.

2. *One must be perfectly competent, adequate, and achieving to be considered worthwhile.* This is a trap into which the beginning criminal justice counselor often falls. You have taken on a very difficult task. A fair percentage of offenders will re-offend

regardless of all your efforts to rehabilitate them. If you regard that circumstance as a personal failure, you denigrate yourself and the offenders' capacity to be responsible for their own lives. A perfectionist will never cut it in correctional work. As long as you have done your best, you are a worthwhile person. We all must develop the courage to be imperfect and not to experience failure as catastrophic.

3. *Unhappiness is caused by outside circumstances over which we have no control.* We allow ourselves to be emotionally upset about outside circumstances caused by our mental interpretations of them. Some outside circumstances constitute such a powerful assault on our lives that it is unreasonable not to expect a negative emotional consequence. However, other circumstances are only as defeating as we let them be. The rational person avoids exaggerating unpleasant\outside circumstances and looks for the growth potential in them. Many offenders find themselves overwhelmed by relatively innocuous unpleasant experiences and turn to the chemical comforts of the bottle or the pill.

4. It is easier to avoid personal responsibilities than to face them. You can hide from your responsibilities only for a short while. When your head does emerge from the sand, the responsibility still is there and may have grown. The rational person knows that it is less painful to attend to a responsibility than it is to deny or avoid it. Offenders are masters at avoiding their personal responsibilities because they often lack the self-confidence to attend to them. It is the counselor's task to make offenders see the logic of the rolling-snowball effect of nonattendance to responsibility.

5. *One must have someone stronger than oneself on whom to depend.* Many offenders are in a dependency mode. They lack the self-reliance to live a responsible, self-motivated life. An over-dependence on others (including a dependence on chemical substances) places the individual at the mercy of life's crutches. Rational people, while they may occasionally depend on others, minimize other-dependence and take charge of their own life.

6. *Past experience determines present behavior, and the influence of the past cannot be eradicated.* Although it is true that our values are largely programmed by our experiences and that it is difficult to overcome their influence, our behavior is not bound by them. We have the capacity to transcend our experiences (and the mindsets they engender) by accepting and analyzing the effect they have on us and by refusing to be determined by them. Typically, offenders have not recognized their capacity for self-directed change and allow themselves to be blown hither and thither by past and present environmental conditions. It is your job to encourage offenders to examine their experiences, make

them realize how they have influenced their negative attitudes and behavior, show them that those past experiences are not acceptable as excuses for present behavior, indicate that they possess the human capacity to break the chains of experience, and activate them toward the goal of self-responsible behavior.

What about Emotions?

According to Dowd (2004: 420), Rational Emotive Behavioral Therapy is at the same time optimistic and pessimistic. Its optimism arises from the demonstrated belief that thinking can be changed even under the most difficult circumstances. "It is pessimistic because Ellis believes that individuals have a strong biological tendency to think irrationally that they can only partially overcome, and then only with effort." In view of this, many people have taken Rational Emotive Behavioral Therapy (and cognitive-behavioral therapies, in general) to task for not being concerned enough with emotion (Slattery 2004).

The champion of the irrational, Sigmund Freud, was aware that humans are capable of logical thought, which he called "secondary process thinking," but the very term *secondary* reveals that he believed that we are overly prone to reverting to immature "primary process" thinking ruled by our irrational emotions (McLeod 2003: 135). Thus, when we engage secondary-process thinking, which for Freud was most of the time, our thoughts are controlled by our emotions, and are thus reflecting a distorted reality.

Of course, emotions range widely in intensity, and, therefore, widely in their ability to distort our thinking. Self-talk and logic may work fine for "cold" cognitions, but not for "hot" cognitions (thoughts with high emotional content). Many people believe that cognitions and emotions are completely separable phenomena, which they are not. We know from brain-imaging studies that thoughts automatically engage emotions and vice versa (Scarpa and Raine 2003). Because emotion is not "rational," it was once thought that emotional activity was a primitive evolutionary "throwback" that was opposed to culture and required inhibition, but the evidence today now points overwhelmingly to the position that the emotions perform many functions vital to social and cultural evolution (Phelps 2006).

Emotions require rational guidance (not inhibition), just as cognitions require emotional guidance. All cognitions have an element of emotion attached to them, and all emotions have an element of cognition attached to them. It is the social emotions such as shame, empathy, and guilt that prevent many of us from following what might be economically more rational (steal), at least in the short term, and it is cognitions that tame and modulate less noble emotions such as anger and hatred (Walsh 2000). Ellis himself wrote that: "RET assumes that human thinking and emotion are not two disparate or different processes, but that they significantly overlap and are in some respects, for all practical purposes, the same thing" (1984: 216). Without the emotions of love, shame, empathy, and guilt, the human social world would be a psychopathic jungle (Walsh and Wu 2008, Wiebe 2004).

Nevertheless, critics do have a point: illogical thought processes are doubtless dealt with more easily when they have little emotional content (are cold) than when they are suffused with emotion (are hot). Yet, a criminal hardly has a deep emotional attachment to his or her lifestyle in the same way that, say, a son has to his mother, a patriot to her country, or religious fundamentalists to their God. Rational-Emotive Behavioral Therapy counselors disputing the primacy of one's mother, country, or

God would be confronted with probably insurmountable emotional barriers to change, whereas confronting criminals with the illogical and self-defeating nature of their criminal lifestyle engages thoughts only slightly tinged with emotion. Thus, because thoughts automatically engage emotions, changing beliefs, attitudes, and perceptions also should automatically change the emotional contents of these things. This is why Ellis (1996) changed his original Rational Therapy to Rational Emotive Therapy in 1961.

A number of meta-analyses (for example, Hofmann and Smits 2008) have shown that cognitive-behavioral therapy has a better track record in therapeutic populations than other methods; but what makes it work in neurological terms? Neuroscientist Richard Restak, quoting Helen Mayberry, writes: "While drugs work on the emotional areas deep in the brain, cognitive therapy exercises the thinking areas of the brain and thereby effects the [cognitive/emotional] balance from top down. Cognitive therapy exercises the cortex and thereby strengthens the [neuronal] pathways by which the thinking brain influences the emotional brain" (2001: 144). Linden (2006) reviewed a wide variety of neuroimaging studies that assessed the effects on the human brain of cognitive-behavioral therapy compared with pharmacological treatment (Prozac, Zoloft, and so forth) for such maladies as depression and obsessive compulsive disorder.

Both types of treatment are found to decrease activity in areas of the brain associated with these problems to the same extent "indicating commonalities in the biological mechanisms of psycho- and pharmacotherapy" (Linden 2006: 528). In other words, the malleable human brain functions analogously to muscles, in that certain pathways can be strengthened by use. But just as muscles need constant and progressive effort to produce desired growth so do the brain's neuronal pathways. Half-hearted, twice-a-week dilly-dallying will not do in the pursuit of either endeavor.

The following case study illustrates the successful use of Rational Emotive Behavioral Therapy with an offender supervised by one of your authors (Walsh). Other examples of specific Rational Emotive Behavioral Therapy techniques are given in the chapter on group counseling.

Case Study
Rational-Emotive Behavioral Therapy with
A Sex Offender

Marc was a tall, good-looking man with an IQ of 119. He also had an attractive wife and a five-year-old son. Nevertheless, his work record was extremely poor. He was mainly a casual laborer. He never kept a job very long because he always seemed to get into an argument with his bosses and get fired or quit. After losing a job, he would go on short drinking binges and then go on to indecently expose himself (he had two prior convictions for indecent exposure). Despite his rather quick temper, his wife said that he was never abusive to her or their young son.

I first met Marc after his conviction for gross sexual imposition. He had been driving around one day in the rain after a minor drinking bout when he came upon two children–a girl age twelve and a boy age eleven–standing at a bus stop in the rain. Marc stopped and offered them a ride, which they accepted. The children later said they had accepted because they had just missed one bus, it was raining heavily, and they apparently felt there was safety in numbers.

After some small talk, Marc took the children into an alley and told them both to take their clothes off. The children refused and started to cry. Marc then verbally abused the children and proceeded to force his hand up the dress of the girl and stick his fingers in her vagina. He also fondled the boy's penis and told them both to keep quiet. The young boy was able to escape and shout for help from a nearby construction team, who apprehended Marc and held him for the police.

Marc told me during his PSI interview that his initial motive was simply to get the children out of the rain (he was trying to make me hear, "I'm really a nice guy, I tried to be helpful"). Once the children were in the car, "I felt an overwhelming urge to expose myself to them" ("I couldn't help myself; I'm a victim of my urges; I need treatment, not punishment"). He admitted frequently exposing himself to children standing at bus stops in the past, and he had two prior convictions for such behavior. He admitted telling the young girl to remove her blouse: "It gave me a feeling of mastery. But I knew she wouldn't do it because of modesty." He denied (there's that awful word) touching the girl's vagina or the boy's penis.

My investigation led me to discover a rape conviction in another state that was not on Marc's FBI rap sheet. He reluctantly admitted this conviction to me, but said that he was wrongfully convicted. This turned out to be the truth, much to my surprise. He has been granted a full governor's pardon and $2,000 compensation for the three years he spent in prison for his conviction. Marc's wife informed me that he had told her that he had been frequently raped in prison, which he described as "a whorehouse where the only thing missing was the women." She felt that many of his sexual problems stemmed from his prison experience.

Continued on the next page

Case Study, *continued*

Marc had referred himself to a private psychiatrist after his arrest and bail. This psychiatrist wrote that Marc's pedophilia was of recent origin and that with "intensive psychotherapy it would never reach a chronic stage." He felt that Marc's desire to expose himself to children was caused by "deep-seated resentment of his mother's early rejection of him," and that he was essentially "thumbing his penis" at his mother. The psychiatrist recommended that Marc be placed on probation and that the county pay for his therapy. Marc never told his psychiatrist about his imprisonment, if he had, I wonder if the psychiatrist's focus on Marc's mother (a favorite whipping boy of classical psychoanalysis) would have changed?

For my part, I reasoned that Marc had kidnapped, terrified, and sexually molested two young children and that nothing less than incarceration could be justified. The judge reasoned otherwise, and placed Marc on probation on the condition that he continue treatment and spend sixty days in jail. Marc did not continue therapy with his psychiatrist. Instead, he opted to attend group counseling at the county court diagnostic and treatment center.

For a variety of reasons, not the least, I suppose, being his ability to make intelligent conversation, Marc's case fascinated and challenged me. During one session in which we were discussing his prison experiences, he told me that other inmates had ridiculed him about the size of his penis and how this used to devastate him. Further discussion led to his telling me that he had measured his erect penis at what was to him an unsatisfactory five inches. As Albert Ellis might have put it, Marc was "catastrophizing" the size of his penis. Ellis might have gone on to say something like: "Yes, I'm sure you would like to have a bigger penis, but there's nothing you can do about it. It's not your penis size that's getting you into trouble, it's your belief that you must have a bigger penis to be a man. You are miserable and feel inadequate, but you make yourself feel that way by irrational and dysfunctional thinking. Your irrational thoughts are leading you to continue your criminal behavior, and that will land you back in the prison environment where you say all your problems stemmed from."

Not being in Ellis' class, I went on to play Dr. Freud (a definite "no-no" for an untrained person) and suggested the possibility that his urge to expose himself to children may have stemmed from an exaggerated concern for the size of his penis. To a young child, an erect adult penis seems gigantic. Marc acknowledged that perhaps he was trying to reassure himself about the adequacy of his penis by shocking his victims with its erect enormity to compensate for the cruel hazing he received about it from his fellow inmates. Latching onto what I thought might be a crucial piece of information, I assigned Marc some Rational Emotive Behavioral Therapy "homework." I instructed him to go to the public library and check out three textbooks on human anatomy and physiology. From these books, he was to look up information on the size of the normal erect penis. He signed a plan saying that he would do this the following morning. This assignment led to Marc's discovery that 95 percent of all males have an erect penis of between five and one-half and six and one-half inches, meaning that Marc was just one-half inch short of being within the average range.

This discovery provided for a fruitful evaluation of just how irrational it was for Marc to get himself into so much trouble for the sake of one-half inch of flesh that no one but his wife and he would ever see if he did not expose himself. He was guided to view his self-esteem in terms of his good looks, his high intelligence, and the love of his supportive wife and dependent child.

Ellis would have added that he will experience anxiety about his perceived inadequacy from time to time and to just accept it as normal. Anxious people tend to get anxious about their anxiety, telling themselves over and again, "I must not be anxious, I must not be anxious!" Being anxious about not being anxious is a self-defeating musturbation ("I must be totally in control of my emotions"). Marc has to learn to accept himself and his anxieties; all that he has to disown are his irrational thoughts and his anxiety will disappear.

Over the next few months, Marc reported that he had experienced urges to expose himself again. However, he had not done so because he reminded himself of the irrationality of the act and of his responsibilities to his family. Marc successfully completed three years of probation without further trouble with the law. I monitored the daily arrest sheet for the two remaining years I spent in probation without ever seeing his name on it. I ran into his wife one day at a shopping center. She told me that everything was going fine, that Marc had been at his job for over a year, that he had drastically cut down on his drinking, and that there did not seem to be any residual sexual problems. Marc's case was the kind that made me feel proud to have been a probation officer, and, for once, glad that my recommendation to the court perhaps had been wrong.

Lifestyle Theory

The interesting thing about the cognitive-behavioral treatment approach is that it is the only approach to have a full-blown criminological theory based on its principles. The theory is known as the lifestyle theory, and has been primarily developed by Glen Walters (1990), a senior psychologist at the U.S. Penitentiary at Leavenworth, Kansas. Walters' theory is more psychological than sociological, and since it was developed in a prison setting, it is of particular interest to corrections workers. The term *lifestyle* appears to have been chosen to let us know that criminal behavior is not just another form of behavior, but rather it is a lifestyle.

Much of the foundation for Walters' theory was laid by Albert Ellis' Rational Emotive Behavioral Therapy and the "criminal mind" or "criminal personality" concept of Samuel Yochelson and Stanton Samenow. Walters borrowed Ellis' ABC concept of personality, which makes the point that people wrongly attribute causal power to situations and circumstances when it should be attributed to our beliefs or perceptions about those events. People respond to events according to the meaning that those events have for them, not according to any intrinsic quality of those events.

Walters also borrowed and further systematized Yochelson and Samenow's list of fifty-two "thinking errors" that help to constitute the criminal personality.

Lifestyle theory contains three key concepts: conditions, choice, and cognition. A criminal lifestyle is the result of choices criminals make, although it is acknowledged that choices take place "within the limits established by our early and current biologic/environmental conditions" (Walters and White 1989: 3). Note that while biological and environmental conditions lay the foundation of future behavioral choices, they do not determine it. Among the most important biological and environmental conditions affecting behavioral choices stressed by Walters are temperament and IQ, as stressed in Agnew's general strain theory, and attachment, as stressed in Hirschi's social control theory.

The third concept, cognition, refers to cognitive styles people develop as a consequence of their biological/environmental conditions and the pattern of choices they have made in response to them. According to this theory, lifestyle criminals display eight major cognitive features, or thinking errors that make them what they are (Walters 1990, Walters and White 1989). Very little can be done to change criminals' behavior until they change this pattern of thinking. Each of these eight interrelated thinking errors is briefly described:

- *Mollification* refers to criminals' rationalizations and excuses designed to mollify (soften) the response of others toward them. Mollification is not simply a ploy to fool others; criminals often believe their own rationalizations.

- *Cutoff* refers to the ability of many criminals to discount the suffering of their victims. Feelings of guilt, sympathy, or empathy would render it difficult for them to victimize others, so they cut off such feelings. Firefighters, police officers, and many other professionals who deal with pain and suffering every day also must "steel" themselves to it if they are to do their jobs properly.

- *Entitlement* refers to criminals' feelings that they are entitled to that which they take from others. Being self-centered creatures, criminals consider themselves "special" people for whom the rules do not (or should not) apply. They believe that the world owes them a living and that they are simply taking their due.

- *Power Orientation* refers to criminals' propensity to view the world in terms of weakness and strength. They desire and understand strength and fear and exploit weakness. They want to dominate and control, and they carry a scorecard into every situation to figure who wins and who loses. They may do whatever they have to not to lose, but if they do lose, they will compensate by exploiting weaker individuals.

- *Sentimentality* refers to criminals' efforts to convince themselves and prosocial others that they are basically good people: "Sure, I've made mistakes, but I've never meant to hurt anyone."

- *Super optimism* refers to criminals' exaggerated sense of self-confidence in their ability to get away with anything. Many criminals retain the adolescent's notion of personal invincibility (nothing will happen to me), which is why they have a strong tendency to discount or downplay the possibility of punishment.

- *Cognitive Indolence* refers to criminals' mental laziness. They are present oriented and concrete in their thinking. They have difficulty understanding abstract moral reasoning, are intellectually immature, easily bored, and crave excitement to fill the shallowness of their inner world.

- *Discontinuity* refers to criminals' inability to integrate their thinking patterns. Their thinking is so compartmentalized that they are overly sensitive to environmental pressures and changes, viewing them as unconnected to any integrated whole. This is why they have difficulty committing themselves to a long course of action such as schooling, training for a skilled occupation, or marriage.

These thinking errors resulting from arrested development of cognitive processes lead to four interrelated behavioral patterns or styles that almost guarantee criminality: rule breaking, interpersonal intrusiveness (intruding into the lives of others when not wanted) self-indulgence, and irresponsibility. Thus, criminality is the result of irrational behavior patterns, which are the result of faulty thinking, which arises from the consequences (reward and punishment) of choices in early life, which are themselves influenced by the individuals' biology and their early environmental conditions.

Note the similarity with Sutherland's differential association theory discussed in Chapter 2: cognition causes conduct. The major difference between the two theories is that Walters' theory stresses that cognitions are caused by individual choices that are in turn caused by early biological and environmental conditions detrimental to the moral development. By contrast, Sutherland's theory explicitly denies biological variables, and considers environmental (cultural) conditions to be simply different rather than deviant. Another difference is that Sutherland does not invest his definitions as "favorable" with any evaluative or moral connotations but Walters does, calling them "thinking errors."

Figure 11.3 illustrates the lifestyle progression toward criminal behavior.

Figure 11.3 Diagrammatic Presentation of Criminal Lifestyle Theory

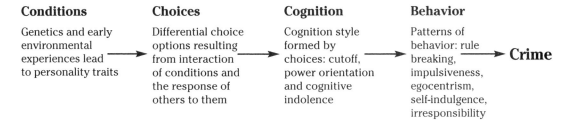

Conditions	Choices	Cognition	Behavior	
Genetics and early environmental experiences lead to personality traits	Differential choice options resulting from interaction of conditions and the response of others to them	Cognition style formed by choices: cutoff, power orientation and cognitive indolence	Patterns of behavior: rule breaking, impulsiveness, egocentrism, self-indulgence, irresponsibility	**Crime**

Read

Summary and Lessons and Concerns

Rational-emotive behavioral therapy emphasizes that problems arise from the faulty operation of that which is unique to humankind: the capacity to think. Ask yourself, however, are emotional problems easily assuaged by pointing out that they are the result of faulty thinking? One philosophical wag opined that the sole function of the neocortex (the thinking brain) is to justify and rationalize the emotions and behaviors generated by the more ancient mammalian and paleo-cortices (the emotional and instinctual centers of the brain, respectively). Freud himself was said to believe that his "talking cures" were effective only with educated, middle-class patients having well-developed capacities for rational thought. This is not an apt description of the typical offender. Nevertheless, Rational Emotive Behavioral Therapy has found a welcome home in corrections.

Are cognitions really more basic and potent than emotions? How often have you realized how utterly stupid it was to feel a certain way, wished very much that you did not, but continued to do so anyway? As Ellis himself frequently points out, we think and emote practically simultaneously, but do we feel bad because we think bad or do we think bad because we feel bad? Certainly, we can change our thoughts regardless of whether they are preceded or followed by our emotions, but we need to address emotions a little more strongly than Rational Emotive Behavioral Therapy does. One way of doing this is to acknowledge that the past is more important to the understanding of the present than is admitted in Rational Emotive Behavioral therapy. It is absolutely and obviously true that we cannot change the past, but invariably it insinuates itself into the present through our memory tapes. Unless we understand why this happens, confront it and move on, we will continue to think irrationally.

Some (but certainly not your authors) criticize Rational Emotive Behavioral Therapy for insisting that rationality and irrationality always be defined from a law-abiding middle-class point of view. The insights of anomie and differential association theories tell us that under certain conditions, crime is a quite rational response (a fit between a goal and the means by which it is sought). Nevertheless, Ellis feels that the counselor's values and attitudes are legitimate therapeutic tools. Many offenders, but by no means all, can learn valuable self-insights from an active and didactic counselor. This is especially true if the counselor also draws lessons from client-centered therapy and establishes a warm relationship before attempting to confront the offender and having the offender confront himself or herself. Finally, Rational Emotive Behavioral Therapy, with its teacher/student relationship, is more realistic and genuine than client-centered therapy in a criminal justice setting, provided that the teacher is not confused with the preacher.

Lifestyle theory's solid concentration on individuals rather than their past and present environments is welcomed by many practically oriented correctional workers. It provides us with a starting point with which to attack criminal behavior with the weapon we know best–talk. We can do nothing about offenders' early conditions or the choices they made in response to them, but we can challenge their cognition. We can attack their thinking errors formed from the rewards and punishment they have experienced in response to their early choices. Many correctional professionals welcome lifestyle, and other similar theories stressing cognitive aspects of the individual, because "they give permission for punishment of offenders, because offenders are responsible for their actions and make purposeful decisions to commit crime" (Williams and McShane 1994: 226).

Note the different conclusions we might draw from anomie/strain theory and lifestyle theory regarding the rationality of offending. The former maintains that offending is fully rational from the offenders' point of view because it is a means by which they attain goals that are (presumably) otherwise unattainable. Lifestyle theorists would not deny that criminal behavior is logical in the sense that it provides means/ends fits that follow from certain premises. Nevertheless, it is irrational because the premises themselves (the faulty cognitions) are seriously flawed. Theories that locate the blame for crime outside the criminal do serious harm to society by providing criminals with authoritative rationalizations for their harmful and irresponsible behavior. If criminals can point to external "causes" of their behavior, they may deny and resist any efforts to correct it.

As welcome as the emphasis on the individual is to the correctional worker, lifestyle theory has its problems. Research in this theoretical tradition has been based overwhelmingly on prison inmates, a focus that excludes nonincarcerated felons and noncriminals. We might wonder how many noncriminals evidence the same thinking patterns. We also might wonder if thinking is not overemphasized at the expense of emotion. Some people are suited temperamentally to quietly "thinking things out," while others are impulsive hotheads. Additionally, Ellis and Walsh's (2000: 317) survey of the literature found sixteen studies showing that moral or prosocial thinking is positively correlated with IQ (the higher the IQ, the greater the moral reasoning), and only one to be nonsignificant. Thus, IQ and temperament may affect the probability of criminal behavior beyond their effects on early life choices. It is all very well to demonstrate that criminals think differently from noncriminals, but science would like to know why they do. However, lifestyle theory is a good "working" theory, and judged on that basis, a good one.

Perspective from the Field
Cognitive-Skills Programs in Correctional Settings

By Bruce L. Bikle, Ph.D.

Bruce Bikle is an Associate Professor in the School of Criminal Justice and the Graduate Program Coordinator at California State University at Sacramento. He began his corrections work as a unit manager in the Hawaii correctional system and has worked in Oregon, Washington, and California in both prisons and jails. He received his Ph.D. from Portland State University in Public Administration and Policy. His areas of specialization are inmate programs, administration and management of correctional facilities, and direct supervision jails.

● ●

Most cognitive-skills programs have as their principal goal to teach offenders to think and act in a prosocial manner. While many cognitive-skills programs are used as stand-alone programs, many jurisdictions have integrated cognitive-skills programming into larger and more comprehensive program

Continued on the next page

Perspective from the Field, *continued*

activities. The doctrine of cognitive thinking or cognitive-skills program centers around the belief that it is "criminal thinking" that leads to criminal acts. Therefore, these programs work toward teaching offenders both the thinking skills and awareness about how thinking influences action.

One such program is the Oregon SUMMIT Boot Camp, which has been in operation since 1994. SUMMIT stands for Success Using Motivation, Morale, Intensity and Treatment. The SUMMIT program is located at the Shutter Creek Correctional Facility on Oregon's central coast. While many boot camps around the country stress the military model, the SUMMIT program stresses the therapeutic and rehabilitative nature of the cognitive skills program in the context of military bearing and discipline (*see* Beers and Duval 1996).

Setting up a program did not come quickly. The 1993 Oregon Legislature in House Bill 2418 mandated a program that would accommodate prisoners who were not sex offenders, or those with mandatory minimum sentences to serve. All fifty-six male participants in SUMMIT are volunteers.

Prior to the arrival of the first platoon of inmates, an extensive amount of research and training went into the program. Staff from Shutter Creek traveled to New York to observe that state's program. Feeling a need to stress rehabilitation, and encouraged by the success of other cognitive-based programs in Oregon (*see* note at the end of this section), the planning staff of the program decided on the "Options" cognitive program that was developed by Jack Bush of Vermont. The Options program had been designed originally for the U.S. Navy and was adopted by Bush and the National Institute of Corrections for the offender population. Bush came to the facility and trained the staff in the principles and practices of the Options program.

The doctrines of the Options program are as follows:

- Choice and noncoercive use of authority: Accountability is stressed and offenders are held accountable in a constructive manner designed to challenge the offenders and motivate them toward change.

- Objectivity: SUMMIT participants are expected to make thinking reports detailing their feelings and thoughts. These are presented without excuses or blame, and are designed to avoid defensiveness and excuse making.

- Thinking Controls Behavior: The program is designed to get offenders to see how their own thinking can shape their behavior

- Cognitive Change is Changing the Thinking Behind the Behavior. The process works by identifying the behavior to be changed, identifying the thinking that influences the behavior to be changed, learning how to stop or interrupt this thinking and replacing it with new thinking and then practicing this new thinking until it becomes ingrained in the individual.

- <u>Self-Awareness and Self-Responsibility</u>: These traits are developed throughout the program through reports, counseling, group meetings, and journals kept by the participants.

The Shutter Creek staff also underwent another cognitive-skills enhancement program when all the staff involved with the program attended "Breaking Barriers" sessions designed to improve the staff acceptance of the boot camp and to develop teamwork. Breaking Barriers has been used in a number of correctional facilities to rehabilitate offenders, and in private industry to improve operations and build a team spirit. Further, since the SUMMIT program was designed to release inmates to parole supervision, parole officers were encouraged to take the training as well. Many of the parole officers attended staff training and participated in military drill and physical training activities so they would know what their charges had experienced at Shutter Creek.

Bill Beers, the Superintendent of the Shutter Creek facility, was determined that this boot camp program would provide the best chance for success on parole for the graduates, and strongly emphasized the necessity of the cognitive-skills piece of the program. Beers states that "the development of cognitive skills to reduce criminal thinking is the primary emphasis of this program."

The first inmates arrived at Shutter Creek in March, 1994 and began their six month program. The regimen is tough–the day goes from 5:30 A.M. until 9:30 P.M., seven days per week, and includes work, physical training, cooperation, teamwork, military bearing, decision making, education, reentry planning, twelve-step classes, alcohol and drug treatment, and daily assessment meetings with staff and each inmates' squad where issues are discussed and lessons are learned in the context of teamwork and self-responsibility.

From March 1984 to April 2000, more than 2,000 inmates entered the SUMMIT program. Of these, 1,172 inmates graduated from the institutional (Shutter Creek) portion of the program and 940 participants completed the community portion of the program. Completion rates were 58 percent for the institutional portion and 49 percent for the entire program.

The program has been successful on several counts. Information provided by the Oregon Department of Corrections shows that the thirty-two platoons who graduated from the program and completed the community reentry phase of the program have demonstrated a lower recidivism rate (measured as a lack of new felony convictions) than individuals who were closely matched to the successful SUMMIT graduates in terms of eligibility for program participation.

The numbers provided by the Oregon Department of Corrections speak for themselves: In the first year following release SUMMIT graduates recidivated at 8.7 percent–the comparable rate for SUMMIT-eligible inmates who did not take the program was 18.1 percent. After two years, SUMMIT graduates showed a 20.4 recidivism rate while the comparison group showed a rate of

Continued on the next page

Perspective from the Field, *continued*

31.7 percent. And, at the three-year mark, SUMMIT graduates' recidivism rate was 28.2 percent while the rate of the comparison group was 40.2 percent.

Not only did SUMMIT graduates stay out of trouble more often and longer than their peers, they also saved the state significant sums of money. Even after accounting for the fact that the SUMMIT program is more expensive to run than the general population program, due to increased program costs, the Department of Corrections estimates that from inception to April 2000, the state had saved more than 14 million dollars with the SUMMIT program (Oregon Department of Corrections).

What lessons can be learned from the Oregon experience with regard to cognitive skills programs?

First, an administrative commitment is essential to a successful program outcome. Oregon invested a lot of time, effort, and money in the development of the cognitive- skills program that is used at SUMMIT, and invests in the Cognitive Skills Network noted below. Cognitive-skills programs are found in most Oregon Department of Corrections' institutions. One might also look at the Correctional Service of Canada, which has adopted a cognitive-skills program at many of their institutions and community corrections centers.

Secondly, we also might look at the SUMMIT program, which closely follows the New York model of boot camps, which makes cognitive skills the centerpiece of the boot camp program. Programs that teach how to recognize thinking errors and how to correct them are of primary importance and demonstrate higher rates of overall success.

Thirdly, the Oregon experience gives weight to the idea that a successful cognitive-skills program needs to involve the staff (all the staff ideally) in the program; thus, "everyone is playing from the same sheet of music." The Canadian experience with their cognitive-skills programs also has demonstrated this is the way to implement programs.

The Oregon SUMMIT boot camp program is one example of how a cognitive- skills based program can contribute to lower recidivism, lower costs, and inmates who have learned how to better manage and control their lives. The success of these programs is contingent on support by administration, and a motivated staff to implement the program. Oregon has demonstrated the hard work is worth it.

Note: Oregon has implemented a number of cognitive-based programs, including: the "Reasoning and Rehabilitation" program developed by Robert R. Ross and Elizabeth A. Fabiano and used extensively in the Correctional System of Canada; "Aggression Replacement Training," developed by Arnold Goldstein and Barry Glick; "Breaking Barriers or Framework for Change," developed by Gordon Graham; and Pathfinders a transition and workforce development program that relies heavily on cognitive skills in the context of preparing inmates for release from prison.

As a result of the popularity of the various programs, a "Cognitive Skills Network" of program providers, facility personnel, counselors, probation and parole officers, program planners and ex-offender graduates of the programs

> meet several times a year to share information, conduct training, and review programs. For more information on cognitive skills program, the reader might go to the National Institute of Corrections (www.nicic.org), the Oregon Department of Corrections,(www.doc.state.or.us) or the Correctional Service of Canada (www.csc.gc.ca), all of which maintain web pages that provide information on various cognitive skills programs.

References and Suggested Readings

Arkowitz, H. and M. Hannah. 1989. Cognitive, Behavioral, and Psychodynamic Therapies. In *Comprehensive Handbook of Cognitive Therapy*, A. Freeman, K. Simon, L. Beutler, and H. Arkowitz, eds. New York: Plenum

Austin, L. 1999. *The Counseling Primer*. Philadelphia: Accelerated Development Group.

Beers, W. and C. Duval. 1966. *The Oregon Summit Program*. In American Correctional Association, ed. *Juvenile and Adult Boot Camps*, Lanham, Maryland: American Correctional Association.

Chavaria, F. 1997. Probation and Cognitive Skills. *Federal Probation* 61: 57-60.

Dowd, E. 2004. Cognition and the Cognitive Revolution in Psychotherapy: Promises and Advances. *Journal of Clinical Psychology* 60: 415-428.

Ellis, A. 1975. *A New Guide to Rational Living*. Hollywood, California: Wiltshire Book Company.

———. 1982. *A Guide to Personal Happiness*. Hollywood, California: Wiltshire Book Company.

———. 1984. Is the Unified-Interaction Approach to Cognitive-Behavior Modification a Reinvention of the Wheel? *Clinical Psychology Review* 4: 215-218.

———. 1989. The History of Psychotherapy. In *Comprehensive Handbook of Cognitive Therapy*. A. Freeman, K. Simon, L.Beutler, and H. Arkowitz, eds. New York: Plenum.

———. 1996. *Better, Deeper, and More Enduring Brief Therapy*. New York: Brunner/Mazel.

Ellis, L and A. Walsh. 2000. *Criminology: A Global Perspective*. Boston: Allyn and Bacon.

Fishbein, D. 2003. The Neuropsychological and Emotional Regulatory Processes in Antisocial Behavior. In *Biosocial Criminology: Challenging Environmentalism's Supremacy*, A. Walsh and L. Ellis, eds. Hauppauge, New York: Nova Science. pp. 185-208.

Glasser, W. 1972. *The Identity Society*. New York: Harper and Row.

Gove, W. and C. Wilmoth. 2003. The Neurophysiology of Motivation and Habitual Criminal Behavior. In *Biosocial Criminology: Challenging Environmentalism's Supremacy*, A. Walsh and L. Ellis, eds. Hauppauge, New York: Nova Science, pp. 227-245.

Hofmann, S. and J. Smits. 2008. Cognitive-behavioral therapy for adult anxiety disorders: A meta-analysis of randomized placebo-controlled trials. *Journal of Clinical Psychiatry* 69: 621-632.

Kohlberg, L.1981. *Essays on Moral Development, Vol. I: The Philosophy of Moral Development*. New York: Harper and Row.

Linden, D. 2006. How Psychotherapy Changes the Brain—the Contribution of Functioning Neuroimaging. *Molecular Psychiatry* 11: 528-538.

Little, G. and K. Robinson. 1988. Moral Reconation Therapy: A Systematic Step-by-Step Treatment System for Treatment-Resistant Clients. *Psychological Reports* 62: 135-151.

McLeod, J. 2003. *An Introduction to Counseling*. Buckingham, England. Open University Press.

Phelps, E. 2006. Emotion and Cognition: Insights from Studies of the Human Amygdala. *Annual Review of Psychology* 57: 27-53.

Restak, R. 2001. *The Secret Life of the Brain*. New York: co-published by Dana Press and Joseph Henry Press.

Ross, R., E. Fabiano, and C. Ewles. 1988. *Time to Think: A Cognitive Model of Delinquency Prevention and Offender Rehabilitation*. Johnson City, Tennessee: Institute of Social Sciences and Arts, Inc.

Samenow, S. 1998. *Straight Talk about Criminals*. Livingston, New Jersey: Jason Aronson.

———. 1999. *Before It's Too Late: Why Some Kids Get Into Trouble and What Parents Can Do About It*. New York: Times Books.

———. 2000. Introduction. In B. Sharp, *Changing Criminal Thinking: A Treatment Program*. Lanham, Maryland: American Correctional Association.

Scarpa, A. and A. Raine. 2003. The Psychophysiology of Antisocial Behavior: Interactions with Environmental Experiences. In *Biosocial Criminology: Challenging Environmentalism's Supremacy*, A. Walsh and L. Ellis, eds. Hauppauge, New York: Nova Science, pp. 209-226

Sharp, B. 2006. *Changing Criminal Thinking: A Treatment Program,* 2nd Ed. Alexandria, Virginia: American Correctional Association.

Slattery, J. 2004. *Counseling Diverse Clients: Bringing Context into Therapy*. Belmont, California: Brooks/Cole.

Vanstone, M. 2000. Cognitive-Behavioural Work With Offenders in the U.K.: A History of Influential Endeavour. *The Howard Journal* 39: 171-183.

Vennard, J., D. Sugg, and C. Hedderman. 1997. The Use of Cognitive-Behavioural Approaches with Offenders: Messages from the Research. In *Changing Offenders' Attitudes and Behavior: What Works?* C. Lewis, ed. London: Home Office Research and Statistics.

Walsh, A. 2000. Evolutionary Psychology and the Origins of Justice. *Justice Quarterly* 17: 841-864.

———. 2002. *Biosocial Criminology: Introduction and Integration*. Cincinnati, Ohio: Anderson.

Walsh, A. and L. Ellis. 2007. *Criminology: An Interdisciplinary Approach*. Thousand Oaks, California: Sage.

Walsh, A. and H Wu. 2008. Differentiating Antisocial Personality Disorder, Psychopathy, and Sociopathy: Evolutionary, Genetic, Neurological, and Sociological Considerations. *Criminal Justice Studies* 21: 135-152.

Walters, G. 1990. *The Criminal Lifestyle: Patterns of Serious Criminal Conduct*. Newbury Park, California: Sage.

Walters, G. and T. White. 1989. The Thinking Criminal: A Cognitive Model of Lifestyle Criminality. *Criminal Justice Research Bulletin*. Huntsville, Texas: Sam Houston State University Press.

Weibe, R. 2004. Psychopathy and Sexual Coercion: A Darwinian Analysis. *Counseling and Clinical Psychology Journal* 1: 23-41.

Williams, F. and M. McShane. 1994. *Criminological Theory*, 2nd ed. Englewood Cliffs, New Jersey: Prentice Hall.

Wilson, D., L. Bouffard, and D. Mackenzie. 2005. A Quantitative Review of Structured, Group-Oriented, Cognitive-Behavior Programs for Offenders. *Criminal Justice and Behavior* 32: 172-204.

Wood, S. and E. Wood. 1996. *The World of Psychology*, 2nd ed. Boston: Allyn and Bacon.

Yochelson, S. and S. Samenow. 1976. *The Criminal Personality: A Profile for Change*. Livingston, New Jersey: Jason Aronson.

Zhu, J. 2003. *The Conative Mind: Volition and Action*. Waterloo, Canada: University of Waterloo.

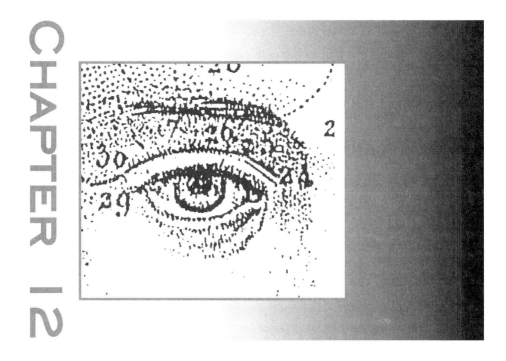

CHAPTER 12

Group Counseling in Institutional Settings

When the prison gates slam behind an inmate, he does not lose his human quality, his mind does not become closed to ideas, his intellect does not cease to feed on a free and open interchange of opinions; his yearning for self-esteem does not end; nor his quest for self-realization conclude. If anything, the needs for identity and self-esteem are more compelling.

—Justice Thurgood Marshall

The Power of the Group

Jails and prisons are not very nice places. They were never meant to be, and they never can be. Whatever euphemisms we dream up for them, they still exist to punish lawbreakers and to separate them from "decent" society. They are prime examples of what Goffman (1961) has called "total institutions."

Total institutions can be mental hospitals, army training facilities, or any other institution where large groups of people live together under tightly restricted and scheduled circumstances and under the control of a central authority. Total institutions are divided into "managers," who control, and "subjects," who are controlled. It is the function of the managers to restrict social interaction between the "subjects" and the outside world. The consequence of such an authoritarian and coercive situation is the development of two antagonistic subcultures within the institution. Social distance between the controllers and the controlled is great, and each group tends to develop hostile attitudes toward the other.

The Inmate Code

The hostility toward the managers is expressed in an informal set of rules known as the inmate code. Gaines, Kaune, and Miller (2000: 493) define the inmate code as: "A system of social norms and values established by inmates to regulate behavior within the correctional institution." The code represents the "model prisoner," in terms of the values and norms of prison society. Of course, it is the inmates who define the values and norms, and decide who is and who is not a "model prisoner." Among the ways of conforming to the inmate code is playing many games with controllers (the "hacks," screws," and "shrinks") that we discussed in the section on transactional analysis. One of those rules is "Don't be a sucker," a rule that warns inmates against granting overt respect and prestige to prison officers and staff and against trusting them.

This rule does not mean that inmates openly defy prison officials and regulations, because overt acts of defiance may bring down the wrath of the managers on the entire group. Rather, it means never be openly friendly to officials unless you can use them for your own ends, never cooperate at a level beyond that which is necessary to avoid trouble, never volunteer for anything simply for the good of the institution, and never show subservience. Unfortunately, the noncooperative inmate code extends to noncooperation with those members of the prison staff whose function it is to aid and counsel inmates. No wonder it has been said that trying to rehabilitate criminals in prison is like trying help alcoholics maintain sobriety in a brewery. Institutional counseling is the ultimate challenge for the correctional helper.

The Origins of the Inmate Code

When we discussed differential association theory, we noted that many criminals develop a set of values and attitudes in opposition to lawful behavior through the frequency, duration, priority, and intimacy of their associations with individuals of like mind. The individuals with whom they most associate, either by choice or by necessity, become their reference group, the group around which they orient their lives, and against whose standards they evaluate themselves. When criminals are incarcerated, the power of the reference group over their lives increases considerably because now it is the only group with which they are able to associate. Within this closed community, antiestablishment values are refined and reinforced. In prison, compliance with antiestablishment values and attitudes can become much more of a survival imperative than it ever was on the outside. This is an important point for any new member of the treatment staff working in a prison.

Prisonization

Not all inmates enter prison with a ready-made set of antisocial attitudes. However, new prisoners, like new immigrants, face a painful process of assimilation into a new culture from which it is difficult to remain aloof. The process of assimilating the norms and values of the prison subculture has been termed *prisonization* by

Clemmer (1958). The basic premise of prisonization is that people who share a common experience, especially one imposed upon them, develop a sense of "we-ness" buttressed by a set of legitimizing attitudes in opposition to those professed by "them." The first steps in the prisonization process are simple acts of behavioral conformity, which occur regardless of how the inmate feels about performing them. The inmate watches and follows the examples of other inmates because conformity makes life easier, avoids conflicts, and enables the inmate to fit in without being conspicuous. Before the inmate knows it, he or she is speaking the language of fellow inmates and beginning to define the inmate world in inmate terms. It requires only a subtle and minute change to make a stated attitude become a "taken-for-granted" perception of reality. When this process is completed, inmates become "cons."

The prison subculture often satisfies the inmates' needs to belong, a need that we all have. To belong, an inmate must be accepted, and to be accepted he or she must live by the inmate code whereby a "wrong" by the standards of the straight world becomes a "right." To the extent that an inmate abides by that code, he or she becomes a "good convict," and is accepted. For an inmate not to be accepted by fellow inmates could be a very dangerous thing indeed for the inmate.

According to Gordon Graham, a hard-nosed ex-con who spent nearly twenty years in various prisons and now is president of the Human Development Training Institute, this need to belong by conforming to the inmate code is the biggest stumbling block to inmate rehabilitation (1992: 62). Through hard experience, observation, and much study, Graham concluded that the establishment of a strong personal identity as a "good convict" in prison becomes more strongly etched into the person's self-concept the longer he (or she) remains in the prison environment.

We all develop what Gordon calls a "comfort zone," which is a set of situations, settings, and circumstances in which we feel confident and comfortable. For instance, a "take charge" police officer might tremble at the thought of giving a lecture, and an erudite professor might tremble if he or she is thrust into the professional world of the police officer. When we are outside of our comfort zones, we get feedback telling us that we are "out of place," and we often retreat back to the psychological safety of the known. Inmates develop a "comfort zone," too, but a very constricted one. When they get back onto the streets, they do not fit in; their much sought after reputations as "good convicts" now become liabilities, their worlds have turned upside down (Graham 1992: 158).

Although all prisoners have to conform behaviorally, not all, perhaps not even most, will conform attitudinally in the sense that they will internalize the inmate code as right and proper. Irwin and Cressey (2004) point out that the attitudes representative of prisonization are not simply responses to prison life but reflect values and norms brought by many inmates into the prison from the free world. The degree of prisonization internalized by inmates thus depends on the attitudes and values brought to the institution with them. Unfortunately, the cliché stating that one bad apple spoils the barrel strongly applies in prison settings in which the worst inmates so often set the ambience. Ways to avoid attitudinal assimilation on the part of prisoners who do necessarily enter prison with strong criminal attitudes suggested by Clemmer (and seconded by Graham) are shorter prison sentences and more frequent contact with the outside world.

Prisoners with strong personalities and those who actively strive to remain aloof from the prison subculture do not succumb to prisonization to the same extent that more pliable individuals do, although trying to remain aloof may subject the inmate to "dangerous ostracism" (Schmalleger 2001: 493). Some take on the values and attitudes surrounding them only as a measure of convenience, being fully aware all the time that their conformity is a temporary condition of their confinement. We can help these individuals to counteract the insidious process of prisonization, and even perhaps those who have already succumbed, by well-run group counseling sessions. Remember, all counseling is designed to challenge what Graham calls our comfort zones. Becoming a better person (attaining psychological growth) requires that we extend those zones as far as we possibly can so that we can be reasonably confident and comfortable in even the most unusual of circumstances.

Group Counseling

A major obstacle to effective institutional counseling is the oppositional stance of the inmate code. Inmates do attend counseling sessions, Alcoholics Anonymous and Narcotics Anonymous meetings, and vocational and educational programs. Attendance at these sessions is not a violation of the inmate code. Indeed, prisoners hear much banter in prisons about the necessity to "get into a program." Unfortunately, the concern for getting into a program is more often than not motivated by efforts to impress the parole board rather than a genuine concern for self-improvement (Berne's "How do I get out of here?" [1964]). If the possibility of the ultimate reward for participation, that of early release, were not a reality, inmates who attended such sessions would be violating the inmate code and branded as "suckers" or "ass kissers." Consequently, inmates who attend sessions aimed at reforming criminal behavior patterns may spend a great deal of time telling other inmates how they are exploiting the sessions for their own ends.

Nevertheless, social- and evolutionary psychology tell us that people tend to function best, are more influenced, and more influential, operating in groups (Gilbert 2001). This is certainly true, and we agree with Tim Lacey when he writes that: "group therapy offers a far more realistic environment for individuals to learn about their behavior and to change it than in individual therapy" (2004: 34). Group counseling is an effective way to combat the negative group pressures that hinder rehabilitative efforts because inmates are more likely to listen to their peers than to representatives of "the system."

Group counseling may be viewed as a type of intellectual jujitsu in which the strength of the group is used against itself. Group counseling uses peer pressure to combat the criminal attitudes and values that many of the group members hold as individuals. The differential association theory of crime stresses the power of peer-group pressure to lead the individual into conformity with antisocial values. Why not use the same pressure for the opposite purpose? If an individual's behavior is an intrinsic part of groups to which he or she belongs, if we want to change that behavior we must direct our efforts at those groups.

However, do not imagine that this is an easy task. As Morgan, Kroner and Mills (2006) point out; if you can facilitate groups counseling in prison, you can do it anywhere. How does one change the criminal attitudes of individuals in a group that, with the exception of the group leader, consists of criminals? Although it is extremely difficult, and realistically you can expect more failures than successes, it is not impossible. Think about the gratifying success rate of Alcoholics Anonymous (AA) groups. Do you think that it is more difficult to rehabilitate the typical alcoholic or the typical criminal? Objectively, the alcoholic presents the more difficult case. After all, there is no biological urge to commit crimes (not that we currently know of, anyway) in the same sense as there is for the alcoholic to drink. The criminal who desists from committing crime does not suffer painful physical withdrawal symptoms that are alleviated only by committing crime. Criminals are not physiologically punished for stopping their activities the way alcoholics are. On the contrary, they run the risk of punishment for continuing with the activity.

Many criminals enjoy the thrills and excitement of the criminal lifestyle just as alcoholics enjoy drinking, but neither alcoholics nor criminals like the negative consequences of their respective activities. Significant emotional events in their lives, the loss of jobs, spouses, and self-respect, and the loss of long periods of freedom constitute powerful motivations for change.

Whatever motivations exist for change must be brought into full consciousness and sharply focused. They then must be carefully cultivated and nurtured. Harking back to our discussion of Motivational Interviewing, discrepancy, dissonance, ambivalence, and tension must be generated in the minds of those whose attitudes are to be modified by forcing them to confront the reality of their behavior. Many criminals are so present-oriented that they fail to consider what five years in prison actually means. It is the group counselor's task, with the cooperation of the group, to bring each member to the realization that powerful motivations for change do exist in every one of them. Specific strategies for achieving this in a group setting are presented later in this chapter. If Alcoholics Anonymous can achieve respectable success rates in groups consisting of members who have all experienced the pleasures and the pains of alcohol, there is no reason to feel that groups consisting of those who have experienced the pleasures and pains of crime could not enjoy similar success.

Characteristics of Effective Correctional Group Counselors

What makes a really effective group counselor in a prison setting? Ed Jacobs and Nina Spadaro (2003: 36-39) offer a list of the characteristics they deem necessary. Pay heed to what they say because each of them has a wealth of experience. Ed Jacobs has taught counseling for more than thirty years, and has served as a trainer for the Federal Bureau of Prisons, and for adult and juvenile corrections in West Virginia. Nina Spadaro was a staff psychologist with the Federal Bureau of Prisons for ten years and continues to train correctional staff in West Virginia. The following are the six characteristics these two experts feel are essential for an effective group leader in a correctional facility.

An Effective Group Leader Understands Prison Culture: You must know what you are getting into; prisons are not monasteries or country clubs. You must understand how the inmate code works, how it influences the behavior of the group toward each other and toward you.

A Skilled Group Leader is not Frustrated by a Lack of Apparent Progress: If you want to see quick results in a prison setting, you will be sorely disappointed. These folks are not inside for singing too loudly at choir practice, and they are not there to learn to modulate the tone of their voices. You are planting seeds that you may or may not see bloom some time down the road.

A Good Group Leader Cares about People who are Hard to Care About: Again, remember what type of people you are dealing with, but also remember the lessons of The Mask presented in Chapter 4. Perhaps some of inmates' nastier characteristics are masks covering up some pretty deep hurts. You do not have to love them—just care about them. If you do not, you are probably doing more harm than good as a group leader.

A Strong Group Leader is Firm yet not Dictatorial: his is "tough love." Inmates need firm boundaries within a flexible foundation if the group is to accomplish its goals.

An Effective Therapy Group Leader Understands Counseling Theories: This one is a "no brainer." Theories anchor your efforts in solid foundation, but without them your efforts will sink in quicksand.

A Skilled Treatment Group Leader has Strong Individual Counseling Skills: This is a corollary of the previous characteristic. There are times in a group setting when only the group leader is able to answer and help a person presenting a particularly difficult problem, and there are times when inmates may need to be counseled in private.

The Power of the Group

A group consists of "a number of persons who communicate with one another often over a span of time, and who are few enough so that each person is able to communicate with all others, not at secondhand, through other people, but face-to-face" (Homans 1950: 1). The prison community is not a group in this sense, but merely an aggregate of people in the midst of which the individual could feel terribly alone. None of us likes to feel alone, and we often will go to great lengths to become part of a group. We are very social animals. Group counseling takes advantage of this human need for social interaction by offering inmates a constructive alternative to the antisocial cliques that form in prisons.

Groups possess dynamics of their own that are relatively independent of the sum of the individual attributes of their members. Much of sociology and social psychology revolves around issues of how group life affects individual behavior. Numerous studies attest to the ability of groups to generate a general conformity to their norms, even among reluctant members. Here we cannot consider in detail the question of why groups possess powers that appear to be greater than the sum of their constituent parts.

Suffice it to say that group conformity is more likely if goals are shared, and goals are more likely to be shared if they are democratically determined. As the group leader, meaning the person who initiates the process and who gives the initial direction and initial suggestions, the counselor is in a position to strongly influence the nature of the goals. Inmates realize, of course, that the ultimate goal is to reeducate them into conformity with society's standards and expectations. Therefore, they are not likely to choose topics that they perceive as being too directly related to this end. As a group counselor, you must make haste slowly. If inmates are to learn new values and unlearn old ones, they will do so only by the process of self-exploration that is of their own choosing.

Planning for Group Counseling: Goals and Operating Philosophy

Group counseling theory takes as an inviolable principle that having a plan is critical (Jacobs, Masson, and Harvill 2002). The first task in the planning for group counseling is to formulate in your own mind the specific aims and goals that you want the group to pursue. Your operating philosophy should be something like that of a professor who has a certain core content of knowledge to impart to the class but who remains flexible enough to let the students dictate the pace of the class. Much student interest and participation is lost in classes where professors refuse to follow a train of thought brought up by a student because "We have to finish Chapter 10 by Thursday." Group interest and participation similarly can be stifled if you do not maintain an attitude of structured flexibility.

Selection of Members

Your next task is the selection of group members from the pool of volunteers. For various reasons, there is rarely any lack of volunteers for group counseling in prisons (Juda 1984: 48). You simply should not throw people together to see what will happen, an all-too-frequent practice in prison settings. An examination of the offenders' classification scales and their psychological profiles obviously will aid you in this endeavor. For instance, it would be extremely unwise to allow anyone in the group who is psychopathic, especially if the counselor is inexperienced. Psychopaths are brilliant game players who will use the group for their own nefarious ends, and counseling tends to make them somewhat worse because they learn more ways to push peoples' buttons (Lee 2007). Needless to say, if the group is to be centered on a specific problem, such as alcoholism, drug addiction, or sexual offenses, then inmates should be selected on the basis of problems they have in the specific area rather than on other considerations.

Each prospective member of the group then should be given an individual screening interview. This practice is laid down as one of the ethical guidelines of the Association for Specialists in Group Work (1980):

The group leader shall conduct a pre-group interview with each prospective member for purposes of screening, orientation, and, in so far as possible, shall select group members whose needs and goals are compatible with the established goals of the group; who will not impede the group process; and whose well-being will not be jeopardized by the group process.

Corey (1983: 102) indicates that the following questions concerning suitability can be explored in about a half-hour interview with each candidate:

1. Why does this person want to join the group?

2. How ready is the person to become actively involved in the process of self-examination that will be part of group?

3. Does the candidate have a clear idea about the nature and purpose of the group? Does he or she have a view of what is expected?

4. Are there any indications that the person might be counterproductive to the development of the cohesion in the group? Might this group be counterproductive to the person?

Such a screening interview not only permits you to choose group members who you feel will strengthen the group's possibilities of success, but it also allows you and individual offenders to become acquainted with one another. Moreover, it gives offenders the opportunity to decide for themselves whether they want to be part of your group after all. Thus, you have a double screening process, yours and theirs. Without the dual checkout process, you and the offenders are on a blind date, and we all know how disastrous blind dates can turn out to be. Except when counseling is mandated, inmates should never be forced into a group against their will. To do so will prove very counterproductive (Alexander 2000).

Components of Group Counseling

Gazda, Duncan, and Meadows provide a clear definition of group counseling:

> Group counseling is a dynamic, interpersonal process focusing on conscious thought and behavior and involving the therapy functions of permissiveness, orientation to reality, catharsis, and mutual trust, caring, understanding, acceptance, and support. The therapy functions are created and nurtured in a small group through the sharing of personal concerns with one's peers and the counselors. The group counselees are basically normal individuals with various concerns which are not debilitating to the extent of requiring extensive personality change. The group counselees may utilize the group interaction to increase understanding and acceptance of values and goals and to learn and/or unlearn certain attitudes and behaviors (quoted in Mahler 1973: 101).

By analyzing the component parts of the definition, we can get a feeling for the process of group counseling, what it is and how it should be conducted.

- *"Group counseling is a dynamic, interpersonal process,"* alerts you to the fact that the process is active, productive, forceful, and energetic. It is not static, but full of continuous verbal movement toward purposeful goals. It can be dynamic only if members of the group put real concerns and problems before the group for open evaluation and discussion.

- *"Interpersonal"* means that it is an activity that takes place between or among two or more people. Advocates of group counseling feel that members learn and/or unlearn attitudes, values, and perceptions better in a group setting because it is similar to their natural interpersonal world (Lacey 2004). Relating to peers is more consistent with normal socialization experiences than relating to a counselor in a situation that can be reminiscent of the teacher/student relationship. Most of all, "interpersonal" means sharing.

- *"Focusing on conscious thought and behavior"* indicates that the topics explored are attitudes and behaviors of which the group members are fully aware and which are problematic. Group counseling is not group therapy. Group therapy is more likely to deal with unconscious motivations. Individuals who conduct it usually have advanced degrees in psychiatry, psychology, or psychiatric social work. The difference is analogous to the distinction made earlier between psychotherapy and individual counseling. Like psychotherapy, group therapy goes into great depth, and it is a process that may last months or years. Group counseling is very short, by comparison, and may be conducted by individuals with minimal specialized skills. Remember, the concerned amateurs of Alcoholics Anonymous conduct the most successful group counseling in the world. Remember also that the personal attributes of the counselor are more important to success than the depth of the counselor's knowledge of the complexities of mental health.

- *"Permissiveness, orientation to reality, catharsis, and mutual trust, caring, understanding, acceptance and support"* are attributes that the counselor must strive to foster in the group. This is no easy task with a prison group! Permissiveness does not mean that the group is allowed to act out, to bully weaker members, or to be otherwise disruptive. It means that the group should be democratic in its choice of problems to discuss, that no one member should be allowed to monopolize the floor, and that no relevant topic should be denied a hearing.

Neither does "permissiveness" mean that the group is run without some basic ground rules. As with the formulation of treatment plans in community corrections, the rules should be determined in concert with the group. However, group counseling is a guided-group experience. Accordingly, during the initial screening interview, the counselor will indicate a series of expectations about what will go on in the group. The counselor basically wants group members to examine their impulses in an atmosphere of acceptance to help them make connections between those impulses and their criminal behavior. Groups function much more effectively if each member is aware of the expectations and has been given an opportunity to participate in their formulation. A democratically determined group structure outlining purposeful goals goes a long way toward developing a feeling of "we-ness" in the group. The essential elements of group interaction–each individual "I," the "we" of the group, and the "it" of the goals–must form an integrated "I-owe-it" triangle if the process is to be useful (Anderson 1984: 13-15).

Take care, however, that democratically derived decisions regarding group topics and issues are not at odds with institutional requirements, are socially acceptable, and are fit for individual members of the group. Neither group nor counselor pressure should be used to cajole individual members into conformity. As Bennett, Rosenbaum, and McCullough (1978: 89) put it: "We cannot continue to coerce offenders into conformity. We must provide those experiences necessary to individual adjustment and a meaningful life. For most people this comes through opportunities for intellectual and emotional growth. Why not for offenders?" Why not indeed?

- *"Orientation to reality"* refers to awareness on the part of all group members that the goals of the group are directed toward the rejection of unrealistic and irresponsible values and behavior and the substitution of realistic and responsible values and behavior. Realistic and responsible here are consistent in meaning with Glasser's usage in his reality therapy. The general goals of a prison group are improved self-awareness, genuine problem sharing, an awareness of the self-defeating nature of a criminal lifestyle, improved coping skills, and an understanding of the benefits and possibilities of the straight life. Specific goals are determined by the makeup of the group (for example, alcohol abusers, exhibitionists, and so forth).

- *"Catharsis"* refers to the release and ventilation of repressed emotions associated with painful experiences. Psychoanalysts feel that much guilt, anger, aggression, and hostility are the result of repressed emotions. If these pent-up emotions can be liberated— that is, brought into consciousness and explored—then much of the negativism they generate will dissipate.

- *"Mutual trust, caring, understanding, acceptance, and support"* are attributes conspicuously absent among prison inmates at anything beyond a superficial level. However, they should not be considered impossible to generate in a prison setting. By and large, inmates do not possess these attributes because they rarely have encountered them in their lives. If you, by your example, can foster such an environment, if you can demonstrate being accepting, understanding, and caring, chances are that some of it will rub off. Here is one inmate's report of her experience in group counseling: "I have felt needed, loving, competent, furious, frantic, anything and everything, but just plain loved. You can imagine the flood of humility, release that swept over me. I wrote with considerable joy, 'I actually felt loved.' I doubt that I shall soon forget it" (quoted in Jarvis 1978: 197-198).

- *"The therapy functions are created and nurtured in a small group,"* says that the size of the group is an important consideration. A group of too few members, say three, is comfortable for the group leader to handle, but it is not very practical in terms of the efficient management of time and resources. Groups this small also have two additional disadvantages that often seem to occur: two members forming an alliance against a third, or members feel too much pressure to speak and thus feel uncomfortable (Jacobs, Masson, and Harvill 2002). Having too many members renders the group unmanageable for the leader. The group begins to act like a class in school, directing communications primarily at the group counselor. This tendency defeats the whole purpose of being in a group. The more people there are in a group, the easier it becomes for some members to hide and avoid discussing their problems. Even if no one wanted to hide, there is just so much "air time" to go around, and the multiplicity of topics may prevent focusing where it is desirable. A generally accepted optimal group size is between five and eight members (Jacobs, Masson, and Harvill 2002).

Even a group of this size can be intimidating and difficult to manage for new counselors. In a one-on-one situation, counselors have the feeling of being in control, because they have to attend to only one individual. It is not unusual for inmate groups to test new counselors by ganging up on them. Having something of a vested interest in maintaining current self-concepts, in demonstrating independence and noncooperation, and in displaying bravado, group members often feel that the best defense is offense.

Confident and self-assured counselors recognize and deal with this obvious game-playing by indicating to the group that they know what is going on, and asking the members why they feel that they have to do it. Counselors never should go on the defensive, but rather, should toss the ball right back at the group, without emphasizing their moral authoritative superiority over the group.

- *"Through the sharing of personal concerns with one's peers and the counselors"* points to the exchange of self-disclosure and feedback among members of the group. This is the essence of group counseling. The success or failure of the group depends almost entirely on the meaningfulness of the self-concerns disclosed and the nature of the feedback.

However, prison is a place where it is often necessary to shut off one's emotions, where inmates are supposed to "do their own time," and where to reveal personal concerns is to open oneself up to possible abuse, derision, or even blackmail. Consequently, inmates in a group session may go to great lengths to lead the group communication away from themselves and toward others, or to general topics. Such ploys may be in evidence in any group setting, but they are especially so in the prison setting. You must learn to identify them and confront members with them, at the same time recognizing the motivations behind them. A prison group is not an encounter group for which members have paid considerable sums of money to seek "self-actualization." You will be setting yourself up for disappointment and failure if you fail to empathize with the special concerns about self-disclosure within a prison setting.

There are several ways to handle the lack of self-disclosure within the group. It is wise not to expect or to attempt to facilitate self-disclosure at all during the first session. Simply give the group members an opportunity to warm up to intergroup communication by venting general non-threatening concerns. Inmates must sense at least a modicum of trust and acceptance before they will risk self-disclosure.

An excellent institutional counseling strategy is to begin the first session with an explanation of Berne's theory of structural analysis (Lester 2000). Its easy terminology and simple diagrammatic presentations of Parent-Adult-Child (PAC) interactions provide a useful shared framework from which all participants can analyze what will go on during future sessions. The various ego states and their transactions can be drawn and explained on the blackboard. You may be surprised how much more easily group members will pick up on game playing and how it quickly will improve understanding when you use this very powerful anchor of shared discourse. However, some experienced prison counselors feel that the transactional analysis approach is not very useful in prison settings beyond the early sessions that introduce terminology. The very simplicity of the approach is tailor-made for inmates who may want to use it to manipulate fellow inmates, and even counselors.

After one or two "getting acquainted" sessions, you may make a statement to the group similar to the following: "You know, we've been talking for quite some time together now, but I haven't heard any of us touch on the topics of 'self' or 'I' yet. Will somebody volunteer to explore the question 'Who or what am I?' with us?"

The first attempt at self-disclosure should be reinforced positively by the use of nonthreatening and nonjudgmental feedback from the counselor. Feedback should reflect the feelings of the discloser, making sure that the reflection is based on accurate perceptions rather than on inferences. If, for instance, Frank responds to your request to explore the question "Who am I?" with the response, "I suppose that by society's standards I am a failure, a no-good screw-up," he is making a statement about his perceptions of how others on the outside view him. You should not infer that he perceives himself that way by asking him why he is a "screw-up." Rather, you should ask him if he agrees with that perception and why he does or does not. Such feedback could lead to an animated group discussion of values and attitudes held by group members.

As a member of the group, the counselor should be prepared to model self-disclosure for the group. Needless to say, the counselor must feel that he or she is fair game in any session and must be prepared to answer uncomfortable questions in an honest and forthright manner. It is not unusual for inmates to test the counselor by asking pointed questions such as "Did you ever steal anything?" Almost everybody has stolen something at one time or another, even if it was only a candy bar or a company pen.

You must not attempt to give the impression that you are a "goody two-shoes" by denying that you have, thereby modeling dishonesty for the group. You could take advantage of such a question by describing how guilty you felt afterwards and asking other members of the group how they feel when they steal and how they themselves have felt when others have stolen from them. You also can use the opportunity to describe your ideas of responsibility, emotional maturity, respect for self and others, and discuss how your values have enabled you to lead a basically happy life. Again, this should not be delivered in a preachy style calculated to impress the group with your moral superiority.

- *"The group counselees are basically normal individuals with various concerns, which are not debilitating to the extent of requiring extensive personality change,"* is a reminder to respect the humanity of the group members. Do not think of them as being sick, evil, beyond help, or radically different in any way from yourself. They are basically unloved individuals with deficiencies that prevent them in one way or another from functioning in a socially acceptable way. Inmates who do have crippling and debilitating concerns do not belong in group counseling. Think of all group members as possessing wholesome potentialities that only need to be recognized and developed. The distortions of reality you encounter are the result of faulty thinking rather than pathological blockages. Your basic task is to reeducate toward responsibility, not to psychoanalyze.

- *"The group counselees may utilize the group interaction to increase understanding and acceptance of values and goals and to learn and/or unlearn certain attitudes and behaviors"* simply restates the goals of any counseling session, group or individual. It is a guided effort to change a failure identity into a success identity through self-disclosure and feedback. The only difference emphasized here is that group counseling makes use of peer feedback and modeling.

Specific Topics and Strategies for Group Counseling

The goal of group counseling is to guide offenders toward change by exploring and assessing their values, attitudes, and behaviors. What follows are some specific strategies for getting started. Additional exercises may be similar to the exercises at the end of some of the chapters in this book, such as exploring general attitudes and values.

Counting the Cost of a Criminal Lifestyle

From the perspective of some criminals, crime may be considered a rational pursuit in the sense that there is a logical fit between the attainment of ends and the means used to achieve them. That is, it gets them what they want at a price that they think they can afford. This group exercise is designed to challenge that perception of rationality through certain cognitive-behavioral techniques. From any objective viewpoint (that is, going beyond the offender's subjective perception of immediate rationality), for all but the "kingpins" of crime, crime simply does not pay in the long run.

You can help your group members discover this for themselves by having them create an inventory of their estimated criminal gains (assuming property offenders) obtained for the crime(s) for which they are doing time. You might go even further by asking them to list their gains from undetected crimes committed during the period between their current arrest and any previous arrest. The list should contain actual cash gains and the "fenced" value of any property taken. A list compiled by an offender who did forty months in prison for three burglaries is presented below. This individual also included in his inventory ten other burglaries for which he was not caught.

Cash	$400
Stereos	$150
TV's	$ 75
Jewelry	$200
Tools	$ 20
Miscellaneous	$180
Total	$1,025

After these lists are completed, divide the monetary gains from crime by the amount of time spent in prison (take along a calculator). For instance, the person in this example received a "paycheck" from his criminal activity of $1,025, for which he did forty months in prison. Therefore: $1,025/40 months = $25.62 per month, $0.82 per day, or $0.10 per hour. The group members will be quite surprised when they discover how little they have been "working" for per hour! Few of the offenders, if any at all, have ever thought along these lines. This revelation should create the discrepancy and ambivalence vital to Motivational Interviewing, as we discussed in

Chapter 9. You then may proceed with what should be an animated discussion of just how smart it is to work for ten cents per hour.

Drive the point home by calculating the possible gains the person would have if he or she had spent forty months in non-criminal activity. Ask each individual to speculate about what portion of his or her prison sentence he or she reasonably could have been expected to work at a regular job on the outside. If our individual doing forty months stated that he would have worked only about one-quarter of the time, multiply this time by the take-home pay he would have received at minimum wage (about $1,100 per month). Thus, $1,100 times ten months = $11,000. Add to this approximately $200 per month he may possibly have received in unemployment benefits during his periods (say six months) of unemployment, and we reach a total of $12,200. This is hardly a princely sum, but considerably in excess of his $1,025. Even if you add the fruits of a criminal lifestyle in the form of prison wages (an average of about 80 cents per hour) for those lucky enough to have a prison job, the contrast will be only slightly diminished.

Other less tangible, but sometimes more important, costs and benefits associated with a criminal lifestyle can be discussed in the group. To start this discussion rolling, have each member divide a sheet of paper into two equal sections. Have them label one column Benefits, and the other Costs. Rather than doing this on an individual basis, consider dividing the group into two sections, one to brainstorm about the benefits of crime and the other to do the same about the costs of crime. They might arrive at a set of costs and benefits like that shown in Table 12.1. Some may even list as a benefit of crime the sheer thrill of committing it. Recall that in Chapter 3 we mentioned that the brain's reward system might kick in with a healthy dopamine buzz when engaging in a risky but thrilling crime (Young 2003).

Figure 12.1 What Do I Gain and Lose From a Life of Crime?

Benefits	Costs
Lots of leisure (not working)	No regular paycheck, little money to spend
The street reputation	The boredom of sitting in a cell
Doing what I want, being free to be my own man	The worry caused to my parents
Lots of girls think I'm cool	Having the screws decide almost all I do and when I should do it
The laughs	No women in the joint
Putting one over on the system	Police hassle and arrest
Money for nothing	Can't get a job because of record
	The whole prison experience
	Appearing in court and paying fines
	This prison is a long way from home, so I rarely see my parents
	My wife divorced me and married another guy while I was away

Other costs and benefits are possible, but almost invariably you will find that members will be able to think of a lot more costs than benefits. Discuss this discrepancy with them, as well as the inconsistency of such items as "being free to be my own man," on the one hand, and having every movement dictated by the "screws" on the other. You even may go further and invite them to rate each item on a scale of one through ten according to how positive they consider each benefit of crime and how negative they consider each cost of crime. They then can sum the columns to arrive at their own numeric evaluation of the costs and benefits of their lifestyles. Since they will have listed the items themselves, as well as deciding what numeric score to assign to them, this exercise can be a powerful tool in getting your group members to realize how destructive to themselves their lifestyles are.

Role Reversal and Empathy Training

Criminals rarely think of the feelings of their victims. One of the ways to encourage such thought is to ask them to compile a list of feelings that they think the victims of their latest crimes may have experienced as a consequence of those crimes. The lists may contain such feelings as anger, revenge, fear, and outrage. Ask the group members if they feel that these responses of the victims are justified. This exercise should not be conducted in the spirit of "How would you like it if . . .?" Most members long ago will have been inured to such moralizing.

Yet, it is highly likely that most group members will have been victims of crimes themselves in the past. Ask them to recall the feelings that they had about their victimizers on those occasions. Also, have them explore feelings they had when a family member or close personal friend was victimized. Such a discussion should lead to the general conclusion that even criminals value justice and "law and order" when the offender/victim roles are reversed. You might even play devil's advocate making justifications for hypothetical crimes you have committed (say child molesting) and have offenders challenge your rationales and excuses.

Sentencing Exercises

Without being explicit, you can further emphasize their beliefs in conventional morality by engaging in the type of sentencing exercises you have been asked to do as students. That is, you could provide the group with hypothetical criminal cases and have the group decide on appropriate penalties for them. You will find that inmates will present arguments similar to those of probation officers at sentencing staffings (meetings at which officers decide together on an appropriate sentencing recommendation) and that they often can be considerably more punitive in their sentencing decisions! What group members will be doing implicitly in these exercises, without fully recognizing it for the moment, is revealing and reflecting on some of their anticriminal and prosocial values.

Reattributing Responsibility

Criminals share with the rest of us a penchant for systematically biasing causal attributions of responsibility for what happens to them. It is generally true that when something good or praiseworthy happens to us, we locate the causal agent in ourselves: "I was able to accomplish this goal because I'm a pretty dependable and neat kind of person." When something bad or blameworthy happens to us, we tend to attribute it to circumstances beyond our control: "I'm branded a criminal because I was never given a chance. My parents beat me and never took an interest in me. Nobody'll give me a job, so I have to steal." In the first instance, we take a free-will perspective by offering "reasons" located within the self for having accomplished a goal. In the second instance, we tend to take a determinist position by offering "causes" external to ourselves that guarantee, "It could not be otherwise."

Such attributions of responsibility are normal, albeit not desirable. They function as defense mechanisms to protect our self-images. Like all other defense mechanisms, they can become pathologically destructive if we deny all responsibility for the negative things that happen to us. Unfortunately, many criminals are remarkably creative in inventing and exaggerating the power of circumstances deemed beyond their control to justify their criminal behavior and their inability to follow the straight and narrow. Your task is to demonstrate the irrationality and lack of responsibility inherent in this attitude. We are not dead leaves blown hither and thither by environmental winds. We do have a hand in what happens to us, and we do possess the capacity to bring those events under our control.

To explore this way of thinking with your group, ask them to draw a large four-celled square like the one in Figure 12.2. Instruct them to list in the windowed cells (1) what good things in their lives are the results of their own actions, (2) what good things in their lives are the results of circumstances outside their control, (3) what bad things in their lives are the results of their own actions, and (4) what bad things in their lives are the results of circumstances outside their control.

The odds are that you will see the great majority of responses in the upper-left and lower-right cells of the square. You might begin the discussion by asking members to volunteer reasons why they have placed a given event in a given cell and then open up those reasons for discussion. You can steer the discussion around to the concept of human autonomy, guided by the insights of Ellis' Rational-Emotive Behavioral Therapy. Emphasize that the subjective reality of free will is extremely useful for individuals if they are to believe that they are capable of initiating actions that will lead to self-improvement. Individuals who insist that they are the directors of their own lives, that they alone are responsible for what they will become, and that they can overcome almost anything through sheer acts of will, are people who will achieve far more than their less active peers who seek excuses for their failures outside of themselves.

Figure 12.2 Reattributing Responsibility

MY LIFE

	Good things that have happened to me	Bad things that have happened to me
The result of my own actions		
The result of circumstances beyond my control		

Of course, things do happen to us that are beyond our personal control. Individuals who blame themselves for events that are clearly outside of their power to influence suffer from low self-esteem (Ickes and Layden 1978). The objective of this exercise is not to move everything into the top two cells. It is rather to explore ways in which some of the bad events could have been brought under the individual's control. The exercise also is designed to enhance the self-esteem of those who masochistically attribute all negative events to themselves and who may tend to attribute the positive events in their lives to outside influences. The idea is expressed in Reinhold Niebuhr's Serenity Prayer: "God grant me the serenity to accept the things I cannot change, the courage to change the things I can, and the wisdom to know the difference."

There are numerous other exercises you can conduct in group counseling. Jacobs and Spadaro (2003) offer a large number of them in their book specifically devoted to the topic. If you are a new, or even a veteran, prison counselor, you cannot afford to miss this dynamic and powerful book.

Difficult Group Members

Despite the screening process designed to gather together a relatively homogeneous group, and despite all the other things you have done to assemble a smoothly running group, you probably will run into members who will be disruptive and/or uncooperative in one way or another. Their behavior may not necessarily be intended as disruption or noncooperation. To prevent such members from hindering the progress of the other members of the group, quickly identify and deal with disruptive behavior. Even if noncooperative behavior affects only the person not cooperating, you also should identify and deal with it. Some of the more usual types of difficult members are described below. Although we begin with the resister as a separate type, all other types are also resisters in one or more respects. Yet, some resistance to change is natural, and as previously pointed out, necessary for health and stability (Harris 1995).

The Resister

Since all group members have volunteered and all have had the opportunity to screen themselves out of the process, you can assume that the resister is experiencing ambivalence about the process. He or she has made a commitment in theory to explore himself or herself but finds it difficult to do so in practice. Because we dealt at some length with resistance when we discussed reality therapy, we will not explore it in detail here. Most authorities on group counseling feel that resistance is easier to deal with in a group setting than it is in an individual setting. This will be particularly true if you have provided the group with a common discourse for identifying resistance, such as structural analysis as outlined in transactional analysis. For instance, in a piece about resistance in groups that has not been said better in the half-century since it was made, Bry states:

> The first and most striking thing in handling of resistance in groups is that frequently resistance does not have to be "handled" at all, at least not by the therapist. The group is remarkably effective in dealing with this phenomenon. Early in the experience of each group, considerable effort is directed toward demonstrating what resistance is and how to become sensitive to its appearance in others as

well as oneself. The group members as well gradually develop ideas as to how to deal with resistance and how to use it productively. In cases of protective talking, sooner or later a group member usually gets sensitive to its resistance character and starts complaining about the "beating around the bush" (1951: 112).

The "Expert"

The "expert " in a group knows the answer to everyone's problems in the group and is not above liberally dispensing advice on how to deal with them. This behavior can be intimidating to the group leader if the advice giver really is an expert, or if everyone believes him or her to be. This author once had a physician in a group of child molesters who knew what was wrong with everyone in the group but himself. He had a doctoral degree, versus this author's master's degree (at the time). The author felt himself relinquishing the group direction to the doctor. Rather than trying to understand his motivations, the author eventually confronted him with a reminder of who was the group leader and of the fact that he was an offender, and that, unlike the doctor, the author had "dealt with hundreds of sex offenders." In other words, the author reduced himself to the doctor's level by puffing up his sense of importance as an "expert" in his own right. This was a very poor way of handling the situation.

Instead, the author should have realized that this man's conviction as a child molester had severely damaged his self-respect and that he was trying to regain some of it by demonstrating his superiority. An empathetic recognition of this would have led to a more sympathetic and understanding resolution of the problem he posed to the group. It is highly likely that he used advice giving to divert attention from his own problems; from letting others help him face and cope with his painful situation. Perhaps, he genuinely even felt that his advice would be helpful to his fellow members.

We all know how unwelcome unsolicited advice is. The group is not meeting for exchange of advice but for self-exploration. When a group member offers advice to another member, you might say something like this to the advice giver: "Charlie, it is obvious that John's problem is of concern to you, and you are concerned enough to offer some suggestions about what he might do."

Without pausing, you could then address John as follows: "John, when you have difficulty in coping, do you like to have someone who cares enough to suggest what you might do? Do you feel that Charlie's suggestion could be of use to you?" These responses indicate to Charlie that you have interpreted his offered advice as a genuine attempt to help John with his problem; you have not put him down. You also have given John an opportunity to respond to Charlie's advice giving, plus a chance to explore his problem further. John probably will put Charlie in his place if he feels he needs to; that is part of the group process of getting feelings out into the open. It is important that any necessary putting down be left to the group members rather than to the group counselor. Only after "experts" are confronted with the unacceptability of their behavior will they start to explore their own problems.

The Monopolizer

The monopolizer shares many of the characteristics of the resister and the expert. He or she tends to be a self-centered recognition seeker who wishes to rule the group. Motivations for monopolizing the group discussion are very similar to the motivations of the expert. Monopolizers really may feel that they are the only ones present with anything meaningful to contribute. However, the monopolizing may be a conscious tactic to steer the group away from discussing uncomfortable topics and toward topics of the monopolizers' choosing: "the best form of defense is offense." Either way, the negative effects on the group are the same.

Bry's statement about the resister is likely to be applicable here. Sooner or later, someone will pipe up with "Why don't you give somebody else a chance to speak?" When a statement such as this emerges, say something like the following to the protester: "Debbie, you feel angry at Sue because you feel that she is not interested in what others have to say and that she may be avoiding topics that are not comfortable for her. Am I right?" If Debbie indicates that you have accurately reflected her feelings, you might go on to say to Sue: "Sue, do you see yourself as monopolizing the conversation? Wouldn't you really like to listen to what others have to say and perhaps learn more about yourself and about others?" Monopolizers lack the important skill of listening. They need feedback from the other members about how their behavior is affecting others, even if the feedback results in a temporary sullen withdrawal from group participation.

The Withdrawn Member

Withdrawn group members either are engaging in passive resistance or may be lacking in confidence and/or the verbal skills to express themselves effectively. They hide in the group and are quite content to let the monopolizer, or anyone else, have the limelight. The group counselor should resist putting such persons on the spot by calling on them as a teacher calls on students in a classroom. As part of the group, however, withdrawn members are fair game for other members to approach. Be ready to help out the withdrawn person on such occasions so that being on the spot does not become too painful.

One way to simultaneously draw out the withdrawn member and minimize his/her embarrassment is to do "rounds." This means addressing each member of the group in turn and asking relatively simple open-ended questions. This tactic also prevents one or two people monopolizing the whole session (Jacobs, Masson, and Harvill 2002).

You might decide that you have made a mistake in allowing the withdrawn person to participate in the group or that the person has made a mistake in deciding to participate. The fact that the person is present, however, can be taken as a sign that he or she desires some form of counseling. You can determine this by the use of a session-evaluation form containing the question: "Would you like an individual session with me?" If the answer is "yes," that person can withdraw from group counseling and enter individual counseling. If it is "no" and he or she continues in the group, make every effort to include that person in the discussions.

The Masochist and the Sadist

Masochists are persons with low self-esteem and ingrained dependency needs who purposely set themselves up as targets for the displaced aggression of others. They doubt their ability to be loved, respected, or accepted by others. Since they desire companionship and relationships, however, they feel that the only strategy available to them is to put themselves into the hot seat where they are the victims of bullying, teasing, receiving sarcasm, and being the butt of bad jokes. They often become welcome targets for sadistic members of a group, and others may follow the sadist's lead to avoid personal exploration.

The group leader should quickly identify both the masochist and the sadistic bully. The feelings of both parties should be reflected so that other group members can suggest better methods for each to relate to others. Under no circumstances should you allow a group member to be set up as a constant target for unproductive criticism and hurtful comments. When other group members realize that such bullying is not acceptable to you, they will rally to the defense of the masochist. They can be relied on to put down the offending party. Allow them to do this for as long as it seems useful. However, if fisticuffs threaten to replace the spoken word, as they may well do with an individual who relies on bullying to get his or her way, bring the put-down to an end. You may offer the offending party an "out" by suggesting that he or she perhaps really did not mean to be hurtful: "Isn't that true, Mike?"

Advantages and Disadvantages of Institutional Group Counseling

There are, then, a number of theoretical and practical reasons why group counseling may be considered superior to individual counseling in an institutional setting. It will not be preferable for all offenders, for some clearly benefit more from private individual sessions. Likewise, many correctional workers are more comfortable conducting private rather than group sessions. Summarized in the following boxes are the major advantages and disadvantages of group counseling in an institutionalized setting.

Some Advantages of Group Counseling in Institutions

1. Time constraints and personnel shortages make it an efficient method of counseling a number of individuals with similar problems at the same time.

2. Groups with prosocial purposes offer inmates a constructive alternative to antisocial inmate cliques that form in response to the need of human beings for social interaction.

3. Because of the sharing of problems with the group members, members learn about alternative coping strategies.

4. Inmates can learn these alternative strategies, which also can be tried out in the abstract by involved discussions with those others who have experienced them.

5. Well-led and democratically run groups tend to develop a feeling of togetherness and "we-ness."

6. This sense of belonging can enable group pressure to change the attitudes of individuals in the direction of the group's purposes—to change antisocial attitudes into prosocial attitudes.

7. Unlike one-on-one counseling sessions with a representative of the "system," group counseling lessens the possibility that an inmate will be intimidated by a perceived authoritarian relationship.

Some Disadvantages of Group Counseling in Institutions

1. Some offenders may be reluctant to explore intimate feelings in the company of peers, although they desperately may want to do so. Some individuals feel much more comfortable speaking in private with an authority figure. Handle this situation by passing out evaluation forms that contain a question such as "Would you like to arrange an individual session with me?" Concerns that have surfaced in the offender's mind during a group session then can be given voice in private.

2. Much time can be wasted pursuing meaningless topics. The snag here is that we can realize that they are meaningless only after they have been fully expressed. Only experience will tell you when to cut off such topics and redirect the session along more meaningful avenues. However, this lost time is more than compensated for by the time saved in counseling a number of individuals at one time.

3. Closely allied to point two is the danger that the means become accepted as the goals. If the group counselor succeeds in generating discussion without reference to where the discussion is leading, nothing much is accomplished. The discussion is the means, not the goal. Group counseling always must be geared to realistic goals.

4. Some group members may take advantage of the numbers in the group to hide. We all are aware of students who select large classes and then sit at the back of the room to avoid class participation. They are missing out on much of the educational experience by doing this. Likewise, offenders who hide miss out on much of what could be meaningful to them. By the use of the same evaluation form, the counselor can determine if a given person is merely a hider or one who really wishes to address problems but who is shy in groups.

Exercises in Group Counseling

One of the best exercises for getting the feel of group counseling is to repeat the exercise in the section on re-attribution of responsibility. Since social psychologists tell us that almost everybody has the tendency to systematically bias causal attributions, this exercise will be more realistic for you than exercises such as counting the cost of a criminal lifestyle because you will be dealing with real issues rather than role-playing criminals.

The instructor may wish to act as the group leader, or he or she may wish to assign this task to someone. Just as in a real group situation, the group leader can begin the process by asking one of the other members to volunteer to explain a life event and to state where he or she has placed it in the 2 x 2 square. The discussion among group members then can begin to explore whether that event (good or bad) could have been brought more under the control of the individual.

This is obviously a time-consuming exercise, and it is likely that not everyone in the class will have the opportunity to offer a life event or serve as the group leader. Given the time constraints, go into some depth with one or two individuals rather than to try to cover everybody superficially. Therefore, the instructor may wish to examine everyone's summary of life events prior to commencing the exercise, and select one or two of the more interesting ones, and ask those people to volunteer.

Summary

Time and cost considerations make group counseling in institutionalized settings attractive. This does not mean that group counseling is "second best" to individualized counseling. Group counseling actually can be more beneficial for some offenders than individual counseling. Group counseling uses the power of the group to achieve its aims. Group counseling offers inmates a constructive alternative to the antisocial cliques that develop in prisons and can function to offset the power of the inmate code. Through the process of sharing, inmates can learn about alternative coping strategies from others who have "been there." A properly run group can develop a feeling of "we-ness," which is not always possible in individual counseling.

It is important to select group members carefully and to plan what is going to happen before starting any new group-counseling program. Even more important are the characteristics that the group counselor brings to the enterprise. These characteristics are taken from the excellent book on inmate group counseling written by Jacobs and Spadaro (2003).

In almost any group setting, there will be members who are disruptive. You can minimize their effect through the proper selection of members based on assessment information and one-on-one interviews with prospective members, but disruptive members, intentional or otherwise, will remain. Group members themselves will take care of much of the disruption, but you retain the ultimate responsibility for recognizing and dealing with disruption.

Disruptive members should be dealt with in a dignified and caring manner. It is possible that disruption is a clear signal that the person doing the disrupting should not be in the group. Approach that person with an offer of individual counseling with you. The insights of Transactional Analysis, Rational Effective Therapy, and reality therapy were presented as discussion topics. The "counting the costs" exercise may be particularly beneficial. Include predetermined topics like this in your counseling strategies. It is too easy to mistake animated discussion on irrelevant topics for progress. Group counseling must have a goal to aim toward. However, any relevant topic raised by a group member should be explored. And, do not forget, you as a member of the group are fair game for discussion.

Perspective from the Field
Group Counseling: Change as a Process Not an Event

By Jeff Lane

Jeff Lane is a program manager at the Idaho State Correctional Institution. He earned a master's degree in psychology from the University of Illinois. He has more than thirty years' experience in the counseling/ mental health program field, with eleven years as a clinician in the Idaho Department of Correction.

● ●

Group counseling in a prison setting is considerably different than group counseling in the community. Individuals in a community setting generally have a pro-social stance and want to deal with a problem. In a prison environment, the motivation can be more complicated. Completing a group or program may be a way to get a parole date or a commutation. There may be a genuine desire to change, or it may be part of a scheme to gain something else.

Although most offenders do not come into groups with a strong motivation to change, it may occur a little bit at a time. It is very difficult to effect change of the criminal personality. Many different types of programs have been developed and tried, but few have obtained any long-term success. In determining what groups are to be offered in prison, I have focused on those behaviors that have brought offenders in conflict with society; anger, problem-solving, sexual behaviors, substance abuse, and the basis for these behaviors, which is criminal logic and criminal thinking. Stanton Samenow and Samuel Yochelson began in the 1950s to develop insight into criminal thinking and the values and belief systems that are the foundation of such thinking. The framework of criminal thinking, or cognitive distortion (thinking errors), gives a good framework for dealing with offenders in groups.

Anyone who has worked in drug and alcohol groups understands that alcohol is a disease of denial. Although criminal behavior, in all of its forms, is not a disease, it is maintained by keeping it secret, calling it something else, rationalizing the effects, or simply pretending it does not exist. This is a type of denial, and presents the biggest challenge in working with offenders. In groups that deal with problems from anger to child molestation, the participants generally will avoid dealing with the behavior and spend time dealing with everything but their own accountability.

The best way to deal with this is by group structure. Without a well-defined and understood structure, a group facilitator can spend a good deal of time redefining boundaries, refocusing on goals, and explaining the process. Offender self-absorption can be counterproductive to the group's goals.

In prosocial groups, individuals usually have problems but do not know why. In offender groups, members know they have problems and tend to

Continued on the next page

Perspective from the Field, *continued*

blame others for those problems. This is counter to the goal of accepting responsibility. If the offender is generally unwilling to talk about his or her problem behavior by using denial, rationalizations, or misrepresentation, then taking responsibility can only occur when an offender remains open to the group process, open to looking at his or her behavior in a different way than is normal. This different view may involve empathy, the cost to the offender regarding the behavior, and evaluating what the behavior has actually given the offender versus his or her perceived gains.

Most groups within the prison system of Idaho are voluntary. We identify what someone wants to get out of the group and what they most value. Examples of what can be valued are family, freedom, recovery, dependent children, helping others, and much more. A person's progress in group can be measured (by themselves) by how openness and behavior brings them closer to or further away from what they say they value. Does their behavior in the group, how they deal with anger, for example, take them closer to their family or further from it? Does this behavior take them closer to their children and the parent they want to be or further from that? This is important in that most offenders are very concrete and look to short-term goals.

The "big picture" is usually something that they do not see, since their values usually get them tied up in the moment. Participant interaction requires offenders to use the words "I" or "me." Their role in groups is to relate their own experience. Lecturing or advising others is not part of the process.

The staff's role is to facilitate. When I have shared in a group, it has been very general and a way to make a point. Staff roles in prisons are very critical and need to be well defined. In offering programs, I know that all change is self-change and groups offer an opportunity to change. That change can be a long process taking years. Each group, each class, each effort to change can be a vital step in the process. Even efforts that may be viewed as failures at the moment may be critical elements that support a later change. This change process that groups offer is probably the most difficult task that an offender ever has undertaken, and the struggles that most offenders go through are normal and not the exception. Supporting them and being aware of where they are in the process is a critical element of any prison group because it is vital to any success that offenders may achieve.

References and Suggested Readings

Alexander, R. 2000. *Counseling, Treatment, and Intervention Methods with Juvenile and Adult Offenders*. Belmont, California: Brooks/Cole.

Anderson, J. 1984. *Counseling Through Group Process*. New York: Springer.

Association for Specialists in Group Work (ASGW). 1980. *Ethical Guidelines for Group Leaders*. Falls Church, Virginia: Association for Specialists in Group Work.

Bennett, L., T. Rosenbaum, and W. McCullough. 1978. *Counseling in Correctional Environments*. New York: Human Sciences Press.

Berne, E. 1964. *Games People Play*. New York: Grove Press.

Bry, T. 1951. Varieties of Resistance in Group Psychotherapy. *International Journal of Group Psychotherapy* 1: 106-114.

Clemmer, D. 1958. *The Prison Community*. New York: Holt, Rinehart and Winston.

Corey, G. 1983. Group Counseling: Being a Counselor: Directions and Challenges. In *Being a Counselor*, J. Brown and R. Pate, eds. Monterey, California: Brooks/Cole.

Gains, L., M. Kaune, and R. Miller. 2000. *Criminal Justice in Action*. Belmont, California: Wadsworth.

Gilbert, P. 2001. *Genes on the Couch*. London: Routledge.

Goffman, E. 1961. *Asylums: Essays on the Social Situation of Mental Patients and Other Inmates*. Garden City, New York: Anchor.

Graham, G. 1992. *The One-Eyed Man Is King*. Seattle, Washington: Graham and Graham Company.

Grayson, Ellis S. 1993. *Short-Term Group Counseling*. Laurel, Maryland: American Correctional Association.

Harkins, L. and A. Beech. 2007. Examining the Impact of Mixed Child Molesters and Rapists in Group-Based Cognitive-Behavioral Treatment for Sex Offenders. *International Journal of Offender Therapy and Comparative Criminology* 30: 1-15.

Harris, G. 1995. *Overcoming Resistance: Success in Counseling Men*. Lanham, Maryland: American Correctional Association.

Homans, G. 1950. *The Human Group*. New York: Harcourt, Brace and World.

Ickes, W. and M. Layden. 1978. New Directions in Attribution Research, vol. 2. In *Attributional Styles*. J. Harvey, W. Ickes, and R. Kidd, eds. Hillsdale, New Jersey: Lawrence Erlbaum Associates.

Irwin, J. and D. Cressey. 2004. Thieves, Convicts and the Inmate Culture. In *The Inmate Prison Experience*, M. Stohr and C. Hemmens, eds. Upper Saddle River, New Jersey: Prentice Hall. pp. 3-16.

Jacobs, E., R. Masson, and R. Harvill. 2002. *Group Counseling: Strategies and Skills*, 4th ed. Pacific Grove, California: Brooks/Cole.

Jacobs, E. and N. Spadaro. 2003. *Leading Groups in Corrections: Skills and Techniques*. Alexandria, Virginia: American Correctional Association.

Jarvis, D. 1978. *Institutional Treatment of the Offender*. New York: McGraw Hill.

Juda, D. 1984. On the Special Problems of Creating Group Cohesion Within a Prison Setting. *Journal of Offender Counseling, Services and Rehabilitation* 8: 47-59.

Lacey, T. 2004. Group Therapy and CBT. *Counseling and Psychotherapy Journal* 15: 34-36.

Lee, C. 2007. The Judicial Response to Psychopathic Criminals: Utilitarianism over Retribution. *Law and Psychology Review* 31: 125-137.

Lester, D. 2000. Group and Milieu Therapy. In *Correctional Counseling and Rehabilitation*, P. Van Vooris. M. Braswell, and D. Lester, eds. Cincinnati, Anderson.

Mahler, C. 1973. Group Counseling: Theory, Research, and Practice. In. *Group Counseling* J. Lee and C. Pulvino, eds. Washington, D.C.: American Personnel and Guidance Association.

McGuire, J. and P. Priestly. 1985. *Offending Behaviour: Skills and Stratagems for Going Straight*. London: Batsford Academic and Educational.

Morgan, R., D. Kroner, and J. Mills. 2006. Group Psychotherapy in Prison: Facilitating Change Inside the Walls. *Journal of Contemporary Psychotherapy* 36, 3. September. pp 137-144.

Morgan, R. and C. Winterowd. 2002. Interpersonal Process-Oriented Group Psychotherapy with Offender Populations. *International Journal of Offender Therapy and Comparative Criminology* 46: 466-482.

Nicholson, R. 1989. Transactional Analysis: A New Method of Helping Offenders. In *Correctional Counseling and Treatment* P. Kratcoski, ed. Prospect Heights, Illinois: Waveland.

Rizzo, N. 1980. Group Therapy: Possibilities and Pitfalls. *International Journal of Offender Therapy and Comparative Criminology* 24: 27-31.

Schmalleger, F. 2001. *Criminal Justice Today*. Englewood Cliffs, New Jersey: Prentice Hall.

Young, J. 2003. Merton with Energy, Katz with Structure: The Sociology of Vindictiveness and the Criminology of Transgression. *Theoretical Criminology* 7: 389-414.

CHAPTER 13

Using Community Agencies and Volunteers in Case Management

Corrections personnel must do more to discover how community and societal resources can be brought to bear on the problems of offenders, bearing in mind that the community is the corrective aspect of the of the correctional process. . . . what helps the offender protects the community.

—Louis Radelet

Community Resources

Providing individual and group counseling for offenders is far from sufficient for good case management. Often the process of changing offending behavior requires accurately assessing offenders' concrete, physical, here-and-now needs and knowing how to go about helping them to meet these needs—and not necessarily deconstructing faulty thinking and attitudes.

The professional correctional worker knows that more concrete help for the offender is often needed and knows where to find it. Attempting to move the offender toward a more responsible lifestyle is a difficult task, which you need not bear alone. Case management consists of you indirectly delivering services by using networks of collaborative providers (Hill 2002). Indeed, no single professional has the expertise needed to provide all the services required by all offenders, so many of whom have multiple problems. As Delany, Fletcher, and Shields (2003: 66) put it: "Without some level of collaboration among agencies, the odds of relapse [into drug or alcohol abuse] and recidivism, which often leads to repeated institutionalization, are high."

All of this means that according to the philosophy of restorative justice, corrections is a community problem, and that you should consider yourself to be in partnership with the various community-supported agencies in the habilitative or rehabilitative endeavor. Probation and parole departments simply do not have the resources to provide for all the needs of offenders. As Carlson and Parks see it: "It is the task of the probation [or parole] officer to assess the service needs of the probationer [or parolee], locate the social service agency which addresses those needs as its primary function, to refer the probationer [or parolee] to the appropriate agency, and to follow up referrals to make sure that the probationer [or parolee] actually received the services" (1979:120).

Carlson and Parks (1979: 121) assert that the correctional workers' relationships with community service agencies are more important than their relationships with offenders. In other words, corrections workers are viewed more as brokers of community services than as counselors. The broker and counselor roles may be of equal importance, although in some cases, one role may be more important than the other. In terms of the emerging case management emphasis in corrections, correctional workers should find themselves as a member of a team of professionals bringing their skills and expertise to bear on creating treatment and service plans for offenders (Healy1999). The corrections worker, having legal authority over the offender, must be the lead person and coordinator of these services (Delany, Fletcher, and Shields 2003).

Unfortunately, many correctional workers are unaware of the help that is available to offenders (and to themselves) within the community. To make proper use of community agencies, you should gain a thorough knowledge of them and an understanding of their functions before you need them. Only with this knowledge and understanding can you decide on the appropriate referral for the specific need.

Correctional workers' ability to provide extended and effective services to offenders is proportional to the scope of their knowledge of available resources in the community. This type of knowledge is helpful in the supervision of all offenders, but it is particularly important for parolees because they have to be integrated back into the community after long absences.

Dean Champion (2005: 45) writes about how important it is for community corrections workers to network with other agencies providing services, which offenders under community supervision need. An important function of community corrections is to network with various community agencies and businesses to match offender-clients with needed treatments and services. Community corrections agencies may not have a full range of services for offenders [this is a definite understatement, community corrections agencies never have a full range of such services]. Cooperative endeavors are necessary if certain offenders are to receive the type of treatment they need most.

With this is mind, here is a brief overview of the types of community resource agencies available in most cities. However, it is important for those who work with offenders to develop their own list of local and state resources.

Mental Health Centers

The mental health center is the community resource with which the criminal justice worker is probably most familiar. Many jurisdictions have a diagnostic and treatment center staffed by social workers, psychologists, and psychiatrists, specifically to assess offenders' mental health and functioning. They deal with competency testing, presentence and postsentencing evaluations, and parole testing and treatment. Specialized individual, group, and family counseling also are provided at many of these centers. Staff in these centers already may be aware of offenders you refer to them, and may have had difficulty treating them because, as we have seen, many mentally ill people are resistant to treatment. However, compliance has been found to greatly increase when the person is ordered to comply under threat of criminal justice sanctions (Lamb, Weinberger, and Gross 2004).

In addition to centers run for and by the court system, there are the more general mental health centers. These centers may be the preferred referrals for the offender because they are not a part of the criminal justice system. Whatever the case may be, you must develop the ability to recognize symptoms of mental illness and/or specific diagnostic and treatment needs that may be best dealt with by a referral to a mental health professional. Never underestimate or downplay symptoms displayed by offenders that lead you to suspect serious mental problems. You may be right or you may be wrong, but err on the side of caution and refer.

Substance Abuse Centers

Recall that the great majority of offenders have some sort of substance abuse problem, a fact that makes it imperative that you be fully aware of centers that deal with substance-abuse issues. Substance-abuse centers can be either private or public agencies. They include hospitals, chapters of Alcoholics Anonymous, Narcotics Anonymous, Volunteers of America, methadone centers, halfway houses, and residential centers specifically designed for offenders. For offenders who are veterans of the U.S. armed forces, various Veterans Administration hospitals provide excellent inpatient substance-abuse treatment free of charge. Many health insurance policies cover the cost of drug and alcohol treatment. If you have offenders who have either of these problems and who are lucky enough to still have a job, check out their insurance with them. It is amazing how often this possibility is overlooked by both officers and offenders.

Educational and Vocational Guidance

Since most convicted criminals tend to be unemployed high school dropouts, education and vocational training should be high on the list of offender needs. Community high schools offer General Equivalency Diploma (GED) preparation classes free of charge, as well as offer some vocational training for minimal fees. One drawback of GED classes at local high schools is their use of traditional teaching methods. Usually, students are taught as a group without much attention paid to individual levels of ability. Because of this problem, some departments set up their own GED programs based on individualized instruction in which students are able to proceed at their own pace without regard to classroom norms. One such program was evaluated and found to significantly reduce recidivism (Walsh 1985). All probation and parole departments should start a program such as this. Money to employ a part-time teacher need not come from tight departmental budgets. The evaluated program was adequately funded by small grants from local churches and other concerned organizations.

The Bureau of Vocational Rehabilitation, a state and federally funded program, provides many opportunities for vocational testing and guidance, on-the-job training, counseling, and a number of other valuable services for qualified applicants. Since this program operates within the prison system and in the community, it is sensitive to the special needs of offenders. It provides offenders with counselors who can assist them with job interviewing and other work-related skills. This is a particularly useful agency with which correctional workers should become fully acquainted.

State employment agencies duplicate, with somewhat less success, many of the functions of the Bureau of Vocational Rehabilitation. Additionally, they maintain lists of currently available employment in the area. In this age of technology, however, it is becoming increasingly difficult to take advantage of the employment office's ever-decreasing job list without adequate vocational preparation. (See *9 to 5 Beats Ten to Life: How to (Re)Enter Society* by Mike Davis, available from the American Correctional Association [2009], for other suggestions to help offenders.)

Welfare Agencies

The local welfare department administers various federal, state, and local welfare programs. Most offenders are better acquainted with "the welfare" than are their officers, but many are not aware of the range of programs available, although recent welfare reforms have severely restricted available funds. In addition to general relief and food stamps, this agency administers aid to the disabled, medical assistance, aid to the aged, and offers family counseling, to name just a few programs. It is useful for probation and parole officers to have a contact at the welfare department who will expedite matters when the need for offender assistance is acute. Such an occasion may arise when a homeless and penniless offender has been released from jail or prison or when young men or women are thrown out of their family home with only the clothes on their back.

Most communities have an agency that specializes in finding accommodations for the homeless. In cooperation with the welfare department, it may provide the offender and his or her family with permanent or temporary accommodation. It often is able to provide the offender or spouse with homemaking skills, such as family planning and balancing a tight budget. Temporary shelter for the real down and out can be found at various religious and secular "missions." These places offer meals, counseling, companionship, as well as accommodations.

Some National Volunteer Groups

A wide variety of regional, national, and even international volunteer groups either specialize in correctional helping or have programs and supply services useful for correctional clientele. Some of these organizations almost definitely have branch offices in your area. If they do not, perhaps a real service you could provide for your department and your community would be to contact these organizations and find out how you might start one. There are far too many organizations to list here, so only those that are national in scope (serving the entire United States as opposed to single counties or states) will be listed. The information given is current, but may change, and you can always visit their websites. Websites listing these and other organizations designed to help offenders and their dependents include the American Correctional Association's site www.aca.org provides links to many other organizations as well.

The Family and Corrections Network

www.fcnetwork.org;
resourcecenter@fcnetwork.org

Ann Adalist-Estrin, Director
e-mail adalist@fcnetwork.org
NRCCFI/FCN
93 Old York Rd, Ste 1 # 510
Jenkintown, PA 19046
(215) 576-1110; Fax (215) 576-1815

Association on Programs for Female Offenders

www.apfonews.org

The National Center for Victims of Crime

www.ncvc.org

This is a nonprofit organization that promotes victims' rights and victim assistance. The center provides programs and services to organizations helping victims and criminal justice-related organizations, and provides information and resources to the media and the public.

National Center for Victims
of Crime
2000 M St.NW, Ste 480
Washington, D.C. 20036
(202) 467-8700; Fax (202) 467-8701

Prison Fellowship

www.prisonfellowship.org.

This nationwide evangelical prison ministry provides seminars and Bible studies focusing on spiritual renewal. Inmates also are offered a correspondence program with pen pals on the outside, and postrelease mentoring, which pairs a volunteer with an ex-offender.

Prison Fellowship
44180 Riverside Pkwy.
Landowsne, VA 20176
(877) 478-0100

The Salvation Army

www.salvationarmyusa.org

This organization works in ninety-seven countries and provides spiritual and practical assistance to inmates and ex-offenders. The Salvation Army offers Bible studies and individual counseling to inmates and provides support services to inmates' families through its corps community centers. Ex-offender services include drug aftercare, employment services, General Equivalency Degree preparation, parenting skills, English as a second language, AIDS counseling, and mental health programs. For more information, contact

The Salvation Army National
Headquarters
PO Box 269
Alexandria, VA 22313
(703) 684-5500

Volunteers of America

www.voa.org

This organization provides inmates throughout the United States with spiritual guidance and opportunities for success. Volunteers of America services include a restitution program, a program for female offenders that houses them with their children, and electronic monitoring for pretrial defendants.

Volunteers of America
Margaret Ratcliff, Director of
Corrections
E-mail mratcliff@voa.org
1660 Duke St.
Alexandria, VA 22314
(703) 341-5039; Fax (703) 341-7002

Resources for Victims

Victims have for too long been the most neglected concern of the criminal justice system. The concept of restorative justice has brought them once again to our attention. Although correctional workers are not trained to address the concerns of victims, one of the things that you can do is to put them in touch with professionals who are aware of the various resources available to them. The following is a list of toll-free numbers of various victims' rights groups

Violence Against Women Online Resources provides materials on domestic violence, sexual assault, and stalking for criminal justice professionals, sexual assault and domestic violence victim advocates, and other multidisciplinary professionals and community partners who respond to these crimes. The materials on this site were developed by organizations with expertise in violence against women and provide technical assistance for grantees funded through the Office on Violence Against Women, U.S. Department of Justice.

http://www.vaw.umn.edu/

Childhelp USA
www.childhelpusa.org
National Hotline: (800) 4-A-CHILD

15757 N. 78th St.
Scottsdale, AZ 85260
(480) 922-8212; Fax (480) 922-7061

There are many regional offices.

"Childhelp® exists to meet the physical, emotional, educational and spiritual needs of abused, neglected and at-risk children. We focus our efforts on advocacy, prevention, treatment and community outreach."

Mothers Against Drunk Driving
www.madd.org
MADD's mission: to stop drunk driving, support the victims of this violent crime, and prevent underage drinking.

MADD National Office
511 E. John Carpenter Fwy, Ste 700
Irving, TX 75062

800-GET-MADD (800-438-6233)
Victim Services 24-Hour Help Line:
877-MADD-HELP; (877) 623-3435;
Fax (972) 869-2206

Child Welfare Information Gateway
http://www.childwelfare.gov/
This is a service of the Children's Bureau, Administration for Children and Families, U.S. Department of Health and Human Services. It provides access to information and resources to help protect children and strengthen families. It offers a wide range of topics from prevention to permanency, including child welfare, child abuse and neglect, foster care, and adoption. It has some Spanish-language resources.

www.ojp.usdoj.gov
This site provides links to the Bureau of Justice Assistance and the Bureau of Justice Statistics.

National Organization for Victim Assistance
www.try-nova.org
(800)-TRY-NOVA (1-800-879-6682)
(703) 535-NOVA (6682);
Fax (703) 535-5550
510 King St,, Ste 424
Alexandria, VA 22314

This is a private, nonprofit, 501(c)(3) organization of victim and witness assistance programs and practitioners, criminal justice agencies and professionals, mental health professionals, researchers, former victims and survivors, and others committed to the recognition and implementation of victim rights and services. It provides information and referrals for victims of crime and disaster.

Parents of Murdered Children
www.pomc.org
> (888) 818-POMC
> National POMC
> 100 E Eighth St., Ste. 202
> Cincinnati, OH 45202

E-mail: natlpomc@aol.com
(513) 721-5683; Fax (513) 345-4489
Toll Free: (888) 818-POMC

It provides support and assistance to all survivors of homicide while working to create a world free of murder. POMC makes the difference through ongoing emotional support, education, prevention, advocacy, and awareness.

In and Out Referrals

You will not always be able to determine the offender's needs and problem areas by yourself. Quite often other agencies—the police, courts, prosecutors, clergy, neighbors, family members, and concerned citizens—will provide information regarding their needs and problem areas. Your task is to act as a broker or go-between matching the complaint or concern referred to you with the appropriate action. You are the hub of a multi-agency service delivery wheel whose task is to keep the offender "rotating" on the road to recovery. The appropriate action will be a referral of your own to another specialized agency.

Figure 13.1 is a flowchart illustrating the in-and out-flow of referrals.

Figure 13.1 Flowchart of In-and-Out Referrals

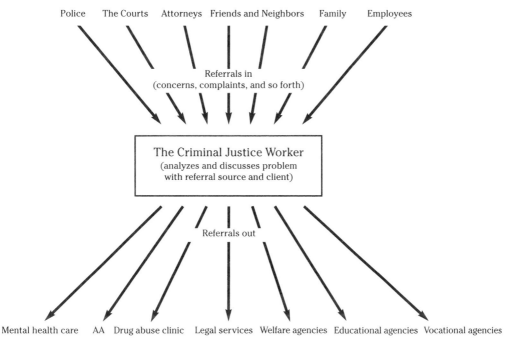

Using and Engaging the Community

The criminal justice system cannot fight the war against crime alone. The police have long recognized that the greatest asset any police department has in its battle is the confidence and cooperation of the community (Thurman, Zhao, and Giacomazzi 2001). Police departments also have discovered that certain members of the community are willing, and often anxious, to aid the police by forming neighborhood watches, engaging in citizens' patrols, or even acting as volunteer officers (police reserves or auxiliaries).

Although the possible roles that members of the general community may play in corrections are not as readily identifiable as their roles in law enforcement, they exist and are much more diverse. We in corrections should follow the example of law enforcement and recognize the tremendously valuable resources that lie untapped in the ordinary men and women who live in our communities. While many agencies and institutions make good use of volunteers, there is always room for new programs and new volunteers. These individuals usually want nothing more out of their efforts than to know that they are helping their community to be a safer place to live by helping those who have victimized it.

Volunteers who assist professionals to combat community problems are critical to a health community. A particularly useful publication for departments thinking about implementing a volunteer program, or for improving and already existing one, is provided by the U.S. Department of Health and Human Services entitled: *Successful Strategies for Recruiting Training and Utilizing Volunteers: A Guide for Faith- and Community-Based Service Providers.* Chapters in this free on-line publication examine planning and recruiting, training, managing, and evaluating volunteers. The booklet also covers background checks for volunteers. Also included: sample mission statements, volunteer application forms and agreements. These various topics and sub-topics are reproduced in Figure 13.2.

Figure 13.2 Steps in Developing a Successful Volunteer Program

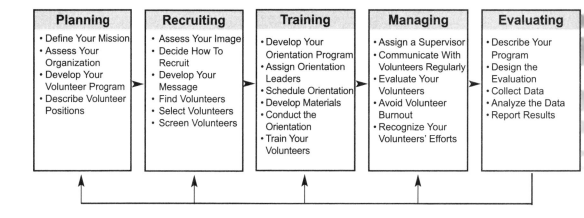

Victim-Offender Reconciliation Programs

Victim-offender reconciliation programs (VORPs) are an integral component of restorative justice philosophy. Many crime victims are less vindictive than commonly supposed and are seeking fairness, justice, and restitution as defined by them (restorative justice), rather than revenge and punishment as defined by the state (retributive justice). In many cases, this can be reasonably accomplished to the satisfaction of all involved.

Central to the victim-offender reconciliation process is the bringing together of victim and offender in face-to-face meetings mediated by a person trained in mediation theory and practice (Trenczek 1990). These meetings are designed to iron out ways in which the offender can make amends for the hurt and damage caused to the victim. The participation of both offender and victim must be voluntary for the process to work, although there is considerable underlying pressure for offender participation in their realization that formal court procedures are the default option for failure to participate.

Victims participating in victim-offender reconciliation programs gain the opportunity to make offenders aware of their feelings of personal violation and loss and to lay out their proposals of how offenders can restore the situation. Offenders are afforded the opportunity to see firsthand the pain they have caused their victims, and perhaps even to express remorse. The mediator assists the parties in developing a contract agreeable to both, which is signed by them and by the mediator, laying out the terms arrived at (such as a schedule of payments). The mediator will monitor the terms of the contract and perhaps schedule further face-to-face meetings. At the satisfactory completion of the contract, the mediator will make a report to the court.

Rarely are victim-offender reconciliation programs used for personal violent crimes—it would be difficult, for instance, to imagine any degree of restoration for the survivors of a murder victim. Such programs work best when the crimes involved are property crimes such as burglary, theft, fraud, and vandalism. A typical finding is that about 60 percent of victims invited to participate in victim-offender reconciliation programs actually become involved, and that a high percentage (mid-to high 90s) result in signed contracts (Coates, 1990). Further, 97 percent of victims involved in victim-offender reconciliation programs in Indiana and Minnesota indicated that the experience was satisfying to them and they would do it again (Coates 1990). Similar positive results have been reported in Britain (Marshall 1990), Germany (Trenczek 1990), and Canada (Pate 1990). Mark Umbreit (1994) sums up the various satisfactions expressed by victims in his study:

1. Meeting offenders helped reduce their fear of being revictimized.

2. They appreciated the opportunity to tell offenders how they felt.

3. Being personally involved in the justice process was satisfying to them.

4. They gained insight into the crime and into the offender's situation.

5. They received restitution.

Victim-offender reconciliation programs are an excellent method of involving the community in the corrections process. Volunteers trained in mediation techniques can relieve overburdened professionals of much of the work of formally dealing with relatively minor property offenders as well as gain personal satisfaction in helping reconcile the offender and the victim. According to Coates, "This participation fosters a significant community stake in VORP as a way of dealing with crime, as well as sensitizing community members to the human nature of crime" (1990: 130). In other words, crime signifies a breakdown of social bonds; victim-offender reconciliation programs are efforts to repair those bonds by bringing people together to work on them. However, do not forget that this model does not suit all victims, especially those who feel that the wrong done to them cannot so easily be "put right," and want the offender punished (Olson and Dzur 2004).

A Community Resource: Volunteer Speakers' Program

Some years ago the Lucas County (Ohio) Adult Probation Department instituted a successful program to help offenders to deal with various problems of living. It provided some useful services for offenders. The program was modeled after the Texas Pre-Release Program designed to prepare inmates for release into the community. Both the Texas program and the Lucas County Adult Probation Department's are based on the recognition that much recidivism could be traced to an inability to cope with what most of us would consider relatively mundane problems.

Inability to cope was, in turn, traced to simple ignorance rather than any lack of native ability or debilitating mental health problems. Consequently, the department developed a Citizens' Volunteer Speakers' Bureau to provide probationers with much-needed guidance and advice on matters of daily living. Each volunteer, and the department itself, never experienced any difficulty recruiting specialists in his or her field. The department's easy successes in getting concerned speakers points to the vast amount of talent "out there" just waiting to be tapped.

Figure 13.3 Community Resource Information Speakers' Program

Week #	Subject	Speaker or Source
1.	Job opportunities and employment aids Finding and keeping a job Social Security benefits Unions and employment	Employment bureau Local employers Social Security Administration Union representative
2.	Sensible spending and budgeting Sensible borrowing Insurance needs Your welfare department	Financial counselor Credit union representative Insurance representative County welfare department
3.	The family Human relationships Reponsible citizenship Veteran's benefits	Family counselor Human relations counselor Leaders in civic affairs Veterans Administration
4.	Personal health Alcohol and drug abuse Educational and vocational opportunities Mental health and general assistance agencies	State and county health departments AA and NA members Bureau of Vocational Rehabilitation Mental health Community Chest professionals

The program worked by first identifying offenders with simple problems of living and getting them to agree to attend a four-week cycle (two nights per week) of informal "resource information" talks conducted by the specialists. If such a program is initiated in your department, you should not require or demand that offenders attend. Insistence could be counterproductive. You should intimate, however, that you will view their attendance very positively as being indicative of their desire to help themselves. Typical topics and sources of speakers are presented in Figure 13.3.

Unfortunately, the program was never formally evaluated for its effectiveness, but the general consensus was that it was extremely helpful to offenders dealing with the problems of living addressed by the various speakers. Officers also learned a great deal about the community resources available to help them help offenders. However, the original Texas Pre-Release Program was formally evaluated. According to Clark (1975), it significantly reduced recidivism among former inmates of the Texas prison system. It is a system well worth instituting in your department or agency.

Volunteer Officers in Corrections

Being a volunteer officer is quite different from being a volunteer who provides some useful service to inmates and offenders. As is a reserve police officer, the volunteer probation/parole officer is invested with many (sometimes, all) of the powers and responsibilities of the professional officer. In some jurisdictions that define their probation and/or parole officers as law enforcement officers, volunteer officers are deputized or sworn in (McShane and Krause 1993). The practice of probation began with volunteers, and to a somewhat lesser extent, so did parole (Allen and Simonsen 2001). Volunteers in probation and parole can be a tremendous aid to the professional officer going far beyond filing cases and licking stamps. This author began his career in probation as a volunteer before accepting a paid position. With proper screening for suitability, initial and ongoing training, and proper matching of offenders and volunteers, volunteers can be a most useful addition to any community corrections endeavor (Champion 2005).

Of course, the successful volunteer program must be well planned and must have the support of the professional staff. As McCarthy and McCarthy (1984: 377) put it: "poor staff-volunteer relations are a frequent cause of program failure," and "positive staff-volunteer relations are essential for program success." As with many areas in which volunteers are involved, the professional staff may view volunteers as "amateurs" sticking their noses in areas in which they have no expertise. There should be a solid training program for volunteers and education for the professionals about the positive things that volunteers can do to help them. Such a program can take care of any staff-volunteer relationship problems.

When good staff-volunteer relationships exist, professional staff tend to be quite positive about volunteer involvement. One evaluation of a volunteer program offered the following conclusion:

> Overall, officers were quite pleased with the quality of volunteers'
> performance. Their ratings suggested satisfaction with VIC [Volunteers in Corrections] service in every activity included in this assessment. While all of the areas examined received average performance ratings of "good" or better, officers were particularly pleased with volunteer services directly delivered to offenders (e.g., high ratings for operation of treatment programs and counseling), as

well as volunteers' direct interactions with officers regarding offender progress (Lucas 1987: 73).

What kind of person is a volunteer, or what kind of person should the volunteer be? According to Henningsen (1981: 119): "Typically, the volunteer is a sensitive and concerned individual with maturity and control over his or her own life. The volunteer relates well to others and is usually a warm and caring person capable of giving and receiving love." In other words, the volunteer's self must be every bit as much "together" as the professional's—neither a naive Pollyanna nor a cynical Cassandra. After all, if volunteers are to be used efficiently and meaningfully by professionals, they have to be very much like professionals. A noncaring and immature dilettante is of no use to either you or the offenders. If such a person manages to slip through the selection net, he or she will not stay long, but can do a lot of damage in the meantime.

What can you as a professional corrections worker expect to gain from the services of volunteers? According to Champion (2005), the two biggest gains lie in the areas of amplification and diversification of services. The volunteer frees professional workers from dealing with a number of less problematic cases so that they can increase meaningful contact time with the remainder of the caseload. Often, offenders accept volunteers more readily than they accept professionals because they see volunteers as less threatening. Some also may view volunteers as more concerned precisely because they receive no financial remuneration for their time and services. A whole host of other benefits accrue for departments and offenders alike from volunteers.

Volunteers can be especially well accepted if you do your best to match offenders and volunteers according to the needs and abilities of each (Lauen 1997). Lauen actually recommends matching professional officers with offenders, but practical considerations preclude such large-scale matching. Although matching treatment modalities and officer/offender types would be an ideal solution, Cullen and Gendreau (2000: 129) opine that this would lead to "an unending permutation of offender-treatment type-setting interactions." We can never "customize" treatment to each offender, but matching is a valid option for volunteers who can devote considerable time to selected offenders.

For example, an older volunteer who is the "nurturing parent" type could be matched with young offenders who have lacked such a person in their own life. Perhaps another offender would be more comfortable with a peer volunteer who is of the same sex and age, who could serve as a role model. Figure 13.4 shows the matching criteria employed in a highly successful volunteer probation officer's program in Lincoln, Nebraska. Notice that the importance of the criteria varies according to the type of offender/volunteer relationship desired. For example, if an adult role model relationship is desired, matching for ethnicity is considered "essential;" if a friend/companion relationship is desired, ethnic matching is seen as "very useful," but it is considered to be only "useful" if a supervisory or counseling relationship is desired. In contrast, counseling skills are essential if a counseling relationship is desired but only "useful" if any of the other three types of relationships is desired. The chart in Figure 13.4, on the next page, may prove valuable to you in matching offenders with volunteers.

With respect to the diversification of services, Scheier (1974) cites one report indicating that a court system made use of fifty different types of skills citizen volunteers brought. Volunteers from all walks of life provide offenders with everything from spiritual guidance to jogging classes. The professional staff most certainly could not

Figure 13.4 Matching Clients with Volunteers by Type of Relationship

Relationship Desired by Usefulness of Match

Volunteer/ Client Match	Adult Role Model	Friend/ Companion	Supervisor	Counselor
Ethnicity	Essential	Very useful	Useful	Useful
Sex	Essential	Essential	Irrelevant	Irrelevant
Age	Essential	Essential	Useful	Irrelevant
Education	Very useful	Very useful	Irrelevant	Irrelevant
Community contacts	Useful	Useful	Very Useful	Irrelevant
Interests	Very useful	Essential	Irrelevant	Irrelevant
Social class	Very useful	Very useful	Irrelevant	Very useful
Counseling skills	Useful	Useful	Useful	Essential

Adapted from: Richard Ku, 1975, *The Volunteer Probation Counselor Program*, Lincoln, Nebraska. Washington, D.C.: U.S. Government Printing Office, p. 48.

have supplied these valuable services. As for the benefit to the department, one retired volunteer with the department at which this author worked put in as much time as any of the paid staff for about ten years. He supervised all of the department's welfare fraud cases, as well as supervised a number of other volunteers.

Volunteers with the Oakland County (Michigan) Adult Probation Department handle about 15 percent of the department's total caseload. Most certainly, this does not mean that potential professional officers are being "robbed" of a job by amateur "dabblers." The typical Oakland County volunteer brings to the position a host of talents and life experiences that young professionals cannot match (Smith 1993). Any corrections agency is remiss if it fails to recognize and use the tremendous variety of skills available in any community. To use volunteers effectively and efficiently not only magnifies the efforts of professional workers, but also can assist the rehabilitative possibilities of the offender. Isn't that what it is all about?

A word of warning is necessary. Make quite sure that offenders are not manipulating volunteers and that volunteers are holding offenders responsible for living up to their conditions of supervision (see Bayse 1993, Cornelius 2009). Problems in these areas can arise with some frequency if volunteers are not screened for suitability, if they are not adequately trained and told what is expected of them, or if they are not matched well with offenders (Sharp and Muraskin 2003). You retain the ultimate responsibility for monitoring the offender's progress. Thus, volunteers should submit a monthly progress report on each of the offenders they supervise for you. Volunteers expect and appreciate this. Volunteers need feedback to improve their services to offenders and to let them know that they are being taken seriously.

Community involvement in corrections is a time that has come. Such involvement is part of the restorative justice ideal and is beneficial to all parties. Lauen calls community involvement "a win-win deal," and adds:

> Lay citizens win by becoming more knowledgeable about crime, corrections, and offenders. In doing so, they reduce their crime fears and increase their power. They begin to take charge. Community corrections offenders, staff, and programs win by building a broader base of support, living and working with people who are more knowledgeable and thereby more supportive, and gaining insights, advice and direct services from citizen volunteers (1997: 218).

Exercises in Community Resource Use

Nearly all communities have a clearinghouse (sometimes referred to as the Community Chest) where you can obtain information about the various types of resources available to help the unfortunate. Identify the needs of the offender on whom you have written a practice PSI report and match him or her with appropriate agencies. Then, find out if your community has an agency that could deal with the offender's particular problem. If your community does not have such an agency, what would your second-best referral or plan of action be?

Devise a resource information speakers' program based on the resources available in your community and on your perception of the needs of offenders. What additional resources not included in this chapter do you think offenders would find useful?

Find out if the community corrections agencies located in your community have volunteer programs. If so, call and ask them about their criteria for volunteer selection, the training offered to volunteers, and whether they attempt to match volunteers with offenders. What did the person you spoke with consider to be the most useful attribute of a prospective volunteer?

Perspective from the Field
Volunteer Probation Work

By Dr. Stephen B. McConnell

Dr. McConnell is a professor of sociology at the University of Toledo, in Ohio. His fields of specialty are criminology and social stratification. He began as a volunteer probation officer with Lucas County supervising adult offenders in 1983. Dr. McConnell also has field experience working in a large California prison.

● ● ● ● ● ● ● ● ● ● ● ● ● ● ● ● ● ● ●

Many things are too important to be left to the professionals alone: defense to the Pentagon, medicine to the doctors, law to legislators and attorneys. If any truth lies in this observation, there well may be a point for volunteerism in criminal justice. For, after all, an array of professional personnel implement correctional policy.

The value that volunteer probation officers bring has little to do with saving a jurisdiction money or sparing regular staff even bigger caseloads. The central contribution of volunteer probation officers derives from the inclusion of ordinary citizens, albeit civic-minded ones, in the operation of justice proceedings. The professionalism of full-time staff is leavened with the innocence of volunteers.

Police officers have a well-documented tendency to develop cynicism as an occupational necessity. Similarly, but to a much lesser extent, probation officers can develop a less-than-sanguine view of offenders and rehabilitation. Volunteers who have developed value systems and understandings outside the criminal justice system, for whom criminal cases have not become routinized affairs, can—and occasionally do—challenge the orthodoxy of the prevailing professional views and ideology. In short, volunteers can ask fresh questions, even provide new insights that do not occur to veteran professionals.

Much of corrections work pivots on anticipating which offenders will or will not repeat crime. Predicting human behavior is a crapshoot at best, and this is especially true concerning criminal recidivism. Some psychologists would have us believe that prediction is a science, but the facts are otherwise. Nobody has a monopoly on predicting what another will do postconviction/postprobation-parole. On this count, the volunteer probation officers whose mature understanding of behavior stems from coping with life itself are on an equal footing with the professionals.

The justice system involves a number of somewhat technical and arcane practices that obscure the big picture of the reality of criminal justice. Informed volunteers can demystify and demythologize the system for the public, which often finds such matters are remote and alien. Likewise, volunteers can step beyond the "trained incapacities" (the inability to see beyond the taken-for-granted realities imposed by professional role socialization) of professionals-as-professionals.

Continued on the next page

Perspective from the Field, *continued*

The motivations of volunteers in criminal justice are very broad. Most of the college students are amassing experience to ease their transition into paid positions upon graduation. Older volunteers have more altruistic and diverse motivations. In this author's own case, the motivation was twofold: he had been teaching in the city for over a decade and wanted to repay in some fashion the community from which he extracted a living. Equally important, he wanted to gain some hands-on experience with offenders, for it has been nearly twenty years since he worked in the field. Direct experience contributes much to the rethinking and refining of the theoretical ideas he teaches in his criminology and corrections classes. In brief, volunteering is a means of keeping fresh in the classroom.

Being a volunteer probation officer involves a host of qualifications. Certainly, one learns to listen with the third ear to detect what offenders are saying indirectly (or trying to conceal) rather than saying directly. And since serving as volunteer probation officers involves making recommendations, even giving direct orders to offenders about intimate aspects of their lives, it behooves the volunteer probation officers to know as much as they can about society. (For this reason, sociology continues to be a valuable study for people in correctional work.) At the broadest level, volunteer probation officers see how the U.S. economic system of capitalism creates a permanent underclass from which the huge majority of garden-variety offenders come. In conjunction, the volunteer probation officer comes to realize how the occupational structure works, how, for example, a drop in the unemployment rate increases the likelihood of offenders getting minimum-wage jobs in the fast food or motel industries.

The volunteer probation officer also comes to understand numerous components of community organization. This information covers everything from local agencies, which may be able to help poor, alcoholic, or drug-addicted offenders, to understanding the subtleties of the operation of the courts, the police department, and the prosecutor's office.

Effective volunteer probation officers must absorb a great deal of information. You can pass this information on to offenders for their benefit, and it enables the volunteer probation officer to understand offenders' behavior in a realistic context.

A cautionary note is in order. Corrections work is not for the fainthearted volunteer, nor is it for people who demand 100 percent success. Offenders can be difficult to work with, and occasionally are outright hostile. Not all offenders make good on probation or parole: some do commit new offenses and are sent to, or back to, prison. Volunteer probation officers adapt to the idea that whatever they do, much of the eventual outcome for an offender lies effectively beyond their control. Respect the fact that offenders are responsible for their own destinies. Maybe it is fair to say that working as a volunteer probation officer lends a humility to one's perspective.

Summary

This chapter has dealt with the very important task of acquainting the corrections worker with the resources, skills, and desires to become involved that exist in the community. Numerous specialized agencies can help offenders with their day-to-day problems. You cannot be expected to have in your head all the information that these community agencies have gathered. Your task is to recognize offender problem areas and to make the appropriate agency referrals if the problems are not within your area of expertise. Your expertise should be that of a broker matching offenders with agencies.

You also can provide offenders and yourself with much-needed information by organizing a community resource information speakers' program. Such a program can operate periodically to accommodate new offenders. Many offenders find themselves in trouble simply because they do not have access to information about the type of help that exists in the community to aid them with their problems. These speaker's programs have proven to be most helpful to offenders and correctional workers alike.

Another valuable resource is the desire of many individuals in the community to be useful and helpful. You can fruitfully incorporate them into the correctional enterprises as volunteers. Probation and parole volunteers provide amplification and diversification of services to offenders. Yet, volunteers must be screened, trained, and matched with offenders. Their performance should be monitored by the professional worker to make sure that they are holding offenders responsible and that they are not being manipulated by offenders. Corrections can be an immensely satisfying career. Your satisfaction will be greatly increased if you learn to use the resources available in your community.

References and Suggested Readings

Allen, H. and C. Simonsen. 2001. *Corrections in America: An Introduction*, 9th ed. Upper Saddle River, New Jersey: Prentice Hall.

Bayse, D. 1993. *Helping Hands: Handbook for Volunteers in Prisons and Jails*. Alexandria, Virginia: American Correctional Association.

Boudouris, J. 1996. *Parents in Prison: Addressing the Needs of Families*. Lanham, Maryland: American Correctional Association.

Carlson, E. and E. Parks. 1979. *Critical Issues in Adult Probation: Issues in Probation Management*. Washington, D.C.: U.S. Government Printing Office.

Champion, D. 2005. *Probation, Parole, and Community Corrections*, 5th ed., Upper Saddle River, New Jersey: Prentice Hall.

Clark, J. 1975. The Texas Pre-Release Program. In L. Hippchen, ed., *Correctional Classification and Treatment*. Cincinnati, Ohio: Anderson.

Coates, R. 1990. Victim-Offender Reconciliation Programs in North America: An Assessment. In B. Galaway and J. Hudson, eds., *Criminal Justice, Restitution, and Reconciliation*. Monsey, New York: Criminal Justice Press.

Cullen, F. and P. Gendreau. 2000. Assessing Correctional Rehabilitation: Policy, Practice, and Prospects. In *Criminal Justice 2000*. Washington, D.C.: National Institute of Justice.

Davis, M. 2009. *9 to 5 Beats Ten to Life: How to (Re)Enter Society*, 2nd ed. Alexandria, Virginia: American Correctional Association.

Delany, P., B. Fletcher, and J. Shields. 2003. Reorganizing Care for the Substance Using Offender—The Case for Collaboration. *Federal Probation* 67: 64-69.

Healy, K. 1999. Case Management in the Criminal Justice System. *National Institute of Justice: Research in Action*. Washington, D.C.: U.S. Department of Justice.

Henningsen, R. 1981. *Probation and Parole*. New York: Harcourt Brace Jovanovich.

Hill, G. 2002. Japan's Volunteer Probation Officers Play Role in Offender Rehabilitation. *Corrections Compendium* 26: 6-7.

LaGrange, R. 1993. *Policing American Society*. Chicago, Illinois: Nelson-Hall.

Lamb, H., L. Weinberger, and B. Gross. 2004. Mentally Ill Persons in The Criminal Justice System. *Psychiatric Quarterly* 75: 107-126.

Lauen, R. 1997. *Positive Approaches to Corrections: Research, Policy and Practice*. Lanham, Maryland: American Correctional Association.

Lucas, W. 1987. Staff Perceptions of Volunteers in A Correctional Program. *Journal of Crime and Justice* 10: 63-78.

Marshall, T. 1990. Results of Research from British Experiments with Restorative Justice. In B. Galaway and J. Hudson, eds., *Criminal Justice, Restitution, and Reconciliation*. Monsey, New York: Criminal Justice Press.

McCarthy, B. R. and B. J. McCarthy. 1984. *Community Based Corrections*. Monterey, California: Brooks/Cole.

McShane, M. and W. Krause. 1993. *Community Corrections*. New York: Macmillan.

Olson, S. and A. Dzur. 2004. Revisiting Informal Justice: Restorative Justice and Democratic Professionalism. *Law and Society Review* 38: 139-176.

Pate, K. 1990. Victim-Offender Reconciliation as Alternative Measures Programs in Canada. In B. Galaway and J. Hudson, eds., *Criminal Justice, Restitution, and Reconciliation*. Monsey, New York: Criminal Justice Press.

Read, E. 1996. *Partners in Change: The 12-Step Referral Handbook for Probation, Parole and Community Corrections*. Lanham, Maryland: American Correctional Association.

Schieier, I. 1974. The Professional and the Volunteer in Probation: An Emerging Relationship. In G. Killinger and P. Crowmwell, eds. *Corrections in the Community*. St. Paul, Minnesota: West Publishing.

Sharp, S. and R. Muraskin. 2003. *The Incarcerated Woman: Rehabilitative Programming in Women's Prisons*. Upper Saddle River, New Jersey: Prentice Hall.

Smith, B. 1993. Probation Department in Michigan Finds Volunteers Make Fine Officers. *Corrections Today* 55: 80-82.

Thurman, Q., J. Zhao, and A. Giacomazzi. 2001. *Community Policing in a Community Era*. Los Angeles: Roxbury.

Trenczek, T. 1990. A Review and Assessment of Victim-Offender Reconciliation Programs in West Germany. In B. Galaway and J. Hudson, eds., *Criminal Justice, Restitution, and Reconciliation*. Monsey, New York: Criminal Justice Press.

Umbreit, M. 1994. Victim Meets Offender: The Impact of Restorative Justice and Mediation. Monsey, New York: Criminal Justice Press.

U.S. Department of Health and Human Services (2008). *Successful Strategies for Recruiting Training and Utilizing Volunteers: A Guide for Faith- and Community-Based Service Providers*. Rockville, MD: National Clearinghouse for Alcohol and Drug Information.

Walker, S. 1993. South Carolina Volunteer Agency Plays Vital Role in Corrections. *Corrections Today* 55: 94-100.

Walsh, A. 1985. An Evaluation of the Effects of Adult Basic Education on Rearrest Rates Among Probationers. *Journal of Offender Counseling Services and Rehabilitation* 9: 69-76.

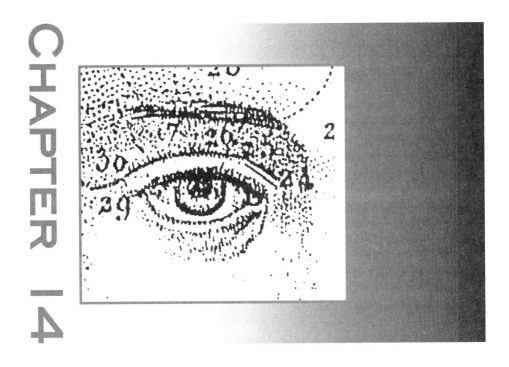

CHAPTER 14

Legal Aspects of Casework and Counseling

By Craig Hemmens, J.D., Ph.D.

Convenience and justice are often not on speaking terms.

—Lord Justice Ackner

Craig Hemmens is a professor in the Department of Criminal Justice at Boise State University. He received his B.A. from the University of North Carolina, his J.D. from North Carolina Central University School of Law, and his Ph.D. in criminal justice from Sam Houston State University. His primary research interests are corrections law and criminal procedure.

Introduction

This chapter examines the legal and ethical issues that frequently confront the criminal justice caseworker in the correctional setting and in the community. It provides an overview of the constitutional rights of prisoners, probationers, and parolees, including the right to treatment, the prohibition on "cruel and unusual" punishment, limitations on probation and parole conditions, due process requirements, and the application of the exclusionary rule and *Miranda* warnings to probationers and parolees. Caseworker liability, an emerging area, also is examined. Finally, ethical issues related to the rights of clients and the duties of caseworkers are discussed.

Leading U. S. Supreme Court cases are discussed, but this area of the law is largely bereft of guidance from the high court. It is therefore essential that caseworkers familiarize themselves with the laws of their respective states. There is a great deal of variation in state laws and administrative regulations, particularly in regards to probation and parole conditions and caseworker immunity from liability.

First, here is a brief note on legal terminology: a criminal offender possesses two types of rights—substantive rights and procedural rights. Substantive rights are those rights created and defined by statute, such as contract law, tort law, and, of course, criminal law. Substantive law prescribes and proscribes various types of conduct. Procedural rights are those rights subsumed under the concept of "due process" in the Fifth and Fourteenth Amendments. When it is said that a person is entitled to due process of law, it means there are certain rules and procedures that the state must follow before depriving a person of his or her rights. Essentially, the substantive law delineates the rules by which all members of society must play, while procedural law delineates the rules by which the government must play.

Historical Background

At common law, and until the middle part of the twentieth century, criminal offenders had few rights. The Bill of Rights, with its protections of individual rights against search and seizure, self-incrimination, and the like, applied only to the federal government, not the states. The exclusionary rule and *Miranda* warnings did not exist. Once incarcerated, individuals lost almost all of their rights and found themselves at the mercy of correctional personnel. Those under community supervision, be it probation or parole, found their rights and opportunities severely circumscribed. Those convicted of crimes often were treated as "slaves of the state" (*Ruffin v. Commonwealth*, 1871). Most states had "civil death" statutes that stripped convicted individuals of most of their civil rights, such as the right to vote or hold elective office. This loss of rights was justified as a part of the punishment for committing a crime.

Courts took what was referred to as a "hands-off" approach to the rights of prisoners (Hemmens, Belbot, and Bennett 2004), choosing not to become involved with the affairs of correctional agencies, which were part of the executive branch of government. Courts reasoned that correctional administrators were better equipped to deal with prisoners than judges, and that judicial involvement, through the hearing of inmate complaints, would unnecessarily complicate relations between the executive and judicial branches of government. If prisoners had no rights, then courts need not oversee correctional agencies dealing with prisoners.

Courts also paid scant attention to the rights of probationers and parolees, treating them as essentially equivalent to inmates. Any number of restrictive probation and parole conditions were upheld, with courts often falling back on the rationale that neither probation nor parole was a right, but merely a privilege, something granted by the state, which could be modified or revoked at any time.

By the 1940s, courts began paying closer attention to the rights of prisoners, as part of a growing trend toward increased protection of individual rights. In 1941, the Supreme Court, in *Ex parte Hull*, held that inmates had a right to unrestricted access to federal courts. This decision signaled the beginning of the end of the "hands-off" doctrine and the beginning of the era of judicial intervention in corrections. In 1944, in *Coffin v. Reichard*, a federal district court expanded the scope of habeas corpus to include lawsuits filed by inmates that challenged not whether the state had a right to confine them, but the conditions of their confinement.

The civil rights movement of the 1960s and a change in the membership of the Supreme Court resulted in tremendous changes in criminal procedure and correctional practices. Under Chief Justice Earl Warren, the Court extended a number of protections to criminal defendants. The Supreme Court also began to extend protection of individual rights to those convicted of crimes. The Court, in a line of cases, required correctional administrators at all levels, from prison to probation and parole, to accord basic procedural (or due process) rights to criminal offenders.

Following the high court's lead, lower federal courts became more receptive to lawsuits brought by prisoners challenging the conditions of their confinement. In *Holt v. Sarver* (1969), a federal district court in Arkansas determined that inmates could challenge as unconstitutional the totality of a prison's conditions. This form of suit became known as the "conditions of confinement" lawsuit. Federal district courts, formerly absolute in their deference to the wisdom of correctional administrators, became intimately involved in the monitoring and operation of entire prison systems.

In 1976, the Supreme Court, in *Estelle v. Gamble*, ruled that correctional administrators could be held liable for injury to an inmate if the administrators displayed "deliberate indifference" to the serous medical needs of that inmate. And in 1992, in *Wilson v. Seiter*, the Supreme Court held that the deliberate indifference standard applied to all conditions of confinement cases, not just those involving claims of medical needs. In *Turner v. Safley* (1987), the Supreme Court held that a prison regulation that limited the constitutional rights of inmates was valid so long as it was "reasonably related" to a "legitimate state interest" (such as prison security),

While the deliberate indifference standard and the *Turner v. Safley* standard have proven to be difficult obstacles for inmate plaintiffs to overcome, it is nonetheless a far cry from the days of *Ruffin v. Commonwealth*, when inmates were treated as "slaves of the state."

Paralleling the increased attention paid by courts to correctional institutions was an increased attention to the rights of those under community supervision. In a series of cases decided during the 1970s, the Supreme Court extended a number of due process rights to probationers and parolees, including the right to a revocation hearing, notice of the charges against the individual, and the right to counsel.

Recently, as the membership of the Supreme Court has become more conservative, the high court has been less receptive to the complaints of inmates, and has declined to extend further the protections accorded inmates and those under community supervision.

Rights of Incarcerated Offenders

The courts have attempted to balance the individual rights of inmates and the authority of correctional administrators. These rights include the Fourth Amendment prohibition on unreasonable searches and seizures, the Fifth Amendment privilege against self-incrimination, the Sixth Amendment right to counsel, and the Fourteenth Amendment's right to be accorded due process of law, whatever that term implies. Other rights examined in some detail by the courts include the right to treatment, and First Amendment rights of association and religious freedom.

Right to Treatment

Treatment involves the cure of a disease or at least the alleviation of pain and suffering. It is a process of diagnosis, intervention, and prognosis (Cohen1995). While a right to treatment is not mentioned in the text of the Constitution, courts have made it clear that inmates and those under civil commitment do enjoy a right to treatment. This treatment need not be the best that science has to offer—rather, it is enough if the state provides reasonable care. Under *Estelle v. Gamble* (1976), the state may not be held liable for mere negligent treatment. Liability attaches only if there is evidence akin to recklessness or intentional disregard for the client on the part of the state— what the Supreme Court termed "deliberate indifference." Furthermore, the Supreme Court held, in *Washington v. Harper* (1990), that an institutionalized person does not have an absolute right to refuse treatment.

The rationale behind mandating a right to treatment for incarcerated persons is that because the state has restricted their liberty, they are unable to obtain medical services on their own initiative—thus, the state must accept responsibility for their medical care. Caseworkers in the institutional setting are not required to do more than is possible, given the limited resources of the institution. For instance, a study of inmates indicated that while approximately 80 percent of all inmates are in need of drug and alcohol treatment, less than 20 percent actually receive treatment while incarcerated, due in large part to the limit on institutional resources (General Accounting Office 1991). Courts have yet to mandate such treatment.

The Eighth Amendment and "Cruel and Unusual" Punishment

The Eighth Amendment prohibits "cruel and unusual" punishment. Exactly what is cruel and unusual has changed as society has evolved. The Supreme Court has applied the standard to a variety of situations in corrections, including the death penalty and the use of force to control inmates, protect other inmates, or to repel an assault by an inmate.

In general, every prisoner has the right to be free of both offensive bodily contact and the fear of it (Palmer 1999). Prison officials are permitted to use reasonable force to enforce discipline and to protect themselves and others. The key here is that the force must be reasonable under the circumstances—thus, prison officials may be justified in using extreme force, even deadly force, if the situation warrants it (Hemmens and Atherton 1999). In addition, the Supreme Court has held that correctional personnel may be liable for failing to prevent harm to an inmate by another inmate, but only if it can be demonstrated that their conduct displayed "deliberate indifference" to the safety of the inmate (*Farmer v. Brennan*, 1994). While prison officials are allowed to use force, when necessary, to enforce prison regulations, courts have backed away from earlier decisions, which upheld the practice of corporal punishment, or the use of physical force to punish inmates for rule violations. While the Supreme Court never has expressly voided the practice, a number of lower courts have declared corporal punishment unconstitutional (see, for example, *Jackson v. Bishop*, 1968).

Related to corporal punishment is the age-old practice of punishing recalcitrant inmates by placing them in solitary confinement. Courts consistently have rejected the contention that solitary confinement is unconstitutional per se, but they have required that: (1) the conditions of solitary confinement must not be disproportionate to the offense; and (2) since solitary confinement is a punishment above and beyond the punishment of incarceration, basic due process protections must be provided, such as the right to a hearing before being sentenced to solitary confinement (Palmer 1999).

Access to Legal Services

Access to the courts was one of the first constitutional rights that the Supreme Court extended to prisoners, in the 1940 case of *Ex parte Hull*. According to the Court, access to the court system is a basic requirement of due process. The question that courts have dealt with since the decision in *Hull* is what constitutes "access?" The major case in this area is *Johnson v. Avery* (1969), in which the Supreme Court held that a prison regulation that prohibited inmates from assisting other inmates in the preparation of legal materials was unconstitutional, if there were no reasonable alternative by which access to the courts could be obtained. The result was that correctional administrators had to either allow "jailhouse lawyers" to help other inmates, or provide some sort of legal assistance program. Prison officials may restrict the amount of legal materials possessed by an inmate, or the time and place for legal assistance, so long as such limitations are reasonable.

Until recently, it was assumed that another decision of the Supreme Court, *Bounds v. Smith* (1977), required prison administrators to provide inmates with either a law library or access to persons with legal training. But in 1996, in *Lewis v. Casey*, the Supreme Court clarified its earlier decision, holding that evidence of inadequacies in the delivery of legal services is not enough to justify remedial action by the courts; such action is justified only when an inmate's efforts to pursue a legal claim, in fact, are impaired by lack of access to legal materials. A number of correctional agencies have responded to this decision by eliminating prison law libraries altogether and instead providing inmates with alternate means of access to legal materials.

Freedom of Religion

The First Amendment includes several distinct individual rights, including the freedom of religion. Regarding the freedom of religion, the Supreme Court has held that prison officials have the right to regulate religious activity to promote valid interests such as security, discipline, and inmate and correctional officer safety (*Turner v. Safley*, 1987). Lower courts generally have deferred to the wisdom of correctional administrators when limitations on religious freedom are based on such grounds. More difficult questions have been what exactly constitutes a "religion," or "religious activity?"

The Fourth Amendment

The right of an individual to be free of unreasonable searches and seizures, provided in the Fourth Amendment and made applicable to the states by the Due Process Clause of the Fourteenth Amendment, obviously has limited application to the institutional setting. Inmates are subject to searches of their person, belongings, and cell without warrant or even probable cause (*Hudson v. McMillan*, 1992). Courts recognize the unique security needs of the institution outweigh the individual rights of the inmate.

Due Process Rights in Disciplinary Hearings

An area of correctional administration that has received much attention from the courts is the process by which inmates are disciplined. Discipline is obviously an important element of maintenance of security in the correctional institution. The courts require correctional administrators to provide "due process of law" to inmates involved in disciplinary proceedings. This means that before punishment can be meted out, certain procedures must be followed, to ensure inmates are not being treated unfairly. In *Wolff v. McDonnell* (1974), the U. S. Supreme Court held that due process in prison disciplinary proceedings entails providing: (1) inmates with written notice of the charges against them; (2) an opportunity for inmates to present evidence and witnesses in their defense; (3) the assistance of staff or a fellow prisoner if necessary under the circumstances; and (4) a written statement by the disciplinary board explaining its findings. The Court did not require that an inmate be allowed to cross-examine witnesses, or to be provided with counsel at the hearing.

Due Process Rights in Parole Hearings

Historically, courts in this country have held that the decision to grant or deny a parole or pardon is a matter of executive discretion, implying that courts should not interfere in administrative decision-making. While there is no constitutional right to parole or sentence commutation, the Supreme Court has held that when parole is a possibility, correctional administrators must accord inmates due process. This merely requires that the parole board hold a hearing, and provide the inmate with written reasons for its decision.

In *Greenholtz v. Inmates of Nebraska Penal and Correctional Complex* (1979), the Court held that an inmate has no right to parole, and that a discretionary parole release determination does not create a protected liberty interest. States are not constitutionally required to provide parole. Because there is no entitlement, no protected liberty interest (such as the right to a parole hearing) is created. In *Connecticut Board of Pardons v. Dumschat* (1981), the Court held that a state's practice of granting approximately three-fourths of the applications for commutation of life sentences did not create either a "liberty interest" or an "entitlement" so as to require the Parole Board to explain its reasons for denying an application for commutation.

Rights of Individuals under Community Supervision

An offender may be released into the community either on probation, or on parole. Probation is a substitute for incarceration of convicted criminals. It is defined as "a sentence imposed for commission of crime whereby a convicted criminal offender is released into the community under the supervision of a probation officer in lieu of incarceration" (Black 2004). Probation has the twin goals of maximizing the liberty of the offender while still protecting the public. It is less costly, and generally more rehabilitative in nature than incarceration (Cromwell, Alarid, and del Carmen 2004).

According to the Supreme Court, the purpose of probation is "to provide an individualized program offering a young or unhardened offender an opportunity to rehabilitate himself [sic] without institutional confinement under the tutelage of a probation officer and under the continuing power of the court to impose institutional punishment for his original offense in the event that he abuse the opportunity" (*Roberts v. United States*, 1943).

Parole is a substitute for, and an extension of incarceration. It is defined as "a conditional release of a prisoner, generally under supervision of a parole officer, who has served part of the term for which he was sentenced to prison" (Black 2004). Parole has the goal of reintegrating the offender into the community while maintaining some degree of supervision over the individual, thus protecting the public.

Conditions of Probation and Parole

Courts consistently have upheld the use of probation and parole conditions. There are several justifications for imposing probation and parole conditions, including protecting the public, reducing recidivism through deterrence of criminal conduct by the client, promoting alternatives to incarceration, and possibly rehabilitating offenders through closer supervision (Palmer 1999).

Probation and parole conditions are imposed either by the judge at sentencing, or by a parole board at the parole hearing. While most states by law suggest conditions to be imposed, the judge or board generally has complete discretion to accept, modify, or reject these conditions.

Surprisingly few statutes specify the goals to be served by probation and parole conditions, but courts have focused on the twin goals of rehabilitation and community protection. The courts see these interests of sufficient importance to meet the "compelling state interest" required for abridgement of "fundamental" constitutional rights (Tribe1988).

While rehabilitation and public safety often are cited goals, defining these terms with precision is difficult. Rehabilitation generally encompasses conditions that involve treatment, education, and reintegration of the offender; public safety involves conditions such as a ban on association with criminals, possession of weapons, and a requirement to obey the law.

Probation and parole conditions are usually classified as either general or specific. General conditions are imposed on all; specific conditions are imposed only on some. While judges and parole boards are given tremendous latitude in establishing conditions; in reality, many use a list of previously adopted standard conditions for every individual. Commonly imposed general conditions include requiring the individual to: (1) make periodic reports to his or her parole officer, (2) notify the officer about changes in employment or residence, (3) obtain permission for out-of-state travel, (4) refrain from possessing firearms, (5) not associate with known criminals, and (6) obey the law (Hemmens 1999).

A special condition is one that is not imposed as a matter of course on all probationers or parolees. Rather, it is applied only to the specific offender. So long as such conditions are reasonable and related to the state's legitimate interest in rehabilitation and/or protection of society, they are likely to be upheld by the courts. A condition that violates a parolee's constitutional rights is invalid even if it has a rehabilitative purpose or protects society.

The imposition of special conditions is not uncommon, as judges and parole boards attempt to tailor the terms of probation or parole to the individual offender. The general rule is that the authority to impose special conditions cannot be delegated to probation officers, although officers are often permitted to determine the precise mode of implementation of a condition. To avoid liability, officers should avoid imposing special conditions, or unilaterally modifying existing conditions.

Considering how many individuals today are on either probation or parole, the amount of litigation concerning the legality of conditions is relatively small. This is likely because the probationer/parolee has agreed to the conditions and is aware of the practical consequences of challenging them. When conditions are challenged, a variety of claims are frequently raised. These include invalid consent, vagueness, unequal enforcement of the law, and infringement upon a fundamental right.

The Due Process Clause of the Fourteenth Amendment prohibits the enforcement of vague laws, on the theory that a person cannot conform his or her conduct if they do not know precisely what is expected of them. Probation and parole conditions often are challenged on the grounds of vagueness, as offenders assert they did not understand the meaning of particular terms. Some conditions are expressed in a very general way, such as "avoid disreputable places" or "do not associate with undesirable individuals." Courts generally have held probation and parole conditions to a lesser standard of clarity than statutory provisions, inquiring only as to whether the phrase in question is of common, everyday English usage (del Carmen 1985).

Unequal enforcement of conditions can be the basis for liability under the Equal Protection Clause of the Fourteenth Amendment. Under this provision, unreasonable distinctions between individuals or classes of individuals are prohibited. The actions of probation and parole officers are sometimes challenged on the grounds of unequal enforcement—the probationer/parolee asserts that he or she has been singled out for harassment by the officer. Courts generally require clear evidence of officer misconduct in these cases (Hemmens and del Carmen 1997).

In general, probation and parole conditions are valid, so long as they: (1) do not violate the constitution, (2) are reasonable, (3) are unambiguous, and (4) are intended to promote the rehabilitation of the offender and/or the protection of society. When a "fundamental right" is abridged, however, the courts will examine the condition more closely, using what is referred to as "strict scrutiny" review. Under this standard of review, a probation or parole condition is valid only if there is a showing of both: (1) a compelling state interest and (2) no less restrictive means of accomplishing the purpose. Rights deemed fundamental by the Supreme Court are found largely in the protections afforded citizens in the Bill of Rights. The First Amendment guarantees of freedom of speech, assembly, and religion are a prime example.

Nonassociation Conditions

A notion likely as old as crime itself is that hanging out with the "wrong crowd" will get a person in trouble. There is support in criminology research for this belief, and it serves as the basis for one of the most common probation and parole conditions, the limitation on association. This condition forbids the offender from having contact with certain persons or types of persons. This limitation is justified on the ground that association with criminals or other "shady" characters will interfere with both the rehabilitation of the offender and reduce public safety. This limitation may apply to a category of persons, such as those with a criminal record, or those who are not "law-abiding" or are of "disreputable or harmful character;" it also may apply to specific, named persons. Nonassociation provisions are authorized by statute in some jurisdictions, and by case law in others.

Nonassociation conditions frequently are challenged as unconstitutional. These challenges fall into one of four categories: (1) the condition is unrelated to the purpose of probation/parole, (2) the condition violates the right of privacy, (3) the language of the condition is too vague, and (4) the condition violates the First Amendment.

Claims that a nonassociation condition is unrelated to the traditional purposes of parole (protection of the public and rehabilitation of the offender) are rarely successful. Courts generally accept without question the assertion that prohibiting contact with criminals and other unsavory types is conducive to public safety and rehabilitation. Claims that a nonassociation condition violates the right of privacy are also rarely successful, except in some limited circumstances where the nonassociation condition infringed on specific familial rights such as prohibiting a person from living with his/her significant other.

Claims that a nonassociation condition is void because it is vague are sometimes successful. Due process requires that probation and parole conditions be stated clearly enough so that the average person can understand them and know what conduct is and is not permitted. Successful challenges have focused on the language of conditions, which prohibit association with all criminals, without regard for whether the probationer/parolee was aware that the person he or she was associating with had a criminal record.

Claims that a nonassociation condition violates the First Amendment are the most likely to succeed. The First Amendment includes the right of freedom of association; a nonassociation condition clearly infringes on this right. This does not necessarily render such conditions invalid, however. Probationers and parolees both enjoy only conditional freedom from confinement, and this freedom comes at the expense of some rights. Courts long have upheld conditions that restrict even "fundamental" rights, such as the freedom of association, so long as the condition is related to a compelling state interest, such as protecting the public or promoting rehabilitation.

The Supreme Court has decided only one case involving the constitutionality of a nonassociation condition. In *Arciniega v. Freeman* (1971), the Court interpreted the meaning of a parole condition which prohibited "association" with other ex-convicts, holding that such a provision did not apply to "incidental" contact that occurs between ex-convicts in the course of work on a legitimate job. Unresolved by the Court's decision in *Arciniega* was the question of exactly what constitutes "incidental" contact in other situations. Lower courts are left to sort out these issues. Generally, courts have treated brief, unplanned contact as "incidental," and have treated repeated, intentional contact as "association."

Several areas pose potential problems regarding limitations on association with other parolees. Often parolees participate in programs composed of individuals with special needs, such as educational programs, vocational training, alcohol and drug treatment, and psychological counseling. Restrictions on association with other parolees presents an obvious problem for these programs. For example, participation in Alcoholics Anonymous by parolees is not uncommon. In this program, members are required to have a sponsor who has similar experiences and maintains a close relationship with the individual. Accordingly, an ex-convict may request another ex-convict to be his or her sponsor. Should this type of association be restricted? If it is not, how would courts differentiate between legitimate self-help organizations and sham organizations created to avoid the restriction on association?

Nonassociation conditions are one of the easiest conditions for probationers and parolees to violate. Most offenders know others with criminal records, or live in an area where they are likely to encounter other offenders. As the facts in *Arciniega* indicate, even offenders who seek to comply with their probation and parole conditions may violate them unintentionally, simply by virtue of working somewhere with other offenders, or by participating in mandatory rehabilitation and reintegration programs.

Clearly, due process requires that offenders be given fair warning as to what conduct will subject them to a deprivation of their liberty. This means probation and parole conditions should be as clear and unambiguous as possible, and that probation and parole officers take steps to ensure that their clients understand their probation or parole conditions. In the context of nonassociation conditions, this means making sure offenders know the legal meanings of terms such as "association," "incidental contact," and "law-abiding."

Travel Conditions

Probation and parole conditions often are categorized into two groups: reform and control. Reform conditions are intended to help in the rehabilitation of the offender, while control conditions are intended to aid in the supervision of the offender (Cromwell, Alarid, and del Carmen 2004). A common probation and parole condition is one which limits in some way the offender's right to travel. Such a limitation is an example of a control condition.

Restrictions on travel, or more generally the offender's freedom of movement, can be divided into three types: (1) those that prohibit the offender from leaving the jurisdiction, (2) those prohibiting an offender from being at a particular location, and (3) those requiring the offender to be somewhere. Often two or more of these restrictions are combined in the conditions of probation or parole.

Conditions prohibiting the offender from being at a particular place may refer to places where criminal activity is known to occur, or where the offender's presence is likely to lead to trouble or criminal involvement, such as a bar, or the residence of the victim of the offender. Conditions requiring the offender to be somewhere include those that require the offender to live in a particular residence or halfway house, and those that require the offender to be present at treatment or counseling sessions.

Perhaps the most common probation and parole condition is one that requires the offender to remain within a certain geographical area, such as the state or county. Such conditions are generally upheld by the courts. The rationale for upholding such restrictions on the ability to travel includes protection of the public and promotion of offender rehabilitation. The public is protected because it is easier to supervise the offender if he or she remains within a limited area. Rehabilitation is fostered because it keeps the offender from going to areas where he or she might be more likely to engage in criminal conduct and because it makes it easier for the probation/parole officer to supervise the offender and help reintegrate the offender into society.

A common condition affecting the freedom of movement is one which requires the offender to be at a particular place at a particular time, such as one in which the offender is required to remain at home during the evening hours. This is a form of curfew. While general curfews for adults are frequently declared unconstitutional by the courts, probation and parole conditions involving a curfew for the offender are often upheld. The justification for upholding a curfew condition is usually that it will protect the public and promote the rehabilitation of the offender by keeping him or her away from places where he or she is more likely to engage in inappropriate and/or illegal behavior.

Probation and parole conditions prohibiting an offender from being in a particular place are not uncommon. For example, an offender might be prohibited from being in a bar, the residence of the victim of his offense, or a school. Courts have struck down such limitations when the state was unable to demonstrate that there is a relationship between the offense and the place prohibited. When the state is able to establish such a relationship, however, courts are likely to uphold the prohibition as fostering rehabilitation and protecting the public.

The right to travel is an ancient one, recognized in English law as early as the Magna Carta (1215). While a right to travel is not specifically mentioned in the Constitution, it is recognized that there exists a constitutional right to interstate travel. The right is derived from Article IV, Section Two of the Constitution, which states that "the citizens of each state shall be entitled to all Privileges and Immunities of Citizens in the several States." The right to travel is a fundamental right, meaning that courts will examine any attempt to restrict it very closely, applying the "strict scrutiny" test, which requires a showing of a "compelling state interest" and that there is no less means of accomplishing the purpose.

There are no U.S. Supreme Court decisions regarding the constitutionality of probation and parole conditions limiting the right to travel. There have been a number of lower federal court decisions and state court decisions involving challenges to such conditions, however. Lower courts long have upheld conditions that restrict even "fundamental" rights, such as the right of travel, so long as the condition is related to a compelling state interest, such as protecting the public or promoting rehabilitation. Probation and parole conditions that impose reasonable restrictions on the ability of the offender to travel or move about usually are upheld, on the ground that it is an appropriate means of both fostering rehabilitation and protecting the public.

While limitations on the freedom of movement are common, such conditions should not be imposed without reason, or without recognition that violation may be all too easy. Requiring an offender to stay away from places where he or she has friends, family, and other ties is an invitation to violation by the offender. Probation and parole officers should work with their clients to ensure the clients fully understand what the limitation on movement means in a practical sense, and to provide ways for clients to conduct activities, which foster their rehabilitation and reintegration into society without leading to an unwitting probation or parole violation.

Speech Conditions

Probation and parole conditions limiting speech are relatively rare, and most involve probationers who committed crimes while engaged in political demonstrations. Typical conditions bar the making of speeches, distributing printed materials, and engaging in public demonstrations or picketing. Such conditions were not uncommon during the Vietnam War, when political protests occurred with some regularity. Courts have seen a recurrence of such conditions in recent years, largely as a result of antiabortion protests. Some conditions have barred nonpolitical speech. These conditions often are intended to limit the ability of offenders to profit from the publication of materials documenting their criminal exploits.

Courts, recognizing the importance of the freedom of speech, tend to examine restrictions on the right very closely. In general, those cases upholding conditions have focused on the relationship between the condition and the goals of rehabilitation and protection of the public. Cases striking such conditions generally have done so on the ground that they are overbroad, and restrict more speech than is necessary. In one case, a court upheld a probation condition prohibiting an antiabortion protestor from entering the establishment that he was picketing against a challenge that such a condition unduly restricted the rights of the offender to engage in a political demonstration. In another case, a court upheld a probation condition preventing an antiabortion protestor from picketing an abortion clinic. The court determined that such a restriction was reasonably related to the goals of probation, including the prevention of further criminal activity and protection of the public.

Conditions Mandating Education or Job Training

Conditions requiring the offender to participate in educational programming or job training are different from previously discussed conditions in several ways, particularly in that they *require* the offender to do something, rather than to refrain from doing something. An affirmative act by the offender is required. A common probation and parole condition is the requirement that the offender attend school or an educational program of some kind. The frequency with which this condition is applied is not surprising, given the high value placed on education in American society and the relatively low education level of most offenders.

The type of education required depends on the offender. Juvenile offenders may be required to attend school; adult offenders generally are required to attend some form of adult education program. Other, offense-related educational programs also may be required, such as attendance at an alcohol and drug awareness class, or driver safety class.

The authority to require the offender to participate in educational programs may be found in specific statutes, or under the court and parole board's general authority to impose any condition that is reasonably related to the primary goals of probation and parole—rehabilitation and protection of the public. While the evidence regarding the rehabilitative effects of education programs on recidivism is mixed, historically there has been strong support for such programs. The assumption is that offenders with basic education are less likely to recidivate and more likely to see themselves as members of law-abiding society.

Offenders who either have completed basic educational programs or are in need of a marketable job skill often are required to obtain some form of job training. The justification for such a condition is also similar to the justification for mandatory education—rehabilitation and protection of the public. The assumption is that offenders with job skills will be less likely to return to their criminal ways as they develop a legitimate means of obtaining money.

Several cautions regarding mandating participation in education and job training programs should be mentioned. First, the course of study must not violate the constitutional rights of the offenders, particularly their First Amendment right of freedom of religion. Requiring an offender to attend religious training would likely be considered a violation of the First Amendment. While offenders on probation or parole retain only limited rights, courts look closely at any conditions that impinge on First Amendment rights. A second caution is that offenders should not be required to participate in educational programs for which they are unprepared or unable to participate in, because of financial constraints or other limitations. This is simply setting the offender up for failure. Probation and parole officers should consider the aptitude and willingness of the offender when making recommendations for educational programming.

Conditions Mandating Medical Treatment

Conditions mandating medical treatment can take several forms, including surgical procedures, psychological treatment, or some type of counseling or therapy. Conditions requiring an offender to undergo some type of surgical procedure are relatively rare, although there have been calls in recent years for greater use of such conditions, at least in regards to offenders with sexual issues.

Challenges to conditions mandating medical treatment are based on several different provisions of the Constitution, including the First and Eighth Amendments, and the general right to privacy. These challenges are relatively rare, no doubt in large part because such conditions are themselves rare. Generally, courts have taken the position that a condition requiring medical treatment is not per se unconstitutional, so long as the treatment is reasonably related to the goal of rehabilitation (*Washington v. Harper*, 1990). Additionally, courts have noted that the offender always has the option of rejecting such a condition.

Conditions mandating some form of therapy or counseling are much more common than those requiring the offender to undergo a medical procedure. Primarily because these conditions are less physically invasive, they are also much more likely to be upheld by the courts. Additionally, it is often easier to establish a connection between the mandated therapy and the goals of probation and parole.

Conditions requiring the offender to receive some form of therapy or counseling may be authorized by a state statute, or by parole authority regulations. This authorization is frequently vague, merely authorizing " psychological or psychiatric treatment" without providing more specifics. A number of states now provide specific authorization for counseling for sexual offenders. Conditions mandating therapy or counseling are quite popular, as there is widespread sentiment that most offenders can benefit from professional attention.

There have been very few challenges to probation and parole conditions mandating therapy or counseling. Courts have routinely rejected such challenges, so long as the treatment is reasonably related to the needs of the offender. Courts have also made it clear that offenders are only required to make reasonable efforts to comply with the treatment condition. Requiring an offender to obtain expensive treatment that he or she clearly cannot afford may be invalidated by the courts.

Conditions Mandating Restitution

A common probation and parole condition is the requirement that the offender make a payment to the victim. Restitution is defined as "an equitable remedy under which a person is restored to his or her position prior to a loss or injury . . . (or) compensation for the wrongful taking of property." It is different from victim compensation, where the money is given to the victim by the state. Restitution is paid by the offender to the victim. It is also different from a fine, which is monies paid by the offender to the state and is not treated as compensation. Restitution serves both as atonement for the offender and rehabilitation for the victim.

Virtually every jurisdiction allows for the imposition of restitution as a probation condition, while twenty-nine states currently require a court to order restitution to the victim. Restitution has been endorsed in the Model Penal Code and by the American Bar Association and the National Council on Crime and Delinquency.

Restitution serves a number of purposes. These primarily include: (1) providing redress for victims of crime; (2) providing accountability for the offender; and

(3) serving as an intermediate sanction that is less severe on the offender. The sanction is used most often for crimes involving damage to property or economic crimes; it is used much less frequently for violent crimes, as it is difficult to determine the appropriate compensation for such injuries, and it is not seen as an appropriate sanction for such serious offenses.

The authority to require an offender to make restitution has been repeatedly upheld by the courts. Ordinarily, there must be a finding or plea of guilty before restitution can be ordered, although this does not apply to cases involving restitution ordered during the pretrial diversion process. Courts may specify the amount, method of payment, and other conditions relating to restitution. However, the U.S. Supreme Court, in *Bearden v. Georgia* (1983), ruled that probation cannot be revoked because of an offender's inability to pay restitution as a condition of probation when the failure to pay is a result of indigence and not a mere refusal to pay. In this case Bearden was ordered to pay a $500 fine and $200 in restitution, but was unable to find employment and consequently failed to pay either the fine or the restitution. His probation was revoked and he was incarcerated. He argued, and the Supreme Court agreed, that the Equal Protection Clause of the Fourteenth Amendment barred the revocation of probation for a non-willful failure to pay restitution. The Court determined that revocation was proper only if the failure to pay was intentional and the offender did not make a good faith effort to obtain the means to pay.

It sometimes seems as though there are as many probation and parole conditions (and challenges to these conditions) as there are individuals under community supervision. Probation and parole officers can do their job well, however, if they keep in mind a few simple points. First, individuals on probation/parole retain a number of rights, and officers must take care not to abridge these rights. Second, officers have a duty to enforce the conditions of probation and parole, and to do so in an evenhanded, consistent manner. Third, many violations may be avoided if officers make clear to their clients the terms of each condition, as well as their intention to enforce these conditions. Fourth, officers will do well to remember that many probation and parole conditions serve two primary functions at the same time: promotion of offender rehabilitation and reintegration, and protection of society.

Sex Offender Registration, Community Notification, and Civil Commitment

Spurred by media accounts of horrible child sexual assault cases, Congress and the state legislatures in recent years have passed a variety of laws affecting the rights of convicted sex offenders. These laws vary in the details, but focus on three primary objectives: (1) requiring sex offenders to register with local authorities; (2) requiring local law enforcement to notify the community about the presence of sex offenders living in the community; and (3) permitting the state to pursue civil commitment of sex offenders after they have served a period of incarceration. Each of these objectives presents potential legal issues.

Laws affecting sex offenders are often referred to as Megan's laws, as many of the laws were passed in response to the rape and murder of Megan Kanka, a seven year-old New Jersey girl, by a twice-convicted sex offender who lived across the street. The New Jersey legislature and Congress responded by immediately passing legislation affecting sex offenders, and other states soon followed. Much of this legislation was spurred by the Jacob Wetterling Crimes Against Children and Sexually Violent Registration Act, which Congress passed in 1994. This legislation established a national registry system for sex offenders, and required states to pass similar registration and tracking systems or face a loss of federal monies. In particular, the legislation required states to release all relevant information necessary to protect the public. Today, every state requires the registration of sex offenders, and at least forty-seven states have some form of notification requirement.

While these laws are obviously popular, they are not without controversy. Social scientists have pointed out that there is little empirical proof that such laws reduce recidivism, while legal scholars have suggested the laws may violate a number of constitutional rights, including the ban on ex post facto laws, the prohibition on double jeopardy, and the right of privacy.

State Sex Offender Registration

Today all fifty states require that convicted sex offenders register with local authorities. States vary in precisely who is required to register: in some states only those convicted of a sex offense after passage of the registration requirement must comply, while in other states the registration requirement is applied retroactively. Some states require anyone convicted of a sexual offense to register; others also require those convicted of a violent crime against a child to register.

Typical registration requirements include requiring released offenders to register with the local law enforcement agency in the jurisdiction where they are living, to verify their address annually, and to do so for a period of years—often between twenty and thirty years. Failure to comply is a felony, punishable as a new offense.

Community Notification

Washington State was the first to pass a notification statute, doing so in 1989. The notification movement gained national attention and tremendous momentum with the passage of New Jersey's notification statute, Megan's law, in 1994. Proponents viewed notification statutes as a necessary supplement to registration laws, many of which already existed.

A variety of methods exist for notifying the public. These include public meetings, provision of a written list of offenders, provision of a list on CD-ROM, news releases, and notices targeted to institutions such as schools. A substantial majority of the states have an Internet site devoted to dissemination of sex-offender information. More than thirty states allow persons to request information on a specific offender, or to view the sex-offender registry at the discretion of local law enforcement officials. States also vary in the determination of which registered sex offenders the public has a right to notice of, with public notice usually limited to those deemed most dangerous.

Civil Commitment

The U.S. Supreme Court upheld the civil commitment of sex offenders in *Kansas v. Hendricks* (1997). Kansas passed legislation in 1994 establishing procedures for the civil commitment of persons who were deemed likely to engage in "predatory acts of sexual violence" due to either a "mental abnormality" or "personality disorder." The statute was applied to Hendricks, after he finished serving a term of imprisonment for child molestation, and he was ordered civilly committed. Hendricks challenged his commitment on double jeopardy, ex post facto, and due process grounds. In a narrow 5-4 decision, written by Justice Thomas, the Supreme Court upheld the civil commitment statute. The high court reasoned that neither the double jeopardy nor ex post facto clauses applied, as civil commitment was not punitive but regulatory, and these clauses apply only to punishment. There was no due process violation because civil commitment for a mental abnormality did not violate the concept of "ordered liberty."

In a subsequent case, the Supreme Court provided further support for states seeking to use civil commitment for sex offenders. In *Kansas v. Crane* (2002), the high court held that civil commitment could be justified upon a mere showing that the offender had a "serious difficulty in controlling [his] behavior." In *McKune v. Lile* (2002), the Supreme Court upheld a requirement that sex offenders could be required to disclose their criminal history (and thus run the risk of providing the authorities with incriminating information) as part of a prison sex offender treatment program. While only a handful of states had enacted civil commitment laws prior to the *Hendricks* decision, a number of states have responded by enacting similar legislation.

How sex offenders are managed and supervised is a matter of great concern to the general public, politicians, and criminal justice professionals. Sex-offender notification and registration is part of a larger trend toward community justice. Supporters of notification often claim that such laws enable individual citizens to protect themselves against criminal activity.

Protecting the public from sex offenders and helping offenders with their rehabilitation and reintegration has taken on even greater importance to probation and parole departments as a consequence of the firestorm over registration and notification. There has been a tremendous increase in the resources needed to supervise sex offenders. Unfortunately, there also have been a number of cases involving claims of improper supervision of sex offenders. As a result, the focus is now on containment and control of sex offenders, rather than on rehabilitation.

The Fourteenth Amendment and Probation and Parole

Individuals convicted of crime, whether incarcerated or on probation or parole, do not retain the privacy rights enjoyed by the average citizen. Indeed, prisoners have no reasonable expectation of privacy and are subject to warrantless searches based on less than probable cause. This limitation also is evident in regards to probation and parole conditions that impinge on the Fourth Amendment right to be free from "unreasonable" searches and seizures. What may be an unreasonable search when the target is an ordinary citizen may be reasonable when the target is a probationer or parolee. Courts frequently base this distinction on the rationale that a probationer or parolee has a lessened expectation of privacy than the ordinary citizen. There are several policy reasons that support allowing searches of probationers and parolees. These include protection of the public, reducing recidivism through deterrence of criminal conduct by the client, promoting alternatives to incarceration, and, hopefully, rehabilitation through reintegration in the community.

Consent to a search is one of the most common conditions of probation and parole. The condition generally covers searches conducted by probation or parole officers, and often allows searches by police officers, as well. The scope of the search usually includes the offender's person and property. The terms of the condition may include blanket permission to be searched by caseworkers or law enforcement personnel, or may be limited to searches conducted by the caseworker. While this condition is widespread, it is rarely specifically authorized by statute (Cohen and

Gobert 1992). Instead, the condition usually is justified under the broad discretionary authority of the sentencing court (for probation) or the parole agency (for parole). While this condition is almost always upheld, some courts have struck it down in specific instances where consent to search was not appropriately related to the offense and background of the offender (Hemmens, Bennett, and del Carmen 1999).

The Fourth Amendment controls all searches and seizures conducted by state actors, be they police or probation officers. All searches and seizures must be conducted either: (1) based on a warrant, issued upon a showing of "probable cause," or (2) without a warrant, so long as the search is not "unreasonable"—meaning there must be a showing of probable cause and an exigent circumstance or exception, which justifies failure to obtain a warrant. Exigent circumstances include such situations as danger to public safety and hot pursuit. Exceptions to the warrant requirement include inventory searches, plain view searches, search incident to arrest, and others. The two exceptions relevant to caseworkers are consent and the special needs of law enforcement.

Another exception to the warrant requirement that comes into play in probation and parole situations is the "special needs of law enforcement" exception. Under this exception, the requirement of a warrant and probable cause are determined to interfere too greatly on the government's objective. Courts must balance the degree of intrusion into an individual's right to privacy with the burden on the government. The Court has upheld searches in schools and drug testing in certain occupations under this exception. In *Griffin v. Wisconsin* (1987), the Court held that a state regulation allowing "reasonable" searches of all probationers was constitutionally valid, on the grounds that the warrant and probable cause requirement would unduly hamper the state's probation system. The Court did not find it necessary to address the issue of the validity of the probationers' consent, since the regulation was upheld under the "special needs" exception.

The Exclusionary Rule and Probation and Parole

Until recently, it was unclear whether the exclusionary rule applied to probation and parole revocation hearings, which are generally considered extrajudicial proceedings. The Supreme Court in *Griffin v. Wisconsin* (1987) held that a state regulation allowing warrantless "reasonable" searches and searches based on "reasonable grounds" of probationers was constitutionally valid, on the ground that the warrant and probable cause requirement would unduly hamper the effectiveness of the state's probation system. Lower courts interpreting *Griffin* were split on the applicability of the exclusionary rule to probation and parole revocation hearings where probation and parole officers conduct illegal searches. Finally, in *Pennsylvania Board of Probation and Parole v. Scott* (1998) the court, in a five to four decision, held that the exclusionary rule does not apply to parole revocation hearings.

Pennsylvania Board of Probation and Parole v. Scott

Keith Scott was released on parole in September 1993, after serving ten years for third-degree murder. One of the conditions of his parole was that he would neither own nor possess any weapons. Another condition was that he consent in advance to warrantless searches of his person, property, and residence by agents of the Pennsylvania Board of Probation and Parole. Furthermore, he agreed that any evidence seized during such searches could be used in a parole revocation hearing.

About five months after Scott was paroled, three parole officers obtained an arrest warrant for Scott, based on evidence that he had violated several terms of his parole. After arresting Scott they went to his residence, where he lived with his parents, and searched it. In a room adjacent to Scott's bedroom they found several weapons. These were introduced at the revocation hearing. Scott objected to the introduction of the evidence seized during the search of his home, claiming the seizure violated the Fourth Amendment because it was conducted without at least "reasonable suspicion" (as required by *Griffin*). He also claimed that his prior consent to a warrantless search was invalid because it was obtained involuntarily, as a requirement of parole eligibility. The hearing examiner rejected his claims, admitted the seized evidence, and recommitted Scott.

On appeal, the Commonwealth Court of Pennsylvania ruled: (1) the search was unlawful because it was conducted without Scott's consent and was not authorized by any state statutory or regulatory framework ensuring the reasonableness of the officers (per Griffin), and (2) the illegally seized evidence should not be admitted at the revocation hearing because the exclusionary rule applied to such proceedings. The Pennsylvania Supreme Court affirmed the lower court, holding that Scott's consent to warrantless searches did not extend to searches conducted without at least "reasonable suspicion," and that the exclusionary rule should apply to parole revocation hearings when parole officers are aware that the subject of their search is a parolee.

The U.S. Supreme Court reversed the decision of the Pennsylvania Supreme Court and held that the exclusionary rule did not apply to parole revocation hearings. Writing for the majority, Justice Thomas emphasized the costs associated with the exclusionary rule, and downplayed the benefits of the rule, particularly in parole revocation hearings. As parole is a "variation on imprisonment of convicted criminals" and parole revocation deprives a parolee "only of the conditional liberty properly dependent on observance of special parole restrictions," Thomas determined that applying the exclusionary rule to parole revocation hearings would significantly alter the revocation process, transforming revocation hearings "from a predictive and discretionary effort to promote the best interests of both parolees and society into trial-like proceedings less attuned to the interests of the parolee."

Thomas stated that the exclusionary rule should not be applied to parole revocation hearings because the purpose of the exclusionary rule is deterrence of unlawful police conduct in the investigation and prosecution of crime, while the purpose of parole is different—to rehabilitate the offender while at the same time to protect the community. Since extension of the exclusionary rule to revocation hearings would not serve these dual purposes, and in fact would hamper the effective administration of a parole system, it has no place in revocation hearings.

The ruling in *Scott* was a major victory for probation and parole officers. It allows the use of evidence, however obtained, in parole revocation hearings. This is an important decision, as parole revocations are becomingly increasingly common as more and more individuals are placed on parole. There are currently in excess of three million people on probation or parole. And while this case dealt only with parole-revocation hearings, it is likely the Court would similarly hold the exclusionary does not apply in probation-revocation hearings.

A subsequent case reaffirmed the Supreme Court's diminished view of the applicability of the Fourth Amendment to probationers and parolees. In *United States v. Knights* (2001), the Court held that a consent search authorized by a probation condition was reasonable. Knights was placed on probation for a minor drug offense.

According to the terms of his probation, he was required to submit to a search at any time, even in the absence of a warrant, probable cause, or even reasonable suspicion, by either a probation or police officer. Shortly after he was placed on probation, Knights became a suspect in an arson investigation. A sheriff's deputy, aware of the search condition in Knights' probation order, conducted a warrantless search of Knights' apartment, where he found material implicating Knights in the arson. The district court conceded that the deputy had "reasonable suspicion" that Knights was involved in the arson, but nonetheless determined that the search of Knights' residence violated the Fourth Amendment because it was conducted for "investigatory" rather than "probationary" purposes. The district court claimed that the search condition in the probation order allowed warrantless searches on less than probable cause only when the purpose of the search was to see if probation was being complied with, not for the investigation of another crime.

The Supreme Court unanimously reversed the lower court and upheld the search of Knights' apartment. Rather than trying to sort out whether the search was investigatory or probationary in nature, the opinion by Chief Justice Rehnquist focused on whether the search was "reasonable" under the Fourth Amendment. The Court held that this particular search, based on reasonable suspicion and authorized by a probation condition, was in fact reasonable. The Chief Justice noted that probation serves several purposes, including rehabilitation of the defendant and protection of the public, and probationers enjoy a lessened expectation of privacy. All of this tilted the balance in favor of the government in this case. While the Court several times focused on the specific facts of this case, some language in the opinion left open the possibility that searches of a probationer might be considered "reasonable" even in the absence of a specific search condition or reasonable suspicion.

In *Samson v. California* (2006), the Supreme Court went a step further and ruled that the Fourth Amendment does not prohibit a police officer from conducting a suspicionless search of a parolee. The case originated in California, which had a statute requiring all parolees to agree, as a condition of their release, to warrantless searches by either parole officers or police officers. The Court, in a six to three decision authored by Justice Thomas, upheld the state law, noting that parolees have a lower expectation of privacy than free citizens or even probationers. The state, on the other hand, has a strong interest in ensuring that parolees do not endanger public safety. Balancing the parolee's low expectation of privacy against the state's interest in public safety, the Court had little difficulty upholding the state suspicionless search statute. Consequently, the Fourth Amendment and the exclusionary rule have little or no application to the rights of parolees.

Privilege Against Self-Incrimination

The Supreme Court has accorded criminal suspects the right to be apprised of their Fifth and Sixth Amendment rights, such as the right to counsel and the privilege against self-incrimination, prior to custodial interrogation. The Court created the so-called *Miranda* warnings because it felt that they were necessary to effectively secure a criminal suspect's privilege against self-incrimination. Prior to the decision in *Miranda v. Arizona* (1966), the Court focused on whether a statement was voluntary—that is, uncoerced by the police. The Court determined in *Miranda* that voluntariness alone was not enough—because an incriminating statement was potentially devastating to a defendant, such statements should be admitted only if it were made freely and with full knowledge of one's constitutional rights.

The Court has refused to extend the *Miranda* warnings to interrogation of probationers or parolees by their caseworkers, however. While the Supreme Court has not directly addressed the issue, most lower courts have held that the *Miranda* warnings are not required before a caseworker speaks with a client, primarily on the rationale that to require the warnings would do serious damage to the relationship between the caseworker and client, creating a law enforcement/interrogation type of atmosphere rather than a counseling type of atmosphere.

While caseworkers are not required to *Mirandize* their clients before engaging in a routine office visit, a different situation arises when the probation or parole officer has placed the client under arrest. *Miranda* warnings are required whenever someone is in custody and interrogation is about to commence. An ordinary conversation between client and caseworker does not fall into this category. However, once a caseworker has begun investigating a possible crime, and has arrested the client, then *Miranda* warnings are required. The same is true if the caseworker is questioning a client who has been arrested by the police and brought to the probation/parole officer for questioning.

Privileged Communications

Courts long have recognized that certain communications should remain confidential, regardless of their probative value in court. Every state has case law and statutes according the privilege of confidentiality to certain relationships, such as doctor-patient, husband-wife, lawyer-client, and clergy-parishioner. Confidentiality is not a constitutional right but an evidentiary privilege. This means that the person who enjoys the privilege must exercise it to keep a communication confidential. In other words, the persons must assert the privilege—it will not be extended to them unless they specifically request it.

The importance of privileged communications for criminal justice caseworkers involves their designation, in some states, as counselors. This designation suggests the caseworker-client relationship may be akin to the doctor-patient relationship and that, therefore, communications between a caseworker and a client may be privileged. Yet, most courts have not taken this view. There are exceptions to the doctor-patient privilege, and courts have declined to extend the common law evidentiary privilege of confidentiality to the caseworker-offender relationship, regardless of whether the caseworker is a probation officer or a parole officer. Thus, conversations between a parolee and his or her caseworker are not treated as confidential. The rationale most often proffered for this distinction is that a criminal justice counselor is not a private counselor, but a counselor and a law enforcement agent (*Fare v. Michael C.*, 1979).

In *Jaffee v. Redmond* (1996), the Supreme Court held that there is a psychotherapist-patient privilege with respect to confidential communications. Furthermore, this privilege extends to communications between licensed social workers and patients, as well. While this decision was in accord with the rule in most states, it is potentially significant in that it may open the door for extension of the privilege to other relationships that involve medical/psychological counseling. This could include criminal justice caseworkers. Courts have not yet taken this step, however, and since most criminal justice counselors are not licensed therapists, courts may distinguish them from social workers and psychotherapists on this basis.

Right to Due Process in Probation/Parole Revocation Hearings

While those convicted of a crime clearly do not retain all of their rights, the Supreme Court has made it clear that the Fourteenth Amendment's Due Process Clause does apply, not only during incarceration but also at probation and parole revocation hearings. This is a significant change from prior practice.

In *Morrissey v. Brewer* (1972), the Court held that due process required that, at a minimum, parole revocation procedures include: (1) written notice of the claimed parole violation; (2) disclosure to the parolee of the evidence against him or her; (3) an opportunity for the parolee to present evidence and witnesses, and to be heard; (4) the right of the parolee to confront and examine witnesses; (5) a neutral and detached hearing committee; and (6) a written statement by the parole board of the evidence and reasons for revoking parole.

In *Gagnon v. Scarpelli* (1973), the Court held that the requirements for a probation-revocation hearing are identical to the requirements for a parole-revocation hearing. While the Court admitted that parole and probation are not identical, revocation of probation where sentence has been imposed previously is fundamentally indistinguishable from revocation of parole. In *Mempa v. Rhay* (1967), the Court held that the Sixth Amendment right to counsel applies to a combined revocation and sentencing hearing, on the grounds that since the right to counsel attaches at any stage in a criminal proceeding where substantial rights of a criminal defendant are involved, the right should include sentencing.

Caseworker Liability Issues

An emerging area of the law of potential concern to criminal justice caseworkers is the issue of liability, both individual and governmental. There has been a tremendous increase in public concern over the release of potentially dangerous offenders, particularly sexual offenders. Every state has enacted legislation requiring public notification of the release of certain offenders, and both individual caseworkers and state governments have been held liable for civil damages for negligent release of criminal offenders. At the same time, caseworkers are faced with maintaining a duty to their clients, be they probationers, parolees, or inmates.

It is important to distinguish the different duties owed by a criminal justice caseworker. The caseworker, as a quasi law-enforcement agent, owes a duty to the public to protect it from harm. This duty applies to caseworkers in both the institutional setting as well as the community. There is an obligation to keep inmates deemed dangerous away from the public. This duty includes keeping such individuals in secure custody to prevent escape, and to keep such inmates incarcerated until it is determined that they pose no future danger to society. There is also the duty to warn the public when a dangerous person is in the community. A number of states recently have enacted legislation requiring the registration of certain released offenders, as well as notification of the public in general and in some cases, notification of individual victims. Furthermore, community-based criminal justice caseworkers owe a duty to supervise offenders under their care and to report potential dangerousness.

Immunity

In common law, the state could not be sued for civil damages as a result of its actions, regardless of the intent of the state. Under the English doctrine of sovereign immunity, the king, as an agent of God, was incapable of doing wrong; hence, there was no possibility of liability, since there could be no wrongdoing. This doctrine has continued, in watered-down fashion, to the present day, under the theory that the government can be sued only if it consents to the suit, either expressly through statute or constitutional provision.

Most states have a statutory provision waiving their sovereign immunity in certain circumstances. This allows lawsuits to be brought in state court relying on state tort law. A tort is a "private or civil wrong or injury other than beach of contract, for which the court will provide a remedy in the form of an action for damages" (Black 2004).

While the federal and state governments all provide for waiver of their sovereign immunity in some circumstances, this waiver is far from complete. There are three forms of immunity defenses invoked in liability suits: absolute, qualified, and quasi-judicial immunity. Under absolute immunity, a lawsuit is dismissed without delving into the merits of the claim itself. Absolute immunity has been applied to legislators, judges, and prosecutors. It generally applies only to officials in the judicial or legislative branches of government.

Where absolute immunity protects officials completely, regardless of motive or intent, qualified immunity protects an official only if the official acted in "good faith." This form of immunity applies only to members of the executive branch of government. Probation and parole officers generally are accorded qualified immunity, although recently some lower courts have become less willing to apply immunity unquestioningly.

Quasi-judicial immunity applies to officials who perform both judicial and executive functions. Under this form of immunity, official duties that are essentially nondiscretionary are not protected from liability, while those official duties that are judicial in nature and involve the exercise of discretion are accorded protection from liability. Courts generally have held that the function must be "intimately associated" with the judicial phase of the criminal process for immunity to apply (Jones and del Carmen 1992). Parole board members generally fall into this protected group. Where qualified immunity is determined by the officer performing the function, quasi-judicial immunity is determined by the function itself (del Carmen 1985).

The importance of the doctrine of sovereign immunity is that it allows a plaintiff to sue not merely the individual caseworker for damages, but to sue the government, as the employer of the individual, under the doctrine of *respondeat superior*. Under this doctrine, an employer may be held liable for the *torts* of an employee, if these torts are committed in the scope of employment. This doctrine allows plaintiffs to go after the one with "deep pockets," as criminal justice personnel, like other employees, are unlikely to have large resources from which a damage award can be obtained.

Generally speaking, for liability to attach, there must be not only a waiver of sovereign immunity, but proof of inappropriate conduct by the caseworker. In tort law, liability may be imposed for several levels of conduct: strict liability, negligence, and recklessness. In strict liability, liability attaches irrespective of the knowledge of the defendant. This very rarely applies to criminal justice personnel. Usually negligence is not enough to impose liability either. Rather, there must be a showing of *recklessness*—conduct, which displays both serious risk-taking and an awareness of the likelihood of harm. While this may be proven by the civil standard of proof by a mere preponderance of the evidence, rather than the criminal standard of proof beyond a reasonable doubt, it is nonetheless a difficult burden for most plaintiffs to meet.

A common issue involves the decision to release an offender, or the decision not to revoke an offender, and a subsequent criminal act by the offender. Can the caseworker who decided to allow the offender to remain in the community be held liable for damages for the future criminal conduct of the offender? Generally, courts have been reluctant to attach liability in such situations absent a showing of recklessness.

In other words, a caseworker who follows established procedure, and who makes an informed discretionary decision will not be held liable if it later turns out to have been a mistaken decision. Courts recognize that predicting future behavior is not foolproof. So long as caseworkers can demonstrate that they have made a good faith effort to make the right decision, liability will not attach. The key is adhering to both existing professional standards and following the legally required steps and procedures. Caseworkers do not always have to be correct, but they do have a duty to acquire and share relevant information, provide the appropriate treatment, and follow any legal requirements (Cohen 1995). In legal terms, caseworkers have a duty to the public to use reasonable care to prevent a foreseeable risk of harm.

Legal Remedies for Harm

There are several bases for caseworker liability. The most common are state tort law, the Federal Tort Claims Act of 1946, and the Federal Civil Rights Act of 1871 (42 U.S.C. Section 1983). The Federal Tort Claims Act of 1946 waives the sovereign immunity of the federal government in a number of areas, and 42 U.S.C. Section 1983 provides a federal law remedy for injury caused by state actors.

For a plaintiff to succeed under a Section 1983 claim, the defendant must be acting "under color of law," meaning that the injury was a result of misconduct by a state agent acting in his or her role as a state agent. Only individuals may be sued under Section 1983, not corrections departments. In addition, the injury must involve a constitutional or federally protected right. While Section 1983 was passed by Congress in 1871, it was not until 1961, in the case of *Monroe v. Pape*, that the Supreme Court held that the law applied to the violation of civil rights of criminal suspects.

State tort law varies a great deal from state to state; consequently, criminal justice caseworkers are advised to familiarize themselves with the law in their jurisdiction. A tort is a civil wrong. Three conditions must exist for a tort to be proven. First, it must be shown that the defendant owed a duty to the plaintiff. This duty may arise from law, as in the case of contracts, or from the relationship of the plaintiff and defendant. It is this situation which is of most concern to criminal justice caseworkers, as the client-counselor relationship and the counselor-public relationship give rise to certain obligations, including the right to privacy and the duty to warn.

It also must be shown that the defendant not only owed a duty to the plaintiff, but that he or she breached that duty. In legal parlance, there are three forms that this breach of duty may take in regards to state agents. If a caseworker takes an improper action, it is termed *misfeasance*. If the caseworker takes no action or takes a required action but performs it inappropriately, it is referred to as *malfeasance*.

The third condition for a tort is a demonstration that the injury suffered by the plaintiff was, in fact, the proximate consequence of the defendant's breach of duty. Proximate cause is a legal creation intended to limit liability for damages to consequences that reasonably are foreseeable and related to the defendant's conduct.

Ethical Issues for Caseworkers

Most state statutes provide only a general outline of the duties of probation and parole officers, often speaking in general terms of supervising, counseling, and assisting the offender. Some statutes classify probation and parole officers as law enforcement personnel, while other statutes classify them as social service personnel. This split indicates the variation in perceptions of what the primary task of caseworkers is, and consequently, how caseworkers should interact with their clients.

Because the statutory goals of probation and parole officers are frequently vague, the manner in which a caseworker deals with his or her clients is likely to be determined in large part by the needs of the local agency and outside factors such as public outcry over individual cases. Commentators have identified three different roles that most caseworkers fall into, based on their education, training, and local agency culture. These are the law enforcement model, the therapeutic model, and the synthetic model (Abadinsky 2005). Under the law enforcement model, caseworkers see their primary role as protecting the public. Under the therapeutic model, caseworkers see their primary role as rehabilitating and aiding the client offender. Under the synthetic model, caseworkers see their primary role as a combination of law enforcement and rehabilitation.

The caseworker is charged, at a minimum, with the twin, and potentially competing, duties of protecting the public by supervising the conduct of the client, and additionally supervising the treatment and rehabilitation of the client. Clearly, there is a potential for role conflict here—what is best for the client may not always be best for the public, and vice versa. How a caseworker reconciles these potentially conflicting goals is determined not only by agency and public pressure, but also by individual ethics. Simply put, the caseworker is faced, on a daily basis, with choosing not just between what is legally required and prohibited, but between what is ethically or morally "right."

The majority of this chapter is taken up with a discussion of the legal rights of criminal justice offenders and the legal duties that these rights create for the criminal justice caseworker. Legal requirements are not the end of the story, however. The law simply provides the parameters of conduct, sketching out the bare minimum that is required of the caseworker. Ethical standards may require more. The caseworker must determine, based on his or her own set of ethics, what sort of conduct is proper. The ethical choices generally break down into two areas: deciding what is owed to the client, and deciding what is owed to the community. Each of these areas require the caseworker to make hard choices, when the two areas come into conflict the choice is even more difficult.

There are several ethical duties the criminal justice counselor owes to his or her client. One is the duty to inform the offender of the limitations of their relationship. Thus, a caseworker should inform a client that total confidentiality cannot be assured. Obviously, this ethical duty may limit the development of the relationship, since clients may decide that they cannot divulge all of their activities to the caseworker if doing so may force the caseworker to report them to the authorities.

Criminal justice caseworkers also owe an ethical duty to the client to act in the best interests of the client. Generally, this means providing the opportunity for rehabilitation and treatment, if necessary. An oft-quoted maxim is that the caseworker should "do no harm" to the client. This is a difficult task for the caseworker who is responsible for both helping and supervising the offender.

Perspective from the Field
Inmate Rights: Getting the Courts to Listen

By Timothy R. McNeese, J.D.

Tim McNeese has been Deputy Attorney General for the Idaho Department of Corrections since 1984. He received his bachelor's degree from New Mexico State University in 1971, his master's degree from the University of Colorado in 1975, and his J.D. from Gonzaga University in Spokane, Washington in 1980. From 1980 to 1984, Mr. McNeese served as a U.S. Army Judge Advocate General. He also serves as an adjunct faculty member at Boise State University.

● ●

In 1984, U.S. District Judge Harold J. Ryan issued a decision in a prisoner civil rights case, which was successfully filed and presented by two inmates, without lawyer assistance, on behalf of the other inmates at the Idaho State Correctional Institution. Judge Ryan found that the Idaho State Correctional Institution was unconstitutionally overcrowded and that "overcrowding brings on many problems, including idleness, frustration, stress, discomfort, edginess, and fear." He issued a decision that placed population caps on the housing units at Idaho State Correctional Institution. He also ordered such reforms as staffing increases, improved medical care, and dietary programs, clothing modifications, and protection for youthful offenders.

From the perspective of the "jailhouse lawyers," this trial was a tremendous victory. It showed that incarcerated persons with time on their hands, a well-supplied prison law library, and a good cause, could exercise the right of access to courts in a highly effective manner. The good quality of legal representation provided by the two inmate litigants did not go unnoticed by Judge Ryan, who also criticized lawyers who practice in the field of prison law.

In the real world of prison law, representing inmates is not a top priority among attorneys. Except for occasional appearances by attorneys for the American Civil Liberties Union, various Legal Aid Societies, and a handful of others, most inmates use prison law libraries and represent themselves, pro se (without a lawyer). The quality and effectiveness of inmate pro se representation can be very good. The primary inmate litigant in the previously described case had a reputation among judges for often dismissing minor legal claims so that he could concentrate on more winnable issues. He also had the exceptional ability to sense the sympathies of the court and the public and to use it for the benefit of the inmate population. Federal court intervention, consent decrees, and court appointed monitors were common in prison cases during the 1980s.

Just a few years ago, the Federal District Court in Idaho estimated that 27 percent of all litigation in federal court involved inmate claims, almost all of which were filed without a lawyer. Although there is no question that many inmate lawsuits have merit, it has been this author's experience that many

Continued on the next page

Perspective from the Field, *continued*

more are meritless, and some are downright frivolous. The frivolous cases, no doubt, are filed by inmates out of frustration and anger and the desire to get even with a correctional employee or "the system." Many see the court system as a more effective tool to get attention and results than simply filing a written grievance with prison officials. Some are simply ignorant of the law and the function of the courts or do not care.

In an effort to bring to the attention of the public the abuses of the court system by inmates, the Idaho Attorney General in 1996 joined Attorneys Generals throughout the country in publishing a list of "most frivolous " inmate lawsuits. A sample of Idaho's most frivolous cases, cited by the Attorney General, include the following:

- An inmate obtained a copy of the American Correctional Association's magazine left in an employee break room. He filled out and mailed to the publisher a card requesting manufacturer's information about prison security and locks. He sued under the First Amendment when the warden refused to let him have the information through the mail.

- One inmate sued under the First Amendment because prison policy recognized as "privileged mail," correspondence from attorneys, doctors, and the governor, but not "dukes, earls, princes, princesses, and the Queen of England." He did not state whether he was expecting any correspondence from these other sources.

- An inmate started a prison riot by shattering the glass window on his cell door and filed an Eighth Amendment lawsuit when he cut his foot on the glass fragments in his cell.

- Another inmate filed a lawsuit because he was ordered to do morning grounds maintenance outside his cell house, but was issued only athletic shoes. He wanted a pair of work boots.

- One of Idaho's most litigious death row inmates has filed so many meritless legal actions that both the state and federal courts have had to impose the extraordinary sanction of refusing to allow him to file any more lawsuits without first obtaining permission of the court to do so. Inmate litigation of this kind also has resulted in recent state and federal legislation designed to curtail frivolous, time-consuming abuses.

Although Idaho law allows for attorney's fees to be awarded to the state's attorneys when an inmate files a frivolous lawsuit, the reality of prison life is that few inmates have any money in their inmate accounts which can be used to satisfy a judgment awarded against them. Thus, until recently, there has been little to deter an inmate from filing a frivolous action.

In 1996, the state legislature adopted a law that allows for disciplinary detention and loss of inmate privileges to be assessed against inmates who bring a lawsuit that is found to be frivolous or malicious. Additionally, it allows prison and jail officials to collect judgments in frivolous cases from money in an inmate's account and even through the sale of his or her personal property.

In April 1996, the U.S. Congress passed the Prison Litigation Reform Act of 1995 (PLRA). Among the highlights of this federal legislation is a requirement that no inmate can bring a prison conditions lawsuit in federal court unless he first has exhausted available administrative remedies such as filing a written grievance with the warden, medical staff, and so forth. The Prison Litigation Reform Act additionally states that an inmate claiming to have insufficient money to pay the filing fee for the lawsuit may still be required to pay a partial filing fee, which can be collected in increments whenever money does appear in his or her inmate account.

It is too early to assess the effects of these legislative attempts to correct abuses of the court system by inmates. Frivolous litigation absorbs the court's time and wastes taxpayer dollars. The abundance of these cases in state and federal courts make it extremely difficult for judges to wade through the pleadings to find the ones that are most egregious. Maybe every American is not entitled to his or her day in court anymore, at least according to those who have to pay for it and listen to it.

Summary

This chapter examined an area of criminal justice casework, which many caseworkers probably would like to avoid entirely. The courts in recent years have made the caseworker's job much more difficult, as the rights of criminal offenders, both incarcerated and in the community, have been expanded dramatically. In addition, caseworkers have been held liable for failing to protect the public from the same clients to whom the courts have been according additional rights.

The day has not yet come that a caseworker needs to think like a lawyer, however. If caseworkers can remember a few main points, they should be able to do their job effectively without infringing on the constitutional rights of their clients or incurring liability. Criminal justice offenders do not enjoy the same rights as ordinary citizens. Yet, where rights have been circumscribed, certain procedures still must be followed. This is the essence of the phrase "due process of law." And while caseworkers need not be lawyers, it would be wise to keep abreast of the latest developments in the legal area.

References and Suggested Readings

Abadinsky, H. 1982. *Probation and Parole: Theory and Practice, 9th ed.* New York: Prentice-Hall.

Black, H. 2004. *Black's Law Dictionary*, 8th ed. St. Paul, Minnesota: West Publishing.

Cohen, F. 1995. Liability and Negligent Release. In B. Schwartz and H. Cellini, eds., *The Sex Offender: Corrections, Treatment, and Legal Practices.* Kingston, New Jersey: Civic Research Institute.

Cohen, N. and J. Gobert. 1992. *The Law of Probation and Parole.* Colorado Springs, Colorado: McGraw-Hill.

Collins, W. 2010. *Correctional Law for the Correctional Officer*, 5th ed. Alexandria, Virginia: American Correctional Association.

del Carmen, R. 1985. *Potential Liabilities of Probation and Parole Officers.* Cincinnati, Ohio: Anderson Publishing Company.

Cromwell, P., L. Alarid, and R. del Carmen. 2004. *Community-Based Corrections*, 6th ed. Belmont, California: Wadsworth.

General Accounting Office. 1991. *Drug Treatment: State Prisons Face Challenges in Providing Services.* Washington, D.C.: U. S. General Accounting Office.

Hemmens, C. 1999. "Probation and Parole Conditions Generally." *Perspectives* 23(1): 12-19.

Hemmens, C. and E. Atherton. 1999. *Use of Force: Current Practice and Policy.* Alexandria, Virginia: American Correctional Association.

Hemmens, C., B. Belbot, and K. Bennett. 2004. *Significant Cases in Corrections.* New York: Oxford University Press.

Hemmens, C., K. Bennett, and R. del Carmen. 1999. The Exclusionary Rule Does Not Apply to Parole Revocation Hearings: An Analysis of *Pennsylvania Board of Probation and Parole v. Scott. Criminal Law Bulletin* 35(3): 388-409.

Hemmens, C. and R. del Carmen. 1997. The Exclusionary Rule in Probation and Parole Revocation Proceedings: Does It Apply? *Federal Probation* 61(3): 32-39.

Jones, M. and R. del Carmen. 1992. When Do Probation and Parole Officers Enjoy the Same Immunity as Judges? *Federal Probation* 56: 36-41.

Palmer, J. 1999. *Constitutional Rights of Prisoners, 6th ed.* Cincinnati, Ohio: Anderson Publishing.

Tribe, L. 1988. *American Constitutional Law.* Minneapolis, Minnesota: West Publishing.

List of Significant Supreme Court Decisions

Arciniega v. Freeman, 404 U.S. 4 (1971).

Bearden v. Georgia, 461 U.S. 660 (1983).

Bounds v. Smith, 430 U.S. 817 (1977).

Coffin v. Reichard, 143 F.2d 443 (6th Cir., 1944).

Connecticut Board of Pardons v. Dumschat, 452 U.S. 458 (1981).

Estelle v. Gamble, 429 U.S. 97 (1976).

Ex parte Hull, 312 U.S. 546 (1941).

Fare v. Michael C., 442 U.S. 707 (1979).

Farmer v. Brennan, 511 US 825 (1994).

Gagnon v. Scarpelli, 411 U.S. 778 (1973).

Greenholtz v. Inmates of Nebraska Penal and Correctional Complex, 442 U.S. 1 (1979).

Griffin v. Wisconsin, 483 U.S. 868 (1987).

Holt v. Sarver, 309 F.Supp. 362 (E.D. Ark. 1970).

Hudson v. McMillan, 503 U.S. 1 (1992).

Jackson v. Bishop, 404 F.2d 571 (8th Circuit, 1968).

Jaffee v. Redmond, 518 U.S. 1 (1996).

Johnson v. Avery, 393 U.S. 483 (1969).

Kansas v. Crane, 534 U.S. 407 (2002).

Kansas v. Hendricks, 521 U.S. 346 (1997).

Lewis v. Casey, 518 U.S. 343 (1996).

McKune v. Lile, 536 U.S. 24 (2002).

Mempa v. Rhay, 389 U.S. 128 (1967).

Miranda v. Arizona, 384 U.S. 436 (1966).

Monroe v. Pape, 365 U.S. 167 (1961).

Morrissey v. Brewer, 408 U.S. 471 (1972).

Pennsylvania Board of Probation and Parole v. Scott, 524 U.S. 357 (1998).

Roberts v. United States, 320 U.S. 264 (1943).

Ruffin v. Commonwealth, 62 Va. 790 (1871).

Samson v. California, 547 U.S. 843 (2006).

Turner v. Safley, 482 U.S. 78 (1987).

United States v. Knights, 534 U.S. 112 (2001).

Washington v. Harper, 494 U.S. 210 (1990).

Wilson v. Seiter, 501 U.S. 294 (1991).

Wolff v. McDonnell, 418 U.S. 539 (1974).

CHAPTER 15

Alcohol and the Criminal Offender

If you treat an individual as he is, he will stay as he is. But if you treat him as if he were what he ought to be, he will become what he ought to be and could be.

—Wolfgang von Goethe

Although we might talk in very broad and general terms about causes of criminal behavior, theorists should acknowledge that their nominated causes are all subject to the deadening qualification "all other things being equal." Criminal behavior is located somewhere in a dense and messy causal maze, and those who become involved in criminal justice system trod many pathways. Many offenders have substance-abuse problems, many have character disorders, a few have chemical imbalances, and some are normally responsible individuals who have succumbed to the pressures and urges of the moment. Without specific proximate causes, the more general ultimate causes (whatever they may be) remain hidden. Note that proximate causes are those things that immediately precede an event. Ultimate causes are those things that are the furthest removed from the present. Although proximate causes may be quite difficult to work with, they certainly are more amenable to identification and treatment than are ultimate causes.

In this chapter, we will explore alcohol use, abuse, and dependence, the problem most commonly found to be the proximate cause of a variety of crimes, especially violent crimes (Schmalleger 2006). Wanberg and Milkman (1998) estimated that at least 70 percent of American prison inmates are alcohol and/or drug addicted, and in Britain, the figure is around 60 percent (McMurren 2003). Alcohol tends to be the drug most often minimized or overlooked by correctional practitioners. We forget that alcohol is a drug, a very powerful and addictive substance, and is a major player in criminal etiology. You will find few recovering heroin addicts who have not had to overcome a latent alcohol dependency, well after their "shooting" years have passed. Just as often, you will run across crack cocaine addicts who discover their addiction to alcohol after trying to put down the pipe. Cross-addiction, cross-tolerance, and multidrug use are the reality of offender substance use and abuse and points to the question of shared causation for criminality and substance abuse (Goldman, Oroszi, and Ducci 2005).

The Scope of the Addiction Problem

We normally think of illegal drugs when it comes to criminal offender behavior. However, we must train ourselves not to lose sight of the greatest substance abuse threat there is today: alcohol, the legal drug. Alcohol is linked to about 85,000 deaths a year versus the "mere" 17,000 fatalities attributable to other drugs (DrugWarFacts.Org 2008). The statistical facts are glaring. City police officers spend more than half of their time on alcohol-related offenses. Estimates are that one-third of all arrests in the United States are for alcohol-related offenses (excluding drunk driving, which would significantly increase the percentage of alcohol-related arrests, if included), and about 75 percent of robberies and 80 percent of homicides involve a drunken offender and/or victim (Schmalleger 2006), and about 40 percent of other violent offenders in the United States had been drinking at the time of the offense (Martin 2001).

Alcohol is, at the same time, the most deadly and the most popular of our chemical comforters. We drink to be sociable, to liven up our parties, to feel good, to sedate ourselves, and to anesthetize the pains of life. Fishman (1986) estimates that about one out of every ten Americans will develop a serious alcohol-related problem sometime during his or her life, and at least a third, and probably closer to half, of all men and women in prison are alcoholic, or at least heavy drinkers. The costs of alcohol abuse to society in terms of crime, health, and family and occupational disruption are nothing less than staggering. Crimes associated with alcohol and drugs combined were estimated to have cost the economy over $205 billion in 2005 (Miller et al. 2006).

Alcohol is a depressant drug that affects our behavior by inhibiting the functioning of the higher brain centers, the locus of our rational thought processes (the conscience or the superego). As we ingest more alcohol, our behavior increasingly becomes less inhibited as the rational neocortex surrenders control to the emotions of the more primitive limbic system. Raw basic emotions then are expressed without benefit of first being channeled to the prefrontal cortex for rational consideration. Given this powerful chemical reaction, and the resultant breakdown in superego functioning, it is no wonder that so much crime is associated with this drug. The rate at which this surrender to raw emotionality occurs depends on a number of variables such as the alcoholic content of the drink and the amount drunk, the speed at which someone drinks, the weight and sex of the drinker, the amount of food in the stomach, and even the time of day.

Abuse versus Dependence

The difference between an alcohol abuser and an alcoholic or alcohol-dependent person is not always easy to discern. There are myriad definitions of alcohol dependence touted by clinicians and academics. The most representative of the crucial diagnostic criteria might read as follows: "Alcoholism is a chronic (it endures or recurs unless treated) condition marked by progressive (it gets worse if left untreated) incapacity to control alcohol consumption despite psychological, spiritual, social, or physiological life disruptions." This simply means, in layperson's terms, that if you cannot reliably predict what happens to you when you do drink and if you repeat the unanticipated negative consequences, you experience after drinking, you are an alcoholic or alcohol dependent. The nonalcoholic heavy drinker will have the wherewithal to stop a self-destructive pattern of drinking in the face of compelling life circumstances such as marital problems, poor job performance, or liver malfunction. The person "dependent" on alcohol (not the occasional "abuser") will be unable to sustain control over time.

Physical dependence means that the body has developed a metabolic demand for a particular substance and rebels violently when you deny it that substance. It is a state of altered cellular physiology caused by the repetitive consumption of alcohol that manifests itself in physical disturbances when alcohol use is suspended (withdrawal syndrome).

Alcoholics are not necessarily or normally using alcohol as a means to achieve a "high," but as a means to avoid the terrible physiological pains of withdrawal, (alcohol withdrawal can be more life-threatening than withdrawal from narcotics). Do not confuse this characteristic dependence with "street bum" behavior. Most street bums in trouble with alcohol are probably physically dependent, but there are many more "functioning" alcoholic offenders who do meet the formal criteria for "dependence" but do not manifest obvious, clearly out-of-control symptoms—at least to all but their innermost circle of family and friends.

Alcohol-dependent offenders also may be maintenance drinkers, adept at keeping sufficient ethanol in their system all day long, so as not to experience withdrawal symptoms. Only rarely might they get "drunk." However, they are seriously alcoholic despite the fact that they do not fit the behavioral stereotype for this form of alcohol dependence.

Causes of Alcohol Abuse and Dependence

The first stage on the road to alcoholism is obviously taking the first drink. People drink alcohol initially to be "with it," to fit in, and to boost confidence and loosen social inhibitions at social gatherings. Alcohol is able to do this because, although it is ultimately a brain-numbing depressant, at low dosage levels it is actually a stimulant because it raises dopamine levels (Ruden 1997). It also reduces anxiety, worry, and tension by affecting the neurotransmitter gamma-aminobutyric acid (GABA), which is a major inhibitor of stimuli (Buck and Finn 2000). The behavioral effect of drinking on GABA is probably "reduced anxiety about the consequences of aggressive [or any other behavior not normally evoked when sober] behavior" (Martin 2001: 41).

Alcohol allows us to reinvent ourselves as superior people; it can thus make those of us with worries and who lack confidence relatively carefree and confident, albeit, for a very short time, making it a powerful reinforcer. The very wise and with it, Benjamin Franklin gave alcohol its ultimate tribute when he supposedly remarked,

"Beer is living proof that God loves us and wants us to be happy." It is no wonder that alcohol is the world's favorite way of drugging itself. Given what alcohol does for us in social situations, it is difficult to think about what it might do to us later on.

This honeymoon phase with alcohol sometimes leads to getting hooked into a horrendously bad marriage to it, and then to a very painful divorce from it, a process that takes the rest of the person's life, with alimony being paid in blood, sweat, and tears.

Type I and II Alcoholics. Given the strong relationship between alcohol and criminal behavior, you may reasonably suppose that both have some common cause. This is not to imply that alcoholism and criminality are synonymous. Researchers have divided alcoholics broadly into Type I and Type II alcoholics. As Crabbe (2002: 449) describes the two types: "Type I alcoholism is characterized by mild abuse, minimal criminality, and passive-dependent personality variables, whereas Type II alcoholism is characterized by early onset, violence, and criminality, and is largely limited to males."

The distinction made between Type I and Type II alcoholics is reminiscent of Terrie Moffitt's distinction between adolescent limited and life-course persistent offenders addressed in Chapter 3 on the biosocial causes of crime. You can liken Type II alcoholics to life-course persistent offenders. They start drinking (and using other drugs) at a very early age and rapidly become addicted, and have many character disorders and behavioral problems that precede their alcoholism. Type I alcoholics are akin to Moffitt's adolescent-limited offenders. They start drinking later in life than type II's and progress to alcoholism slowly. Type I's typically have families and careers, and if they have character defects, these typically are induced by the alcohol and not permanent (Crabbe 2002). Because of the greater vulnerability of the adolescent brain (see Chapter 19), the likelihood of alcoholism (and drug addiction) is increased by about 4 to 5 percent the earlier the onset of use. For instance, someone who starts drinking or taking drugs at age thirteen is 20 to 25 percent more likely to become addicted than someone who starts at eighteen given the same level of genetic vulnerability (Goldman, Oroszi, and Ducci 2005).

BIS/BAS and Alcoholism. Another similarity between criminological and alcoholism theorizing is the similarity between reward dominance theory in criminology and the "craving brain" concept in alcoholism theory. The concept of BIS/BAS introduced in Chapter 3 indicated that the behavioral activating system (BAS) is primarily dopamine dominated, that the behavioral inhibiting system (BIS) is primarily serotonin dominated, and that these two systems are "bio-balanced" in most people most of the time. There is an old saying among alcoholics that one drink is one too many, and that a hundred drinks are not enough. This seemingly contradictory statement informs us that a single drink activates the pleasure centers in the nucleus accumbens by activating dopamine, but that one drink leads to such a craving for more that even a hundred drinks will not satiate. The saying is a metaphor for the "craving brain" (Ruden 1997).

The craving brain is a reward-dominant brain because it is unbalanced, with the need for dopamine, the "go get it" neurotransmitter being unopposed by serotonin, the "got it, now stop it" neurotransmitter (Yacubian et al. 2007). Alcohol initially increases serotonin, but then rapidly decreases it, thereby allowing the increasing affects of dopamine and thus reducing the impulse-control capacity of the prefrontal cortex (Badawy 2003). The craving brain concept is common to all craving behaviors (eating, gambling, engaging in promiscuous sex, taking drugs, smoking), and not just to alcoholism, which is probably why few people are addicted to just one substance or behavior, and why individuals easily addicted are also ripe candidates for criminal behavior (Ellis 2003).

For example, a large study of twins found that factors accompanying externalizing disorders such as antisocial personality disorder and conduct disorder accounted for 71 percent of the genetic liability to alcoholism (Kendler et al. 2003). Fishbein (1998) proposes that Type II alcoholics have inherited abnormalities of the serotonin and dopamine systems that may be driving both their drinking and their antisocial behavior. Figure 15.1 identifies the areas of the brain involved in the rewarding aspects of alcohol consumption.

Figure 15.1 Brain Involvement in Alcohol Consumption

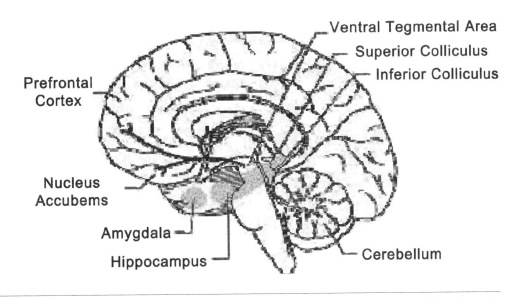

Source: National Institute on Drug Abuse (1996). The Brain's Drug Reward System (*NIDA Notes* 11). Washington D.C.. U.S. Department of Heath and Human Services.

Genetics and Alcoholism. Accumulating research increasingly points to the conclusion that vulnerability to alcohol addiction is strongly related to genetics (Slaught, Lyman, and Lyman 2004). The degree to which anything is influenced by genes is quantified by a measure called a heritability coefficient, which ranges in value between 0.0 (no genetic influence) and 1.0 (entirely genetic). Various estimates of the heritability of alcoholism range between 0.49 and 0.64, which means that between about one-half and two-thirds of the variance of the risk for alcoholism is related to genetic factors (McGue 1999). Researchers base these heritability estimates on Type I and Type II alcoholics combined; for Type II alone it is about 0.90 and less than 0.40 for Type I alcoholics (McGue 1999). This indicates that environmental factors are much more important to understanding Type I alcoholism than Type II alcoholism (Crabbe 2002).

Heritability estimates only tell us that genes are involved; they do not tell us what genes are involved and what their mechanisms are. An ever-growing body of literature seeks to identify these genes and their function. A bewildering number of genes make and control neurotransmitters and enzymes implicated in alcoholism. For instance, a large meta-analysis of 2,343 lines of evidence from peer-reviewed journals identified 316 alcohol addiction-related genes and 13 addiction-related pathways (the molecular routes and interactions among neurotransmitters and enzymes to produce the effect) to alcohol addiction (Li, Mao, and Wei 2008).

One such pathway to alcoholism is related to differential enzyme functioning and the biosynthesis of neurotransmitters such as GABA, dopamine, and serotonin (Buck and Finn 2000). Enzymes are protein molecules that serve as catalysts in the chemical conversion of molecules into other types of molecules. Ethanol alcohol is broken down in the liver by the enzyme alcohol dehydrogenase into a molecule called acetaldehyde (ADH). ADH produces unpleasant reactions to drinking, such as nausea and headaches, if the body does not convert it through other enzymes into molecules excreted in the urine. People who metabolize alcohol rapidly but who have metabolisms that allow for the buildup of ADH will quickly be sensitized to its unpleasant effects. This natural punishment for drinking makes them less likely to over indulge in the future. ADH, as the first metabolite of alcohol, is thus a built-in guardian against alcoholism. In fact, drug programs use disulfiram (Antabuse®) as a treatment for alcoholics because it functions to maintain high levels of ADH in the body by retarding further metabolic reactions (Mann 2004).

ADH combines with several neurotransmitters such as dopamine and serotonin to produce a family of chemicals known as isoquinolines, one of which is a morphine-like substance called tetrahydropapaveroline (THP) (Myers 2004). People whose metabolisms rapidly convert ADH into a number of highly addictive substances (including THP) are far more likely to become alcoholics than people whose metabolisms are less efficient at breaking down ADH. This biophysical line of inquiry could lead to the explanation of why the vast majority of those who drink over a lifetime never become addicted. The road to alcohol addiction is thus a meandering one that depends largely (but not completely) on how well an individual's metabolic system for processing alcohol functions. This is not the complete story of the etiology of alcoholism. It only states that among those who do turn to drink, some have an inherited predisposition to become addicted.

Assessment, Treatment, and Counseling

In view of the high social and financial costs of alcoholism, it is imperative that you make every effort to identify offenders with these problems. Most alcoholics will not readily admit to their condition. They cannot admit, even to themselves, that they have relinquished, or have started to relinquish, control of their lives to alcohol. Their disease tells them so, tells them they have no problem at all. Most are not lying in the traditional sense of the term. They really do believe they are all right. Alcoholics typically lack the choice of accepting reality: every muscle, molecule, and enzyme in their body demands more and more of the substance that carries them forth with life. In contrast, some offenders will overemphasize their drinking, hoping that you and the judge will regard it as a mitigating factor when considering sentencing alternatives. Most often, however, offenders will minimize their consumption pattern.

The ability to identify the alcohol abuser and the alcohol-dependent offender is a skill all correctional counselors should strive to acquire. The most obvious indicator of a drinking problem is an arrest record of alcohol-related offenses (drunk driving, drunk and disorderly conduct, and so forth). Ask about the offender's drinking patterns. The frequency and amount of alcohol consumed on a weekly basis, the frequency of legal problems due to drinking, and the amount of time and money spent on drink are all indications of the depth of the problem.

Remember, far more than quantity or frequency of consumption, what really is important is what alcohol does to the person who consumes it. If you discover such patterns, you have an ipso facto case to present to offenders showing that they do have a problem. Point out to offenders that to continue to deny it in the face of such evidence is irrational and unacceptable to you. You are encouraged not to discuss offender alibis designed to convince you that factors other than drinking are responsible for irresponsible behavior. Doing so will result in an argument over the merits of the alibi, possibly leading to reinforcement of the alibi. Moreover, the more persons defend their position, the more difficult it becomes to relinquish it.

If you suspect offenders have a drinking problem and you want them to admit this problem to themselves, the CAGE Screen Test (Ewing 1984), Table 15.1, affords you this opportunity to confirm it both for yourself and for the offender. CAGE is an acronym for Cut Down, Annoyed, Guilty, and Eye-opener. If a person answers "yes" to two or more of the following questions, an 88 percent likelihood exists that the person has an alcohol problem.

Table 15.1 CAGE Screen Test

1. **C**=Have you ever felt you should CUT DOWN on your drinking?

When a person feels the need to control drinking, and actually takes steps such as making vows to stop, switching brands, limiting drinking to certain times and places, he or she already has recognized the presence of a problem.

2. **A**=Have people ANNOYED you by criticizing your drinking?

Having someone close to you express anger certainly means that they consider the drinker's behavior upsetting and problematic, thus providing a basis for the drinker to consider his or her behavior. Typical social drinkers do not end up with spouses or others expressing this type of concern.

3. **G**=Have you ever felt bad or GUILTY about your drinking?

Guilt is the psychological equivalent of physical pain—not very pleasant, but very useful. Guilt, like pain, tells us that something is wrong that we should put right. The guilty person knows that his or her life would be better without alcohol, and feels guilty and ashamed about what he or she is doing.

4. **E**=Have you ever had a drink first thing in the morning (an EYE-OPENER) to steady your nerves or to get rid of a hangover?

Number 4 is a sure giveaway, but two or more positive responses are suggestive of alcoholism.

You may use a number of more formal screening tools to help to identify the offender in trouble with alcohol. One frequently used tool is the Michigan Alcoholism Screening Test (MAST). Use this twenty-four-item yes/no questionnaire only as a corroborative diagnostic aid. Yet, do not rule out alcoholism if the scale score is negative for alcoholism. Offenders certainly can lie on the questionnaire, and verbal and nonverbal cues, such as alcohol-related arrests (which you will know about independently of offenders' responses), may be more valuable with offenders reluctant to disclose the requested information. Best practice is to administer the questionnaire in your presence so that the offender can clarify the items, if necessary. There are numerous other substance abuse assessment tools available, such as the Adult Substance Use Survey (ASUS), Addiction Severity Index (ASI), and, of course, our old friends the CMC and LSI-R.

Skilled interviewing is often the most effective way to ascertain whether someone is manifesting signs of alcohol dependence. Do not be afraid to ask very specific questions about the offender's drinking history, weekly pattern, and attitude toward consumption. Focus on using open-ended questions (such as "Tell me exactly what you had to drink Saturday") designed to encourage dialog and expression that may reveal clues about their relationship to the drug, rather than yes or no queries. Do not be shy about getting specific about the amount a person consumes. An offender's interpretation of "a beer" could be that forty-two ounce "bumper" of malt liquor, nearly equal to an entire six-pack of regular beer. Most community corrections' personnel, including probation and parole officers, use their interviewing, investigative, and assessment skills more than anything else prior to an initial referral for treatment. Often, they have time for little else, let alone the administration of a test instrument, no matter how simple.

Treatment for the alcoholic or problem drinker is a complex affair that may include both medical treatment and psychosocial counseling (McCaul and Petry 2003). The goal is recovery as defined by abstinence, sobriety, and an interest in personal growth. Even more will depend on the relative progression of that person's disease and whether there are complicating coexisting disorders such as depression or antisocial personality disorder. Much will depend on the level of the offender's drinking and motivation at the time that you first meet him or her.

If the offender is in the chronic stage of alcoholism, hospitalization for detoxification will be necessary. Most likely, however, detoxification took place in the jail or at a hospital after the offender's arrest, and you will not have to concern yourself with it. If it did not, secure inpatient medical treatment for the offender. Detoxification in a medical environment is a prerequisite to any future treatment. However, recently, very capable "social" detoxification programs, not located in a medical setting—some even conducted on an outpatient basis—have arisen to provide less costly solutions. If the offender does not have insurance that provides for such treatment, or if welfare authorities cannot provide it, organizations such as the Salvation Army and the Volunteers of America often are successful in securing the necessary treatment (see Chapter 13). Detoxification is not a treatment for alcoholism, which is a long and difficult process of learning how to sustain and have complete abstinence from all mood-altering substances.

Mutual Self-Help Groups: Alcoholics Anonymous

Many different professional addictions treatment resources are available and reflect particular individual treatment needs: individual counseling, group therapy, Motivational Interviewing, intensive outpatient facilities, day-treatment programs, longer-term residential programs, and many others. However, and despite all these different therapeutic approaches, most, if not all good clinicians, regardless of their professional orientation, will stress the importance of making good self-help group referrals as a complement to the professional treatment most offenders will require (Lemieux 2009).

The best-known mutual self-help group, of course, is Alcoholics Anonymous or AA. AA has been called "one of the great success stories of our century" by a group of World Health Organization researchers after studying AA groups in eleven different countries (cited in Alexander 2000: 20). This AA fellowship (a strange "non-organization" organization really) is a very supportive and totally nonprofessional support group of other human beings in trouble with alcohol. They often go to great lengths to help one another and if used appropriately by the corrections worker, AA groups can assist in helping the offender work through his/her denial (Read 1996). AA is not a class. AA is not treatment. Moreover, AA is not a quick fix. It is a lengthy and often lifetime process of personal transformation.

"Old timers" in AA will say to the newcomer, "Sobriety is a process and not an event." The principles of AA eventually become a way of life for many. Initially, there is emphasis only on not drinking one day at a time. Then, the focus shifts toward learning how to achieve sobriety in the sense of balance and serenity. Finally, note that AA is not a religious program. It is, however, a spiritual process, a spiritual program of self-help. Agnostics, atheists, and true believers are all welcome. Unlike religious movements, sects, or denominations, AA holds no preconception or demand for a belief in God.

A great deal of typical Rogerian empathy occurs in the meeting rooms of AA. There can be no skirting of the issue in such company. Alcoholic offenders cannot reasonably tell their "bottle-wise" compatriots that they "just don't understand," the way they could their nonalcoholic corrections counselors. Fellow AA members will provide offenders not only with support but also with visions of the possible. They are role models whose presence serves to emphasize much more strongly than the counselor could that recovery is possible (this role modeling is the social learning component of cognitive-behavioral therapy). People, who have successfully dealt with their alcoholism, discuss methods of dealing with specific alcohol-related problems. When a peer offers the solution to a problem, it is more likely to carry weight than if it is posed by "the Man," who many offenders instinctively distrust and resent.

Genuineness is another Rogerian principle that is a hallmark of AA groups. Most AA participants strongly encourage members to confront honestly their problems, their shortcomings, their responsibilities, and their realities. Although there are no formal leaders, manipulation and game playing are quickly recognized and rejected: "You can't con the cons." Members are encouraged to share with the group their fears, anxieties, hopes, and self-evaluation. This self-disclosure provides the offender with the opportunity to share genuine feelings with others and to build self-esteem and a group identity, qualities sorely lacking in the lives of many persons in trouble with alcohol. As a real added bonus, researchers report that attending AA actually raises serotonin levels (Gogek 1994). Not only do raised serotonin levels counteract craving, they also reduce the dysphoric feelings (depression, agitation, hopelessness) described among alcoholics as a "dry drunk" (Ruden 1997).

The Role of Personal Characteristics in Alcoholism Treatment

AA is a marvelous tool, but that amorphous quality we call "character" affects treatment outcomes, as it affects everything else in life. Baeklund, Lundwall, and Kissen (1975: 305) state it well when they write about their experiences in treating alcoholics: "Over and over we were impressed with the dominant role of the patient, as opposed to the kind of treatment used on him, played both in his persistence in treatment and his eventual outcome."

Even Herbert Fingarette, who calls the disease model of alcoholism a myth, supports this view: "The consensus of scientific researchers is that willpower and personal strengths do affect the course of a heavy drinker's efforts to control his drinking" (1988: 72). So, we return to a central thesis of the various directive-counseling theories: the individual, alcoholics, drug addicts, criminals, or whatever only can change their destructive behavior by resolving to accept personal responsibility for their behavior. This might be a good point to remind you of Jack Powell's (2004) five-stage model (willingness, responsibility, knowledge, application, and maintenance) discussed in Chapter 10. AA is one vehicle with demonstrated success in helping alcoholics to develop and maintain that resolve. As William Glasser states: "The alcoholic must regain control over his life to satisfy his needs. AA, by itself, cannot satisfy his needs, but it is a way—probably the best way we have available—to get the process started" (1984:132).

Glasser views diseases as falling on a continuum in terms of the amount of control we have over them. At one end of the continuum is a disease like Huntington's chorea, which is totally genetic. It does not matter how healthy, fit, and strong you otherwise may be, or what you do to try to avoid it, if you have the gene for Huntington's chorea, eventually you will get it. Further down the continuum is cancer. Cancer is a disease with genetic vulnerability, but we can take certain steps to lessen our chances of falling afoul of it by altering our environment (eating right, not smoking, and so forth). Further along the continuum are the various cardiovascular diseases that may be equally under genetic and environmental control. Living a healthy life dramatically reduces our risk of such diseases, even if genetic predisposition exists.

At the other end of the continuum is alcoholism. Glasser insists that although alcoholism is a disease, we have considerable control over it. Even if a person has a genetic predisposition, if he or she learns to resist the temptation to drink, the disease cannot manifest itself. Glasser's approach appears to be an eminently sensible compromise between the disease and no-disease models of alcoholism.

The debate about whether addiction, particularly alcoholism, is a "disease-based" condition continues to rage. Most chemical dependency experts, including physicians who are certified addictionologists accept it as such with few questions. Among the others, though, there is a real sense of frustration at not being able to identify a single medically scientific and proven cause for the disease of addiction, although scientists are closing in on the elusive cause(s). Based on a Supreme Court ruling that the Veterans Administration (VA) may deny certain benefits to alcoholics because their behavior was thought to be the result of "willful misconduct," we sometimes hear that the Supreme Court has ruled that alcoholism is not a disease. The Court is not qualified to rule on such matters, it simply ruled on a matter of law that had to do with the benefit guidelines of the VA. As mentioned earlier, the problem is that addiction simply does not have one single cause; it is multifaceted. It is complex, and we do not yet fully understand it.

Whether it is "really" a disease, some feel that the disease model "has little clinical utility, and in fact may interfere with assisting the individual in successfully modifying his or her behavior through implicit communication that substance use is something that is happening to their body rather than something that is within their voluntary control" (Weekes, Moser, and Langevin 1999: 6). Others, who assert that the disease model fosters dependency and passivity (Parks and Marlatt 1999), share this opinion. Both these sets of researchers are cognitive-behavioral adherents who strongly support self-reliance and the acceptance of responsibility, thus they believe that defining alcoholism as a disease and admitting of "powerlessness" (step one of the 12-step program) is counterproductive.

From our perspective, we do not doubt that alcoholism is a disease that alters the brain's physiology and functioning. We can even see the differences in the brains of alcoholics versus nonalcoholics through brain-imaging techniques (Kalivas and Volkow 2005, Koob and Le Moal 2008). We see no contradiction in asserting that it is a disease—a self-induced disease for which the person must accept full responsibility for recovery. Surely admitting being "out of control" and deciding to do something about it is accepting responsibility for changing one's life—a direct confrontation with one's self if there ever was one. Surely, believing that one has a disease does not contravene personal efforts to combat it, as legions of cancer and heart patients, among others, can attest.

We urge that all persons with alcohol-related disorders caught up in the criminal justice system be strongly encouraged to participate in AA (Lemieux 2009). Based on reviews of empirical studies, experts estimate that about half of those who regularly attend AA meetings with serious intent maintain several years of total abstinence, and that about 60 percent of the remainder "improve to some extent" (U.S. Department of Health and Human Services 1990: 265).

Although no figures are available specific to criminal justice offenders in AA, one would not expect their success rate to be this high. Yet, offender motivation remains a crucial variable. As a correctional worker, you have a professional responsibility to do your best to generate this motivation. Other studies of large groups of alcoholics have found that AA members experience more positive outcome than those only receiving cognitive-behavioral therapy, although subjects who received both AA and cognitive-behavioral therapy did better than those who only participated in one of the modalities (Moos 2008). Other studies show that those individuals who enter AA earlier after recognizing their alcoholism had better outcomes than those who delayed participation (Moos and Moos 2006). The lesson is clear: Get your offenders into 12-step programs as soon as possible.

Community corrections professionals have recognized the power of these "free" community-based self-help programs for many years. In fact, Ed Read, a federal probation officer for the U.S. District Court, in Washington D.C., who has written and published extensively on addictions, has written a full-length book devoted solely on how to access, use, and make proper 12-step self-help group referrals within the criminal justice system. He is adamant that making these referrals, sometimes repeatedly with the same offender in the course of his or her casework, is an irrefutable professional obligation of the corrections worker. In his indispensable book, *Partners in Change*, Read writes:

> Why refer every addict or alcoholic? It is almost so simple we forget. We do it because we want to capitalize on what we know is successful, on what we know works out there beyond our office doors (Read 1996: 5).

Catherine Lemieux has updated the concepts of Read's book in *Offenders and Substance Abuse: Bringing the Family into Focus* (2009) and offers suggestions on how to involve the family in the offenders' recovery.

Do not hesitate to make attendance at AA (or some alternative sobriety program') meetings a condition of probation or parole. Experiencing the warm support and caring of fellow travelers may well turn the resistant offender into a motivated client. Insisting that the offender attend AA is another instance of the constructive use of authority.

To those with legal concerns about whether mandatory self-help group attendance violates the Establishment Clause of the First Amendment to the U.S. Constitution, please note: In June 1994, U.S. District Judge Gary L. Taylor of the Central District of California (*O'Conner v. State of California*) ruled in favor of the state's Driving Under the Influence (DUI) education and treatment programs that routinely refer offenders to AA and other self-help groups. Significant to this ruling was that the element of personal choice remained intact. Offenders were mandated to attend self-help group meetings, and AA was the recommended vehicle for satisfaction of this condition; however, they were not prevented from using alternative programs, such as Rational Recovery (RR). However, in *Kerr v. Farley* (1996), a federal court judge ruled that offenders' rights are violated by coerced treatment at AA and NA (Narcotics Anonymous) programs.

An alternative to AA meetings outside the probation or parole office is an in-house alcohol program (AA programs in jails, prisons, and halfway houses are "in-house" by definition). The advantage of an in-house program is that officers can closely monitor attendance, participation, and progress. Volunteer members of AA and/or community corrections workers who are thoroughly versed in alcohol counseling make the best group leaders for in-house counseling.

The Lucas County Adult Probation Department (Toledo, Ohio) has an in-house program called STOP (Sobriety Through Other People). It requires STOP clients to (1) attend one in-house AA meeting and at least three others outside the department, (2) attend biweekly in-house group meetings, (3) submit to weekly urinalysis, and (4) meet with the program coordinator once per month. Latessa and Goodman (1989) compared 102 STOP probationers with a control group of 101 other probationers matched for sex, race, and supervision level. STOP clients had more serious criminal histories and much more serious substance-abuse problems. STOP offenders had a higher rate of absconding and of technical probation violations, although the authors stress that given the intensity of the treatment regimen and level of surveillance for this group, this was to be expected. The bright spot was that the STOP offenders had 9.2 percent fewer arrests than the regularly supervised offenders, a relatively small difference, but one put in proper perspective when we realize that alcoholic offenders are particularly susceptible to frequent arrests. The authors conclude: "The STOP program has demonstrated it is possible to select special-need offenders and deliver increased services in an effective manner" (Latessa and Goodman 1989: 42).

Self-Help Options for Nonbelievers

There are instances when we encounter offenders who legitimately oppose and resist involvement in the traditional Twelve Step AA model of self-help. Some, usually a distinct minority, base their opposition not on denial but on genuine philosophical convictions about the recovery process. They may have tried AA but were unable to reconcile their own beliefs about religion and/or spirituality with the Twelve Step model.

Rational Recovery (RR) first appeared in the 1980s, founded by recovering alcoholics who rejected both the spiritual foundation of the AA Steps and the disease concept of alcoholism. RR patterns itself after the writings of Albert Ellis, a pioneer in the field of cognitive psychology and Rational Emotive Behavioral Therapy. Like AA, RR groups vary widely, but they differ in some key respects (Lemieux 2009).

Most RR members attend meetings only once a week, as opposed to the daily attendance schedule encouraged for newcomers to AA. Meetings generally are limited to no more than twelve participants. RR participants believe that problem drinkers make incorrect or shortsighted choices based on emotional states. RR is more time-limited while AA prefers to view itself as indefinite. RR members attend for six-to-ten-months and then often stop, sometimes returning to deal with specific crises or relapse. RR members emphasize coming to an understanding of the psychological precursors of their drinking as opposed to developing a relationship with a higher power. Figure 15.2, on the next page, provides a comparison of AA and RR principles.

Secular Sobriety (SS) provides another alternative. James Christopher, who was in AA but left over his objection to the spiritual orientation of the Steps and the program's reliance on a higher power, founded SS. Christopher believes that individuals can attain sobriety best through an emphasis on self-reliance and self-knowledge. SS meetings resemble AA discussion groups. Like AA, the basic premise of SS is that alcoholism is a chronic and progressive disease. Therefore, unlike RR members, participants feel they cannot drink because of a physiological rather than psychological abnormality. Additionally, SS groups do not place as much value as AA on the role of sponsorship in the recovery process.

Recognize that few offenders are "believers" in the traditional sense. This is no problem–the majority of all people coming to AA meetings for the first time fit into this category. It is much easier to find an AA meeting these days; RR never has achieved the prominence and widespread availability that AA has realized. Actually, AA's tremendous availability is the biggest difference between it, RR, and Secular Sobriety groups. AA groups are very tolerant of different spiritual beliefs or nonbeliefs, so do not prematurely refer to RR based on an offender's initial expression of resistance.

Medication and Recovery

Disulfiram (Antabuse®) treatment, as a type of aversion therapy, can be a very useful adjunct to other treatment modalities. As indicated earlier, Antabuse works by maintaining high levels of ADH in the body by retarding its metabolism (DuPont 1997). Begin Antabuse treatment, under medical supervision because it can have

Continued on page 339

337

Figure 15.2 A Comparison of AA's Twelve Steps to Sobriety and Rational Recovery's Equivalents

Alcoholics Anonymous	**Rational Recovery**

Alcoholics Anonymous

1. We admitted we were powerless over alcohol—that our lives had become unmanageable.

2. We came to believe that a Power greater than ourselves could restore us to sanity.

3. We made a decision to turn our lives over to the care of God as we understood Him.

4. We made a searching and fearless moral inventory of ourselves.

5. We admitted to God, to ourselves, and to other human beings, the exact nature of our wrongs.

6. We were entirely ready to have God remove all these defects of character.

7. We humbly asked Him to remove our shortcomings.

8. We made a list of all persons we had harmed, and became willing to make amends to them all.

9. We made direct amends to such people wherever possible, except when to do so would injure them or others.

10. We continued to take personal inventory and when we were wrong, promptly admitted it.

11. We sought through prayer and meditation to improve our conscious contact with God, as we understood Him, praying only for knowledge of His will for us and the power to carry that out.

12. Having had a spiritual awakening as a result of these steps, we tried to carry the message to alcoholics and to practice these principles in all our affairs.

> * The Twelve Steps are reprinted with the permission of Alcoholics Anonymous World Services, Inc. Permission to reprint the Twelve Steps does not mean that A.A. has reviewed or approved the contents of this publication, nor that A.A. agrees with the views expressed herein. A.A. is a program of recovery from alcoholism *only*—use of the Twelve Steps in connection with programs and activities which are patterned after A.A., but which address other problems, or in any other non-A.A. context, does not imply otherwise.
>
> ** Material from RR reprinted with permission from Rational Recovery Systems, Inc.

Rational Recovery

1. I admit that I have become chemically dependent, and the consequences of the dependency are unacceptable.

2. I accept that, to get better, I will have to refrain from the use of alcohol, because any use very likely will lead to more, and then a return to my previous addiction.

3. I accept that I will likely benefit from some outside help in accomplishing this, because I have been unsuccessful in previous attempts to resist my desire to drink.

4. Although I may have serious personal problems, I still have the capacity to learn about myself, and new ideas and how to achieve a durable and meaningful sobriety.

5. The idea that I need something other than myself upon which to rely is only another dependency idea, and dependency is my original problem.

6. I surrender all ideas of perfection for myself, as I am a fallible, yet very worthwhile, human being.

7. I place a high value on the principles of rationality, learning, objectivity, self-forgiveness, and on my own self-interest.

8. With the passage of time, I will find that refraining from mind-altering drugs is no big thing because they have little intrinsic appeal to a physically and mentally healthy person.

9. Recognizing that there is much more to life than a constant struggle to remain sober, and having gained a reasonable expectation that I can live a meaningful life without alcohol or drugs, I will gradually separate myself from my RR group or therapist, with the understanding that I may return at any time I wish.

10. I accept that there are no perfect solutions to life's problems, and that life is in part a matter of probability and chance, so, therefore, I am willing to take risks to achieve my own self-defined goals.

11. Now certain of my inherent worth, I can take the riskes of loving, for loving is far better than being loved.

12. I recognize the desperate need of others for a rational recovery plan, so I will take these ideas to them, as a way of creating a larger society of sober, rational people.

harmful, even fatal, effects for people with heart problems, after detoxification. The client takes the drug for several consecutive days along with small doses of alcohol. The unpleasant feelings that accompany drinking alcohol while ADH levels are high act as negative reinforcers. The treatment goal is that these highly unpleasant consequences associated with alcohol ingestion will be sufficiently aversive to condition the patient against future abuse.

Realize, however, that Antabuse treatment is voluntary on the patient's part. You cannot require it as a condition of supervision. A client who does make the voluntary decision to take Antabuse is taking his or her treatment seriously because he or she also, in effect, has made the decision not to drink during the period that this highly aversive drug remains effective. The body eliminates Antabuse very slowly, leaving it sensitive to alcohol for six to ten days after Antabuse ingestion (Mann 2004).

Like most other conditioned responses, however, the effects of Antabuse effects are extinguished with the passage of time. It does provide a strong and immediate reason not to drink and thus buys time for the implementation of other types of treatment. It appears to be quite successful when used in conjunction with psychosocial counseling. Billet (1974) reports that 64 percent of a sample of patients who were administered Antabuse in addition to undergoing a comprehensive psychosocial rehabilitation program showed "marked improvement." Only 31 percent of those who were in the same program did not show positive effects (U.S. Department of Health and Human Services 1990: 266). Even among alcoholics who relapse, those taking Antabuse had fewer drinking days and fewer drinks than did alcohol relapsers not on Antabuse (Mann 2004).

In 1996, the U.S. Food and Drug Administration approved the pharmacologic agent naltrexone as a safe and effective adjunct to psychosocial treatments for alcoholism (also for opiate addiction). While certainly not considered a "magic bullet," naltrexone (sold under the trade-name ReVia®), promises help to many offenders in their struggle against chronic relapse. Some claim that the drug reduces craving and relapse by 50 percent (DuPont 1997). The National Institute on Alcohol Abuse and Alcoholism (NIAA) recommends that for now, until further study is completed, that only physicians familiar with addiction treatment should prescribe this medication, and only in the context of an alcoholism treatment program. Naltrexone is antagonistic to the chemicals in the brain that generate feeling of pleasure and thus it appears to reduce craving in abstinent persons and blocks (by binding to the receptor sites that targeted by the drug) the reinforcing effects of alcohol in patients who drink (Schmitz et al. 2004). This latter effect lessens the likelihood that persons who drink a small amount of alcohol will return to heavy drinking.

As with other chronic diseases such as cardiovascular conditions or diabetes, medication by itself is never enough—there must be sometimes drastic life changes to go along with it. Apart from counseling and attendance at self-help groups, you should train alcoholics to identify environmental triggers that lead them to thinking about, and thus wanting, a drink. Triggers leading to relapse can be such simple external things as walking past their former "watering holes," meeting an ex-drinking buddy, hearing the clinking of glasses, or seeing a beer commercial. A number of studies have demonstrated how powerful these cues can be in bringing on craving and increasing the heart rate and pupil dilation, which are indicators of increased interest and attention (McCaul and Petry 2003, McGue 1999). Triggers also can be internal, such as feelings of loneliness, sadness, anger, and/or dwelling on problems. You must teach alcoholics and other addicts to recognize these internal and external triggers and take evasive action whenever they threaten to appear.

The increasing evidence that alcoholism has a strong biological basis is not cause for despair. Marc Schuckit, one of the leading researchers in the biology of alcoholism, writes, "It is unlikely that anyone is predestined to alcoholism or that all those predisposed exhibit the same mechanism of risk" (1989: 297). Even those individuals genetically identified as at-risk obviously will not succumb to the disease if they never drink, and individuals who have succumbed can be spared its further ravages if, with the help of caring others, they can move toward sobriety "one day at a time."

Perspective from the Field
Working with the Alcohol-Dependent Offender

By Sandra Tebbe

Sandra Tebbe is a probation officer who specializes in working with offenders in trouble with alcohol. She holds master's degrees in both sociology and rehabilitation counseling, and she is a Certified Alcoholism Counselor. In the past, Ms. Tebbe has specialized in counseling compulsive gamblers on probation.

● ● ● ● ● ● ● ● ● ● ● ● ● ● ● ● ● ● ●

Alcoholics usually will not recognize that they have a drinking problem. Many cannot recognize it because they find satisfaction in the "loving" concern of those around them. They use this "love" as a means of manipulating their way through an addictive lifestyle. The alcoholics' skillful maneuvers and manipulations do not stop when they commit a crime. Most alcoholic probationers come under supervision expecting the same "loving" concern and the same ignoring, overlooking, and excusing to which they are accustomed.

To help the alcoholic offender, you have to be willing to be rejected. That is what "tough love" is all about, caring enough about clients to hold them totally responsible for their behavior, regardless of whether they like you. Tough love is making each decision carefully to assure that you are not enabling probationers to continue their drinking. This will not make you popular, and it certainly will not make you loved. It is all too easy to ease up a little, to give them some slack, so that they will like you. However, you are not the issue. You demonstrate your love for them by holding them responsible for the defeat of their alcoholic conditions.

I started working as a probation officer eight years ago. I coordinate a special state-funded in-house alcohol program. This program provides one of the highest levels of supervision in community corrections and provides for strict and unambiguous correctional consequences for every misbehavior. This good program teaches what tough love is.

People often ask me, "How can you spend so much time working with alcoholics without getting burned out?" I entered the probation profession at a young age and with idealistic attitudes. It did not take me long to learn how to adapt and survive. Counseling alcoholics means learning how to let go. It does not mean that you stop caring. It means that you must learn that you cannot do it for someone else. It is the realization that you cannot control another person's life or fix his or her defects. Only they can do that. You have to respect their capacity for control and choice, and allow them to learn from the natural consequences of their behavior.

Most alcoholics have had someone to enable, or make possible, their drinking behavior from the very start. For this reason, the alcoholic's family, and most everyone else influenced by him or her, becomes "sick." Enabling is usually in the form of continually making excuses for and rescuing the alcoholic from distress. Unfortunately, it is not until alcoholics experience the real pains of their disease that they get around to making a decision to change their lifestyles.

You easily can fall into rescuing behavior with your alcoholic offenders, but you are not doing them any favors if you continue with the enabling patterns they have come to expect. You are not being "nice," "neat," or "loving" to those who need tough love by allowing them to manipulate you and to continue to ruin their lives. Confront them, challenge them, educate them, and help them!

Alcoholics almost always will deny their alcoholism. Take Jim, a high-risk probationer of mine. He had been in prison for threatening the life of his baby when police arrived at his home on a domestic dispute call. During the alcohol-screening period, Jim stated repeatedly that he was not an alcoholic: "I don't have to wake up to a drink every day like the drunks on the street. I'm not a weak man. There's lots of times I don't drink."

Jim's defensiveness was a reaction to the many myths associated with alcoholism. Many people think of alcoholics as weak, low-class moral degenerates who lack willpower. My job as his probation officer was to educate him about his disease so that he would open up his mind to treatment. Jim learned through my efforts and through mandatory participation in AA that alcoholism is primarily a physiological disease and that he became addicted because his body is incapable of processing alcohol normally. He also learned that alcoholism is a disease that affects all classes and races. Jim's many family and financial problems did not cause his alcoholism. Rather, his alcoholism undermined his ability to cope, and this inability then exacerbated his problems.

Once Jim learned about his disease, he was better able to deal with it. Jim had to realize that to admit his alcoholism was not to admit that he was a weak or bad person. Through small-group participation and AA attendance, Jim found comfort and support from others with the same problem. These folks "tough loved" Jim into sobriety. Jim has been sober for more than two years now. He has chosen a new life for himself. Although not all of his other problems have disappeared, he is learning how to cope with them without alcohol.

Jim was relatively easy to deal with as alcoholic probationers go. Often, I find that supervising alcoholic probationers means long periods waiting for them to "hit bottom." "Hitting bottom" is the term for when alcoholics come to realize that they have gotten about as low as they can go, and that they must change or be forever lost.

Continued on the next page

Perspective from the Field, *continued*

A few months ago, one of my probationers hit his bottom while sitting in the county jail. John was doing thirty days for his second probation violation, a violation that I easily could have ignored. He had continually denied having a drinking problem, refused to go to AA meetings, and was resentful of authority. This time, however, something was different about John when I visited him in jail. For the first time, he did not attempt to rationalize his behavior or blame it on someone else. He was physically sick from withdrawal, homeless, and his wife had left him (a natural consequence of his behavior) because she could not handle his drinking anymore.

With a broken spirit, John started to take a hard look at himself and finally asked for help. John is now doing something about his problem. He is one of the several sober probationers in the program, and is one of the many probationers who have learned to love and respect themselves through an officer's use of tough love.

Summary

This chapter addresses the most common problem you will encounter in corrections: alcohol use disorders. We defined and discussed the significant challenges posed by offenders in trouble with alcohol. Although researchers have not identified one single cause for alcoholism and consider it a complex and multifaceted condition, it undoubtedly has a strong genetic underpinning. We noted the similarity between certain biosocial criminological theories and theories of alcoholism. Alcoholism seems to be at one level a function of the "craving brain," a concept close to reward dominance theory in criminology.

Other scientific evidence on the cause of alcoholism points strongly to the role of the production and metabolism of acetaldehyde (ADH). Antabuse, a drug used in treating alcoholism, functions to maintain high levels of ADH in the bloodstream. This causes the alcoholic to experience the "punishing" physical feelings associated with high alcohol intake. Antabuse is administered to chronic alcoholics in association with intensive psychosocial counseling.

The most successful self-help program that you always should use as a complement to professional treatment is Alcoholics Anonymous (AA). You should endeavor to place every offender with a drinking problem in this organization. It provides members with all the components of a successful counseling relationship (even though it is not "treatment" per se) as outlined by Rogers: positive regard, genuineness, and empathy. Some people, however, object to the "spiritual" nature of AA. For those that are truly resistant, and although not nearly as widely available, you could refer offenders to Rational Recovery or other strictly nonspiritual support groups.

Professionals use various pharmacological aids to treatment such as Antabuse and Naltrexone in conjunction with AA and other forms of psychosocial counseling. These medications provide strong punitive reasons for not drinking (Antabuse), or block the reinforcing effects of alcohol (Naltrexone). However, these medications are never enough by themselves to combat the intense psychological craving for alcohol.

References and Suggested Readings

Alexander, R. 2000. *Counseling, Treatment, and Intervention Methods with Juvenile and Adult Offenders.* Belmont, California: Brooks/Cole.

Alexander, R. and G. Pratsniak. 1992. *Understanding Substance Abuse and Treatment.* Alexandria, Virginia: American Correctional Association.

____. 2002. *Arresting Addictions: Drug Education and Relapse Prevention in Corrections.* Alexandria, Virginia: American Correctional Association.

American Psychiatric Association. 1994. *Diagnostic and Statistical Manual of Mental Disorders,* Fourth Edition, Text Revised. Washington, D.C.: American Psychiatric Association.

Badawy, A. 2003. Alcohol and Violence and the Possible Role of Serotonin. *Criminal Behaviour and Mental Health* 13: 31-44.

Baeklund, F., L. Lundwall, and B. Kissen. 1975. Methods for the Treatment of Chronic Alcoholism: A Critical Approach. In R. Gibbons, Y. Israel, H. Kalant, R. Popham, and R. Smart, eds., *Research Advances in Alcohol and Drug Problems.* New York: Wiley.

Billet, S. 1974. Antabuse Therapy. In R. Cantanzaro, ed., *Alcoholism: The Total Treatment Approach.* Springfield, Illinois: Charles C. Thomas.

Buck, K. and D. Finn. 2000. Genetic factors in addiction: QTL mapping and candidate gene studies implicate GABAergic genes in alcohol and barbiturate withdrawal in mice. *Addiction* 96: 139-149.

Crabbe, J. 2002. Genetic Contributions to Addiction. *Annual Review of Psychology* 53: 435-462.

DrugWarFacts. 2008. Annual causes of death in the United States. http://drugwarfacts.org/cms/?q=node/30

DuPont, R. 1997. *The Selfish Brain: Learning from Addiction.* Washington, D.C.: American Psychiatric Press.

Ellis, A. and E. Velten. 1992. *When AA Doesn't Work for You: Rational Steps to Quitting Alcohol.* Fort Lee, New Jersey: Barricade Books.

Ellis, L. 2003. Genes, Criminality, and the Evolutionary Neuroandroangenic Theory. In A. Walsh and L. Ellis, eds., *Biosocial Criminology: Challenging Environmentalism's Supremacy*, Hauppauge, NY: Nova Science. pp.15-34.

Ewing, J. 1984. Detecting Alcoholism: The CAGE Questionnaire. *Journal of the American Medical Association* 252: 1905-1907.

Fingerette, H. 1988. *Heavy Drinking: The Myth of Alcoholism as a Disease.* Berkeley, California: University of California Press.

Fishbein, D. 1998. Differential Susceptibility to Comorbid Drug Abuse and Violence. *Journal of Drug Issues* 28: 859-891.

Fishman, R. 1986. *Alcohol and Alcoholism.* New York: Chelsea House

Galanter, M., S. Egelko, and H. Edwards. 1993. Rational Recovery: Alternative to AA for Addiction. *American Journal of Drug and Alcohol Abuse.*19: 499-510.

Glasser, W. 1984. *Control Theory.* New York: Harper and Row.

Gogek, E. 1994. The Dry Drunk Syndrome: Subtype of Depression. *American Journal of Psychiatry* 151: 947-948.

Goldman, D., G. Oroszi and F. Ducci. 2005. The Genetics of Addictions: Uncovering the Genes. *Nature Reviews/Genetics* 6: 521-532.

Kalivas, P. and N. Volkow. 2005. The neural basis of addiction: A pathology of motivation and choice. *American Journal of Psychiatry* 162: 1403-1413.

Kendler, K., C. Prescott, J. Myers, M. Neale. 2003. The Structure of Genetic and Environmental Risk Factors for Common Psychiatric and Substance Use Disorders in Men and Women. *Archives of General Psychiatry* 60: 929-937.

Kerr v. Farley, 95 F.3d 472 (1996).

Koob G. and M. Le Moal M. 2008. Review. Neurobiological mechanisms for opponent motivational processes in addiction. *Philosophical Transactions of the Royal Society of London: Biological Science* 363: 3113-3123.

Latessa, E. and S. Goodman. 1989. Alcoholic Offenders: Intensive Probation Program Shows Promise. *Corrections Today* 51: 3 June. 38-42.

Lemieux, C. 2009. *Bringing the Family into Focus: Substance Abuse and Corrections.* Alexandria, Virginia: American Correctional Association.

Leshner, A. 1998. Addiction Is a Brain Disease–and It Matters. *National Institute of Justice Journal* 237: 2-6.

Li, C., X. Mao, and L. Wei. 2008. Genes and (Common) Pathways Underlying Drug Addiction. PLoS *Computational Biology* 4: 28-34.

Mann, K. 2004. Pharmacology of Alcohol Dependence: A Review of the Clinical Data. *CNS Drugs* 18: 485-504.

Martin, S. 2001. The Links between Alcohol, Crime and the Criminal Justice System: Explanations, Evidence and Interventions. *The American Journal on Addictions* 10:136-158.

McCaul, M. and N. Petry. 2003. The Role of Psychosocial Treatments in Pharmacotherapy for Alcoholism. *The American Journal on Addictions* 12: S41-S52.

McGue, M. 1999. The Behavioral Genetics of Alcoholism. *Current Directions in Psychological Science* 8: 109-115.

McMurren, M. 2003. Alcohol and Crime. *Criminal Behaviour and Mental Health* 13: 1-4.

Miller, T., D. Levey, M. Cohen and K. Cox 2006. Costs of Alcohol and Drug-Related Crime. *Prevention Science* 7: 333-342.

Moffitt, T. 1993. Adolescent-Limited and Life-Course Persistent Antisocial Behavior: A Developmental Taxonomy. *Psychological Review* 100: 674-701.

Moos, R. 2008. Journal Interview: Conversation with Rudolf Moos. *Addiction* 103: 13-23.

Moos, R. and B. Moos. 2006. Participation in Treatment and Alcoholics Anonymous: a 16-Year Follow-Up of Initially Untreated Individuals. *Journal of Clinical Psychology* 62: 735-750.

Myers, R. 2004. Neurobiological Basis of Alcohol Reinforcement and Drinking. http://www.Indiana.edu/~engs/cbook/chap4.hthl. Retrieved November, 2004.

O'Connor v. California, 855 F. Supp. 303, 1994.

Parks, G and G. Marlatt. 1999. Keeping "What Works" Working: Cognitive-Behavioral Relapse Prevention Therapy with Substance Abusing Offenders. In E. Latessa, ed., *Strategic Solutions: The International Community Corrections Association Examines Substance Abuse*. Alexandria, Virginia: American Correctional Association.

Powell, J. 2004. Five Stages to Responsible Human Behavior. *International Journal of Reality Therapy* 23: 27-30.

Read, E. 1996. *Partners in Change: The 12-Step Referral Handbook for Probation, Parole and Community Corrections*. Lanham, Maryland: American Correctional Association.

Read, E. and D. Daley. 1990. *Getting High and Doing Time: What's the Connection?* Lanham, Maryland: American Correctional Association.

Ruden, R. 1997. *The Craving Brain: The Biobalance Approach to Controlling Addictions*. New York: Harper/Collins.

Schmalleger, F. 2006. *Criminal Justice Today*, 8th ed. Upper Saddle River, New Jersey: Prentice Hall.

Schmitz, J., A. Stotts, S. Sayre, K. DeLaune, and J. Grabowski. 2004. Treatment of Cocaine-Alcohol Dependence with Naltrexone and Relapse Prevention Therapy. *The American Journal on Addictions* 13: 333-341.

Schuckit, M. 1989. Biomedical and Genetic Markers of Alcoholism. In H. Goedde and D. Agarwal, eds., *Alcoholism: Biomedical and Genetic Aspects*. New York: Pergamon Press.

Slaught, E., Sue Lyman, and Scott Lyman 2004. Promoting Healthy Lifestyles as a Biopsychosocial Approach to Addictions Counseling. *Journal of Alcohol and Drug Education* 48: 5-16.

U.S. Department of Health and Human Services. 1990. *Alcohol and Health*. Washington, D.C.: U.S. Government Printing Office.

Wanberg, K. and H. Milkman. 1998. *Criminal Conduct and Substance Abuse Treatment: Strategies for Self-Improvement*. Thousand Oaks, California: Sage Publications.

Weekes, J., A. Moser, and C. Langevin. 1999. Assessing Substance-Abuse Offenders for Treatment. In E. Latessa, ed., *Strategic Solutions: The International Community Corrections Association Examines Substance Abuse*. Alexandria, Virginia: American Correctional Association.

Yacubian, J. T. Sommer, K. Schroeder, J. Glascher, R. Kalisch, B. Leuenberger, D., F. Braus, and C. Buchel. 2007. Gene-Gene Interaction Associated with Neural Reward Sensitivity, *Proceedings of the National Academy of Sciences* 104: 8125-8130.

CHAPTER 16

Illegal Drugs and the Criminal Offender

The descent to Hell is easy; the gates stand open day and night; but to climb the slope and escape to the upper air, this is labor.

—**Virgil**

Introduction

Although alcohol is a mind-altering drug in common with other drugs, we discussed it separately because of the attitude of American society toward alcohol relative to its attitude about "street" drugs. Alcohol is a legal and socially acceptable form of drugging oneself; marijuana, heroin, LSD, cocaine, and so on are not. People once thought that respectable middle-class people drink, but only criminals took drugs. Today, we see sports and entertainment figures and supposedly "respectable" professionals arrested for drug abuse with some regularity. So many of us swallow, sniff, and inject such a variety of mind-altering substances, and have done so for centuries, that it suggests that we humans find sobriety a difficult state to tolerate.

According to the U.S. Department of Justice (1991: 17), drugs relate to crime in three ways: psychopharmacological, economic-compulsive, and systemic. Most drug-related crimes are crimes committed to obtain money to buy drugs, which are very expensive because of their illegal status (the economic-compulsive component). Other crimes are those committed as part of "doing business" in the drug culture

345

(the systemic component). The National Institute of Justice (1991: 17) estimated that about 80 percent of the homicides in the District of Columbia in 1988 were drug-related, a staggering increase from the 1985 estimate of 21 percent. The dramatic decline in homicides in the United States, including the District of Columbia, during the 1990s may have a lot to do with the consolidation of drug gangs (particularly those in the lucrative crack market) and the subsequent end to the territorial wars (Witkin 1998).

Crimes committed under the influence of drugs (the psychopharmacological component) have less impact on the overall relationship between drugs and crime than the economic compulsive and systemic connections. That is, unlike the direct link between alcohol consumption and crime, the link between drug abuse and crime is more indirect. We are not concerned with systemic drug-related crime here; that is more a social and political issue than a corrections issue. We are concerned with the demand side—the users and pushers who will be on our caseloads.

The psychopharmacological link means that crimes are committed because of drug-induced changes in mood and cognitive functioning. According to Seiter (2005: 432), 67 percent of state and 56 percent of federal prison inmates were regular drug users before incarceration. Because most drug addicts commit crimes, we should not fall into the trap of concluding from this, that drug abuse "causes" criminal behavior. A large body of research (reviewed by McBride and McCoy 1993) indicates that drug abuse does not appear to initiate a criminal career, although it does increase the extent and seriousness of one. Drug abusers are not "innocents" who are propelled into a criminal career by drugs. Rather, both drug abuse and criminality are part of a broader propensity of some individuals to engage in a variety of deviant and anti-social behavior. Menard, Mihalic, and Huizinga (2001: 295) explain the reciprocal (feedback) nature of the drugs/crime connection as follows:

> Initiation of substance abuse is preceded by initiation of crime for most individuals (and therefore cannot be a cause of crime). At a later stage of involvement, however, serious illicit drug use appears to contribute to continuity in serious crime, and serious crime contributes to continuity in serious illicit drug use.

Fishbein (2003) and McDermott et al. (2000) have shown that traits characterizing antisocial individuals (ADHD, conduct disorder, impulsiveness, and high scores on the Hare Psychopathy Checklist) also characterize drug addicts.

Figure 16.1 presents data from the Office of National Drug Control Policy (ADAM II) that shows that up to 87 percent of persons arrested in each of the ten cities studied tested positive for an illegal drug. These data forcefully point to the link between drug use and crime in our largest cities. Although there is considerable variability among the drugs used within the various cities, marijuana is the most commom drug used with between one-third to one-half of arrestees testing positive for it. Cocaine is the second most commonly detected substance among arrestees in 2008 in all but Sacramento where methamphetamine is more common and in Atlanta where cocaine is the most commonly detected substance.

Figure 16.1 Percent of Arrestees Testing Positive for Any Drug in Ten American Cities

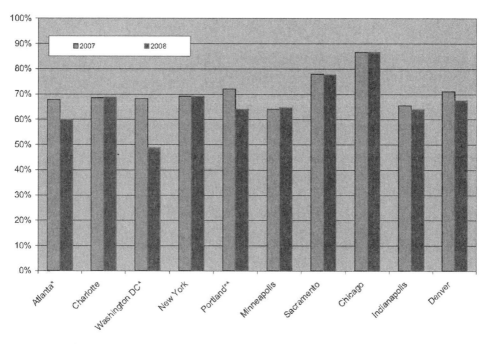

Significant at the .10 level (*), .05 level (**), or .01 levels (***).

Source: Office of Drug Control Policy (2009) *ADAM II 2008 Annual Report.*

Defining Drug Addiction

The Drug Enforcement Administration defines drug addiction as "compulsive drug-seeking behavior where acquiring and using a drug becomes the most important activity in the user's life" (2003: 13). As with alcoholism, this definition implies a loss of control and the continual use of drugs despite the serious medical and social consequences that arise from doing so. Physical dependence on a drug refers to changes to the body that have occurred after repeated use of a drug, and necessitate the continued administration of the drug to avoid a withdrawal syndrome.

Physical dependence on a drug is not synonymous with addiction as commonly thought. However, psychological dependence (the deep craving for the drug and the feeling that one cannot function without it) is synonymous with addiction. Actually, "psychological" dependence is traceable to deregulation of the brain's reward system, and is thus ultimately physical; there are no "ghosts in the machine" (Koob and Le Moal 2008). Detoxified addicts have no drugs in their bodies, and are thus not experiencing any withdrawal symptoms, but frequently return to their drugs because of psychological, not physical, demands (Pinel 2000). Reports estimate five million Americans suffer from drug addiction as defined by the Drug Enforcement Administration's criteria (Drug Enforcement Administration 2003: 13).

Regardless of the type of drug, addiction is not an invariable outcome of drug usage any more than alcoholism is an invariable outcome of drinking. The Drug Enforcement Administration (2003: 14) estimates that the majority (about 55 percent) of today's youths has used some form of illegal substance, but few descend into the

347

hell of addiction (Kleber 2003). As with almost all other forms of antisocial behavior, an age curve is associated with drug usage, with many young people experimenting with various substances. Figure 16.2 shows a sharp increase during the teen years of people using drugs over the past month in 2007 and then a rather sharp decrease with increasing age.

Figure 16.2 Past Month Illicit Drug Use among Persons Aged 12 or Older, by Age: 2007

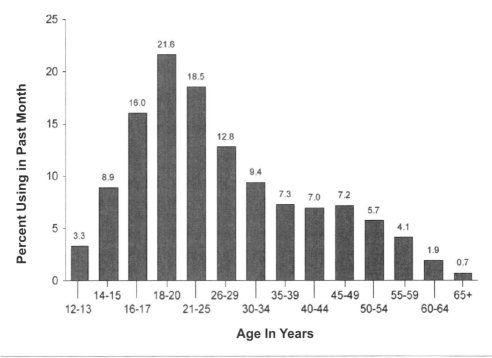

Source: U.S. Department of Health and Human Services, 2008. *National Survey on Drug Use and Health.*

As is the case with alcohol, genetic differences relate to a person's chances of becoming addicted given the same amount of a drug and the same frequency with which they take it. People differ in the degree of pleasure obtained by a drug, the rate of tolerance, and the type of effect produced (Pinel 2000). For instance, ADHD (attention disorder with hyperactivity disorder) children are at double the risk of non-ADHD children for serious substance abuse, particularly the abuse of stimulants such as cocaine and amphetamines (Restak 2001).

Some Causes of Illegal Substance-Related Disorders

Drugs affect brain functioning in one of four ways:

1. They inhibit or slow down the release of chemical neurotransmitters.

2. They stimulate or speed up their release.

3. They prevent the re-uptake of transmitters after they have stimulated neighboring neurons.

4. They break down the transmitters more quickly.

Note that all addictive drugs mimic the actions of normal brain chemistry (Koob and Le Moal 2008). Virtually all illegal drugs "have common effects on a single pathway deep within the brain, the mesolimbic reward system" (Leshner 1998: 4). These drugs hijack the brain and produce more powerful, rapid, and predictable effects on the brain's pleasure centers than are obtained by the normal reward system (the natural action of neurotransmitters in response to our pleasant experiences). As Hyman (2007: 10) explains: "unlike natural rewards, addictive drugs always signal 'better than expected.' Neural circuits 'over-learn' on an excessive and grossly distorted dopamine signal." Depending on the type of drug taken, the individual's behavior and/or feelings are speeded up or slowed down, intensified or reduced, or stimulated or mellowed. In short, drugs allow us to change an undesirable mood state to one perceived of as more desirable. Figure 16.3 shows the brain areas targeted by the opiates and the stimulants cocaine and amphetamines.

Figure 16.3 Reward Areas of the Brain Targeted by Opiates and Stimulants

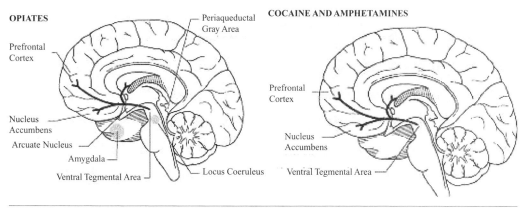

Source: National Institute on Drug Abuse (1996). "The Brain's Drug Reward System" (*NIDA Notes* 11). Department of Heath and Human Services. Washington D.C..

People turn to illegal drugs for many of the same reasons that people turn to alcohol. They may take them initially to be "with it," to be sociable and to conform, to induce pleasure, to escape psychic stress, or to escape chronic boredom. Others perhaps are genetically predisposed to develop dependency rapidly–much the same way some people, given their genetic background, are "sitting ducks" for addiction. Their bodies, their metabolism, and their brain functioning may be different from that of the "normal" person (Robinson and Berrridge 2003). In these cases, a little experimentation with an illegal drug, especially during the teen years, may have far greater negative long-term consequences (Schepis, Adinoff, and Rao 2008). Many abuse them and become dependent on them because they find little pleasure, comfort, solace, or meaning in their lives. People who confront more pain than pleasure in their daily lives tend to pursue all the artificial comfort they can get. Addicts can become emotionally attached to their substances the way most of us become attached to other people because, generally, their experiences have not prepared them for intimate relationships with others.

A study of drug usage and sexual promiscuity found that lack of parental attachment was a better predictor of both behaviors for men and women than a number of other possibilities (Walsh 1995). Similarly, looking at the family backgrounds of addicts, Chein and his colleagues (1964: 273) note "In almost all addict families, there was a disturbed relationship between the parents, as evidenced by separation, divorce, open hostility, or lack of warmth." Burnett expresses a similar sentiment (1979: 354): "Drug abusers often complain of lack of love and warmth in their homes. An absence of parent 'stroking' in the home will lead to low self-image, which contributes to the susceptibility to drug abuse." Lacking this inner sense of warmth, and self-esteem, addicts think of their pharmacopoeia of fake happiness not in terms of what it does "to" them, but rather in terms of what it does "for" them.

However, let us not get carried away, many of the negative observations about addict's lives could be, and probably are, the effects of their abuse rather than the causes. Drug addicts are no fun to live with when using, and during periods of abstinence, they are even worse because of their negative emotional states due to the depletion of natural reward neurotransmitters (Koob and Le Moab 2008). Nevertheless, we have to break through all their rationalizations, projections, and denials to make them understand the profound difference between what drugs are doing for them and what they are doing to them. As the ancient Roman poet Virgil so well put it in this chapter's epigraph; it is so very easy to descend into hell (and addiction is just that), but to climb the slope and escape it, "this is labor."

Illegal Drug Classification

As a correctional worker, you should become familiar with all types of illegal drugs and their effects. However, our mission here precludes any attempt at an exhaustive treatment. What follows is a brief description of the different classes of drugs.

The Narcotics

The narcotics include drugs that range from relatively mild medications such as codeine all the way to the insidious heroin. All drugs in this category have the potential for physical and psychological dependence, and all produce tolerance (the tendency to require larger and larger doses to produce the same effects after the body adjusts to lower dosages), and to induce withdrawal symptoms (adverse physical reactions when the body is deprived of the addicting drug). This class of drugs tends to appeal to individuals whose characteristic coping style leans toward isolation, withdrawal, and indifference because they reduce tension, anxiety, and aggression. We begin with heroin, the drug that leads to addiction in about 23 percent of the people who try it (Kleber 2003).

Heroin is a derivative of morphine, a powerful pain-killer. It is a white or brownish powder that usually is dissolved in water and injected. Heroin wafts the individual into a euphoric state of sweet indifference, a state that heroin users describe as the "floats." Intravenous injection of heroin ("mainlining") used to be the most popular method of administering the drug among hard-core addicts. This produces the famous rush, a warm skin flush and orgasmic feeling. After the initial rush, the addict drifts off into a private carefree world for anywhere from three to twelve hours. Needless to say, the problems are still around after the effects wear off, not the least of which is the problem of securing the next rush. Walsh once supervised a heroin addict who had a $300-per-day (in 1980 dollars) habit and who challenged this author's characterization of him as lazy. He said, "Man, addicts work harder than anybody you know. You try to hustle the streets to come up with that kind of bread every day."

Given the AIDS epidemic and the increasing awareness of the dangers of sharing contaminated "works," many heroin-dependent offenders have shifted to snorting or even smoking heroin and opium. Very disturbing indeed are the reports we receive that indicate heroin smoking and snorting are on the rise, and interestingly, that this increase is not limited to the poor or disenfranchised: middle-income suburban youth are visiting the emergency rooms as well. Another related trend has been the increasing potency of the heroin and opium available on the street. It now is possible to achieve a significant state of intoxication without having to "mainline" (Drug Enforcement Administration 2003). Recent data show that opium (which almost always means heroin) use among arrestees remained fairly stable from 1990 to 2000, going up in some cities, down in others, and remaining more or less the same in others (Office of Drug Control Policy 2009).

This "hustle" is the main reason for heroin addiction's close association with criminal activity. The euphoric sleeplike state achieved under the influence of heroin is not conducive to effort, criminal or otherwise. Narcotics users are significantly less likely to commit violent crimes than are users of alcohol or stimulants, particularly methamphetamine and cocaine. In fact, many advocates of decriminalizing or legalizing some or all drugs point to lower levels of drug-related crimes in those countries where habitual abusers received free narcotics (Walker 2001).

The brain has its own pain-killing substances that do naturally, if far less effectively, what heroin does. These substances are the endorphins (for "endogenous morphine-like substances"), which are larger and more complex neurotransmitters than those previously discussed, such as dopamine. The presence of naturally occurring analgesics provides clues to the addictive process. Some have suggested that some individuals become heroin addicts because they have insufficient endorphins in the brain to anesthetize naturally the pains of life. In other words, it is not that heroin addicts experience more pains of living than the rest of us, but that they have fewer endorphins. Lacking normal amounts of nature's "tonic" precipitates a search for artificial substitutes to make up the deficit. Frequent injections of heroin affects the body's natural capacity to release endorphins in much the same way that giving individuals too much thyroid extract will eventually cause the body to cease its own production of the thyroid-stimulating hormone, thus turning them into "thyroid junkies." An addict's lower level of natural endorphins is therefore considered a consequence rather than a cause of addiction (Pinel 2000).

A great deal of evidence exists for this. As already mentioned, the brain releases neurotransmitters synthesized by genes that have the same mood-altering effects (although much weaker) than drugs do. When persons ingest drugs, they initially enhance neurotransmission rates, but protracted usage eventually leads to neurotransmitter depletion and ultimate suppression (Franken et al. 2004, Robinson and Berridge 2003). In effect, the genes responsible for synthesizing the particular neurotransmitter(s) affected by the drug shut down because they have been fooled into "thinking" that the brain has all that it needs. This inoperative endogenous-reward system makes withdrawal from drugs so physically and psychologically painful.

The Stimulants

The stimulants, primarily amphetamine, methamphetamine, and cocaine, have effects opposite to those of the narcotics. These drugs increase arousal and a sense of well being. The stimulants increase the action of norepinepherine and dopamine (the "fight or flight" and "pleasure" chemicals), and, thus, are often the drugs of choice for individuals who seek excitement and adventure, who are bored, driven, and who are chronically under-aroused (Grabowski 1984). The stimulant class of drugs includes everything from the $3.95 over-the-counter diet pills to the $150 per gram powdered cocaine.

Cocaine: Along with the depressant, alcohol, the use of amphetamine and cocaine has the most immediate association with violent criminal behavior (Fishbein 2000). Holden (1989: 1378) has characterized cocaine as "the most powerful reinforcer known." Cocaine works by blocking the reuptake of the neurotransmitters dopamine and norepinephrine at the synaptic terminals, thus keeping the body in an extended state of arousal. Being highly soluble in fatty tissue, the brain takes up coke quickly, producing the familiar euphoric rush. When an individual takes cocaine intravenously, the "rush" or "flash" takes only about fifteen seconds. The strongest and fastest rush comes from smoking "freebase" (the cocaine alkaloid it frees from its acid salt to produce pure cocaine).

A form of smokeable cocaine, known as "rock" or "crack," produces intense craving and may be the most addictive substance known (Read 1992). Kleber (2003) indicates that only 17 to 23 percent of those who try cocaine become addicted, but we do not know whether crack addiction is contained in these percentages. Crack is manufactured by combining cocaine, baking soda, and water. This mixture is then heated, allowed to cool, and broken into tiny pieces resembling gray slivers of bar soap. Without the elaborate and sometimes dangerous preparations necessary to produce free-base cocaine, crack produces the same high, and its relatively low price makes it attractive to those who formerly resisted the more expensive powdered cocaine. Crack prices range from $5 to $25 for 300 milligrams as opposed to about $150 for a gram (a gram is about the amount of artificial sweetener contained in the typical Equal or NutraSweet packet) of powdered cocaine. People smoke crack in cigarettes or in small pipes, and the high, which lasts only about five to ten minutes, comes within eight seconds.

Cocaine addiction is extremely difficult to treat because use of the drug is so rewarding in that it quickly, powerfully, and most importantly, directly affects the brain's pleasure receptors. In the case of crack, it takes effect within seconds (crack is a real shortcut to the nucleus accumbens) of users inhaling it, with the high maintained from five-to-thirty minutes. Most addicts who have been involved with other types of drugs will tell you that cocaine is by far the most desirable. One of the authors once had an offender who spent nine days locked in her room living on only cocaine and water. Her nine-day cocaine holiday cost her $5,000, which she had obtained by trafficking the stuff among her middle-class friends. Cocaine addiction is also very difficult to treat because its nonuse after prolonged use produces a devastating "crash." This period of intense anxiety, irritability, and depression lasts about four days. After prolonged use, the natural activation of the brain's pleasure centers does not occur (depletion and suppression have occurred), making the brain dependent on cocaine to feel any pleasure at all (Gove and Wilmoth 2003).

People used to think that although cocaine quickly produced tolerance, requiring increasingly greater amounts to obtain the same effects, it did not produce physical dependence. Many individuals do use cocaine on a "recreational" basis without suffering major withdrawal symptoms when not using, but few researchers today deny its addictive power, a power that is especially strong where crack is concerned. Crack addiction develops and progresses faster than any other kind of addiction (Read 1992). The depression and fatigue resulting from overstimulation of the nervous system creates a tremendous desire for more cocaine to counteract these effects. Since smoking cocaine produces a quicker and stronger high than snorting it, its effect is of shorter duration, and the crash is more devastating. If more cocaine is not immediately available, some may resort to alcohol ingestion to help ease the crash.

The number of arrested suspects testing positive for cocaine (including crack) is down dramatically, although it is still the most frequently used of the illegal drugs after marijuana (Office of Drug Control Policy 2009). We may attribute this decrease to several factors, including severely increased penalties for sale and possession of crack and the extreme danger from others trafficking in the same market. It also shows that many individuals have made a rational decision not to try crack in the first place after surveying the ravages visited on addicts they know. The emerging norm that tells many inner city youth that crack is not "cool," has been attributed to what some researchers call the "younger brother" syndrome (Witkin 1998). That is, younger members of the community have seen relatives and friends killed or permanently disabled in drug deals gone wrong, and they see others serving long prison sentences or old and emaciated before their time because of their addiction. There are still plenty of crack heads around for us to deal with, however.

Methamphetamine

Methamphetamine or "speed" is the most dangerous of all illegal drugs in terms of its psychopharmacological association with violence. Speed, in its various forms, has reached near-epidemic proportions in some parts of the country, especially the West. It operates on the limbic system to accentuate and accelerate the visual, tactile, auditory, and olfactory impulses. The onset of the effects of methamphetamine are slower in coming than they are for cocaine, but the effects last longer. When methamphetamine is taken, users become "wired." They have boundless energy, are super alert, and feel on top of everything. The effects feel so good that they often go on what is called a "run." A run consists of several days on speed without pausing for sleep. Speed is considerably less expensive than cocaine, so a run of five days will cost "only" a few hundred dollars. The price to be paid for the run is that the longer it lasts, the more the feelings of well-being turn to hyperactive aggressiveness. The accentuated sensitivity to stimuli, intermixed with fatigue, very easily can produce psychotic like reactions. This is especially true if the run is conducted, as it usually is, with several others, all of whom are similarly hypersensitive. Love, beauty, and clever conversation will become paranoia, ugliness, hostility, and violent disagreement. This result becomes increasingly more likely as they extend the run and as the available supply of speed peters out.

Offenders dependent on methamphetamine are especially dangerous after the run is over. They find themselves in deep post-high depressions, their nerves are badly frayed, and they are in desperate need of sleep. They become very argumentative and are susceptible to explosive violence. Any confrontation worsens the depression and leads them on a desperate search for more speed to alleviate the feeling. They will do almost anything to get the next fix and start the vicious cycle spinning again. Chronic abuse of methamphetamine may produce schizophrenic-like effects (for example, having paranoia and auditory and visual hallucinations, picking at one's skin, and being preoccupied with one's inner thoughts) that can last for months or years after withdrawal from the drug (Drug Enforcement Administration 2003).

Ice, or crystal. This more potent and more addictive form of methamphetamine is now part of America's ever-growing illicit pharmacopoeia. Ice is chemically identical to methamphetamine, but, as its name implies, is crystalline in its appearance rather than powdered. It is popular among users of stimulant drugs because of its low price relative to cocaine/crack, its intense and long-lasting high (a high lasting anywhere from seven to twenty-four hours), because it can be smoked rather than injected, and because it is virtually odorless, making for a reduced chance of detection (Nugent 1990a).

The Hallucinogens

The hallucinogens are mind-altering drugs such as marijuana and lysergic acid diethylamide (LSD). The smoking of marijuana is so pervasive today that some pay little attention to it; yet, it is safe to say that most offenders have tried or continue to smoke marijuana. Readers can discern its quasi-acceptance by reading PSI reports that frequently contain such statements as "With the exception of marijuana, the defendant denies any drug usage." Offenders are often ordered into treatment for marijuana dependency but rarely sent back to prison solely because of such illicit use. There is a tendency on the part of the entire correctional system, sometimes unwittingly, to minimize marijuana use relative to the heavy hitters who use cocaine, crack, and heroin. This is a mistake and we should be doing better.

Those who consider marijuana to be merely a "simple natural weed" akin to tobacco fail to realize the ever-increasing potency of the modern product. Unlike alcohol, which is water soluble and quickly metabolized and excreted from the body, cannabinoids, such as tetrahydrocannabinol (THC), are fat-soluble. They penetrate the fatty areas of the body—notably in the brain and the gonads—and remain there for long periods. Since only about 10 percent of the THC crosses the blood-brain barrier to produce the marijuana "high," one shudders to think of the damage that the other 90 percent of this powerful chemical is doing to the body. Marijuana is anything but harmless. It has a wide range of subtle, insidious physical and psychological effects, many of which we still need to discover.

Additionally, marijuana contains hundreds of other chemicals, with unknown effects on the body. The fact that increasing numbers of adolescents are experimenting with marijuana, and the research identifies it as a "gateway" drug to other illegal substances, makes minimization of marijuana a dangerous proposition. The percentage of arrestees testing positive for marijuana increased considerably from 1990 to 2000 (Office of Drug Control Policy 2009).

A more immediately dangerous form of hallucinogen is LSD. In its unadulterated form, LSD is a clear, odorless, and tasteless liquid. It is sold soaked in sugar cubes, in tiny pills, or on saturated blotting paper (microdots). LSD has been termed a psychomimetic drug because its effects sometimes mimic psychosis.

After a period of decline, LSD's usage appears to be increasing again. Today's LSD, however, is only about half as potent as it was during the hippie period in the 1960s-1970s. LSD is a drug primarily favored by individuals seeking intellectual adventure, the inward-lookers who want to increase awareness rather than escape it. It causes hyperawareness and a greatly enhanced appreciation of stimuli in the user's perceptual field, but it also causes sensory/perceptual distortions, which lead users to great risk of personal injury ("Look guys, I can fly!"). LSD does not cause physical dependence, but psychological dependence may occur, and the drug produces tolerance rapidly.

Look-alike drugs, drugs of deception, and designer drugs are ones that fall within the general family of psychoactive substances affecting the brain and central nervous system. We distinguish them from those listed above because they tend to be ever changing and very hard to pinpoint. Some are not new at all, but are substances from the existing pharmacological pool adapted for street use and abuse. Some are modified "look-alike" drugs made up of nonprescription substances. Most are entirely synthetic, made by underground chemists using increasingly sophisticated equipment and techniques.

A fairly well known drug on the street today that fits this category is "Ecstasy," a street name and a far more pronounceable, name for 3, 4 methylenedioxymethylamphetamine (MDMA). It is a synthetic substance synthesized from methamphetamine and safrole, which comes from sassafras, nutmeg, or is made from another synthetic called piperonylacetone. Its effects are similar to those produced by both psychedelic drugs such as LSD (mild hallucinations) and stimulants such as methamphetamine (increased sensual arousal). Some say that persons who enjoy amphetamine-like stimulation and euphoria will gravitate toward "Ecstasy." Young people are doing a great deal of "E" at "raves," their surreptitious (at least to parents!) all-night dancing parties. As is the case with almost all illegal stimulant drugs, extended use of Ecstasy can lead to psychosis and long-term cognitive impairment (Pinel 2000).

Table 16.1 published by the Drug Enforcement Agency offers information on the most common drugs of abuse.

Table 16.1 Drugs of Abuse/Uses and Effects

Drugs	CSA Schedules	Trade or Other Names	Medical Uses	Dependence		Tolerance	Duration (Hours)	Usual Method	Possible Effects	Effects of Overdose	Withdrawal Syndrome
				Physical	Psychological						
Narcotics											
Heroin	Substance I	Diamorphine, Horse, Smack, Black tar, Chiva, Negra (black tar)	None in U.S., Analgesic, Antitussive	High	High	Yes	3-4	Injected, snorted, smoked	Euphoria, drowsiness, respiratory depression, constricted pupils, nausea	Slow and shallow breathing, clammy skin, convulsions, coma, possible death	Watery eyes, runny nose, yawning, loss of appetite, irritability, tremors, panic, cramps, nausea, chills and sweating
Morphine	Substance II	MS-Contin, Roxanol, Oramorph SR, MSIR	Analgesic	High	High	Yes	3-12	Oral, injected			
Hydrocodone	Substance II, Product III, V	Hydrocodone w/Acetaminophen, Vicodin, Vicoprofen, Tussionex, Lortab	Analgesic, Antitussive	High	High	Yes	3-6	Oral			
Hydromorphone	Substance II	Dilaudid	Analgesic	High	High	Yes	3-4	Oral, injected			
Oxycodone	Substance II	Roxicet, Oxycodone w/Acetaminophen, OxyContin, Endocet, Percocet, Percodan	Analgesic	High	High	Yes	3-12	Oral			
Codeine	Substance II, Products III, V	Acetaminophen, Guaifenesin or Promethazine w/Codeine, Fiorinal, Fioricet or Tylenol w/Codeine	Analgesic, Antitussive	Moderate	Moderate	Yes	3-4	Oral, injected			
Other Narcotics	Substance II, III, IV	Fentanyl, Demerol, Methadone, Darvon, Stadol, Talwin, Paregoric, Buprenex	Analgesic, Antidiarrheal, Antitussive	High-Low	High-Low	Yes	Variable	Oral, injected, snorted, smoked			
Depressants											
gamma Hydroxybutyric Acid	Substance I, Product III	GHB, Liquid Ecstasy, Liquid X, Sodium Oxybate, Xyrem®	None in U.S., Anesthetic	Moderate	Moderate	Yes	3-6	Oral	Slurred speech, disorientation, drunken behavior without odor of alcohol, impaired memory of events, interacts with alcohol	Shallow respiration, clammy skin, dilated pupils, weak and rapid pulse, coma, possible death	Anxiety, insomnia, tremors, delirium, convulsions, possible death
Benzodiazepines	Substance IV	Valium, Xanax, Halcion, Ativan, Restoril, Rohypnol (Roofies, R-2), Klonopin	Antianxiety, Sedative, Anti-convulsant, Hypnotic, Muscle Relaxant	Moderate	Moderate	Yes	1-8	Oral, injected			
Other Depressants	Substance I, II, III, IV	Ambien, Sonata, Meprobamate, Chloral Hydrate, Barbiturates, Methaqualone (Quaalude)	Antianxiety, Sedative, Hypnotic	Moderate	Moderate	Yes	2-6	Oral			
Stimulants											
Cocaine	Substance II	Coke, Flake, Snow, Crack, Coca, Blanca Perico, Nieve, Soda	Local anesthetic	Possible	High	Yes	1-2	Snorted, smoked, injected	Increased alertness, excitation, euphoria, increased pulse rate & blood pressure, insomnia, loss of appetite	Agitation, increased body temperature, hallucinations, convulsions, possible death	Apathy, long periods of sleep, irritability, depression, disorientation
Amphetamine/ Meth-amphetamine	Substance II	Crank, Ice, Cristal, Krystal Meth, Speed, Adderall, Dexedrine, Desoxyn	Attention deficit/hyperactivity disorder, narcolepsy, weight control	Possible	High	Yes	2-4	Oral, injected, smoked			

(continued)

Drugs	CSA Schedules	Trade or Other Names	Medical Uses	Dependence (Physical)	Dependence (Psychological)	Dependence (Tolerance)	Duration (Hours)	Usual Method	Possible Effects	Effects of Overdose	Withdrawal Syndrome
Stimulants (cont)											
Methylphenidate	Substance II	Ritalin (Illy's), Concerta, Focalin, Metadate	Attention deficit/hyperactivity disorder	Possible	High	Yes	2-4	Oral, injected, snorted, smoked	same as noted above	same as noted above	same as noted above
Other Stimulants	Substance III, IV	Adipex P, Ionamin, Prelu-2, Didrex, Provigil	Vasoconstriction	Possible	Moderate	Yes	2-4	Oral			
Hallucinogens											
MDMA and Analogs	Substance I	(Ecstasy, XTC, Adam), MDA (Love Drug), MDEA (Eve), MBDB	None	None	Moderate	Yes	4-6	Oral, snorted, smoked	Heightened senses, teeth grinding and dehydration	Increased body temp, electrolyte imbalance, cardiac arrest	Muscle aches, drowsiness, depression, acne
LSD	Substance I	Acid, Microdot, Sunshine, Boomers	None	None	Unknown	Yes	8-12	Oral	Illusions and hallucinations, altered perception of time and distance	(LSD) Longer, more intense "trip" episodes	None
Phencyclidine and Analogs	Substance I, II, III	PCP, Angel Dust, Hog, Loveboat, Ketamine (Special K), PCE, PCPy, TCP	Anesthetic (Ketamine)	Possible	High	Yes	1-12	Smoked, oral, injected, snorted		Unable to direct movement, feel pain, or remember	Drug seeking behavior *Not regulated
Other Hallucinogens	Substance I	Psilocybe mushrooms, Mescaline, Peyote Cactus, Ayahuasca, DMT, Dextromethorphan* (DXM)	None	None	None	Possible	4-8	Oral			
Cannabis											
Marijuana	Substance I	Pot, Grass, Sinsemilla, Blunts, Mota YerbaGrifa	None	Unknown	Moderate	Yes	2-4	Smoked, oral	Euphoria, relaxed inhibitions, increased appetite, disorientation	Fatigue, paranoia, possible psychosis	Occasional reports of insomnia, hyperactivity, decreased appetite
Tetrahydrocannabinol	Substance I, Product III	THC, Marinol	Antinauseant, Appetite stimulant	Yes	Moderate	Yes	2-4	Smoked, oral			
Hashish and Hashish Oil	Substance I	Hash, Hash oil	None	Unknown	Moderate	Yes	2-4	Smoked, oral			
Anabolic Steroids											
Testosterone	Substance III	Depo Testosterone, Sustanon, Sten, Cypt	Hypogonadism	Unknown	Unknown	Unknown	14-28 days	Injected	Virilization, edema, testicular atrophy, gynecomastia, acne, aggressive behavior	Unknown	Possible depression
Other Anabolic Steroids	Substance III	Parabolan, Winstrol, Equipose, Anadrol, Dianabol, Primabolin-Depo, D-Ball	Anemia, Breast cancer	Unknown	Yes	Unknown	Variable	Oral, injected			
Inhalants											
Amyl and Butyl Nitrites		Pearls, Poppers, Rush, Locker Room	Angina (Amyl)	Unknown	Unknown	No	1	Inhaled	Flushing, hypotension, headache	Methemoglobinemia	Agitation
Nitrous Oxide		Laughing Gas, balloons, Whippets	Anesthetic	Unknown	Low	No	0.5	Inhaled			
Other Inhalants		Adhesives, spray paint, hair spray, dry cleaning fluid, spot remover, lighter fluid	None	Unknown	High	No	0.5-2	Inhaled	Impaired memory, slurred speech, drunken behavior, slow onset vitamin deficiency, organ damage	Vomiting, respiratory depression, loss of consciousness, possible death	Trembling, anxiety, insomnia, vitamin deficiency, confusion, hallucination, convulsions
Alcohol											
Alcohol		Beer, wine, liquor	None	High	High	Yes	1-3	Oral			

Source: U.S. Department of Justice Drug Enforcement Administration

Case Study
Confessions of a Recovered Addict

Anonymous

The writer of this piece, one of the author's ex-students, found that love, both tough and tender, was the answer to her many addictions. She is now a drug abuse counselor—and a good one.

We all know what drug and alcohol addiction is, but I was addicted to just about everything that kicked my pleasure centers into gear—booze, drugs of all kinds, food, tobacco, and sex. You might say that I have an addictive personality. This is no story about a ghetto child, for I'm the product of an upper middle-class background.

At my "sweet sixteen" stage of life, I discovered men. I was fresh out of a private Catholic girls' school, and men, a lot of them, were what I wanted. I would go out to the naval air station in Lemore, California, to dance, drink, and to find a man who would go to bed with me while the rest of my chums were at a high school football game or at some other "square" function.

I was drinking heavily by the time I was eighteen, and I was also beginning to turn on to various drugs. When I graduated from high school, I didn't go onto college like most of my friends. I went to a home for unwed mothers. We were counseled there for our promiscuous ways, but the subject of drug and alcohol abuse was never addressed. However, this was 1968, and nobody thought about addiction among "young ladies." After all, heroin addiction belonged in the ghetto, and alcoholics were all dirty old men rolling in the gutters of skid row.

At this period in my life, I sought men out only for sex; "meaningful relationships" were for squares. Besides, who would want to love a 280-pound woman anyway? (Remember, food was another of my addictions). Not too many wanted to sleep with one either, so I found myself "buying" a man for a gram of coke or a few drinks. I didn't really get pleasure from sex, and often I actually would get physically sick when thinking about what I was doing. I realize now that I just wanted someone to hold me, and if sex was the price, so be it. This is not much different from being willing to suffer hangovers and withdrawal pains from my other addictions.

Throughout the late sixties, through the seventies and into the eighties, sex, drugs, and rock n' roll were a way of life for me. I was desperate for love, but thought I could only get it from stuffing myself with food, booze, pills, or penises. I spent my entire inheritance of $250,000 (I told you I was no pauper) in the mad service of these addictions. It's a horrible feeling to wake up in the morning thinking that the only things that would make the new day bearable were my addictions. This lifestyle cost me my health, the respect of my family, my self-respect, and the opportunity to get an education and lead a normal life. I can't even bear children now because the various venereal diseases I've had have destroyed this capacity.

One event in my life was instrumental in turning it around for me. I was in an automobile accident in which both the driver and I were drunk and high. I received a broken jaw and a few other things, but was out of the hospital and back running the bar I owned within six weeks. However, by now, the cops were on to me. I was doing a little drug dealing from my bar, and was stupid enough to sell $1,800 worth of coke to an undercover officer. I was busted the next day and held in jail until my trial date. There, I spent three months without drugs, alcohol, sex, or excessive amounts of food.

The judge sentenced me to five years probation, a $4,000 fine, and 120 hours of community service. I also was ordered to pay back the "buy money." My probation officer was a real "knuckle dragger," an ex-cop. He made it plain to me that his only job was to put me back in jail if I screwed up. I did my community service hours and visited my parole officer weekly. I began to see him as the caring father who I never had, actually enjoying the discipline involved in doing my community service and following my parole officer's orders. He and I became as friendly as a probationer and her officer could be. He was a very positive influence in my life, getting me interested in enrolling in college and pursuing a career in criminal justice.

I am now off probation, have my degree in criminal justice, and am married to a very loving man. I have not touched either alcohol or drugs since I was busted, have given up smoking, am down to a respectable weight of 165 at 5' 6", and my husband is the only man I've had sex with, or wanted to have sex with, in the past six years. I still see and talk with my probation officer, and I still volunteer at the agency where I did my community service. I want to devote my life's work to helping those poor lost souls on the same mad path to hell that I once walked, a path now made even more dangerous by the appearance of the AIDS virus.

There is a life after addiction if only you can find love and give it in return. I first found it in the cold stare of my probation officer, and then in the arms of my loving husband and the soft smiles of his two children.

Identification and Treatment Considerations

The National Institute of Drug Abuse (NIDA) has produced a guide specifically designed to aid criminal justice professionals to understand drug abuse treatment (*Principles of Drug Abuse Treatment for Criminal Justice Populations: A Research-Based Guide* [2006]). Table 16.2 reproduces the basic principles. The full report is available online at www.drugabuse.gov/PODAT_CJ/. These principles will be the guide for our discussion of identification and treatment of drug abuse.

Table 16.2 The Principles of Effective Drug Abuse Treatment

1. **No single treatment is appropriate for all individuals.** Matching treatment settings, interventions, and services to each individual's particular problems and needs is critical to his or her ultimate success in returning to productive functioning in the family, workplace, and society.

2. **Treatment needs to be readily available.** Because individuals who are addicted to drugs may be uncertain about entering treatment, taking advantage of opportunities when they are ready for treatment is crucial. Potential treatment applicants can be lost if treatment is not immediately available or is not readily accessible.

3. **Effective treatment attends to multiple needs of the individual, not just his or her drug use.** To be effective, treatment must address the individual's drug use and any associated medical, psychological, social, vocational, and legal problems.

4. **An individual's treatment and services plan must be assessed continually and modified as necessary to ensure that the plan meets the person's changing needs.** A patient may require varying combinations of services and treatment components during the course of treatment and recovery. In addition to counseling or psychotherapy, a patient at times may require medication, other medical services, family therapy, parenting instruction, vocational rehabilitation, and social and legal services. It is critical that the treatment approach be appropriate to the individual's age, gender, ethnicity, and culture.

5. **Remaining in treatment for an adequate period of time is critical for treatment effectiveness.** The appropriate duration for an individual depends on his or her problems and needs. Research indicates that for most patients, the threshold of significant improvement is reached at about three months in treatment. After this threshold is reached, additional treatment can produce further progress toward recovery. Because people often leave treatment prematurely, programs should include strategies to engage and keep patients in treatment.

6. **Counseling (individual and/or group) and other behavioral therapies are critical components of effective treatment for addiction.** In therapy, patients address issues of motivation, build skills to resist drug use, replace drug-using activities with constructive and rewarding nondrug-using activities, and improve problem-solving abilities. Behavioral therapy also facilitates interpersonal relationships and the individual's ability to function in the family and community.

7. **Medications are an important element of treatment for many patients, especially when combined with counseling and other behavioral therapies.** Methadone and levo-alpha-acetylmethadol are very effective in helping individuals addicted to heroin or other opiates stabilize their lives and reduce their illicit drug use. Naltrexone is also an effective medication for some opiate addicts and some patients with co-occurring alcohol dependence. For patients with mental disorders, both behavioral treatments and medications can be critically important.

8. **Addicted or drug-abusing individuals with coexisting mental disorders should have both disorders treated in an integrated way.** Because addictive disorders and mental disorders often occur in the same individual, patients presenting for either condition should be assessed and treated for the co-occurrence of the other type of disorder.

9. **Medical detoxification is only the first stage of addiction treatment and by itself does little to change long-term drug use.** Medical detoxification safely manages the acute physical symptoms of withdrawal associated with stopping drug use. While detoxification alone is rarely sufficient to help addicts achieve long-term abstinence, for some individuals it is a strongly indicated precursor to effective drug addiction treatment.

10. **Treatment does not need to be voluntary to be effective.** Strong motivation can facilitate the treatment process. Sanctions or enticements in the family, employment setting, or criminal justice system can increase significantly both treatment entry and retention rates and the success of drug-treatment interventions.

11. **Possible drug use during treatment must be monitored continuously.** Lapses to drug use can occur during treatment. The objective monitoring of a patient's drug and alcohol use during treatment, such as through urinalysis or other tests, can help the patient withstand urges to use drugs. Such monitoring also can provide early evidence of drug use so that the individual's treatment plan can be adjusted. Feedback to patients who test positive for illicit drug use is an important element of monitoring.

12. **Recovery from drug addiction can be a long-term process and frequently requires multiple episodes of treatment.** As with other chronic illnesses, relapses to drug use can occur during or after successful treatment episodes. Addicted individuals may require prolonged treatment and multiple episodes of treatment to achieve long-term abstinence and fully restored functioning. Participation in self-help support programs during and following treatment often is helpful in maintaining abstinence.

Everything said about alcoholism treatment has general application to other drug treatment. Pessimistic attitudes such as "once an addict, always an addict" have impeded attempts to rehabilitate drug abusers. This attitude partly may be a function of society's more negative perceptions of drug addicts in relation to its perceptions of alcoholics. Although addiction is certainly a chronic condition, and periods of relapse are to be expected, the correctional worker should not share the common attitudes of hopelessness and stigma (Epstein and Preston 2003).

Like alcoholics, many drug abusers and addicts are reluctant to admit that they have the problem unless they feel that you may consider their problem to be a factor militating against some form of punitive reaction. If drug abusers do not admit their dependency during the initial interview, they will tend to do whatever they can to hide it while under supervision. It is important that you identify any existing drug problem during your initial contacts. Several signs can assist you in this endeavor. Some researchers (Weekes, Moser, and Langevin 1999), however, feel that denial is not such a problem with hard-core offenders, who are largely inured to concerns of stigma.

The most obvious first step is to check the record for a history of drug-related arrests or previous drug treatment. Ask the offender to explain involvement with drugs at those times. This may lead into an admission of current usage. If you suspect narcotics usage, look for tracks on their hands and arms, which they conceal, even in summer, by wearing long sleeves. Does the offender wear sunglasses to your office to conceal constricted and fixed pupils? Is the offender drowsy and "laid back" during visits? If the offender's nose is frequently running or eyes watering, it may indicate that he or she is late in getting a fix. Does the offender scratch himself or herself and complain of frequent sickness? Does the offender have difficulty concentrating and frequently arrives late or misses appointments?

The abuser of stimulants is somewhat harder to detect by behavior in your office. As opposed to the narcotic addict, the stimulant abuser may display an excited, hyperactive, and talkative demeanor, which may sometimes degenerate into hostility and irritability. This will be particularly in evidence if you tell offenders that you suspect their drug abuse and order them to go to a clinic for urinalysis. All offenders whom you suspect of drug abuse should be made to undergo urinalysis at frequent but always random intervals (Bouffard and Taxman 2004).

Research studies strongly suggest that regular urine testing in conjunction with intensive supervision is more effective in reducing recidivism among probationers and parolees than if intensely supervised without urine testing (Speckart, Anglin, and Deschenes 1989).

As indicated above, urinalysis should be performed on a random basis because veteran users know how to beat it for most drugs. Cocaine, for instance, is detectable in the urine for only up to forty-eight to seventy-two hours, often even less if the user "flushes" (consumes large quantities of water to dilute the concentration of foreign substances per unit of urine). Relatively cheap drug adulteration tests can be used to discover either flushing or the contamination of a specimen with various substances.

The onsite, relatively immediate, drug-testing methodology has advanced rapidly in recent years. There are "kits," portable machines, and testing cups, all with various advantages and disadvantages in terms of practical value. Staff must determine their particular office's needs, meet the various company representatives, and do the cost-pricing research, accordingly. Although still fairly expensive, and this may change over time, hair analysis shows promising results. Unlike most all the other drug-testing methodology, examining hair samples can provide information about an offender's drug use over time, often dating back years. One popular company that provides onsite kits for numerous common substances is Expomed; their website is http//www.expomed.com/drugtest/adcheck.htm.

An even better alternative may be the sweat patch. The supervising officer may apply this patch to the offender's arm, and the offender may wear it for up to fourteen days. The patch is resistant to environmental contaminants and is tamper-evident (no one can tamper with it undetected). The pad collects and contains various residues from the offender's sweat left behind after it evaporates, including residues from consumed drugs (Baerand and Booher 1994). Probation and parole officers taking part in a field trial of the patch conclusively endorsed it over traditional urinalysis because of its gender-neutral convenience and the elimination of the need to handle urine samples. The patch is more expensive than urinalysis, but since it may cover the same period as two or three analyses, it may be more cost effective over the long run (Vito 1999).

Self-Help Support Groups

The results indicated above underscore the need for ongoing treatment and support for drug addicts over an extensive period. Those addicts who abstain with relative ease while in closely supervised programs with others battling the same problem may find it extraordinarily difficult once out in the world by themselves. Addicts in therapeutic communities obtain reinforcements for abstaining from others, but such reinforcements are not forthcoming outside where they will find stimuli conducive to taking up with drugs again. Thus, relapse prevention is the biggest issue correctional workers face with their drug-addicted offenders after completion of a residential program (Litt and Mallon 2003).

Among the many nonresidential mutual support options available today are Narcotics Anonymous (NA) and Cocaine Anonymous (CA), two 12-step fellowship groups located throughout the world and modeled after AA. No matter what your evidence, if you have the slightest suspicion that someone is in trouble with illegal drugs, refer them to these experts. They have been there. They know how to achieve abstinence, and they know how to sustain their positive arrest-free lifestyle. The author recommends Catherine Lemieux's *Offenders and Substance Abuse: Bringing the Family into Focus* for a complete and very practical explanation of how these programs function. Programs such as Rational Recovery (RR) and Secular Sobriety also are available for referrals.

Self-help support groups are not sufficient by themselves for offenders with multiple needs; social support means more than the empathetic support of the similarly afflicted. It is the correctional worker's role to coordinate and broker several other sources of potential social support. For instance, you should try to enlist the help of concerned family members in getting offenders to stay clean and to obtain educational and job opportunities for them. Being socially connected to family and working colleagues has long been considered of the utmost importance in the treatment armamentarium available to correctional workers in dealing with drug-abusing offenders (Boufard and Taxman 2004, Leukeford et al. 2003, Moos 2008, Lemieux 2009).

Pharmacological Treatments

Arguing that addiction is a brain disease, Alan Leshner, Director of the National Institute on Drug Abuse, states that: "If we understand addiction as a prototypical psychobiological illness, with critical biological, behavioral, and social context components, our treatment strategies must include biological, behavioral, and social context elements" (1998: 5). The biological elements are the various drug antagonists (drugs that inhibit the effects of other drugs). Opponents of pharmacotherapy argue that it merely substitutes one drug for another and it, therefore, is not a treatment. However, advocates of this method of treatment counter that it enhances and augments, not replaces, traditional methods of treatment and is more cost effective and immediate.

363

Nugent argues that "Drug users are often emotionally unstable; pharmacotherapeutics regulate them, making them more receptive to counseling and rehabilitation" (1990b: 6). We agree; after all, we pharmacologically attempt to regulate schizophrenics and others suffering from syndromes associated with chemical imbalances in the brain. First, we try to stabilize their brain chemistry, and then their lives; one logically precedes the other.

Among the various drug therapies, the best known and most widely used is methadone maintenance. Some authorities feel that this method should be used only after psychotherapeutic methods have been tried and failed because methadone creates its own dependence. However, it is extremely successful in blocking the withdrawal pains of heroin without producing any rewarding euphoria or rush of its own. Best of all, the heroin addict on a methadone program can function normally in the community. Although addicts retain their physical dependence on a narcotic (methadone), they defeat their psychological craving for heroin and no longer have to engage in criminal activity to avoid withdrawal (Kleber 2003). Addicts typically report to a clinic daily to drink their methadone mixed with orange juice. Methadone appears fairly successful as a treatment method. Kaplan (1991: 3) states that "Methadone maintenance 'works' for around 30 or 40 percent of the addicts who undergo treatment. Moreover, the arrest rate of addicts drops dramatically when they enter methadone treatment."

If psychological craving for heroin exists, narcotic antagonists such as Cyclazocine and Naltrexone are available to offset the craving. They do not possess the narcotic like properties of methadone, but they do produce rapid detoxification. These antagonists block the desirable effects of heroin. Like Antabuse, they should be used in conjunction with intensive counseling designed, as always, to get offenders to exert control over their own lives, and to behave responsibly. A recent study of more than 1,600 cocaine addicts in treatment in eleven U.S. cities found that 77 percent remained cocaine free in the year following treatment, with relapse incidents being highly related to severity of patient problems and shorter stays (less than ninety days) in treatment (Simpson et al. 1999). A study of drug addicts on federal probation found that roughly two-thirds of those who received only counseling for their problem relapsed versus one-third of those who received counseling plus naltrexone (Kleber 2003). Based on studies such as these, one has to wonder with Kleber why (with few exceptions) the criminal justice system is relatively uninterested in using pharmacological treatments.

Desipramine is a drug that has been used experimentally in the treatment of cocaine addicts within the context of a full treatment plan that may include counseling and dietary changes. It has a claimed success rate in keeping addicts from craving the drug for up to nine months. This is quite an advance over the use of other methods, which have reported records of only fifteen days (Koob and Le Moal 2008). However, desipramine is not a magic bullet, and must be used as an adjunct to other therapies.

The newest antagonistic drug is buprenorphine, which can be used to treat both cocaine and heroin addiction, and potential addiction to other drugs as well. It has several other advantages, not the least of which is that it is nonaddictive and safe (Ling et al. 1996). Unlike methadone and other therapeutic drugs, buprenorphine is not likely to create an illicit drug market because its opiate effects are weak (Drug Enforcement Administration 2003).

Interestingly, the effects of the various antagonists differ across genders. For males, methadone is more effective than buprenorphine in treating opiate addiction, while for females the opposite is the case. For cocaine addiction, buprenorphine was superior to methadone for males, but methadone was superior to buprenorphine for females (Oliveto et al. 1999).

There are quite a few complications involved with the pharmacological treatment of drug addiction. These complications are not your affair, however. Your responsibility is to become familiar with medical facilities that dispense these antagonistic drugs for a particularly intractable offender with whom all else has failed.

Do not be put off by arguments that these drugs "only treat symptoms, not the cause." The symptoms are precisely those aspects with which we are most immediately concerned. Much of medicine is concerned with "treating symptoms" while the body marshals its natural defenses to attack the cause. In fact, apart from the infectious diseases, wounds, and breaks, medicine has very few "cures." Ailments such as heart disease, diabetes, and arthritis, just like alcoholism and drug addiction, are never cured. Drugs designed to alleviate these medical problems help people cope by minimizing the destructive effects of symptoms associated with the problems in people's lives.

Further, do not be disheartened by those who tell you that it is practically "impossible" to wean substance abusers successfully from their problems, or by those who will assert that voluntary acquiescence on the part of the offender is "absolutely necessary" for successful treatment. A number of studies of troops returning from Vietnam show that many men were able to kick their habits regardless of whether they were treated. One study found that 43 percent of a sample of 600 returning soldiers reported an addiction to heroin. Although some reported occasional use in the United States, only 12 percent of those reporting addiction in Vietnam relapsed to addiction levels back in the United States. Once they returned home, "removed from the pressures of war and once more in the presence of family and friends and opportunities for constructive activity, these men felt no need for heroin" (Peel 1978: 65). This is an instructive statement about the power of attachment, commitment, and involvement to generate responsible behavior and the stabilizing effects of a supportive environment. However, recall that only some users of illicit drugs have the genetic predisposition for drug addiction, so do not take this optimistic statement to mean that it applies to everyone

Of the second pessimistic assertion, the majority of chemically dependent people who were successfully treated were forced into treatment against their wills. They did not necessarily want to discontinue their chemical usage, but certain crises in their lives forced them to accept help. It is true that the vast majority of people treated for substance abuse have very large boot prints impressed on their backsides. But, so what? Being involved with the criminal justice system because of substance abuse should be crisis enough to generate the beginnings of motivation in some offenders, and the experiences undergone in the treatment program may motivate others. Two reviews of the U.S. (Farabee, Pendergast, and Anglin 1998) and U. K. (Barton 1999) literature on coerced substance-abuse treatment concluded that such treatment leads to positive reductions in abuse, even greater reductions in some cases than among voluntary clients, presumably because of the threat of criminal justice sanctions.

As a correctional worker who is probably not trained in direct clinical techniques, most likely you will not be directly involved in the treatment of alcohol or other drug-dependent offenders. However, you will be indirectly involved by being a knowledgeable broker about available programs in your community, insisting on frequent urine testing (or other equivalent test) of offenders not in residential treatment, and above all, by holding offenders strictly responsible for remaining alcohol and drug free. Treating offenders with substance-abuse problems is a team effort, and you do your part by effective offender monitoring and liaison with treatment agencies according to the principles of good case management.

Summary

Looking at illegal drug abuse and addiction, we noted that illegal drug users bear the added burden of the crime associated with their use. Illegal drugs cost a lot of money and generally precipitate great risks on the part of the dependent or potentially dependent offender.

Drug classification is important to understand. The depressants range from the relatively mild analgesic sedatives to the more challenging narcotics such as heroin and opium. Since purity levels have risen, and offenders are worried about dirty needles, many more are snorting or smoking these drugs as opposed to injecting them intravenously. The stimulants, of course, have the opposite effect. Crack cocaine and methamphetamine are powerfully addictive substances ravaging some parts of the country with their enticing capacity to generate a stimulating sense of well being. Marijuana, actually classified as a hallucinogen, is far more potent today than ever before. Unfortunately, studies are showing that young people and others, including a very large segment of the offender population, are heavily involved with marijuana.

Identification and assessment of offenders in trouble with illegal drugs and alcohol is a critical component of your job. Although drug-dependent offenders respond to the full range of treatment resources available, therapeutic communities (TCs) seem particularly suited to many of them. As always, referral to mutual self-help support groups such as Narcotics Anonymous (NA), Cocaine Anonymous (CA), and Rational Recovery (RR) should be routine in every case, and accompany any other professional treatment referral.

The criminal justice system under-uses pharmacological therapy although a wide variety of studies show that medication plus counseling provides better treatment outcomes than does counseling alone. Do not be overly pessimistic about drug treatment; it can and does work for at least one-third of addicts, which is not all that bad. If we do try to treat addicts at all, that one-third success rate turns into hundreds of thousands of extra addicts not on the streets.

References and Suggested Readings

Anglin, M., G. Speckart, and E. Deschenes. 1989. *Reexamining the Effects of Probation and Parole on Narcotics Addiction and Property Crime: Final Report.* National Institute of Justice, Washington, D.C.: U.S. Department of Justice.

Baerand, J. and J. Booher. 1994. The Patch: A New Alternative for Drug Testing in the Criminal Justice System. *Federal Probation* 58: 29-33.

Barton, A. 1999. Breaking the Crime/Drugs Cycle: The Birth of a New Approach? *The Howard Journal* 38: 144-157.

Bogdanovich, P. 1985. *The Killing of the Unicorn: Dorothy Stratten 1960-1980.* New York: Bantam.

Bouffard, J. and F. Taxman. 2004. Looking Inside The "Black Box" of Drug Court Treatment Services Using Direct Observation. *Journal of Drug Issues* 22: 195-218.

Burnett, M. 1979. Understanding and Overcoming Addictions. In S. Eisenberg and L. Patterson, eds., *Helping Clients with Special Concerns*. Chicago: Rand McNally.

Chein, I., G. Gerhard, R. Lee, and E. Rosenfeld. 1964. *The Road to Narcotics, Delinquency and Social Policy*. New York: Basic Books.

Drug Enforcement Administration. 2003. *Drugs of Abuse*. Arlington, Virginia: U.S. Department of Justice.

DuPont, R. 1997. *The Selfish Brain: Learning from Addiction*. Washington, D.C.: American Psychiatric Press.

Epstein, D. and K. Preston. 2003. The Reinstatement Model and Relapse Prevention: A Clinical Perspective. *Psychopharmacology* 168: 31-41.

Farabee, D., M. Pendergast, and M. Anglin. 1998. The Effectiveness of Coerced Treatment for Drug-Abusing Offenders. *Federal Probation* 109: 3-10.

Fishbein, D. 2000. Neuropsychological Function, Drug Use, and Violence. *Criminal Justice and Behavior* 27: 139-159.

———. 2003. Neuropsychological and Emotional Regulatory Processes in Antisocial Behavior. In A. Walsh and L. Ellis, eds., *Biosocial Criminology: Challenging Environmentalism's Supremacy*, Hauppauge, NY: Nova Science, pp. 185-208.

Franken, I., C. Stam, V. Hendriks, and W. van den Brink. 2004. Electroencephalographic Power and Coherence Analyses Suggest Altered Brain Function in Abstinent Male Heroin-Dependent Patients. *Neuropsychobiology* 49: 105-110.

Gove, W. and C. Wilmoth. 2003. The Neurophysiology of Motivation and Habitual Criminal Behavior. In A. Walsh and L. Ellis. eds., *Biosocial Criminology: Challenging Environmentalism's Supremacy*. Hauppauge, NewYork: Nova Science. pp. 227-245.

Grabowski, J. 1984. *Cocaine: Pharmacology, Effects and Treatment of Abuse*. Washington, D.C.: National Institute of Drug Abuse.

Holden, C. 1989. Street-Wise Crack Research. *Science* 246: 1376-1381.

Hooper, R., D. Lockwood, and J. Inciardi. 1993. Treatment Techniques in Corrections-Based Therapeutic Communities. *The Prison Journal* 73: 290-306.

Hyman, S. 2007. The Neurobiology of Addiction: Implications for Voluntary Control of Behavior. *The American Journal of Bioethics* 7 :8-11.

Kaplan, J. 1991. *Heroin*. National Institute of Justice Crime File (NCJ # 97225). Washington, D.C.: U.S. Department of Justice.

Kleber, H. 2003. Pharmacological Treatments for Heroin and Cocaine Dependence. *The American Journal on Addictions* 12: S5-S18.

Koob, G. and M. Le Moal 2008. Review. Neurobiological mechanisms for opponent motivational processes in addiction. *Philosophical Transactions of the Royal Society of London: Biological Science*. 363: 3113-3123

Lemieux, C. 2009. *Offenders and Substance Abuse: Bringing the Family into Focus*. Alexandria, Virginia: American Correctional Association.

Leshner, A. 1998. Addiction is a Brain Disease—And It Matters. *National Institute of Justice Journal* 237: 2-6.

Leukefeld, C., H. McDonald, M. Staton, A. Mateyoke-Scrivner, M. Webster, T. Logan, and T. Garitty. 2003. An Employment Intervention for Drug Abusing Clients. *Federal Probation* 67: 27-32.

Lightfoot, L. 1999. Treating Substance Abuse and Dependence in Offenders: A Review of Methods and Outcomes. In E. Latessa, ed., *Strategic Solutions: The International Community Corrections Association Examines Substance Abuse*. Alexandria, Virginia: American Correctional Association.

Ling, W., D. Wesson, C. Charuvastra, and J. Klett. 1996. A Controlled Trial Comparing Buprenorphine and Methadone Maintenance in Opioid Dependence. *Archives of General Psychiatry* 53: 401-407.

Litt, M. and S. Mallon. 2003. The Design of Social Support Networks for Offenders in Outpatient Drug Treatment. *Federal Probation* 67: 15-22.

Marlatt, G., J. Baer, D. Donovan, and D. Kivlanhan. 1989. Addictive Behaviors: Etiology and Treatment. *Annual Review of Psychology* 39: 223-252.

McBride, D. and C. McCoy. 1993. The Drugs-Crime Relationship: An Analytical Framework. *The Prison Journal* 73: 257-278.

McDermott, P., A. Alterman, J. Cacciola, M. Rutherford, J. Newman, and E. Mulholland 2000. Generality of Psychopathy Checklist Revised Factors over Prisoners and Substance-Dependent Patients. *Journal of Consulting and Clinical Psychology* 68: 181-186.

Menard, S., S. Mihalic, and D. Huizinga. 2001. Drugs and Crime Revisited. *Justice Quarterly* 18: 269-299.

Narcotics Control Technical Assistance Program. 1990. Future Drug Testing Kits. *NCTAP News*. October. 4: 1.

National Institute of Drug Abuse. 1996. The Brain's Drug Reward System. *NIDA Notes, 11: Tearoff Sheet*. Washington, D.C.: National Institutes of Health, U. S. Department of Health and Human Services.

———. 2006. *Principles of Drug Abuse Treatment for Criminal Justice Populations: A Research-Based Guide*. Washington, D.C.: National Institutes of Health, U. S. Department of Health and Human Services. Also available online at www.drugabuse.gov/PODAT_CJ/

———. 2008. *Principles of Drug Addiction Treatment: A Research Based Guide*. Retrieved February 25, 2009 from www.nida.nih.gov/podat?PODAT2.html

National Institute of Justice. 1991. *Annual Report on Adult Arrestees: Drugs and Crime in America's Cities*. Washington, D.C.: U.S. Department of Justice.

———. 2003. *Drug and Alcohol Related Matters Among Arrestees*. Washington, D.C.: United States Department of Justice.

Nugent, E. 1990a. Ice: The New Cold War. *NCTAP News*. January. 3: 1-4.

———. 1990b. Pharmacotherapy. *NCTAP News*. April. 3: 6-7.

Office of National Drug Control Policy. 2009. *Adam II 2008 Annual Report*. www.whitehousedrug policy.gov/publications/pdf/adams2008.pdf

Oliveto, A., A. Feingold, R. Schottenfeld, P. Jatlow, and T. Kosten. 1999. Desipramine in Opioid-Dependent Cocaine Abusers Maintained on Buprenorphine vs. Methadone. *Archives of General Psychiatry* 56: 812-820.

Parks, G. and G. Marlatt. 1999. Keeping "What Works" Working: Cognitive-Behavioral Relapse Prevention Therapy with Substance Abusing Offenders. In E. Latessa, ed., *Strategic Solutions: The International Community Corrections Association Examines Substance Abuse*. Alexandria, Virginia: American Correctional Association.

Peel, S. 1978. Addiction: The Analgesic Experience. *Human Nature* 1: 61-66.

Pinel, J. 2000. *Biopsychology*, 4th ed. Boston: Allyn and Bacon.

Read, E. 1992. Euphoria on the Rocks: Understanding Crack Addiction. *Federal Probation* 56: 3-11.

———. 1996. *Partners in Change: The 12-Step Referral Handbook for Probation, Parole and Community Corrections*. Alexandria, Virginia: American Correctional Association and Hazelden Foundation.

Restak, R. 2001. *The Secret Life of the Brain*. New York: co-published by Dana Press and Joseph Henry Press.

Robinson, T. and K. Berridge. 2003. Addiction. *Annual Review of Psychology* 54: 25-53.

Schepis, T., B. Adinoff, and U. Rao. 2008. Neurological Processes in Adolescent Addictive Disorders. *The American Journal of Addiction* 17: 6-23.

Seiter, R. 2005. *Corrections: An Introduction*. Upper Saddle River, New Jersey: Prentice Hall.

Simpson, D., G. Joe, B. Fletcher, R. Hubbard, and D. Anglin. 1999. A National Evaluation of Treatment Outcomes for Cocaine Dependence. *Archives of General Psychiatry* 56: 505-514.

Speckart, G., M. Anglin, and E. Deschenes. 1989. Modeling the Longitudinal Impact of Legal Sanctions on Narcotics Use and Property Crime. *Journal of Quantitative Criminology* 5: 33-56.

United States Department of Health and Human Services, 2008. *National Survey on Drug Use and Health*. Washington, D.C. Department of Health and Human Services

United States Department of Justice. 2000. *1999 Violent Crime in the United States*. Washington, D.C.: Bureau of Justice Statistics.

———. 1999. *Annual Report of Drug Use among Adult and Juvenile Arrestees*. Washington, D.C.: Bureau of Justice Statistics.

Vito, G. 1999. What Works in Drug Testing and Monitoring. In E. Latessa, ed., *Strategic Solutions: The International Community Corrections Association Examines Substance Abuse*. Alexandria, Virginia: American Correctional Association.

Walker, S. 2001. *Sense and Nonsense about Crime and Drugs*. Belmont, California: Wadsworth.

Walsh, A. 1995. Parental Attachment, Drug Use, and Facultative Sexual Strategies. *Social Biology* 42: 95-107.

Weekes, J., A. Moser, and C. Langevin. 1999. Assessing Substance-Abusing Offenders for Treatment. In E. Latessa, ed., *Strategic Solutions: The International Community Corrections Association Examines Substance Abuse*. Alexandria, Virginia: American Correctional Association.

Witkin, G. 1998. The Crime Bust. *U.S. News and World Report*. May 25.

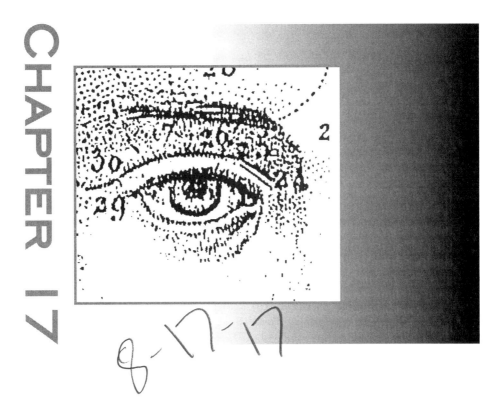

Therapeutic Communities in Correctional Institutions: Something Works

Introduction

Therapeutic communities and their reported successes in reducing recidivism, and its associated costs, epitomize the promise of treatment for a whole new generation of practitioners, researchers, and policymakers. As was discussed in Chapter 9, the effect of the Martinson (1974) article, in addition to a political shift to the right, spurred disillusionment about the ability to treat offenders successfully in the 1970s and 80s. Still, even during these dark days for treatment in corrections, most of the U.S. population believed in the "idea" of rehabilitation (Cullen and Gilbert 1982).

While this disillusionment with the effects of treatment in practice (though not in theory) continued, the need to deal with addicts' involvement in crime only increased. In most cases, we dealt with those addicts by incarcerating them without treatment. In a recent study by the Urban Institute (Bhati, Roman, and Chalfin 2008: xiv), the researchers estimated that 1.5 million arrestees are at risk of drug abuse or dependence. "We find that several million crimes could be averted if current eligibility limitations were suspended and all at-risk arrestees were treated."

Certainly at least some of the stakeholders' new enchantment with treatment is driven by the escalating costs of "locking 'em up and throwing away the key." However, as the Urban Institute reported, policymakers and practitioners are beginning to appreciate the successes of treatment in turning some offenders into pro-social members of society or at least non-criminally engaged ones. Rather than "nothing works" as the damning and partially misleading mantra for treatment programming after the publication of the Martinson report (1974), the research on therapeutic communities and certain treatment practices indicate that "something works."

The "something" that works, however, is carefully structured and targeted programming such as in the best run therapeutic communities (discussed in this chapter). Even these programs, which employ the "best practices" as identified through scientific study, only work for some offenders. So, as Palmer (1995[first published in 1983]) and Gendreau and Ross (1995[first published in 1983]) essentially argued in their rebuttals to the Martinson report and to the pessimism about rehabilitation programming generally, "some programs work for some offenders some of the time." Current research indicates that therapeutic communities can be operated so that they work for some clients, some of the time.

The problem appears to be that people engaged in criminal activity are diverse with multiple reasons associated with their deviance. Some have engaged in serious criminal acts from their teen years, others are dabblers in minor and/or assorted criminal acts. Some have psychological difficulties in recognizing the pain they cause others, while others are addicts who commit crimes to support their habit. Therapeutic communities are not geared to address all of the attributes of all offenders and their criminality. Rather, they tend to address the problems of substance abusers and their related criminal behavior. Interestingly, research and experience shows that since many criminal offenders addicted to illegal drugs are also struggling with character or personality disorders, including an antisocial personality, longer-term residential treatment facilities seem to offer the best hope for treatment success. Many disenfranchised offenders within this population need habilitation rather than rehabilitation. They need a total long-term cultural change, with the opportunity to learn new values, behavior, and cognitions (Litt and Mallon 2003).

In this chapter, we discuss the attributes of therapeutic communities and the research on them. We explore strengthening therapeutic communities through both process and outcome evaluations, which allow the stakeholders to assess their relative worth and weaknesses. We then distill from the research, best practices for the operation of therapeutic communities. The chapter ends with a review of where we have been and where we might go in the evolution of therapeutic communities.

History and Nature of Therapeutic Communities

The use of therapeutic communities in the treatment of alcohol and drug abuse has been popular since 1958. At this time, its most famous representative, Synanon, was established. However, some of the elements of therapeutic communities reportedly developed in Europe during the Second World War (Broekaert, Vandevelde, Soyez, Yates, and Slater 2006).

Therapeutic communities are total treatment environments isolated from the rest of society, as far as is practical. According to a leading researcher on therapeutic communities, their essential dynamic is mutual self-help. Thus, the day-to-day activities are conducted by the residents themselves. In their jobs, groups, meetings, recreation, personal, and social time, it is residents who continually transmit to each other the main messages and expectations of the community" (cited in Hooper, Lockwood, and Inciardi 1993: 291).

The amount of time residents spend in therapeutic communities ranges from six months to two years, but typically residents stay six-to-twelve months. In such settings, addicts receive support, feedback, and information in an accepting, caring, honest, and empathetic way.

They learn that if tensions and stresses arise, a refocusing of the primary stress in their lives (addiction) will place the secondary tensions and stresses in proper perspective. The therapeutic community is expected to help them increase their self-esteem and provide them with renewed feelings of self-control. Researchers consider the regaining of self-esteem and a sense of self-control essential for drug addicts (Leukefeld et al. 2003, National Institute on Drug Abuse [NIDA] 2002). Addicts learn self-forgiveness through positive and negative peer pressure, and they learn from the positive examples of those peers. This enables them to focus their anger and negative talk on the substance that holds them in its grip, rather than on themselves. Self-worth, the product of both self-forgiveness and the elimination of negative self-talk, eventually will emerge. In therapeutic communities, the community acts as a "change agent" to help members face their addiction and related foibles, while the individual also focuses on "self-help" (NIDA 2002).

As discussed in Chapter 11, cognitive restructuring and cognitive skill-building are processes based on the principle that the way individuals think has a great deal to do with their behavior. Therefore, changing risk and problematic thinking is fundamental to long-term behavioral change. Therapeutic communities are devoted to the importance of practicing new behaviors and adopting new values through social learning in a community environment. An individual's ability to learn, cope, and engage in recovery is dependent upon a proper blend of these two very important concepts and practices.

Cognitive-behavioral programs merely used as parts of a learning experience or as static groups are not very useful. Therapeutic community practitioners argue that cognitive-behavioral programs should be a part of the overall structure and strategy of treatment (Gornik and Bush 2000, Gornik et al. 1999). Practitioners and researchers agree that therapeutic community programs should be carefully planned and approached systematically. They also realize that as offenders build pro-social competence in knowledge, skills, and attitude, the staff builds competence in delivery techniques.

Therapeutic communities are considered to be the most successful of drug rehabilitation programs, but they typically require:

> a highly structured, long-term (eight to twelve month) residential program, which includes a highly confrontational form of group therapy, resocialization, progressive responsibility, and gradual reentry into the community (Lightfoot 1999: 55).

They are not panaceas, nor are they suited for all addicts. As with treatment for alcoholism, success or lack of success will depend a great deal on the personal attributes addicts bring with them to the therapeutic process.

A Day in the Life of a Therapeutic Community Participant

As indicated in Table 17.1, (on page 371) the therapeutic community participant has a very structured day, filled with group meetings, phase (treatment) meetings, work, recreation, individual counseling sessions, and journaling (written reflections on treatment assignments) although, not all of these activities occur each day. Activities and their duration will vary by whether the therapeutic community is located in the community or in a correctional institution and by where the participants are in their treatment plan.

However, some activities do occur every day (for example, morning and night community meetings, AA/NA, and phase meetings). Participants are unlikely to have individual counseling sessions or group confrontations every day, and most individuals involved in treatment programming do no work. Other activities that participants might be involved in, while in therapeutic communities, include educational, family or psychological services programming. For those incarcerated in correctional facilities, therapeutic community participants must regularly submit to "counts" to make sure they are where they are supposed to be.

The morning meeting is usually a rousing wake-up call so participants start their day on a positive and enthusiastic note. Typically, program participant leaders (with staff present) lead the session, which covers everything from the positive activities and actions of community members, to world events, community plans and changes, and respectful chiding of some members by others or the leaders, regarding behaviors that violate the rules. All participants have or have access to a manual on community operation. Sometimes participants perform a skit or sing a song to illustrate a point or to set the right tone. In a meeting one of the authors attended, she heard *America the Beautiful* sung at the end of the morning meeting.

Phase meetings focus on the treatment stage of a participant. A person can be in each phase for a month to three months (often the treatment regimen has three-to-four phases), depending on the structure of the program, its length, and the progress of a given participant. As most therapeutic communities have a cognitive self-change component, these phases focus on addictive behaviors and thinking that are associated with using/dependence and criminality.

Usually, these phase meetings are very participative. They are led by staff but require the involvement of participants to be successful. Staff ask participants to either create or respond to scenarios to identify thinking or behavioral errors, and then to propose alternative actions. Relating these errors to their own cognitive processes and behaviors is a key element of making progress in treatment. The leaders use active learning in the form of speaking and journaling to push participants to process not just what they are doing, but why they are doing it (for example, what might be the tipping points that lead to criminal engagement or substance abuse), so that they may take an alternative path when such situations arise again.

Some programs build in recreation and work as part of the daily activity. However, the opportunity to work depends on what might be available for therapeutic community participants in a correctional institution, though it might be required for those in a community-based therapeutic community. Weightlifting or other forms of physical activity and recreation might also support the positive and healthful message, which therapeutic communities try to convey. A healthy body aids a healthy mind. Moreover, team recreation might build group cohesion and teach participants how to control their anger and frustration when a game does not go their way.

Staff also counsel participants individually so they can develop treatment plans. These counseling sessions provide staff with an opportunity to address any concerns they have with the individual's progress. They also give staff the opportunity to interact with their clients individually and as persons separate from the group.

Institutional and community therapeutic communities have inmate/offender leaders who are given the responsibility to make important decisions about the community and its operation. They address community plans, positive events, and negative behaviors of participants. If there are recurring or serious violations of rules, these inmates lead the group meeting and respectfully confront offending participants with their rule-violating or questionable behavior. (These are the group conflict-resolution meetings referred to in Table 17.1). If someone has questioned the objectionable behavior before, or if it is serious enough, the group can kick a participant out of the therapeutic community and/or, if need be, staff can do this.

Alcoholics Anonymous and Narcotics Anonymous are key aspects of most recovery programs for addicts. Going through the 12 Step process requires recognition of one's addiction and the need to repair, or at least recognize and repent for the damage caused to others because of one's behavior.

The purpose of the night meeting is to close the day positively. Residents and staff review community events and decisions and community members have an opportunity to both complement and correct the behavior of others. When a correction is mentioned, the offending party usually acknowledges the violation of rules and tells the group that he or she will get right on that behavior (change it). Such meetings might also close with an upbeat song or inspirational words to give participants hope about their treatment and their ability to change.

Table 17.1 A Day in the Life of a Therapeutic Community:

Participant's Activity List

6-7 a.m.	Get up, eat breakfast, tidy living area
8-8:30 a.m.	Morning meeting
8:30-10:00 a.m..	Phase meeting
10:00 a.m.-11:30 a.m.	Recreation/work/individual counseling
11:30-1:00 p.m.	Lunch
1:00-2:00 p.m.	Phase meeting
2:00-4:00 p.m.	Journaling/work/individual counseling/community leader meetings or group conflict resolution
4:00-5:00 p.m.	Dinner
5:30-7:00 p.m.	AA/NA meetings
7:00-7:30 p.m.	Night meeting
7:30-10:00 p.m.	Free time
10:00 p.m.	Lights out

Note: We created this activity list from therapeutic communities in Pennsylvania (Young and Porter 1999) and observations in Idaho (Stohr et al. 2000).

Evaluation of Therapeutic Communities

Fashioning a valid evaluation of therapeutic community programming is doable, but problematic. Research tells us that we must temper any treatment program success by institutional factors. These include such items as: the pay, training, and turnover of staff, the relative seclusion of the therapeutic community, and the support the program enjoys from the rest of the institution and its key players (such as the warden and heads of treatment and security) (Ruefle and Miller 1999). As Linhorst and his colleagues (2001) indicate in an article on the implementation of a prison-based therapeutic community, a number of situational factors (such as the enactment of a no-smoking policy and the change in treatment providers) can also influence the viability of a treatment program.

Clearly, programs falter because of external factors, some of which they have little or no control over. As mentioned, funding shortfalls, a lack of leadership and support by administrators, or crowding are some of the types of factors that could inadvertently sink the success of a program.

Therapeutic community programs are likely to face many challenges at first which, if supported, they can overcome in the long term. Leukefeld and Tims (1992) argue that therapeutic communities must be given time to succeed or fail on their merits. They note that to succeed, programs must have sustained adequate funding over time and their design must consider evaluation. Such design should be realistic in scope and timeline on outcomes and subject participation (Leukefeld and Tims 1992; Schuiteman and Bogle 1996).

Lipton and his colleagues (1992) found in their review of evaluations of two well-studied correctional therapeutic community substance-abuse programs, the New York Stay'n Out and the Oregon Cornerstone programs, that recidivism in crime and substance abuse decreased for participants compared to control groups. They note, however, that the history of therapeutic-community-program demise over the past two decades oftentimes relates to factors external to those programs such as administrative changes and funding reductions.

For instance, Stohr and some colleagues found in a process evaluation of a therapeutic communities that the treatment and security staff were particularly concerned about the turnover of key staff, training of treatment providers, communication between the treatment program and the security program, and mishaps in referrals to the program (Stohr, Hemmens, Baune, Dayley, Gornik, Kjaer, and Noon 2000). The program itself was sound, but funding shortfalls and personnel factors (often tied to funding) and miscommunications and misunderstandings presented threats to its ability to deliver treatment effectively.

Establishing and maintaining program integrity requires rigorous examination of a number of program components and provider and participant activity and preparedness over time. We expect that the initial graduates will not be as "pure" a product of the therapeutic community as will those who follow them a year or so later. This is likely because the program will evolve once implemented and the staff will adjust and mature organizationally when they become accustomed to programmatic requirements.

A process evaluation provides the opportunity for providers to become attuned to the basic strengths and weaknesses of the program during and after this initial implementation period. Key to this type of evaluation is attention to the details of program's goals and objectives, admittance and release criteria and procedures, program requirements of participants, treatment and custody staff training and perspective, program content connection to established and viable treatment protocols, administration involvement and support, parole board or judicial commitment (when applicable), and provision for aftercare treatment (Andrews 2006).

The methods used by process evaluators to investigate such matters include a review of program training, inmate assessment, intake and exit instruments; data from the inmate management system; and aftercare procedures and content. Process evaluators might also want to interview key actors, participants, survey staff, and participants generally about the substance and operation of the program. The point of a process evaluation is to determine if the program is operating as expected. Andrews (2006) and others argue that programs should be devised with an evaluator already on board so that key indicators of program integrity and efficacy can be collected and observed from the beginning.

Once the program has been "process evaluated," it does not remain statically situated. Issues associated with its viability, such as staff training and turnover, budgetary and organizational support may shift in the time between a process and an outcome evaluation. Moreover, those programs not previously process evaluated will need a more intensive outcome evaluation to give those findings a context. For these reasons, some researchers believe that evaluations of the effectiveness of programs should continue to employ some "process" measures so that treatment outcomes might be better understood. Moreover, determining the effect of programming on an institution (its role) and the reciprocal impact of the program on the institutional and external environment (which houses it) requires that researchers conducting an outcome evaluation stay attuned to the likely obstacles that programs might face in delivering effective treatment.

Outcome evaluations, as opposed to process evaluations, are more focused on the results of programming. Of interest for the correctional-program manager and researchers doing an outcome evaluation are whether the program affected recidivism and other behaviors and attitudes of participants. Certainly, they will want to know, as will policymakers funding the program the following things about whether participants:

- Recidivate less

- Associate less with those involved in crime

- Are less likely to use illegal substances and drink alcohol to excess

- Are employed more

- Have more pro-social attitudes than similar persons not involved in programming

An experimental design is used to test whether the programs obtained these outcomes. In this case, people who need treatment are randomly assigned to the program or to the control group (not to the program). The greater the number of people in the experimental group (the program participants) and the non-experimental or control group (the nonparticipants), the more likely the researcher will be able to generalize, or apply, the findings more broadly. Therefore, if only ten people are assigned to each group, the findings that emanate from comparing these groups are likely to be less important for everyone concerned than if 200 people were in each group. Unfortunately, it is not always possible in social service agencies to arrange and complete an experimental design. For one thing, agency heads and program managers are reluctant to withhold treatment, even untested treatment, from people who clearly need it.

For this, and related reasons, researchers and program managers often sponsor (in the case of managers) a quasi-experimental design. In this case, program participants are matched demographically (for example, by age, gender, race/

ethnicity, education, income) and criminogenically (for example, by type of offense, criminal history) with a similarly addicted comparison group and are compared to them on those outcomes mentioned earlier. Another form of quasi-experimental design, used separately or in addition to the matching, would be to compare outcomes of those who complete all or more of the program with those who complete less of it. Researchers and policymakers have concerns with bias inherent in quasi-experimental designs (for example, those who choose to participate in programming and to complete more of it might differ in other important respects that might affect their ability and willingness to change and which may have nothing to do with the efficacy of the program itself). However, sometimes such designs are the best that researchers or practitioners can do when assessing the outcomes of therapeutic communities or other such programs.

To some extent, the methods employed in an outcome evaluation depend on the outcomes of interest, the nature of the program and its setting, and the unique attributes of the participants. Typically, researchers examine correctional clients' post-program arrest and conviction records and any community corrections reports. Researchers might do interviews of key stakeholders and surveys of staff and participants to assess perspectives on outcomes, changes in attitudes, and other outcomes of interest.

The types of questions that researchers are typically interested in scientifically exploring include:

1. *During treatment*, did antisocial attitudes change for program completers?

2. *During treatment* or *post-release* who is most likely to benefit from the program (based on distinguishing offender characteristics)?

3. Are changes in criminal thinking or prosocial attitudes related to *post-release* decreases in drug use and recidivism?

4. Did *post-release* drug use and recidivism decrease for those exposed to, or who completed, treatment?

5. Is exposure to, or completion of aftercare, associated with favorable *post-release* outcomes?

6. What role did the treatment program have, if any, in affecting the organizational milieu where the program is located (from the perspective of the treatment providers, security, correctional officers, counselors, and the program participants)?

7. What organizational factors at the institution and during aftercare are associated with favorable *post-release* outcomes?

8. Was the length of aftercare associated with favorable *post-release* outcomes?

Research on Therapeutic Communities

The literature on substance abuse and related programming is replete with research evaluations that indicate successful treatment programming can be designed and implemented in the correctional environment (Andrews et al. 1990, Applegate, Langworthy and Latessa 1997, Lipton 1998, Office of Justice Programs 1998, Wexler, DeLeon, Thomas, Kressel and Peters 1999). The science, mostly in the form of quasi-experimental designs, indicates that cognitive-self-change programming and therapeutic communities both are positively associated with reductions in criminal offending and drug abuse (Andrews et al. 2001, Henning and Frueh 1996, Knight, Simpson, and Hiller 1999, Lipton 1998, Martin, Butzin, Saum and Inciardi 1999, Pearson and Lipton 1999, Siegal, Wang, Carlson, Falck, Rahma, and Fine 1999, Bhati, Roman and Chalfin 2008, Wexler, Melnick, Lowe, and Peters 1999), but, as mentioned earlier, this may not be true for any given program for any number of reasons.

Andrews (2006: 250-255) has noted that rehabilitation programming targeted to high-risk offenders (the "risk principle"), that targets "crime-producing needs" (the "need principle"), and that matches the "offenders' needs and learning styles" with "cognitive and behavioral treatment" (the "responsivity principle") are the best suited to achieve the desired effects. These include reducing recidivism and understanding of criminal thoughts and desired changes in attitudes and behaviors.

The most successful programs, then, are those that combine the delivery of substantive knowledge in an environment suited to therapeutic change. Research also indicates that cognitive attributes (as discussed in Chapter 11), positive modeling, behavioral redirection, emotional therapy, a treatment environment engendering trust and empathy, and intensive involvement in problem-solving by clients in their own treatment are also key to attaining actual behavioral change upon release (Andrews et al. 1990, Antonowicz and Ross 1997, Gendreau and Ross 1987, 1995, Henning and Freuh 1996, Inciardi 1995, McMurran 1995). Treatment programs directed at drug offenders also appear to achieve greater success in reducing recidivism when services are continued post release or at the completion of the program (Andrews 2006).

Research by Pearson and Lipton (1999) indicates that large effect sizes are associated with cognitive-based programs in changing criminal activity. Now, a substantial body of literature documents the success of prison-based therapeutic community programs in reducing substance abuse and recidivism, especially when combined with an aftercare component (Gendreau 1996, Knight, Simpson, Chatham and Camacho 1997, Knight, Simpson, and Hiller 1999, Linhorst, Knight, Johnston, and Trickey 2001, Martin, Butzin, and Inciardi 1995, Martin, Butzin, Saum, and Inciardi 1999, NIDA 2002, Pearson and Lipton 1999, Peters and Steinberg 2001, Wexler, Melnick, Lowe, and Peters 1999).

In a number of studies by the National Institute on Drug Abuse on therapeutic communities and other treatment programs (2002) that included data collected at admission, during treatment, and follow-ups of a year or more after treatment, the researchers found that participation in therapeutic communities led to positive outcomes. These studies found that participation in a therapeutic community was associated with several positive outcomes. For example, the Drug Abuse Treatment Outcome Study showed that those who successfully completed treatment in a therapeutic community had lower levels of all the followoing: cocaine, heroin, and alcohol use; criminal behavior; unemployment; and indicators of depression than they had before treatment (NIDA 2002: 2).

In addition to therapeutic communities themselves, many correctional agencies are attempting to implement cognitive-behavioral and social-learning approaches because they believe these treatment components answer the question "What Works?" to change offender behavior (Andrews, Zinger, Hoge, Bonta, Gendreau, and Cullen 2001). However, these same jurisdictions may be frustrated in their ability to combine these "best practices" in a complementary continuum of services. Yet, correctional agencies must understand how to integrate best practices to produce optimum-treatment outcomes. It is becoming the norm for therapeutic communities to include cognitive self-change programming as part of the treatment regimen.

The structure and intense pressure experienced in the therapeutic community leads to a large number of dropouts (either voluntary or removal initiated by staff or peers in the community). In one study of a prison-based therapeutic community, even among those who did complete the program, only 54.5 percent were drug free after six months of completion. This was significantly better than the 34.4 percent in a work-release control group, however. On a more positive note, 90.9 percent who completed the therapeutic community and were part of a postrelease outreach program were drug free during the same period (Hooper, Lockwood, and Inciardi 1993: 305).

An interesting treatment program, for addicts in a prison setting and then transitioned into the community upon their release, is the Delaware Multistage Program (Mathias 1997). At the beginning stage of the program, offenders spend twelve months in a prison-based therapeutic community called Key; in phase two they spend six months in a pre-release therapeutic community Crest; and finally in phase three, they receive an additional six months of counseling while on parole or in work release. Figure 17.1 compares drug use and arrest outcomes for offenders completing all phases (Key-Crest), Crest only, Key only, and a comparison group eighteen months after release from prison. It is heartening to see that 76 percent of the Key-Crest group remained drug free during the period and that 71 percent remained arrest free. Treatment participants in all phases did well compared with the control group, among whom only 19 percent remained drug free in the same period and only 30 percent remained arrest free.

Figure 17.1 Delaware Multistage Correctional Treatment Program Eighteen Months after Release from Prison

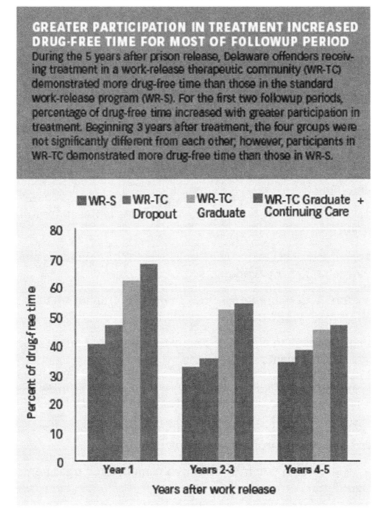

GREATER PARTICIPATION IN TREATMENT INCREASED DRUG-FREE TIME FOR MOST OF FOLLOWUP PERIOD

During the 5 years after prison release, Delaware offenders receiving treatment in a work-release therapeutic community (WR-TC) demonstrated more drug-free time than those in the standard work-release program (WR-S). For the first two followup periods, percentage of drug-free time increased with greater participation in treatment. Beginning 3 years after treatment, the four groups were not significantly different from each other; however, participants in WR-TC demonstrated more drug-free time than those in WR-S.

Source: R, Mathias, 1997. National Institute on Drug Abuse and Addiction: *National Institute of Drug Abuse Notes*, July.

Best Practices in Therapeutic Community Operation

As the research demonstrates, therapeutic communities when constructed and operated appropriately are more likely to produce the desired results. Not surprisingly, some of these practices also "work" for other treatment programs.

1. Adoption of therapeutic community programming that has achieved positive outcomes in other jurisdictions (learn from others' successes and failures)

2. Setting program funding at a level that ensures integrity in operation and staffing

3. Selection of staff with the requisite academic and experiential background to run, or work in, a therapeutic community

4. Compensation for staff that allows the program to attract and keep those who are qualified to deliver and maintain the program

5. Involvement of an outside research entity in program setup, operation, and review

6. Clear and complete (as much as is possible) separation of therapeutic community participants from other correctional clientele

7. Pre-training for treatment and correctional staff that covers the full gamut of setup, operation, and teamwork in a therapeutic community

8. Establishment of clear communication lines between treatment and security staff

9. Involvement of security, when possible, in therapeutic community treatment for participants

10. Assignment of only therapeutic community-trained security staff to work in the therapeutic community

11. Use of established classification instruments that target risk and need of participants

12. Careful selection of participants based on screens for participants' need for the program and its type of operation

13. Provision of therapeutic community rules and procedures manuals for staff and program participants

14. Staff supervision and intensive involvement in all treatment programming

15. Staff modeling of pro-social and community-oriented behaviors

16. Ongoing staff training that focuses on the development of community, program maintenance, and enhancement of skills

17. Cognitive-program components that focus on the recognition of thinking errors and cognitive restructuring

18. Participant community-leadership opportunities that build trust and responsibility

19. Positive community building opportunities (for example, group meetings and activities)

20. Opportunities for genuine engagement and problem solving for participants

21. Active learning opportunities for participants that involve speaking and writing, knowledge building and reflection

22. Weekly treatment-staff meetings that focus on treatment goals of participants and program operation. If the work environment is such that people can air mistakes, acknowledge them, and all learn from them, it is more likely that the program and staff can evolve to be more responsive to the needs of the participants.

23. Opportunities for participants to engage in co-programming (for example, anger or stress management, education or other skills development or parenting classes) or work, when appropriate

24. Regular and ongoing self-assessment by staff regarding program components and implementation

25. Provision of aftercare for participants that continues for a year or more after program completion

26. Process and outcome evaluations of the therapeutic communities at prescribed periods of time (for example, a process evaluation after one year, three years, and five years, and at regular intervals thereafter and an outcome evaluation at one year post-completion of the program, two and three years post-completion, and at regular intervals thereafter)

27. Use of multi-method assessment techniques in these evaluations, which include review of archived data, official reports, staff and participant interviews, observation of program operation and treatment delivery, and surveys of staff and participants. Collection of data pre- and post-treatment and comparison of like treatment participants with a control group would also tend to bolster any claims of program success and highlight areas needing remedial attention.

Resources

You could contact a number of agencies regarding therapeutic community establishment and operation, including the following:

Center for Substance Abuse Treatment, www.samhsa.gov/csat

National Clearinghouse on Alcohol and Drug Information, www.health.org

National Institute of Justice, www.ojp.usdoj.gov/nij

National Institute of Corrections, www.nicic.org

National Institute on Drug Abuse, www.drugabuse.gov

Summary: Where Do We Go From Here?

Wherever we go from here with correctional populations, it is clear that we cannot long sustain where we have been. The numbers of incarcerated people in this country have spiraled far beyond the ability of states and localities to maintain them decently. The Urban Institute report indicated that many of these addicted and incarcerated or supervised persons would benefit from treatment either in lieu of incarceration or in addition to it (Bhati et al. 2008). They also found, as have a number of researchers cited in this chapter regarding therapeutic communities, that treatment when done right has the potential to reduce recidivism.

Clearly, then, where we go from here is toward treatment. Therapeutic communities provide the type of structured, long-term, and intensive habilitative experience that yields reductions in substance abuse and dependency and, collaterally, crime. If operated with an eye to risk, need, and responsivity and with the integrity of treatment components in mind (for example, see the list of best practices delineated in this chapter), correctional program managers are more likely to achieve success with some correctional clients, some of the time.

Perspective from the Field
Therapeutic Communities

By Scott Brooks

Scott Brooks is Program Coordinator with the Idaho Department of Correction. He has worked as a Certified Alcohol and Drug Counselor for fourteen years in inpatient and outpatient treatment settings. Mr. Brooks co-authored Cognitive Self-Change—The Idaho Model. *He has worked exclusively with therapeutic communities for the past ten years. In conjunction with private contract and Idaho Department of Correction's staff, he began the first therapeutic community program in Idaho. He was instrumental in the development of the treatment and clinical manuals that have established the standard operating procedures for therapeutic community programs in Idaho.*

● ●

Whenever someone asks me the question, "What makes therapeutic communities work?" the first thing that comes to mind is the concept of community.

Community is the essential element of the therapeutic community that distinguishes therapeutic communities from other treatment models. Treatment participants are accustomed to the staff being the change agent. In the therapeutic communities, the community acts as the change agent.

Addicts and alcoholics who enter therapeutic communities have long-term substance-use histories that have affected all life areas. Most were raised in or became part of a counterculture. To survive in this counterculture, they are secretive and deceptive. In the counterculture, detection hinders substance use and related criminal acts; hence, secrecy is imperative to the lifestyle. Even within the counterculture, friendships and alliances are grounded in a mutually accepted level of mistrust and deception that they describe as "just the way things are." Lying is a primary tactic of survival that has worked in acquiring short-term gains, just as it may for all of us under the rationalization of "social necessity."

Think of it this way, not everyone who has secrets or lies is a criminal; the problem is that secrets and lying are woven together to continue a lifestyle, which results in use and harm to others. Consequently, therapeutic community participants have to learn trust and honesty, not just acquire it. Within other treatment settings, staff assume they must restore qualities lost in addiction to the participant's life. A challenge for staff is to recognize that qualities of community participation, self-esteem, work ethic, and family leadership have never been present in the first place. We do not restore, we introduce for the first time, experiences which are unfamiliar to our population.

In the therapeutic communities, social learning occurs within the context of everyday life as perceived and experienced by members of the community. Community members are placed within roles that are loosely defined by specific rules and tightly defined by values, creating situations where they must learn by failing.

A key difference from other residential substance use programs is that the therapeutic community supports trial-and-error learning. This provides an environment in which one can fail safely. Contrast this with the outside world that harbors greater risk of loss, humiliation, or punishment from performance failure. Remember, despite the feigned indifference or defensiveness, the substance user is embarrassed about his or her self-perceived deficits. To avoid participants focusing on only themselves and "working their own program," therapeutic communities evaluate not only the effect of the participant's behaviors and actions, but also the impact these behaviors and actions have on other community members. This concept of community acts as the antidote to selfishness and secrecy.

In therapeutic communities, individuals are placed in a position of being responsible for their own actions, and for the actions of others. This creates a well-focused awareness of self and others. This awareness strips away the ability to hide in secrecy and lies. The social-learning process extends to all activities within the therapeutic communities.

For example, at South Idaho Correctional Institution, due to the dormitory-style living areas, most residential interaction occurs within the confines of their living space. Daily operations of the therapeutic communities are held in the living space. These tasks may be as simple as participants being responsible for the cleanliness of their personal living area, to scheduling rotation of cleaning with twenty-five other participants. Over time, the level of responsibility is increased. A key factor is that attitude and commitment to the community are weighted more than skill level in determining increased levels of responsibility within the community.

I have seen several "treatment smart" individuals enter the therapeutic communities, read the participant manual, go to orientation and immediately think, "I've got this down." They will then become "therapeutic community machines" confronting their peer's behavior, attempting to gain staff favor, or giving the impression of compliance. The same individuals are always brought

Continued on the next page

Perspective from the Field, *continued*

to encounter group in front of all of their peers. Participants alert staff to the offense, and the process allows the accused to confront the confronter. This illustrates the strength of the therapeutic community process. Even when an individual attempts to subvert it, what "does not come out in the wash comes out in the rinse."

"People need people" is a common concept in therapeutic communities. Family, brotherhood, and a feeling of fellowship are essential to the functioning of a community. Without this, the community becomes hollow and has no heart. Fellowship assists the growth process and creates a spiritual nature to a community. The community will develop its own culture, language, lore, and history; in a sense, it will create its own culture. To achieve this, the individual must be an active, successful participant—people support what they build.

The therapeutic community elements and activities such as rules, daily meetings, groups, and overall process, focus upon reinforcing positive perceptions of the community—enhancing the feeling of fellowship. These perceptions include nurturing (providing for daily maintenance), hope, and possibility (perceived in staff and peer role models), safety (maintaining the cardinal rules against violence or other threats), trust (perceived acceptance for self-disclosure), bonding (positive interpersonal perceptions), and alliances (for example, friendships and affection). As participants progress in therapeutic communities, they feel the positive effects of fellowship and, in turn, impart this experience to the newly arrived participant. This creates a feedback loop sustaining the culture of fellowship within the community.

References and Suggested Readings

Andrews, D.A. 2006. The Principles of Effective Correctional Programs. In *Correctional Contexts: Contemporary and Classical Readings*, 3rd ed., E. J. Latessa and A. M. Holsinger, eds. Los Angeles, California: Roxbury Publishing Company.

Andrews, D. A., I. Zinger, R. D. Hoge, J. Bonta, P. Gendreau, and F. T. Cullen. 2001. "Does Correctional Treatment Work? A Clinically Relevant and Psychologically Informed Meta-Analysis." In E. J. Latessa, A. Holsinger, J. W. Marquart and J. R. Sorensen, eds. *Correctional Contexts: Contemporary and Classical Readings*. Los Angeles: Roxbury Publishing Company.

Andrews, D. A., I. Zinger, R. D. Hoge, J. Bonta, P. Gendreau, and F.T. Cullen. 1990. Does Correctional Treatment Work? A Clinically Relevant and Psychologically Informed Meta-Analysis. *Criminology* 28: 369-404.

Antonowicz, Daniel H. and Robert R. Ross. 1997. Essential Components of Successful Rehabilitation Programs for Offenders. In J. W. Marquart and J. R. Sorensen, eds. *Correctional Contexts: Contemporary and Classical Readings*. Los Angeles: Roxbury Publishing Company.

Applegate, B. K., R. H. Langworthy, and E. J. Latessa. 1997. Factors Associated with Success in Treating Chronic Drunk Drivers: The Turning Points Program. *Journal of Offender Rehabilitation* 24: 19-34.

Bhati, A., J. K. Roman, and A. Chalfin. 2008. *To Treat or Not to Treat: Evidence on the Prospects of Expanding Treatment to Drug-Involved Offenders*. Justice Policy Center, Urban Institute. Washington D.C.: Urban Institute.

Broekaert, E., S. Vandevelde, V. Soyez, R.Yates, and A. Slater. 2006. The Third Generation of Therapeutic Communities: The Early Development of the Therapeutic Communities for Addictions in Europe. *European Addiction Research* 12: 1-11.

Cullen, F. T. and K. Gilbert. 1982. *Reaffirming Rehabilitation*. Cincinnati, Ohio: Anderson.

Gendreau, P. 1996. The Principles of Effective Intervention with Offenders. In *Choosing Correctional Options that Work*, A. Harland, ed. Newbury Park, California: Sage Publications.

Gendreau, P. and R. R. Ross 1987. Revivification of Rehabilitation: Evidence for the 1980s. *Justice Quarterly* 4: 349-407.

———. 1995. Correctional Treatment: Some Recommendations for Effective Intervention. In *The Dilemmas of Corrections: Contemporary Readings*, 3rd ed. K. C. Haas and G. P. Alpert, eds. Prospect Heights, Illinois: Waveland Press.

Gornik, M. and D. Bush. 2000. Design and Implementation of a Cognitive Community. Research Brief submitted to the Maine Department of Corrections.

Gornik, M., D. Bush, and M. Labarbera. 1999. Strategies for Application of the Cognitive Behavioral/Social Learning Model to Offender Programs. Technical Assistance Proposal. Washington, D.C.: National Institute of Corrections.

Henning, K. R. and B. C. Frueh.1996. Cognitive-Behavioral Treatment of Incarcerated Offenders: An Evaluation of the Vermont Department of Corrections' Cognitive Self-Change Program. *Criminal Justice and Behavior* 23: 523-541.

Hooper, R., D. Lockwood, and J. Inciardi. 1993. Treatment Techniques in Corrections-Based Therapeutic Communities. *The Prison Journal* 73: 290-306.

Inciardi, J. A. 1995. The Therapeutic Community: An Effective Model for Corrections-Based Drug Abuse Treatment. In K. C. Haas, and G. P. Alpert, eds. *The Dilemmas of Corrections: Contemporary Readings*, 3rd ed. Prospect Heights, Illinois: Waveland Press.

Knight, K., D. D. Simpson, L. R. Chatham, and L. M. Camacho. 1997. An Assessment of Prison-Based Drug Treatment: Texas' In-Prison Therapeutic Community Program. *Journal of Offender Rehabilitation* 24: 75-100.

Knight, K., D. D. Simpson, and M. L. Hiller. 1999. Three Year Reincarceration Outcomes for In-Prison Therapeutic Community Treatment in Texas. *The Prison Journal* 79: 337-351.

Leukefeld, C., H. M. McDonald, A. Staton, M. Mateyoke-Scrivner, T. Webster, T. Logan, and T. Garitty. 2003. An Employment Intervention for Drug Abusing Clients. *Federal Probation* 67: 27-32.

Leukefeld, C. G. and F. M. Tims, eds. 1992. *National Institute on Drug Abuse Research Monograph Series: Drug Abuse Treatment in Prisons and Jails*. Rockville, Maryland: National Institute on Drug Abuse.

Lightfoot, L. 1999. Treating Substance Abuse and Dependence in Offenders: A Review of Methods and Outcomes. In E. Latessa, ed., *Strategic Solutions: The International Community Corrections Association Examines Substance Abuse*. Alexandria, Virginia: American Correctional Association.

Linhorst, D. M., K. Knight, J. S., Johnston and M. Trickey. 2001. Situational Influences on the Implementation of a Prison-Based Therapeutic Community. *The Prison Journal* 81: 436-453.

Lipton, D. S. 1998. Treatment for Drug Abusing Offenders During Correctional Supervision: A Nationwide Overview. *Journal of Offender Rehabilitation* 26: 1-45.

Lipton, D., G. P. Falkin, and H. K. Wexler. 1992. Correctional Drug Abuse Treatment in the United States: An Overview. In *National Institute on Drug Abuse Research Monograph Series: Drug Abuse Treatment in Prisons and Jails*, C.G. Leukefeld and F. M. Tims, eds. Rockville, Maryland: National Institute on Drug Abuse.

Litt, M. and S. Mallon. 2003. The Design of Social Support Networks for Offenders in Outpatient Drug Treatment. *Federal Probation* 67: 15-22.

Martin, S. S., C. A. Butzin, and J. A. Inciardi. 1995. Assessment of a Multi Stage Therapeutic Community for Drug-Involved Offenders. *Journal of Psychoactive Drugs* 27: 109-116.

Martin, S. S., C.A. Butzin, C.A. Saum, and J. A. Inciardi. 1999. Three-Year Outcomes of Therapeutic Community Treatment for Drug-Involved Offenders in Delaware: From Prison to Work Release to Aftercare. *The Prison Journal* 79: 294-320.

Martinson, R. 1974. What Works? Questions and Answers about Prison Reform. *The Public Interest* 35: 22-54.

Mathias, R. 1997. National Institute on Drug Abuse and Addiction: *National Institute of Drug Abuse Notes*, July.

McMurran, Mary. 1995. Alcohol Interventions in Prisons: Towards Guiding Principles for Effective Intervention. *Psychology, Crime and Law* 1: 215-226.

National Institute on Drug Abuse. 2006. *Principles of Drug Abuse Treatment for Criminal Justice Populations: A Research-Based Guide*. Washington, D.C.: National Institutes of Health, U. S. Department of Health and Human Services.

———. 2002. *Therapeutic Community: Research Report Series*. Washington, D.C.: National Institutes of Health, U.S. Department of Health and Human Services.

———. 1996. The Brain's Drug Reward System. *National Institute of Drug Abuse Notes*, 11: Tear off Sheet. Washington, D.C.: National Institutes of Health, U.S. Department of Health and Human Services.

Office of Justice Programs. 1998. *Residential Substance Abuse Treatment for State Prisoners*. Washington, D.C.: U.S. Department of Justice.

Palmer, T. 1995. The "Effectiveness" Issue Today: An Overview. In *The Dilemmas of Corrections: Contemporary Readings, 3rd ed.* K. C. Haas and G. P. Alpert, eds. Prospect Heights, Illinois: Waveland Press.

Pearson, F. S. and D. S. Lipton 1999. A Meta-Analytic Review of the Effectiveness of Corrections-Based Treatments for Drug Abuse. *Prison Journal* 79: 384-410.

Peters, R. H. and M. L. Steinberg. 2001. Substance Abuse Treatment in U.S. Prisons. In *Correctional Contexts: Contemporary and Classical Readings*, E. J. Latessa, A. Holsinger, J. W. Marquart and J. R. Sorensen, eds. Los Angeles: Roxbury Publishing.

Ruefle, W. and J. M. Miller. 1999. *Final Report: Evaluation of the South Carolina Residential Substance Abuse Treatment Program for State Prisoners*. Washington, D.C.: National Institute of Justice.

Schuiteman, J. G. and T. G. Bogle. 1996. *Evaluation of the Department of Corrections' Indian Creek Therapeutic Community: Progress Report*. Richmond, Virginia: The Criminal Justice Research Center, Virginia Department of Criminal Justice Services.

Siegal, H. A., J. Wang, R. G. Carlson, R. S. Falck, A. M., Rahman, and R. L. Fine. 1999. Ohio's Prison-Based Therapeutic Community Treatment Programs for Substance Abusers: Preliminary Analysis of Re-Arrest Data. *Journal of Offender Rehabilitation* 28: 33-48.

Stohr, M. K., C. Hemmens, D. Baune, J. Dayley, M. Gornik, K.Kjaer, and C. Noon. 2000. *Final Report: Residential Substance Abuse Treatment for State Prisoners (RSAT) Partnership Process Evaluation*. Washington, D.C.: National Institute of Justice.

Wexler, H. K., G. DeLeon, G. Thomas, D. Kressel, and J. Peters. 1999. The Amity Prison Therapeutic Communities Evaluation. *Criminal Justice and Behavior* 26: 147-167.

Wexler, H. K., G. P. Falkin, D. S. Lipton, and A. B. Rosenblum. 1992. Outcome Evaluation of a Prison Therapeutic Community for Substance Abuse Treatment. In *National Institute on Drug Abuse Research Monograph Series: Drug Abuse Treatment in Prisons and Jails*. C. G. Leukefeld and F. M. Tims, eds. Rockville, Maryland: National Institute on Drug Abuse.

Wexler, H. K., G. Melnick, L. Lowe, and J. Peters. 1999. Three-Year Reincarceration Outcomes for Amity In-Prison Therapeutic Community and Aftercare in California. *The Prison Journal* 79: 321-336.

Wexler, H. K. and R. Williams 1986.The Stay 'N Out Therapeutic Community: Prison Treatment for Substance Abusers. *Journal of Psychoactive Drugs* 18: 221-230.

Young, D. and R. Porter. 1999. *A Collaborative Evaluation of Pennsylvania's Program for Drug-Involved Parole Violators*. Washington, D.C.: National Institute of Justice.

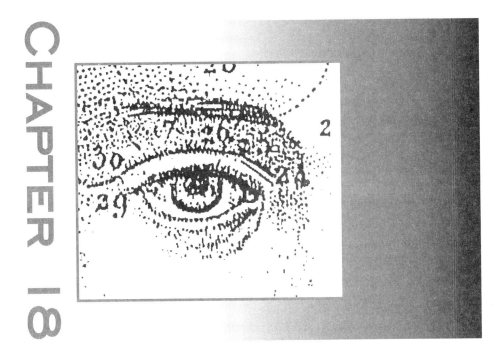

CHAPTER 18

The Sex Offender

Sex offenders had better not be viewed as horrible, villainous criminals who have to be harshly punished. . . . They can, rather, be diagnosed either as relatively healthy individuals who are rash enough to get into occasional difficulty, or a more seriously disturbed persons whose sexual behavior puts them in frequent conflict with the law.

—**Albert Ellis**

Sex and American Society

Sexual offenses encompass such a wide range of behaviors that you reasonably may question the wisdom of placing all of them in a single polyglot category. After all, the exhibitionist is as different from the rapist as the check forger is from the armed robber. Up until 2003, if you lived in a state that has anti-sodomy laws you may even have committed a felony if you had engaged in oral or anal sex (in some states, with a member of either sex), even with your consenting spouse. In 2003 the U.S. Supreme Court ruled Texas' anti-sodomy law unconstitutional in *Lawrence v. Texas*, which means sex offenses are now offenses that only involve a true offender/victim relationship, such as rape and child molesting; that is, behavior that is almost universally considered to be a serious breach of lawful behavior.

We have to view the sex offender and his behavior in the context of his culture (we use the male personal pronoun because sex offenders are almost invariably male, although there may be more female perpetrators than is generally suspected [Denov

2003]). Few things interest Americans more than sex. Our culture is shot through with sexual themes. Americans spend billions of dollars every year on cosmetics, hair styling, breath mints, health spas, and so forth, to make us appear sexually attractive. Ears (as well as other sundry parts of the body) are pierced, lips painted, underarms sprayed, necklines lowered, and skirts raised, and young men advertise their wares by pouring their salon tanned limbs into shrunken jeans. Goaded on by the wizards of Madison Avenue, many of us have fallen prey to the notion that we are less than good Americans if we are not supremely sexual beings.

The Public Image of the Sex Offender

Americans do not like sex offenders. They are the only group of offenders we keep in prison under indefinite civil commitment laws after they have completed their criminal sentences, a practice given the seal of approval by the U.S. Supreme Court in *Kansas v. Hendricks* (1997). This remedy is well applied to sexual predators (and Henricks was certainly that), but there is a danger that it may be applied to less serious sexual offenders in the future. Practices such as this, as well as notification and registration laws, set sex offenders apart from other offenders (all fifty states now have such laws on the books [Talbot et al. 2002]). These laws apply to adjudicated juvenile delinquent sex offenders as well as adult offenders, which means that they will have to register as convicted sex offenders for the rest of their lives unless the law changes. This may be appropriate for a seventeen-year-old youth who rapes toddlers, but it has been applied to a twelve-year old boy who mooned a group of younger children, and a fifteen-yerar-old boy who grabbed the breasts of a female classmate (Trivits and Repucci 2002). Applying draconian measures such as these across the board trivializes the horrible experiences of real victims.

As a society, we appear to be convinced that the sex criminal is a brutally depraved and oversexed monster who spends his time haunting dirty movies and teenage hangouts; an incurable, spiritually disfigured "dirty old man." He is a "species apart," either a "super male" in an interminable state of tumescence or a pathetic and evil old man searching for sparks of sensuality in the unwilling arms of a child (Quinn, Forsyth, and Mullen-Quinn 2004). Although such characteristics are sometimes true, all "sex offenders," unfortunately, tend to be defined by the very worst of their kind. According to Quinn, Forsyth, and Mullen-Quinn (2004) current American attitudes about sex offenders have been formed by sensationalized news media accounts of extremely atypical sex offenders, and Brian Francis (2002) describes a similar situation of "moral panic" existing in Britain.

No common denominator distinguishes all sex offenders. Unlike the typical robber or burglar, sex offenders are businessmen, physicians, teachers, attorneys, police officers, and ministers, as well as unskilled laborers and "street people." In terms of their crimes, a sex offender can be everything from a sexual sadist who uses his penis to defile and degrade his victim to the gentle and unassuming church deacon who "playfully" touches a neighborhood child where he should not. There are certainly differences between the sex offender whose passion for his new date exceeds her expectations and the rapist who attacks with equal intensity the nubile homecoming queen and the octogenarian cripple—differences that will affect your sentencing recommendations and treatment strategies. Likewise, there is the father who feels that he has the lordly "right of the first night" with a succession of his offspring versus the father who offends once and is then mortified by what he has done.

Rape and Rapists

Forcible rape is defined in the Federal Bureau of Investigation's *Uniform Crime Reports* (UCR) as: "the carnal knowledge of a female forcibly and against her will" (Federal Bureau of Investigation 2007: 27). According to this report, there were 93,934 reported rapes in 2006. Even though rape rates have been decreasing steadily since 1990, rape is still perhaps the most underreported of all crimes, probably because of the fear and embarrassment suffered by its victims. According to the 2009 National Crime Victimization Survey (NCVS), there were an estimated 203,830 sexual assaults in 2008 against victims age twelve and older (Rand, 2009). In other words, approximately three times as many rapes occur for every rape reported to the police. No doubt that rape is an excruciatingly traumatic event for its victims, the effects of which may last long after any physical scars have healed. This can be true even if the perpetrator is an acquaintance, boyfriend, date, or even the spouse of the victim.

The views of the rapist in the professional literature run the gamut, with many of the opinions being strongly colored by such nonobjective factors as personal morality and sexual politics. Each view, of course, fits some rapists, but no view fits all rapists. There are those who regard rape as being symptomatic of some dark psychological disturbances and others who see it simply as part of a complex of cultural values that emphasize macho masculinity, power, aggression, and violence. The first of these views is exemplified by the work of Drzasga, who explains rape as an act performed by "degenerate male imbeciles" seeking to satisfy "sadistic and aggressive desires for sexual dominance" (1960: 57). In this perspective, rape is a violent rather than a sexual act in which the penis substitutes for the gun or knife.

This view may be accurate in some unknown percentage of rape cases, but to ascribe such motivations across the board is to commit what philosophers call the logical fallacy of affirming the consequent. *Affirming the consequent* means that having observed the consequences of an action, we infer that they were the motivations of the actor. Thus, we observe that the rapist asserts his dominance over his victim and in doing so humiliates, defiles, and degrades her. It is unwarranted, however, to assume that this outcome necessarily constituted his motivations for his crime.

The common assertion that "there is nothing sexual about rape" may be politically correct, but it ignores the fact that if intercourse were accomplished, the sexual component of the act is the only one of which we can be sure everything else is conjecture. We have no direct access to a rapist's motivations beyond the sexual. Many imprisoned rapists will eventually convince a counselor that their motivations were to degrade and defile their victims. However, do they do this because those were indeed their motivations, or do they do it because they have learned that the way to obtain parole points is to tell officials what they think the officials want to hear? "Confess your crime, confront your crime, understand the motives for your crime, and show remorse for your crime:" These are the conditions of the parole game that inmates soon learn. Is it really only coincidence that sophisticated criminals always seem to explain their behavior in accordance with the contemporary academic explanation?

While it is true that the feminist perspective generally rejects the idea of sexual motivation for rape, some feminists now recognize the sexual motivation for rape, claiming that the "not sex" argument was initially necessary to emphasize that women got no pleasure out of being raped (Gilmartin 1994; Herman 1990; Mealey 2003). Very few American females (about 18 percent) and even fewer males (about 9 percent) believe that rape is committed because of nonsexual motives such at hatred and anger (Hall 1987).

The clinical perspective (the perspective of those engaged in the assessment and treatment of rapists) remains tied to the notion that rape is primarily sexually motivated (Barbaree and Marshall 1991). The contemporary treatment literature is replete with studies that explicitly or implicitly view rape as sexually motivated. This is evident by the treatment modalities, which emphasize cognitive restructuring for deviant sexual fantasies and/or medications designed to reduce sexual arousal (Bogaerts et al. 2008; Dreznick 2003; Giotakos et al. 2003; Grubin 2007; *Harvard Mental Health Letter* 2004; Howard 2002; Lindsay, Maletzky, and Field 2003). Science rather than sexual politics should be the guide to the "true" nature of this horrible crime. In a plea to de-politicize rape, Craig Palmer asserts that the "not sex" explanation prevents researchers from learning more about the phenomenon of rape, and this occurs "at the expense of an increased number of rape victims" (1994: 59). Palmer's point is that if we misidentify the motives of rapists, we compromise treatment plans for the rapist as well as efforts at rape prevention. This is what should concern us most as correctional workers.

Lee Ellis supplies voluminous evidence to support his contention, that rape is "sexually motivated, and that aggressiveness and dominating behavior exhibited by rapists largely reflect tactics rather than goals" (1991: 632). However, he agrees that the drive to possess and control is a motive, although it is secondary to the sex drive. He states that in the overwhelming majority of acquaintance rapes, force is used only after other tactics (pleading, use of alcohol, claims of love) have failed, which makes it difficult to claim that rape is "nonsexual." Similarly, Figueredo and his colleagues (2000: 315) write that "Coercive sexual strategies" are engaged in "when the major noncoercive and prosocial avenues of sexual expression fail." Additionally, the nonhuman equivalent of rape exists in a number of animal species, making it difficult to claim that similar behavior in humans is motivated by hatred of females, or is the result of socialization (Thornhill and Palmer 2000).

While Ellis (1991) claims that the motivation for rape is unlearned (the sex drive and the drive to possess and control are considered the products of evolutionary selection forces), the specific behavior surrounding it is learned. The mechanisms he proposes are those of operant conditioning. The raw basics of operant conditioning boil down to stating that behavior that is rewarded tends to be repeated, and punished behavior tends to become extinguished. He contends that males who have successfully employed "pushy" tactics to gain sexual favors have been reinforced in that behavior. The early reinforcements may have been little more than a necking or petting session, but if he learns that each time he escalates his pushiness that he gains greater sexual access, his behavior will gradually be shaped in ways that eventually could lead to rape.

It appears that the majority of rapes are motivated by misdirected and misguided sexual desires rather than by dark, sadistic, and disturbed psychological motivations far removed from sex. We readily grant, however, that male dominance feelings are an integral part of sexual relations, whether consensual or otherwise. Perhaps rape is best viewed as a fusion of sex and aggression because both sexual and aggressive behavior is mediated by the same neurological substrates, and both are facilitated and activated by the same sex steroids (Grubin 2007; Marshall and Barbaree 1990; Pinel 2000).

As a correctional worker, you will be doing offenders a disservice if you succumb uncritically to pat interpretations that sound esoteric but may well be empty. Perhaps the best way to view someone accused of rape is suggested by Albert Ellis in the epigraph to this chapter; that is, unless there is evidence to the contrary (for example, the perpetrator is a repeat offender), you should view him as a relatively psychologically healthy individual who has committed a very odious crime.

Most rapes involve offenders and victims who are acquainted with one another. Many men who are convicted of rape under these circumstances are enamored of traditional masculine values. They value sexual prowess and tend to hold the "whore/Madonna" image of women. They have difficulty understanding how their victims could be so ungrateful as to accuse them of rape. They feel that once a woman's initial protestations are overcome in a forceful "masculine" way, just like the romantic heroes in the movies, then she should just melt into their arms. After all, in the world of veiled sexual messages it is "common knowledge" to them that "no" really means "yes," or at least "Maybe, if I push hard enough."

Here is an excerpt from a presentence investigation report in which the processing officer is commenting on the statement of a defendant convicted of raping his sister in law. This defendant came home drunk one night (rape is often associated with alcohol), dragged his seventeen-year old sister-in-law into his bedroom, told his sleeping wife to get up and get out, and proceeded to rape her sister:

> It is clear from the defendant's explicit statement that he does not deny the charge. On the contrary, one almost gets the impression that he rather enjoyed writing his statement, which depicts him as an accomplished lover and mentor to the sexually naive.
>
> "How can this be rape?" he asks in an aggrieved tone of voice. He believes that his amorous designs were pursued fully in accord with the rules of the game; i.e., in the "masculine" way of his subculture. For him the crime was little more than an "assault with a friendly weapon." It strains this officer's imagination to think of the defendant as venting his sexual passions on an unwilling girl whose mother was in the next room fully aware of what was going on. Not only that, he had the audacity to ask his wife to vacate her bed so that he could do his thing in comfort.

After this young man was placed on probation, he actually divorced his wife and married his victim! This event corresponds to one of the strangest (yet consistently found) findings related to date rape, to wit: "a significant percentage [of date rape victims] continue to date a date rapist after the rape," and that, "a larger percentage of women continue to date the perpetrator of a completed rape than of an attempted but uncompleted rape" (Mealey 2003: 91, emphasis original). We wonder what Freud would make of such findings? Perhaps it is explicable in terms of the same mechanisms that lead many battered women to remain with their spouses and boyfriends.

Rapists, such as the above young man, use aggression as a means to an end, not as an end in itself. Many of them might not have gone on to complete the act if they did not harbor stereotypes of women as sexual playthings who "really" want to "be taken," even if they do put up a little token resistance. Many date rapes and acquaintance rapes would not occur if males who engage in this type of behavior rid themselves of such stereotypes. Females also would do well to divest themselves of their own stereotypes of femininity. Talking to many victims of date and acquaintance rape often reveals that they tend to be passive, nonassertive types with traditional views of the relationship between the sexes. Counselors at rape crisis centers will frequently state that many rapes can be avoided if women forcefully assert their rights to their own bodies.

There are predatory rapists who do become more sexually aroused when victims fight back, and may even be impotent without such stimuli. They may prefer violent to consensual sex and defiling and humiliating their victims may be "necessary" for them to achieve sexual satisfaction. Such rapes tend to be stranger rapes and are thus more terrifying and physically injurious to the victim. Rapists of this type tend to have marked feelings of inadequacy, inferiority, and powerlessness, and tend to be highly sexed and socially inadequate, especially in terms of heterosocial competence—they lack the ability "to interact with a person of the opposite sex in an actual, hypothetical, or potentially romantic situation, or the ability to correctly interpret a woman's affective cues" (Dreznick 2003: 177).

Unlike the typical date or acquaintance rapist, stranger rapists tend to have histories of other violent crimes (Freeman 2007; Mills, Anderson, and Kroner 2004). Most studies of rapists concentrate on the violent rapist. We do know with relative certainty that among these subjects violence is an important component of the sexual excitement they obtain from their crimes, just as whips and other devices are important to masochists and sadists, and enema hoses are to klismaphiliacs. This pattern of preferential violence is determined by comparing penile responses of convicted rapists with those of nonrapists when exposed to sexual stimuli with a strong content of violence. A device called a penile plethysmograph, which is rather like a blood pressure gauge, measures penile response. The penile plethysmograph measures the pressure of blood in the penis to ascertain how sexually excited subjects become when exposed to auditory and/or visual stimuli depicting various sexual situations. Violent rapists become significantly more aroused than nonrapists or nonviolent rapists when exposed to this material (Robertiello and Terry 2007; Tong 2007).

Most men will show some penile response to a variety of sexual stimuli, especially novel stimuli, even if they consider it deviant and would not engage in such behavior. The value of the penile plethysmograph lies not only in comparing the responses of convicted rapists with those of "normal" males, but also in comparing rapists' penile responses to stimuli depicting violent sex to their responses to stimuli depicting nonviolent consensual sex. For instance, if a rapist achieves a 30 percent erection when viewing nonviolent sex and one of 80 percent when viewing violent sex, we can conclude both that he is more interested in violent than consensual sex and that he is probably a dangerous individual. Likewise, if a man has a 90 percent erection in response to sexual stimuli involving young boys and one of only 5 percent to stimuli involving adult females, we can conclude that he is a homosexual pedophile. The penis, unlike its owner, finds it difficult to lie.

Such findings do seem to indicate that the violent rapist is "sick" in that he apparently needs violence to complete the sexual act. Strangely enough, although rape was once considered for inclusion in the 1985 edition of the American Psychiatric Association's *Diagnostic and Statistical Manual*, it has never been listed as a sexual deviation in any edition thus far (Janus 2004). The American Psychiatric Association apparently does not see any clearly defined syndrome associated with rape that could be called "rapism" in the same way that they identify conditions such as exhibitionism and pedophilia. Violent rapists simply may be violent men who take what they want, whether it is money, or sex, or anything else (Mills, Anderson, and Kroner 2004). Their sexual offenses appear to be part of a pattern of violent criminality. However, the correctional worker's primary concern should be the safety of the public. Accordingly, individuals who exhibit patterns of violent behavior should be placed in custodial care for as long as the law allows.

A Look at Stranger versus Date/Acquaintance Rape

Data on sex offenders reveal some remarkable differences between stranger and date/acquaintance rape that suggest that quite different men commit these offenses. Victims of stranger rape tend to range more broadly in age, typically from about ten to seventy. The age range of victims of date/acquaintance rape is typically much smaller (fourteen through forty-four), as would be expected in a dating context. Stranger rapists have significantly more serious criminal histories, are of significantly lower class, and are much younger (Figueredo et al. 2000; Mills, Anderson, and Kroner 2004). In one study, 80 percent of the victims of stranger rape were physically harmed, as opposed to 33.3 percent of the date/acquaintance category; 73 percent of the stranger rapists used some kind of weapon, as opposed to 21 percent of the acquaintance rapists, and 66.7 percent were drug and/or alcohol addicts, as opposed to 12 percent of the others (Walsh 1983).

Unlike stranger rape, which almost by definition involves the perpetrator's expectation of violence, in most instances of date rape, force is used only after various other nonviolent tactics have been tried (Ellis 1991, Figueredo et al. 2000, Mealey 2003). Of course, you should not construe this data as minimizing date rape. Date rape can cause injuries that go beyond the physical. The betrayal of trust that is inherent in date rape may be psychologically more deleterious to the victim than the physical and psychological pains of stranger rape.

Assessment and Treatment of Sex Offenders

It is part of popular lore that sex offenders are untreatable and cannot prevent their compulsive offending. For instance, Fortney and his colleagues (2007) conducted a study of attitudes about sex offenders among community members and sex offenders and found huge differences in the perceptions of both groups on a variety of sex offender-related questions. For example, the published data on sexually reoffending for convicted sex offenders shows that about 14 percent will re-offend, but the estimate of their sample of sex offenders was that 21 percent will, and the community sample estimated that 74 percent will. Fortney et al. (2007: 1) commented: "Common misconceptions may interfere with offenders' treatment and reintegration into society as well as influence legislatures to pass laws that are misguided and inefficient (2007: 1). Indeed, many of the laws that apply only to sex offenders seem almost purposely designed to prevent rehabilitation and reintegration.

Thus, taken as a whole, sex offenders are less likely to re-offend than any other type of offender. Researchers looking at years of British crime statistics found that sex offenders were the least likely (19 percent) to recidivate within two years of being released from prison, and that burglars (76 percent) were the most likely (Mawby 2001: 182). Reviews of U.S. studies conducted by the Center for Sex Offender Management (Bynum, et al. 2006) examining recidivism of sex offenders broken down by different types of offenders found the following ranges of recidivism:

- Child molesters with male victims (13 - 40 percent)
- Child molesters with female victims (10 - 29 percent)

- Rapists (7 - 35 percent)

- Incest offenders (4 - 10 percent)

Different studies find different rates of re-offending because of different defini-tions (do we include all offenses or only sex offenses as a measure of recidivism?) and different follow-up periods. Of course, recidivism rates include only those of-fenders who have been caught, so the above rates should be considered only as bare minimum figures. This, of course, is also true of recidivism studies of all offenders.

Perhaps the most instructive study of recidivism conducted to date was a study by the Bureau of Justice Statistics whose researchers tracked 9,691 sex offenders re-leased from prisons in fifteen states in 1994 (Langan, Schmitt, and Durose 2003). These men were followed for a period of three years after release. As with the British data reported by Mawby (2001), over the three-year period sex offenders had a lower rate of rearrest (43 percent) than 272,111 non-sex offenders released at the same time in the same states (68 percent). The 43 percent re-arrest rate for sex offenders included all types of crimes and technical violations such as failing to register as a sex offender or missing appointments with their parole officers; only 3.5 percent were reconvicted of a new sex crime during the follow-up period. We should repeat and underscore that: only 3.5 percent were reconvicted for a new sex offense. Of course, this is not to deny that there are true sexual predators, who will indeed continue to prey while at liberty to do so.

Public outrage at rapists and child molesters has made the idea of treatment rather than administration of swift punishment for sex offenders a very unpopular idea. However, Quinn, Forsyth, and Mullen-Quinn (2004) point out that the realization that most incarcerated sex offenders will eventually be released has generated a de-mand for treatment to insure a successful reintegration into the community, and from their review of a number of studies dealing with sex-offender treatment programs, they are cautiously optimistic. Most studies did report a gratifying rate of success when comparing results from treated versus untreated offenders. Although none of these studies dealt with the violent rapist, the general impression gleaned from their totality is that incest and heterosexual child molesters showed the most treatment success, and homosexual child molesters performed worst (Gendreau and Ross 1987).

A review of twelve meta-analyses covering 356 different studies found that nine of the meta-analyses were positive (treatment "works"), three were inconclusive, but none was negative (Lotke 1996: 2). Another review of seventy-nine studies with a total of 10,988 sex offenders found an overall recidivism rate of 13 percent among treated offenders compared to 18 percent for untreated offenders (Alexander 1999). Recidi-vism was defined as rearrest for a sexual offense (although follow-up periods differed greatly). While this percentage difference does not seem much, it still represents a lot of women and children who remained unvictimized. Quinn, Forsyth, and Mullen-Quinn (2004) cite federal statistics from a three-year follow-up study that show sex of-fenders reoffend at a much lower rate than other offenders convicted of other types of assaultive crimes.

The assessment and treatment of sexual offenders is almost always conducted by mental health teams; your job as a correctional worker is to refer offenders to them and to monitor their treatment. If an offender's crime or his record of sexual offenses warrant it, you should refer him to a diagnostic center, or to individual psychologists or psychiatrists in communities lacking such a specialized center. Typically, the offender is administered a series of tests such as the MMPI and an IQ test, and he undergoes a series of psychosocial interviews. The judge and the PSI investigator receive the results of these tests, a diagnosis, treatment prognosis, and a sentencing recommendation. One study suggests that the diagnosis tends to be a reflection of behavior (such as a nonviolent child molester labeled as a "passive aggressive pedophile"), and the prognosis and sentencing recommendation are entirely a function of the severity of the offense and of the offender's criminal history (Walsh 1990).

Treatment for the violent rapist (the stranger rapist) is extremely difficult and the results discouraging. Alexander's (1999) study cited above found a recidivism rate of 20.1 percent for treated rapists compared to 23.7 percent for untreated rapists. These rates went up to 29.3 percent after five years for treated offenders (no data were available for untreated offenders). Many treatments such as aversive conditioning (a method of treatment by which an offender is shown sexually arousing pictures in conjunction with some sort of punishing stimuli, such as an electric shock or some foul-smelling substance) have been drastically curtailed in the United States because of civil rights considerations (Marsh and Walsh 1995).

Therapeutic castration (surgical removal of the testes) appears to be the most effective form of treatment. A review of European literature involving 2,055 sex-offending castrates followed over time—as long as twenty years—found extremely low recidivism rates ranging from zero to 7.4 percent (Bradford 1990). A later review of more studies from the early to mid-twentieth century (surgical castration has since been discontinued in all European Union countries) found similar lifetime low recidivism rates (Harrison 2007).

As we have seen, studies of violent rapists in the United States show that they have much higher rates of known recidivism regardless of whether treated (with methods other than surgical or drug intervention) or not (Alexander 1999). Another review of a number of castration studies of men with high pre-surgery recidivism show post-surgery recidivism rates in the 2-to-3-percent range (Maletzky and Field 2003). The castration research offers strong support for those who favor theories of rape that emphasize hormonal factors (coupled with inadequate socialization) in the etiology of rape, such as Ellis (1991) and Thornhill and Palmer (2000). Although surgical castration has been tried in the United States in the past and has been largely discontinued for civil rights reasons, Texas surgically castrated three offenders between 1997 and 2005 (Harrison 2007).

It remains to be seen how the courts will ultimately view chemical castration by the use of drugs, such as medroxyprogesterone (Depo Provera) or cyproterone acetate (Andocur), on offenders with excessive sex drives that place them at risk for reoffending. Depo Provera reduces libido by drastically reducing testicular production of testosterone, and Andocur does the same thing by blocking testosterone receptors (Maletzky and Field 2003). People call such drugs "limbic hypothalamic tranquilizers" because they "allow the offender to concentrate on his psychosocial problems without the distracting fantasies and urges accompanying androgen driven limbic hypothalamic activity" (Marsh and Walsh 1995: 87). Grubin (2007: 442) makes a similar statement: "By blocking testosterone receptors, cyproterone [acetate] lowers both psychological arousal and interest (libido) and the physical ability to an erection, with a reduction in the frequency of masturbation, 'sexual tension,' and sexual fantasies." He also adds that selective serotonin reuptake inhibitors such as Prozac and Zoloft (these drugs inhibit impulsivity) and cognitive-behavioral therapy should be part of a comprehensive treatment regimen.

In other words, these drugs reduce the effects of the male sex hormone, testosterone, which leads to a diminution of sexual arousal. With the activity of the more primitive brain area (the limbic system) dampened, the counselor can concentrate on combating neocortical weaknesses ("thinking errors") with cognitive behavioral therapy. We should note that castration does not eliminate the sex drive, and that a castrate can become aroused with a willing partner's patient stimulation. What are greatly reduced are sex offenders' excessive and compulsive sexual fantasies and desires.

Chemical castration was mandated into law in California in 1997 and several other states (such as Iowa, Florida, Montana, and Texas) and many countries (such as Belgium, Germany, Sweden, Hungary, and Italy) have similar laws (Harrison 2007). Some states require it for repeat offenders, some for first-time offenders if the offense was particularly heinous, and some as a condition of probation or parole

Not all sex offenders need to be treated with such drugs, however. Most therapists believe that they should be reserved for the most chronic and recalcitrant offenders who have previously failed cognitive-behavioral treatment. A pilot program run by the Oregon Department of Corrections uses a weighted 13-point scale called the Depo-Provera Scale to assess suitability for this type of treatment. According to the lead researchers in this program: "Those with hypersexuality, impaired impulse control, developmental disabilities, or homosexual pedophilia were deemed particularly appropriate [Depo-Provera treatment targets]" (Maletzky and Field 2003: 399). The authors emphasize that pharmacological treatment should always be accompanied by intense cognitive-behavioral counseling.

Whereas the convicted violent rapist nearly always is incarcerated, the date or acquaintance rapist tends to get probation more often than imprisonment. The treatment of the latter type of rapist while on probation should center on group counseling sessions to correct "thinking errors" in which stereotypical images of women are brought out into the open and discussed. Educating males to accept women as equals who have the right to say "no" can go a long way toward preventing a reoccurrence.

As we have seen, it is a sad fact that many men do actually believe that women "ask for it" if they accept a date or willingly engage in any physical behavior. Egocentric thinking (believing that everyone thinks as we do) leads some men to the conclusion that, "Hey, I'm aroused and ready to go so she must be, too." The type of men who tend to believe these things and to commit date rape are masculine males in the traditional "macho" sense of the word (Bernard et al. 1985) "Real men don't take no for an answer." Given this, it would not hurt to also explore thinking errors as they relate to the date rapist's conceptions of what a "real man" is. The questioning and challenging techniques of Rational Emotive Behavior Therapy (REBT) and a healthy dose of bibliotherapy (both discussed in Chapter 11) should prove useful in this regard.

Exercises such as the one concerning the victim experience (empathy training) in the chapter on institutional counseling can be used fruitfully here. You can show videos that reveal the psychological trauma that accompanies rape. In the spirit of restorative justice, it is better yet to have a rape victim speak to the group about her experience and about how it affected her life. Select the victim carefully, however. You do not want one who spouts trendy sexual politics and who defines rape as everything from violent sexual assault to sexual innuendo and jokes. Nor do you want one who flays the group and denigrates all men because of her experience. Although such a response from a victim is quite understandable, the group will act defensively against her and refuse to take her seriously. If this does become the group's reaction, the whole exercise probably will have done more harm than good. Local rape crisis centers usually have a number of strong victims willing to talk to various groups about their experiences in a dispassionate way. Certainly, if alcohol were involved in the incident, attention to that problem area also should be part of the offender's treatment.

Child Molesters

Child molesters are persons who use children to gratify their sexual urges. Robertiello and Terry (2007: 512) provide a general thumbnail sketch of child molesters' common characteristics, which include:

> poor social skills, low self-esteem, feelings of inadequacy, a sense of worthlessness and vulnerability, a hindrance to normal adult relationships or previously frustrating experiences with adult relationships...physically unattractive, have problems with potency, and they have feelings of inadequacy, humiliation, and loneliness.

Approximately two-thirds of all sex offenders in state prison offended against children (Talbot et al. 2002).

A child molester may or may not be a true pedophile (a person who is literally a "lover of children"). Most individuals convicted of molesting children apparently prefer adult sex but have opportunistically taken advantage of a child, but pedophiles are preferentially sexually attracted to children, sometimes exclusively (*Harvard Mental Health Letter* 2004). Some child molesters are offenders who take advantage of any form of sexual gratification immediately available to them, regardless of age, sex, or even, at times, of species. Child molestation tends to be associated with three age categories: the teen years, the mid to late thirties, and the mid fifties and older.

Teenage molesters tend to be socially withdrawn and of lower intelligence than the average teenager. Young molesters rarely attempt intercourse. Sexual activity tends to take the form of kissing and the digital manipulation of the genitals. The victim most often is known to the offender, and the act can be viewed as a form of sexual curiosity on the part of a teenager who is too self effacing to attempt to satisfy it with consenting persons of his own age. Estimates are that juveniles commit about one-half of all child molestation in the United States (Talbot et al. 2002).

Offenders in their mid-to-late thirties are more likely than not to be married, and quite often the victim is a stepchild of the offender. Having a stepfather is the strongest single predictor of sexual abuse for girls, and the greatest predictor for boys is living in a father-absent home (Glaser and Frosh 1993). A nationwide study of children ages two through nine found that children of single parents were 6.7 times more likely to witness family violence, 3.9 times more likely to be maltreated, and 2.7 times more likely to be sexually assaulted than children with both biological parents present. The figures for stepparent families were even worse at 9.2, 4.6, and 4.3, respectively (Turner, Finkelhor, and Ormond 2006).

Not infrequently, the molestation can go on for quite some time. The offender usually is able to maintain the ongoing "relationship" by telling his victim that the child's mother would get mad if she found out, or that the child probably would be placed in a juvenile detention center or a foster home if the offense became known. The initial act of molestation is likely to occur when the offender finds himself unemployed for an extended period of time, has been drinking, or finds that his normal sex life has soured. One study of child molesters found that 34.3 percent of them were unemployed at the time of their offense (Walsh 1994). This is about five times the average unemployment rate for males over a six-year period in the jurisdiction from which the data were obtained.

The molester of fifty-five and older is usually a man without any prior contact with the law. He recently may have suffered the loss of his wife by death or divorce and finds himself quite lonely. It is extremely rare that such offenders will use any kind of force to gain compliance. They usually will use promises of rewards, such as money or candy, to persuade victims to do their bidding. As with teenage molesters, but not middle-aged molesters, actual intercourse rarely figures in the sexual activity of this group. Also, they tend to be deeply ashamed and remorseful when their activity is discovered, and they are the least likely of all offenders to offend again.

Molesters who offend against male children tend more to be true pedophiles than are their heterosexual counterparts (*Harvard Mental Health Letter* 2004). Walsh (1994) found that 34.7 percent of the homosexual molesters were diagnosed as pedophiles, as opposed to 13.2 percent of the heterosexual offenders. They were also more likely to be strangers to their victims (26.5 percent, versus only 4.8 percent of the heterosexual offenders). On the one hand, homosexual offenders were much less likely (4.1 percent) to use force or the threat of force to gain compliance than were the heterosexuals (19.2 percent). On the other hand, they were more than twice as likely to have a prior conviction for molesting (49 percent versus 22.1 percent). However, in 21.6 percent of those prior molestations, the victims were females. It may be thus more accurate to call these men bisexual pedophiles.

Rapists Versus Child Molesters

According to Groth (1979), both rapists and child molesters are threatened by normal adult sexuality, but the rapist attacks the source of the threat and the child molester retreats from it by turning to safer substitutes (children). Compared with non-sex offenders and rapists, child molesters tend to be shy and introverted and haunted by feelings of inadequacy, which may prevent them from interacting sexually with mature adults (Dreznick 2003). It is not unusual to see cases in which an offender carried on an affectionate "affair" with a child for long periods of time (Walsh 1988). The emotional investment quite often appears to extend beyond sexuality. However misdirected the attachment, the child is valued as a person and a "lover." In contrast, the target for the rapist is just an object upon whose body he seeks to satisfy his selfish needs. It is rare that the child molester attempts sexual penetration, whereas such penetration, as the primordial symbol of conquest, is the ultimate aim of the rapist. Only 14 percent of the author's sample of child molesters vaginally or anally penetrated their victims, as opposed to 69 percent of the combined stranger and date/acquaintance rapists. Oral sex (61 percent) was the primary type of sexual activity engaged in by the molesters, with 25 percent having only digital sexual contact with their victims.

Among other interesting comparisons in the above study, were that rapists had far more serious criminal histories despite being significantly younger (average age of twenty-eight versus an average of thirty-seven for the molesters). The child molesters were of significantly higher social class. Occupationally, molesters ranged from laborers to ministers and physicians. The rapists were almost all in lower status occupations, if working at all, which is consistent with later studies (Figueredo, et al. 2000; Mills, Anderson, and Kroner 2004). Seventy two percent of the molesters had been married at some stage in their lives, with 42 percent being married at the time of their offenses. The identical marriage figures for the rapists were 58 and 30 percent, respectively. Ninety percent of the child molesters were related to or acquainted with their victims, as opposed to 61 percent of the rapists, and 63 percent had previous sexual contact with their victims, as opposed to 23.8 percent of the rapists. None of the molesters used a weapon; 30 percent of the rapists did. Judging from these data, it is clear that a sharp line divides the rapist from the child molester.

Most child molesters, with the exception of child rapists (strangers who attempt or accomplish genital intercourse), tend to have a strong stake in conformity, and "the majority of them do not have extensive criminal histories or 'traditional' criminal lifestyles" (Carter and Morris 2002: 3). If the offense were not violent or if the offender has no previous record of similar behavior indicative of an abiding interest in children as sexual targets, he usually can be considered a good probation risk. However, given the level of seriousness attached to this type of behavior, it is imperative that you conduct a thorough investigation into his background prior to making any recommendations to that effect. Obviously, the findings and recommendations of mental health professionals should be read and considered very carefully.

Assessment and Treatment of Child Molesters

Some estimate that one in five women and one in seven men was sexually abused at some point during their childhood. With estimates this high, the problem of the sexual assault of children is obviously an urgent one. Unfortunately, as we have seen, an aura of "nothing works" pessimism surrounds the treatment of child molesters. Laws, mandating registration for convicted child molesters and requiring that neighbors be informed when a convicted child molester moves into a neighborhood, make it clear that the public is more concerned with punishment and surveillance than with treatment.

Nevertheless, about 60 percent of all convicted sex offenders are in the community as probationers or parolees at any one time (Carter and Morris 2002), making the issue of their treatment of the utmost importance. Most probation and parole officers have neither the time nor the training to counsel child molesters, and even those whose exclusive role is to supervise sex offenders will find it difficult to treat them without more expert help. Therefore, it is necessary to gain some idea of the treatment modalities available for sex offenders in your community.

Public and private agencies have implemented a variety of treatment modalities, although those most frequently implemented rely almost exclusively on group therapy, interpersonal communication skills, and psycho-educational programs. Some researchers question the efficacy of such modalities in terms of recidivism rates (Grubin 2007, Studer and Aylwin 2006). They have failed to find statistically significant differences in recidivism rates between sex offenders on probation who received treatment and control groups of offenders who did not. This would seem to indicate that either the treatment modalities themselves are not successful, or else treatment was initiated without a proper assessment of the condition to be treated. Psychometric assessment by itself is of limited utility for the assessment, classification, and treatment of sexual offenders (Hall and Proctor 1987, Maletzky and Field 2003).

According to Greer and Stuart (1983) a "state of the art" sexual-abuse treatment program would include tools for physiological assessment of sexual-arousal patterns in addition to psychosocial assessment and treatment. Such tools are the penile plethysmograph and the polygraph. Several researchers have reported the superiority of penile tumescence measures to assess and classify sex offenders, as well as a tool for treatment (Gannon, Beech and Ward 2008, Tong 2007). The rationale for the use of these tools is simple: an adequate assessment of an offender and his full and open disclosure of the nature and extent of his sexual proclivities must precede any meaningful treatment. As Lundell (1987: 2) states: "All therapists concur that effective treatment only can begin when the full extent of the offender's history of sexual deviant behavior is known."

Without polygraph information, it is doubtful if the treatment providers will get the full extent of this history. For instance, one study found that the number of victims admitted by child molesters increased from an average of 1.87 at the intake interview to 2.85 when required to take a polygraph (Lester and Hurst 2000). A survey of two decades of research comparing self-reports, pre- and post-polygraph testing, found more dramatic results overall. This review found that molesters will understate by a factor of five or six times the number of sexual crimes they have committed, and will overstate their own childhood victimization (an effort to gain sympathy and understanding—"I'm a victim too") by two-to-three times (Hindman and Peters 2001).

Self disclosure does not mean that if the offender discloses his sexual sins and peccadilloes that he will necessarily benefit from the emotional "catharsis," although he may well do so. While it is axiomatic that the offender cannot be properly confronted (nor can he confront himself) until the full extent of his offending behavior is out in the open, other purposes are attached to the effort to elicit full disclosure. Additional victims identified through the disclosure process may be contacted and invited to come in for victim counseling. Many sexual-abuse treatment centers consider the contacting of previously unknown victims to be a vital part of their mandate since it is well known that untreated victims are candidates for future psychological problems, including becoming offenders themselves (*Harvard Mental Health Letter* 2004, Walsh 1988).

The SANE Therapeutic Program

This section briefly outlines one such "state of the art" treatment program known as SANE (Sexual Abuse Now Ended) that has gained national attention (Marsh and Walsh 1995). SANE is a victim-oriented program based on the philosophy of "restitution therapy," a concept that falls under the umbrella of restorative justice. The program views treatment for the offender as a privilege, which is designed to repair the damage done to the sexually abused victim through "clarification." Clarification is the process by which the sex offender accepts and communicates to his victim his responsibility for his crime, thereby eliminating much of the shame and guilt that victims of sexual abuse experience. Through treatment of one-to-five years in duration, the offender learns to restructure the thought processes that have allowed him to commit his crime, and to develop a genuine empathy for how his victim experienced the sexual abuse he perpetrated. The program employs Rational Emotive Behavior Therapy and group counseling to help offenders unlearn thinking errors and to acquire more appropriate thinking patterns.

The SANE program does not accept offenders who are violent, who show clear evidence of brain damage or psychosis, or who deny the charge against them. Because this is a confrontational program, it is of little use to confront offenders who deny the existence of anything to confront. Offenders who deny accusations of child molestation generally have higher recidivism rates than either treated or nontreated offenders who admit their offenses (Marshall and Barbaree 1988).

Upon intake, the offender completes a demographic and sexual history questionnaire (augmented by his presentence investigation report), and is required to complete a battery of psychological tests. These tests are sent to one of SANE's consulting psychologists to determine diagnosis, amenability to treatment, appropriate treatment modality, and reoffending risk. Then, clinical staff ascertain whether the offender has given his therapists a complete accounting of his sexual history. Periodic polygraph assessments aid this process. The offender then must recognize and diminish his sexual arousal to deviant sexual activity as assessed through periodic penile plethysmograph testing. This should show a progressive decrease in penile blood volume when he is exposed to deviant sexual stimuli.

The offender is terminated from the program successfully only when he completes the following:

1) Reveals all victims as indicated by passing his polygraph examinations

2) Recognizes and confronts his deviant arousal patterns revealed by plethysmograph tests

3) His penile arousal to nondeviant sexual material is greater than it is to deviant sexual arousal, and

4) When his therapist has determined that the offender accepted his full responsibility for his actions and has made "emotional restitution" to his victim or victims.

Perspective from the Field—One
SANE Solutions to Sexual Offending

By Jeffrey Betts, M.S., LMFT, LCPC

Jeffrey Betts is a treatment specialist providing outpatient therapy for juveniles who have committed sexual offenses and their families. He holds a master's degree in marriage and family therapy from Azusa Pacific University in California. In the State of Idaho he is a Licensed Marriage and Family Therapist (LMFT), and a Licensed Clinical Professional Counselor (LCPC). He is a current member of the Association of the Treatment of Sexual Abusers (ATSA), and was the president for the Idaho chapter of Association for the Treatment of Sexual Abusers. He is a past executive committee member of the Los Angeles Sex Offender Round Table and a past member of the California Coalition on Sexual Offending. He has worked in his current position with SANE Solutions in Boise, Idaho for the past eight years. For five years prior to this, he provided treatment for juvenile sexual offenders in a residential treatment facility in California.

Continued on the next page

Perspective from the Field—One, *continued*

In more than thirteen years of working with juvenile sexual offenders, I have come to many conclusions. Most people, including myself, never imagined that they would one day be remotely interested in working with this population. I held many of the same misconceptions that I routinely see from others in the field and in the community. Fourteen years ago, when approached about providing treatment services to juvenile sex offenders, I turned down the offer very quickly. Over the following year, after having the opportunity to interact with the therapists providing treatment, and after talking to the juveniles themselves, I ventured into the field.

I realized that I lacked sufficient knowledge and experience to work effectively with juvenile sex offenders. I endeavored to read everything I could. I spent hours in university libraries researching journal articles. I read the few available books on the subject. I attended as many conferences and trainings as finances allowed. In particular, I reviewed the literature on clinical work with juvenile sex offenders. I also searched out and joined professional organizations that focused on the treatment of sexual abusers and networked with other treatment providers.

In reality, the field was still in its infancy and much was yet to be learned about this population. Fortunately, I also had the opportunity to receive helpful supervision while learning on the job. I have since concluded that what I learned in graduate school did not fully prepare me for working with juvenile sex offenders. Most individuals who enter the field do so without direct clinical training or experience specific to this population. On a good note, additional educational opportunities are now available in response to this need, including specialized classroom training and certificate programs.

I learned rapidly that critical aspects of juvenile sex-offenders' treatment rely on effective evaluation, intervention, and risk management of juvenile sex offenders in the community. This treatment relies heavily on current research, and the ethical and moral conduct of those who provide this service. Juvenile sex-offenders' treatment and evaluation is a specialized field that requires the implementation of good practice standards and guidelines. For example, juvenile sex-offenders' treatment seeks to help individuals manage their risk of re-offense and helps them live safely and in a healthy manner in their community. Juvenile sex-offenders' treatment seeks to prevent future sexual offenses by employing a team of individuals to effectively manage juveniles who commit sexual offenses.

Another major goal of juvenile sex-offender treatment is the protection of the community. This is done through responsible, moral, and ethical treatment of juvenile sex offenders; by developing effective risk-management strategies; and by providing public awareness and education that reflects the best available clinical and research knowledge. The Association for the Treatment of Sexual Abusers (ATSA) has adopted and promoted these and other goals of treatment.

Some of the specific goals of treatment include developing relapse-prevention strategies, enhancing empathy, employing interpersonal skills training and cognitive restructuring, teaching effective management of emotions and sexual-arousal control, using family therapy, and developing family and other social support networks. Due to the inherent risks involved in working with this population in the community and the need for specialization, many local, state, and federal jurisdictions are creating and adopting minimal requirements for evaluators and providers of treatment for sexually abusive adults and youth.

After providing treatment services with juvenile sex offenders for a period of time, I was surprised at how much I enjoyed the work. In reflection, I identified three important reasons why this is so.

1. First, children in general know when the adults in their life value them. Over time, no adults will be successful in working with any juvenile population unless they genuinely like them and like to be around them. I have witnessed many educators, youth leaders, counselors, and so forth, who clearly did not like kids or teens and it showed in the results of their work.

2. Secondly, it is important for anyone working with juvenile sex offenders to be able to have solid emotional boundaries due to the horrific subject matter that must be processed, not only by the juveniles, but also by the therapists working with them. To the degree that the therapists are successful with this, they will have a higher degree of satisfaction and longevity in the field.

3. Thirdly, the satisfaction gained from being a part of a growing field of knowledge and experience is worthwhile. The opportunity to make a significant contribution to the field, and to the juvenile sex offenders and their families is rewarding. In all, I find that work with juveniles who have committed sexual offenses is an interesting, satisfying, and challenging field of therapy.

ACA has a juvenile sex offender treatment book available by Christopher Frey, MSW, LCSW: *Double Jeopardy: A Counselor's Guide to Treating Juvenile Male Sex Offenders/Substance Abusers* and an accompanying workbook for the juveniles themselves. For information log onto ACA's website: www.aca.org/bookstore.

Perspective from the Field—Two
Adult Sex-Offender Treatment: An Inside View

By Raymond W. Schuenemann

Ray Schuenemann is a prison inmate serving a sixty-nine-year sentence in Arizona. An obsessive-compulsive neurosis stemming from childhood abuse was both the motivator for his adult offenses as well as his lifelong successes. Active in high school sports and student government, he was a senior class officer. Within sixteen months of enlisting in the Marines, he was promoted to sergeant. He graduated summa cum laude from the University of Houston, is a licensed plumber in two states, and has held a Secret Security clearance. His eight-year marriage was solemnized in the Salt Lake Temple and produced one son. He exposed himself compulsively from the age of four. Nine days after returning from Vietnam, he entered a woman's apartment for sex. A year later, he confessed this to authorities and they charged him with burglary. He spent the next eight years (1971 to 1979) on Texas prison farms, followed by six months on parole. In 1987, at the age of thirty-eight, he was convicted of five sexual assaults, four attempts, and three related burglaries. The sixty-nine-year sentence was too long to allow him into treatment, but he cooperated by admitting to offenses for which others were doing time, and he was admitted into the Fairbanks program. He graduated from the Sex Offender Treatment Program in 1992 and is now serving the remainder of his sentence. He will be eighty-four years old when he gets out.

● ● ● ● ● ● ● ● ● ● ● ● ● ● ● ● ● ● ● ●

Fairbanks Correction Center's (FCC) sex-offender treatment program (SOTP) combines education and therapy enabling men to grow from past conditioning to learn self-management. Core subjects, program format, and key features are described to inform the public, policymakers, victims, and prospective offenders about what goes on in a successful treatment program. Prior to the sex-offender-treatment program, I was skeptical about sex-offender treatment, which looked like a waste of time and money. Sex offenders were "other people" who deserved prison punishment to deter (magical thinking) them from offending.

In truth, offenders grow only through education with professional help in order to develop self-control. Each offender's personal motivation for offending must be diagnosed and specifically treated. Without professional help and deliberate social training, offenders have no chance of defying the laws of human behavior to miraculously change for the better. My gratitude for the sex-offender-treatment program comes from perspectives denied to therapists because I know what it is like to be forcibly separated from family, to be an abused child, a perpetrator, and an adult living in either self-disgust or in prison. In healing, I also rely on my religious faith.

A sex crime is a symptom of a problem within a perpetrator. Sex, itself, is never the root cause. Offenses are the byproduct of poor self-esteem, lack of social skills, faulty attitudes, childhood abuse, mental illness, misdirected legitimate needs, and causes generally summed up as inappropriate behavior connected to sex and aggression. Offenders are made, but, fortunately, they can be unmade with proper diagnosis and training.

The Fairbanks Correction Center's sex-offender-treatment program is composed of four parts, three in-jail phases: I-beginner, II-intermediate, III-advanced, with Phase IV-aftercare in the community for a year. The in-jail portion was designed to last eighteen months, six in each phase, but the few men who graduated generally needed two years or longer to complete all the requirements. In the fifteen-year history of the sex-offender-treatment program in Alaska, there only have been about fifty graduates from Phase III. It took me three years to graduate. Twenty-four hours a day, each offender lives under intense scrutiny by peers, therapists, and prison employees. Three years is comparable to the total actual number of months spent in high school, or in college gaining a bachelor's degree. Think of your growth and quantum leaps of development during those periods of your own life.

Core Subjects: Prison-based sex-offender-treatment programs in different states teach common fundamentals such as victim awareness, behavior patterns, unresolved childhood issues, relapse prevention, and thinking errors. Each core subject holds different value in treatment depending on what motivated an offender. The backbone of the Fairbanks Correction Center's sex-offender-treatment program was cognitive- behavioral therapy concerning thinking errors. It involved weekly homework, monthly presentations, and phase assignments. The premise underlying thinking errors is that behavior follows from thoughts; therefore, conscious thinking guides us to better choices. Each offender learns to recognize both his/her thought patterns and their consequences.

Victim awareness is a study of the harmful effects our behavior can have on others. People can be harmed physically, mentally, emotionally, spiritually, socially, and have their lives drastically altered. Rarely is harm intentional in sex offenses, but serious harm is almost always the outcome. This has to be brought to men's attention, and for this sensitivity to develop there are two prerequisites. First, a man has to recognize his own emotions and understand their function. Offenders are stunted emotionally, generally due to childhood abuse. Second, before a man can feel empathy for others, he has to feel sympathy for himself.

People are creatures of habit; our behavior follows cycles. Poor self-image leads to being depressed, withdrawing, acting out, feeling guilt, pushing guilt away, having false confidence, and beginning another turn of the cycle. The sex-offender-treatment program helps each man identify his pattern and then teaches him coping skills to get out of unhealthy spirals. Self-understanding was the goal, for as Carl Rogers said, "The degree of self-understanding is perhaps the most important factor in predicting the individual's behavior."

Offenders are made by their childhood experiences. To some degree, all of us are products of a community. There are specific reasons why some abused children grow up to be offenders while others do not. Offenders learn

Continued on the next page

Perspective from the Field—Two, *continued*

a different code of right and wrong from what happened to them and what they saw modeled. It is okay for offenders to learn that they were victims and that they must take responsibility to counteract those adverse affects by wholesome, growth-developing self-management. These offenders have learned faulty attitudes that erroneously gave them permission to act-out. Some children are abused to such a degree that major mental illness is inflicted. In my case, treatment for an obsessive-compulsive disorder was essential for reformation.

Relapse prevention is an itemized plan for wholesome living. The plan reviews an offender's strengths and weaknesses, and then lists tempting situations, which he must avoid. Allowing for mistakes (called "lapses"), the plan calls upon the offender's known coping skills to get him out of lapses so they do not escalate into a relapse, a law violation.

Program Format. Sex-offender-treatment program offenders are taught in more than one way. Repeated learning events reinforce the lessons. Offenders are organized into closed groups of ten, which meet for an hour, five days a week. Ten minutes at the beginning of each group session is allocated for "individual issues" in which men are called to task by their peers for any misconduct. With twenty group-working days per month, each member is responsible for two days of presentations on subjects assigned by a therapist. Day and night group members monitor other members' behavior throughout the institution.

Every month each of the three therapists hold a private office meeting with each offender. One-on-one sessions focus on any issue the therapist chooses. Therapists take time with each man to determine why he has gone wrong, and then tailor an individualized treatment plan, as well as talk about individual concerns. The therapist takes meeting notes, which are kept in each offender's file.

Each individual must complete a daily treatment journal. All individuals record events, thoughts, and feelings of that day along with examinations of past trauma. This journal is a key to discovery, insight, and growth. Each month, a therapist reviews the journals and writes comments and suggestions. Also, for that phase, group members, therapists, and the treatment team perform evaluations. Treatment team evaluators include the prison classification officer, a parole officer, and sometimes ranking correctional officers. Questions from these savvy average citizens reflect society's concerns. All aspects of the offender's life are subject to inquisitorial inspection.

Small groups of four-to-fifteen men convene on their own time in personal rooms, the dayroom, or classrooms, on weekends and evenings for further study. Topics include: human sexuality, goal imagery, childhood abuse, motivation, and gaps in the sex-offender-treatment program itself. Leading a subgroup gives each Phase III client-facilitator the additional experience of mastering the subject, because nobody learns like the teacher.

The sex-offender-treatment-program office is filled with pertinent reading material. Bibliotherapy is great for those men who can learn from self-help psychology books, including articles from victims. More texts and publications are available from the staff psychologist.

Informal socialization is perhaps the most subtle and effective way of teaching prosocial behavior. Prison employees and therapists maintain wholesome living conditions in the wing where all thirty-one program participants live apart from the 200-man general population. This provides an oasis for repentance and rehabilitation, because each man adhered, more or less voluntarily, to the same values and goals and was committed to the same ways and means of achieving them. Everybody worked on everybody else to file off the rough edges. Conversations and publications were kept to wholesome standards, in contrast to elsewhere in prison.

Key Features Some features of sex-offender-treatment programs deserve specific recognition for their effectiveness. Upon entering the program, each offender takes a battery of tests that provide a psychological profile. In Phase III, all program participants retake the same battery to measure any improvement. Explaining your test results to the group requires a two-day presentation, scheduled after privately reviewing your scores with a therapist.

Classes promoted by prison administrators dovetail with the sex-offender- treatment program. Each support program teaches correct principles and gives offenders an opportunity to serve and to practice prosocial behavior. A list of supporting classes includes: drug and alcohol counseling, Adult Children of Alcoholics, alternatives to violence, the learning center, religious services, assertiveness training, institutional jobs, talking circle, craft shop, Jaycees, veteran's affairs workshops for war veterans and others suffering from posttraumatic stress disorder (PTSD), peer group counseling, and others.

Some people learn the value of talking in their family. Others do not; it is not modeled for them. They learn to keep their mouths shut, to be secretive, or simply not to talk. Until a person learns how to listen actively and how to talk assertively, expressing true feelings, and verbally processing the day's events, he does not know how wonderful it is, how it paves the way for meeting daily needs. Legitimate emotional needs motivate every bit of human behavior. People sometimes resort to indirect means such as crime to meet their needs. Awareness of legitimate needs helps men to fulfill them directly through socially approved channels.

Sex-offender-treatment-program offenders have to perform different behaviors, practice them in real situations, such as using coping skills and being properly confrontational in crises. Demonstrating change is a phase requirement judged by group members and therapists. This is not just an academic program; practical skills such as demonstrating work responsibility and getting along well with others have to be proven over years. When I asked the therapists if this treatment works, they gave me a printed article, which said that our FCC sex-offender-treatment program was based on one in Oregon where the overall program effectiveness was 95 percent of the offenders were free of new sex- crime convictions and 96 percent were free of any new felony.

Summary

Few types of criminals arouse our passion for punishment more than do the sex offender. Sex offenses are perhaps the most underreported of all major crimes, but we should not put all sex offenders into a common basket. The rapist differs dramatically from the child molester, and stranger rapists and acquaintance rapists also differ considerably. The majority of rapists appear to be traditional macho males who hold onto the notion that "no" means "yes." They rarely respect women as autonomous human beings who have absolute rights to their own bodies. There are those rapists (usually strangers to their victims) who do appear to require violence and victim degradation for their perverted satisfaction. This type of rapist is rare in comparison with the acquaintance/date rapist.

Treatment of rapists in community corrections should focus on discussions of sex roles, images of women, and the victim's experience. Usually, rapists who are imprisoned are those who are violent. Their treatment must be more intense and specialized, and, therefore, tends to be administered by psychiatrists and psychologists.

Child molesters are, in the main, weak and lonely individuals. Only occasionally will you run into a true pedophile. Child molesters tend to be concentrated in three age categories: the teens, mid to late thirties, and the mid fifties and older. Usually some special conditions contribute to child molestation, such as mental deficiency, unemployment, and loneliness. Just as there are some major demographic differences between acquaintance and stranger rapists, major differences exist between rapists and child molesters. The biggest differences are the average ages of the two groups and the rapists greater propensity to use force.

The treatment of child molesters is best accomplished within specialized sex-abuse clinics. One such program we examined uses physiological assessment tools (the penile plethysmograph and the polygraph) to assess, treat, and monitor the offender.

References and Suggested Readings

Alexander, M. 1999. Sexual Offender Treatment Efficacy Revisited. *Sexual Abuse: A Journal of Research and Treatment* 11: 101-116.

Barbaree, H. and W. Marshall. 1991. The Role of Male Sexual Arousal in Rape: Six Models. *Journal of Consulting and Clinical Psychology* 59: 621-630.

Bartol, C. 2002. *Criminal Behavior: A Psychosocial Approach*, Sixth Ed. Englewood Cliffs, New Jersey: Prentice Hall.

Bernard, J., S. Bernard, and M. Bernard. 1985. Courtship Violence and Sex Typing. *Family Relations* 34: 573-576.

Bogaerts, S., A. Daalder, S. Vanheule and F. Leeuw. 2008. Personality Disorders in a Sample of Paraphilic and Nonparaphilic Child Molesters. *International Journal of Offender Therapy and Comparative Criminology* 52: 21-30.

Bradford, J. 1990. The Antiandrogen and Hormonal Treatment of Sex Offenders. In W. Marshall, D. Laws, and H. Barbaree, eds., *Handbook of Sexual Assault: Issues, Theories, and Treatment of the Offender*. New York: Plenum.

Brecher, E. 1978. *Treatment Programs for Sex Offenders*. Washington, D.C.: U.S. Government Printing Office.

Bynum, T., M. Carter, S. Matson, and C. Onley. 2006. Recidivism of Sex Offenders. In E. Latessa and A. Holsinger, eds, *Correctional Contexts*. Los Angeles: Roxbury. pp. 277-296.

Carter, M. and L. Morris. 2002. *Managing Sex Offenders in the Community*. Washington, D.C.: Center for Sex Offender Management.

Cummings, G. and M. Buell. 1997. *Supervision of the Sex Offender*. Safer Society Press and American Correctional Association. Available from the American Correctional Association, Lanham, Maryland.

Clark, L. and D. Lewis. 1977. *Rape: The Price of Coercive Sexuality*. Toronto: The Woman's Press.

Denov, M. 2003. The Myth of Innocence: Sexual Scripts and the Recognition of Child Sexual Abuse By Female Perpetrators. *The Journal of Sex Research* 40: 303-314.

Dreznick, M. 2003. Heterosexual Competence of Rapists and Child Molesters: A Meta-Analysis. *The Journal of Sex Research* 40: 170-178.

Drzasga, J. 1960. *Sex Crimes*. Springfield, Illinois: Charles C. Thomas.

Ellis, A. 1986. The Sex Offender. In H. Toch, ed., *Psychology of Crime and Criminal Justice*. Prospect Heights, Illinois: Waveland Press.

Ellis, L. 1991. A Synthesized (Biosocial) Theory of Rape. *Journal of Consulting and Clinical Psychology* 59: 631-642.

Emory, L., C. Cole, and W. Meyer. 1992. The Texas Experience with DepoProvera: 1980 1990. *Journal of Offender Rehabilitation* 18: 125-139

Federal Bureau of Investigation. 2007. *Uniform Crime Reports: 2006*. Washington, D.C.: U.S. Department of Justice.

Figueredo, A., B. Sales, K. Russel, J. Becker, and M. Kaplan. 2000. A Brunswickian Evolutionary-Developmental Theory of Adolescent Sex Offending. *Behavioral Sciences and the Law* 18: 309-329.

Fortney, T. J. Levenson, Y. Brannon, and J. Baker. 2007. Myths and Facts about Sexual Offenders: Implications for Treatment and Public Policy. *Sexual Offender Treatment*, 2: 1-17, http://sexual-offendertreatment.org/55html/retrieved February 2010.

Francis, B. 2002. Moral Panics and the Aftermath: A Study of Incest. *Journal of Social Welfare and Family Law* 24: 1-18.

Freeman, N. 2007. Predictors of Rearrest for Rapists and Child Molesters on Probation. *Criminal Justice and Behavior* 34: 752-758.

Gannon, T., A. Beech, and T. Ward. 2008. Does the Polygraph Lead to Better Risk Prediction for Sexual Offenders, *Aggression and Violent Behavior* 13 (1): 29-44.

Gendreau, P. and R. Ross. 1987. Revivification of Rehabilitation: Evidence from the 1980s. *Justice Quarterly* 4: 349-406.

Gilmartin, P. 1994. *Rape, Incest, and Child Sexual Abuse: Consequences and Recovery*. New York: Garland.

Giotakos, O., M. Markianos, N. Vaidakis, and G. Christodoulou. 2003. Aggression, Impulsivity, Plasma Sex Hormones, and Biogenic Amine Turnover in a Forensic Population of Rapists. *Journal of Sex and Marital Therapy* 29: 215-225.

Glaser, D. and S. Frosh. 1993. *Child Sex Abuse*. Toronto: University of Toronto Press.

Greer, J. and I. Stuart. 1983. *The Sexual Aggressor: Current Perspectives and Treatment*. New York: Van Nostrand Reinhold.

Groth, A. 1979. *Men who Rape*. New York: Plenum

Grubin, D. 2007. Sexual Offending and the Treatment of Sex Offenders. *Psychiatry* 6: 439-443.

Hall, E. 1987. Adolescents' Perceptions of Sexual Assault. *Journal of Sex Education and Therapy* 13: 37-42.

Hall, G. and W. Proctor. 1987. Criminological Predictors of Recidivism in a Sexual Offender Population. *Journal of Consulting and Clinical Psychology* 55: 111 112.

Harvard Mental Health Letter. 2004. Pedophilia 20: 1-4.

Harrison, K. 2007. The high risk offender strategy in England and Wales: Is chemical castration an option? *The Howard Journal*, 46: 16-31.

Herman, J. 1990. "Sex Offenders: A Feminist Perspective." In W. Marshall, D. Laws, and H. Barbaree, eds., *Handbook of Sexual Assault: Issues, Theories, and Treatment of the Offender*. New York: Plenum.

Hindman, J. and J. Peters. 2001. Polygraph Testing Leads to Better Understanding Adult and Juvenile Sex Offenders. *Federal Probation* 65: 1-15.

Howard, R. 2002. Brain Waves, Dangerousness and Deviant Desires. *The Journal of Forensic Psychiatry* 13: 367-384.

Janus, E. 2004. Sexually Violent Predator Laws: Psychiatry in Service to a Morally Dubious Enterprise. *Medicine, Crime, and Punishment* 364: 50-51

Kansas v. Hendricks 138 U.S. 521 (1997).

Koss, M. and K. Leonard. 1984. "Sexually Aggressive Men: Empirical Findings and Theoretical Implications." In N. Malamuth and E. Donnerstein, eds., *Pornography and Sexual Aggression*. New York: Academic Press.

Langan, P. E. Schmitt and M. Dunrose. 2003. *Recidivism of Sex Offenders Released from Prison in 1994*. Washington, D.C.: U.S. Department of Justice, Bureau of Justice Statistics.

Langavin, R. 1990. "Sexual Anomalies and the Brain." In W. Marshall, D. Laws, and H. Barbaree, eds., *Handbook of Sexual Assault: Issues, Theories, and Treatment of the Offender*. New York: Plenum.

Lawrence v. Texas. 539 U.S. 558 (2003).

Lester, D. and G. Hurst. 2000. "Treating Sex Offenders." In P. Van Voorhis, M. Braswell, and D. Lester, eds., *Correctional Counseling and Rehabilitation*. Cincinnati, Ohio: Anderson.

Lindsay, W. 2002. Research and Literature on Sex Offenders with Intellectual and Developmental Disabilities. *Journal of Intellectual Disability Research* 46: 74-85.

Lotke, E. 1996. Sex Offenders: Can Treatment Work? *Corrections Compendium* 21: 1-3.

Lundell, R. 1987. The Utility of Polygraph Testing in the Treatment of Sex Offenders. Paper presented at the annual conference of the Association for the Behavioral Treatment of Sexual Abusers. Portland, Oregon.

Maletzky, B. and G. Field. 2003. The Biological Treatment of Dangerous Sexual Offenders, a Review and Preliminary Report of the Oregon Pilot Depo-Provera Program. *Aggression and Violent Behavior* 8: 391-412.

Marsh, R. and A. Walsh. 1995. Physiological and Psychosocial Assessment and Treatment of Sex Offenders: A Comprehensive Victim Oriented Program. *Journal of Offender Rehabilitation* 22: 77-96.

Marshall, W. and H. Barbaree. 1988. The Long Term Evaluation of a Behavioral Treatment Program for Child Molesters. *Behavior Research and Therapy* 26: 499-511.

———. 1990. An Integrated Theory of the Etiology of Sexual Offending. In W. Marshall, D. Laws, and H. Barbaree, eds., *Handbook of Sexual Assault: Issues, Theories, and Treatment of the Offender*. New York: Plenum.

Mawby, R. 2001. *Burglary*. Colompton, Devon, England: Willan Publishing.

Mealey, L. 2003. "Combating Rape: Views of an Evolutionary Psychologist." In R. Bloom and N. Dess, eds., *Evolutionary Psychology and Violence*, Westport, Connecticut: Praeger. pp. 83-113.

Mills, J., D. Anderson, and D. Kroner. 2004. The Antisocial Attitudes of Sex Offenders. *Criminal Behavior and Mental Health* 14: 134-145.

Palmer, C. 1994. "Twelve Reasons Why Rape Is Not Sexually Motivated: A Skeptical Examination." In R. Francoeur, ed., *Taking Sides: Clashing Views on Controversial Issues in Human Sexuality*. Guilford, Connecticut: Dushkin.

Pinel, J. 2000. Biopsychology, 4th ed. Boston: Allyn and Bacon.

Quinn, J., C. Forsyth, and C. Mullen-Quinn, 2004. Societal Reaction to Sex Offenders: A Review of the Origins and Results of the Myths Surrounding Their Crimes and Treatment Amenability. *Deviant Behavior* 25: 215-232.

Rand, M. S. 2009. *Criminal Victimization, 2008*. Washington, D.C.: Bureau of Justice Statistics.

Robertiello, G. and K. Terry. 2007. Can we Profile Sex Offenders? A Review of Sex Offender Typologies. *Aggression and Violent Behavior* 12: 508-518.

Robinson, M. 2005. *Justice Blind: Ideals and Realities of American Criminal Justice*. Upper Saddle River, NJ: Prentice Hall.

Romero, J. and L. Williams. 1983. A Comparative Study of Group Psychotherapy and Intensive Probation Supervision with Sex Offenders. *Federal Probation* 47: 36-42.

Schmalleger, F. 2001. *Criminal Justice Today*, Sixth Ed. Upper Saddle River, New Jersey: Prentice Hall.

Smith, W. and C. Monastersky. 1986. Assessing Juvenile Sexual Offenders' Risk for Reoffending. *Criminal Justice and Behavior* 13: 115-140.

Studer, L. and S. Alywin. 2006. Pedophilia: The Problem with Diagnosis and Limitations of CBT in Treatment. *Medical Hypotheses* 67: 774-781.

Talbot, T., L. Gilligan, M. Carter, and S. Matson. 2002. *An Overview of Sex Offender Management*. Washington, D.C.: Center for Sex Offender Management.

Thornhill, R. and C. Palmer. 2000. *A Natural History of Rape: Biological Bases of Sexual Coercion*. Cambridge, Massachusetts: MIT Press.

Tong, D. 2007. The Penile Plethysmograph, Able Assessment for Sexual Interest, and MSI-II: Are They Speaking the Same Language? *The American Journal of Family Therapy* 35: 187-202.

Trivits, L. and N. Repucci. 2002. Application of Megan's Law to Juveniles. *American Psychologist* 57: 690-704.

Turner, H., D. Finkelhor, and R. Ormrod. 2006. The Effects of Lifetime Victimization on the Mental Health of Children and Adolescents. *Social Science and Medicine* 62: 13-27.

U.S. Department of Justice. 2003. *Criminal Victimization in the United States, 2002*. Washington, D.C.: Bureau of Justice Statistics.

Walsh, A. 1983. *Differential Sentencing Patterns among Felony Sex Offenders and Non Sex Offenders*. Ann Arbor, Michigan: University Microfilms International.

———. 1988. Lessons and Concerns from a Case Study of a "Scientific Molester." *Corrective and Social Psychiatry and Journal of Behavior Technology, Methods, and Therapy*. 34: 18-23.

———. 1990. Twice Labeled: The Effects of Psychiatric Labeling on the Sentencing of Sex Offenders. *Social Problems* 37: 375-389.

———. 1994. Homosexual and Heterosexual Child Molestation: Case Characteristics and Sentencing Differentials. *International Journal of Offender Therapy and Comparative Criminology*. 38: 339-353.

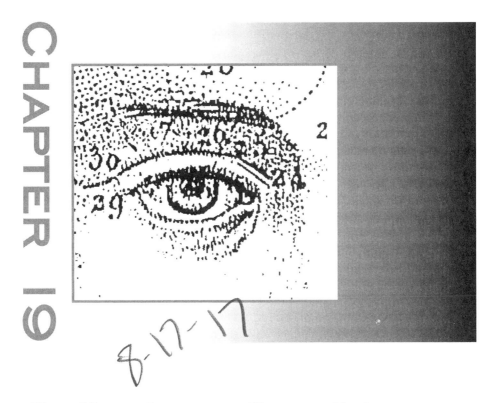

CHAPTER 19

8-17-17

Mentally Ill and Mentally Deficient Offenders

Our task now is to begin to understand that the causes of mental health problems are as varied as their manifestations. Some are physical. Some are emotional. Some are rooted in social and environmental conditions. Most are a complex combination of these and other factors, some of which are unknown.

—**President's Commission on Mental Health**

Mentally ill and mentally deficient (low IQ) offenders pose a particularly difficult set of challenges for the correctional worker. A survey of New York probation officers found that working with mentally ill and mentally deficient offenders presented them with their greatest difficulties (Wertlieb and Greenberg 1989). For new correctional workers used to dealing with only "fully rational" people in their daily lives, their first acquaintance with mentally ill or deficient offenders comes as quite a shock, even experienced officers report being ill at ease with them (Skeem and Louden 2006). Nevertheless, correctional workers must be prepared to deal effectively with offenders who are especially ill equipped to respond positively to their problems.

Figure 19.1, on the next page, presents the highlights of a Bureau of Justice Statistics report on the mental health problems of prison and jail inmates that provides a preliminary idea of the problem faced in corrections (James and Glaze 2006).

Figure 19.1 Prevalence of Mental Health Problems of Prison and Jail Inmates

	Percent of inmates in			
	State Prison		Local Jail	
Selected characteristics	With mental problem	Without problem	With mental problem	Without problem
Criminal record				
Current or past violent offense	61%	56%	44%	36%
3 or more prior incarcerations	25	19	26	20
Substance dependence or abuse	74%	56%	76%	53%
Drug use in month before event	63%	49%	62%	42%
Family background				
Homelessness in year before arrest	13%	6%	17%	9%
Past physical or sexual abuse	27	10	24	8
Parents abused alcohol or drugs	39	25	37	19
Charged with violating rules*	58%	43%	19%	9%
Physical or verbal assault	24	14	8	2
Injured in a fight since admission	20%	10%	9%	3%
*Includes items not shown				

• Nearly a quarter of both state prisoners and jail inmates who had a mental health problem, compared to a fifth of those without, had served three or more prior incarcerations.

• Female inmates had higher rates of mental health problems than male inmates (state prisons: 73 percent of females and 55 percent of males; local jails: 75 percent of females and 63 percent of males).

• About 74 percent of state prisoners and 76 percent of local jail inmates who had a mental health problem met criteria for substance dependence or abuse.

• Nearly 63 percent of state prisoners who had a mental health problem had used drugs in the month before their arrest, compared to 49 percent of those without a mental health problem.

• State prisoners who had a mental health problem were twice as likely as those without to have been homeless in the year before their arrest (13 percent compared to 6 percent).

• Jail inmates who had a mental health problem (24 percent) were three times as likely as jail inmates without (8 percent) to report being physically or sexually abused in the past.

• More than one in three state prisoners and one in six jail inmates who had a mental health problem had received treatment since admission.

• State prisoners who had a mental health problem were twice as likely as state prisoners without to have been injured in a fight since admission (20 percent compared to 10 percent).

Source: D. James and L. Glaze. 2006. *Mental Health Problems of Prison and Jail Inmates*. Bureau of Justice Statistics, U.S. Department of Justice.

This study found that 24 percent of state prison inmates, 14 percent of federal prison inmates, and 21 percent of jail inmates had a recent history of mental health problems, with female inmates more like to have such problems than male inmates. The 2006 study did not address probation and parole populations, but a 1999 Bureau of Justice Statistics report indicated that 547, 8000 (about 14 percent of the total) probationers/parolees had some form of mental illness (Ditton 1999). These figures do not include mentally deficient (IQ 70 or below) offenders, who are estimated to constitute 10 percent of the jail and prison populations (Schmalleger 2001). The Judge David L. Bazelon Center for Mental Health Law estimates that about 16 percent of individuals on probation or parole have some form of mental illness (2008).

Although no similar figures are available for the number of community corrections' offenders who are mentally deficient rather than mentally ill, many are functioning at an intellectual level that makes them difficult and frustrating people with whom to work, and almost all of them will have IQ's below the general population average of 100. To be forewarned is to be forearmed, so the more you learn about such offenders before meeting them the better prepared you will be. Some of you might even find the challenge so interesting and rewarding that you might decide to specialize in this type of offender.

Schizophrenia

You will run into a variety of mentally ill offenders in corrections. This is not the place to conduct a comprehensive overview of mental illness, so we concentrate on the syndrome illnesses most associated with offending (psychopathy is not considered an illness since psychopaths are able to function well, if not morally, in society). According to Palermo, Gumz, and Liska (1992), schizophrenics probably account for more criminal offenses than all other mental patients combined do. Thus, we limit our discussion of mental illness to this group.

Schizophrenia is the most widespread of the psychotic disorders, affecting perhaps as much as 1 percent of the population (Mueser and McGurk 2004). With an incidence of this magnitude, you can expect to have to supervise at least a few diagnosed schizophrenic offenders on your caseload at some time or another. With the evolution of concerns for patients' rights and the accompanying deinstitutionalization movement, many schizophrenics previously hospitalized are now living on the streets. For instance, in 1955 there were 339 per 100,000 individuals in state mental hospitals compared with 20 per 100,000 in 2001 (Lamb, Weinberger, and Gross 2004). This, combined with the elevated risk of criminal behavior among this population, leaves the criminal justice system as the only system left to absorb much of the mentally ill population (Lamb, Weinberger, and Gross 2004). Robinson (2005) reports that there are now about three-and-one-half times more mentally ill people in American prisons and jails as there are in psychiatric hospitals.

Schizophrenics are extremely difficult to supervise in a community corrections setting, and they frequently end up seriously violating their conditions of probation or parole and being consigned to prison. Schizophrenics are not, however, a homogeneous category of individuals. There are various medically defined subtypes, which need not concern us here. The most severely impaired schizophrenics are hospitalized, so those with whom you may be dealing are able to function minimally in the community (Lurigio 2001).

415

As well as being differentiated behaviorally and symptomatically, schizophrenics also may be differentiated by the pathway they took to their condition. The most serious and most typical type of schizophrenic is the process schizophrenic. Process schizophrenia develops insidiously over a long time. The histories of individuals with process schizophrenia show an early inability to function normally, to make friends, to handle schoolwork, and to behave acceptably.

The second type of schizophrenic is the reactive schizophrenic. People with reactive schizophrenia may not have a history of psychological and social dysfunction. Their descent into schizophrenia is usually marked by the onset of an acutely stressful experience. The psychological evaluation of Bill Bloggs described him as "being in the early stage of reactive schizophrenia," related to the stress of his arrest and incarceration (sometimes termed "jailhouse psychosis"). Research evidence bears out the proposition that incarceration for the first time, along with other profoundly stressful experiences, can bring out symptoms of mental disorder not previously in evidence (Walker et al. 2004).

The "four A's" are readily observed symptoms used by mental health professionals to make a preliminary diagnosis of schizophrenia (American Psychiatric Association 2001). These are the following:

1. Autism (living in a subjective fantasy world)

2. Ambivalence (simultaneous conflicting feelings)

3. Inappropriate affect (emotions and feelings that are not congruent with the situation)

4. Loose associations (the connection of an experience or idea with an unrelated experience or idea).

Although offenders are probably diagnosed with schizophrenia before community corrections workers see them, be on the lookout for evidence of any of these four A's. Many people suffering from psychosis are not identified/diagnosed unless their symptoms are explicitly part of their offenses (Lurigio 2001); so, if you encounter them, make a referral to the local diagnostic and treatment center.

It is extremely difficult for the average person to have any idea what the schizophrenic experience is like. To obtain an inkling of what it might be like, think of the scariest and most vivid dreams you have ever had. When we are in a dream state, our neurons are active making random connections. We do not make these connections in response to external stimuli as occurs when we are awake; since we are unconscious during sleep, there are no external stimuli. The brain has an inherent need for structure, to make sense of the information coming into it from the outside in the form of electrochemical impulses. During sleep, it does the best that it can to generate order from this chemical chaos by drawing on experiences stored in its memory.

However, since the brain impulses are largely haphazard, darting from one memory to others that may be quite unrelated, the images they generate are less than coherent. As Garrett (2009: 474) describes the process: "the brain engages in a sort of confabulation [a process of filling in gaps in one's memory with fabrications that one believes to be true] using information from memory to impose meaning on nonsensical random input." Based on brain imaging studies, some hypothesize that this "confabulation" is the result of abnormal interactions between the prefrontal cortex and other brain areas (Lawrie et al. 2008).

Individuals evoke their dreams and schizophrenic states from a very private reality, which may be scary and quite incoherent. The difference—and what a difference it is—is that when we dream, we wake up, are aware that we were dreaming, and begin to respond "normally" to stimuli from the outside world. Schizophrenics must remain in the scary and incoherent private world with their brain trying to make sense out of a neurochemical cascade that has little or no connection with external reality. In sum, schizophrenics have great difficulties in filtering information and focusing their attention and responding appropriately to environmental stimuli (Pinel 2000).

Causality

The causes of schizophrenia have long been hotly debated. In this author's undergraduate days, radical environmentalists dismissed schizophrenia as a myth, or as a diagnostic "grab bag" used against poor people of whose behavior we disapproved. This viewpoint was radically wrong, for schizophrenia is an identifiable entity that we can "see" with the use of positron emission tomography (PET) and functional magnetic resonance imaging (fMRI) scans. PET and fMRI scans provide information about brain functioning and produce distinct neurological maps of normal, schizophrenic, and manic depressive individuals (Walker et al. 2004). These identifiable differences in brain functioning indicate an objective physical reality corresponding to the observable behavioral symptoms that describe the condition we call *schizophrenia*.

Experts now know that schizophrenia has a genetic basis, but just how strong that basis is remains an open question. As we have seen, the heritability of a trait is most often determined by comparing its incidence among identical twins, who share 100 percent of their genes, with fraternal twins, who share only 50 percent, on average. According to the logic of behavioral genetics, if genes influence a trait, we should see stronger similarities between individuals who share more of their genes than among people who share fewer of their genes. All studies show a much larger concordance rate (about 50 percent) or more for identical twins than for fraternal twins (about 12 percent) (Mueser and McGurk 2004, Walker et al. 2004). In other words, if one of a pair of identical twins has schizophrenia, about half of the time so will the co-twin, but if one of the fraternal twins has it, the co-twin has only about a 12 percent risk of having it. Note that both percentages are considerably greater than the general-population-risk rate for schizophrenia of 1 percent.

An earlier clue to the chemical basis for schizophrenia came with the advent of the antipsychotic drugs, such as haloperidol and clozapine, which work by blocking the neurotransmitter dopamine at the synapse. All antipsychotic drugs are effective, but a number of patients are neurologically treatment-resistant. Clozapine, works well in such cases but carries a significant risk of seizures (Hales, Yudofsky, and Talbot 1996). The new generation antipsychotic drugs include risperidone and aripiprazole, which are more powerful and have fewer side effects (Buckley 2004).

A literature review of the various antipsychotic drugs concluded that they have differing effects on the various cognitive deficits suffered by schizophrenics, and thus medication should be specifically tailored to the severity of each individual's symptoms (Meltzer and McGurk 1999). All antipsychotic drugs work more effectively for symptoms such as hallucinations, delusions, and incoherence, which represent increased neural activity, than for symptoms such as decreased neural activity, such as withdrawal, lack of warmth, and blunted emotions (Buckley 2004, Pinel 2000).

Schizophrenia, viewed at the molecular level seems to be a function of one of three possible conditions: (1) an excess of dopamine, (2) a deficiency of enzymes that remove dopamine after it has performed its excitatory function, or (3) an excess of dopamine receptors in the brain (Pinel 2000). Any one of these conditions (or a combination of all three) would cause the hyper-stimulation of the brain characteristic of schizophrenics.

Other researchers note that high doses of amphetamines can produce symptoms mimicking psychosis by stimulating the secretion of dopamine (Mueser and McGurk 2004). If any offenders show schizophrenic symptoms, it is a good idea to check their substance abuse history for excessive use of stimulants and hallucinogens; substance abuse may induce and/or exacerbate schizophrenic symptoms (Buckley 2004).

The Diathesis/Stress Model

Linking the schizophrenic syndrome to brain structure and functioning and genetic predisposition does not preclude strong environmental input. After all, if only one-half of a genetically identical twin pair falls afoul of the disease, on average, then there must have been something in the environment of the afflicted twin that was not in the environment of the unafflicted twin that caused the schizophrenia. The 1995 International Congress on Schizophrenia Research summarized a decade of research by concluding that: "genetic factors determine predispositions to schizophrenia, but environmental factors are required for expression of the illness" (Buckley et al. 1996: 458).

The diathesis/stress model is a biosocial model that has dominated the schizophrenia research field for a long time. This model posits that a congenital predisposition (diathesis) combined with environmental stressors is necessary for the syndrome to occur. In other words, persons can possess constitutional vulnerability for the disease but not succumb to it unless they are exposed to one or more major environmental stressors. The list of potential environmental stressors is seemingly endless: genetic mutation suffered during embryonic development, rubella, maternal influenza, birth complications such as oxygen deprivation, exposure to abuse and neglect, poverty, and extremely traumatic environmental events (Buckley 2004, Mueser and McGurk 2004). A number of researchers have hypothesized that the hormonal surges of puberty (adolescence is the most common time of the onset of schizophrenic symptoms) trigger the expression of liability genes and the brain malfunctions that underlie the syndrome (Walker and Tessner 2008).

There are thus many possible pathways to schizophrenia, and we certainly do not want to fall into the trap of blaming every developmental outcome on parental behavior as used to be the case when strict environmentalism ruled the causal roost. Many of the negative parental events observed among families of schizophrenics are more likely to be effects of schizophrenia rather than a cause. Even the most loving of parents may become frustrated and eventually turn away when their mentally ill children continually rebuff their best efforts. Schizophrenia can develop even in "model" loving families.

The Link Between Mental Illness and Crime

After several decades of denying that there was any link between mental illness and crime, the psychiatric community has reversed its stance. Many of the studies that led to the conclusion that there was no link between crime and mental illness were conducted during the period when individuals with serious mental illnesses were routinely institutionalized for very long periods, and often even for life. As we have seen, the deinstitutionalization movement in the 1960s shifted many such persons into the community and resulted in greater visibility and higher arrest rates for the mentally ill (Bartol 2002, Marzuk 1996).

Even with the new evidence, there is some reluctance to affirm the link between crime and mental illness out of fear of further stigmatizing an already highly stigmatized group. However, the evidence cannot be dismissed or ignored, especially by correctional workers charged with supervising the mentally ill. In one review of eighty-six studies that examined the relationship between mental illness and criminal/antisocial behavior, seventy-nine (92 percent) found the relationship to be positive, six studies were nonsignificant, and only one study was negative; that is, mental illness was associated with lower levels of criminal and antisocial behavior in this study (Ellis and Walsh 2000).

Two studies found that the incidence of violence was up to five-times greater among people with serious mental problems (mostly schizophrenics and manic-depressives) than among people with no diagnosis of mental illness after controlling for many demographic factors (Link et al. 1992, Swanson 1994). Researchers in Denmark looking at more than 300,000 individuals followed to age forty-three found that persons with histories of psychiatric hospitalization were three to eleven times more likely to have criminal convictions than people with no psychiatric history (Hodkins et al. 1996).

Similarly, a Swedish study reported that people with psychosis are about four times more likely to have a criminal record than members of the general population (Tuninger et al. 2001), and an American study (Buckley 2004) found that schizophrenics were far more like to be imprisoned for assaultive crimes than for any other type of crime. A well-controlled British study found that male schizophrenics had three times as many convictions for violent crimes than nonpsychotic criminals in a control group (Beck and Wencel 1998).

After reviewing many studies of the link between mental illness and violence, Marzuk concluded that:

> [W]e must recognize that the link is a real one and that it persists even after controlling for demographic . . . variables. The link appears strongest for the severe mental illnesses, particularly those involving psychosis, and, as for those persons without diagnosed mental illness, it is increased by the use of alcohol and other psychoactive substances. It is likely that active symptoms, particularly distorted perceptions, faulty reasoning, and distorted modulation of affect are more important than the label of a specific diagnosis (1996: 484).

However, the vast majority of the mentally ill are nonviolent, and they are more likely to be victims of violence than perpetrators (Marzuk 1996). The mentally ill most at risk include the homelessness, those who use alcohol and other drugs, and those who do not take their antipsychotic medication (Buckley 2004).

As is the case with sex offenders, all mentally ill persons are usually defined by the worst amongst them. Patients who remain connected to other human beings and who faithfully take their medication are probably less dangerous than the average person is (Bartol 2002). Most of the worst killers in American history were morally rather than mentally "sick." Most of the truly scary people one of the authors has met in his days in the field were not mental patients, and most of the mental patients he has met seemed much more scared and anxious than dangerous. Nonetheless, the correctional worker must be aware that if the situation is right, the mentally ill offender is at greater risk for committing violence than is the typical offender.

Treatment

The treatment of schizophrenics is primarily a medical concern. The correctional worker is involved as a community resource broker and as a medication monitor. Most schizophrenics are quite manageable and cooperative as long as they are taking their antipsychotic medication. The difficulty has always been to make sure that they take it. They are quite prone to "forgetting" their daily dose, and some who may be willing to take it one day will be unwilling to take it the next day for fear that they are being "poisoned," or because of its side effects. You may be able to circumvent schizophrenic offenders' ambivalence about daily pill taking by negotiating an agreement to treatment with the long-acting drug risperidone. This drug is injected every two or three weeks, and the medication is gradually released over that time (Buckley 2004). You usually can enlist the help of a family member to drive the patient to the community health clinic for this treatment every two weeks or so.

Again, be cautioned against the old "treating symptoms rather than causes" argument. Drugs no more cure schizophrenia than insulin cures diabetes. Yet, who would deny insulin to the diabetic? Antipsychotic drugs do for schizophrenics what insulin does for diabetics. They stabilize biological functions, and by doing so, they help them to cope and enable them to control desires to act out their delusions. The combination of appropriate medication and individual and family counseling has shown good results with schizophrenics who have been properly assessed as being able to benefit from such a regimen (Lamberti 2007, Spaulding et al. 1999).

Sometimes schizophrenics who do not suffer too severely from the disorder are able to stabilize their lives through a supportive marriage and the acquisition of some work skills. You cannot play Cupid, but you can try to obtain employment for schizophrenic offenders in sheltered workshops. Sheltered workshops provide an opportunity for individuals to learn work skills, gather self esteem, and become somewhat independent in a protective work setting that is not as demanding as a regular work setting. Such work shelters also provide counseling and instruction on such work related activities as grooming, timekeeping, learning work habits, following instructions and orders, and getting along with fellow employees.

Most large cities have at least one such workshop in the community, but the final decision about admissions belongs to their administrators. If you have an offender who you feel is a likely candidate for admission to a work shelter, you should accompany the offender on a visit so that you can learn about its program and of the administrator's reasons for granting or denying the offender a place.

Remember, schizophrenics' perceptions of reality, however distorted, are as real to them as your vivid dreams are to you while you are experiencing them. Schizophrenics have withdrawn from the common reality because it is too painful and threatening, so they have a stake in maintaining their own. You should not argue with their reality, but this restraint does not preclude your pointing out its disadvantages or comparing it with your own reality in a gentle and reassuring manner. You should not validate their reality by pretending to participate in it, and you should not accept their condition as hopeless. Involving family members of schizophrenics in their treatment (Heinssen and Cuthbert 2001) and using cognitive-behavioral therapy while they are on their medication is beneficial (Muesser and Bond 2000).

Milwaukee's Community Support Program

A "model" community based program for schizophrenics is Milwaukee's Community Support Program (CSP). The program's primary objective "to keep persons afflicted with chronic mental illnesses out of local jails and hospitals and to help them live independently" (McDonald and Teitelbaum 1994: 8). The program receives most of its clients from the courts and probation agencies in the area, although some are referred from elsewhere. Like all good criminal justice programs, the Community Support Program adopts a "carrot and stick" approach to managing its clientele. It does everything that it can to help offenders live independently and within the law, but noncompliance with directives often results in withdrawal of services or a new court appearance. The principal kinds of services provided to Community Support Program participants are therapeutic, financial management, and housing assistance.

Therapeutic services include both medical and psychosocial services. Offenders receive a full medical examination upon entry; they receive close monitoring thereafter. The primary medical service is the provision of antipsychotic medication five days per week. After nurses verify that offenders have taken their medication, offenders receive a chit, which they turn in at the cashier's window where they receive their daily monetary allowance. Failure to take medication results in nonpayment of this allowance. It is surprising how many notoriously reluctant patients suddenly become motivated to take their medication when there is an immediate cash reward for doing so.

The Community Support Program is able to reward offenders for taking their medication because it is the legal recipient of each offender's social security and disability benefits. The program pays all offenders' fixed expenses such as rent and utilities, with the rest doled out after each dose of medication. Financial management services are particularly useful for mentally ill offenders who are poorly prepared to manage their own finances and often are preyed on by thieves who know when social security checks are delivered. Full time financial advisers maintain offenders' accounts and work out budgets and other money management techniques with them to maintain the relative stability of their cash flow.

The third major component of the program is housing assistance. Many offenders come to the program lacking any type of stable accommodation. Housing specialists at the Community Support Program indicate that they are able to find stable housing for offenders with relative ease because property owners like the idea of regular payments coming directly from the program rather than having to chase down renters every month.

Space does not permit more than this barebones description of this program that appears to be the probation/parole officer's dream. Such a program in any jurisdiction would prove a tremendous asset to correctional workers who could not possibly supply the services supplied by Community Support Program. The program illustrates that it is possible to supervise mentally ill offenders in the community quite successfully and relatively inexpensively. While this program (which began in 1978) has not been formally evaluated, its continued funding from state and local government as well as high praise from the local judiciary and probationary agencies, speak of the high esteem in which the program is held (McDonald and Teitelbaum 1994).

The National Institute of Corrections document, *Mentally Ill Offenders in the Community*, provides descriptions and evaluations of a number of other similar community programs in various states (Veysey 1995). The conclusions made following these evaluations are as follows:

- Cross training of probation and mental health staff is crucial to develop an understanding of the complex needs of individual probationers and of the systems involved in providing services.

- Probation programs that contract for or provide mental health services in conjunction with special revocation or supervision practices show great promise.

- Integration of services is critical to meet the many needs of probationers with mental illness. Intensive case management programs that link mental health, substance-abuse treatment, and other social support services with housing and entitlements are effective mechanisms to promote integration of services. Caseworkers can use mechanisms that encourage integration of systems, such as community planning boards and memoranda of understanding, to identify and overcome barriers to the provision of services, particularly concerning fiscal and turf issues.

The Mentally Deficient Offender

Although there are high IQ offenders (for example, corporate criminals and some serial killers), the great majority of the criminal offenders you will be dealing with will have IQ's below the general population average of 100. The relationship between IQ and crime can be visualized in the form of the normal (bell-shaped) curve. Very low IQ (50 and below) are at very low risk for committing crimes; the risk climbs steadily from there and peaks with IQs in the "dull-normal" category (IQ in the range 80-90). The risk then declines with increasing IQ (Ellis and Walsh 2003). In other words, very low and very high IQ individuals are underrepresented in the criminal population, and those with IQs from about 70 to 90 are overrepresented.

Mental deficiency (also sometimes called intellectual disability) is defined as having an IQ score under 70 together with poor social functioning (Petersilia 2004). Although people fitting this description constitute only about 2 1/2 percent of the population, they are overrepresented in prisons and community corrections in many Western countries (McBrien 2003). These people are childlike in their thinking and are easily manipulated by their more intelligent (albeit, below average) peers. The definition of mental deficiency may be extended to include anyone whose level of intelligence makes it difficult for him or her to function adaptively and pro-socially in our increasingly complex world. We will thus look at the impact of low IQ in general, and not confine ourselves to offenders with IQs below 70.

Intellectual functioning, as measured by IQ tests, is making a strong comeback after a long period of neglect in terms of its relationship with criminal activity (Ellis and Walsh 2003). We agree with Wilson and Herrnstein's opinion that:

> Criminology acted rashly when, in the 1930s, it virtually ceased considering IQ as a significant correlate of criminal behavior, for it was just at that moment in the evolution of mental testing that the tests were beginning to yield solid data on the cognitive predispositions toward offending (1985: 159).

Although many criminologists still believe that IQ tests are biased, a decade's worth of research conducted by geneticists, psychometricians, developmental psychologists, and neuroscientists led the prestigious National Academy of Sciences to insist that they are not (Seligman 1992), and an overwhelming proportion of more than 1,000 experts surveyed by Snyderman and Rothman (1988) agreed. More recently, the American Psychological Association's Task Force on Intelligence reiterated that IQ tests were not biased, and that variation in genes has a very large influence on variance in intelligence (Neisser et al. 1995).

Although some people are still loath to admit the role of genes in intelligence, evidence from behavioral genetics indicates that about 60 percent of the variance in IQ scores is attributable to genetic factors, which leaves about 40 percent attributable to environmental factors (Dickens and Flynn 2001, Neisser et al. 1995). Additionally, numerous brain-imaging studies Posthuma, de Geus and Boomsma (2003) reviewed show the relation of IQ to a number of anatomical and physiological features of the brain.

However, no matter what our part our genes play, our intelligence is stretched or suppressed by a host of environmental factors such as low birth weight, poverty, malnutrition, lack of stimulation, and abuse and neglect, all of which modify gene expression and thus heritability estimates (Turkheimer et al. 2003). For instance, one study found that abused and neglected illegitimate children had both the lowest average VIQ (83.02) and highest average PIQ (102.24) among four cross-classified groups of juvenile delinquents (Walsh 1990). These findings lend support to the hypothesis developed in Chapter 3 that abuse and neglect can lead to elevated PIQ scores relative to VIQ scores through the possible effect of abuse and neglect in dampening autonomic nervous system response. A review of the literature by Salzinger and her colleagues (1991) found across various studies that abuse and neglect has a serious negative impact on IQ levels.

The Intelligence Tests and What They Mean

Given this new interest in IQ, and given that IQ scores are the assessment measurements most readily available (and probably one of the most useful) to correctional workers, it is necessary to know what these scores have to tell us. The most widely used IQ tests are the Revised Wechsler Intelligence Scale for Children (WISC R) and the Wechsler Adult Intelligence Scale (WAIS).

As we saw in Chapter 3, these scales are divided into verbal and performance subtests, providing measures of verbal IQ (VIQ) and performance IQ (PIQ). PET scan studies have shown that the neurological processes engaged when subjects were administered the different IQ subscales and were lateralized to opposite hemispheres of the brain (Chase et al. 1984, Duara et al. 1984). In other words, different sides of the brain are involved depending on whether the individual is working a problem that engages verbal or performance IQ skills. VIQ and PIQ subtests are alternated and are administered in the following order:

Verbal Scale	**Performance Scale**
1. Information	2. Picture completion
3. Similarities	4. Picture arrangement
5. Arithmetic	6. Block design
7. Vocabulary	8. Object assembly
9. Comprehension	10. Coding (or mazes)

All ten subtests as a whole are measures of general intelligence in that they measure an individual's capacity to think rationally, act purposefully, and to deal effectively with his or her environment. They attempt to measure such things as long- and short-term memory, concentration, computational skills, verbal abstractions, awareness of and openness to one's culture and its norms, manual dexterity, visual/spatial acuity, and adaptability. However, there is no one to one relationship between the two subscales; they measure somewhat different domains of intelligence, with the performance scale providing an assessment for those whose family backgrounds do not promote verbal skills. Both subscales contribute about equally to an individual's full scale IQ score.

Most studies linking IQ to crime and delinquency have viewed IQ as a unitary phenomenon. That is, IQ studies have tended to correlate full scale IQ with various measures of crime and delinquency. Such a conceptualization of IQ may obscure as much about the IQ/delinquency relationship as it reveals. You can obtain full scale IQ (FIQ) by summing VIQ and PIQ scores and dividing by two. For example, if an individual has a VIQ score of 100 and a PIQ score of 90, his or her FIQ is $(100 + 90)/2 = 95$. The reason that the use of FIQ might distort the IQ/delinquency relationship is that offenders typically show a greater deficit in VIQ than they do in PIQ relative to general population norms. Combining the two subscales to obtain FIQ has the effect of making the overall IQ mean scores for the general and delinquent populations somewhat more equal than they would otherwise be (Walsh 2003), thus leading to the underestimation of the influence of cognitive variables on delinquency.

You may view low VIQ individuals as somewhat more prone to violence and aggression because they lack verbal skills that mediate between a stimulus and a response. Restak (2001) tells us that the motor areas of the cortex mature earlier than areas involved with thought processes, making for speedy responses to stimuli on the part of infants and young children that are not mediated by thought processes. As children mature, increasing communication occurs between the verbal and motor hemispheres of the brain, and their responses to stimuli slow while the left-brain processes and interprets motor behavior initiated by the right brain. Initially, this is an "after the fact" interpretive process, but with increasing language acquisition and socialization, children eventually are able to foresee their response before they react. In other words, there is an ever increasing engagement of the left hemisphere in the processing, organization, and appropriate inhibition, of emotional transmissions received from the right brain.

The efficiency with which the left hemisphere performs its interpretive and inhibitory task varies considerably from person to person. Early environmental experience greatly influences this variability. There is stiff competition within the infant's rapidly branching neurons for synaptic connections, and those neurons activated most frequently are those that firmly establish themselves (Kolb, Gibb, and Robinson 2003). To borrow a couple of metaphors from transactional analysis, established neuronal connection patterns function as "memory tapes" playing over and over in the head until they become a "life script" governing our interactions with others.

Children who have strong visual spatial capabilities relative to their verbal capabilities may tend to retain some of the unmediated rapidity of response to stimuli that is characteristic of the immature brain. As such, when these children grow older, they retain their childhood priorities for instant pleasure and self-gratification without having developed the "self-talk" necessary to generate a sense of discipline, responsibility, and recognition of the rights of others. When we have a young child who processes information this way, we have a "brat" who slaps playmates and steals their candy. A juvenile or an adult using similar cognitive processes may be a delinquent or a criminal, who steals, assaults, robs, and rapes. The cognitive processes of the immature child and the delinquent or criminal are the same, but the content of those cognitions becomes much more threatening as the person becomes older, stronger, and more ambitious in the pursuit of instant self gratification.

Low IQ indexes a low level of social and interpersonal maturity, which means that individuals with low IQs will need somewhat different treatment modalities. Researchers have linked low IQ (particularly VIQ) to levels of interpersonal maturity using the I level ("I" for "interpersonal maturity") system. This system proposes that cognitive and personality integration follows a sequential pattern in normal human development, and sets up seven I levels. Level one is the most basic (the character Lenny in *Of Mice and Men* is an example of I-level 1 functioning), and the extremely rare level seven is considered the ideal (perhaps only someone such as Mother Theresa fall into this category). Criminals generally are levels two through five, with level five so rarely found among them that only levels two through four usually are used to assess delinquent and criminal subjects. Bartollas and Miller (2005) point out that the I-Level system has been widely used, particularly in training schools for delinquents, throughout the United States.

As might be expected, interpersonal maturity varies positively with VIQ. In Andrew's (1980) study, level two subjects, subjects in which the only system of cognitive reference appear to be themselves and their personal needs, had a mean VIQ of 78.7. Level three subjects, those who have internalized some social rules but who use them to manipulate, had a mean VIQ of 90.4. Level four subjects, who tend to be neurotic and acting out because of conflicts between personal needs and social rules that have been more strongly internalized than other I level subjects, had a VIQ mean of 98.4.

In an earlier study of probationers, Andrew (1974) found that interpersonal maturity was even more closely related to the P>V discrepancy marker (described in Chapter 3). The most mature probationers (I level four) had a mean P > V discrepancy of 4.41 points, the I level three probationers had a mean discrepancy of 7.33 points, while the I level two's had a mean of 17.78. It is clear that low verbal intelligence alone cannot account for interpersonal immaturity, and that a high PIQ relative to an individual's VIQ also plays an important part.

Overall, it is probable that intellectual maturity is a necessary, if not sufficient, condition for moral maturity. Researchers consistently find moderate correlations (in the mid .40s range) between moral reasoning and IQ (Ellis and Walsh 2000). Moral reasoning involves making decisions about what is acceptable behavior and what is not. A deficit in moral orientation also means a mental fixation on egocentric thinking and short run hedonism, patterns of thought more congruent with infantile and early childhood brain development than that of the mature adult. What this suggests is that individuals with a deficit in left brain VIQ relative to right brain PIQ have a tendency to act out rather than think out in a variety of situations. In a sense, then, violent and aggressive behavior is a form of visual/spatial ability that is unregulated by verbal ability among individuals lacking in internal moral standards of conduct.

Mental deficiency does not necessarily have to mean mental retardation. The former term connotes a correctable deficiency in mental functioning; the latter connotes a congenital impairment of the ability to learn. Relatively large numbers of offenders with mental deficiencies will be on correctional caseloads. These people have the mental capacity to commit crimes but are deficient in the capacity to forge a responsible lifestyle.

The Impact of IQ on Life Outcomes

IQ is related to a wide range of life outcomes, many of which are related to criminal behavior such as low level of education, unemployment, and poverty. The data presented below in Figure 19.2 come from 12,686 white males and females in the *National Longitudinal Study of Youth*. Respondents were first tested in 1979 when they were fourteen to seventeen years old; the outcome data were collected in 1989 when they were twenty-four to twenty-seven years old. Subjects were divided into the bottom 20 percent on IQ (scores of 87 and below) and the top 20 percent (scores 113 and above). The data represent the percentage of subjects in each category with the indicated life outcome and the ratios between the two percentages. Of most immediate concern to this chapter, note that thirty-one low-IQ subjects were interviewed in jail or prison for every one high-IQ subject interviewed in jail or prison. Thus, low IQ affects many areas of life that increase the probability of offending. If we had taken the bottom and top 10 percent rather than the bottom and top 20 percent, the results would have been even more dramatic.

Figure 19. 2 IQ Level and Social Behavior

	IQ Level		
Social Behavior	Bottom 20%	Top 20%	Ratio
Dropped out of high school	66%	2%	33.0:1
Living below poverty level	48%	5%	9.6:1
Unemployed entire previous year*	64%	4%	16.0:1
Ever interviewed in jail or prison	62%	2%	31.0:1
Chronic welfare recipient	57%	2%	28.5:1
Had child out of wedlock**	52%	3%	17.3:1

*Males only **Females only. Bottom 20 percent = IQ 87 and below; Top 20 percent = IQ 113 and above.

Source: National Longitudinal Study of Youth. Data taken from various chapters in Herrnstein and Murray (1994), *The Bell Curve.*

How Does IQ Affect the Probability of Offending?

A number of reviews over the decade have characterized the IQ criminality relationship as ubiquitous and robust (Stattin and Klackenberg Larsson 1993, Walsh 2003. Nevertheless, perhaps because of mainstream sociology's distaste for explanations of individual differences, some criminologists have tended to avoid the issue of the link between IQ and criminality, or have even considered the topic taboo. Some consider it particularly distasteful if those individual differences are linked to genetic factors. Ellis and Walsh (2000) report that 130 out of 159 studies (82 percent) found a negative relationship between IQ and criminal and antisocial behavior (the lower the IQ the greater involvement in such behavior), twenty-four found nonsignificant results (mostly in self-report studies), and five actually reported a positive relationship. Demonstrating a link between IQ and crime is not the same as demonstrating a causal link.

We have already seen how the effects of IQ on the probability of offending can be underestimated by combining verbal IQ with performance IQ given that offenders are almost invariably below average on the former but not on the latter. Another is to estimate the effects of IQ on offending by combining youths who limit their offending to adolescence (Moffitt's adolescent-limited offenders) with those who commit offenses across the lifespan (Moffitt's life-course persistent offenders). Moffitt (1993) reports that there is only about a 1-point deficit between adolescent-limited offenders and nonoffenders, but about a 17-point deficit between life course-persistent offenders and nonoffenders. Analyzing these groups as if they constituted a homogeneous whole obviously diminishes the estimated effects of IQ on offending. Other studies have found the same 17-point difference (Gatzke-Kopp et al. 2002).

Perhaps intelligence is only linked to crime because only the less intelligent criminals are caught. The so called differential-detection hypothesis proposes exactly that; in other words, lower IQ offenders are overrepresented in the criminal justice system because of their inability to avoid detection. Moffitt and Silva's (1988) review of the evidence does not support this hypothesis. To explore this issue further, Moffitt and Silva obtained juvenile arrest and IQ data for every male born in a certain area of New Zealand over one year. They divided the males into three groups:

(1) self-reported delinquents who actually had a juvenile record, (2) self-reported delinquents who officially were undetected (they were unknown to the police), and (3) self-reported nondelinquents. They cross-checked all self-reports with police records for accuracy. They found that the two delinquent groups (detected and undetected) did not differ significantly from each other on mean FIQ, VIQ, or PIQ. This indicates that undetected delinquents were no "brighter" than their detected peers were. Both delinquent groups, however, had significantly lower FIQ and VIQ means than the non-delinquent group. The two delinquent groups did not differ from the nondelinquent group on PIQ, however, which again emphasizes the superiority of PIQ relative to VIQ among delinquents.

This still does not demonstrate a direct effect of IQ on crime and delinquency. Rather, low intelligence may exert its influence indirectly through a long chain of other negative factors. Figure 19.3 shows the most likely sequence of events.

Figure 19.3 Possible Sequence of the Effect of IQ on Crime and Delinquency

Low IQ → Poor school performance → Negative teacher evaluations → Dropping out of school → Associating with delinquent peers → Offending behavior

This chain indicates that individuals with low IQs tend to do poorly in school, which may lead to frustration, low self-esteem, and negative labeling by teachers. These outcomes have the effect of increasing the probability that low IQ people will drop out of school and associate with others ("bad company") with similar characteristics and experiences. This results in a number of frustrated and alienated young men (and increasingly, young women) of limited intelligence and achievement hanging around together on street corners with nothing to do, and as we all know, "The devil finds work for idle hands."

The other possibility is that IQ has a more direct effect. A national cohort study found that IQ scores at age four (long before children accumulate school experiences) predict later delinquency (Lipsitt, Buka, and Lipsitt 1990). In other words, poor cognitive skills and conduct problems are evident before children enter school, and poor school performance is another manifestation of these disabilities. This evokes the cognitive and temperamental deficits of Terrie Moffitt's life-course persistent offenders discussed in Chapter 3. In fact, a California Youth Authority study showed that early delinquency starters were much more likely to continue their criminal activity into their twenties and thirties than late starters, and that low IQ was a significant predictor of both early offending and offending into the thirties (Ge, Donnellan, and Wenk 2001).

A Look at the Intellectual Functioning of Correctional Offenders

Table 19.1 compares percentages in a sample of 376 Ohio adult male felons and a sample of 513 Idaho juvenile delinquents with percentages of the general population within seven IQ levels. The table provides some indication of the distribution of IQ levels with which the correctional helper can expect to work, although neither sample constitutes a random sample of the general population of offenders. The mean IQ of the adult sample is 93.5, and the mean IQ of the delinquent sample is 93.7.

Table 19.1 Comparison of Population IQ Norms with Scores of Criminal and Delinquent Samples

IQ Level	Descriptions and Anticipations	Percentage of General Population	Percentage of Criminal Sample	Percentage of Delinquent Sample
65 and below	Defective: needs special education, can function in protected situation.	2.2	0.5	3.5
66-79	Borderline: slow learner, can perform routine work under close supervision	6.7	13.3	10.2
80-90	Dull normal: can function independently but needs vocational training.	16.1	25.0	23.2
91-110	Normal: can complete high school and some college-level work, has few vocational limitations.	50.0	56.6	51.6
111-119	Bright: no limitations	16.1	2.4	9.2
120-127	Superior: no limitations	6.7	2.1	1.2
128 >	Very superior	2.2	0.5	0.4

* General population norms adapted from Wechsler, *The Measurement of Adult Intelligence* (Baltimore: Williams and Wilkins 1944).

These figures are somewhat higher than the 10 point gap (100 being the American mean IQ), which Wilson and Herrnstein (1985) say is consistently found between offenders and nonoffenders. However, the national mean includes the offender population, which means that if we excluded offenders in the calculation of the national mean, it may be close to 103 (Herrnstein 1989). In light of what we said earlier about the problem of combining VIQ and PIQ to obtain FIQ, note that the mean VIQ and PIQ scores of the juvenile sample were 90.5 and 97.6, respectively. The former is significantly different from the population mean, but the latter is not. Separate VIQ PIQ scores were not obtained from the adult sample.

The table provides comfort for those of us who believe in the concept of rehabilitation. Mindful of the limitations of the samples, what conclusions can we draw? It is clear that more than half of the subjects in both samples are within the normal range (90-110) of intelligence. Also, note that above-average intelligence (IQs more than 110) is relatively incompatible with the criminal activity with which most of us will be dealing. This is not to deny that many consider corporate crime, committed by high-IQ executives to be more costly than street crime, but administrative rather than criminal law usually deals with such activity.

Only 5 percent of the adult criminals and 4 percent of the delinquents had IQs more than 110, whereas 25 percent of the population has IQs that high. At the other end of the scale, those with IQs less than the normal range are overrepresented in both samples. They constitute 38.3 and 37.6 percent of the adult and juvenile samples, respectively; as opposed to the 25 percent we would expect if IQ and criminal activity were unrelated variables. Nevertheless, with the possible exception of the "defectives," all the offenders in the samples possess the intellectual capacity to be educable and/or trainable. This also means that they have the capacity to be taught to act responsibly.

We advise correctional workers to consider offenders' IQ scores, especially at the lower levels, as a reflection of their minimal rather than their maximal level of functioning. Of course, low intelligence does place limitations on what a person can achieve, but with a caring, involved, optimistic, and demanding helper, most offenders can be taught to behave responsibly and can be motivated to make the best of their capacities. If you do not make this belief an integral part of your operational style, then perhaps you could employ your talents better in some other line of work.

Special Problems Working with Mentally Deficient Offenders

For this discussion, "mentally deficient" are those at any level below the "dull normal" cutoff IQ score of 80. There are no glaring differences between mentally deficient offenders and other offenders; intellectual functioning is a matter of degree, not of kind. Yet, because of their deficiencies, many such offenders cannot express themselves adequately or indicate their needs, which often makes it difficult for correctional workers to identify the appropriate services they may require. Realizing this, some probation/parole agencies have special MRO (mentally retarded offender) units staffed by officers specially trained in mental retardation issues. According to Bowker and Schweid (1992), this is the "optimal" solution to supervising such offenders. Unfortunately, many departments do not have the resources to develop and train yet another "specialized" unit requiring relatively small caseloads. Given this situation, all correctional workers should be aware of the following concerns and difficulties when dealing with mentally deficient offenders.

The Nature of Today's Economy: People define terms such as retardation or mental deficiency relative to the level of intellectual functioning needed for meaningful participation in society. In labor intensive agricultural and industrial societies, low IQ individuals have many opportunities to earn a living wage, and thus participate meaningfully in their societies. However, as we move into the less labor intensive postindustrial age, the intellectual demands of the workplace have become increasingly complex. The more difficult those demands become, the level of intellectual functioning required to meet them becomes higher. The American economy has been bleeding manufacturing jobs overseas for the last two or three decades, and the competition for those jobs that remain leads employers to demand ever-increasing educational achievement to enter them, regardless of whether higher levels of educational preparation are really required to do the job. Thus, for those at lower levels of IQ, it becomes more frustrating for them to find and maintain employment that pays a living wage. Such unfortunate facts about the modern economy make the community brokerage aspect of correctional work more difficult, but not impossible.

Self-Esteem Maintenance: Most people are well aware of their limitations and do not need others to remind them of what they are. Few things are more self-esteem deflating than being told you are "stupid." Many offenders adopt their tough and aggressive veneer to resist others applying the "stupid" label to them (Carbonell and Perkins 2000). You must never imply by word, deed, or gesture, that mentally deficient offenders are anything less than valuable human beings. It is particularly important that you establish a warm supportive relationship with mentally deficient offenders because they tend to operate more from an emotional rather than an intellectual frame of reference (but take care that they do not become overly dependent on you).

Offenders are easier to deal with if they feel that you value their humanity. However, it is easy to become frustrated and angry with offenders who continually fail to follow instructions. You must hold them accountable for such failures, but you should never say things like, "God! I've told you over and over; wassamatter, are you stupid or somethin'?" Be firm, but be cognizant of the person's need to maintain his or her sense of self-worth.

The Self-Consistency Motive: Have you ever nodded knowingly in class when catching your professor's eye to acknowledge that you are following what he or she is saying when, in fact, you did not have a clue? Although you missed the chance to have the point clarified, it was probably more important to you to maintain the impression for yourself and others that you are a person who "catches on."

Some low-functioning offenders, likewise, are inclined to nod in response to what you might consider simple instructions when they actually are quite confused. They fear that to ask constantly for clarification would upset their (and your) tenuous hold on the image of themselves as "not stupid." One study of New York probation officers found that many of them complained that "special needs" offenders frequently did not understand their instructions (Wertlieb and Greenberg 1989: 10-17). So, do not assume that mentally deficient offenders fully understand your instructions just because they smile and nod at you.

Proctor and Beail frequently found that people with intellectual disabilities fail to develop a "theory of mind," which is your comprehension that others have a mind and mental states separate from your own (2007). That is, people who lack an adequate theory of mind tend to believe that others think exactly as they do and thus they have difficulty taking the perspectives of others that do not cohere with their own reality.

Patience is a Virtue: It should be obvious that patience is especially virtuous in dealing with such offenders. Because of their limited ability to take the perspective of others, you cannot assume that offenders with mental deficiencies appreciate what you are telling them. You should impart instructions slowly in simple language; that is specific and concrete. You should ask offenders to repeat instructions one at a time "just to make sure I know I'm telling you right, Jack." Remember, limited intelligence usually means a limited time horizon, so make sure that offenders can fulfill any instructions in reasonably short order. Make sure that you pay special attention to balancing (not overtaxing) treatment efforts, that you are especially concrete and specific, and that you proceed slowly.

The techniques of reality therapy are perhaps best suited to working with the mentally deficient offender. Its emphasis on specificity, concreteness, and "one step at a time" appears tailor-made for offenders lacking in the type of talking and reasoning skills required for Rational Emotive Therapy counseling or the analytical skills required for doing structural analysis in transactional analysis.

Personal Hygiene: Bathing and other habits or personal hygiene are not particularly important items on the agendas of most mentally deficient offenders. Ignorance of such matters often leads to disgust and ostracism from others. This may further exacerbate the person's low self-esteem. Poor hygiene and dress can prevent a person from obtaining even the most menial of jobs. There is no excuse for poor hygiene habits in today's society. Make sure that the offender understands this. It would be especially useful in this regard to be aware of special community agencies that work with such problems among the mentally deficient.

Case Study
Portrait of a Schizophrenic

Greg was a frail, good looking man of twenty-four when I first met him. He had two prior convictions for misdemeanor vandalism and was in my office now convicted of felony vandalism. Greg had this nasty habit of throwing chunks of rock through plate glass windows.

He was extremely difficult to interview for he manifested all the classic symptoms of the schizophrenic. He sat staring at me with flat affect, his hygiene was poor, and he did not particularly care what I had to say to him.

I was able to find out that his life revolved around the TV set, in front of which he spent practically every waking hour. He was not fussy about which programs he watched, but he was concerned that whatever channel it happened to be, it must not be changed. Each of his vandalism charges stemmed from arguments with his mother or some other family member over changing channels. The upshot of those arguments was that his mother would throw him out of the house. When that occurred, Greg would proceed to the closest business establishment with a big glass window, put a brick through it, and sit down among the debris to await the arrival of the police. This tactic yielded him a place to sleep and another TV at which he could stare.

I took Greg back home after the presentence investigation interview since he had just been released from the county jail and was penniless. I also wanted to get a feel for his environment. Upon meeting his mother, I soon formed an opinion of her as a dominating, egocentric, and manipulative shrew. She flatly informed me that the only reason that her son was welcome in her house was his $200 monthly disability check.

His four brothers were likewise unfriendly and cruel. Since Greg was much smaller than his brothers, and a "wacko" to boot, he was a convenient target for their verbal and physical aggression. It seemed to me that rather than involving himself with those who rejected him and offered him no love, Greg had withdrawn into a semicatatonic world of dials and plastic people. The characters on the screen could not rebuff him as real people could. I came to view his reactions to channel switching as an attempt to protect somehow the existence of those benign characters on the screen.

I learned that Greg was seeing a psychiatrist at a local center who was prescribing Thorazine for him. Unfortunately, family members never made it much of their business to make sure that Greg took his medication as directed. I was able to persuade his mother to request that his psychiatrist place him on Prolixin if medically advisable, arguing that for a small investment of her time (driving Greg to the center for his injection twice a month), she could enjoy a semblance of peace in the house. Additionally, more important for her, she could be assured of the uninterrupted flow of his disability checks. I also suggested that to avoid future problems she might consider buying Greg his own TV set.

Greg's mother did both of these things, and peace reigned for about nine months. Greg reported at my office on time twice a month and was fairly agreeable. Visits to his home revealed that things were still the same in terms of the family's treatment of Greg. They still picked on and rejected him. He was even beaten by other family members, even though his own behavior had improved rather remarkably.

Then, I received a call from the mental health center informing me that Greg had missed his last two appointments with them. He was also a week late reporting to me. I decided to go to his home to find out what was happening. I was informed that two weeks prior to my visit Greg had gotten into a fight with his older brother and had stabbed him. Although the wound was superficial and the police had not been called, Greg panicked and fled from the house. I never heard from Greg again. Had he remained in my city, he surely would have been arrested again and I would have seen him. As far as I know, Greg is still out there somewhere among the hordes of loveless and rejected individuals who aimlessly wander the streets of our big cities. Greg's case is an example of how one's best efforts can sometimes come to less than an ideal ending. We have to accept failures as well as successes and learn from them both.

Perspective from the Field
Never a Dull Moment with a Mental Health Caseload

By William D. Smith

For the past eleven years, William Smith has been an adult supervision probation officer in Santa Cruz County, California. A graduate of San Francisco State University in psychology, Mr. Smith formerly worked as a group counselor at Juvenile Hall in Santa Cruz.

● ● ● ● ● ● ● ● ● ● ● ● ● ● ● ● ●

My job as a probation officer with a mental health clientele involves intense supervision of fifty-five individuals suffering from various types of schizophrenia and bipolar disorders. They all are court-ordered to take their prescribed psychotropic medications, to follow all mental health directives, and to follow all the usual probation terms and conditions. Their crimes range from relatively minor misdemeanors to bank robbery and assault with a deadly weapon. In this unique position, I work closely with a variety of mental health professionals to prevent recidivism and relapses into chronic states of mental deterioration. I spend about 70 percent of my time in contact with probationers in my office or in the field, about 20 percent in court appearances and writing probation violations, and about 10 percent in meetings with mental health staff.

Bipolar individuals are most problematic when they are in their manic phase. During this phase, they are hyper, "on top of the world," and have delusions of grandeur. A term that best describes the manic person is "in your

Continued on the next page

Perspective from the Field, *continued*

face." Such people sometimes can go without sleep for several days and not realize they have deteriorated. A few of my bipolar probationers can function fairly well at their "baseline" level of functioning, and a few can maintain part-time jobs or attend college. However, most of them are chronic sufferers who are unemployed and on Social Security.

The two most common reasons mental health offenders relapse are that they fail to take their medication and/or they abuse alcohol and/or drugs. Such relapses often lead to reoffending or expensive inpatient stays at mental health facilities. People choose not to take their medication for a variety of reasons, but mostly because of the many negative side effects. This can include abnormal weight gain, liver and kidney damage, male impotency, and a general impairment of functioning. Manic patients may go off their medication just to experience the manic high, and others to avoid the stigma of the "mentally ill" label. Some offenders who begin to fell "normal" while on their medication will stop because they feel that they do not need it any more. Yet, the vast majority of schizophrenics and those with bipolar disorders need to be on medication for the rest of their lives.

One patient/offender with a long history of failing to take her medication because of side effects and denial is Jan, a forty-year-old paranoid schizophrenic who was diagnosed in her early twenties. She was on probation for setting fire to her parents' curtains believing that she was ridding the house of demons. After she had been on my caseload for about two months, I paid a home visit and found her wearing a robe and a white towel wrapped around her head. She claimed that she was "Queen Holiness Heinous," queen to "David Shang-Hai-Shek."

I tried to get her into a short-term treatment program, but they turned her away after she claimed to be "Mrs. Jesus Christ." Because of this, I had to arrest her and place her in the mental health unit at the county jail so that we could stabilize her and get her back on medication. Several weeks after her jail stay, I had to arrest her again for failing to take her medicine. Her brother had called me because she had fixated on watching the "Chinese T.V. station," although she does not understand a word of Chinese.

Following this and other such incidents, I asked that her medication be administered by injection. It has now been approximately seven months since she started receiving her monthly shots without any further incidents of instability.

Another chronic schizophrenic on my caseload is a forty-two-year-old male named Doug. He has been on probation for about two years for abusing his wife, who is also schizophrenic. Six months ago, Doug was admitted into the local mental health unit after trying to commit suicide by swallowing his bottle of psychiatric pills. Doug told me that he had done this because he had abused his wife again, felt guilty about it, and was afraid of going back to jail. The combination of fear and guilt caused him to experience hallucinations regarding jail inmates who were threatening that they were going to eat him alive. I assured him that I would not send him back to jail, as he was already in his own mental prison. After his release from the hospital, he was transferred to an open psychiatric facility for one month. Doug is presently living with his wife in a board and care facility. They both attend couples counseling, and so far, this appears to have had a positive impact on their relationship.

Other outcomes are not so positive. For example, take twenty-seven-year-old Steve who was placed on probation in 1995 for shattering his college professor's jaw and cheekbone with an axe handle. Steve had done this because he thought that the professor was spreading rumors about him. Although placed in a state mental hospital for six months and in the county jail for one year, he continued to harbor animosity against the professor. After several months on probation and employed part-time as a gas station attendant, I received calls from others telling me that Steve was acting outlandishly and was telling everyone that he wanted to hurt the professor again. Additionally, Steve was observed on the professor's college campus, which was a violation of his "stay away" order. Because of this, Steve was arrested and ordered to complete six months in the state hospital. Stories such as this are worrisome and feed into the popular belief that the mentally ill are violent and dangerous. However, this is the exception, not the rule, and for the most part, the mentally ill are nonthreatening.

In summary, there is literally never a dull moment on my job. The key assets to doing this job are patience and a sense of realism about what you can and cannot accomplish. At least 80 percent of the offenders on my caseload have violated their probation at least once during the five years I have been working this caseload. However, I do not view this as indicative of low success. My success indicators are the safety of the public and the safety and welfare of the offenders.

Summary

Unless their departments have a specialized caseload of mentally ill offenders, most probation and parole officers are likely to get at least one or two individuals of this type on their caseloads at any one time. Schizophrenics are identified by the "four A's" autism, ambivalence, inappropriate affect, and loose associations. Schizophrenia also can be identified today by the use of the PET scan, which reveals the brain's functioning, as opposed to its structure.

At the physiological level, schizophrenia appears to be a function of an excess of various chemical neurotransmitters, or perhaps an excess of receptors for those neurotransmitters. There are also strong indicators that the development of schizophrenia requires environmental as well as biological input. The most common background item associated with schizophrenia is a history of childhood love deprivation, although schizophrenia may appear in the most loving of families. Your job in dealing with schizophrenics is to act as a medication monitor and to put them in touch with various community agencies, such as sheltered workshops and specialized counseling services.

Intelligence, as measured by IQ tests, once again is becoming of interest to criminologists. Modern research has determined fairly reliably that IQ tests are not biased and that intelligence levels are strongly influenced by genetics. High IQ tends to be relatively incompatible with crime (at least with street-level crime), and the mentally deficient commit a disproportionate amount of crime. Nevertheless, most delinquents and criminals are in the normal (90-110) range of intelligence, and, therefore, intellectually capable of profiting from counseling, education, and training.

Low IQ offenders present some special supervision difficulties. One of the major problems you may face is helping them to secure work in an increasingly technological, and thus intellectually demanding, society. Pay special attention to the self-esteem and self-consistency needs of such offenders, and be very patient with them. All instructions should be phrased as simply and as concretely as possible to avoid misunderstanding.

References and Suggested Readings

American Psychiatric Association. 2001. *Diagnostic and Statistical Manual of Mental Disorders, 5th ed.* Washington, D.C.: American Psychiatric Association.

Andrew, J. 1974. Delinquency, the Wechsler P>V Sign, and the I Level System. *Journal of Clinical Psychology* 30: 331-335.

———. 1980. Verbal IQ and the I Level Classification System for Delinquents. *Criminal Justice and Behavior* 7: 193-202.

Bartol, C. 2002. *Criminal Behavior: A Psychosocial Approach.* Englewood Cliffs, New Jersey: Prentice-Hall.

Bartollas, C. and S. Miller. 2005. *Juvenile Justice in America*, 4th ed., Upper Saddle River, New Jersey: Prentice Hall.

Bazelon Center for Mental Health Law. Individuals with Mental Illness in Jail and Prison. http://www.bazelon.org/issues/criminalization/factssheets/criminal3.html Accessed March 30, 2008.

Beck, J. and H. Wencel. 1998. Violent Crime and Axis I Psychopathology. In *Psychopathology and Crime*, A. Skodel, ed. Washington, D.C.: American Psychiatric Press.

Bowker, A. and R. Schweid. 1992. Habilitation of the Retarded Offender in Cuyahoga County. *Federal Probation* 56: 48-52.

Buckley, P. 2004. Pharmacological Options for Treating Schizophrenia with Violent Behavior. *Psychiatric Times* (supplement), October: 1-8.

Buckley, P., R. Buchanan, S. Schulz, and C. Tamminga. 1996. Catching up on Schizophrenia: The Fifth International Congress on Schizophrenia Research. Warm Springs, Virginia. April 8 12, 1995. *Archives of General Psychiatry* 53: 456-462.

Canales Portalatin, D. 1995. Comorbidity of Mental Illness and Substance Use in Jail Populations. *Journal of Offender Rehabilitation* 22: 59-76.

Carbonell, J. and R. Perkins. 2000. Diagnosis and Assessment of Criminal Offenders. In *Correctional Counseling and Rehabilitation*, P. Van Voorhis, M. Braswell, and D. Lester, eds. Cincinnati, Ohio: Anderson.

Chase, T., P. Fedio, N. Foster, R. Brooks, G. Di Chiro, and L. Mansi. 1984. Wechsler Adult Intelligence Scale Performance: Cortical Localization of Fluorodeoxyglucose F 18 Positron Emission Tomography. *Archives of Neurology* 41: 244-247.

Dickens, W. and J. Flynn. 2001. Heritability Estimates Versus Large Environmental Effects; The IQ Paradox Resolved. *Psychological Review* 108: 346-349.

Ditton, P. 1999. *Mental Health and Treatment of Inmates and Probationers.* Washington, D.C.: Bureau of Justice Statistics.

Duara, R., C. Grady, J. Haxby, D. Ingvar, L. Sokoloff, R. Margolin, R. Manning, N. Cultler, and S. Rapoport. 1984. Human Brain Glucose Utilization and Cognitive Function in Relation to Age. *Annals of Neurology* 16: 702-713.

Ellis, L. and A. Walsh. 2000. *Criminology: A Global Perspective.* Boston: Allyn and Bacon.

———. 2003. Crime, Delinquency and Intelligence: A Review of the Worldwide Literature. In *The Scientific Study of General Intelligence: Tribute to Arthur Jensen*, H. Nyborg, ed. Oxford, UK: Elsevier Science. pp. 343-365.

Garrett, B. 2009. *Brain and Behavior.* Thousand Oaks, California: Sage.

Gatzke-Kopp, L., A. Raine, R. Loeber, M. Stouthamer-Loeber, and S. Steinhauer. 2002. Serious Delinquent Behavior, Sensation Seeking, and Electrodermal Arousal. *Journal of Abnormal Child Psychology* 30: 477-486.

Ge, X., M. Donnellan, and E. Wenk. 2001. The Development of Persistent Criminal Offending In Males. *Criminal Justice and Behavior* 28: 731-755.

Hales, R., S. Yudofsky, and J. Talbot. 1996. *Textbook of Psychiatry*. Washington, D.C.: American Psychiatric Association Press.

Heinssen, R. and B. Cuthbert. 2001. Barriers to Relationship Formation in Schizophrenia: Implications for Treatment, Social Recovery, and Translational Research. *Psychiatry* 64: 126-131.

Herrnstein, R. 1989. *Biology and Crime*. National Institute of Justice Crime File, NCJ 97216. Washington, D.C.: U.S. Department of Justice.

Hirschi, T. and M. Hindelang. 1977. Intelligence and Delinquency: A Revisionist Review. *American Sociological Review* 42: 571-587.

Hodkins, S., S. Mednick, P. Brennan, F. Schulsinger, and M. Engberg. 1996. Mental Disorder and Crime: Evidence from a Danish Birth Cohort. *Archives of General Psychiatry* 53: 489-496.

James, D. and L. Glaze. 2006. *Mental Health Problems of Prison and Jail Inmates*. Bureau of Justice Statistics, U.S. Department of Justice.

Kolb, B., R. Gibb, and T. Robinson. 2003. Brain Plasticity and Behavior. *Current Directions in Psychological Science* 12: 1-5.

Lamb, H., L. Weinberger, and B. Gross. 2004. Mentally Ill Persons in the Criminal Justice System. *Psychiatric Quarterly* 75: 107-126.

Lamberti, J. 2007. Understanding and Preventing Criminal Recidivism among Adults with Psychotic Disorders. *Psychiatric Services* 58: 773-781.

Lawrie, S., A. McIntosh, J. Hall, D. Owens, and E. Johnson. 2008. Brain Structure and Function Changes During the Development of Schizophrenia: The Evidence from Studies of Subjects at Increased Genetic Risk. *Schizophrenia Bulletin* 34: 330-340.

Link, B., H. Andrews, and F. Cullen. 1992. The Violent and Illegal Behavior of Mental Patients Reconsidered. *American Sociological Review* 57: 275-292.

Lipsitt, D., S. Buka, and L. Lipsitt. 1990. Early Intelligence Scores and Subsequent Delinquent Behavior: A Prospective Study. *American Journal of Family Therapy* 18: 197-208.

Lurigio, A. 2001. Effective Services for Parolees with Mental Illness. *Crime and Delinquency* 47: 446-461.

Marzuk, P. 1996. Violence, Crime, and Mental Illness: How Strong a Link? *Archives of General Psychiatry* 53: 481-486.

McBrien, J. 2003. The Intellectually Disabled Offender: Methodological Problems in Identification. *Journal of Applied Research in Intellectual Disabilities* 16: 95-105.

McDonald, D. and M. Teitelbaum. 1994. Managing Mentally Ill Offenders in the Community: Milwaukee's Community Support Program. Washington, D.C.: National Institute of Justice.

Meltzer, H. and S. McGurk. 1999. The Effects of Clozapine, Risperidon, and Olanzapine on Cognitive Function in Schizophrenia. *Schizophrenia Bulletin* 25: 233-255.

Moffitt, T. 1993. Adolescent Limited and Life Course Persistent Antisocial Behavior: A Developmental Taxonomy. *Psychological Review* 100: 674:701.

Moffitt, T. and P. Silva. 1988. IQ and Delinquency: A Test of the Differential Detection Hypothesis. *Journal of Abnormal Psychology* 97: 330-333.

Moffitt, T. and A. Walsh. 2003. The Adolescent-Limited/Life-Course Persistent Theory of Antisocial Behavior: What Have We Learned? In *Biosocial Criminology: Challenging Environmentalism's Supremacy*, A. Walsh and L. Ellis, eds. Hauppauge, New York: Nova Science. pp. 123-144.

Mueser, K. and G. Bond. 2000. Psychosocial Treatment Approaches for Schizophrenia. *Current Opinion in Psychiatry* 13: 27-35.

Mueser, S. and S. McGurk. 2004. Schizophrenia. *The Lancet* 363: 2063-2073.

Neisser, U., G. Boodoo, T. Bouchard, A. Boykin, N. Brody, S. Ceci, D. Halpern, J. Loehlin, R. Perloff, R. Sternberg, and S. Urbina. 1995. *Intelligence: Knowns and Unknowns: Report of a Task Force Established by the Board of Scientific Affairs of the American Psychological Association*. Washington, D.C.: American Psychological Association.

Palermo, G., E. Gumz, and F. Liska. 1992. Mental Illness and Criminal Behavior Revisited. *International Journal of Offender Therapy and Comparative Criminology* 36: 53-61.

Petersilia, J. 2004. Justice for All? Offenders with Mental Retardation and the California Correctional System. In *The Inmate Experience*, M. Stohr and C. Hemmens, eds., Upper Saddle River, New Jersey: Prentice Hall. pp. 269-288.

Pinel, J. 2000. *Biopsychology*, 4th ed. Boston: Allyn and Bacon.

Posthuma, D., E. de Geus, and D. Boomsma. 2003. Genetic Contributions to Anatomical, Behavioral, and Neurophysiological Indices of Cognition. In *Behavioral Genetics in the Postgenomic Era*, R. Plomin, J. Defries, I. Craig, and P. McGuffin, eds. Washington, D.C.: American Psychological Association. pp. 141-161

Proctor, T. and N. Beail. 2007. Empathy and Theory of Mind in Offenders with Intellectual Disability. *Journal of Intellectual and Developmental Disability* 32: 82-93.

Restak, R. 2001. *The Secret Life of the Brain*. New York: co-published by Dana Press and Joseph Henry Press.

Robinson, M. 2005. *Justice Blind: Ideals and Realities of American Criminal Justice*. Upper Saddle River, New Jersey: Prentice Hall.

Salzinger, S., R. Feldman, M. Hammer, and M. Rosario. 1991. Risk for Physical Child Abuse and the Personal Consequences for its Victims. *Criminal Justice and Behavior* 18: 64-81.

Schmalleger, F. 2001. *Criminal Justice Today*, 6th ed. Upper Saddle River, New Jersey: Prentice Hall.

Seligman, D. 1992. *A Question of Intelligence: The IQ Debate in America*. New York: Birch Lane.

Skeem, J. and J. Louden. 2006. Toward Evidence-Based Practice for Probationers and Parolees Mandated to Mental Health Treatment. *Psychiatric Services* 57: 333-342.

Snyderman, M. and S. Rothman. 1988. *The IQ Controversy, the Media, and Public Policy*. New Brunswick, New Jersey: Transaction Books.

Spaulding, W., S. Fleming, D. Reed, M. Sullivan, D. Storzbach, and M. Lam. 1999. Cognitive Functioning in Schizophrenia: Implications for Psychiatric Rehabilitation. *Schizophrenia Bulletin* 25: 275-289.

Stattin, H. and I. Klackenberg Larsson. 1993. Early Language and Intelligence Development and their Relationship to Future Criminal Behavior. *Journal of Abnormal Psychology* 102(3): 369-378.

Swanson, J. 1994. Mental Disorder, Substance Abuse, and Community Violence. In *Violence and Mental Disorders: Developments in Risk Assessment*. J. Monahan and H. Steadman, eds. Chicago, Illinois: University of Chicago Press.

Tuninger, E., S. Levander, R. Bernce, and G. Johansson. 2001. Criminality and Aggression among Psychotic In-Patients: Frequency and Clinical Correlates. *Acta Psychiatrica Scandinavica* 103: 294-300.

Turkheimer, E., H. Andreana, M. Waldron, B. D'Onofrio, and I. Gottesman. 2003. Socioeconomic Status Modifies Heritability of IQ in Young Children. *Psychological Science* 14: 623-630.

Veysey, B., ed. 1995. *Mentally Ill Offenders in the Community*. Washington, D.C.: National Institute of Corrections.

Walker, E., L. Kestler, A. Bollini, and K. Hochman. 2004. Schizophrenia: Etiology and Course. *Annual Review of Psychology* 55: 401-430.

Walker, E. and K. Tessner. 2008. Schizophrenia. *Perspectives on Psychological Science* 3: 30-37.

Walsh, A. 1990. Illegitimacy, Child Abuse and Neglect, and Cognitive Development. *Journal of Genetic Psychology* 151: 279-285.

———. 1991. *Intellectual Imbalance, Love Deprivation and Violent Delinquency: A Biosocial Perspective*. Springfield, Illinois: Charles C. Thomas.

———. 2003. Intelligence and Antisocial Behavior. In *Biosocial Criminology: Challenging Environmentalism's Supremacy*, A. Walsh and L. Ellis, eds. Hauppauge, New York: Nova Science. pp. 105-124.

Wechsler, D. 1944. *The Measurement of Adult Intelligence*. Baltimore: Williams and Wilkins.

Wertlieb, E. and M. Greenberg. 1989. Strategies for Working with Special Needs Probationers. *Federal Probation* 53: 10-17.

Wilson, J. and R. Herrnstein. 1985. *Crime and Human Nature*. New York: Simon and Schuster.

CHAPTER 20

The Juvenile Delinquent

The logic of concentrating on treating the youngest of offenders is inescapable. There is almost universal agreement by crime experts of every persuasion that the roots of criminal behavior are often embedded in very early life. If past experience piles up around the offender in cumulative fashion, early roots can soon grow too large to unearth.

—Hans Toch

Legal Background

Those who aspire to work in juvenile probation services must become familiar with the differences between the adult and juvenile systems. In the juvenile system, juveniles are never called "criminals," even when they commit acts defined as criminal. "Delinquent" acts are juvenile acts forbidden by law. The term *delinquent* comes from a Latin term meaning to "leave undone." The connotation is that the juvenile delinquent has not done something that he or she was supposed to (behave lawfully) rather than done something he or she was not supposed to do. The difference is subtle, but reflects the rehabilitative rather than punitive thrust of American juvenile justice. In fact, in some states, juveniles are not put on probation but enrolled in aftercare, and their probation officer becomes their aftercare worker or counselor.

Juveniles enjoy or, depending on your perspective, suffer, a special status in society and in its justice system. They are expected not to do a number of things adults have a right to do, such as smoke, drink, drive automobiles, leave home, and ignore the wishes of their parents. They also are expected to do a number of things that adults may ignore, such as attend school, obey curfews, and obey their parents. If juveniles violate any of these do and don't rules, they can be charged with a *status offense* an act of commission or omission applicable only to juveniles. Status offenses are the most frequently dealt with offenses in the juvenile system (Heck 2000).

The special status of juveniles in the juvenile justice system rests on the concept of *parens patriae*. This term literally means "father of his country," and practically means that the state may take over the supervision of a child under legal disability and act as a substitute for his or her parents. Underlying this concept is the philosophy that if the child misbehaves his or her parents are to blame. In such an event, the state may assume responsibility for the child, diagnose the problem, and take appropriate remedial action. This responsibility can be in the form of juvenile probation services, with the child remaining in the parental home, or a court order may be issued removing the child from the parental home and placing him or her in a state facility (training school, detention center, or group home).

All actions of the juvenile courts and its officers, at least in theory, are supposed to be "in the best interests of the child." The juvenile courts do not have trials. They have "hearings" or "adjudication hearings." The child does not plead guilty or not guilty; he or she "admits" or "denies" the charge. The court never finds the child "guilty," but rather makes "a finding of fact." The "finding of fact" can be either that he or she is delinquent (that is, in a condition requiring the intervention and care of the state), or is not delinquent. A presentence investigation report is not written, a "predisposition" or "social inquiry" report is. The courts never sentence the child, rather they "dispose" of the matter, and they seek rehabilitation rather than punishment (Heck 2000). Despite all these euphemisms, you should hold juveniles responsible for their conduct.

Figure 20.1 shows the juvenile proportion of all reported arrests in 2005 (Snyder 2007). Juveniles accounted for 16 percent of all violent crime arrests and 26 percent of all property crime arrests. According to the U.S. Census Bureau (2004), the percentage of the population between ten and seventeen years of age, inclusive, was about 11.5 percent in 2005. Juveniles are thus overrepresented in most of the crime categories shown in Figure 20.1 (note that juveniles have a particular propensity to engage in maliciously destructive behaviors such as arson and vandalism). Statistics such as these are troubling, but we should realize that while not welcome or excusable, antisocial behavior is normative for juveniles; juveniles who do not engage in it are statistically abnormal (Moffitt and Walsh 2003). Adolescence is when youths are "feeling their oats" and temporarily stressing parental bonds in their own personal declaration of independence.

Why Delinquency?

The last four years of the twentieth century saw eleven school-shooting incidents that resulted in the deaths of thirty-eight victims (Lawrence and Mueller 2003). Unusual incidents such as these tend to fuel our perceptions of juvenile offending and offenders. Krisberg (2005) decries the media-induced notion of juvenile "super-predators," and indicates that we have actually witnessed a steady decline in juvenile offending since 1994. Nevertheless, as made plain in Figure 20.1, juveniles are still greatly overrepresented among those arrested for both property and violent offenses.

Figure 20.1 Proportion of Juvenile Arrests by Offense, 2005

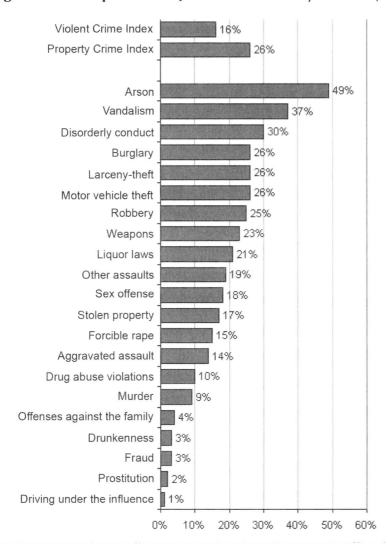

Source: H. Snyder, *Juvenile Arrests 2005.* [2007]. Washington, D.C.: Office of Juvenile Justice and Delinquency Prevention.

A large surge in antisocial behavior of all sorts begins around puberty. This situation is not unique to the contemporary United States; juvenile misbehavior occurs everywhere, and everyone bemoans it. In the *Republic*, Plato soundly condemned the behavior of the youth of his time; and William Shakespeare puts the following words into the mouth of a shepherd in *The Winter's Tale*:

> I would there be no age between ten and three-and-twenty, or that youth would sleep out the rest; for there is nothing in the between but getting wenches with child, wronging the ancientry, stealing, fighting (Act III, Scene III).

However, these observations do not diminish the urgency of the problem in the contemporary United States. Whatever else they may have done, those ancient Greek or Elizabethan English youngsters never ran around drugged to their eyeballs, wielding automatic weapons, and killing, raping, and robbing for fun.

Antisocial behavior is generated by the various factors discussed in Chapters 2 and 3, so we will not be fishing in that pond again. Rather, we will explore certain factors unique to juvenile delinquency. A look at graphs depicting age-related crime rates from around the world, and as far back as such graphs have been drawn, show a dramatic surge in offending shortly after the average age of male puberty, a peak at ages sixteen and seventeen, and a slow, steady decline thereafter (Ellis and Walsh 2000). Most juveniles involved in delinquency (about 85 percent of them) happily do not become adult criminals (Moffitt and Walsh 2003), so there must be something special requiring its own explanations that is going on during the youthful period of life that dramatically, albeit temporarily, increases the probability of antisocial behavior.

Causality: Biological Factors

It is impossible to begin to understand juvenile delinquency unless we understand what is going on biologically during the teenage years. Aaron White (2004: 4) sums up four key messages from the 2003 conference of the New York Academy of Sciences, which focused of the maturation of the adolescent brain:

1. Much of the behavior characterizing adolescence is rooted in biology intermingling with environmental influences to cause teens to have conflicts with their parents, take more risks, and experience wide swings in emotion.

2. The lack of synchrony between a physically mature body and a still maturing nervous system may explain these behaviors.

3. Adolescents' sensitivities to rewards appears to be different than that in adults, prompting them to seek higher levels of novelty and stimulation to achieve the same feeling of pleasure.

4. With the right dose of guidance and understanding, adolescence can be a relatively smooth transition.

The most obvious and dramatic event affecting behavior at this point in life is puberty, an event that marks the beginning of the rocky road from childhood to adulthood. Puberty does not just signal outward physical changes, but also changes in the endocrine (hormonal) system and in the brain. There is a large increase of testosterone at puberty, particularly in males, who have about twenty times the female level of "free" testosterone; that is, testosterone that is unbound to globulins that prevent the activating effects of the hormone. Scientists link testosterone to a variety of behaviors (sexual, aggressive, and competitive) that emerge most strongly in adolescence, and which are related to offending (Ellis 2003).

Testosterone, by itself, cannot explain adolescent offending since offending behavior declines rapidly in early adulthood without an accompanying decline in testosterone. There is another half of the biological equation, and that is the physical immaturity of the adolescent brain.

The pubertal hormonal surges prompt the increase of gene expression in the brain. This then plays its part in slowly refining the neural circuitry to its adult form (Walker 2002). As Steinberg (2005: 70) explains: "Significant changes in multiple regions of the prefrontal cortex [occur] throughout the course of adolescence, especially with respect to the processes of myelination and synaptic pruning." Functional magnetic resonance imaging (fMRI) studies reveal that the prefrontal cortex undergoes a wave of synaptic overproduction just prior to puberty, which is followed by a period of pruning during adolescence and early adulthood (Giedd 2004, Sowell et al. 2004). Thus, fMRI studies confirm what "nagging" parents have always known—adolescents are a couple of doughnuts shy of a dozen in the cognitive area. These studies show that the prefrontal cortex is the most immature area of a teen's brain.

As we saw in Chapter 3, the prefrontal cortex functions include such things as making reasoned judgments and modulating emotions arising from the limbic system. FMRI data show that this link between the limbic system and the prefrontal cortex is often tenuous among adolescents (Walker 2002), which is probably why they rely more on raw emotions to evaluate situations than adults do. Perhaps it is no wonder that teens so often misinterpret the intentions of others, and often seem to be moody. The adolescent brain is simply physically immature relative to the adult brain. This may facilitate a tendency to assign faulty attributions to situations superimposed on an unfamiliar and diffuse state of physiological arousal induced by the hormonal surges of puberty. A brain on "go slow" combined with physiology on "fast forward" may explain why many young persons find it difficult to accurately gauge the meanings and intentions of others, and experience more stimuli as aversive during adolescence than they did as children or will do so again when they are adults.

Richard Restak explains the relationship between brain and behavior (2001: 76): "The immaturity of the adolescent's behavior is perfectly mirrored by the immaturity of the adolescent's brain." It has long been known that early-maturing boys confronting their "raging hormones" with a less mature brain than their age mates do engage in more antisocial behavior than late maturing boys (Buchanan, Eccles, and Becker 1993), and the same finding has also been reported for girls (Caspi et al. 1993). Studies such as these suggest that the age effect on offending is a function of two biosocial processes on opposite trajectories, one of which (pubescent hormonal surges) holds temporary sway over the other (neurological maturity). Consistent with this suggestion, scientists found that testosterone levels at puberty do affect future problem behavior, but only for boys entering puberty significantly earlier than is the norm (Drigotas and Udry 1993).

Adolescence is a particularly stressful time because of the brain "resculpting" (the adding and eliminating of various neuronal pathways) that occurs during this period (Spear 2000a). As noted in Chapter 18, these neurological changes may be what trigger "vulnerability genes" for a number of mental disorders that are first evidenced during adolescence such as schizophrenia and depression (Spear 2000b). Not only that, a generalized decrease in behavior-inhibiting serotonin and an increase in behavior-activating dopamine occurs during this period (Walker 2002). In light of what we read about these neurotransmitters and the BIS/BAS system in Chapter 3, we might well agree with Martin Daly (1996:193) when he writes: "There are many reasons to think that we've been designed [by natural selection] to be maximally competitive and conflictual in young adulthood."

Table 20.1 Delinquency Risk Factors by Domain

Domain	Early Onset (ages 6 –11)	Late Onset (ages 12 -14)	Protective Factors

Individual	Being male
	ADHD/impulsivity
	Medical, physical problems
	Aggression
	Low IQ
	General offenses
	Problem (antisocial behavior)
	Substance abuse
	Exposure to TV violence
	Antisocial attitudes, beliefs
	Dishonesty*
		Restlessness
		Difficulty concentrating*
		General offenses
		Risk taking
		Aggression*
		Being male
		Physical violence
		Antisocial attitudes, beliefs
		Crimes against persons
		Low IQ
		Substance abuse
			Intolerant attitude
			  toward deviance
			High IQ
			Being female
			Positive social orientation
			Perceived sanction for
			  transgressions

Family	Low socioeconomic status
	Antisocial parents
	Poor parent/child relationship
	Harsh, lax, or inconsistent
	  parenting
	Broken home
	Separation from parents
	Abusive parents
	Neglect
		Poor parent-child relationship
		Low socioeconomic status
		Harsh, lax, or inconsistent
		  parenting
		Poor monitoring, supervision
		Antisocial parents
		Broken home
		Abusive parents
		Family conflict*
			Warm, supportive
			relationship with
			parents and other adults
			Parent's positive
			  evaluation of child's
			  peers
			Parental monitoring

School	Poor attitude and
	performance
		Poor attitude and
		  performance
		Academic failure
			Commitment to school
			Recognition for
			  involvement in
			  conventional activities

Peer Group	Weak social ties Antisocial peers	Weak social ties Antisocial, delinquent peers Gang membership	Friends who engage in conventional behavior
Community		Neighborhood crime, drugs Neighborhood disorganization	Stable, organized neighborhood

* Males only

Adapted from Office of the Surgeon General, 2001. U.S. Department of Health and Human Services.

Delinquency Risk Factors

Table 20.1 presents a number of risk and protective factors for delinquency compiled by researchers at the Office of the Surgeon General of the United States (2001). A risk factor is something in a person's individual traits or in his or her environment that increases the probability of offending. These factors are dynamic in that their predictive value changes according to what stage of a person's development they occur in, the presence of other risk and protective factors, and the immediate social circumstances. For instance, low socioeconomic status (SES) is a family risk factor, but a juvenile with a high IQ who enjoys a warm relationship with parents is "inoculated" against the risks low SES poses, and will doubtless attain a higher SES position in adulthood. Similarly, low SES exposes a child to medical problems such as low birth weight and birth complications due to poor maternal health, and maternal smoking, drinking, drug taking, and so on. These problems can lead to low IQ, which leads to poor school performance, which can lead to offending. The Surgeon General's report (2001) indicates that a ten-year-old child with six or more risk factors is approximately ten times more likely than a ten-year-old child with only one risk factor to be violent by the age of eighteen. We examine here those individual-level factors that have their onset early in life and become more salient in adolescence.

ADHD. Among the many other problems associated with delinquency is attention deficit with hyperactivity disorder (ADHD). Despite the tendency of some to dismiss ADHD as the medicalization of childish "high spirits," it is clearly identifiable as much more than that. In fact, brain-imaging studies find differences in brain anatomy and physiology between ADHD and non-ADHD children (Raz 2004). Ellis and Walsh (2000) found ninety-nine studies in which attention deficit with ADHD was positively related to delinquent and criminal behavior, and only one (for drug offenses) in which no significant relationship was reported.

Children affected by attention deficit with ADHD have extremely short attention spans and are prone to extreme boredom, are restless, have low levels of inhibitory control and great impulsiveness, have difficulties with peers, frequently exhibit disruptive behavior, and are academic underachievers. Although it is true that most children manifest some of these symptoms at one time or another, and it is probably true that ADHD is over diagnosed, the symptoms of children affected by ADHD amass to form a syndrome. Eight out of fourteen symptoms are required for diagnosis, and their symptoms are chronic and more severe than are those of children who are simply high-spirited (Restak 2001).

ADHD affects somewhere between 2 and 6 percent of the childhood population and is four or five times more prevalent in males than in females (Raz 2004). Although the precise cause of attention deficit with hyperactivity disorder is not known, fifteen twin studies and two adoption studies show that genetics is a factor (Ellis and Walsh 2000). The heritability estimate of ADHD is exceptionally high compared to other behavioral disorders. It is reported to range between .75 and .91, and the findings are robust regardless of whether the disorder is considered to be a categorical (a discrete, either/or disorder) or continuous (a matter of degree) trait, and regardless of the cutoff criteria applied (Levy et al. 1997).

Some children diagnosed with ADHD show EEG patterns of underarousal (slow brain waves) similar to adult psychopaths (Lynam 1996). Youth experience such a brain-wave pattern subjectively as boredom, which motivates them to seek or create environments containing more excitement. ADHD symptoms can be normalized temporarily by methylphenidate (Ritalin), which is a mild stimulant drug, and nonstimulant drugs such as atomoxatine. Although stimulants have the effect of increasing activity for non-ADHD individuals, they have a calming or normalizing affect on suboptimally aroused individuals by raising the activity of the brain's sensory mechanisms to normal levels. This relieves boredom because the brain becomes more attentive to features of the child's environment previously ignored, and the child becomes less disruptive, less obnoxious to peers, and can focus more on schoolwork.

Child delinquents affected by ADHD are more likely than delinquents not affected by it to persist in their antisocial ways as adults, but this probability rises dramatically for affected children also diagnosed with conduct disorder (CD). *Conduct disorder* is defined as "the persistent display of serious antisocial actions [assaulting, stealing, setting fires, behaving with cruelty toward animals] that are extreme given the child's developmental level and have a significant impact on the rights of others" (Lynam 1996: 211). ADHD and CD occur together in 30 to 50 percent of cases (reviewed in Lynam 1996). Lynam (1996: 22) describes the trajectory from ADHD/CD to criminality, stating that the co-occurrence of ADHD and CD:

> may tax the skills of parents and lead to the adoption of coercive child rearing techniques, which in turn may enhance the risk of antisocial behavior. Entry into school may bring academic failure and increase the child's frustration, which may increase his or her level of aggressive behavior. Finally, the peer rejection associated with hyperactivity may lead to increased social isolation and conflict with peers.

ADHD does not represent some form of hopeless pathology that leads those with it down the road to inevitable criminality. Many ADHD individuals have very high IQs and are loving and creative. Perhaps, the symptoms of ADHD are only problematic in the modern context in which we expect children to sit still for long periods striving to learn subjects that they do not find interesting. ADHD-like symptoms may have even been adaptive in our evolutionary history when restless boldness and curiosity meant exploring beyond the boundaries of the taken-for-granted (Lakoff 2000). Nevertheless, the symptoms of ADHD often do have negative consequences in the modern world, and thus the juvenile caseworker must be cognizant of the syndrome.

Causality: Psychological Factors

As we have seen, neurological and hormonal changes during adolescence often make the period between childhood and adulthood stressful and confusing for many teens. In the United States, where we keep individuals in the dependent role of childhood longer than any other nation, it is a particularly trying period. This strange and sometimes frightening stage of life we call "adolescence" has been considered everything from a normal developmental period accompanied by a few mild disturbances experienced by about half of all teenagers to a stage of life that is very emotionally disturbing for just about all teenagers (Wood and Wood 1996). From a review of the literature, Udry (1990: 2) lists the following changes that typically occur among high school age adolescents:

> They complete puberty, [have] lower academic achievement values, increase values of independence, increase tolerance for violation of adult standards, decrease religiosity, decline in church attendance, increase reported alcohol and drug use, and increase sexual activity.

Except for the completion of puberty, parents and other authority figures are not likely to welcome these changes, and they certainly represent a gap between biological and social maturity that must be bridged.

In psychologist Erik Erikson's (1963) *Eight Ages of Man* model of human psychosocial development, he identifies eight stages in the human life cycle in which individuals are confronted with new challenges and interactions with themselves and with their environment. Each of these stages involves crises that can lead to opposite (positive or negative) personality outcomes depending on how we confront and re-solve the crises. He identifies adolescence as the transition from childhood to adult-hood (no longer a child, but not yet a man or woman) and a stage in which the two polar outcomes are identity versus role confusion. In reality, these outcomes are never either/or dichotomies. Most teenagers emerge from this stage situated some-where on a shifting continuum.

During this stage, young people start asking philosophical questions about themselves: "Who am I?" "What is my place, and where am I going?" These questions asked, consciously or subconsciously, identity development and role confusion is-sues that need resolution for healthy development (Hall and Brassard 2008). Teenagers also start to form opinions and theories and ask questions about many as-pects of their environment that they formerly took for granted. Their surging hor-mones, abundant energies, and new questioning orientation make them impatient, action orientated, and imbued with an aura of omnipotence. If, thanks to loving par-ents, they were successful in navigating previous developmental states (trust versus mistrust, autonomy versus doubt, initiative versus guilt, and industry versus inferi-ority), they will emerge with a positive identity ("I'm OK, you're OK") and very little role confusion. If mistrust, doubt, guilt, and inferiority were previous outcomes, role confusion is the likely outcome of this stage.

Although adolescents naturally turn more toward peer influences than parental influences, secure attachment to parents appears to be vital to healthy identity for-mation (Hall and Brassard 2008). Teens lacking such attachment will turn away from parents and toward others in the same sorry boat as themselves to sort out their identity. Such a strategy is not a good one, for these groups come with negative iden-tities "delinquent," "doper," "punk," but even a negative identity is better than no identity at all as long as it is accepted by the groups to which we belong.

Freed from the apron strings of childhood and freed of the necessities of adult commitment, adolescence is a wonderful time to experiment with all sorts of roles, fads, tastes, and attitudes. Unfortunately, some of these experiments include drugs, alcohol, weird cults, unprotected and irresponsible sex, and delinquent behavior (Berzonsky 2008). Even well-adjusted youths from well-adjusted homes often con-form more to their peers' expectations than to their parents' during adolescence. This is a normal part of growing up and part of finding one's own way in life. The trick is to find the right set of peers. Well-loved youths generally will be prosocial and will seek the company of others like themselves, but children who do not find love, sup-port, and supervision at home may resort to groups outside the family, and these groups are often deviant (Rodkin et al. 2000). Rejected children, being unsure of them-selves, will often overidentify with the heroes of cliques and crowds, or with the he-roes, the media provides for them to hold themselves together.

We emphasize that the great majority of delinquents (adolescent-limited) are "normal" youths whose offending reflects adaptive responses to conditions that have temporarily diverted them from their prosocial life trajectories. Unlike life-course persistent offenders, they have built up enough "social capital" that they can cash in when they mature. It would seem that youths (particularly males) who abstain from delinquency altogether are less psychologically "healthy" than their more behav-iorally obnoxious peers are. They tend to be extremely self-controlled, timid, fearful, socially inept, and latecomers to sexual experiences. However, they all tend to lead successful and satisfactory adult lives, are typically well educated, and tend to hold high status jobs (reviewed in Moffitt and Walsh 2003). They may well be individuals with hyperarousable autonomic nervous systems, which would account for their fear, timidity, and excessive conformity to adult norms. We mention delinquency abstainers only to reinforce the point that the great majority of delinquents are healthy and normal individuals who will mature out of their youthful high jinks.

Causality: Environmental Factors

Messner and Rosenfeld write that the American "fetishism of money" (2001: 68) has produced an institutional imbalance of power by the subjugation of other social institutions to the economy. What this essentially means is that American culture tends to devalue the non-economic function and roles of other social institutions and obliges them to accommodate themselves to economic requirements. A great deal of the focus of the family, religion, education, law, and government is thus brought to bear on instilling in Americans the beliefs and values of the marketplace to the detriment of the institution-specific beliefs and values they are supposed to inculcate, such as nurturance, spirituality, love of learning, justice, and democratic principles, respectively. The dominance of the economy thus disrupts the prosocial functioning of the other institutions and substitutes an overweening concern for the pursuit of monetary rewards.

With our country's diminishing emphasis on the institution of the family (according to Messner and Rosenfeld, many parents are too busy meeting the demand of the economy to pay much attention to their children), increasingly behavior, attitudes, and values have come under the influence of other less benign forces. Likewise, with the declining emphasis on religion, many become moral relativists who believe that no one system of values is inherently superior to another. The moral vacuum that our society has created produces more than one million illegitimate births each year in the United States to teens barely past menarche. Eventually, many of these children become part of the horde of gang members who infest our cities and bankrupt our hospitals' trauma centers (Lykken 1995). Figures from 2007 indicate that 72.5 percent of black infants, 47.6 percent of Hispanic infants, and 24.4 percent of white infants were born out of wedlock (Camarota 2007).

In some ways, the demands of the economy have a direct effect on the probability of youthful offending. As Terrie Moffitt said: "adolescent-limited offending is a product of an interaction between age and historical period" (1993: 692). Moffitt means that there are two trajectories—one biological and one social-economic—operating in opposite directions. The first is the increasingly lower age at which youths enter puberty, which is largely a function of better health care and nutrition. The other is the increasingly complex nature of today's economy, which necessities longer periods of educational preparation to engage in it. Compulsory education and child labor laws kept our grandparents and great grandparents out of the labor market for a while, but because they entered puberty later and required less education to enter the job market, the gap between puberty and the acquisition of a socially responsible role was perhaps no more than two years. Today, this gap is upwards of ten years, and it is within this gap that so much adolescent-limited offending grows.

Thus, just when we need to exercise more control over our young, we seem to have abrogated much of the responsibility for socializing them to peer groups and to television, both of which represent immature and often antisocial visions of reality. Groups have a morality and direction of their own that is often radically different from the sum of their individual parts. Already unsure of identity and direction, being juiced up on hormones and having a brain undergoing a major overhaul, juveniles in peer groups defer to the collective judgment. With internalized standards submerged in groups, and with responsibility diffused among them, sometimes we see horrible manifestations of antisocial "group think" such as "gang banging" and "wilding."

Television, the other half of the socialization equation, provides youth with models and standards of behavior, selling greed, hedonism, impatience, and impulsivity ("Go out and buy this or that and you will feel great and the boys/girls will love you. Do it now!"). Our youth grow up seeing a variety of complex problems solved in one hour (often by violent means) with six commercial breaks designed to sell children TV land's version of the good life. Is it any wonder that our children and youth become narcissistic, lower their thresholds for violence, become desensitized to the suffering of others, and have difficulty delaying gratification? Do not forget, these cultural factors are superimposed on an adolescent neurophysiology designed for action.

The themes of many television programs and movies often seem produced by some malignant "juvenocracy" specifically to challenge traditional notions of decency and good character. Teachers are portrayed as helpless, bumbling idiots who are easily manipulated, intimidated, and outsmarted by crude (but "cool") teenagers. Youths who study and behave respectably are characterized as "nerds" or "geeks," and are ostracized by the Gossip Girl in-crowd. Either parents are archetypal versions of the 1950s "square" or they are hypocrites (which in reality, unfortunately, is all too often the case) who indulge their own hedonistic impulses (sexual, chemical, and so forth) while condemning those of their children, such as the dysfunctional family portrayed in the movie *Napoleon Dynamite*. The family warmth (although Pollyannaish) of the Waltons and Ozzie and Harriet of yesteryear has been replaced by the dysfunctional pairings of Ozzy and Sharon Osbourne and Homer and Marge Simpson.

To this equation, add the music that interests teens nowadays—a metallic cacophony that revels in undisguised misogynistic and violent lyrics. We used to hear songs of love and romance, now we hear "Rape the bitch!" And after we've done that, we might play "Kill the cops!" just to make our day complete. No one contends that these cultural artifacts "cause" the negative behavior of those who partake in them. We form music and entertainment tastes by our own preferences and by cultural pressures. For instance, people with a propensity for violence are naturally drawn to violent video games (Anderson, Gentile, and Buckley 2007), have lower SES, and people inclined to be antisocial are drawn to rap, particularly "gangsta rap" (Mulder et al. 2007, North and Hargreaves 2007). There is ample evidence, however, that violent video games and rap music exacerbate the violent and antisocial propensities of the fans of these things via mechanisms such as desensitization to the suffering of others and the cementing of the attitude that violence is an acceptable and manly way to deal with one's problems. We tolerate all this in the name of moral relativism and the demands of the economy (they sell stuff, so sell it, period!). Within this cultural, psychological, and biological context, the juvenile caseworker is supposed to work his or her magic.

Effective Supervision of the Juvenile Delinquent

A child's psychosocial development must involve at least the nine requirements outlined below. Love is essential, of course, but it is not enough. Although the primary responsibility for meeting these requirements rests with the parents, when a child is placed in the care of the state, responsibility partly rests on the juvenile probation officer and/or detention officer/group home counselor/care worker. The requirements presented below should serve juvenile correctional workers as a minimal working model for understanding their juvenile offenders and for meeting their needs. *Child* is the usual term in juvenile probation for an offender of any age who has not reached the age of majority.

1. Children Need Discipline

The cornerstone of raising children to healthy and responsible adulthood is discipline. An undisciplined child is either smothered with unconditional love, making the child a spoiled brat who excuses himself or herself for anything, or is an unloved child, an unruly child, and probably a child who will grow up to be an unconscionable adult. This author considers discipline to be *applied love* (or "tough love," if you prefer).

Although there are components of punishment in discipline, the two terms are not synonymous. Juvenile delinquents have suffered far more than their share of punishment, but have received little discipline. Forcing children to follow rules by inflicting pain hitting, punching, yelling, screaming, hog tying, and other forms of humiliation is punishment. Looking into the family histories of delinquents, you will find many arbitrary rules have been applied inconsistently. If mom or dad feels good on Friday (payday), the violation of rule X perhaps is overlooked. If they feel bad on "blue" Monday, the same violation is severely punished. No wonder the child is confused and comes to view punishment more as a function of parental mood than of rule violation. Children soon learn that being caught rather than breaking rules is the thing to be avoided.

On the other hand, discipline "always starts with trying to teach children to follow reasonable rules through negotiation. . . . Discipline involves the sanctions of the loss of either freedom or privileges until the child is willing to negotiate" (Glasser 1984: 197). Children must know the rules, what is expected of them, and the guidelines they must follow.

This does not imply that the household should be democratic in that the child's wishes are given equal status to those of the parents. Children lack the maturity to receive such privileges. Rather, it should be a benevolent dictatorship in which the best interests of the child are given every consideration. Few children would not benefit from increased expectations such as doing chores around the house, having more common courtesy, and participating in family functions. Living up to reasonable expectations gives children a sense of participation in common goals, a sense of accomplishment, a sense of being needed for one's contributions, and the beginnings of a success identity.

If children violate any of these expectations, they must be allowed to suffer the natural consequences. Although these sanctions should not be severe or designed to humiliate, they should be applied swiftly and with absolute certainty. Of course, the imposed sanctions are punitive in the sense that the children do not welcome them. However, since both the rules and the consequences of violating them are agreed to before the violation occurs, children retain feelings of control over their life that are absent in households that alternate arbitrarily between permissiveness and punishment. If delinquents lack this sense of control, Glasser asserts that they should be "treated with strict but creative probation where they would learn to regain control of their lives" (1984: 198).

2. Children Must Learn To Understand and Accept Themselves.

The development of a realistic and positive self-concept (identity) is a must for all of us, and is the goal of all counseling. It is the juvenile probation officer/aftercare worker's role, in corroboration with children's families, teachers, and other interested parties, to help them to accomplish this. These efforts should be coordinated by the juvenile probation officer/aftercare worker, with special attention to assure that individual efforts are not working at cross purposes. Consistent discipline related to reasonable rules gives children structure, predictability, and the ability to think about an outcome in the abstract and then to select a behavior that will achieve it. This is self-discipline. The sooner this structure and predictability is in place, the sooner the children can build their self-concept around it.

3. Children Must Become Aware of and Understand their Emotions and Feelings.

This is, of course, part of the process of acquiring a realistic sense of self and of self-control the ability to select the appropriate response to a feeling from a number of possibilities. When children are aware of their feelings and understand them for what they are, they can respond to them more appropriately. For instance, a frustrated adolescent may respond with terms such as, "I hate you," or, "I could kill you." They pluck these immature labels from their immature brain and place them on feelings they do not understand well. We hope, what they mean is that "I don't like what you've done," rather than "I hate you, "and "I would very much like you to stop," rather than "I could kill you." Whenever children inappropriately label their emotional feelings, you should help them explore these feelings in a patient, caring, and nonauthoritarian fashion. Even more than an adult offender, juveniles will "shut down" if they perceive an attitude of "I know best." You do "know best," but children must come to this conclusion themselves. The better children relate to you, the sooner this will happen.

4. Children Must Understand the Feelings and Emotions of Others.

This involves the ability to empathize with the feelings and concerns of others. Several studies have shown that the lack of empathy is strongly related to criminal and delinquent behavior (Ellis and Walsh 2000, Tibbetts 2003).

As Granello and Hanna (2003: 14) nicely put it: "Empathy is the intrinsic enemy of the criminal. If one were to feel a victim's pain, it would surely hinder the performance of criminal acts." Inappropriately socialized children live only in their own emotionally egocentric worlds, and they blame other people or circumstances for their antisocial behavior. If such children constantly feel angry, hostile, mean, and uncaring, they will take it for granted that it is natural to feel that way, and, therefore, think everyone else feels that way, too. With the realization that this is not so, the children perceive alternatives and pay attention to positive role models who can exchange their caring, compassion, and understanding for the children's anger and hostility.

All children know when they have been hurt, and they all know that they do not like it. They must learn that other people have feelings too, and that these feeling must be respected. Sometimes their lack of maturity does not allow them to realize that they may deeply hurt mom and dad by their troublesome behavior. This is more often the ignorance of immaturity than the "I don't care" of malice. Empathy training in group sessions may afford them this realization. Getting a child enrolled in team sports, a religious group, or organizations such as scouts, or if appropriate, a Big Brother/Big Sister program, goes a long way to show them that many people do care.

All communities contain their share of truly physically and mentally disadvantaged youngsters. A program that would be advantageous to both these youngsters and to delinquents could be to set up some kind of program, supervised by a probation officer, in which delinquents were assigned to help handicapped youngsters. This could involve everything from wheeling chair-bound youngsters around the local shopping mall to helping them to read. Handicapped youngsters obviously would benefit, and so would their delinquent helpers. They would achieve a measure of empathy with the truly disadvantaged, would gain a feeling of accomplishment, community involvement, and enhanced self-esteem. As a lot of us know, it is often much more rewarding to give than to receive, and research supports the notion that empathy training is useful in reducing aggressive behavior (Romig, Cleland, and Romig 1989).

5. Children Must Learn to Establish Positive Interpersonal Relationships.

Parents often blame "bad companions" for their children's problematic behavior (of course, to other parents their children are the bad companions). The obvious answer to this is to forbid juvenile delinquents from associating with other juvenile delinquents. However, like so many other things, this is much easier said than done. As with adolescent romantic relationships, to forbid is to drive the parties further into each other's arms (the "Romeo and Juliet" effect). Birds of a feather do flock together, and if we want to stop the flocking, we have to clip some feathers. We have to teach children, and provide them with positive prosocial alternatives to the birds with whom they are currently flying. We have to discover their prosocial interests and make them as exciting as "raising hell." They have to learn to relate to more mature peers, to cooperate through teamwork, and learn how to settle conflicts peacefully.

Sports, such as those offered at Police Athletic Leagues and at various probation departments, are an excellent vehicle for teaching a child teamwork, competence, and self-esteem through positive and constructive endeavors. Bill Wakefield (1991) provides us with information on a low-cost athletic program for delinquents, which significantly increased these positive attributes among participants. He organized a running program staffed by volunteer coaches, and with running gear donated by local athletic stores, (you will be surprised how generous businesses can be when asked for a good cause). He reports increased pride in the youths, both in terms of achievement and body image, as they covered increasing distances, developed a greater sense of group cohesion, and had less "acting out." Successfully completing a run of some distance garners the all-important approval of their peers for socially acceptable behavior, and, at the same time, the approval of authority figures. Wakefield's study shows that "treating" troubled children means more than just sitting in an office trying to reason with them.

6. Children Must Understand the Processes Involved in Making Choices and Decisions and in Solving Problems.

We are all constantly making choices and decisions; delinquents just make too many bad ones. Making positive choices depends on the knowledge we have of the consequences of making these decisions (the remote as well as the immediate consequences) rather than of making an alternative decision, and on the control we feel that we have over our lives that allows us to make relatively independent choices.

As we have pointed out, an unloved and undisciplined child will turn to peer groups for affiliation and attention. The members of these groups have had similar experiences and, likewise, will lack the ability to make positive decisions. Choices and decisions within such a peer group will be made under antisocial pressure, and based on gut emotions unalloyed by thoughts of remote consequences. Children must be taught to make their own decisions. The task of parents and probation officers is to seek and achieve a sound balance between supporting the child's decision and making sure these decisions are responsible ones.

7. Children Need Positive Values and Ideals with which to Guide their Lives.

Values are the vital core of society, the cement that holds it together, without which social life would be literally meaningless ("anomie"). Values have to be taught; children need to know what goals are worth striving for, what ideas are worthy of being preserved, what is important in life, and how they should lead a good life. As we have seen, the popular media assaults many positive values. Some people view values such as the golden rule, honor, and personal integrity as hopelessly old fashioned and restrictive of personal liberty. On the contrary, values set us free by anchoring our lives in a meaningful sense of community and provide us with guidelines for social living. Children who never learn the value of values trudge through life caring for little else other than the immediate gratification of their selfish impulses.

Juvenile careworkers should serve as role models for their offenders by emphasizing in word and deed that positive prosocial values are indispensable. In an effort to "identify" with offenders, you should never except perhaps jokingly adopt their mannerisms and speech. This does not mean that you always look cold and professional and use language that smells of old books. A little contemporary vernacular is fine, but stay away from delinquent slang that expresses antisocial values such as "fink," "NARC," "pigs," and "bad mutha." The use of such language by the correctional worker gilds it with an aura of legitimacy. This might be "identifying" with offenders, but the point of the whole process is to get them to identify with you and the prosocial values you are supposed to embody.

8. Children Must Learn to Appreciate the Value of Education and Work.

We all know the tremendous value of education and work, but we will never get the message over to delinquents (who are convinced otherwise) by preaching to them. They have heard it all before and rejected it, so they are not likely to buy it from you. We tend to reject and belittle the things we feel that we do not understand or feel we cannot master. This happens even in college, where presumably students do have a belief in the value of education.

Although many delinquents have attention deficit disorders and other learning disabilities, there are few reasons why healthy children should not be able to master the typical American high school curriculum. However, students need to know and understand why education is important and what it can do for them. Many barely literate student athletes knuckle down to study under "no pass, no play" rules. A 1999 television news item reported that youths who drop out of school in Virginia cannot obtain a driver's license. Given the importance of driving for teenagers, no prizes are offered for guessing what has happened to Virginia's dropout rate it declined substantially. Yes, it is coercion (discipline), but we are all coerced to some extent. How many of you reading this are in college for no other reason than being possessed of an insatiable desire to acquire knowledge for its own sake? You are probably in college because you have made a contract with yourself to forego immediate gratification for the greater rewards that you know education brings with it. You have learned the lesson; others can too.

We often think of police officers as "bustin' 'em" and probation officers as "trustin' 'em." Yet, police officers and probation officers can work, in conjunction with school authorities, as a three-pronged team to help troubled children. An innovative program implemented by the Boise (Idaho) Police Department has been in operation for more than twenty-five years in various Boise elementary and high schools. Plainclothes Boise police officers are assigned to schools as school resource officers. These officers, because of the authority inherent in the police role, often can be more effective than school authorities are in dealing with hostile and uncooperative youths and parents because they cannot be intimidated by them in a way that teachers and school counselors can.

School resource officers are very effective in not only detecting and deterring school crime, but also in counseling and helping many troubled youths. As for the attitude of the youth toward the police in these schools, the interviews with students revealed a positive humanistic view of police and their role in society. They showed a high degree of trust in the resource officer, and a clear indication that many students have altered their attitudes concerning wrong doing as well as how they think about the functions and motives of the police (Scheffer 1987: 85).

This is a heartening attitude from teenagers, many of whom have had little contact with caring police officers, whose attitudes toward the police are usually ones of fear, contempt, and disrespect. Turning kid's heads around about the most visible symbols of authority goes a long way to turning their heads around about all reasonable authority. If your city has such a program, as a juvenile probation officer, you should find out all you can about it and use this valuable resource to its fullest.

9. Children Need a Sense of Responsibility for their Actions and Lives.

This whole book is more or less about the development of a sense of responsibility. *Responsibility* means disciplined action doing chores around the house, doing your schoolwork, occupying your time with meaningful activities, giving to others, and so on. It means having a positive self-concept around which you can organize your life and pursue meaningful and socially useful goals. It also means you have the maturity to know when you are wrong and are willing to accept the consequences for your actions without rancor. Even some law-abiding adults have problems with this, so be patient with your young delinquent charges.

Imposition of community service and restitution orders go a long way to help juvenile offenders develop a sense of responsibility. Repaying the community through putting in useful work hours with a nonprofit organization can give children a sense of usefulness as contributing members to the community they have offended. It also places the children in the company of prosocial others from whom they may learn valuable lesson. Both community service and restitution are integral components of the restorative justice philosophy.

Restorative justice principles mandate that monetary restitution in the amount the child appropriated also should be assessed. Restitution is reparation ("repairing" damage done) performed for justice's sake and for teaching juveniles moral values (Bartollas and Miller 2005). In other words, in addition to being simple justice for the victim, the child learns that you cannot get something for nothing. Sometimes the payment of restitution presents a problem for a child who is below the age requirement for legal employment. If children cannot pay restitution themselves, the court may order the parents or guardians to do so because they are financially and legally responsible for their children. Research indicates that relatively mature offenders identify restitution as right and proper and see its reparative and rehabilitative intent, while low-maturity offenders tend to see it as punitive (Van Voorhis 1985). Your task is to convince all offenders ordered to pay restitution of the morality and responsibility of such an order.

Different Strokes for Different Folks

Nothing works uniformly for everyone. This is particularly true of juveniles who come to you in various stages of maturity and from various backgrounds. You need to treat subcultural delinquents who view the gang as an extension of the family differently from neurotic delinquents, who may be from fairly functional families, and then, both these types have to be treated differently from sociopathic delinquents. From the well-established finding that delinquents who begin offending before puberty become the most frequent and serious offenders, you should certainly be aware that these children need very special attention.

Delinquents may be classified for treatment purposes in many ways; far too many, in fact, for an attempt at any exhaustive coverage here. Unless your department has routine testing of its children by psychologists, and unless you are well versed in interpreting these tests and translating the information imparted into treatment action, you may be in the self-defeating position of treating all offenders alike. It is useful, however, to know something about offenders' treatment potential and how they might differ among themselves vis-à-vis this potential. For instance, take the differences between extroverts (people whose attention and interests are directed predominantly toward what is outside the self) and introverts (people who are predominantly inward looking and introspective). Extroverts condition less well than introverts do, because typically they are suboptimally aroused. For this same reason, extroverts do less well in school and are more likely to be delinquent than introverts (Scarpa and Raine 2003). Just in terms of the extroversion/introversion dimension, then, you would expect different treatment strategies to follow.

Yet, how do you know at what level of maturity offenders are, or if they are introverts or extroverts? You could learn the dynamics of I level interviewing as described by Ruth Masters (1994) if you have the time, or you could read a book or article or two on the subject to sensitize yourself to this system. In addition, various scales in the literature tap the concepts of sensation seeking and introversion/extroversion. However, unless your department allows for time and funds to pursue these strategies, you are on your own. This is not as bad as it sounds. After two or three sessions with offenders, you should have a good idea about their maturity levels and how they are situated along the introversion/extroversion continuum. Additionally, you usually will have access to a piece of information that may serve as an adequate proxy for these intellectual and personality attributes.

As indicated in Chapter 3, one of the most readily available tests for correctional workers is the Wechsler performance verbal IQ profile, which correlates with the I level classification system (Masters 1994). Although the V > P intellectual profile (high maturity level/introvert) is rare among delinquent and criminal populations, if a child with such a profile becomes seriously delinquent, he or she may be more psychologically disturbed than other delinquents. Walsh, Petee, and Beyer (1987) found that V > P children who do become delinquent are more seriously involved in it than are intellectually balanced (P = V) children, but less so than P > V children. The implication is that while subcultural delinquents may be "normal" children reacting to criminogenic environments, the delinquency of V > P children may have its origins in some psychological disturbance rather than in outside factors. You should have children with a significant V > P profile psychologically tested by a competent psychologist. If the examining mental health professionals uncover some disturbance, they are the ones to treat it. You also need to get their input on how you should handle the child.

However, the Wechsler test is not a classification panacea. Interpret it with caution, and only if the subscale scores are significantly discrepant (twelve to fifteen points or higher). Even then, the discrepancy is only meaningful in terms of predicting antisocial behavior if we have a fairly normal PIQ combined with a significantly below normal VIQ. Scientists and engineers tend to have a large P > V discrepancy because PIQ signals strong visual-spatial ability, but in the case of such people, VIQ would also be significantly above average. With so many factors to consider, you can see why prediction and classification is such a tricky business.

Family Counseling

An added dimension of difficulty in juvenile probation work not encountered in adult correctional work is the necessity of dealing with the children's parents, who can be more difficult to handle than their children. As a juvenile probation officer/caseworker, you may receive resistance and hostility from the child but also from the child's parents. If the child comes from a negative family situation in which there is parental criminality and substance abuse, you are not likely to receive voluntary cooperation. If the parents care little or not at all for the child or his or her future, such children are not likely to understand why you should, and if they come to believe that you do, they may consider you a "sucker." Your home visits and telephone calls may be considered just another hassle they have to endure. They also may be concerned that you might uncover many negative aspects of the family's lifestyle (such as drug dealing or physical and sexual abuse) that may further incur the wrath of the adult authorities.

You may experience some parental hostility and resistance even if the child comes from a relatively healthy family. Parents may feel threatened by your probing of the family dynamics. They may feel it an unwarranted intrusion into their private lives, and perhaps as an effort to pin the blame for their child's predicament on them. They also may seek to protect the child from you, believing that he or she is a blameless victim of circumstances or the bad influence of friends (it is always someone else's kid who causes the trouble). This is particularly devastating to your efforts to help the child who may come to view the relationship as "us against them" (he or she and the parents against you and probation services, in general). This reinforces any feeling that the child has that he or she is being picked on. After all, "mom and dad think so." Such parents are enabling their children's delinquent behavior.

Nevertheless, the juvenile probation officer needs, and should insist on, parental support in working with children. Your task is to help parents understand that their role and responsibility is not diminished when their children are placed on probation. On the contrary, parental supervision is even more critical during this period. It is the parents, not the probation officer, who handle routine day to day discipline in the home. Parents have to realize that their cooperation during this period is of the utmost importance, and you should supply them with general guidelines relating to the direction that this cooperation should take. It includes such things as attending appointments with the juvenile probation officer when requested, arranging transportation for their child's appointments, reporting violations of probation rules, enforcing consistent discipline, and working with their child on the conditions of probation, including family counseling.

Experts believe the involvement of the family in the rehabilitative effort is necessary" (Bleckman and Vryan 2000). The child is embedded in a family, so if the family system is dysfunctional, it is of little use concentrating on the individual child, who is only a minor part of the whole. If the juvenile court is to function "in the best interests of the child," it must have jurisdiction over the family so that it can enforce its decisions. The juvenile court has authority to order parents, under pain of contempt of court, to receive counseling. This could take the form of simple Parental Effectiveness Training (PET) in which parents receive schooling in the art of parenting, or it could explore, in conjunction with their child, the family dynamics contributing to the child's misbehavior. Bartollas and Miller (2005: 384) recognize this: "Family therapy appears more likely to be successful when it is focused on teaching parents communication, problem solving, and discipline skills."

Because the family is an interlocking system containing a number of complicated relationships, effective family counseling is more difficult than individual counseling. The maximum number of paired relationships in any family can be obtained by total pairs = $[N (N - 1)]/2$, where N is the number of people in the family. If the Evans family consists of mom, dad, and five children, the total number of possible paired relationships existing in that family is $[(7)(6)]/2 = 21$. This is twenty one interacting pairs! That is just the beginning; there are many other combinations consisting of groups greater than two. These relationships may include everything from genuine love to genuine hatred, all existing within a single household. Therefore, you can see why family counseling is a specialty that only those with training in this field should employ. Any attempt to engage in it on the part of a correctional worker unschooled in its techniques may do more harm than good.

Some well-funded jurisdictions have family crisis units directly responsible to the juvenile court, but if your department lacks such a luxury, you must be aware of counselors in the community to whom you can refer the family. Even short-term family counseling—focusing on clarity of family communication, limit setting, contract negotiation, conflict resolution, and the presentation of alternative problem solving strategies—show progress in decreasing delinquent behavior (Robins and Szapocznik 2000). These same types of programs also have positive effects on the prevention of younger sibling delinquency. In other words, an improvement in family dynamics spills over to prevent delinquency in younger children who, while not delinquent at the time that the counseling took place, are at risk of becoming so. The (relatively) short-term Prosocial Family Therapy System described by Bleckman and Vryan (2000) is a comprehensive system with very encouraging results. However, it works on a family-by-family basis and requires master's level counselors. The great majority of juvenile probation departments have neither the time for such individualized counseling nor the appropriate treatment staff. As frequently stressed, if the child's family is in need of such counseling, refer, refer, refer!

When all is said and done, how successful is family counseling? One study comparing recidivism rates among first-time juvenile offenders on probation found that juveniles placed in a family-group-intervention program were an astonishing 9.3 times less like to reoffend than other first-time youth placed on probation without family counseling (Quinn and Van Dyke 2004). Even youths whose families initially enrolled in the program but subsequently dropped out were 4.4 times less likely to reoffend. Since families could drop out of the program, there is an obvious self-selection factor involved here.

Nevertheless, the family is a natural resource and buffer against the stresses of the world, and if the relationships that exist within the family are healthy, family counseling will be a very useful tool and clearly a very valuable part of delinquency prevention and treatment. It is more realistic than individual counseling in a juvenile setting because it takes place in a context in which children are fully immersed, and because it enlists the treatment aid of (hopefully), more mature adults who are in full legal control of the delinquent child. It often forces parents and children to engage in what they both want (parent/child reconnection), but lack the knowledge and insight to initiate themselves.

Assessing the Child's Needs

The first thing you have to do when you are presented with new juvenile offenders is to find out as much as you can about them. In addition to the information you may have at your disposal from various sources, such as school counselors, teachers, and parents, you need to get a "feel" for your offenders from an assessment interview. Table 20.2 provides a suggested interview guide by which you can learn something about the children, their family, and peers. We developed the interview topics around the nine components for healthy psychosocial development, previously addressed.

When you have learned something about the children's needs, you will have to obtain a commitment from the children and their family to cooperate with you in the rehabilitative effort. You then have to match the children's needs with the available resources in your community whose business it is to address these needs, making very sure that you do not undertax or overtax the children's coping resources or those of the family. Treatment plans for juveniles then can be developed and implemented in a fashion similar to the process outlined in this chapter.

Table 20.2 An Assessment Guide on Juvenile Delinquents and Their Needs, Attitudes, and Attributes

1. What is your perception of the child's self-worth?
2. Does the child frequently feel depressed, angry, or rejected?
3. Does the child lie and/or manipulate facts and situations?
4. Does the child accept the validity of society's value system?
5. Does the child express empathy toward others?
6. What are the child's full scale, verbal, and performance IQ scores, and is there a significant (12 or more points) discrepancy between his/her verbal and performance scores?
7. Does the child have any positive goals in life?

Behavior

8. Do the child's behavior patterns indicate an age-appropriate maturity and sense of responsibility?
9. Do the child's behavior patterns indicate extroversion/introversion?
10. Does the child show the ability to defer gratification and control impulses?
11. Does the child show appropriate remorse for delinquent acts?
12. Does the child abuse alcohol/drugs, and why (peer pressure, reduce inhibitions, kill emotional pain)?
13. What is the child's offense pattern (violent, sexual, stealing, related to substance abuse, status offenses) and does it evidence an increasing pattern of seriousness?
14. Does the child have any hobbies or engage in sports?
15. Is the child sexually active?

School Behavior and Attitudes

16. How does the child perform in school? Does the child live up to his/her potential as indicated by IQ scores and teachers' perceptions?
17. Does he/she put adequate effort into studies?
18. Does the child have a learning disability that contributes both to low self-esteem and school difficulties?
19. What is the child's attitude toward school and his/her teachers?
20. Does the child have frequent absences (excused or unexcused)?
21. Does the child sufficiently appreciate the value of education?

Family Dynamics

22. Does the child feel attached to parents and siblings or does he/she feel rejected?
23. What is the attitude of parents toward the child?
24. Is there evidence of abuse and neglect in the family?
25. Do parents know the difference between punishment and discipline, and which do they use?

Continued on the next page

Table 20.2 An Assessment Guide on Juvenile Delinquents and Their Needs, Attitudes, and Attributes, *continued*

26. Does the child speak and behave very differently when in the company of parents from when he/she is not?
27. What family stresses (financial, occupational, legal, emotional, and so forth) exist, and how are they being dealt with?
28. Do parents and siblings model illegal and irresponsible behavior?
29. Do parents encourage, support, and reinforce desired behavior?
30. Do parents monitor school performance and take an active part in the child's school interests?
31. Do adequate communications skills exist in the family?
32. Do parents expect too little or too much from the child?

Peer Groups

33. Does the child associate with delinquent peers?
34. Does the child have any nondelinquent friends?
35. Do the child's peers model illegal behavior?
36. How dependent on the peer group is the child for his/her feelings of support, attachment, acceptance, and direction.
37. Has there been a recent drastic change in the child's dress and appearance (tattoos, colors, hair style) suggesting a deepening integration into a gang subculture?
38. What are the peer group's typical nondelinquent activities, and are they constructive or destructive?
39. What was the peer influence (if any) on the current offense?

Perspective from the Field
The Workaday World of a Juvenile Probation Officer

By Grace J. Balazs

Grace J. Balazs is a juvenile probation officer in Ada County, Idaho. A graduate of Boise State University in Criminal Justice, Ms. Balazs formerly worked as a presentence investigator for Ada County's Fourth District Felony Court and as a co-counselor for a sexual abuse clinic

● ●

I wrote a *Perspective from the Field* for the first edition of this book shortly after I became a juvenile probation officer, more than ten years ago. In reviewing that perspective, I was surprised and pleased that my attitude and commitment has not changed. I still believe that the profession is full of challenges, and is not the typical 8:00 to 5:00 job. The pay is not exceptional, the stress is high, and time constraints and paperwork abound. I believe I have become wiser and more effective in doing my job, but I am perhaps still a bit naive in my belief that the kids we see at "juvey" are basically good kids who have made bad choices. Juveniles have not changed much over the past ten years; many of their crimes are still committed out of stupidity and peer pressure, and they want acceptance and self-esteem. There are those juveniles who commit crimes because it is in their nature, and there are those who commit them because of environmental conditioning. I believe that the child's home environment and his or her parents' lifestyles play a major role in determining the child's behavior.

What I have observed over the years is that children sorely lack self-respect, and have little respect for parents (and adults in general), authority (police, courts), or the rights and property of others, and there is little comprehension of conscience, or healthy guilt and remorse. In addition, I see lack of respect for education. It is sad to see a child's commitment to school erode because of poor attendance, poor grades, and poor behavior. Parents often seem helpless to do anything to make their children appreciate education or make them comply with rules. Every day I see children as old as seventeen who can hardly read or write. I hear young girls calling themselves "sluts" and "whores," and permitting themselves to be sexually active, the only way they know to gain acceptance. Altercations between children and (step) parents are common. I wonder if "respect" will ever again be something we will value.

The responsibilities of a probation officer are not only to the court, but to the juvenile, his or her parents, and to the community. Probation officers attempt to redirect the juvenile's behavior by offering him or her and their families a variety of resources both within and outside of the probation offices. The Ada County Juvenile Court uses the balanced approach, which incorporates accountability, community protection, and competency development, with victim's rights, compensation, and protection being a priority.

Continued on the next page

Perspective from the Field, *continued*

A juvenile probation officer's work is extremely necessary. I can think of nothing more worthwhile than contributing toward turning around a troubled child's life. However, the job is also very tough, and sometimes frustrating. Juvenile probation officers run into many absurd situations that make them shake their heads and wonder how children and families are able to cope. For instance, I have had one seventeen-year old girl who has already had three pregnancies, and one fourteen-year old girl who explained with relish, and perhaps a little pride, that she had been tested for the HIV virus! Most juveniles that come through "juvey" already have experienced many trials and traumas on a fairly regular basis. Many of these youths are survivors of dysfunctional families with a wide range of problems. These problems may be anything from physical abuse and neglect, to parents who enable their kids' delinquency by not providing them with behavioral boundaries.

I have a boy on probation who has experienced physical, mental, and chemical abuse for most of his life. His mother abandoned this sixteen-year old when he was four. He was raised by a "wicked stepmother" who did not want him in her home, and did all she could to deprive this youngster of love and affection. The boy's father had a serious alcohol problem, which interfered with employment and added to the family's stress. More stress led to more drinking and to more anger, which was directed at the boy. Consequently, the boy became a user of chemicals himself, got into fights, had numerous problems in school, and constantly ran away from home. After being labeled as a "worthless no account," he was told that he was no longer welcome in their home.

It seemed almost inevitable that this child would be turned over to the custody of the state; however, after some telephone investigation, I located his biological mother's whereabouts in another state. That was the easy part; the challenge was yet to come, for how do you attempt to reunite a relationship after twelve years? How does a child talk comfortably with a woman who abandoned him twelve years ago, and his only knowledge of her reflects a criminal record for drug abuse and prostitution? A lesson learned you never assume anything. This woman, a recovering alcoholic, was turning her life around and had been steadily employed for four years. She was overjoyed at the prospect of seeing her son again. The "official" story was that she had abandoned her son. Her story was that her husband had taken him from her because of her chemical abuse, and that she did not know how to go about getting him back. Through an Interstate Compact (an agreement by one state to take over the supervision of another state's case), the boy was reunited with his mother after twelve years without contact and with a head full of questions and misinformation. It appears to be a happy conclusion, but who knows what will happen in both their lives?

As a juvenile probation officer, I have to work with families to support their efforts to rehabilitate their children. Probably one of the most challenging tasks of the juvenile probation officer is working with dysfunctional and difficult families. Such families are a problem because, even if the child is afforded the resources to help facilitate positive change, he or she must return to a family environment where our best efforts may be sabotaged.

Unlike dealing with adult offenders, where you need only to attend to the adults themselves, when dealing with juvenile delinquents, you must face their parents as well. This is no easy task, for many are hostile toward the system, including the juvenile probation officer. Many of them provide slim sources of strength, tough love, or guidance to their offspring. It is common for parents simply to want the court to lock up their children and to throw away the key. They may be angry and frustrated with their children, but this is no solution. Other parents will take the opposite stance, claiming that their child is without flaw of character, and dispute the evidence against him or her. There are also parents who will fight and argue against every effort you make toward helping their child.

Occasionally, some parents will take the initiative and seek help for their children. Some appreciate what you are doing, will cooperate with your efforts, and perhaps even give you a "thanks." Such instances almost seem unnatural. Parents present the juvenile probation officer with as much of a problem as the youths in many instances.

The family of an offender who was molested by her "Uncle Jose" when she was six-years-old, contains a father who is a homosexual, and whose sister is brain damaged because of being dropped on her head as an infant. This fourteen-year-old girl hates her mother for reasons she will not articulate, but whom she identifies as the source of her troubles. This offender is recovering from a major chemical dependency, but insists "I don't need counseling; I've worked it all out." I know this is not true, and that it is imperative to work through feelings and issues and to establish new boundaries through counseling. She has lived with a series of foster families, and although she wears a fake smile, I wonder what is going on in her mind and how psychologically sound she really is.

Not all case scenarios are as interesting or challenging as these are. Most of my offenders are youths who have made mistakes, but are quite pleasant. They will never see the inside of "juvey" again after their probation has expired. Although many of the kids I meet are able to creatively manipulate and twist the facts, and some are cons in the making, I can honestly say that I have not met a kid yet who I did not believe had some type of saving quality. Only once have I had an offender who made me so angry that I lost my "cool." At the next meeting, however, he was a pussycat, so I assume that I said something right to him to bring the relationship back to a working situation.

The agency here in Boise is a small community working for the best interests of the juvenile. We are a close knit group, and the camaraderie I feel is one of the best experiences I have known. I believe that the prosecutors, public defenders, judges, clerical staff, juvenile probation officers, intake staff, and detention staff, are all here because they care about young people. I have personally received much satisfaction knowing that I am doing my part assisting young offenders with their rehabilitation and making my community a safe and pleasant place to live.

Summary

A correctional professional in juvenile services has perhaps the most demanding and important job in the criminal justice field. As Hans Toch indicated in the epigraph of this chapter, the juvenile officer gets individuals at a crucial juncture; the time before their criminal roots are too deeply embedded. If through your caring efforts you can wrench these roots from their criminogenic soil, you have performed a great service both to the child and to your community. Edwards and Nuckols (1991: 40) provide us with a statement that all juvenile officers should stamp in their minds:

> Working with high risk children and adolescents is a long, long walk with many disappointments. It is important to know that no matter how horrible the environment, the fact remains that children respond to love, although it's a cliché, one person can make a difference in the life of a child.

Working with juveniles presents some special problems (and opportunities) not found among adult criminal populations. Despite the sometimes overwhelming nature of working with juvenile delinquents, the official ideology of the juvenile court is frankly rehabilitative and avoids many of the stigmatizing terms ("criminal," "defendant," "trial," "guilty," and so forth) used in the adult system.

With the realization that most delinquents do not become adult felons, we identified certain psychological and environmental factors as possible causal factors in delinquency. We described adolescence as a trying time for many youngsters, caught as they are in a "time warp" between childhood and adulthood. During this time, they are trying to distance themselves from the authority of their parents and to find their own identities. They make this attempt often under the influence of the peer group and the entertainment media, both of which often model antisocial attitudes and behaviors. We also cited the "hardening" of poverty, especially in our ghettoes, as a factor in many of the worst manifestations of modern American delinquency.

Then, we discussed the effective supervision of juveniles and placed emphasis on the essential requirements for the healthy psychosocial development of children. Loving discipline is the first essential requirement. Such discipline differs from punishment, and lays a foundation for a responsible lifestyle. Other requirements addressed were the children's acceptance of themselves and of their emotions and feelings, their understanding of the feelings of others, and the process of making decisions, problem solving, and establishing positive interpersonal relationships. We also addressed values, education, and a responsible lifestyle. Then, we expanded on the idea of treating different individuals differently, addressed in earlier chapters, with emphasis on two dimensions: maturity level and extroversion/introversion, and on the Wechsler P > V test to form a preliminary impression of where the child fits along these dimensions. We urged caution when making interpretations, noting that any interpretation should account for the environmental context.

Family counseling is the most important component of a delinquent's treatment. We cannot deal effectively with delinquency until we define and confront delinquency-generating factors in the family. Although many families are reluctant to get involved in counseling, they must be involved in it, and the juvenile probation officer/caseworker's task is to make sure that they do become involved and come to appreciate its values. Many families and delinquents welcome the opportunity to learn how to communicate more effectively, and studies have shown that family counseling is useful and productive.

The chapter ended with a guide for a needs assessment interview to help correctional workers get a feel for offenders and their environmental situations. After making an assessment, the next step is to match the children's needs with available community resources to help them.

References and Suggested Readings

American Correctional Association. 1996. *Correctional Issues: Juvenile Justice Programs and Trends*. Lanham, Maryland: American Correctional Association.

Anderson, C., D. Gentile, and K. Buckley. 2007. *Violent Video Game Effects on Children and Adolescents: Theory, Research, and Public Policy*. New York: Oxford University Press.

Bartollas, C. and S. Miller. 2005. *Juvenile Justice in America*, 4th ed. Upper Saddle River, New Jersey: Prentice Hall.

Berzonsky, M. 2008. Identity Formation: The Role of Identity Processing Style and Cognitive Processes. *Personality and Individual Differences* 44: 645-655.

Bleckman, E. and K. Vryan. 2000. Prosocial Family Therapy: A Manualized Preventative Intervention for Juvenile Offenders. *Aggression and Violent Behavior* 5: 343-378.

Buchanan, C., J. Eccles, and J. Becker. 1993. Are Adolescents the Victims of Raging Hormones? Evidence for Activational Effects of Hormones on Moods and Behavior at Adolescence. *Psychological Bulletin* 111: 62-107.

Camarota, S. 2007. Illegitimate Nation: An Examination of Out-of-Wedlock Births Among Immigrants and Natives. Center for Immigration Studies, Washington, D.C. Online at www.cis.org.

Caspi, A., D. Lynam, T. Moffitt, and P. Silva. 1993. Unraveling Girls' Delinquency: Biological, Dispositional, and Contextual Contributions to Adolescent Misbehavior. *Developmental Psychology* 29: 19-30.

Clark, M. 2001. Influencing Positive Behavioral Change: Increasing the Therapeutic Approach of Juvenile Courts. *Federal Probation* 65: 18-28.

Cullen, M. and J. Wright. 1996. *Cage Your Rage for Teens: A Guide to Anger Control*. Alexandria, Virginia: American Correctional Association.

Daly, M. 1996. Evolutionary Adaptationism: Another Biological Approach to Criminal and Antisocial Behavior. In *Genetics of Criminal and Antisocial Behaviour*. G. Bock and J. Goode, eds., Chichester, England: Wiley. pp. 183-195.

Drigotas, S. and J. Udry. 1993. Biosocial Models of Adolescent Problem Behavior: Extension to Panel Session. *Social Biology* 40: 1-7.

Edwards, D. and C. Nuckols. 1991. Identifying Kids at High Risk. *Adolescent Counselor* 3: 25-40.

Ellis, L. 2003. Genes, Criminality, and the Evolutionary Neuroandrogenic Theory. In *Biosocial Criminology: Challenging Environmentalism's Supremacy*, A. Walsh and L. Ellis, eds. Hauppauge, New York: Nova Science. pp. 13-34.

Ellis, L. and A. Walsh. 2000. *Criminology: A Global Perspective*. Boston: Allyn and Bacon.

Erickson, E. 1963. *Childhood and Society*. New York: Norton.

Farrington, D. 1989. Psychobiological Factors in the Explanation and Reduction of Juvenile Delinquency: Genetics, Intelligence, Morality, and Personality. *Today's Delinquent* 8: 37-51.

Giedd, J. 2004. Structural Magnetic Resonance Imaging of the Adolescent Brain. *Annals of the New York Academy of Science* 1021: 77-85.

Glasser, W. 1984. *Control Theory: A New Explanation of How We Control Our Lives*. New York: Harper and Row.

Glick, B. and A. Goldstein. 1995. *Managing Delinquency Programs that Work*. Lanham, Maryland: American Correctional Association.

Granello, P. and F. Hanna. 2003. Incarcerated and Court-Involved Adolescents: Counseling an At-Risk Population. *Journal of Counseling and Development* 81: 11-19.

Hall, S. and M. Brassard. 2008. Relational Support as a Predictor of Identity Status in an Ethnically Diverse Early Adolescent Sample. *Journal of Early Adolescence* 28: 92-114.

Heck, C. 2000. Civil Law and Juvenile Justice. In A. Walsh and C. Hemmens, eds., *From Law to Order: The Theory and Practice of Law and Justice*. Lanham, Maryland: American Correctional Association.

Krisberg, B. 2005. *Juvenile Justice: Redeeming our Children*. Thousand Oaks, California: Sage.

Lakoff, A. 2000. Adaptive Will: The Evolution of Attention Deficit Disorder. *Journal of the History of the Behavioral Sciences* 36: 149-169.

Levy, F., D. Hay, M. McStephen, C. Wood, and I. Waldman. 1997. Attention-Deficit Hyperactivity Disorder: A Category or a Continuum? Genetic Analysis of a Large-Scale Twin Study. *Journal of the American Academy of Child and Adolescent Psychiatry* 36: 737-744.

Lawrence, R. and D. Mueller. 2003. School Shootings and the Man-Bites-Dog Criterion of Newsworthiness. *Youth, Violence, and Juvenile Justice* 1: 330-345.

Lykken, D. 1995. *The Antisocial Personalities*. Hillsdale, New Jersey: Lawrence Erlbaum.

Lynam, D. 1996. Early Identification of Chronic Offenders: Who Is the Fledgling Psychopath? *Psychological Bulletin* 120: 209-234.

Masters, R. 1994. *Counseling Criminal Justice Offenders*. Thousand Oaks, California: Sage.

Mednick, S., T. Moffitt, and S. Sack, eds. *The Causes of Crime: New Biological Approaches*. Cambridge: University of Cambridge Press.

Messner, S. and R. Rosenfeld. 2001. *Crime and the American Dream*, 3rd ed. Belmont, California: Wadsworth.

Moffitt, T. 1993. Adolescent-Limited and Life-Course-Persistent Antisocial Behavior: A Developmental Taxonomy. *Psychological Review* 100: 674-701.

Moffitt, T. and A. Walsh. 2003. The Adolescent-Limited/Life-Course Persistent Theory of Antisocial Behavior: What Have We Learned? In *Biosocial Criminology: Challenging Environmentalism's Supremacy*, A. Walsh and L. Ellis, eds. Hauppauge, New York: Nova Science. pp. 123-144.

Mulder, J., T. ter Bogt, Q. Raaimakers, and W. Vollebergh. 2007. Music Taste Groups and Problem Behavior. *Youth and Adolescence* 36: 313-324.

Nachshon, I. and D. Denno. 1987. Violent Behavior and Cerebral Hemisphere Function. In S. Mednick, T. Moffitt, and S. Sack, eds. *The Causes of Crime: New Biological Approaches*. Cambridge University Press, Cambridge, England. pp. 185–217.

North, A. and D. Hargreaves. 2007. Lifestyle Correlates of Musical Preference: Relationships, Living Arrangements, Beliefs, and Crime. *Psychology of Music* 35: 58-87.

Office of Juvenile Justice and Delinquency Protection. 1996. *Juvenile Offenders and Victims: 1996 Update on Violence*. Washington, D.C.: U.S. Government Printing Office.

Office of the Surgeon General. 2001. *Youth Violence: A Report of the Surgeon General*. Washington, D.C.: U.S. Department of Health and Human Services. Retrieved from www.surgeongeneral.gov/library/youthviolence.

Quinn, W. and D. Van Dyke. 2004. A Multiple Family Group Intervention for First-Time Juvenile Offenders: Comparisons with Probation and Dropouts on Recidivism. *Journal of Community Psychology* 32: 177-200.

Raz, A. 2004. Brain Imaging Data of ADHD. *Neuropsychiatry* August: 46-50.

Restak, R. 2001. *The Secret Life of the Brain*. New York: co-published by Dana Press and Joseph Henry Press.

Robins, M. and J. Szapocznik. 2000. Brief Strategic Family Therapy. *Juvenile Justice Bulletin* April: 1-11.

Rodkin, P., T. Farmer, R. Pearl, and R. Van Acker. 2000. Heterogeneity of Popular Boys: Antisocial and Prosocial Configurations. *Developmental Psychology* 36: 14-24.

Romig, D., C. Cleland, and L. Romig. 1989. *Juvenile Delinquency: Visionary Approaches*. Columbus, Ohio: Merrill.

Scarpa, A. and A. Raine. 2003. The Psychophysiology of Antisocial Behavior: Interactions with Environmental Experiences. In *Biosocial Criminology: Challenging Environmentalism's Supremacy*, A. Walsh and L. Ellis, eds. Hauppauge, New York: Nova Science. pp. 209-226.

Scheffer, M. 1987. *Policing from the Schoolhouse: Police School Liaison and Resource Officer Programs*. Springfield, Illinois: Charles C. Thomas.

Snyder, H. 2007. *Juvenile Arrests, 2005*. Washington, D.C.: Office of Juvenile Justice and Delinquency Prevention.

Sowell, E., P. Thompson, and A. Toga. 2004. Mapping Changes in the Human Cortex throughout the Span of Life. *Neuroscientist* 10: 372-392

Spear, L. 2000a. Neurobehavioral Changes in Adolescence. *Current Directions in Psychological Science* 9: 11-114.

———. 2000b. The Adolescent Brain and Age-Related Behavioral Manifestations. *Neuroscience and Biobehavioral Review* 24: 417-463.

Steinberg, L. 2005. Cognitive and Affective Development in Adolescence. *Trends in Cognitive Science*, 9: 69-74.

Tibbetts, S. 2003. Selfishness, Social-Control, and Emotions: An Integrated Perspective on Criminality. In *Biosocial Criminology: Challenging Environmentalism's Supremacy*, A.Walsh, and L. Ellis, eds. Hauppauge, New York: Nova Science. pp. 83-101.

Udry, J. 1990. Biosocial Models of Adolescent Problem Behaviors. *Social Biology* 37: 1-10.

U.S. Census Bureau. 2004. *The Population of the United States*. U.S. Census Bureau: Washington, D.C..

Van Voorhis, P. 1985. Restitution Outcome and Probationers' Assessments of Restitution. *Criminal Justice and Behavior* 12: 259 287.

Wakefield, B. 1991. Delinquency, Exercise, and Self Esteem: A Look at a New Program for High Risk Youth. Paper presented at the 1991 annual meeting of the Academy of Criminal Justice Sciences, Nashville, Tennessee.

Walker, E. 2002. Adolescent Neurodevelopment and Psychopathology. *Current Directions in Psychological Science* 11: 24-28.

Walsh, A. 1990. Illegitimacy, Child Abuse and Neglect, and Cognitive Development. *The Journal of Genetic Psychology* 15: 279-285.

———. 1991. *Intellectual Imbalance, Love Deprivation and Violent Delinquency: A Biosocial Perspective*. Springfield, Illinois: Charles C. Thomas.

Walsh, A., T. Petee, and J. Beyer. 1987. Intellectual Imbalance: Comparing High Verbal and High Performance IQ Delinquents. *Criminal Justice and Behavior* 14: 370 379.

Weiss, G. 1991. Attention-Deficit Hyperactivity Disorder. In *Child and Adolescent Psychiatry: A Comprehensive Textbook*, M. Lewis, ed. Baltimore: Williams and Wilkins.

White, A. 2004. *Substance Use and the Adolescent Brain: An Overview with the Focus on Alcohol*. Durham, North Carolina: Duke University Medical Center.

Wood, S. and E. Wood. 1996. *The World of Psychology*, 2nd ed. Boston: Allyn and Bacon.

The Female Offender

Counselors of women must intervene with delicate balance. The goal is to help women adapt to transitions and resolve ambiguities in their own individual ways and according to their values while also helping them move beyond where they are in order to become independent, autonomous human beings.

—Nancy Schlossberg and Laura Kent

Gender Differences in Criminal Behavior

Across time, national boundaries, and type of crime, females commit far fewer crimes than males. Moreover, the more serious, brutal, and violent the offense the more males dominate in its commission (Campbell 2009). Prostitution (which is male driven) is the only crime for which females are arrested more frequently than males. The lower crime rate among females is reflected in their incarceration rates. The latest figures from the Bureau of Justice Statistics (Sabol, Couture, and Harrison 2007) reported that in 2006, 112,498 women were incarcerated in state and federal prisons in the United States (7.2 percent of all incarcerated adults) compared with 1,458,363 men. Incarceration rates for women are growing faster than they are for men. From 2000 to 2005 the increase in incarceration was 1.9 percent for men and 2.9 percent for women (Sabol, Couture, and Harrison 2007). Women were 24 percent of the probation and 12 percent of the parole populations in 2006 (Glaze and Bonczar 2007).

Figure 21.1 Female/Male Crime Rate Comparisons: 2006 Uniform Crime Report Data

Source: *FBI Uniform Crime Reports: Crime in the United States, 2006* (2007).

Figure 21.1 shows male/female differences in number of arrests in 2006 for seven of the eight FBI index crimes (FBI 2007); rape is not included because we cannot graph the 77-fold difference without distorting the remaining comparisons. The graph shows the number of males arrested for each crime as multiples of the female number. For instance, the number of males arrested for murder and robbery are approximately eight times the number of females, and the male larceny/theft number is about 1.5 times the female number.

Are these large differences in male/female arrests an accurate reflection of actual sex differences in behavior or of something else? Some feminist criminologists view the relationship between gender and crime as largely a function of differential reporting and differential application of formal arrests rather than actual differences in male and female criminality. In other words, there is a bias in favor of women that dispose individuals victimized by women not to report crimes and a similar bias in the "chivalrous" criminal justice system revealed in the unwillingness of police to arrest women and in the unwillingness of the courts to convict them.

Researchers tested and rejected this male-chivalry hypothesis by comparing Uniform Crime Report (UCR) data and National Crime Victimization Survey (NCVS) data in which victims are able to identify the sex and race of their victimizers for researchers. Researchers find that official and victimization data agree extremely well with one another. In fact, the first such test of this hypothesis found that women perpetrators appeared more in the official arrest data than in the victimization surveys, a finding that runs directly contrary to the chivalry hypothesis (Hindelang 1979). Similar findings have been consistently found (Steffensmeier and Allan 1996). Most feminists now assert that the chivalry hypothesis is dead and that the courts now appear to have gone the other way (arresting and incarcerating more women), mainly due to the war on drugs (van Wormer and Kaplan 2006).

The Female Offender

Why are females so much less prone to criminal behavior than men are? Proposing a structural explanation for the differences is difficult because female offenders are found in the same places as their male counterparts: they are "typically of low socioeconomic status, poorly educated, under- or unemployed, and disproportionately from minority groups" (Steffensmeier and Allan 1996: 465). As Bennett, Farrington, and Huesmann (2005: 280) state: "Males and females are not raised apart and exposed to an entirely different set of developmental conditions."

The correlations between male and female rates strongly support this contention. For instance, Campbell, Muncer, and Bibel (2001: 484) report correlations between male and female violent and property crime rates in the United States of .95 and .99, respectively; and that the average correlations across a number of countries for a variety of crimes are all in the mid to upper .90s. What these correlations tell us is that no matter how wide the gender gap and crime rates are, they go up or down together. Additionally, the individual predictors of male offending (for example, low self-control, conduct disorder, attention deficit hyperactivity disorder) also predict female offending, although more males than females have these traits and are more affected by them (Moffitt et al. 2001).

It would seem to follow from the above that females who become criminal are more atypical of their gender than criminal males are atypical of theirs. Herrnstein (1989: 20) opines that: "there are fewer female offenders than male, but they are more deviant [than nonoffending females—not more deviant than offending males] psychologically, both intellectually and in personality." The reasoning is that since females generally tend to be more conformists in their behavior than males, the threshold for crossing the line from conforming to criminal behavior is much higher for females than for males. That is, it takes greater frequency and/or severity of the risk factors typically related to criminal behavior to push females over the line dividing prosocial from antisocial behavior.

Although there is a relative dearth of studies of female crime and delinquency, what studies there are tend to support the contention that female offenders tend to come from more dysfunctional families than their male counterparts do. For instance, one study found that: "There was more mother-adolescent conflict/hostility and a trend for more parental conflict/hostility in families of female delinquents than in the families of male delinquents" (Henggeler, Edwards, and Borduin 1987: 206).

Other studies among female prison inmates found that they had been subjected to physical and sexual abuse (either as children or by husbands and boyfriends) at rates exceeding three to four times the national rate (Chesney-Lind 2000, Van Voohris et al. 2003). Women's offending is more likely to involve relationship issues, such as parental and/or spousal/lover abuse, and ensnarement into the antisocial activities by criminal males (Van Voorhis et al. 2003). Because females are more resistant to criminogenic environmental influences (it takes more of an environmental push to make them "cross the line"), a number of theorists have hypothesized about a probable stronger genetic component involved for females who engage in crime than there is for males who engage in crime (Campbell 1999, Mealey 1995, Raine 1993). This does not mean, of course, that females are more genetically prone to criminal behavior than males; quite the opposite is true. It simply means that just as females require a stronger environmental push than males to cross the line to criminal activity, they also apparently need a stronger genetic push than males.

Recalling the material on intellectual imbalances among males in Chapter 3, note how the delinquent girls compare with the boys in terms of intellectual imbalance. Of the seventy-four girls in the sample, forty-five (60.8 percent) were P=V, and twenty-nine (39.2 percent) were P>V imbalanced. None of the girls showed the V>P imbalanced profile, further emphasizing the atypicality of female delinquents. Since the P>V profile is also overrepresented among female delinquents, with the V>P profile being completely absent, we have further evidence that P>V is a marker of antisocial behavior, and V>P is a marker of conforming behavior (Walsh 1991).

Causality: Cultural and Structural

As we have seen, female crime rates are as sensitive to shifting cultural and structural factors, as are male rates. The correlations between male and female rates reported above by Campbell, Muncer, and Bibel (2001) mean that we can predict the female assault rate from the male rate, and vice-versa, with almost complete accuracy. Thus, as previously noted, while we can use structural variables to predict fluctuations in crime rates for both sexes, it is difficult to formulate a viable structural explanation for the differences between the rates.

As in so many "sensitive" areas of criminology, heated debate surrounds the issue of why we observe such a criminality gender gap. Some writers, citing the ideology that always seems to intrude into the issue of gender difference, indicate that to even to explore the issue borders on the taboo (Scarr 1993). Not to explore an issue because it may cause psychic pain for some is to agree with those who feel that ignorance might be bliss, which is sheer nonsense. The best approach is to admit that no single cause of the gender gap exists, and that the issue is not one of nature versus nurture but rather nature via nurture, as it is in all human behavior. Let us first look at typical feminist explanations.

Feminist criminology has two major concerns: (1) Do the traditional male-centered theories of crime apply to women? (2) What explains the universal fact that females are far less involved in crime and other forms of antisocial behavior than males (Price and Sokoloff 1995)? Only the second concern is relevant to us here. Feminist criminologists' explanations for the large gender gap in criminality rest heavily on traditional sociological notions of the power of socialization. Males are socialized to be assertive, aggressive, ambitious, and dominant. These are admirable qualities if pro-socially directed, but also may be conducive to crime in some situations. Females, on the other hand, are socialized to be passive, nurturing, "ladylike," and home- and family-oriented; these qualities are negatively related to criminality. This viewpoint suggests that if we socialized females in the same way as males and gave them similar roles and experiences, gender differences in criminality would disappear. We will address this point later, but for now, we briefly will examine what feminists mean by examining female criminal behavior from a feminist point of view.

In asserting the inadequacy of mainstream ("malestream"?) theories to explain female crime, feminists are not saying that females do not face, nor are they insensitive to, the same kinds of pressures that influence male criminality. What they are saying is that females often face situations that are more or less specific to their gender that may lead to crime but which mainstream criminology ignores too often. For instance, some consider shoplifting an extension of the legitimate shopping role of females (Smart 1976), and prostitution as an illegitimate extension of the legitimate role of a wife (Morris 1987). While these examples may seem to stretch concepts to a breaking point (and the second one is downright insulting to married women), some feminists take them very seriously.

Two gender-specific accounts of female criminality are criminalizing girls' survival and victim-precipitated homicide. In the first instance, research shows that girls are far more likely than boys are to be sexually victimized, especially by family members (Chesney-Lind 2000). This victimization leads to a variety of psychological and behavioral responses such as depression, anger, anxiety, promiscuity, truancy, and running away from home (Chesney-Lind, 1995). The first runaway offense probably will result in the girl being returned to the conditions she sought to escape, reinforcing her belief that "nobody cares," and strengthening her resolve not to be caught again. In order not to be caught again and to survive, the girl may steal food, money, or clothing, may use and sell drugs, and may prostitute herself. These "survival behaviors" probably will result in arrest and may precipitate lifetime patterns of criminal behavior. According to Chesney-Lind, patriarchy (as expressed in male-centered family dynamics) combines with paternalism (as expressed in official reactions to female runaways) to force girls into "lives of escaped convicts" (1995: 84).

Victim-precipitated homicide (a homicide in which the victim initiates the sequence of events leading to his or her murder) is a second gender-specific theory. This concept begins with the fact that homicides committed by males are mostly intrasexual (male/male) while most committed by females are intersexual (female/male). This suggests that the causes of homicide might be very different for females and males.

Researchers have long noted that African-American women are second only to African-American men in the rate of arrest for homicide in the United States (Barak 1998, Mann 1995). Most instances of black female homicide involve women killing their husbands or lovers in self-defense situations (Mann 1995). Assaults by African-American males on their wives and lovers tend to be more frequent, violent, and injurious than assaults by males of other races (Rasche 1995), but black victims are less willing or able to make use of agencies dealing with spousal abuse (Rasche 1995). Consequently, African-American women often resort to the use of deadly weapons to protect themselves.

The sequence of events leading to victim-precipitated homicide typically is described as follows: The frustrations experienced by African-American males in American society often lead to violent assaults on their wives/lovers. Because these wives/lovers have less access to social agencies, and may be taken less seriously if they have, they may have to resort to violence to protect themselves (Mann 1995, Rasche 1995). Thus, feminist criminologists consider women who kill in self-defense situations to be victims of a classist, racist, and sexist society, as well as victims of a black subculture that has a high level of tolerance of violence.

Causality: Biosocial

As long as we continue to view the commission of any crime as simply a function of differential opportunities and/or differential socialization and ignore biological differences between the sexes, we will remain puzzled regarding the gender gap. Males are simply more "prepared" to do violence than females whether we look at children, adolescents, or adults, and regardless of the culture in which it takes place (Barash and Lipton 2001, Campbell 2008). As Dianna Fishbein (1992: 100) summed up the issue of socialization versus biology as it pertains to male/female differences in crime rates "[C]ross cultural studies do not support the prominent role of structural and cultural influences of gender-specific crime rates as the type and extent of male versus female crime remains constant across cultures."

In her presidential address to the American Sociological Association, Alice Rossi (1984) admonished her colleagues to pay attention to the findings of the biological and neurological sciences if their theories about sex and gender are to be viable. Rossi's admonition is particularly important if the sex difference we are attempting to understand is a propensity for violence. From a biosocial perspective, gender differences are the result of differences in neurological organization due to the influence of prenatal hormones, which, in turn, reflect sex-specific evolutionary pressures.

Most gender differences are small and inconsequential, but the largest differences are those at the center of one's identity as male or female (Hines 2004). These core differences are the traits most strongly related to criminal behavior, such as aggression, dominance, empathy, nurturance, and impulsiveness, all of which reflect sex-specific evolutionary pressures. According to Doreen Kimura, evolutionary pressures assure that males and females come into, this world with "differently wired brains," and these brain differences "make it almost impossible to evaluate the effects of experience independent of physiological predisposition" (1992: 119). Sarah Bennett and her colleagues (2005: 273) augment Kimura in explaining the pathways from sex-differentiated brain organization to antisocial behavior:

> Males and females vary on a number of perceptual and cognitive information-processing domains that are difficult to ascribe to sex-role socialization . . . the human brain is either masculinized or feminized structurally and chemically before birth. Genetics and the biological environment in utero provide the foundation of gender differences in early brain morphology, physiology, chemistry, and nervous system development. It would be surprising if these differences did not contribute to gender differences in cognitive abilities, temperament, and ultimately, normal or antisocial behavior.

Biological gender differences are especially pertinent when we consider life-course persistent versus adolescent-limited offenders (see Chapter 3) of either gender. Moffitt and Walsh (2003: 137) tell us that the sex ratio for life-course persistent offenders (LCP) is ten males for every one female, and add that:

> Much of the gender difference in crime is attributed to sex differences in the risk factors for LCP antisocial behavior. Girls are biologically less likely to encounter the putative neurophysiological links that initiate the causal chain for LCP antisocial development. Girls are at lower risk for symptoms of nervous system dysfunction, difficult temperament, late verbal and motor milestones, hyperactivity, learning disabilities, reading failure, and childhood conduct problems. In other words, more girls than boys lack the congenital elements of passive, reactive, and active person/environment correlations and interactions that initiate and maintain LCP antisocial behavior.

Taken as a whole, the evidence points to a neuro-hormonal foundation for sex-typical (not sex-specific) social behavior, including criminal behavior. A review of the behavior and personality characteristics of the various types of genetic and chromosomal pseudo-hermaphrodites (Klinefelter's and XYY syndromes, androgen insensitivity syndrome, and congenital adrenal hyperplasia) concluded that the further we depart from "pure" femininity (defined as the complete absence of androgen activity) along the intersex continuum, the more deviant and antisocial both personality and behavior tend to become (Walsh 1995). This should not be taken to mean that hormonal factors determine antisocial behavior, but rather as underlining the point that androgens that organize the male brain differently early in the second trimester of pregnancy and activate it further at puberty cannot be ignored in the study of human behavior.

One of the benefits of examining female criminality separately from male criminality is that it cautions against simplistic biological or environmental determinism. Both biological and environmental factors contribute to criminality, and always act in tandem. The black/white comparison of homicide rates highlights the role of the biology of sex differences (in both black and white communities, males have a much higher homicide rate than females), and the role of sociocultural factors (black females have a higher homicide rate than white males).

Case Study

"Dr. Jekyll and Ms. Hyde": Portrait of a Violent Woman

One of the most memorable cases I ever had was that of a well-educated thirty-year-old 5' 1", 110 pound woman, "Jane." She had gotten into a vicious fight with her husband, and with the help of a butcher knife, which she embedded in his chest, she got the better of him. She then left the house, and returned some minutes later to have another go at him. By that time, her husband had staggered into a bedroom for his pistol, with which he shot her in the chest and shoulder. Both parties were taken to the hospital, he with a collapsed lung, she to have her right breast removed. Jane was arrested for aggravated assault.

Looking at Jane's record, it was clear that until the age of twenty-seven she was the picture of propriety and conformity, with only two traffic tickets on her rap sheet. After the age of twenty-seven, her sheet began to resemble that of an aggressive psychopath, with ten assaults recorded (including the present offense). The stories behind those assaults revealed that she had assaulted her parents several times, driven her car at police officers when they attempted to arrest her, chased a woman whom she accused of having an affair with her husband with an ice pick, and threatened her husband's employer with a gun. These attacks had grown in number and severity over the several months before the stabbing of her husband.

To all who knew her, it seemed as though this sweet and dedicated daughter, wife, and mother had been transformed overnight into a raging

Continued on the next page

Dr. Jekyll and Ms. Hyde, *continued*

monster. She was only an occasional drinker, but her aggressive outbursts did not coincide with her drinking; she did not use any kind of illicit substances, and her family could not identify any tension or stresses in her environment that had occurred prior to the onset of her bizarre behavior. Yet, she certainly had them now. Her husband was awarded custody of their children, her right breast had been shot off, and she was facing sentencing for aggravated assault for which she could receive four to twenty-five years in prison.

I met Jane in the county jail in the course of conducting a PSI interview. She was quite depressed, but articulate and cooperative, and she did not seem the least bit dangerous. Before being placed in jail, she had been placed in a local psychiatric hospital for ten weeks. They had done the usual psychiatric workups on her and concluded that she was "rather severely maladjusted, extremely impulsive, and in dire need of psychiatric care." There was no attempt to explain Jane's apparent "Dr. Jekyll and Ms. Hyde" behavior or its rather abrupt onset at age twenty-seven. Instead, they had chosen a series of adjectives describing her emotional state at the time of the commission of her assaults in terms describing her behavior but that did not explain that behavior.

In a conclusion consistent with Jane's diagnosis, the psychiatric team recommended "due process" (which meant incarceration) with extensive psychiatric treatment. Initially, this author agreed with them, but Jane said one thing that made him reconsider. Her assaultive behavior always seemed to occur around the time of her menstrual period. She also had mentioned this to her psychiatrist, but since this was the late 1970s, the heyday of strict environmentalist explanations for all kinds of behavior, he dismissed it as an "old wife's tale." I was aware of studies by psychiatrist Katharina Dalton (1964) and her colleagues that implicated the role of premenstrual tension syndrome (PMS) in violent crime among women.

Further reading revealed that PMS had been successfully used as a defense in many European courts. I discussed these things with the sentencing judge and indicated that we might have the basis for medical treatment. The judge allowed two extra weeks to complete the PSI report, during which I sought a physician to corroborate "this PMS stuff" and to treat her. Although PMS is a well-known syndrome today, there were still a lot of physicians in the 1970s who agreed with her psychiatrist that PMS was an old wife's tale. One biologically oriented psychiatrist prescribed progesterone hormone therapy for Jane. She remained in the county jail for an additional two months while the psychiatrist assessed the effectiveness of the treatment. Her behavior during that time was sufficiently good for the judge to take a chance with her, and, much to the chagrin of her husband, she was released on probation.

While on probation, Jane received physical therapy for her arm, which had withered somewhat due to the effects of her gunshot wound, and she continued with her progesterone treatments. She obtained employment, and she became reconciled with her parents. Although her husband retained custody of their children, Jane was allowed previously denied visitation rights. Not once during her four-year period of probation did Jane feel the urge to assault anyone, and she was a very cooperative probationer.

> Looking back on this case, I was glad that I was successful in sustaining my point of view, but from Jane's perspective, the whole thing was a tragedy. Because of an accident of physiology, she lost her husband and the custody of her children, became estranged from her parents, had her right breast shot off, and had been imprisoned in a psychiatric ward and jail. Her unpleasant story may well have continued on the same track had the author been unable to find a psychiatrist not afraid to go up against the conventional wisdom of the time. The simple administration of progesterone turned Ms. Hyde back into the much more appealing Dr. Jekyll. It is indeed a pity that it came so late.

Counseling Female Offenders

Some readers may wonder why it is necessary to devote a separate chapter to the female offender: "Aren't women people too, with the same motives and frailties of men?" Doesn't it 'ghettoize' females to treat them separately?" Can't women benefit from the same kinds of counseling and treatment that men get?" Judith Resnik (1983: 109) goes so far as to say that prison inmates should not be classified by sex because, "sexual segregation does harm to the emerging, but still fragile, societal value of sexual equality," and some counseling theorists believe that men and women should not be treated differently in counseling for much the same reasons (Spiegel 1979). Although these arguments have some validity, few people take this view today, either in terms of sex segregation or in terms of the use of different counseling modalities for women. These folks seem to believe that equitable means identical, which it certainly does not. Like it or not, women are different from men in certain respects that demand different (but not unequal) treatment. The American Psychological Association (APA) recognizes this, and has set forth a series of principles that they consider essential for the counseling of women. Based on Corey (1986: 341), we summarize and paraphrase those principles having applicability to correctional settings.

First and foremost, any individual counseling women should be knowledgeable and sensitized to the biological, psychological, and social issues that have an impact on women. In other words, there are differences between the sexes that make a difference, and these differences should not be ignored in the name of political correctness. It follows from this, according to the American Psychological Association that the counselor must be aware that models and treatment modalities developed for male offenders may not be applicable to females. This obviously does not mean that females do not benefit from the counseling skills of a warm and concerned counselor in the same way that men do; indeed, the relationship aspect of counseling is even more important for females (McLeod 2003). It simply means that there are additional considerations.

Counselors must be sensitive to issues of sexism in their language and behavior. Male counselors must be as professional with their female offenders as they are with their male offenders. Using such endearments as "honey" or "sweetheart" or offering fond embraces send messages that women may not receive in the same spirit with which you sent them. Women who are sensitive to the women's movement will take this as a sexist attempt to denigrate them and keep them in their place. More traditional women may take it as a sexual come-on; in either case, you have damaged the professional relationship. A power relationship exists between the correctional worker and the offender, and males supervising and counseling females should be aware of the possibility of sexual activity between the worker and his offender. You must avoid this possibility, but it will be more difficult to accomplish if male counselors give female offenders the impression that they have more than a professional interest in them. These are all points made previously in this book, but they are well worth repeating here.

Edward Scott's long experience with counseling female offenders leads him to believe that they present special and unique challenges. He writes that he has never met a female criminal in a counseling setting with a healthy attitude about human relationships. In agreement with many feminist criminologists, Scott believes that this is primarily due to the negative experiences with males that most female offenders have had. He also feels that many such women may be hostile toward male counselors, making the male counselor the target for past abuses (this is not necessarily open hostility, but rather an attitude of "passive aggressiveness"). However, he further believes a male counselor is preferable to a female counselor because female offenders must be allowed to work through their relationship problems, which he considers the main obstacle that they have to circumvent (1977).

Writing from a radical feminist perspective, Jeanne Slattery (2004: 156-157) both agrees and disagrees with Scott when she states that: "a same-gendered therapeutic relationship can increase therapists' understanding of their clients' lives and can create a more nurturing and empowering therapeutic environment." However, she also writes, "it can sometimes be empowering to have a positive therapeutic relationship with someone [a male] of an oppressive group."

Feminist Counseling

Kathy Evans and her colleagues (2005: 269) define feminist counseling thusly: "Feminist therapy incorporates the psychology of women, developmental research, cognitive-behavioral techniques, multicultural awareness, and social activism in a coherent and therapeutic package." Mirroring the feminist complaint about male dominance in criminology, McLeod (2003: 208) states, "Virtually all the key historical figures in counseling and psychotherapy have been men, and they have written, whether consciously or not, from a male perspective." Feminist counselors want to rectify this, and most would strongly disagree with Scott on at least two issues. First, they insist that female counselors (of a feminist persuasion) are more effective with female offenders than males.

According to Jocelyn Chaplin, the first phase of feminist counseling is the "mothering" phase. Although she asserts that men are just as capable of mothering as women are, because only females have been socialized into that role in our patriarchal society, only female counselors can adequately engage in this trust-building phase (1988). Second, feminist counselors would argue that it is precisely because female offenders have had such bad experiences with male relationships that male counselors would be ineffective in building trust. They also might fear that Scott's "working through their relationship problems" means that women will be persuaded to further adjust to the status quo and remain in subordinate positions (Enns 1993). Women certainly have issues with power imbalances, and they probably will perceive the counseling relationship as just another instance in which the offender is in a subordinate position (Alexander 2000).

A number of important differences exist between traditional and feminist counseling. Feminist counselors use a number of traditional counseling theories, which they tailor to fit feminist philosophy by stripping them of what they consider their male-centered biases (Slattery 2004). Another important difference is that while traditional counseling theories encourage their adherents to adopt a value-free stance, feminist counseling is unabashedly ideological and encourages its adherents to adopt a value-laden activism (Enns 1993, Evans et al. 2005). They consider "consciousness raising" as necessary to free women from the shackles of patriarchy, which many feminists see as the "cause" of women's offending. On the other hand, confrontational methods appear to threaten women because of past confrontations with men (Shearer 2003). The best programs for women appear to be those that empower them; in other words, programs that help them to build skills and competencies to achieve independence (Bloom 2000).

A corollary of consciousness raising is that offenders are taught how to separate the external and internal sources of their problems. In other words, offenders should not blame themselves for the problems they have, which arise from institutionalized sexism, sex-role socialization, patriarchy, and so forth (Worell and Remer 1992). Recognizing external sources of our problems is an aid in both reducing guilt and anxiety associated with self-blame and in knowing what steps to take to change those sources. Research indicates that most (about 60 percent) of the females in prison or on probation/parole have experienced physical and sexual abuse (Prichard 2000). When women are empowered by the knowledge that they are not to blame for their victimization, and come to value themselves as independent persons who do not need their batterers' "support," they may take steps to terminate the relationship before either they murder their batterer or their batterer murders them.

Externalizing blame is not always an inappropriate defense mechanism, nor is it "copping out." It is entirely appropriate to divest yourself of responsibility for bad things that happen to you if they are truly the result of the actions of others. As discussed earlier, the trouble is that many of us have a built-in bias to accept readily suggestions that exonerate us. Women never should blame themselves for their own abuse, or for using whatever methods they must to defend themselves. However, we have severe reservations about any counselor telling a female thief, forger, drug addict, child abuser, or whatever, that she can lay all her actions and problems at the door of our sexist and patriarchal society. There is a real danger that such "consciousness raising" will serve as an exculpatory factor, and thus be counterproductive. If the offender is truly blameless, however, the question for the feminist counselor becomes "Now that you have correctly attributed blame, what are you going to do about it?"

Feminist Counseling Techniques

Feminist counselors employ a variety of techniques in common with traditional counselors such as role-playing and bibliotherapy. This description is limited to only those techniques relatively unique to feminist theory as described by Judith Worrell and Pam Remer (1992) and Brenda Wiewel and Toni Mosley (2006). These descriptions demonstrate that feminist counselors must have knowledge of the sociology of sex roles and be conversant in assertiveness-training skills.

Sex-Role Analysis: Counselors often conduct sex-role analysis in a group context. This analysis explores sex roles and the messages they imply and shows how the consequences of these roles (both positive and negative) affect women. It invites offenders to identify how they have internalized these messages and then decide which of these messages they would like to change. Women may ask themselves questions such as "What are the costs and benefits of continuing to adopt this particular sex role for me?" "Are the internalized messages related to this role really congruent with my innermost feelings, or are they strongly at odds with them?"

Power Analysis: Power analysis extends sex-role analysis by increasing offenders' awareness of sex-based power differentials (how do sex-role stereotypes affect the male/female use of power?). It also empowers offenders to be able to influence factors external to themselves that are affecting their lives.

Assertiveness Training: To become empowered is to stand up for yourself, to refuse to be exploited psychologically or physically by others who have influence on your life. To achieve this goal, it is necessary to receive assertiveness training. Being assertive is not the same as being aggressive. Indeed, asserting one's right to be treated with respect may be the very thing needed to avoid aggressive confrontation in the future. It always struck us that women who killed their husbands or lovers were typically (but not always) very passive types who finally snapped under frequent abuse (see also Wojda and Rowse 1997).

Reframing and Relabeling: Reframing refers to a shift in the frame of reference used to view the offenders' problems. Feminists want to shift from a diagnosis-based "What is wrong with this woman?" to an experience based "What has happened to this woman?" (Scott 2004: 256). There is a definite danger in this since it focuses the offender on the past rather than the present or the future. However, it is a useful starting point for the counselor to explore what issues the offender has. *Relabeling* refers to a change in the name or evaluation of offenders' characteristics and behaviors, usually from negative (based on male-centered norms) to positive (based on female-centered norms). From the feminist perspective, *reframing* concerns a shift from the individual to the sociopolitical system. This is the most controversial aspect of feminist counseling. It would be unacceptable by other counseling theories; not because our sociopolitical system is beyond criticism, but because if blame lies outside of ourselves, then change only can come when that external thing changes, which may be never. Blame shifting to the sociopolitical system is not the same as identifying specific relationships negatively affecting one's life. An individual can change relationships with specific persons readily; the "system" obviously cannot be changed as easily. Furthermore, are there gender-specific norms about what is good, desirable, and positive behavior or personal characteristics? We think not.

Special Concerns of Women in Prison

As of 2006, 112,498 women were imprisoned in state and federal prisons. Drug-related offenses landed the majority of these women behind bars (Wiewel and Mosley 2006). Women seem particularly susceptible to cocaine abuse (mostly in the form of crack). The ADAM drug-use data discussed in Chapter 16 (although we did not break the data down by gender there) showed that in almost every reporting city, the percentage of female arrestees testing positive for cocaine was greater than the percentage of male arrestees. This does not mean that more women abuse cocaine than men do. It means that among the much lower number of arrested women, a greater percentage test positive than among the arrested men.

We see a reflection of the growing number of women using drugs in the fact that females who abuse drugs are the fastest growing segment of the correctional system

(Shearer 2003). Because female drug users are likely to engage in unprotected sex in exchange for money or drugs, they are in great need of safe-sex education as well as drug treatment (Shearer 2003). Women are more likely to contract HIV during sex than men are because of the internal nature of female genitalia, and a recent report indicates that the number of HIV-positive women is almost equal to that of men today (Mestel 2004).

Those who believe that separate standards for males and females perpetuate sexism may be happy to learn that few special efforts have been made to design prison classification systems for females. Only four states (Idaho, New York, Massachusetts, and Ohio) had separate classification systems for women in 2001 (Van Voorhis et al. 2003). The typical strategy is to apply systems designed for male prisoners to women without change (Bloom 2000). This "benign neglect" reflects the reality that only about 7.2 percent of incarcerated individuals are women, and that female inmates are less violent, more cooperative, and less escape prone than men are (Van Voorhis et al. 2003). The attitude seems to be, "Why make special efforts for such a small and relatively well behaved group when we are faced with the horrendous problems of male inmates." It is not that female inmates cause staff no trouble at all. It appears from a number of studies that female inmates commit more disciplinary offenses than male inmates do during the first year of incarceration, although these offenses are far less serious and may reflect less tolerance of female misbehavior on the part of correctional staff (Lindquist 1980).

Part of the reason that females may commit more disciplinary offenses is the abysmal state of correctional programs available for females in prison, and for the special pains of imprisonment, they may feel (Pollock-Byrne 1990). Programs for women tend to be overwhelmingly sex stereotyped. They emphasize clerical work, food service, and cosmetology, or are aimed at housekeeping skills, such as cooking and sewing, with few programs offering better-paying employable skills (Kratcoski and Babb 1990). According to some critics, such programs serve to reinforce social roles and expectations of women as servants of others, feelings of dependency in women, and low self-esteem (Welch 1996). There obviously is nothing remiss, however, in providing Parental Effectiveness Training for women who may be deficient in this area. As opposed to being sexist, this simply reflects the fact that women do the vast majority of parenting, and the fact that female offenders are not the best parents in the world (Stawar and Stawar 2008, Flanagan 1996, Boudouris 1996).

Adding to the normal pains of imprisonment is the fact that most female inmates have children under the age of eighteen. Approximately 75 percent of incarcerated women have children (Chapple 2000), and 72 percent of women on probation have children (Bloom 2000); yet, most of them (about 63 percent) are single mothers (Hoskins 2000). Vetter and Silverman describe the pains of imprisonment for inmate mothers.

> Imprisonment for the inmate mother has a twofold adverse effect. In addition to the emotional loss and pangs of separation suffered by the mother, she faces the prospect of endless worry over the care and custody of her children. . . . If there is no father or close relative to assume responsibility for looking after the children, the most likely result is that the children's care will be taken over by a social welfare agency and the children may be placed in a foster home or put up for adoption (1986: 228).

In general, male inmates do not suffer the same emotional pangs over separation from their children. Writing of the male inmate's separation from his children, Scott (1977: 219) says: "He walks away with ease–and at times, pride–from children he has fathered." Moreover, while some husbands and boyfriends take responsibility for their children while the children's mothers are incarcerated, they are exceptions to the rule (Schmalleger 2003). Institutional counselors and caseworkers should keep the special concerns of inmate mothers foremost in their minds. The discussion of unwed motherhood raises a particularly thorny issue for the correctional worker with female offenders of childbearing age. Out-of-wedlock births present the United States with a tremendous burden, and have been called "the new American dilemma" (Garfinkel and McLanahan 1986: 1).

Illegitimacy brings with it a plethora of problems for both mother and child, not the least of which is the huge increase in the probability of lifelong poverty (Wilson 1993). Conservatives traditionally have placed the blame for illegitimacy on moral irresponsibility and "generous" welfare payments that enable jobless women to bear illegitimate children and still get by. Liberals talk about the hardening of poverty in this country that has produced unemployable males who are poor marriage prospects, or on the horrendous homicide rate among young black males, leaving black women with fewer prospective spouses.

These structural arguments doubtless have merit, but, once again, offer no help to the correctional worker. Yet, we may be able to do our bit in preventing at least some out-of-wedlock births by keeping in mind Gottfredson and Hirschi's (1997: 33) focus on illegitimacy as the policy recommendations deducible from their self-control theory. They write "Delaying pregnancy among unmarried girls would probably do more to affect the long-term crime rates than all the criminal justice programs combined." This is not a statement of moral condemnation. Rather, this statement recognizes the importance of the reproductive team of mother and father to the healthy development of offspring.

It seems that young girls and women who consciously chose to bear illegitimate children without adequate means to support them, or who irresponsibly fail to take proper precautions, are in need of intensive counseling. As emphasized by many sociologists, the breakdown of the family and traditional morality has turned values on their head. Just as it is "cool" for many males to deal drugs and father numerous illegitimate offspring, it is a mark of status for some females to become mothers (Anderson 1999). A young girl lacking in love and affection now has her own child upon whom she can pour out her love, and who has to love her in return. Otherwise stated, she is getting her love and worthiness needs met in the best way she knows how.

Some, who consider *morality* to be a quaint, old-fashioned word with little modern relevance, will consider any efforts to try to change reproductive behavior an intrusion of privacy. However, attempting to inculcate some sort of responsibility as it is defined by therapists such as Ellis and Glasser, discussed previously, is not simply morality. Clearly, it is irresponsible and irrational (in the reality-therapy sense of long-term consequences) to produce illegitimate children for most women. Research indicates that among many unwed mothers, there is much pride and love initially, but that when the child begins to explore and put verbal demands on them, love gives way to "rather severe rejection" (Wilson and Herrnstein 1985: 239). The effects of this rejection and other factors typically surrounding illegitimate birth among the poor are severe and criminogenic (Cleveland et al. 2000, Walsh 2003). Parenting skills and an understanding of healthy sexuality is considered a "must" for female offenders (Wiewel and Mosley 2006).

Without moralizing about sexual behavior (a lost cause, anyway), the correctional worker might point out the many downsides of unwed motherhood. Many unwed mothers already know who they are emotionally, but they may lack the verbal skills to bring them fully to conscious realization. These young women and others who are not yet mothers have to find alternative means to fulfill their needs for love and worthiness, and to realize that it is not smart to reproduce without thinking of what the future holds for them and their offspring. If their pregnancies are more a functional lack of taking proper precautions than a conscious desire to reproduce, a referral to the local family planning agency for counseling and birth-control devices may be appropriate. Community agencies offering parenting skills also are useful in this context. Given the cultural pressures arrayed against you, however, do not expect much success in your efforts.

For a variety of reasons, female inmates are more isolated from the outside world than male inmates. Kratcoski and Babb's study of seven U.S. Bureau of Prison facilities found that 50 percent of female inmates never had visitors compared with 25 percent of the men (1990: 269). This may be due to a greater number of married male inmates compared to female inmates, a greater propensity among women to visit their men in prison, or perhaps a greater geographical isolation of women's facilities. The isolation of female inmates from significant others is particularly disturbing in light of findings indicating that female self-esteem is more dependent on loving relationships than is male self-esteem (McLeod 2003).

Whatever the reasons may be for greater female isolation: "correctional experts agree that inmates who maintain contact with their spouses and families are likely to experience fewer adjustment problems than those who do not have family support" (Kratcoski and Babb 1990: 278, Lemieux 2009). Correctional counselors and caseworkers should be sensitive to the visitation patterns of female inmates and attempt to compensate through the provision of some sort of alternative pattern of interpersonal interaction for their isolation from the outside world. This could be in the form of trying to involve them more in group discussions/counseling and perhaps getting them involved with volunteer visitors, such as members of volunteer ministries.

Positive Rehabilitative Aspects of Female Offenders

So far, all seems negative. As a group, female criminals have suffered more abuse and neglect than male criminals have. They appear to be more atypical of their sex than males are of theirs. If imprisoned, they seem to adjust less well initially, have fewer programs to occupy their time, and have emotional problems involving separation from their children and other loved ones that apparently exceed the pain felt by men similarly separated. What are the positive aspects of dealing with female offenders?

First, in general, females tend to possess more of the attributes that contribute to a prosocial lifestyle, such as empathy and altruism, than males. For instance, genetic studies have shown that females are inherently more altruistic than males (Rushton et al. 1986). The authors attribute this difference to the influence of genes on sex-hormone secretion patterns. In every study surveyed by Campbell she found females more empathetic than males regardless of the tools and methods used to assess empathy (2006).

The "male" hormone testosterone dampens empathy (Knickmeyer et al. 2006), and the neuropeptide oxytocin, found in much higher levels in females, enhances empathy (Taylor 2006). For instance, women who received a single sublingual dose of testosterone showed a statistically significant reduction in empathetic responses to experimental stimuli than women in a control group who were administered a placebo (Hermans, Putman, and van Honk 2006). On the other hand, males given a single intranasal dose of oxytocin significantly enhanced their ability to infer the mental states of others (empathy) relative to a placebo control group (Domes et al. 2007). In other words, studies such as this show that males become more empathetic with the administration of "female" oxytocin, and females become less so with the administration of "male" testosterone.

We see evidence of a greater "decency" among women even when we compare interpersonal relationship patterns in male and female institutions. Within male prisons, rape and brutality are rife, with rape used to humiliate and dominate as much as to relieve sexual tension. On the other hand, coerced sexuality in female prisons is a rare thing. Female inmates tend to form close emotional relationships, get "married," and form "families." Additionally, "much of what has been described as prison homosexuality does not even include a sexual relationship. Rather, the women involved receive the affection and attention they need in a dyad with sexual connotations" (Pollock-Byrne 1990: 144).

Second, females receive very little peer support for their criminality. There are no accolades for being tough and street smart for females as there often are for males. As destructive as they may be, males do receive some psychic rewards from like-minded others, but such rewards are not forthcoming for females. Consequently, females are less comfortable with a deviant identity, less committed to criminal values, less likely to rationalize their antisocial behavior, and psychologically more motivated to change their behavior (Van Voorhis et al. 2003).

Third, female offenders appear to have better intellectual skills than male offenders do. Studies involving the I-level classification system (see Chapter 19) indicate that, as a group, female offenders tend to fall into higher maturity levels than male offenders (Warren 1986). Similarly, a study of all male and female inmates in North Carolina (Joesting, Jones, and Joesting 1975) found that female inmates had a significantly higher mean IQ (100.5) than male inmates (85.5). This study also found that males scored significantly higher on all except three of the MMPI subscales indicative of psychological and characterological problems. In no instance was the female mean significantly higher than the male mean. Perhaps, best of all, female prisoners are less involved in the inmate code than males prisoners, which allows them to focus their psychic energies on confronting and changing their behavior (McKenzie 2004).

We can safely generalize these studies to all female offenders because they reflect general sex differences typically found among nonoffender samples. Research fairly well establishes that the female brain matures earlier than the male brain: girls talk earlier than boys do; there are fewer mentally retarded females than mentally retarded males; and females of all ages generally do better than males on standardized tests of verbal skills (Moir and Jessel 1991). Thus, most females will be better candidates for counseling methods that emphasize cognitive skills. As a result, female offenders seem to be in a better position intellectually than male offenders are to seek and to use information about themselves and their situations so that they may change and become prosocial and independent human beings. You can help them to do this if you understand the special disabilities and stresses suffered by women in a society that still tends to afford women second-class status.

Perspective from the Field
The Special Challenge of the Female Offender

By Cydnee J. Heyrend

After a career in a variety of criminal justice positions, Cydnee Heyrend became the superintendent of the Boise Community Work Center for Women in 1988. The Work Center functions as a halfway house providing a safe, secure, and humane environment that promotes respect and dignity for inmates and staff while recognizing the need to provide programs that specifically address women's issues. This facility is the first in Idaho committed to providing a comprehensive program for the needs of female offenders and served as the model for Idaho's women's prison, which opened in 1993.

● ● ● ● ● ● ● ● ● ● ● ● ● ● ● ● ● ●

The Idaho Department of Corrections has challenged itself to not only redesign our female offender program but also, through a National Institute of Corrections' grant, to develop a new risk and needs classification instrument designed specifically for the female offender, thus acknowledging that prior male measurement tools served little benefit when applied to the female offender. Once recognizing that the female offender is cut from a different cloth than the male, it offers a unique opportunity for professionals in our field to increase their repertoire of counseling and security abilities.

In dealing with the female offender, one of the most compelling issues and differences between the male and female is the "processing" of information. The male inmate appears to have been socialized and trained more easily to accept a monosyllabic answer. However, the female offender demands processing and dialog about any given situation. This necessitates a staff that is open to explaining the reasons for a "no;" the reasons for policies and procedures, rules and regulations, or referrals. In an institution, if the staff does not take the time to give the offender these explanations, you can pretty well bet that within a course of one hour, you will not have just one upset, disgruntled, or frustrated woman, but an entire tier.

Female offenders tend to be very literal. Besides extended explanations, simple verbal comments by staff members can upset or defuse a situation dramatically. Emotional issues of women are close to the surface and variable. Therefore, prior to making a judgment or answering a question, it is paramount that the staff member should assess the situation and the female's emotional and cognitive level and endeavor to determine the ramifications of their interaction.

For the male staff members, this type of interaction becomes even more complex. Knowing that a great percentage of female offenders are dealing with codependency issues and a strong probability of prior abuse by male family members, training for male staff members becomes a critical issue. Training must include progressive and active approaches to determine a

Continued on the next page

Perspective from the Field, *continued*

healthy role model and training in the subtleties of manipulation that these women have used with males to survive.

When a woman enters a correctional institution, the staff must be prepared to deal with her complexities. Women need programs in anger management and stress reduction to resolve bitterness, anxiety over the loss of her children, shame, and the fear of the future. The staff must be alert to the physical health of the woman, gynecological status, prenatal and postpartum care, birth control, and, of course, the AIDS virus. Also, staff must place an emphasis on the sensitive issues of physical and sexual abuse or domestic violence. It is important to remember that the majority of female offenders, like men, are alcohol and substance abusers and should receive appropriate programming. Additionally, a well-balanced mental health treatment program will maintain the appropriate security concerns, primarily because female offenders become more self-abusive rather than destructive toward the facility or staff.

Realizing that the female offender will most likely become the sole support of her family and children, programming must address educational and vocational training. Emphasize placement in these programs as part of their return to the community. These are as important as improvement emotionally. Female offenders' individualized program plan should include parenting skills, child development, and educational programs. Facilities should include a parent-child visitation room and a children's playroom to provide training for both mother and child in a supervised program.

From the authors' experience in dealing with offenders of both sexes, we believe that the female offender is more complex and demanding than the male offender. Working with female offenders, therefore, requires great attention and appropriate decision making. It focuses on creativity and demands changes from the predominant male system. Interaction is more intense with female offenders but allows the largest opportunity for their change. To make this interaction successful, the caseworker or staffer should have both knowledge of the offender and knowledge of the community to help the women accomplish the transition from incarceration to resocialization.

The future for female offenders will be determined in large measure by the professional staff. Staff need the cognizance and dedication to realize that the female offender is different and deserves specific programs to answer her long-unaddressed needs.

Summary

Although some women can be as dangerous and as criminal as men are, females, in general, are much less crime prone. However, greater participation in the workforce provides women with increasing opportunities to commit crimes such as fraud and embezzlement. While female rates of such "economic" crimes are increasing faster than male rates, their numbers are still much smaller.

Although the demographic profile of the typical female offender matches that of the typical male, numerous studies have shown that females who do become criminal have suffered a greater frequency and/or intensity of many of the negative environmental factors said to increase the probability of criminal activity than do male criminals. They tend to have suffered more physical, sexual, and psychological abuse, parental substance abuse, parental neglect, and come from poorer homes and homes that are more likely to be broken. Yet, it appears that women have a higher threshold against antisocial behavior than men do.

Feminist criminologists wish to look at female criminality in light of the experiences that color the female world. Some feminists view female crime as extensions of normal female roles, while others concentrate on how patriarchy and sexism can lead to female criminality. We examined "criminalizing girls' survival" and "victim-precipitated homicide" as examples of the latter.

In all cultures and at all time, males commit far more crimes than females, and the more serious the crime the greater the gap. This suggests that we have to go beyond culture to explain this gap. Mountains of data from the biological sciences tell us that females are less biologically "prepared" to do violence than men are. Greater nonviolence among women is probably attributable to neuro-hormonal factors.

Although there is some disagreement as to whether female offenders should be treated differently in terms of counseling, the American Psychological Association and feminist counselors believe that they should. Many problems leading females to commit crimes are the result of their relationships with males, making it unreasonable to expect female offenders to respond positively to male counselors. Feminist counseling tailors traditional counseling theories to feminist philosophy and is unabashedly ideological. Such counseling seeks to raise consciousness among its clientele by techniques such as sex role and power analysis, assertiveness training, and reframing and relabeling.

Females appear to have greater adjustment problems when incarcerated. Unwed motherhood, the lack of meaningful programs, and a greater isolation from the outside world than that suffered by males are reasons for this situation. We emphasized the disabilities of unwed motherhood, both for the mother and her child, and emphasized the attention of the correctional worker.

On the positive side, many female characteristics make female offenders better candidates for rehabilitation than male offenders. Females are less comfortable with a deviant lifestyle, are more altruistic, have higher maturity levels, and higher IQ's than male offenders. Thus, although women suffer greater social disabilities than men suffer and are less well serviced by the criminal justice system, we may view their personal characteristics as affording them greater rehabilitative potential.

References and Suggested Readings

Alexander, R. 2000. *Counseling, Treatment, and Intervention Methods with Juvenile and Adult Offenders*. Belmont, California: Brooks/Cole.

American Correctional Association. 1990. *Female Offender: What Does the Future Hold?* Laurel, Maryland: American Correctional Association.

———. 1993. *Female Offenders: Meeting the Needs of a Neglected Population*. Lanham, Maryland: American Correctional Association.

Anderson, E. 1999. *Code of the Street: Decency, Violence, and the Moral Life of the Inner City*. New York: W. W. Norton.

Barak, G. 1998. *Integrating Criminologies*. Boston: Allyn and Bacon.

Barash, D. and J. Lipton. 2001. Making Sense of Sex. In *Understanding Violence*, D. Barash, ed. Boston: Allyn and Bacon.

Bennett, S., D. Farrington, and L. Huesman. 2005. Explaining Gender Differences in Crime and Violence: The Importance of Social Cognitive Skills. *Aggression and Violent Behavior* 10: 263-288.

Bloom, B. 2000. Gender-Responsive Supervision and Programming for Women Offenders in the Community. In *Responding to Women Offenders in the Community*, Washington, D.C.: National Institute of Corrections. pp. 11-18.

Boudouris, J. 1996. *Parents in Prison: Addressing the Needs of Families*. Lanham, Maryland: American Correctional Association.

Campbell, A., 1999. Staying Alive: Evolution, Culture, and Women's Intrasexual Aggression. *Behavioral and Brain Sciences* 22: 203-214.

———. 2006. Sex Differences in Direct Aggression: What are the Psychological Mediators? *Aggression and Violent Behavior*, 6: 481-497.

———. 2009. Gender and Crime: An Evolutionary Perspective. In *Criminology and Biology: New Directions in Theory and Research*, A. Walsh and K. Beaver, eds. New York: Routledge. pp. 117-136.

Campbell, A., S. Muncer, and D. Bibel. 2001. Women and Crime: An Evolutionary Approach. *Aggression and Violent Behavior* 6: 481-497.

Chaplin, J. 1988. *Feminist Counseling in Action*. Beverly Hills, California: Sage.

Chapple, K. 2000. Community Residential Programming for Female Offenders and Their Children. In *Responding to Women Offenders in the Community*. Washington, D.C.: National Institute of Corrections. pp. 31-35.

Chesney-Lind, M. 1995. Girls, Delinquency and Juvenile Justice: Toward a Feminist Theory of Young Women's Crime. In *The Criminal Justice System and Women: Offenders, Victims, and Workers*, B. Price and N. Sokoloff, eds. New York: McGraw Hill. pp.71-88.

———. 2000. Women and the Criminal Justice System: Gender Matters. In *Responding To Women Offenders in the Community*. Washington, D.C.: National Institute of Corrections. pp. 7-10.

Cleveland, H., R. Wiebe, E. van den Oord, and D. Rowe. 2000. Behavior Problems among Children from Different Family Structures: The Influence of Genetic Self-Selection. *Child Development* 71: 733-751.

Corey, G. 1986. *Theory and Practice in Counseling and Psychotherapy*. Monterey, California: Brooks/Cole.

Daley, M. and M. Argeriou. 1997. Characteristics and Treatment Needs of Sexually Abused Pregnant Women in Drug Rehabilitation: The Massachusetts MOTHERS Project. *Journal of Substance Abuse Treatment* 14: 191-196.

Dalton, K. 1964. *The Premenstrual Syndrome*. Springfield, Illinois: Charles C Thomas.

Domes, G., M. Heinrichs, A. Michel, C. Berger, and S. Herpertz. 2007. Oxytocin Improves "Mind-Reading" in Humans. *Biological Psychiatry* 61: 731-733.

Ellis, L. and A. Walsh. 2000. *Criminology: A Global Perspective*. Boston: Allyn and Bacon.

Enns, C. 1993. Twenty Years of Feminist Counseling and Therapy: From Naming Biases to Implementing Multifaceted Practice. *The Counseling Psychologist* 21: 3-87.

Evans, K., E. Kincade, A. Marbley, and S. Seem. 2005. Feminism and Feminist Therapy: Lessons from the Past and Hopes for the Future. *Journal of Counseling and Development* 83: 169-277.

Federal Bureau of Investigation. 2007. *Uniform Crime Reports 2006*. Washington, D.C.: U.S. Government Printing Office.

Festervan, E. 2003. *Women Probationers: Supervision and Success*. Alexandria, Virginia: American Correctional Association.

Fishbein, D. 1992. The Psychobiology of Female Aggression. *Criminal Justice and Behavior* 19: 9-126.

Flanagan, L. 1996. Meeting the Special Needs of Females in Custody: Maryland's Unique Approach. *Federal Probation* 59: 49-53.

Garfinkel, I. and S. McLanahan. 1986. *Single Mothers and their Children: A New American Dilemma*. Washington, D.C.: The Urban Institute.

Glaze, L. and T. Bonczar. 2007. Probation and Parole in the United States. Washington, D.C.: Bureau of Justice Statistics.

Gottfredson, M. and T. Hirschi. 1997. National Crime Control Policies. In *Criminology 97/98*, M. Fisch, ed. Guilford, Connecticut: Dushkin Publishing.

Henggeler, S., J. Edwards, and C. Borduin. 1987. The Family Relations of Female Juvenile Delinquents. *Journal of Abnormal Child Psychology* 15: 199-209.

Hermans, E. J., P. Putman, and J. van Honk. 2006. Testosterone Reduces Empathetic Mimicking in Healthy Young Women. *Psychoneuroendocrinology* 31, 859–866

Herrnstein, R. 1989. The Individual Offender. *Today's Delinquent* 8: 5-35.

Hindelang, M. 1979. Sex Differences in Criminal Activity. *Social Problems* 27: 143-154.

Hines, M. 2004. *Brain Gender*. Oxford: Oxford University Press.

Hoskins, R. 2000. Partnership Network Responds to Female Substance Abusers in the Criminal Justice System. In *Responding To Women Offenders in the Community*. Washington, D.C.: National Institute of Corrections. pp. 19-22

Joesting, J., N. Jones, and R. Joesting. 1975. Male and Female Inmates' Differences on MMPI Scales and Revised Beta IQ. *Psychological Reports* 37: 471-474.

Kimura, D. 1992. Sex Differences in the Brain. *Scientific American* 267: 119-125.

Knickmeyer, R., S. Baron-Cohen, P. Raggatt, K. Taylor, and G. Hackett. 2006. Fetal Testosterone and Empathy. *Hormones and Behavior* 49: 282-292.

Kratcoski, P. and S. Babb. 1990. Adjustment of Older Inmates: An Analysis of Institutional Structure and Gender. *Journal of Contemporary Criminal Justice* 6: 264-281.

Lemieux, K. 2009. *Substance Abusing Offenders: Bringing the Family into Focus*. Alexandria, Virginia: American Correctional Association.

Lindquist, C. 1980. Prison Discipline and the Female Offender. *Journal of Offender Counseling, Services and Rehabilitation* 4: 305-318.

Lopreato, J. and T. Crippen 1999. *Sociology in Crisis: The Need for Darwin*. New Brunswick, New Jersey: Transaction.

Mann, C. 1995. Women of Color in the Criminal Justice System. In *The Criminal Justice System and Women: Offenders, Victims, and Workers*, B. Price and N. Sokoloff, eds. New York: McGraw Hill.

McKenzie, D. 2004. Age and Adjustment to Prison: Interactions with Attitudes and Anxiety. In *The Inmate Prison Experience*, M. Stohr and C. Hemmens, eds. Upper Saddle River, New Jersey: Prentice Hall. pp. 104-117.

McLeod, J. 2003. *An Introduction to Counseling*, 3rd ed. Buckingham, England: Open University Press.

Mealey, L. 1995. The Sociobiology of Sociopathy: An Integrated Evolutionary Model. *Behavioral and Brain Sciences* 18: 523-59.

Mestel, R. 2004. HIV among Females, *Idaho Statesman*, November 24, p. 10.

Moffitt, T., A. Caspi, M. Rutter, and P. Silva. 2001. *Sex Differences in Antisocial Behaviour: Conduct Disorder, Delinquency and Violence in the Dunedin Longitudinal Study*. Cambridge: Cambridge University Press.

Moffitt, T. and A. Walsh. 2003. The Adolescent-Limited/Life-Course Persistent Theory of Antisocial Behavior: What Have We Learned? In *Biosocial Criminology: Challenging Environmentalism's Supremacy*, A. Walsh and L. Ellis, eds. Hauppauge, New York: Nova Science. pp.123-144.

Moir, A. and D. Jessel. 1991. *Brain Sex: The Real Differences Between Men and Women*. New York: Lyle Stuart.

Morris, A. 1987. *Women and Criminal Justice*. Oxford: Basil Blackwell.

Morton, J. 1998. *Complex Challenges, Collaborative Solutions: Programming for Adult and Juvenile Female Offenders*. Alexandria, Virginia: American Correctional Association.

———. 2004. *Working with Women Offenders in Correctional Institutions*. Alexandria, Virginia: American Correctional Association.

Moynihan, D. 1992. How the Great Society Destroyed the American Family. *Public Interest* 108: 53-64.

Pollock-Byrne, J. 1990. *Women, Prison, and Crime*. Pacific Grove, California: Brooks/Cole.

Price, B. and N. Sokoloff. 1995. Theories and Facts about Women Offenders. In *The Criminal Justice System and Women: Offenders, Victims, and Workers*, B. Price and N. Sokoloff, eds. New York: McGraw-Hill. pp.1-10.

Prichard, D. 2000. Project Reconnect: Responding to Women Offenders on a Personal Level. In *Responding To Women Offenders in the Community*, Washington, D.C.: National Institute of Corrections. pp. 7-10.

Raine, A. 1993. *The Psychopathology of Crime: Criminal Behavior as a Clinical Disorder*. San Diego: Academic Press.

Rasche, E. 1995. Minority Women and Domestic Violence: The Unique Dilemmas of Battered Women of Color. In *The Criminal Justice System and Women: Offenders, Victims, and Workers*, B. Price and N. Sokoloff, eds. New York: McGraw Hill.

Resnik, J. 1983. Should Prisoners Be Classified by Sex? In *Criminal Corrections: Ideals and Realities*, J. Doig, ed., Lexington, Massachusetts: Lexington Books.

Rossi, A. 1984. Gender and Parenthood: American Sociological Association, 1983 Presidential Address. *American Sociological Review* 49: 1-19.

Rushton, J., D. Falker, M. Neale, D. Nias, and H. Eysenck. 1986. Altruism and Aggression: The Heritability of Individual Differences. *Journal of Personality and Individual Differences* 6: 1192-1198.

Sabol, W., H. Couture, and P. Harrison. 2007. *Prisoners in 2006*. Washington, D.C.: Bureau of Justice Statistics.

Scarr, S. 1993. Biological and Cultural Diversity: The Legacy of Darwin for Diversity. *Child Development* 63: 1-9.

Schmalleger, F. 2003. *Criminal Justice Today*, 7th ed. Upper Saddle River, New Jersey: Prentice Hall.

Scott, E. 1977. Women Criminals: Therapy with Female Offenders. *International Journal of Offender Therapy and Comparative Criminology* 21: 208-220.

Scott, S. 2004. Opening a Can of Worms? Counseling for Survivors in UK Women's Prisons. *Feminism and Psychology* 14: 256-261.

Shearer, R. 2003. Identifying the Special Needs of Female Offenders. *Federal Probation* 67: 46-52.

Simon, R. 1975. *Women, Crime, and Criminology*. London: Routledge and Kegan Paul.

Slattery, J. 2004. *Counseling Diverse Clients: Bringing Context into Therapy*. Belmont, California: Brooks/Cole.

Smart, C. 1976. *Women, Crime, and Criminology: A Feminist Critique*. London: Routledge and Kegan Paul.

Sokoloff, N. and B. Price. 1995. The Criminal Law and Women. In *The Criminal Justice System and Women Offenders, Victims and Workers*, B. Price and N. Sokoloff, eds. New York: McGraw Hill. pp. 11-29.

Spiegel, S. 1979. Separate Principles for Counseling Women: A New Form of Sexism. *The Counseling Psychologist* 8: 49-50.

Stawar, D. and T. Stawar. 2008a. *How to Be a Responsible Mother: A Workbook for Offenders*. Alexandria, Virginia: American Correctional Association.

————. 2008b. *How to Be a Responsible Mother: Instructor's Manual*. Alexandria, Virginia: American Correctional Association.

Steffensmeier, D. and E. Allan. 1996. Gender and Crime: Toward A Gendered Theory of Female Offending. *Annual Review of Sociology* 22: 459-487.

Taylor, S. 2006. Tend and Befriend: Biobehavioral Bases of Affiliation Under Stress. *Current Directions in Psychological Science* 15: 273-277.

Urquhart, J. and M. Cullen. 2003. *Cage Your Rage for Women*. Alexandria, Virginia: American Correctional Association.

Van Voorhis, P., J. Peiler, L. Presser, G. Spiropoulis, and J. Sutherland. 2003. *Classification of Women Offenders: A National Assessment of Current Practices and the Experience of Three States*. Report to the National Institute of Corrections. Washington, D.C.: Government Printing Office.

Van Wormer, K. and L. Kaplan. 2006. Results of a National Survey of Wardens in Women's Prisons: The Case for Gender-Specific Treatment. *Women and Therapy* 29: 133-151.

Vetter, H. and I. Silverman. 1986. *Criminology and Crime: An Introduction*. New York: Harper and Row.

Walsh, A. 1990. Illegitimacy, Child Abuse and Neglect, and Cognitive Development. *Journal of Genetic Psychology* 151: 279-285.

————. 1991. *Intellectual Imbalance, Love Deprivation and Violent Delinquency: A Biosocial Perspective*. Springfield, Illinois: Charles C. Thomas.

————. 1995. Genetic and Cytogenetic Intersex Anomalies: Can They Help Us to Understand Gender Differences in Deviant Behavior? *International Journal of Offender Therapy and Comparative Criminology* 39: 151-166.

————. 2003. The Sex Ratio: A Biosocial Explanation for Racial/Ethnic Variation in Crime Rates. In *Biosocial Criminology: Challenging Environmentalism's Supremacy*, A.Walsh and L. Ellis, eds. Huntington, New York: Nova Science Publishers. pp. 61-82.

Warren, M. 1986. The Female Offender. In *Psychology of Crime and Criminal Justice*. H. Toch, ed. Prospect Heights, Illinois: Waveland.

Weis, J. 1982. The Invention of the New Female Criminal. In *Contemporary Criminology*, L. Savitz and N. Johnson, eds. New York: Wiley.

Welch, M. 1996. *Corrections: A Critical Approach*. New York: McGraw Hill.

Welo, B. 2004. *Picking Up the Pieces: A Workbook for Incarcerated Women*. Alexandria, Virginia: American Correctional Association.

Wiewel, B. and T. Mosley. 2006. Family Foundations: A New Program for Pregnant and Parenting Women Offenders with Substance Abuse Histories. *Journal of Offender Rehabilitation* 43: 65-91.

Wilson, J. 1993. On Gender. *Public Interest* 112: 3-26.

Wilson, J. and R. Herrnstein. 1985. *Crime and Human Nature*. New York: Simon and Schuster.

Wojda, R. and J. Rowse. 1997. *Women Behind Bars*. Lanham, Maryland: American Correctional Association.

Worell, J. and P. Remer. 1992. *Feminist Perspectives in Therapy: An Empowerment Model for Women*. New York: John Wiley.

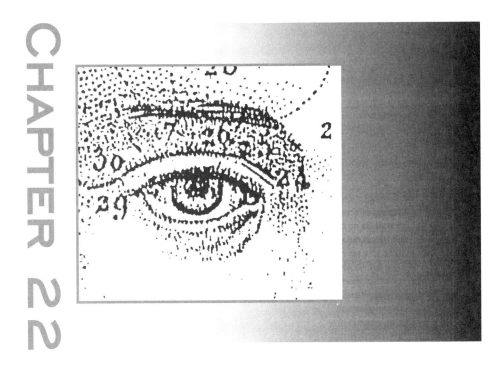

CHAPTER 22

The Elderly Offender

If society has little place for the elderly man/woman in general, it has even less place for the elderly prisoner or ex-convict.

—Delores Golden

Scope of the Problem

The elderly criminal offender is perhaps the most under-researched topic in the criminological literature (Curtice et al. 2003). This neglect is understandable because so few older people commit crime and there are so few elderly offenders under correctional supervision relatively speaking. However, we can expect an increase in interest in the elderly offender as the American population ages. Demographers estimate that 25 percent of the American population will be fifty-five years of age or older by the year 2010 (Feldmeyer and Steffensmeier 2007).

There is a problem in defining the term "elderly" in a criminal justice context. In the larger society, elderly usually describes those who have achieved senior citizen status; that is, those aged sixty-five or older. However, age is relative, and anyone over the age of thirty is considered "old" in prison settings (Chaiklin and Fultz 1985). In some systems, the term *geriatric* is applied to inmates as "young" as fifty-nine, regardless of the presence or absence of health problems (Snarr 1996). Alston points

493

out that the literature on the "older offender" has referred to age groups ranging from forty to sixty-five, and adds that these discrepant definitions make generalizations difficult (1986). The Uniform Crime Report (FBI 2006) defines older offenders as those fifty-five years of age or older. Given the overabundance of definitions, we variably define the term "elderly" in this chapter.

According to a U.S. Department of Justice report (Beck and Mumola 1999), the proportion of inmates aged thirty-five to fifty-four ("old" by prison standards) grew from 25 percent in 1986 to 40 percent in 1998, and has increased to 43 percent in 2003 (Harrison and Karberg 2004). However, inmates fifty-five years and over constituted only 3.5 percent of the prison population in 2003 (Harrison and Karberg 2004). The neglect of the elderly offender in terms of criminal justice policy also can be attributed to the reluctance of criminal justice administrators to allocate scarce funds for special programs aimed at a small category of offenders who present them with few supervision problems. As McCarthy and Langworthy (1987: 8) point out: "As we have found from research on female offenders, small numbers and the designation of an offender group as a 'nonproblem' may lead to a lack of agency attention." Being widely seen as basically nonproblems also makes the crimes of the elderly less of a sexy research topic for criminologists than alternative topics. In fact, a search of *Books in Print* and Amazon.com revealed only one book-length treatment of the elderly in corrections—*Aging Prisoners: Crisis in American Corrections* (Aday 2003)—published so far this century.

According the latest *Uniform Crime Report* statistics, elderly males (defined in this instance as sixty-five years or older) accounted for only 0.6 percent of male arrests and elderly females only 0.4 percent of female arrests (FBI 2006). Similar figures are cited for the United Kingdom (Curtice et al. 2003). Of course, far fewer people in society are sixty-five or older than those who are younger than that, so we must take the age distribution of the population into account. According to the U.S. Census Bureau (2005), those over sixty-five accounted for only 12.0 percent of the total U.S. population, so even when we adjust for the number of over sixty-fives in the general population, they still are massively underrepresented among criminal offenders.

However, evidence shows that elderly criminal activity has increased steadily over the past few decades given the recent large increases in the over-fifty-five prison population. The latest national figures show that the number of male inmates more than age fifty-five increased 244 percent from 1996 to 2003 (from 18,064 to 62,200) and female inmates more than age fifty-five increased 491 percent (from 643 to 3,800) (Harrison and Karberg 2004).

Do these huge increases mean that we have a geriatric crime wave going on in the United States? No, however, we must interpret the huge percentage increases in elderly incarceration rates in light of the much lower base rates of the elderly. Better health care and awareness of health issues among the older population mean that more people are becoming old enough to be called "elderly," and we are witnessing the graying of the huge post WW II baby-boomer generation. Thus, the increasing number of older people in America is reflected in the increasing numbers of them in prison. A study of the elder crime trends from 1980 through 2004 found that: "Elder crime rates have not increased in level or seriousness in recent decades. Instead, for almost all offenses, elderly arrest rates have been either stable or have fallen over time" (Feldmeyer and Steffensmeier 2007: 317). Feldmeyer and Steffensmeier (2007) indicate that the elderly have the lowest arrest rate of any segment of the population with the exception of children under twelve.

The increase in the number of elderly persons in the general population comes nowhere near to matching their increase in the prison population. Much of the increase in the elderly behind bars, beyond the increase of the elderly in the general population, can be attributed to tougher sentencing policies such as the three-strikes laws, mandatory-minimums, and truth in sentencing legislation. They capture more offenders in the net and keep them for longer periods. In addition, the prison building booms in the 1980s and 1990s reduced the need to release prisoners early to alleviate crowding (Rikard and Rosenberg 2007). However, with the current crowded prison conditions and budget cutbacks, things may change.

Very few older people are arrested for committing the major index offenses (murder, rape, robbery, and so forth). In 2003, males fifty-five and over constituted only 3.2 percent of the homicides committed by males, and females over fifty-five committed 4.1 of all female homicides (FBI 2004). In fact, more than 85 percent of elderly arrests in 2003 were for either alcohol-related offenses such as driving while intoxicated or petty thievery, with males accounting for most of the drinking arrests and females for most of the petty theft offenses (FBI 2004).

Some Causes of Elderly Crime

If we examine the causes of crime among elderly offenders with long criminal histories, the social or personal situations that moved them in criminal directions when they were young are presumably the same ones that influence them today. They may be successful career criminals who continue to receive psychic and financial rewards from crime, which they consider to be preferable to those they feel that they could receive from leading a "straight" life. Since most criminals "mature" out of crime by the time they are forty, if not well before that (Sampson and Laub 2005), we have to assume that offenders who continue the criminal lifestyle past this age are either "successful" criminals or else are psychologically immature individuals who lack the requisite insight to engage in the midlife reassessment process that most of us go through, criminal or not. Of course, some elderly criminals simply have found their "comfort zone" in prison, and are proud of their criminal exploits and values (McKenzie 2004). One researcher described many long-term older prisoners as "jitterbug celebrities proud of their fifty-year mandatory minimums" (Chaneles 1995: 556).

What about offenders who enter the criminal justice system for the first time at an advanced age? Why, after presumably leading a conventional life up to that point, do they become involved with crime for the first time long after most former criminals have matured out of it? Interestingly, a greater percentage of older offenders than younger ones report problems with alcohol and have been convicted of sexual offense in the United States (Schmalleger 2003), Canada (Brown and Brozowski 2003), and the United Kingdom (Curtice et al. 2003). This suggests that there may be special considerations concerning the causes of crime among the elderly just as there are for juvenile crime. Some suggest that certain brain syndromes associated with age may lead to loss of inhibitions against illegal sexual behavior, such as exhibitionism and child molestation, and against aggression. However, this explanation would account for only a very small proportion of elderly criminal behavior. Abnormal brain functioning that is secondary to old age (such as Alzheimer's disease) is far less common than many people think, and has a typical onset age of around age seventy (Restak 2001).

From a psychological point of view, many of the frustrations of old age—poverty, loss of occupational status, and boredom—combined with situational factors such as loneliness and liquor, create opportunities for sexual acting-out and/or violence. The problem also may be associated with a declining range of personal contacts, which may lead to emotional intensity and conflict. As Curtice and his colleagues (2003: 261) put it: "Elderly sex offenders may have a long lasting 'Achilles heel' normally held in check by compensatory satisfactions or pressures but liable to emerge in times of stress." Fazel and Jacoby (2000: 201) write in a similar vein:

> The need to compensate for a 'collapse of narcissism'—the loss of the outward symbols of masculinity such as work, physical health, sexual activity—could also contribute to an explanation as to why men with previously unblemished records commit sexual offenses in old age.

Thinking about the correctional population in chronological terms is not useful. For instance, Rikard and Rosenberg (2007: 151) write "The combination of physical and mental declines makes aging inmates, on average, ten to eleven and a half years older physiologically than their unincarcerated age peers." Thus, in addition to role losses and the natural decline in physical health, the unhealthy lifestyles these men have led make them a lot older than their chronological age suggests. Accompanying all these declines and deficits is a loss of self-esteem. A study of self-esteem across the lifespan among 326,641 individuals found that self-esteem is high in childhood, drops during adolescence, rises gradually throughout adulthood, and declines sharply in old age (Robins et al. 2002). This finding held true for both genders, across socio-economic classes, and in every racial and nationality grouping.

However, Robins and his colleagues suggest that this loss of self-esteem might not mean the same thing for the elderly as it does for younger people. They suggest that relatively low self-esteem scores among the elderly reflect a more realistic appraisal of themselves to a more balanced and modest view, less use of defense mechanisms used to inflate feelings of self-worth, and less need for self-promotion. In short, all of the things that artificially boost reports of self-esteem among younger respondents have been shelved in favor of acceptance of self, warts and all. It may be among the elderly who commit criminal acts that they have not reached this stage of self-acceptance and that their crimes reflect efforts to regain feelings of mastery.

The theme of age-related stressors is also found in a study of MMPI profiles of older prison inmates that found them to be less psychopathic than younger inmates, but much more neurotic. Commenting on these profiles, Panton states: "They appeared to have limited ability to cope with emotional stress and appeared to have difficulty in personal adaptability and resourcefulness" (1976/1977: 207). Since elderly first-time offenders apparently have led conventional lifestyles up to the point of committing their crimes, it is possible that any and all of these causal factors may have contributed to the sudden onset of their criminal behavior. The spontaneity and impulsiveness of the crimes of the elderly first offender also point to the possibility that the cognitive infirmities of age play an important role in the criminal act.

Maturing Out of Crime

Why are the elderly, even the elderly who were formerly criminals, less crime-prone than the young? Some of us may think of crime as a physical occupation requiring strength and stamina, attributes that decline with age, so criminals desist from crime as they age because they no longer can cut the mustard. As appealing as this simple explanation may be, it widely misses the mark. Maximum endurance can be maintained into the mid-thirties; strength does not usually peak until the late thirties to early forties; and the coordination of a fifty-year-old man is about on par with that of a man half his age (Donnelly et al. 1991). In most cases, most formerly criminal men withdraw from crime before the age of forty; an age long before any normal person becomes infirm or enfeebled (Jolin and Gibbons 1987). However, given the health-destroying lifestyles that many folks who land in the lap of Lady Justice have led, they probably become enfeebled long before the average person does.

All countries note the accelerating decrease in criminal activity after its peak during the mid-teens–ever since crime statistics have been kept (Ellis and Walsh 2000). This suggests that something "law like" akin to the increase in offending among adolescents is occurring. Baldwin (1990) addresses this issue by focusing on average age-graded levels of arousal at different developmental periods, and finds that these levels closely mirror the age/crime curve. Infants are often confronted by novel stimuli that surpass their optimal arousal level and become distressed as a result. Children become habituated to more and more stimuli and need higher levels of sensory input to be optimally aroused as they age.

The need for arousal is greatest during adolescence when ratios of behavior-facilitating dopamine and the behavior-moderating serotonin favor dopamine. As we age, habituation sets in as formerly novel occurrences become commonplace. As we age further, even formerly optimal levels of neurological arousal become aversive to many, and we take pains to reduce the level of stimuli to more tranquil levels. Baldwin does not claim that the neurohormonal mechanisms underlying sensory reinforcement and habituation is all that we need to know to understand the age-related crime levels.

Related to Baldwin's theory are findings from five different countries showing that age brings with it a decrease in personality traits positively related to antisocial behavior and increases in personality traits negatively related to antisocial behavior (McCrae et al. 2000). McCrea and his colleagues state:

> From age eighteen to thirty there are declines in Neuroticism, Extraversion, and openness to experience, and increases in Agreeableness and Conscientiousness; after age 30 the same trends are found, although the rate of change seems to decrease (2000: 183).

Thus, shifting neurohormonal ratios are related to shifting personality patterns as we age, and these shifting patterns are in the direction of prosocial behavior.

Testosterone also decreases considerably with age, with seventy-year-old males having levels on par with pre-pubescent boys (Ellis 2003). Testosterone is the great facilitator (not cause) of much aggressive and dominance-seeking behavior (Walsh 2002) and its decline should be expected to bring with it a decline in behaviors that can often lead to antisocial behavior. Of course, one can exhibit aggressive and dominant behavior without normal adult male levels of testosterone, as many women and pre-pubescent boys demonstrate. We simply assert that older males have less of a hormone that constitutes a risk factor for such behavior among younger males.

From a social-psychological perspective, there are some significant insights as to why the elderly are so much less crime-prone than the young. The elderly are likely to experience changes in role expectations and in their aspirations and goals, so that they no longer strive for the same level of material fulfillment and recognition that they sought when younger. In effect, the major sources of reinforcement for criminal behavior—money, sex, status, intense and lasting hostility toward others, and anti-social peer pressure—are absent or relatively weak in old age.

Shifting contingencies and opportunities thus result in decreasing reinforcements for antisocial behavior and increasing reinforcements for prosocial behavior. The physiological and social/psychological explanations complement each other. We would expect to witness a reduction in the kinds of behavior mentioned above on the basis of neurohormonal changes alone. Along with these changes there is a growing psychological maturity, more opportunities to develop ties with the conventional world, more reasonable (scaled-down) ambitions, and an increase in conservatism that most aging individuals seem to develop (McCrae et al. 2000).

The Elderly Behind Bars

Although based on minimal evidence, there is some indication that elderly offenders, all other things being equal, are treated more leniently than their younger counterparts, and that the general public expects it to be so (McCarthy and Langworthy 1987). For instance, Stephen Hucker's (1984) comparison of elderly and younger minor sex offenders found that older offenders were less likely to be sent to prison (1 percent versus 27 percent), but also less likely to receive counseling (33 percent versus 50 percent) in either prison or community-based settings. Of course, the criminal justice system has limits to its sentencing flexibility for the elderly who violate societal rules and regulations. The elderly do not expand these limits merely because of their age and the perplexities that accompany the aging individual.

Surprisingly, a relatively large proportion of incarcerated elderly offenders, particularly first offenders, are there for committing violent offenses, at least in proportion to their numbers relative to their youthful peer inmates (Chaiklin and Fultz 1985). Regardless of the crimes that put them in prison, the management of the elderly is an issue with which correctional institutions must contend. The prison milieu adds to physical and psychological woes, and to the confusion and disorder of the truly geriatric individual. On the other hand, the elderly are not generally a management problem, are generally quite cooperative with the prison staff, get along well with other inmates, and accumulate significantly lower numbers of disciplinary write-ups than youthful and middle-aged inmates (McKenzie 2004).

Prison Programs for the Elderly

Public representatives and correctional leaders are hard pressed to support specific programs designed for the incarcerated elderly offender. Such tailor-made programs are considered unrealistic, and are low on the hierarchy of priorities in a system in which the bulk of its offenders are young men. There is also the constant strain on the correctional budget and its other resources, including community services, volunteers, and counseling programs. The expense of medical care and maintenance of the elderly inmate already constitutes a severe strain on the correctional budget quite apart from any special geriatric nonessential services and programs. Additionally, complying with the Americans with Disabilities Act, which disproportionately applies to older offenders, is a major financial and management burden on the correctional system (Morton and Anderson 1996). According to Rikard and Rosenberg (2007), it costs about three and one-half times as much to incarcerate a man over fifty-five years of age than it does the young offender, or about $72,000 per year. Of course, many students of the elderly-inmate experience feel that prison programs for the elderly are necessary. For instance, Chaiklin and Fultz write:

> The emphasis in most correctional training and placement programs often has been on youthful offenders. As an unfortunate consequence, older offenders experience proportionately greater hardship in the civilian labor force. There is an obvious need for special programs emphasizing job placement and community-based treatment to aid older offenders (1985: 27).

One serious problem associated with the lack of programs for the elderly is that it can hurt their chances of parole. Participation in prison programs contributes greatly to positive parole decisions for inmates (Champion 2005). Of course, this is not a problem for older offenders who are fit and who enjoy good health, but basketball and boxing are programs that do not appeal to our older population either inside or outside prison walls. Additionally, the elderly offender is not particularly motivated to participate in vocational-type programs because they feel that they have "done their time" in the workforce already (Goetting 1983: 298).

A study by C. Eamon Walsh (1992) found that elderly inmates express different prison environment needs from those expressed by younger inmates. Whereas younger inmates wanted lots of activity and stimulation in prison, the elderly sought more structure and predictability, and wanted to be insulated from the noise and intrusion of the younger inmates. Their main concerns were for more preventive medical attention and help in maintaining family ties and support. In short, Walsh (1992) found that the differing needs and concerns of the old and the young in prison are essentially the same differences as that between the young and old on the outside.

As it is now, the elderly are not seen as constituting a unique group of individuals, as are women and juveniles, for instance. Once upon a time, both women and juveniles were not treated differently from male offenders either, but as we began to realize their unique situations, we started to deal with them differently. Perhaps we will view the elderly as a unique population some time in the future also. We certainly do appear to need such special programs, for as Krajick has written: "They are a corrections problem, they are a parole problem, they are a welfare problem, they are a mental health problem, and no one takes care of them" (1979: 36).

Psychological Aspects of Incarceration

Being sentenced to prison has to be a traumatic experience, especially for the elderly first-time offender. The elderly are supposed to be wise, serene, and to have reached a point in their lives at which respect and deference is expected from the young. However, elderly inmates find themselves in an environment in which they are constantly ordered around by young correctional officers, and "constantly hustled and cheated by younger inmates" (Chaneles 1987: 51). Elderly offenders have reached a stage in life in which they are compelled to look back on their lives and arrive at some sort of evaluation, as we all must do eventually. The need to evaluate oneself must be felt more intensely for the incarcerated geriatric offender whose life has been turned upside down.

Erik Erikson best described this process of self-evaluation in his "eight ages of man" model of socialization (in Yablonsky and Haskell 1986). According to Erikson, after individuals have proceeded through multiple stages of life in which they have to establish new basic orientations to the self and to the social world, they are ultimately confronted with conceptualizing their entire life and being. Erikson refers to this particular facet as the stage of ego identity versus despair. Undergoing this stage, individuals find a sense of resignation and perhaps wisdom from the circumstances of their lives. Alternatively, they may find only disgust or bitter resentment. The prison environment in which elderly offenders find themselves obviously can have a substantial effect on how they resolve this final life-stage.

As we have seen, Panton's research (1976/1977) has shown that the elderly criminal is more likely to be psychologically characterized as neurotic rather than psychotic or psychopathic. Their psychological problems are more ones of loneliness, self-esteem, and ones associated with medical disabilities. Chaiklin and Fultz's (1985) sample of older inmates found that half of them had IQs below 90, and that 25 percent were receiving some sort of psychiatric treatment. They further indicated that: "A comprehensive workup on this group would show that their mental health is as poor as their physical health. They survive because, in its own way, prison provides a supportive and structured life" (1985: 29).

Inabilities, such as decreased stamina and strength, the inability to endure discomfort, and fatigue and memory loss are additional disabilities that may be suffered by the elderly. Health problems, such as arthritis, strokes, infections, imbalanced blood chemistries, and insufficient and improper medications are daily concerns (Kuhlman and Rudell 2005). The inability to deal with such problems and concerns may become preoccupations of the elderly, which may plunge them further into depression and despair. On the other hand, Goetting (1983: 295) indicates that several studies have shown that elderly inmates report only slightly less life satisfaction than do senior citizens in free society. However, this could be because elderly inmates have learned to have fewer expectations about themselves and their lot in life.

Female inmates fifty-five and older constitute a much smaller percentage of all female prisoners than do their male counterparts. For white males, the rate is 162 per 100,000, while for white females it is only 8 per 100,000 (Harrison and Karberg 2004). The corresponding figures for African-Americans are 842 and 28, respectively (Harrison and Karberg 2004). However, although there are far fewer older female inmates than older male inmates, they appear to have more difficulty adjusting to institutional life. Kratcoski (2000) points out that older females are less likely than their male counterparts to receive visitors, participate in structured activities, less likely to form friendships with other inmates, and are more likely to have health problems. All of this is exacerbated by the general tendency of prison authorities to concentrate resources on programs for males, who are perceived as being in greater need of them.

Supervising the Elderly Offender on Probation/Parole

Most elderly offenders are given a suspended sentence and placed on probation, as are most other convicted offenders (Champion 2005). At least four elderly offenders are under community supervision for every one elderly offender in prison (McCarthy and Langworthy 1987). In general, probation and parole departments find no difficulty in maintaining supervision of the elderly offender (Ellsworth and Helle 1995). Basically, the elderly do not cause much trouble, and often are placed on inactive supervision status (mailed-in reports). However, at times, the truly geriatric offenders are senile, thus causing a different type of problem for their probation and parole officers.

Most are on probation or parole for crimes against persons, primarily sexual crimes such as child molestation, and many are granted probation for crimes, which probably would have resulted in incarceration for younger offenders (McCarthy and Langworthy 1987). However, there is evidence that elderly sex offenders are now dealt with more harshly than younger offenders (Yorston and Taylor 2006).

Female elderly offenders constituted about one-fourth of the offenders in these studies, and were convicted primarily of welfare fraud. About two-thirds of the elderly offenders in these studies never finished high school, and more than half were unemployed and had incomes below the poverty level. Another study found that 85 percent of probationers older than fifty-five have no previous felony convictions (100 percent of those seventy-five or older), and that most of them had relatively stable family relationships (Ellsworth and Helle 1995).

Although most elderly offenders present few supervision problems, the correctional worker should be aware of certain aspects of their supervision. Foremost among these aspects is that you should be on guard against negative or preconceived stereotypical attitudes toward them based on their age ("ageism").

As in any other instance of bias based on visible characteristics, such as sex or race, harboring age bias severely limits a counselor's effectiveness. This does not mean that you should not be aware of and pay attention to real differences that separate the aged from the young. Ageism, as well as sexism and racism, does not mean that you ignore basic differences. Rather, these "isms" reflect attitudes that go beyond what the data warrant to assert some type of inferiority in the class of people identified. In other words, you should be aware of the limiting factors involved with advanced age, but by no means must you assume that advanced age automatically limits offenders in their activities (some sixty-five-year-olds are physically and mentally more fit than some twenty-five-year-olds), their attitudes toward change, or their ability to change.

Active listening is particularly important with very elderly offenders. Many of the concerns voiced in the discussion of the mentally deficient offender are applicable to the elderly offender, albeit for different reasons. You must be prepared to take more time with them because decreased speed in processing information is one of the most universal facts of aging (Fozard and Gordon-Salant 2001). Although elderly offenders' verbal skills are little affected by aging, they need just a little more time to process what you are saying, so your normal rate of discourse may present a problem for them. They may be reluctant to ask you to frequently repeat what you have said, so you must anticipate this need for greater time for them. If you do not, you may be faced with a lot of miscommunication and confusion. As Giordano (2000: 318) puts it: "When older adults receive negative or passive acknowledgment to their verbalization, this will obstruct communication or will produce information intended to please the listener."

Also, be aware of the possibility of some hearing loss among elderly offenders, many of whom may not be able to afford corrective devices. If this is the case, you will have to moderate the tone of your speech somewhat without giving offenders the impression that you are shouting at them. Elderly people are prone to more anxiety than the young (Fozard and Gordon-Salant 2001), so you must be careful that your efforts to make yourself heard are not reflected in your agitated looks or your barking tone. Many older people try to cover up hearing loss by faking or "bluffing" hearing because they fear negative ageist reactions from others. Such people have been found to have significantly more negative self-concepts than older people who realistically accept their impairment (Blackwell and Levey 1986).

Some elderly offenders play on hearing loss, whether or not it is an impairment that they actually have. Many of them try to use hearing impairment as an excuse for infractions, claiming that it caused them to misunderstand a situation or instruction or to make a bad decision based on misperceived information. Do not add to the negative self-concepts of "bluffers" by ridiculing them in pointing out their bluffs, neither should you allow hearing impairment to constitute an excuse for not following instructions. Rather, you might point out that there is no need to engage in such behavior, that you fully understand and accept their impairment, and that you do not mind repeating yourself any time that is necessary. Make sure they also know that it is their responsibility to ensure that they have heard and understood your instructions.

Older people quite rightly feel that they have achieved a stage in life that entitles them to a certain special respect and dignity. As we have seen, many elderly offenders often feel especially poorly about themselves for having acquired a criminal label. Along with this loss of self-respect, imagine how embarrassing it must be to have a great part of their lives controlled by an officer who, in all likelihood, is half his or her age. Never subject elderly offenders to condescension by talking down to them as if they were children, although extra patience sometimes may be required when dealing with those who may have some impairment in their cognitive functioning.

Unless requested to do otherwise, always show your respect by referring to older inmates as "Mr.," "Mrs.," or any such title they may prefer. While it is necessary to respect the dignity of all offenders, it is especially necessary to respect the dignity of those who have come to expect it in their "golden years."

Traditional counseling techniques must be geared (the responsivity principle) to the special needs and characteristics of the older offender. According to Lynskey, Day, and Hall (2003: 131), counseling should include: "Non-confrontational approaches, cognitive-behavioral interpersonal and supportive approaches, slower pace and attention to medical needs and issues specific to the population such as bereavement, loneliness, boredom and isolation." This does not mean, of course, that you should not use confrontational approaches when they are clearly required.

If you are supervising elderly parolees, be aware of some of the special difficulties they face. The imprisoned elderly offender's reentry into the community is a matter that can be quite confusing, filled with anxiety, embarrassment, and a mixture of excitement and depression. The readjustment problem was dramatically presented in the movie, *Tough Guys*. In this movie, two legendary bank robbers—Harry Doyle (Burt Lancaster) and Archie Long (Kirk Douglas)—are released into a world that bewildered them after serving thirty years inside. A similar theme occurs for Brooks and Red in *The Shawshank Redemption*.

If parolees lack support from family, friends, and significant others, their re-assimilation into the community can be painful and difficult. This is true for parolees of any age, but perhaps particularly so for elderly parolees. Carroll states:

> Many have lost or outlived their families. They may have no homes or job skills. Who hires an older person anyway, much less an ex-con? They have no savings or medical insurance, and may not know how to take advantage of welfare programs (1989: 70).

The ability of the elderly offender to function outside the criminal justice system is of great concern, especially if they have become institutionalized. Consequently, being set free with next to no resources poses a threat for these individuals because of their dependency on the institution. Many have a natural impulse to want to go that extra mile for an older person, but you must not let them transfer their dependency on the institution to dependency on you. As is the case with your other offenders, do things with them rather than for them. Elderly individuals must learn to draw on reserves of physical and mental attributes, which do not come easily to them anymore. The parole agent must be aware of this and of the resources in his or her community that may ease the elderly parolee's transition into a world that may be quite different from the one left behind some years ago.

Alcoholism and problem drinking are a particular problem among elderly criminal justice offenders (McCarthy and Langworthy 1987). According to Fishman (1986), increasing age leads to an increasing likelihood of alcohol abuse among the elderly, who are suffering problems of social isolation, bereavement, ill health, low self-esteem, and the side effects of medication. Many elderly people take to drinking much more frequently than they did when younger because it serves as a substitute for what they have lost. Alcohol may be seen as replacing lost friends, dulling the psychic pains of bereavement, and the physical pains of ill health, and temporarily bolstering self-esteem.

Fishman (1986) believes that problem drinking among the elderly ideally should not be treated in mainstream alcoholism programs (this is particularly true if the problem drinking is of recent onset, situational, and related to the problems of old age). He feels that elderly drinkers are best treated through counseling and increased social involvement with age peers. Furthermore, he feels that the prognosis for successful treatment is good for late-onset elderly problem drinkers if treated in this fashion. Fishman's message to correctional workers emphasizes that narrow and uniform approaches to alcohol treatment will not suffice, and that you must be sensitive to special classes of offenders who need to be treated outside the usual methods. Part of the reason for this is that alcoholism is particularly dangerous for the elderly. Because of age-related physiological changes, older people will metabolize alcohol more slowly; in other words, the same amount of alcohol will result in a higher blood-alcohol concentration (BAC) for the elderly than for younger drinkers. Additionally, alcohol withdrawal will take longer, be more severe, and be more dangerous for the older individual (Lynskey, Day, and Hall 2003).

Another aspect of ageism is the notion that "you can't teach old dogs new tricks." While it is true that older individuals tend to resist change more than younger individuals, it is wrong to assume that older people cannot develop new components of their lives if enough motivation is generated. You just need a bit more flexibility in your approach with older inmates. As Twining (1988: 177) puts it: "It is no good having a few standard solutions to problems and then just picking the one that seems to fit best. This might not work too badly for younger people, but it is no good for people who are older." Whatever your "solutions" might be, above all treat elderly inmates with the dignity they especially deserve, while remembering that the elderly are your future.

Case Study: The Elderly Inmate
A View from the Inside

By Grace Jean Balazs

Mr. "Frank James" is a sixty-three-year-old inmate at the Idaho State Correctional Institution. He began his term of incarceration in August of 2005 for the sexual abuse of his fifteen-year-old stepdaughter, for which he is serving a sentence of five-to-ten years. Frank believes that he is serving a life sentence because of his age and poor health. Mr. James has severe emphysema, which requires him to be practically inseparable from an oxygen supply day and night. He does not berate the court for his incarceration, but questions the severity of his sentence given his lack of previous convictions.

Mr. James is a personable gentleman; he is quiet and courteous, and does not appear to be disturbed in his present environment. His social history reflects only a tenth-grade education, and he admits that he has a bad-conduct discharge from the Army. He has been married five times, with the longest marriage lasting nine years and the shortest lasting just over one year. He is presently unmarried, and has no communication with any of his ex-wives or nine children. His victim is presently living in a foster home in another state, and he resents the fact that he was not consulted on this matter.

Presently, he is in denial about the offense, and he stated that he had told his daughter that if the occasion should arise where he was confronted with such an accusation, he simply would deny the charge. He is involved in a sex-offender therapy group under Dr. John Mills, and states that he knows the psychologist thinks he is lying and that no progress will be made until he admits the offense, yet Mr. James remains consistent in his denial.

When asked to describe the world of an elderly offender, one of the first things he said was that most offenders do not have a support system of individuals on the outside. This is even more evident for the elderly, whether they are incarcerated or not. Many times, families neglect their elderly for many different reasons. He identifies himself as one of those neglected individuals. His sole contact is his elderly mother who lives in Nebraska and is seriously ill.

Mr. James says that he functions quite well in prison and gets along with both older and younger prisoners. He finds that the prison provides adequate accommodations for his medical needs, although he states that it is often a "hassle" to obtain medical care, and thus not worth the effort to seek it out. He sees a doctor in prison much less frequently than he did on the outside, indicating that he spent thirty days in the hospital before being sent to prison while the institution made arrangements for his health care.

Mr. James has taken the attitude of "live and let live" at the institution. He cooperates with prison officials, and does not pry into the business of other offenders. He also has not let the prison environment affect his state of mind. He says that he feels and functions much the same as he did on the outside, and never suffers from depression, although he acknowledges that this is unusual for the elderly offender.

Mr. James is housed with a group of fifteen-to-twenty individuals who range between sixty and eighty years old. Their age does not exclude these men from associating with other inmates at the institution, but many just seek to be left alone to serve out their sentence. Television and cards are popular pastimes among these men. He has not explored the entire facility, choosing to restrict himself to the area of his cellblock. He chooses to take his meals at his cellblock because this is more convenient for him in terms of mobility and personal comfort. He seldom finds it necessary to visit the commissary at the institution. He receives no money from outside the prison, which would allow him to make purchases there. He does not feel particularly deprived, however, and feels that his needs are adequately met without having to supplement them.

Mr. James does not think that it is necessary to have correctional institutions designed specifically for the elderly, especially not if the purpose is to separate them from younger offenders. He feels that younger inmates have a positive affect on the older inmates because morale is usually higher among the older men when free association is permitted. Mixing with younger men, says James, is uplifting, and provides the elderly offender with mental and physical stimulation. He also feels that older offenders act as a "stabilizing influence" on the "younger bucks" inside the walls. This mixture of ages is the closest thing the inmates have to a community atmosphere, the likes of which, many of these men may not see for some time. However, James says that the prison environment can get you down quick enough in one way or another.

Mr. James' time is pretty much his own, with his day beginning when he chooses. Breakfast is served at the dining room at 7:00 A.M., but he rarely gets up that early. Instead, he asks for his breakfast to be brought to the cellblock around 9:00 A.M., after he is up and about.

His day is not demanding. He functions at his own pace because many of the prison's activities are of no interest to him, with the exception of working with leather. He seems quite proud of the fact that he has learned to work leather into many practical articles, and is disappointed that the items cannot be put up for sale at the prison site or in the community, stating that it would be nice to have some extra cash created by the motivation that comes from his sense of accomplishment. This hobby is the only pastime that adds variety to his day. The rest is routine: get up, watch television, play cards, eat meals, lights out. Although lights are out officially at 10:00 P.M., he reads until 1:30 A.M., thanks to the individual lights that are in each room.

Mr. James stated several times that his routine does not vary much from what it did at home. He was relatively inactive then, with limited employment

Continued on the next page

Case Study: The Elderly Inmate, *continued*

because of his disability. The lack of privacy is the thing that bothers him most, "but what can be done about that in a place like this when one is under continual guard?" He does not care much for his cell mate either, but goes with the flow and does not make an issue about something he cannot change. He does not want to cause trouble, stating that it is better to work together and avoid controversy so that correctional officers do not lock down the cell block.

Frank James will continue to serve his time with little change in his routine until his five years are up. He says that he has little to worry about inside or outside the institution since he lacks personal obligations outside the prison that require his attention. When he is released, he plans to live in Nebraska with his mother, if she is still alive. If not, he is familiar with the services available through the housing authorities, food programs, welfare, and Medicare, to adequately sustain him for the rest of his life.

Perspective from the Field
Golden Years and Iron Gates

By Kenneth L. Faiver, MPH, MLIR

Kenneth L. Faiver is president of Correctional Health Resources, Inc., a firm which recruits doctors and other health care staff for prisons and jails. Active as a consultant in correctional health care issues, he is an auditor for the American Correctional Association and a senior accreditation surveyor for the National Commission on Correctional Health Care and the author of Health Care Management Issues in Corrections, *available from the American Correctional Association. In addition, he was the administrator of health services for the Michigan Department of Corrections for sixteen years and served as chief medical coordinator for Puerto Rico's prison system for three years. He holds master's degrees in theology, labor and industrial relations, and in public health, and was a Pew doctoral fellow in public health.*

● ●

Until a very few years ago, even large prison systems had only a handful of inmates above seventy-five years of age. In fact, there were not very many prisoners older than sixty. The median age of most prison populations was in the mid-twenties. It is a relatively new phenomenon in the United States to find large numbers of elderly persons behind bars.

The few gray heads and wrinkled faces belonged to old-timers serving life sentences who already had spent many years behind bars. "Prisonwise" and mellowed by their years, they wanted to do "quiet time." They often were respected and looked up to by the younger crowd. Indeed, the old-timer sometimes became a "pet" of staff and of other inmates, as well. People made allowances when they were slow in line or became mixed up or confused. There were willing hands to push wheelchairs or to assist with other needs.

Things are different today. Not only are there more elderly prisoners than ever before, they are aging, or "graying" as it has been called. Judges are giving felons longer sentences. Parole and pardon boards are reluctant to release inmates to the community. With the growing number of senior citizens in the free world, the number of those who commit crimes will increase, as well. Some older persons suffering from mental problems used to live out their days in state mental institutions. However, now that most mental hospitals across the country have been closed, many of these people are homeless. They sleep on park benches, in doorways, in abandoned houses, or under bridges. When they become too much of a public nuisance, they are arrested. Several such arrests incur longer sentences. Sometimes elderly persons who lack adequate means of support intentionally seek shelter from the cold and from hunger by committing acts that are likely to result in arrest and incarceration.

Whatever the reason—and there are many—elderly inmates are no longer the rare exceptions, which used to inspire respect, assistance, and protection. Instead, they have become a "bother"—a nuisance. In addition, they themselves are annoyed by the loud voices and loud music so common among younger inmates. These younger, predatory types show little respect and take advantage of older inmates, hurting or abusing them, teasing them, and taking or damaging their property. Moreover, officers are required to enforce rules equitably and may not be able to allow for special accommodations due to the slowness, confusion, or disability that frequently accompanies the aging process.

Besides the increasing number of elderly in prisons, one must take into account the past lifestyles of those elderly inmates (smoking, having a poor diet, living in poverty with minimal access to health care), and then the need for increased resources—to include personnel, funding and facilities—to care for them, in record numbers, becomes obvious. According to Jonathan Turley, the founder of Project for Older Prisoners (POPS), a Washington, D.C. advocacy group,

> The geriatric prison population has very specialized needs that most facilities are very poorly suited to handle. The result is that most gerontological problems go untreated until they are chronic (Schreiber 1999).

One elderly inmate costs an average of $69,000 per year to care for, which is two to three times the cost for other inmates (Drummond 1999). Although the percentage of prisoners age fifty and older is estimated at only 5.7 percent, more than 55 percent of inmates are between the ages of thirty and forty-nine, and are serving, on average, twenty-four year sentences (Schreiber 1999, Hollis 1999). In Virginia, more than $61 million annually is

Continued on the next page

Perspective from the Field, *continued*

spent on only 891 inmates, or 3 percent of the total inmate population, and a special facility to house the infirm and elderly inmate population has room for 200—about one-fourth of Virginia's eligible inmates (Holman 1999).

Some states have begun addressing the issue. For instance, in Columbia, South Carolina the first private medical prison opened in October 1999. Pennsylvania quickly followed suit by contracting out the building and operation of a 700-inmate medical prison for an estimated price tag of $45 million. Texas currently is converting part of a state prison into a sixty-bed geriatric center. An example of how the influx of elderly inmates is affecting states that are less prepared is Michigan. In 1996, their only facility equipped to accommodate elderly offenders had eighty-five beds; yet, more than 600 prisoners in the state qualified to be there (French 1996).

Some Solutions

The number of inmates requiring assistance with activities of daily living (dressing, feeding, bathing, using the toilet, and walking) will continue to increase. Some of these will require nursing home care. Those who are incontinent will need to be diapered and bathed frequently. These are costly, highly labor-intensive services. Disorders such as Alzheimer's disease and organic brain syndrome resulting from the aging process also place major burdens on caregivers. The Americans with Disabilities Act makes it clear that appropriate accommodations must be made, even in prisons, to meet the needs of physically and mentally disabled persons.

More and more persons will reach the end of their lives while under sentences. Some of them do not need to die in prison. Especially as they become disabled or terminally ill, depending on a number of factors, many no longer will represent a real threat or danger to society. Under such circumstances, consideration should be given to seeking approval from the parole board or the governor for release in a time-sensitive manner. Special laws may be necessary in some states to enable or facilitate compassionate release.

For those who cannot be released, humane environments should be prepared for the terminally ill. Hospices in the free world can serve as a model. People associated with the hospice movement are often happy to provide advice and valuable assistance for replication of features of this program in the prisons.

Prisons need a specific policy concerning "do not resuscitate" orders, advance directives, and durable power of attorney. It is appropriate to respect the inmate's wishes and to permit death with dignity. Legal advice should be sought in preparing the policy, and due care must be observed to ensure that the terminal patient (or properly constituted representative) provides witnessed informed consent and that there is no coercion. Where feasible, you should consult family members. The chaplain also may be helpful. It is clearly unacceptable to do as one facility administrator recently said: "We don't bother with DNR orders here. We just run a slow code."

Secure extended-care facilities, or nursing homes, may need to be developed. A number of systems already have done this. However, if these were planned and established at a time when the number of elderly and chronically disabled inmates was far less, they are likely no longer adequate. Besides in-house units, nursing home beds also can be contracted in the community. It also may be feasible to parole them to a secure nursing home—possibly with an electronic tether.

Specialized housing for the elderly, perhaps in a low-security unit constructed near a prison medical complex, may be a cost-effective solution to some difficult management problems. One or more social workers should be assigned to assist in prerelease research and preparations for discharge, including Medicaid/Medicare enrollment, identifying shelter and support systems, or reestablishing linkage with family members.

Summary

Until quite recently, little attention has been paid to the elderly offender. Because they are very much underrepresented among our criminal population, they have been considered something of a "non-problem." However, the proportion of our elderly citizens under some form of correctional supervision is rising as our society ages.

We raised several issues regarding the elderly offender, including the definition of "elderly," which varies among studies. Given the youthful nature of our criminal population, anyone more than thirty is considered old in prison, but we have not considered anyone below fifty as old. We also looked at some possible reasons why, after a lifetime of noncriminal behavior, many elderly individuals commit crime. These reasons ranged from the biological impairments sometimes accompanying old age, to the social and psychological problems of the elderly.

The elderly behind bars are not considered to be a behavioral problem. Probably for this reason (and in common with female inmates), there are very few programs specifically aimed at them. The main problem for the institutional correctional people presented by the elderly is financial. Because of the plethora of health problems suffered by the elderly, it costs about three and one-half times more to maintain a person in prison who is fifty years of age or older than other inmates.

Perhaps partly because of this, many elderly offenders, who otherwise may have been incarcerated, are diverted into community corrections. Yet, they present relatively few supervision problems to probation/parole officers. We noted some specific aspects of community supervision, such as problem drinking and hearing impairment, as well as the importance of treating elderly offenders with respect and dignity while also holding them accountable.

References and Suggested Readings

Aday, R. 2003. *Aging Prisoners: Crisis in American Corrections*. Westport, Connecticut: Praeger.

Alston, L. 1986. *Crime and Older Americans*. Springfield, Illinois: Charles C. Thomas.

Baldwin, J. 1990. The Role of Sensory Stimulation in Criminal Behavior, with Special Attention to the Age Peak in Crime. In *Crime in Biological, Social, and Moral Contexts*, L. Ellis and H. Hoffman, eds. New York: Praeger.

Beck, A. and C. Mumola. 1999. *Prisoners in 1998*. Washington, D.C.: Bureau of Justice Statistics.

Blackwell, D. and L. Levey. 1986. Hearing Impairment, Self-Concept and Morale Among the Elderly. *Free Inquiry in Creative Sociology* 15: 21-26.

Brown, G. and K. Brozowski. 2003. Golden Years? The Incarceration of the Older Offender. *Geriatrics Today* 6: 32-35.

Carroll, G. 1989. Growing Old Behind Bars. *Newsweek* November 20.

Chaiklin, H. and L. Fultz. 1985. The Service Needs of Older Offenders. *The Justice Professional* 1: 26-33.

Champion, D. 2005. *Probation, Parole, and Community Corrections*, 5th ed. Upper Saddle River, New Jersey: Prentice Hall.

Chaneles, S. 1987. Growing Old Behind Bars. *Psychology Today* 21(10), 47-51.

Curtice, M., J. Parker, F. Wismayer, and A. Tomison. 2003. The Elderly Offender: An 11-Year Survey of Referrals to a Regional Forensic Psychiatric Service. *Journal of Forensic Psychiatry and Psychology* 14: 253-265.

Donnelly, S., J. Kane, M. Thigpen, and D. Thigpen. 1991. It's Coming Back to Me Now. *Time* 22: 78-80.

Drummond, T. 1999. Cellblock Seniors: They Have Grown Old and Frail in Prison. Must They Still Be Locked Up? *Time Magazine*, June 14-21. Reprinted at www.mapinc.org/drugnewsv99/n653/a12.html

Ellis, L. 2003. Genes, Criminality, and the Evolutionary Neuroandrogenic Theory. In *Biosocial Criminology: Challenging Environmentalism's Supremacy*, A.Walsh and L. Ellis, eds. Hauppauge, New York: Nova Science. pp. 13-34.

Ellis, L. and A. Walsh. 2000. *Criminology: A Global Perspective*. Boston: Allyn and Bacon.

Ellsworth, T. and K. Helle. 1995. Older Offenders on Probation. *Federal Probation* 58: 43-51.

Favier, K. 1998. *Health Care Management Issues in Corrections*. Alexandria, Virginia: American Correctional Association.

Fazel, S. and R. Jacoby. 2000. The Elderly Criminal. *International Journal of Geriatric Psychiatry* 15: 201-202.

Federal Bureau of Investigation. 2004. *Uniform Crime Report 2003*. Washington, D.C.: U.S. Government Printing Office.

Feldmeyer, B, and D. Steffensmeier. 2007. Elder Crime: Patterns and Current Trends. *Research on Aging* 29: 297-322.

Fishman, R. 1986. *Alcohol and Alcoholism*. New York: Chelsea House.

Fozard, J. and S. Gordon-Salant. 2001. Changes in Hearing and Vision with Aging. In *Handbook of the Psychology of Aging*, J. Birren and W. Schaie, eds. San Diego: Academic Press. pp. 241-266.

French, R. 1966. State Taxpayers Feel Pinch of Aging Prison Population. *The Detroit News*. www.detnews.com/menu/stories/42072.htm.

Giordano, J. 2000. Effective Communication and Counseling with Older Adults. *International Journal of Aging and Human Development* 51: 15-324.

Goetting, A. 1983. The Elderly in Prisons: Issues and Perspectives. *Journal of Research in Crime and Delinquency* 20: 291-309.

Harrison, P. and J. Karberg. 2004. Prison and Jail Inmates at Midyear 2003. *Bureau of Justice Statistics Bulletin*, May.

Hollis, M. 1999. Tough Sentences Leave Florida with Prisons Filled with Aged, Ailing Criminals. *The Sun Sentinel*. www.sunsentinel.com/news/daily.

Holman, B. 1999. Old Men Behind Bars. *The Washington Post*. July 25. Reprinted at www.sentencing.org/v212.html.

Hucker, S. 1984. Psychiatric Aspects of Crime in Old Age. In *Elderly Criminals*. E. Newman et al. eds. Cambridge: Oelgeschlager, Gunn and Hain.

Jolin, A. and D. Gibbons. 1987. Age Patterns in Criminal Involvement. *International Journal of Offender Therapy and Comparative Criminology* 31: 237-260.

Krajick, K. 1979. Growing Old in Prison. *Corrections Magazine*. March: 5: 33-39.

Kratcoski, P. 2000. Older Inmates: Special Programming Concerns. In *Correctional Counseling and Treatment*, P. Kratcoski, ed. Prospect Heights, Illinois: Waveland Press.

Kratcoski, P. and S. Babb. 1990. Adjustment of Older Inmates: An Analysis of Institutional Structure and Gender. *Journal of Contemporary Criminal Justice* 6: 264-281.

Kuhlmann, R. and R. Ruddell. 2005. Elderly Jail Inmates: Prevalence and Public Health. *California Journal of Health Promotion* 3: 49-60.

Lynskey, M., C. Day, and W. Hall. 2003. Alcohol and Other Drug Use Disorders among Older-Aged People. *Drug and Alcohol Review* 22: 125-133.

McCarthy, B. and R. Langworthy. 1987. Older Offenders on Probation and Parole. *Journal of Offender Counseling, Services, and Rehabilitation* 12: 7-25.

McCrae, R., P. Costa, F. Ostendorf, A. Angleitner, M. Hrebickova, M. Avia, J. Sanz, M. Sanchez-Bernardos, M. Kusdil. R. Woodfield, P. Saunders and P. Smith. 2000. Nature Over Nurture: Temperament, Personality, and Life Span Development. *Journal of Personality and Social Psychology* 78: 173-186.

McKenzie, D. 2004. Age and Adjustment to Prison: Interactions with Attitudes and Anxiety. In *The Inmate Prison Experience*, M. Stohr and C. Hemmens, eds. Upper Saddle River, New Jersey: Prentice Hall. pp. 104-117.

Morton, J. and J. Anderson. 1996. Implementing the Americans with Disabilities Act for Inmates. *Corrections Today October* 86, 58, 90, 140-141.

Panton, J. 1976/1977. Personality Characteristics of Aged Inmates within a State Prison Population. *Offender Rehabilitation* 1: 207.

Restak, R. 2001. *The Secret Life of the Brain*. New York: co-published by Dana Press and Joseph Henry Press.

Rikard, R. and E. Rosenberg. 2007. Aging Inmates: A Convergence of Trends in the American Criminal Justice System. *Journal of Correctional Health Care* 3: 150-162.

Robins, R., K. Trzesniewski, J. Tracy, S. Gosling, and J. Potter. 2002. Global Self-Esteem Across The Lifespan. *Psychology and Aging* 17: 432-434.

Sampson, R. and J. Laub. 2005. A Life-Course View of the Development of Crime. *American Academy of Political and Social Sciences* 602:12-45.

Schmalleger, F. 2003. *Criminal Justice Today*. Upper Saddle River, New Jersey: Prentice Hall.

Schreiber, C. 1999. Behind Bars: Aging Prison Population Challenges Correctional Health Systems. *Nurse Week*. www.nurseweek.com/features/99-7/prison.html

Shichor, D. 1984. The Extent and Nature of Lawbreaking by the Elderly: A Review of Arrest Statistics. In *Elderly Criminals*, E. Newman, D. Newman, and M. Gerwitz, eds. Cambridge, Massachusetts. Oelgeschlager, Gunn, and Hain.

———. 1988. An Exploratory Study of Elderly Probationers. *International Journal of Offender Therapy and Comparative Criminology* 32: 163-174.

Snarr, R. 1996. *Introduction to Corrections*. Madison, Wisconsin: Brown and Benchmark.

Twining, C. 1988. *Helping Older People: A Psychological Approach*. New York: Wiley.

U.S. Census Bureau. 2005. *65+in the United States: 2005*. U.S. Department of Commerce. Washington, D.C.: U.S. Government Printing Office.

U.S. Department of Justice. 1989. *Monday Morning Highlights*. Washington, D.C.

Walsh, A. 2002. *Biosocial Criminology: Introduction and Integration*. Cincinnati, Ohio: Anderson Publishing.

Walsh, C. 1992. Aging Inmate Offenders: Another Perspective. In *Correctional Theory and Practice*, C. Hartjen and E. Rhine, eds. Chicago: Nelson/Hall.

Yablonsky, L. and M. Haskell. 1988. *Juvenile Delinquency*. New York: Harper and Row.

Yorston, G. and P. Taylor. 2006. Commentary: Older Offenders—No Place to Go? *Journal of the American Academy of Psychiatry and Law* 34: 333-337.

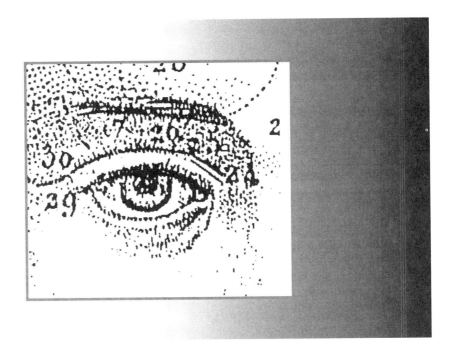

Epilog

The professional application of the knowledge, tools, and techniques presented in this book, we believe, will assist you in supervising and helping those unfortunate lives that it one day may be your privilege to touch. It is an awesome responsibility to be charged with helping, befriending, and rectifying the attitudes and behaviors of another human being. Never cease examining and improving yourself or learning everything you can about your profession. Make wise use of the numerous community resources available to aid you in this endeavor.

However, never lose sight of the fact that the most important person in the rehabilitative effort is the offender. You must not fall into the trap of doing things for and to offenders; rather, you should do things with them. We wish to foster offender responsibility through self-reliance. An overemphasis on providing everything for the offender, beyond the initial stage, is not congruent with this aim and tends to encourage offender dependence. It is fine if offenders lean on you a little, but only if they learn to lift themselves up to responsibility.

The experienced worker may be excused for asking how all these concepts, suggestions, and techniques realistically can be put to work given the constraints imposed by time and large caseloads. The judicious management of caseloads requires organization and a thorough knowledge of clientele. This is best accomplished by proper offender classification based on presentence investigation information. Proper classification and risk and needs assessment enable officers to determine which offenders are most in need of their attention. Many offenders on the average caseload require little, if any, "treatment" beyond occasional reporting and the officer's monitoring of daily arrest sheets. These low-risk/low needs offenders are often "situational" offenders whose trip through "the system" can be sufficient to teach them the errors of their ways.

The time you save by having minimal contact with these offenders can be put to good use by concentrating on more problematic offenders. Knowledge and proper use of community resources, and of the skills and motivations of volunteers, will strengthen your efforts. There is always enough time for organized, efficient, and caring criminal justice workers to do the job they have chosen. Few vocations are more psychologically rewarding and uplifting.

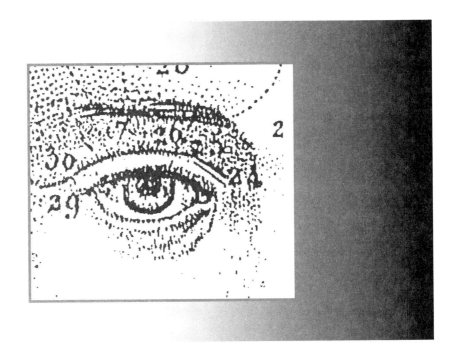

Appendices

SOCIAL HISTORY QUESTIONNAIRE _____

Prior to your next appearance in court for final disposition, the Adult Probation Department must complete a presentence investigation for the judge. This presentence investigation includes information about your background that the judge will take into consideration when deciding whether to place you on probation or not. Please completely fill out this questionnaire, and if you have any questions concerning the questionnaire, feel free to ask. The information that you provide will be confidential in that only the Probation Department and the judge will be allowed to see it. Upon completion of this questionnaire, please return it to the person who gave it to you.

GENERAL INFORMATION:

FULL NAME:_____

PRESENT ADDRESS:_____

TELEPHONE #:_____

PLACE OF BIRTH:_____

DATE OF BIRTH:_____

SOCIAL SECURITY NO.:_____

SOCIAL HISTORY QUESTIONNAIRE (continued) _____

FAMILY:

Please list the members of your family, including parents, brothers, sisters, spouse, and children.

NAME	RELATIONSHIP	AGE	ADDRESS
PARENTS:			
BROTHERS & SISTERS:			
WIFE/HUSBAND:			
CHILDREN:			

Have you ever been married before? Yes / No

Date of wedding:

Date of divorce:

SOCIAL HISTORY QUESTIONNAIRE (continued)_____

EDUCATION:
Please list what schools you have attended (elementary, secondary, college, and job training programs).

SCHOOL	DATES ATTENDED	HIGHEST GRADE COMPLETED

EMPLOYMENT:
Please list in order your job history. If employed at the present time, please note where and the name of your supervisor.

EMPLOYER	ADDRESS	DATE STARTED	DATE LEFT	REASON

Spouse's Current Employer:

SOCIAL HISTORY QUESTIONNAIRE (continued) _____

MILITARY HISTORY:
Please note the following information:

Branch of Service:_____

Date of Entry:_____

Date of Discharge:_____

Type of Discharge:_____

Location of Service:_____

_____

HEALTH:
Please make a statement as to your general state of health. Do you have any medical problems, are you under a doctor's care, or are you on medication? Please note below:

PRIOR RECORD: **BIR #**   **FBI #**

If you have been arrested before, either as a juvenile or adult, please list these arrests. Also, please note what happened in court after these arrests. Please note if you have been on probation or parole before, or if you are under any supervision at the present time.

SOCIAL HISTORY QUESTIONNAIRE (continued)_____

Please fill in the following list of information:

1. Housing costs: Weekly:_____ or monthly: _____

2. Food costs: Weekly: _____ or monthly: _____

3. **Approximate Monthly Cost of Utilities:**

    A. Telephone: _____
    B. Gas: _____
    C. Water: _____
    D. Electric: _____

4. **Loan Payments:**

    A.

    B.

    C.

    D.

    E.

5. **Other Miscellaneous Costs:**

    A.

    B.

    C.

    D.

    E.

Print in your own words a statement concerning the offense. What did you do, when, who was involved, why, did you repay the victim?, etc.

CLIENT MANAGEMENT CLASSIFICATION ASSESSMENT INSTRUMENT _____

The purpose of CMC is to provide the probation professional with an efficient and effective case management system. CMC includes procedures for developing individualized strategies for the quality supervision of adult offenders. This process is accomplished through the completion of the three system components: an assessment procedure, a supervision planning process, and supervision according to one of five distinct strategies, depending on individualized case needs. It is not to be used with juveniles nor for any other than its stated purpose.

CMC INSTRUCTIONS

There are four parts to the CMC assessment instrument. Whenever possible, the following sequence (A to D) should be followed.

A. Attitude interview (45 items)
B. Objective history (11 items)
C. Behavioral observations (8 items)
D. Officer impressions of contributing factors (7 items)

The Attitude Section

Column One:

A SEMI-STRUCTURED INTERVIEW with suggested questions has been developed to elicit attitude information about the offense, the offender's background, and about present plans and problems. The average interview takes about forty-five minutes and the scoring about five minutes.

Use a **natural, open** conversational style of interviewing that is comfortable for both you and the probationer. If the probationer presents some important or interesting information requiring follow-up, feel free to do so before returning to the structured sequence. While stressing free-flowing communication, some structuring is required to ensure the reliability and validity of the instrument. Therefore, make every effort to **preserve the meaning of the questions** when transposing them into your own words.

In the interview, each section is introduced by one or two open-ended questions, which are intended to encourage discussion on a particular subject. If the information needed to score the items is not obtained from the open-ended questions, one or two specific questions are provided for each item. If those questions fail to elicit the needed information, continue to inquire with increasingly direct questions unless you see the word -STOP-. "-STOP-" means to discontinue inquiry (except to repeat or clarify a misunderstood question).

For some items, "a" and "b" questions are included. If the "b" question is asterisked (*), always ask it unless the answer to the "a" makes the "b" questions meaningless (e.g., "no" to question 10a). If question "b" is not asterisked, ask it if the needed information was not elicited from question "a."

Column Two:

THE ITEM OBJECTIVES AND RESPONSES are listed in column two. Many times the suggested questions will approach the item objective in an indirect manner in order to elicit the most valid response.

Column Three:

A SCORING GUIDE is included to provide criteria and assistance in scoring ambiguous responses. When scoring, you must choose only one alternative for each item. If you cannot choose an alternative, do not rate the item.

CMC (continued) _____

Attitudes About Offense

Could you tell me about the offense that got you into trouble?

QUESTIONS	RESPONSES	SCORING GUIDE
1a. How did you get involved in this offense?	1. Motivation for committing the offense (a) emotional motivation (e.g., anger, sex offense, etc.)	1. a. -Using drugs -Assault (not for robbery)
1b. (If denied) What did the police say that you did?	(b) material (monetary) motivation	b. -Prostitution -Car theft (except for joy riding) -Selling drugs (including to support a habit)
	(c) both emotional and material motivation	c. -Stealing from parents for revenge -Stealing primarily for peer acceptance -Man who won't pay alimony primarily because he's angry with his ex-wife
2a. How did you decide to commit the offense? 2b. Could you tell me more about the circumstances that led up to the offense?	2. Acceptance of responsibility for current offense (a) admits committing the offense and doesn't attempt excuses (b) admits committing the offense but emphasizes excuses (e.g., drinking, influence by friends, family problems, etc.) (c) denies committing the offense	2. a. Explains circumstances but takes responsibility b. Blames circumstances and does not take responsibility c. Probationers who deny any significant aspect of the offense are scored "c" (e.g., the probationer admits that he helped to jimmy a car window but denies responsibility for removing valuables because his friends removed them).

CMC (continued) _____

QUESTIONS	RESPONSES	SCORING GUIDE
3a. Looking back at the offense, what is your general feeling about it? -STOP-	3. Expression of guilt about current offense (a) expresses guilt feelings or spontaneous empathy toward victim (b) expresses superficial or no guilt (c) victimless crime	3. a. Probationer must feel some personal shame and regret (not just verbalization to impress the officer). b. -"I feel bad because now I have a record." -"People are disappointed in me." (Indicates some regret but not necessarily guilt.) -"I know it was wrong." (Emphasis is on having done wrong, but not on feeling bad because one has done wrong.) c. -Using drugs -Sexual activities between consenting adults

Offense pattern

I'd like to talk to you about your prior offenses. Have you been in trouble before? (Obtain a *complete* picture of probationer's offense style, including current offense, when scoring items 5-8.)

QUESTIONS	RESPONSES	SCORING GUIDE
4a. What prior offenses have you been convicted of? *4b. Were you ever in trouble as a juvenile?(List on grid below)	4. Offense and severity (a) no prior offenses (Skip items 5, 6, 7, and 8.) (b) mainly misdemeanors (c) no constant pattern (d) mainly felonies	4-8. Include juvenile and serious traffic offenses (e.g., drunk driving). Don't count dismissals. 4. Use only prior offenses. b. Should not be used if probationer has more than two serious felonies. (Use choice "c" or "d.") d. Over 50% of probationer's offenses are felonies.

CMC (continued) _____

QUESTIONS	RESPONSES	SCORING GUIDE
5a. Have you ever been armed or hurt someone during these offenses? *5b. Did you ever threaten anyone?	5. Was probationer ever involved in an offense where he (she) was armed, assaultive, or threatened injury to someone? (a) yes (b) no	5-8. Use current and prior offense factors to score 5-8.
6a. How did you decide to commit these offenses? 6b. Did you plan these offenses beforehand? (Discuss offenses individually until a clear pattern emerges).	6. Offenses were *generally* (a) planned (b) no consistent pattern (c) impulsive	6. Officer's judgement based on all factors. a. -Exhibitionist who drives around in a car looking for a girl to whom to expose himself. b. -Person who decides to commit an offense, then drinks to build courage. c. -Exhibitionist who is driving to work, suddenly sees a girl, and pulls over and exposes himself. -Person gets drunk and into a bar fight.
7. Were you drinking or on drugs when you committed this offense?	7. Percent of offenses committed while drinking or on drugs (a) never (b) 50% or less (c) over 50%	7. Count offenses where there was *any* chemical use regardless of whether person was intoxicated or not.
8. Did you do the offense alone or with others?	8. Offenses were *generally* committed (a) alone (b) no consistent pattern (c) with accomplices	

CMC (continued) _____

Offense	(Item 4) Fel./Misd.	(Item 5) Assaultive?	Circumstances of Offense	(Item 6) Planned?	(Item 7) Chemicals?	(Item 8) Accomplices?

School and Vocational Adjustment

Now, I'd like to find out some things about your background. Let's begin with school. How did you like school?

QUESTIONS	RESPONSES	SCORING GUIDE
9. What was your favorite subject in school? -STOP-	9. Favorite subject (a) vocational (b) academic (c) gym (d) no favorite subject	9. a. -Business course. b. -Music or art.
10a. Did you have a favorite teacher in high school? 10b. What did you like about him (her)?	10. Attitude toward teachers (a) no favorite teacher (b) teacher chosen because of certain qualities that the probationer admired (c) teacher chosen because of close personal relationship with the teacher	10. b. -"She would help kids." c. -"She would help me."

CMC (continued)

QUESTIONS	RESPONSES	SCORING GUIDE

11a. How far did you go in school?

11b. Did you have any problems with schoolwork? (If probationer did not graduate from high school, find out why not.)

11. Probationer's school performance
  (a) no problems
  (b) learning problems (difficulty performing schoolwork)
  (c) lack of interest, behavior, or other problems

11. a. Don't use for probationer who didn't complete high school.
  b. For probationer whose learning problems result from a lack of capacity (not just from lack of interest or behavioral problems). If probationer has both a lack of capacity *and* behavioral problems, score "b." Lack of capacity takes precedence when scoring.

12. Now, I'd like to know about your work history. What kinds of jobs have you had? (Find out actual job responsibilities. Use grid on next page.)

12. Primary vocation
  (a) unskilled labor
  (b) semi-skilled
  (c) skilled labor or white collar
  (d) no employment history (homemaker) (Skip 13 & 14)
  (e) student or recent graduate (Skip 13 & 14)

12. a. -Average person could do job without training.
    -Probationer's been in the job market for over six months, but has no employment history. (Also score items 13 and 14.)
  c. Job requires some training and/or experience.
  d. For homemaker, use prior vocational history, if any. If none, check "d" and skip items 13 and 14.
  e. Probationer was recently (within six months) a student and hasn't had the opportunity to establish an employment pattern. (Skip items 13 and 14.)

CMC (continued) _____

QUESTIONS	RESPONSES	SCORING GUIDE
13a. How long did you work on your most recent job? 13b. How long between that job and your previous job? (Start with most recent job and go backwards, until a clear pattern emerges. Use grid for 12 - 14.)	13. Percent of working life where probationer was employed full-time (a) over 90% (b) over 50% to 90% (c) 50% or less	13. "Working Life..." i.e., time period society would expect one to be working. Subtract time in school, institutions, etc.
14a. What was your reason for leaving your most recent job? 14b. Have you had any trouble getting jobs?	14. Primary vocational problem (a) none (Can be used only if item 13 is scored "a.") (b) problems due to lack of skills or capacity (c) attitude or other problems	14. a. Don't use "a" if working less than 90% c. -"Because of my drinking problem."

(Item 12) (Start with most recent) Jobs and Job Responsibilities	(Item 13a) Duration	(Item 14a) Reason for Leaving
(Item 13b) Unemployment Interval		
(Item 13b) Unemployment Interval		
(Item 13b) Unemployment Interval		

CMC (continued) _____

QUESTIONS	RESPONSES	SCORING GUIDE
15a. Where do you live now? 15b. Have you moved around much? (Deal with time period after probationer turned 18.)	15. Living stability background (a) essentially stable living arrangements (b) some unstable periods (c) essentially unstable living arrangements	15. Consider what is stable for the probationer's age group.
16a. Have you had any trouble supporting yourself or received welfare? 16b. (If applicable) How did you support yourself when you were unemployed?	16. History of being self-supporting (a) probationer has usually been self-supporting (b) probationer has had several periods where he (she) wasn't self-supporting (c) probationer has essentially not been self-supporting	16. Illegal activities and welfare are not counted as self-supporting. For probationer who has not had the opportunity to support her/himself (e.g., homemaker or person living with relative), estimate the likelihood of (her) his being able to support (her) himself.

CMC (continued) _____

FAMILY ATTITUDES

Now I'd like to know about your childhood. Can you tell me what it was like?

QUESTIONS	RESPONSES	SCORING GUIDE
17a. How do (did) you get along with your father? 17b. How do you feel about your father?	17. Present feelings toward father (a) close (b) mixed or neutral (c) hostile	17. In multi-father families, use the person whom the probationer identifies as father. b. -"We get along" (without implication of closeness)
18a. If you did something wrong as a teenager, how did your father handle it? 18b. What kind of discipline did he use?	18. Type of discipline father used (during probationer's teenage years) (a) verbal or privilege withdrawal (b) permissive (generally let probationer do as he (she) pleased) (c) physical	18. If the probationer didn't live with father or father figure during at least part of his (her) adolescent years, do not rate item 18. b. -"He always left it to mom."
19a. How do (did) you get along with your mother? 19b. How do you feel about your mother?	19. Present feelings towards mother (a) close (b) mixed or neutral (c) hostile	19. In multi-mother families, use the person whom the probationer identifies as mother. b. -"We get along" (without implication of closeness).
20a. If you did something wrong as a teenager, how did your mother handle it? 20b. What kind of discipline did she use?	20. Type of discipline mother used (during probationer's teenage years) (a) verbal or privilege withdrawal (b) permissive (generally let probationer do as he (she) pleased) (c) physical	20. If the probationer didn't live with mother or mother figure during at least part of his (her) adolescent years, do not rate item 20. b. -"She always left it to Dad."

CMC (continued) _____

QUESTIONS	RESPONSES	SCORING GUIDE
21a. Were you ever abused by either of your parents? 21b. Did either of them ever go overboard on the punishment? -STOP-	21. Was probationer ever physically abused by a biological, step, or adoptive parent? (a) yes (b) no	21. Item 21 should be based on facts described and not whether the client felt abused. a. -cuts on face -severe body bruises -sexual abuse -locked in closet or starved for unusual periods of time
22a. How would your parents have described you as a child (before you were a teenager)? *22b. Did both of your parents see you the same way?	22. Parental view of probationer (prior to adolescence) (a) good child (b) problem child (c) parents differed	22. a. -No special problems. -"Like anybody else." b. -"My parents were always complaining about me." -Seen as "strange kid."
23. How would you describe yourself as a child (before you were a teenager)?	23. As a child, probationer describes self as (a) good child (normal or average) (b) problem child	23. Accept what the probationer says even if his (her) behavior does not match his (her) perception. (Examples from item 22 apply here.)
24a. How do you get along with your brothers and sisters? 24b. How do you feel about them?	24. General feelings toward siblings (a) close (b) neutral or mixed (c) hostile (d) no siblings	24. Include half-siblings; exclude step-siblings. b. -"Like some, not others."
25. Would you describe your early childhood (before you were a teenager) as happy or unhappy? -STOP-	25. General attitude toward childhood (a) happy (b) not happy	25. Accept the probationer's view.

CMC (continued) _____

QUESTIONS	RESPONSES	SCORING GUIDE
26. If you could change anything about your childhood, what would you change?	26. Satisfaction with childhood (a) basically satisfied (would change little) (b) dissatisfied with material aspect (c) dissatisfied with self, family, or emotional climate	26. c. -"I should've gone to school."
27. Can you describe your father's personality? (If answer is unclear, ask probationer to describe another person he (she) knows well.)	27. Probationer's description of personality (a) multi-faceted (b) superficial (e.g., "good," "bad," "nice," etc.)	27. The focus of this item is the *complexity* with which the probationer views people. The ability to describe attributes, or explain the reasons for behavior, is being measured. "Superficial" indicates a lack of capacity to perceive depth in personality and not just an evasion of the question. One or two complex statements are sufficient for an "a" score. a. -"Ambitious and honest." -"Sensitive to others." -"Dad was strict because that is the way he was brought up." b. -"No good drunk" (with no further explanation). -"Kind." -"Don't know."

CMC (continued)

Interpersonal Relations

Let's talk about your friends. Do you spend much time with them?

QUESTIONS	RESPONSES	SCORING GUIDE
28a. What are your friends (associates) like? *28b. Have any of them been in trouble with the law? (If probationer has no current associates, use prior associates.)	28. Probationer's associates are (a) essentially non-criminal (b) mixed (c) mostly criminal	28. Don't count marijuana use (alone) as criminal. a. Don't use "a" if probationer committed offense(s) with accomplices.
29a. How do you get along with your friends? *29b. How do they act toward you?	29. In interaction with friends, probationer is (a) used by others (b) withdrawn (c) other problems (d) normal	29. This item should be based on *officer's judgement* of the quality of the probationer's interactions. If the officer thinks the probationer is used by friends even though the probationer thinks he (she) gets along "ok," check choice "a."
30a. Do you have a closest friend? *30b. What do you like best about him (her)? -STOP-	30. Description of probationer's relationship with his (her) closest friend (a) talk (share feelings) or help each other (b) do things together (less emphasis on talking or sharing feelings) (c) has none	30. a. -"We do things for each other." -"We're like brothers." b. -"He's a hunter too."
31. Are you satisfied with the way you get along with people?	31. Satisfaction with interpersonal relationships (a) feels satisfied (b) feels dissatisfied	31. Accept the probationer's statement.

CMC (continued) _____

QUESTIONS	RESPONSES	SCORING GUIDE
32. In general, do you tend to trust or to mistrust people? -STOP-	32. General outlook toward others (a) basically trusting (b) mixed or complex view (c) basically mistrusting	32. b. A complex view of people (e.g., trusts in some situations and not in others) -"I trust people too much." -"It takes a while to get to know them."
33a. Can you tell me about your relationships with women (men)? *33b. Do you generally go out with a lot of women (men) or date the same person for long periods?	33. Probationer's opposite sex relationship pattern generally is (a) long-term (over six months) or serious relationships (b) short- and long-term relationships (c) short-term, less emotionally involved relationships, or little dating experience	33. c. Short-term relationships with no solid commitments to persons of the opposite sex
34. In your relationship with your wife/girlfriend (husband/boyfriend), who tends to make the decisions?	34. In opposite sex interactions, probationer generally (a) dominates (b) is average or adequate (c) is nonassertive or dominated	34. *Officer's judgement:* Do not accept the probationer's response without exploring his (her) relationships or seeing how some specific decisions are made (e.g., who decides what to do or with whom to socialize; who controls the money).

CMC (continued) _____

Feelings

Now, I'd like to ask you about your feelings. Have you had any problems handling your feelings?

QUESTIONS	RESPONSES	SCORING GUIDE
35. Do you consider yourself to be a nervous (or anxious) person? -STOP-	35. Does probationer view self as a nervous person? (a) yes (b) no	35. Accept the probationer's statement. a. -"I worry a lot." -"I'm hyperactive."
36a. What kind of things get you depressed? 36b. What do you do when you're feeling depressed? (If denies, find out how he (she) keeps from getting depressed.)	36. What does probationer do when feeling depressed? (a) seeks someone to talk to, or tries to figure it out (b) seeks an activity to distract self (c) drinks or uses drugs (d) isolates self	36. b. -"Forget about them." -"Watch T.V." d. -"I pray." -"I go to sleep."
37a. Have you ever thought seriously about hurting or killing yourself? 37b. (If probationer says yes to above) Have you ever tried it?	37. Self-destructive behavior (a) never seriously contemplated suicide (b) has had definite thoughts of suicide (c) has attempted it	37. c. Requires overt action that resulted in self-harm or clear intent toward suicide.
38a. What do you do when you are feeling angry with people? 38b. Have you ever hurt anybody when you were angry?	38. In handling anger, probationer (a) is physically aggressive (b) avoids expression to others or has trouble expressing anger appropriately (c) responds appropriately	38. Based on all sources of reliable information (e.g., offense history) and not just on probationer's statement: Physically aggressive problems should take precedence in scoring. If probationer says, "I leave," find out if/how he (she) deals with the anger later. b. -"I break things."

CMC (continued) _____

QUESTIONS	RESPONSES	SCORING GUIDE
39a. Can you describe your personality? 39b. What do you like and what do you dislike about yourself? -STOP-	39. In describing self, probationer (a) emphasizes strength (b) emphasizes inadequacy (probationer tends to downgrade self) (c) can't describe self	39. If the probationer gives both positive and negative statements about (him) herself, *choose the one emphasized most*. If the positive and negative have equal emphasis, choose the first response given. c. Choice "c" is designed to identify the probationer who is incapable of showing *insight* or *complexity* into (him) herself; e.g., "I'm okay" (and can't elaborate); "I'm nice"; "I get into too much trouble"; etc.
40. (No questions asked. Rate your impression of probationer's openness in discussing feelings.)	40. Openness in discussing feelings (a) discusses as openly as able (b) is evasive or superficial	40. a. If the officer felt that the probationer was fairly straightforward in talking about his (her) feelings. b. If the officer thought the probationer was evasive or superficial.

CMC (continued) _____

Plans and Problems

QUESTIONS	RESPONSES	SCORING GUIDE
41. Aside from your legal problems, what is the biggest problem in your life right now? -STOP-	41. What does the probationer view as his (her) most important problem area right now? (a) personal (b) relationships (c) vocational-educational (including employment) (d) financial (e) no big problems presently (Score item 42 as "a")	41. a. Probationer names several important problems -Drinking or drugs -"Get my head together." b. -"Get things straightened our with my fiancee." -"Try to get along better with my parents."
42. How do you expect this problem (from item 41) to work out?	42. Attitude toward solving problems (a) optimistic; expects to succeed (Include 41. e) (b) unclear (c) pessimistic; expects to fail	42. a. -"O.K., because I've got a better paying job." b. -"O.K., I hope." -"I'll be O.K. if I get a better paying job." c. Probationer is pessimistic about outcome or can't figure out a solution.
43a. What goals do you have for the future? *43b. What are your plans for achieving your goals? -STOP-	43. Future plans (a) short-term goals (most goals can be fulfilled within about six months) or no goals (b) unrealistic goals (c) realistic, long-term goals (most goals are well-developed and extend beyond six months)	43. a. -"Just live day to day." Poorly developed goals with no plans for achieving them b. -Strange, way-out, or impossible-to-achieve goals c. Probationer is able to (1) set a goal within the realm of possibility and (2) list the steps necessary to achieve the goal.

Correctional Assessment, Casework and Counseling

QUESTIONS	RESPONSES	SCORING GUIDE
44. (No question asked. Rate the item based on follow-through on jobs, education, training programs, treatment programs, etc., based on all sources.)	44. Probationer usually sticks with, or completes, things he (she) begins. (a) yes (b) no	44. Compare to the average probationer.
45a. How will being on probation affect your life? 45b. What do you expect to get from being on probation? -STOP-	45. Probationer's general expectations about supervision (a) no effect (b) monetary, counseling, or program help (c) hopes supervision will keep him (her) out of trouble (d) negative expectations (e) mixed or unclear expectations	

CMC˙ (continued) _____

Objective Background Items

Instructions: Ask direct questions to obtain the following information.

QUESTIONS | SCORING GUIDE

Legal History

1. Age of earliest court appearance:
    (a) 14 or younger
    (b) 15-17
    (c) 18-22
    (d) 23 or older

46. Include juvenile offenses and serious traffic offenses (e.g., drunk driving, hit and run). Exclude divorce, custody proceedings, etc.

2. Number of prior offenses:
    (a) none
    (b) 1-3
    (c) 4-7
    (d) 8 or more

47. Exclude the probationer's present offense in rating this item. Include juvenile and serious traffic offenses.

3. Number of commitments to state or federal correctional institutions:
    (a) none
    (b) 1
    (c) 2 or more

48. Include juvenile commitments.

4. Time spent under probation or parole supervision:
    (a) none
    (b) 1 year or less
    (c) over 1 year; up to 3 years
    (d) over 3 years

49. Include juvenile supervision.
    a. Use "a" for new probationer.

Medical History

5. (Circle all applicable choices.)
    (a) frequent headaches, back, or stomach problems
    (b) serious head injuries
    (c) prior psychiatric hospitalization
    (d) outpatient psychotherapy
    (e) none of the above

50. a. Vague complaints not diagnosed by a physician
    b. Skull fractures
       Head injuries that required treatment (beyond X-ray)
    d. Professional inpatient or outpatient drug/alcohol treatment

539

CMC (continued) _____

QUESTIONS   **SCORING GUIDE**

School History

6.   Highest grade completed:
     (a) 9th or below
     (b) 10th to 12th
     (c) high school graduate (exclude GED)
     (d) some post-high school training leading
          toward a degree

7.   Did probationer ever receive special educa-   52.   Include special programs for learning
     tion or remedial help in school?   deficiencies (rather than behavior problems).
     (a) yes   Do not include English-as-a-second-language
     (b) no

Family History

8.   Probationer was raised primarily by: 53.   Choice "a" requires *both natural parents* in
     (a) intact biological family   an intact home until probationer reached
     (b) other   about 16 years of age.

9.   Did either parent have a history of   54.   Includes step and adoptive parents.
     (Circle all applicable choices):
     (a) being on welfare
     (b) criminal behavior
     (c) psychiatric hospitalization
     (d) suicide attempts
     (e) drinking problems
     (f) none of the above

10. Have siblings (including half- and step-
     siblings) ever been arrested?
     (a) none
     (b) some
     (c) most
     (d) not applicable

Marital Status

11. Currently probationer is:
     (a) single (never married)
     (b) single (separated or divorced)
     (c) married (including common-law)

─────────────── END INTERVIEW ───────────────

540

CMC (continued) _____

Behavioral Patterns

Instructions: Rate the following behaviors as observed during the interview. Use (b) for the average probationer. Use (a) and (c) for distinct exceptions to the average.

1. **Grooming and Dress**

   (a) Below Average   (b) Average   (c) Above Average

2. **Self-confidence**

   (a) Lacks Confidence   (b) Average   (c) Overly Confident

3. **Attention Span**

   (a) Easily Distractable   (b) Average   (c) Very Attentive

4. **Comprehension**

   (a) Below Average   (b) Average   (c) Above Average

5. **Thought Processes**

   (a) Sluggish   (b) Average   (c) Driven (Accelerated)

6. **Affect**

   (a) Depressed   (b) Average   (c) Elated

7. **Self-disclosure**

   (a) Evasive   (b) Average   (c) Very Open

8. **Cooperation**

   (a) Negativistic   (b) Average   (d) Eager to Please

CMC (continued) _____

Impressions

Instructions: On the continuum below, rate the significance of each factor with regard to the probationer. Did (does) this problem contribute to the probationer's legal difficulties? At least one item must be rated a "1" and at least one item must be rated a "5."

A. SOCIAL INADEQUACY

Socially inept. Unable to perceive the motives and concerns of others. Unable to survive in society and care for self. (1) (2) (3) (4) (5) Socially adept. Able to assert self and to perceive the motives and concerns of others. Able to survive in society and care for self. *Do not merely rate performance on social situations. Rate ABILITY.*

B. VOCATIONAL INADEQUACY

Lacks the capacity to obtain and maintain relatively permanent and reasonably paying employment. (1) (2) (3) (4) (5) Has the capacity to obtain and maintain relatively permanent and reasonably paying employment. *Do not merely rate job performance. Rate CAPACITY.*

C. CRIMINAL ORIENTATION

Criminal behavior is an acceptable and common part of the probationer's life and s/he attempts to live off crime without trying to make it in a pro-social way. (1) (2) (3) (4) (5) Criminal behavior is not an acceptable nor common part of his/her life, nor does s/he attempt to live off of crime without trying to make it in a pro-social way. *Do not merely rate the frequency of offenses. Rate VALUES and ORIENTATION.*

D. EMOTIONAL FACTORS

Emotional problems (e.g., chemical dependency, sex, fear, depression, low self-esteem, anxiety, self-destructiveness) contributed highly to the offense (pattern). (1) (2) (3) (4) (5) Emotional factors did not contribute significantly to the offense (pattern).

CMC (continued) _____

E. FAMILY HISTORY PROBLEMS

Parental family problems in childhood and adolescence contributed significantly to the offense (pattern).

(1) (2) (3) (4) (5)

Parental family problems of childhood and adolescence did not contribute significantly to the offense (pattern).

F. ISOLATED SITUATIONAL (TEMPORARY CIRCUMSTANCES)

Unusual or temporary circumstances in the probationer's life, which are unlikely to be repeated, contributed significantly to the offense.

(1) (2) (3) (4) (5)

Offense is not a result of unusual or temporary circumstances (i.e., offense is part of a continuing pattern).

Do not merely rate infrequency of offenses. Rate OVER-ALL PATTERN.

G. INTERPERSONAL MANIPULATION

Uses, controls, and/or manipulates others to gain his/her own ends with little regard for the welfare of others.

(1) (2) (3) (4) (5)

Misuse of others, manipulation, and control did not contribute significantly to offense (pattern).

CMC (continued) _____

Supervision Planning

STEP 1: FORCE FIELD ANALYSIS: Using all resources available, identify the strengths/resources and problems/weaknesses, if any, that pertain to each area in reference to the probationer and his (her) primary environment.

Area	Rank	Strength/Resource	Problem/Weakness	Rank
Present offense				
Offense pattern				
Correctional history				
Education				
Mental ability				
Employment record				
Vocational skills				
Finances				
Residential stability				
Family history				
Interpersonal skills				
Companions				
Intimate relationships				
Emotional stability				
Drugs & alcohol				
Plans & goals				
Probation expectations				
Sexual behavior				
Health				
Values & attitudes				

STEP 2: PRIORITIZATION: Apply the following criteria to the above in order to rank the four most important areas relative to the probationer's legal difficulties: the relative strength, the alterability, the relative speed with which change can occur, and the interdependency with other areas.

CMC (continued) _____

STEP 3: TENTATIVE SUPERVISION PLAN: Using the priority areas from step B, "pencil in" tentative goals, objectives, and action plans. Use Supervision Guidelines as a resource.

1. Problem Statement: _____
    _____

    Long-range Goal: _____
    _____

    Short-range Objectives: _____
    _____ Date Achieved: _____
    _____ Date Achieved: _____

    Probationer Action Plan: _____
    _____
    _____
    _____
    _____

    Officer/Referral Action Plan: _____
    _____
    _____

2. Problem Statement: _____
    _____

    Long-range Goal: _____
    _____

    Short-range Objectives: _____
    _____ Date Achieved: _____
    _____ Date Achieved: _____

    Probationer Action Plan: _____
    _____
    _____
    _____
    _____

    Officer/Referral Action Plan: _____
    _____
    _____

STEP 4: FINAL PLAN: Negotiate the above with the probationer and modify accordingly.

CMC (continued) _____

REASSESSMENT PLAN: Revise at routine intervals or when special circumstances so indicate.

1. Problem Statement:_____

    Long-range Goal:_____

    Short-range Objectives:_____

    _____ Date Achieved:_____

    _____ Date Achieved:_____

    Probationer Action Plan:_____

    _____

    Officer/Referral Action Plan_____

2. Problem Statement:_____

    Long-range Goal:_____

    Short-range Objectives:_____

    _____ Date Achieved:_____

    _____ Date Achieved:_____

    Probationer Action Plan:_____

    _____

    Officer/Referral Action Plan:_____

FELONY SENTENCING WORKSHEET

Defendant's Name:_____ Case No. _____

OFFENSE RATING	OFFENDER RATING

OFFENSE RATING

1. Degree of Offense

Assess points for the one most serious offense or its equivalent for which offender is being sentenced, as follows: 1st degree felony = 4 points; 2nd degree felony = 3 points; 3rd degree felony = 2 points; 4th degree felony = 1 point. _____

2. Multiple Offenses

Assess 2 points if one or more of the following applies: (A) offender is being sentenced for two or more offenses committed in different incidents; (B) offender is currently under a misdemeanor or felony sentence imposed by any court; or (C) present offense was committed while offender on probation or parole. _____

3. Actual or Potential Harm

Assess 2 points if one or more of the following applies: (A) serious physical harm to a person was caused; (B) property damage or loss of $300 or more was caused; (C) there was a high risk of any such harm, damage, or loss, though not caused, (D) the gain or potential gain from theft offense(s) was $300 or more, or (E) dangerous ordnance or a deadly weapon was actually used in the incident, or its use was attempted or threatened. _____

4. Culpability

Assess 2 points if one or more of the following applies: (A) offender was engaging in continuing criminal activity as a source of income or livelihood, (B) offense was part of a continuing conspiracy to which offender was party, or (C) offense included shocking and deliberate cruelty in which offender participated or acquiesced. _____

5. Mitigation

Deduct 1 point for each of the following, as applicable: (A) there was substantial provocation, justification or excuse for offense; (B) victim induced or facilitated offense, (C) offense was committed in the heat of anger, and (D) the property damaged, lost, or stolen was restored or recovered without significant cost to the victim. _____

NET TOTAL = OFFENSE RATING _____

OFFENDER RATING

1. Prior Convictions

Assess 2 points for each verified prior felony conviction, any jurisdiction. Count adjudications of delinquency for felony as convictions. _____

Assess 1 point for each verified prior misdemeanor conviction, and jurisdiction. Count adjudications of delinquency for misdemeanor as convictions. Do not count traffic or intoxication offenses or disorderly conduct, disturbing the peace, or equivalent offenses. _____

2. Repeat Offenses

Assess 2 points if present offense is offense of violence, sex offense, theft offense, or drug abuse offense, and offender has one or more prior convictions for same type of offense. _____

3. Prison Commitments

Assess 2 points if offender was committed on one or more occasions to a penitentiary, reformatory, or equivalent institution in any jurisdiction. Count commitments to state youth commission or similar commitments in other jurisdictions. _____

4. Parole and Similar Violations

Assess 2 points if one or more of the following applies: (A) offender has previously had probation or parole for misdemeanor or felony revoked; (B) present offense committed while offender on probation or parole, (C) present offense committed while offender free on bail; or (D) present offense committed while offender in custody. _____

5. Credits

Deduct 1 point for each of the following as applicable: (A) offender has voluntarily made bona fide, realistic arrangements for at least partial restitution; (B) offender was age 25 or older at time of first felony conviction; (C) offender has been substantially law-abiding for at least 3 years; and (D) offender lives with his or her spouse or minor children or both and is either a breadwinner for the family or, if there are minor children, a housewife. _____

NET TOTAL = OFFENDER RATING _____

FELONY SENTENCING WORKSHEET (continued) _____

Indicated Sentence

Circle the box on the chart where the offense and offender ratings determined on the previous page intersect. This indicates a normal sentencing package. If the indicated sentence appears too severe or too lenient for the particular case, do not hesitate to vary from the indicated sentence. In that event, however, list the reasons for the variance in the space provided on the next page.

OFFENSE RATING		OFFENDER RATING				
		0 - 2	3 - 5	6 - 8	9 - 11	12 OR MORE
6 OR MORE		Impose one of three lowest minimum terms. No probation.	Impose one of three highest minimum terms. No probation.	Impose one of three highest minimum terms. No probation.	Impose one of two highest minimum terms. Make at least part of multiple sentences consecutive. No probation.	Impose highest minimum term. Make at least part of multiple sentences consecutive. No probation.
5		Impose one of three lowest minimum terms. Some form of probation indicated only with special mitigation.	Impose one of three lowest minimum terms. No probation.	Impose one of three highest minimum terms. No probation.	Impose one of three highest minimum terms. No probation.	Impose one of two highest minimum terms. Make at least part of multiple sentences consecutive. No probation.
4		Impose one of two lowest minimum terms. Some form of probation indicated.	Impose one of three lowest minimum terms. Some form of probation indicated only with special mitigation.	Impose one of three lowest minimum terms. No probation.	Impose one of three highest minimum terms. No probation.	Impose one of three highest minimum terms. No probation.
3		Impose one of two lowest minimum terms. Some form of probation indicated.	Impose one of two lowest minimum terms. Some form of probation indicated.	Impose one of three lowest minimum terms. Some form of probation indicated only with special mitigation.	Impose one of three lowest minimum terms. No probation.	Impose one of three highest minimum terms. No probation.
0 - 2		Impose lowest minimum term. Some form of probation indicated.	Impose one of two lowest minimum terms. Some form of probation indicated.	Impose one of two lowest minimum terms. Some form of probation indicated.	Impose one of three lowest minimum terms. Some form of probation indicated only with special mitigation.	Impose one of three lowest minimum terms. No probation.

FELONY SENTENCING WORKSHEET (continued)_____

PROBATION AVAILABILITY

Sometimes the preceding chart will indicate probation when it is forbidden by law in the particular case. Before recommending or imposing sentence in any case, consult the statutes for probationability and check the boxes below if applicable.

☐ **OFFENDER IS A REPEAT OFFENDER OR A DANGEROUS OFFENDER.** See RC 2929.01 for definitions. Probation for drug treatment permitted in limited cases under RC 2951.04 (B) (3).

☐ **OFFENSE IS NON-PROBATIONAL PER SE.** Indicates aggravated murder, murder, rape, felonious sexual penetration, any offense committed while armed with a firearm or dangerous ordnance, and any offense in which a sentence of "actual incarceration" is required.

SENTENCE IMPOSED; VARIANCES

ACTUAL SENTENCE IMPOSED
Term imposed each count, and fine if any

_____

_____

_____

_____

☐ Committed to serve sentence.

☐ Committed but shock probation possible.

☐ Other probation granted (describe)

_____

_____

REASONS FOR VARIANCE
If the actual sentence imposed varies from the disposition indicated on the chart in any respect, state the reasons for the variance.

_____

_____

_____

_____

_____

_____

_____

_____

549

CLIENT RISK AND NEED ASSESSMENT SURVEY _____

DEPARTMENT OF CORRECTIONS
DIVISION OF PROBATION & PAROLE

Client No. _____   Client Name: _____

Officer No. _____

CLIENT RISK ASSESSMENT

Instructions: Enter numerical rating in box at right.

1. **TOTAL NUMBER OF PRIOR FELONY CONVICTIONS:**
   (include juvenile adjudications, if known):
   a. None. .... Enter 0
   b. One... Enter 2
   c. Two or more .... Enter 4

2. **PRIOR NUMBER OF PROBATION/PAROLE SUPERVISION PERIODS:**
   (include juvenile, if known):
   a. None .... Enter 0
   b. One or more... Enter 4

3. **PRIOR PROBATION/PAROLE REVOCATIONS:**
   (adult only)
   a. None .... Enter 0
   b. One or more .... Enter 4

4. **AGE AT FIRST KNOWN CONVICTION OR ADJUDICATION:**
   (include juvenile, if known)
   a. 24 years or older .... Enter 0
   b. 20 through 23 years .... Enter 2
   c. 19 years or younger... Enter 4

5. **HISTORY OF ALCOHOL ABUSE:**
   a. No history of abuse.. Enter 0
   b. Occasional or prior abuse .... Enter 2
   c. Frequent current abuse.. Enter 4

6. **HISTORY OF OTHER SUBSTANCE ABUSE:**
   (prior to incarceration for parolees):
   a. No history of abuse.. Enter 0
   b. Occasional or prior abuse .... Enter 1
   c. Frequent current abuse.. Enter 2

CLIENT RISK AND NEED ASSESSMENT SURVEY (continued)_____

7. AMOUNT OF TIME EMPLOYED IN LAST 12 MONTHS:
(prior to incarceration for parolees; based on 35-hr. week):
a. 7 months or more ....Enter 0
b. 4 months through 6 months ....Enter 1
c. Less than 4 months ....Enter 2
d. Not applicable..Enter 0

8. AGENT IMPRESSION OF OFFENDER'S ATTITUDE:
a. Motivated to change; receptive to assistance ....Enter 0
b. Dependent or unwilling to accept responsibility...Enter 3
c. Rationalizes behavior, negative; not motivated to change.....................................Enter 5

9. RECORD OF CONVICTION FOR SELECTED OFFENSES:
(include current offense; add categories and enter total):
a. None of the following...Enter 0
b. Burglary, Theft, Auto Theft, Robbery .... Add 2
c. Forgery, Deceptive Practices (Fraud, Bad Check, Drugs) .... Add 3

10. ASSAULTIVE OFFENSES:
Crimes against persons, which include use of weapon, physical force, threat of force, all sex crimes, and vehicular homicide. Yes/No (circle one)

Total Score (Range: 0-34):

CLIENT RISK AND NEED ASSESSMENT SURVEY (continued) _____

CLIENT NEED ASSESSMENT

Instructions: Enter numerical rating in box at right.

1. ACADEMIC/VOCATIONAL SKILLS:
    a. High school or above skill level .... Enter 0
    b. Has vocational training, additional not needed/desired .... Enter 1
    c. Has some skills; additional needed/desired... Enter 3
    d. No skills; training needed... Enter 5

2. EMPLOYMENT:
    a. Satisfactory employment for 1 year or longer.. Enter 0
    b. Employed; no difficulties reported; or homemaker, student, retired, or disabled and
        unable to work ....Enter 1
    c. Part-time, seasonal, unstable employment or needs additional employment; unemployed, but
        has a skill .... Enter 4
    d. Unemployed & virtually unemployable; needs training .... Enter 7

3. FINANCIAL STATUS:
    a. Longstanding pattern of self-sufficiency... Enter 0
    b. No current difficulties... Enter 1
    c. Situational or minor difficulties.. Enter 4
    d. Severe difficulties ....Enter 6

4. LIVING ARRANGEMENTS (within last six months):
    a. Stable and supportive relationships with family or others in living group .... Enter 0
    b. Client lives alone or independently within another household... Enter 1
    c. Client experiencing occasional, moderate interpersonal problems within living group ..... Enter 4
    d. Client experiencing frequent and serious interpersonal problems within living group....... Enter 6

5. EMOTIONAL STABILITY:
    a. No symptoms of instability... Enter 1
    b. Symptoms limit, but do not prohibit adequate functioning .... Enter 5
    c. Symptoms prohibit adequate functioning.. Enter 8

6. ALCOHOL USAGE (Current):
    a. No interference with functioning.. Enter 1
    b. Occasional abuse; some disruption of functioning; may need treatment .... Enter 4
    c. Frequent substance abuse; serious disruption; needs treatment........................... Enter 7

7. OTHER SUBSTANCE USAGE (Current):
    a. No interference with functioning.. Enter 1
    b. Occasional substance abuse, some disruption of functioning; may need treatment........... Enter 4
    c. Frequent substance abuse; serious disruption; needs treatment........................... Enter 6

CLIENT RISK AND NEED ASSESSMENT SURVEY (continued)_____

8. REASONING/INTELLECTUAL ABILITY:
  a. Able to function independently .... Enter 1
  b. Some need for assistance; potential for adequate adjustment............................ Enter 4
  c. Deficiencies suggest limited ability to function independently .... Enter 7

9. HEALTH
  a. Sound physical health, seldom ill.. Enter 1
  b. Handicap or illness interferes with functioning on a recurring basis .... Enter 2
  c. Serious handicap or chronic illness; needs frequent medical care...................... Enter 3

10. AGENT'S IMPRESSION OF CLIENT'S NEEDS:
  a. None.. Enter 0
  b. Low .... Enter 1
  c. Moderate .... Enter 4
  d. High .... Enter 6

Total Score (Range 5-61)

SCORING AND OVERRIDE

Instructions: Check appropriate block.

SCORE-BASED SUPERVISION LEVEL: ☐ Maximum ☐ Medium ☐ Minimum

Check if there is an override: ☐ Explain: _____

FINAL CATEGORY OF SUPERVISION: ☐ Maximum ☐ Medium ☐ Minimum

APPROVED:_____
        (Supervisor Signature and Date)   Agent

Date Supervision Level Assigned: MONTH: DAY: YEAR:

553

RISK ASSESSMENT SCORING GUIDE

This scale emphasizes behavior while on supervision. The reassessment is based on behavior since the last classification form was completed.

1.   Total number of prior felony convictions (include juvenile adjudications if known).

   A.   Do not count present offense. The item refers to prior convictions.
   B.   Multiple convictions are counted as separate offenses.
   C.   For juveniles, this includes only behavior that would be a felony if committed by an adult.

2.   Prior number of probation/parole supervision periods (include juvenile, if known).

   A.   Revocation hearings that result in a continuance are not counted as a new period of probation/parole.
   B.   For juvenile records count only those periods of probation that follow an actual adjudication.
   C.   Note: The officer needs only one prior probation/parole in order to move client out of the 0 category. It is not necessary to know the total number of revocations that may have occurred.

3.   Prior probation/parole revocations - (adult only)

   A.   Disposition of the court or board must be revocation, even though the client may later be reinstated or immediately granted a new parole/probation.

4.   Age at first known conviction or adjudication, include juvenile if known.

   A.   Convictions may be for a felony or misdemeanor.
   B.   Exclude routine traffic, such as: speeding, stop sign, parking violations, etc. Include convictions for DUI, Reckless Driving, Careless Driving, etc.
   C.   For juvenile, include only those instances where a person has actually been adjudicated for a crime they could be convicted of if they were an adult.

5.   History of alcohol abuse.

   A.   This item should be interpreted to mean "in the last 36 months."
   B.   The officer is not to make a judgment based simply on number of drinks consumed per day or information of that nature; rather, does the client's drinking interfere with his/her ability to function and meet day-to-day demands. Indications of problems in this area would thus include such things as arriving for work late due to a hangover, frequent drunken quarrels at home or work, excessive expenditure on alcohol, etc. Alcohol-related arrests should generally be coded as indications of serious problems.

RISK ASSESSMENT SCORING GUIDE (continued) _____

    C. Probationers/parolees being supervised for a crime such as DUI Manslaughter should automatically be scored as 4.

6.   History of other substance abuse.

    A. The officer should interpret this item to mean "in the last 36 months." The scoring of this item is similar to that of the alcohol item with one difference. The officer must bear in mind that drug usage may, in itself, be a violation of the law and thus is much more threatening to the client's remaining out of legal trouble. The officer should be attuned to other problems stemming from legal drug use as well. In this regard, prescriptions that the client has should be scrutinized in terms of both frequency and duration of usage.

7.   Amount of time employed in the last 12 months (prior to any incarceration based on a 35-hour week).

    A. A person will receive a 0 in this category if he has been employed for seven or more months, averaging at least 35 hours per week during the last 12 months.

        A person will receive a score of 1 if he has been employed four to six months, averaging a 35-hour week during the last 12 months.

        A client will receive a 2 if he has been employed less than four months throughout the past twelve months.

    B. Part-time employment should be averaged. If a client has been employed for the past twelve months working 20 hours per week, he would receive a score of 1.

    C. Students are scored non-applicable, even though they may have been working part-time. Use non-applicable if in the officer's judgment, there are valid reasons why the client could not have been employed, as in situations of extended illness, disability, or are retired and receiving a monthly retirement check.

8.   Current Living Situation: This area can only be determined after a home visit has been conducted.

    A. A person will receive a 0 in this category if his present living situation is stable. There must be an adequate income and no serious family disturbances such as fights that require law enforcement or outside parties to calm the incident. Takes pride in the appearance of his/her residence.

    B. A person will receive a 3 if there is an inadequate income in the home, occasional serious argument, which may require outside assistance to calm, and/or cluttered living area.

RISK ASSESSMENT SCORING GUIDE (continued) _____

    C. A person will receive a 5 if any of the following conditions exist: (1) there is little, if any, income coming into the home; (2) there are fights that require law enforcement assistance to calm; (3) there is separation or divorce; (4) there is a dirty, cluttered home; (5) child protective has investigated abuse or neglect or any other serious incident that creates disorganization or stress.

9.   Agent's impression of offender's attitude.

    A. This term is inherently subjective. The officer will find scoring easier if he/she focuses on the phrase "motivated to change." Does this client recognize the need for change, and does he/she accept the responsibility for change? Are there any indications that he/she is beginning to make initial behavior changes? The difference between a score of 3 or 5 would be the client's motivation to change.

10.   Record of conviction for selected offenses (include current offense—add categories and enter total).

    A. This category includes convictions, felony or misdemeanant, during the past five years.

    B. The only possible answers are 0, 2, 3, or 5. If the item does not apply, enter 0. The only way to receive 5 points is to have at least one offense that receives 2 points plus one that receives 3 points.

11.   Violent or assaultive offenses within the last five years.

    A. This category receives no points. If yes is checked, the client may be classified maximum regardless of the number of points acquired.

    B. If a client was committed to a treatment for custody, exclude the time spent in those facilities as part of the last five years, unless the client was convicted for a new offense.

    C. For parolees, count assaultive offenses occurring five years prior to incarceration.

    D. An assaultive offense is defined as an offense against a person that involves the use of a weapon, physical force or threat of force, all forcible felonies, and all sex crimes.

    E. The current offense is counted if it is assaultive.

NEEDS ASSESSMENT SCORING GUIDE _____

INTRODUCTION

The needs assessment form has been constructed to provide a standardized information base from which programs may be developed. Its purpose is to serve as a tool in making objective classification decisions.

The items and scores on the instrument are based on agent's time required to deal with the various problem areas and levels. The basic idea behind the scoring of each item is the same: to what extent, if any, is the client's ability to function in the day-to-day world impaired. The needs assessment instrument differs from the risk assessment instrument in that both positive and negative points are awarded.

The form is designed to indicate areas of programming need and to distinguish among those clients who definitely need programming, those that may require some programming, and those who need no programming in each designated area. The needs assessment form has not been designed to make classification a more rigid, mechanical, or routine process, nor is its purpose to eliminate client input. In those areas where programming is definitely needed or may be needed, the agent should discuss with the client the various program options and the nature of each program. After reviewing the needed programming and the options available, the probation/parole officer should formulate a supervision plan.

The usefulness of the needs assessment instrument is largely dependent on the quality of information relied upon.

The goal of the needs assessment instrument is to eliminate subjectivity and the personal interpretation from the classification decision-making process. The new classification process will consist of decisions based on objective criteria. It is believed that this process will be beneficial to both the probation and parole officer who must justify their decisions and to clients being classified who demand fairness.

1. ACADEMIC AND VOCATIONAL SKILLS

The item focuses on functional skills rather than actual academic credentials. Therefore, a skilled craftsman may receive zero even though he or she may have little formal education. The individual's ability to make his or her way in the world is an important consideration. College, high school diploma, or G.E.D. may not be enough—ability must be shown.

    (a) High school or above skill level (demonstrates ability) ....Enter 1
    (b) Has vocational training; additional not needed/desired (adequate skills)...........................Enter 1
    (c) Has some skills; additional needed/desired, low skill level, may have high school diploma
       or G.E.D. but demonstrates difficulty reading and writing. Real difficulty filling out writ-
       ten reports or job applications. Has ability to do better...Enter 3
    (d) No skills; training needed, minimal-retarded, special education classes or unable to read,
       write, or do simple mathematical computations..Enter 5

2. EMPLOYMENT

The probation/parole officer must look beyond simple employment/unemployment in rating the item. Under-employment should be taken into account as should "unsatisfactory" employment. An example of "unsatisfactory"

NEEDS ASSESSMENT SCORING GUIDE (continued) _____

employment would be a client with a serious alcohol problem and repeated alcohol-related offenses who is employed as a bartender. In order to score this item, the probation/parole officer must establish a firm employment chronology. While attempting to do so, the agent should be particularly sensitive to gaps in employment.

   (a) Satisfactory employment for one year or longer, likes the job, salary sufficient to pay for basic needs, education or vocational background. ....Enter 0
   (b) Employed; no difficulties reported, or homemaker, student, retired, or disabled and unable to work, chance for upward advancement with current employer. ....Enter 1
   (c) Part-time, seasonal, unstable employment and needs additional employment; unemployed, but has a skill, job has no future. ....Enter 4
   (d) Unemployed and virtually unemployable; needs training, large gaps in employment, culturally handicapped, self-employment highly questionable. ....Enter 7

3. FINANCIAL STATUS

Does the client have the skills to handle the simple financial responsibilities of everyday life such as maintaining a checking account and preparing a personal budget?

   (a) Long-standing pattern of self-sufficiency, well-off. ....Enter 0
   (b) No current difficulties, providing—not overextending, no serious indebtedness. ....Enter 1
   (c) Situational or minor difficulties, employed but not making it, difficulty in paying court obligations, overextending, difficulty paying bills...Enter 4
   (d) Severe difficulties, welfare, can't pay court obligations, bankruptcy. ....Enter 6

4. LIVING ARRANGEMENTS (Within the last six months)

   (a) Stable and supportive relationship with family or other living group, marriage intact—no history of separation; both parents together, no prior criminal record for other family member, good attitude toward spouse/parents..Enter 0
   (b) Client lives alone or independently within another household, relatively stable, getting along, no noticeable problems. ....Enter 1
   (c) Client experiencing occasional, moderate interpersonal problems with living group, disorganized, recognize problems exist, motivated to change. ....Enter 4
   (d) Client exhibiting frequent and serious interpersonal problems within living group, children removed, recently separated or divorced (within two years); history of bad marriage; extensive prior criminal records of family members; sexual abuse; lack of control; abusive drinking; domestic violence. ....Enter 6

5. EMOTIONAL STABILITY

Guides for the probation/parole officer in regard to this item are as follows: Does the client deal with anger appropriately? Does he/she exhibit excessive anxiety or become immobilized by stress? Ability to cope with day-to-day life situations is a concern here. The 5 score would be used for a neurotic client, with 8 reserved for those with psychotic characteristics.

NEEDS ASSESSMENT SCORING GUIDE (continued) _____

(a) No symptoms of instability; no apparent stress, well-adjusted ....Enter 1

(b) Symptoms limit, but do not prohibit adequate functioning; neurotic, mild symptoms of
depression, anxiety, or acting out, occasional abuse of alcohol or other drugs ....Enter 5

(c) Symptoms prohibit adequate functioning; psychotic, severe symptoms of depression,
anxiety, or acting out, frequent use of alcohol or other drugs; suicidal ....Enter 8

6. ALCOHOL USAGE (Current)

As on the risk assessment instrument, "interference with functioning" is the key here. Parole/probation officers are to avoid moral judgments regarding alcohol use and focus instead on the role of alcohol in the client's life. Alcohol-related driving offenses receive a 7.

(a) No interference with functioning, no alcohol abuse..Enter 1

(b) Occasional abuse; some disruption of functioning; may need treatment; gets
"drunk" by own definition twice a month or more; some disruption in functioning
when drinking (whether or not "drunk") with family, work, socially, etc. Minor al-
cohol-related offenses ....Enter 4

(c) Frequent abuse; serious disruption; needs treatment; drinks regularly although never or
rarely gets "drunk"; has withdrawal symptoms if stops drinking; has physical symptoms of
alcoholism; memory lapse, blackouts, passing out; serious disfunction at work; absen-
teeism, fired, fights with co-workers or other supervisors or customers; with family, becomes violent, neglectful, abusive toward spouse, children, parents, can't pay bills,
separation occurrence; past driving record involving alcohol; present offense or any arrests
within the past five years involving alcohol before or during ....Enter 7

7. OTHER SUBSTANCE ABUSE (Current)

The scoring of this item is to be accomplished in the same manner as the "drug usage" item in the risk assessment instrument. A 4 score would apply to clients convicted of marijuana possession while the 6 would refer to present involvement with the drug.

(a) No interference with functioning, no abuse..Enter 1

(b) Occasional substance abuse; some disruption of functioning; may need treatment; convicted of marijuana possession, but no longer using..Enter 4

(c) Frequent substance abuse; serious disruption; needs treatment; addiction or recent use of
marijuana, narcotics, medication as not prescribed; conviction for possession or intent to
deliver; deals in selling of drugs..Enter 6

8. REASONING/INTELLECTUAL ATTITUDE

This item looks at organic cognitive capacity as opposed to emotional ability, hence the problem level relates to the possibility of retardation. Is the client mentally alert or able to function effectively?

(a) Able to function independently; appears to be average intelligence. Can comprehend
what is being said in normal conversation. Can read and comprehend rules of proba-
tion/parole ....Enter 1

NEEDS ASSESSMENT SCORING GUIDE (continued) _____

     (b) Some need for assistance; potential for adequate adjustment; has difficulty in completing forms without assistance; has difficulty understanding written or verbal communication; has difficulty using or reading a clock, ruler, calendar, dictionary; has difficulty in following directions; emphasis on difficulty in comprehension ....Enter 4
     (c) Deficiencies suggest limited ability to function independently; borderline mental retardation; client cannot function independently; client receives SSI benefits for reason due to developmental disabilities; client is employed in shelter work house ....Enter 7

9. HEALTH

The probation/parole officer should take mental health into account (particularly in the case of the substance abuser), as well as the presence of physical handicaps. Alcoholism or drug abuse is automatically 2 points.

     (a) Sound physical health; seldom ill; no problems. ....Enter 1
     (b) Handicap or illness interferes with functioning on a reoccurring basis; client may have a condition that restricts employment, requires occasional medical attention (high blood pressure, heart condition, epilepsy, missing limb, back problems, etc.) ....Enter 2
     (c) Serious handicap or chronic illnesses; needs frequent medical care; client has a condition that severely restricts employment and program participation. He/she requires frequent medical attention and may be on medication (blindness, serious heart conditions, terminal illness, deafness, paralysis, etc.) ....Enter 3

10. AGENT'S IMPRESSION OF CLIENT'S NEEDS

This is designed to accommodate the agent's subjective impressions.

     (a) None. ....Enter 0
     (b) Low ....Enter 1
     (c) Moderate...Enter 4
     (d) High..Enter 6

PRINCIPLES OF CLASSIFICATION

The foundation of classification is a system—the organized and established procedure for combining an interdependent group of events into a unified whole. A system entails the coming together of all components to produce a product: classification. The type of system that exists will determine the type of classification that exists. The *process* by which classification is effected is an integral part of the product. If the process (embodied in the policy and procedure manual) changes, then the classification decisions will change.

Any classification system must operate on the basis of valid principles; those presented below describe the factors necessary for a classification system to exist (Solomon 1980). (In addition, the 14 principles listed below make up the criteria for a classification system assessment tool for evaluating basic system functioning. Specific methods for use of the principles as an assessment tool are discussed in Section 5, *Prison Classification: A Model Systems Approach*.) It is important to note that the following principles must apply to the *entire* prison system, including women and youthful offender institutions and programs.

1. There must be a clear definition of goals and objectives of the total correctional system.

Traditionally, security and custody have been the primary goals and objectives of correctional systems. While most also have rehabilitation as a goal, it is secondary to security and custody, as the latter comprise the primary public mandate to corrections. Humane care and treatment, however, should be integral to all systems.

Prior to attempting to design a classification process or other system-wide program, the Department of Corrections must be very clear as to its own goals and objectives (its function, purpose, and priorities). These should be realistic and understandable to both staff and inmates.

Within these goals, a classification system can be developed to sort those inmates whose identified needs fall within the agency's objectives. Only after conceptualizing its own goals can a correctional system develop a rational classification process.

2. There must be detailed written procedures and policies governing the classification process.

An essential component for a classification decision-making model is a policy statement that sets forth the Department of Corrections' goals, objectives, and purposes for the new classification system. For example, when developing its new classification system in 1979, the Minnesota Department of Corrections based the system on eight departmental "principles" regrading classification. These principles, in order of importance to Minnesota's Department of Corrections, are:

- Minimize risk to the public
- Minimize risk to other inmates and institution staff
- Minimize breaches of security
- Minimize system risk
- Minimize security levels
- Maximize fairness (similar offenders treated in a similar manner)
- Maximize the objective and quantitative nature of all classification criteria
- Maximize inmate understanding of the classification system and inmate participation in program decisions

PRINCIPLES OF CLASSIFICATION (continued)

Policies such as Minnesota's should be included in a comprehensive departmental classification policy manual. The American Correctional Association (ACA) Manual of Standards for Adult Correctional Institutions (1977) calls "essential" (Standard No. 4373) a ". . . classification manual containing all the classification policies and detailed procedures for implementing policies; this manual is made available to all staff involved with classification and is reviewed at least annually and updated as necessary."* The manual must be written clearly and concisely and *must* be understood by classification personnel. The policies contained in the manual should deal with such classification issues as:

- Initial inmate classification and reclassification
- Instructions regarding the makeup of classification committees, units, and teams and the full responsibilities of each
- Definitions of various committees' responsibilities for custody, employment, and vocational/program assignments
- Instructions concerning potential changes in an inmate's program
- Procedures relating to inmate transfer from one program to another and from one institution to another
- Content of the classification interview
- Method of documentation of decisions made

Since classification policies must be dynamic, constantly subject to change and revision as the classification process is continuously evaluated, the classification manual should be prepared in such a manner as to provide for easy update. (An important caution here is that the length of the manual is not necessarily correlated with its quality.)

3. The classification process must provide for the collection of complete, high-quality, verified, standardized data.

The classification system must define the data needed and the format in which it is to be collected and analyzed. High-quality, standardized data is essential to a valid statistical base for classification decision making and for correlation of prediction and need factors.

Complete and verified data permits:

- Equitable determinations based on particular factors of individual cases
- Similar decisions among individual classification analysts on roughly comparable cases
- Quantitative analysis of trends in classification decision making for individual facilities or the Department of Corrections as a whole

Through its technical assistance projects, NIC has found that the quantity and quality of offender data (criminal history, personal and family background, etc.) available to teams when the classification decision must be made are frequently less than adequate, and sometimes entirely unusable. Forms often are incomplete, some data collected are of questionable relevance, and much information is subject to broad interpretation because of its qualitative (narrative) nature.

---

*This standard has since been superseded by Standard 3-4282, which states: "Written policy, procedure, and practice provide for a written inmate classification plan. The plan specifies the objectives of the classification system and methods for achieving them, and it provides a monitoring and evaluation mechanism to determine whether the objectives are being met. The plan is reviewed at least annually and updated as needed." Standards for Adult Correctional Institutions, Third edition, 1990.

PRINCIPLES OF CLASSIFICATION (continued) _____

In many of the systems studied, NIC found that no specific guidelines were given to field staff regarding the collection of offender background data necessary for a valid classification decision. Without specific and objective guidelines, field staff are not likely to prepare reports sufficiently comprehensive and reliable to be used in an empirically valid statistical analysis.

4. Measurement and testing instruments used in the classification decision-making process must be valid, reliable, and objective.

The numerous legal grievances filed by inmates in recent years charging that classification decision-making processes are discriminatory, biased, or invalid point up the necessity to ensure that any tests administered to inmates have been validated for reliability as predictors of custody and/or program needs. In addition, correctional departments must be able to demonstrate that the testing processes are objective, logical, and fundamentally fair and are designed to meet the needs of both the inmates and the institution. By the same token, tests designed for other purposes should not be used to classify inmates (I.Q. tests, personality inventories).

In mid-1979, NIC sponsored a national survey of screening and classification processes, which assessed the current state-of-the-art in the design and utilization of classification instruments for decision making (American Justice Institute 1979). The survey found that correctional agencies have been shifting from subjective judgments to standardized instruments for classification decision making. The instruments being used are printed forms containing a fixed set of weighted criteria that provide an overall offender summary score. Considerations of this score in the process assists the classification team in making more uniform and consistent decisions that are less subject to legal challenge. (North Carolina and Minnesota submitted their instruments for legal review prior to implementation.) In some states, the forms are used both for custody and needs decision making.

5. There must be explicit policy statements structuring and checking the discretionary decision-making powers of classification team staff.

A corrections department must establish clear guidelines governing the discretionary decision-making powers of classification team staff. Otherwise, the department leaves itself open to allegations of unfairness, arbitrariness, and bias.

Discretionary powers of classification staff remain unstructured in too many systems. One example of the resultant problems was provided by a state corrections department in a grant application to NIC: "There is a very broad range of subjective and informal criteria used by those responsible for the classification of inmates; each person involved in the classification process has internalized his own set of significant variables, has established the relative importance of each of these variables according to his own value scale, and applies these standards in the classification decision on a case-by-case basis.

While discretion cannot and should not be completely eliminated, steps can be taken to designate boundaries within which classification decisions will be made, thus eliminating too broad discretionary power of individuals. A system in which the classification processes, rules, policies, findings, and reasons are open to scrutiny can further serve to check discretion.

Structuring and checking discretion is the responsibility of the Department of Corrections' central office. This responsibility is carried out by:

- Direction and supervision of the classification process by high-level central office personnel
- Establishment of procedures for interinstitutional transfer, including review by central office staff and an appeal procedure and administrative review of difficult cases
- Establishment of procedures for central office monitoring and evaluation of the classification process to ensure that it is operating according to policy
- Establishment of procedures for consideration of mitigating or aggravating factors in decision making
- Initiation of policy pertaining to classification, inmate programs/treatment, and casework, including a classification manual
- Selection, training, and supervision of counselors and other classification staff members

6. **There must be provision for screening and further evaluating inmates who are management problems and those who have special needs.**

   This necessary function, also the responsibility of the Department of Corrections' central office, must be included in any model classification system.

   Inmates who are management problems and require special considerations in placement and programming fall into several categories:

   - Those who require protection and separation because they may be in danger from other inmates
   - Those who, by reason of their offense, criminal record, or institutional behavior require particularly close supervision
   - Those who received unusual publicity because of the nature of their crime, arrest, or trial or who were involved in criminal activities of a sophisticated nature, such as organized crime

   The most dangerous inmates must be separated from the less violent individuals; thus, the classification process, by necessity, needs to include procedures to determine which inmates are potentially dangerous, such as those who have a history of assaultive or predatory behavior.

   In addition to screening and further evaluating inmates who are management problems, the correctional system's central office must provide for inmates who have special needs. Those individuals who, through effective screening, are shown to require special program assignments and monitoring include, but are not limited to, the aged and infirm, the mentally ill and retarded, and those with special medical problems.

7. **There must be provisions to match offenders with programs; these provisions must be consistent with risk classification needs.**

   This process involves the establishment of clear, operational definitions of the various types of offenders and available institutional programs. But risk as well as need factors must be considered when decisions are being made.

   Thus, NIC recommends that the classification process be directed toward:

   - Identifying and evaluating the factors underlying each inmate's needs
   - Recommending programs and activities for inmates according to their *specific* needs and the availability of resources

PRINCIPLES OF CLASSIFICATION (continued) _____

- Developing and recording the necessary data to support services and long-range program planning

To fulfill these tasks, it is necessary to identify and utilize *all* programs that are available to each individual inmate. This function can be accomplished through a systematic classification of the offender and subsequent development of a program plan specifically designed for him/her.

8. There must be provision to classify each inmate at the least restrictive custody level.

This model classification system component targets the prevalent problem of overclassification. Eliminating overclassification is among the most significant objectives of new classification systems being designed and implemented in Minnesota, Tennessee, New York, and other states.

The first step involved here is developing specific criteria for differential custody assignments. Equally crucial is the second step of ensuring that both staff and inmates are aware of these criteria.

NIC recommends that clearly understandable custody definitions and supervision guidelines be applied system-wide. At a minimum, definitions should be given for (1) the traditional levels of custody—maximum, close, medium, and community and (2) the different uses of segregation (especially disciplinary segregation). A basic premise is that every inmate should be in the lowest custody believed suitable for adequate supervision and warranted by his/her behavior.

9. There must be provision to involve the inmate in the classification process.

Each new inmate should be provided with a copy of the custody criteria; a written explanation of the classification process; and a written explanation of the health care, employment, vocational training, education, transfer, and special programs available, including the selection criteria for each.

In addition, the correctional system should provide for classification teams at each institution so the inmate can participate in the classification decision-making process. ACA standard No. 4374 [Standard 3-4284, Third edition, 1990] calls for "maximum involvement of . . . the inmate in classification reviews." The inmate should be present except, perhaps, during deliberations of the classification team.

10. There must be provisions for systematic, periodic reclassification hearings.

Providing for reclassification on a regularly scheduled basis is another "essential" standard (No. 4376)[Standard 3-4287, Third edition, 1990] recommended by the ACA. Periodic review and reclassification is a cornerstone of any model classification system.

In reporting on its study of the classification process at the Tennessee Department of Corrections, NIC suggested the adoption of the following reclassification guidelines:

- Review/reclassification within two weeks following the inmate's transfer from another institution within the system
- Review every three months for inmates serving terms of 18 months or less
- Review every six months for inmates serving terms of 18 months and one day to five years
- Annual review for inmates serving terms of five years of more (NIC now recommends review every six months.)

565

PRINCIPLES OF CLASSIFICATION (continued) _____

If suitable manpower is available, reviews can be conducted on a more frequent basis. Optimally, inmates should be permitted to initiate reviews of their progress, status, and programming (ACA "important" Standard No. 4379)[Standard 3-4290, Third edition, 1990].

11. The classification process must be efficient and economically sound.

An empirically based classification system should enable the Department of Corrections to handle large numbers of offenders efficiently through a grouping process based on needs and risk. This can be accomplished by using modern technology to assist in the storage, correlation, and retrieval of data, although use of a computer should not be essential.

An efficient, economically sound classification system also makes effective use of other components of the criminal justice system, as well as social service agencies, for the provisions of offender data (such as information obtained for pre-sentence reports).

The development of a model classification system should involve cooperating with other agencies to devise a standard reporting format for offender information, preferably one that elicits quantitative data insofar as possible.

12. There must be provisions to continuously evaluate and improve the classification process.

Any true process continuously strives to improve itself through feedback, evaluation, and action to correct deficiencies. Thus, the model classification system, if it is to be effective, must be able to continuously improve to meet the changing needs of the inmate population and the correctional system as a whole. It must be responsive to emerging knowledge and professional understanding of the classification process. The system must also be responsive to staff and inmate input.

13. Classification procedures must be consistent with constitutional requisites.

The central office must keep abreast of litigation applicable to its jurisdiction in order to ensure the continued legality of its classification policies, procedures, and decisions. Most state Departments of Correction have a legal section that can be of assistance in this area.

14. There must be an opportunity to gain input from administration and line staff when undertaking development of a classification system.

In summary, the hallmark of classification is *the non-capricious assignment of individuals*. In order to accomplish equity in custody, security, program and treatment determination, and placement, a system reflecting the above principles must exist. Furthermore, it must be utilized.

A basic tenet to classification takes the idea of non-capricious placement a step further. As stated earlier, classification seeks to determine the placement of individuals in accord with their various correctional needs. Each of these outcomes may be accomplished separately, but it is only when they are combined into a comprehensive process that strives for equity and objectivity that we define it as classification. Since equity and objectivity are goals, principles and procedures should be employed that reflect these aims.

INITIAL INMATE CLASSIFICATION_____

Custody

Name:_____ Number:_____

       Last   First   MI

Classification Caseworker:_____ Date:_____

1. HISTORY OF INSTITUTIONAL VIOLENCE   Score:_____

(Jail of Prison, code most serious within last five years)

None 0

Assault and battery not involving use of a weapon or resulting in serious injury 3

Assault and battery involving use of a weapon and/or resulting in serious injury or death 7

2. SEVERITY OF CURRENT OFFENSE   Score:_____

(Refer to the *Severity of Offense Scale* on p. 303. Score the most serious offense if there are multiple convictions.)

Low... 0

Low moderate 1

Moderate.. 2

High 4

Highest... 6

3. PRIOR ASSAULTIVE OFFENSE HISTORY   Score:_____

(Score the most severe in inmate's history. Refer to the *Severity of Offense Scale*.)

None, low, or low moderate 0

Moderate.. 2

High 4

Highest... 6

4. ESCAPE HISTORY (Rate last 3 years of incarceration)   Score:_____

No escapes or attempts (or no prior incarcerations) 0

An escape or attempt from minimum or community custody, no actual or threatened violence:

     Over 1 year ago 1

      Within the last year.. 3

An escape or attempt from medium, or above custody, or an escape from minimum or community custody with actual or threatened violence:

     Over 1 year ago 5

     Within the last year..7

CLOSE CUSTODY SCORE (Add items 1 through 4)

(If score is 10 or above, inmate should be assigned to close custody. If score is under 10, complete items 5 through 8 and use medium/minimum scale.)

INITIAL INMATE CLASSIFICATION (continued)_____

5. ALCOHOL/DRUG ABUSE   Score:_____
   None 0
   Abuse causing occasional legal and social adjustment problems 1
   Serious abuse, serious disruption of functioning 3

6. CURRENT DETAINER   Score:_____
   None 0
   Misdemeanor detainer 1
   Extradition initiated - misdemeanor 3
   Felony detainer 4
   Extradition initiated - felony 6

7. PRIOR FELONY CONVICTIONS   Score:_____
   None 0
   One 2
   Two or more 4

8. STABILITY FACTORS   Score:_____
   (Check appropriate box(s) and combine for score.)
   Age 26 or over .... -2
   High school diploma or GED received .... -1
   Employed or attending school (full or part-time) for six months or longer at time of arrest .... -1

MINIMUM/MEDIUM SCORE (Add items 1 through 8.)   **Total**
                                                                                                                        Score:_____
MEDIUM/MINIMUM SCALE:
   Medium Custody 7-22
   Minimum Custody .... 6 or less

INITIAL INMATE CLASSIFICATION (continued) _____

Severity of Offense Scale

(From Massachusetts Superior Court Sentencing Guidelines Project, 1979)

6 POINTS:

- Armed assault in a dwelling
- Armed robbery while masked
- Armed robbery
- Arson in a dwelling place, night, occupied
- Burglary, being armed
- Kidnapping to extort
- Murder*
- Rape
- Robbery
- Stealing by confining or putting in fear

5 POINTS:

- Extortion
- Incest
- Kidnapping
- Manslaughter
- Mayhem

4 POINTS:

- Arson (Note: not Arson as listed above)
- Breaking and entering, nighttime
- Burglary, not being armed
- Burning to defraud
- Burning insured property
- Burning real property
- Carrying a firearm+
- Common receiver
- Indecent A&B child under 14
- Mfg., dist., or poss. with intent to dist., Class A&B

INITIAL INMATE CLASSIFICATION (continued)_____

3 POINTS:
- Assault and battery to collect a loan
- Assault and battery with a dangerous weapon
- Assault with intent to murder, maim
- Assault with intent to rob while being armed
- Attempt to murder by poisoning
- Breaking and entering in the daytime

_____

Attempt or accessory before the fact of an offense receives the same score as the substantive offense.

*Score only if prior offense.

+If present offense, score only if *not* most serious offense.

INITIAL INMATE CLASSIFICATION (continued) _____

Assessment of Needs

NAME:_____ NUMBER:_____
     Last   First   MI

CLASSIFICATION CHAIRMAN:_____

DATE:_____

TEST SCORES: I.Q.:_____

                                                                                 Reading:_____

                                                                                  Math:_____

NEEDS ASSESSMENT: Select the answer that best describes the inmate.

HEALTH: Code:_____

1. Sound physical health, seldom ill.
2. Handicap or illness that interferes with functioning on a recurring basis.
3. Serious handicap or chronic illness, needs frequent medical care.

INTELLECTUAL ABILITY: Code:_____

1. Normal intellectual ability, able to function independently.
2. Mild retardation, some need for assistance.
3. Moderate retardation, independent functioning severely limited.

BEHAVIORAL/EMOTIONAL PROBLEMS: Code:_____

1. Exhibits appropriate emotional responses.
2. Symptoms limit adequate functioning, requires counseling, may require medication.
3. Symptoms prohibit adequate functioning, requires significant intervention, may require medication or separate housing.

ALCOHOL ABUSE:

                                                                              Code:_____

1. No alcohol problem.
2. Occasional abuse, some disruption of functioning.
3. Frequent abuse, serious disruption, needs treatment.

INITIAL INMATE CLASSIFICATION (continued)_____

DRUG ABUSE: Code:_____

1. No drug problem.   2. Occasional abuse, some   3. Frequent abuse, serious
                          disruption of functioning.   disruption, needs treatment.

EDUCATIONAL STATUS: Code:_____

1. Has high school diploma 2. Some deficits, but potential for 3. Major deficits in math and/or
   or GED.   high school diploma or GED.   reading, needs remedial programs.

VOCATIONAL STATUS: Code:_____

1. Has sufficient skills to 2. Minimal skill level, needs 3. Virtually unemployable, needs
   obtain and hold   enhancement.   training.
   satisfactory employment.

INITIAL INMATE CLASSIFICATION (continued) _____

Initial Classification Summary

1. Override Considerations   Code:_____
   - Custody Classification
      1. None
      2. Inmate Needs Protection
      3. Temporary Placement-Pending Investigation
      4. Temporary Placement-Punitive Isolation
      5. Temporary Placement-Suicide Threat   Score:_____
      6. Other, Specify:
                                                                  I.Q._____

      _____   Score:_____   Reading:_____

      _____   Math:_____

2. Custody Level Assignment: Code:_____
      1. Community
      2. Minimum
      3. Medium
      4. Close
      5. Maximum
      6. Protective Custody
      7. Other, Specify:
                                                                  Code:_____

      _____   Score:_____

                                                                  Code:_____

      _____   Score:_____

3. Facility Assignment: Code:_____

4. Program Recommendations   Score:_____
      (In order of priority)
                                                                  Code:_____

                            Program   Enrollment
                              Code   Code*
                                                  ☐
      _____   ____   ____   Code:_____
      _____   ____   ____
      _____   ____   ____   Score:_____   Code:_____
      _____   ____   ____

573

INITIAL INMATE CLASSIFICATION (continued)_____

5. Work Recommendations:

Work Code		Inmate Skills	Skill Code		
_____	___	_____	___	Score:_____	Code:_____
_____	___	_____	___		
_____	___	_____	___		
_____	___	_____	___		
_____	___	_____	___	Score:_____	Code:_____

Score:_____

TOTAL SCORE:_____

*Enrollment Code
Program available = 1
Program currently at capacity/unavailable = 2
Program needed but does not exist at required custody level = 3
Inmate refuses program = 4

CORRECTIONAL ADJUSTMENT CHECKLIST (CACL) _____

Name and number of inmate:_____

Name of person completing this checklist: _____

Your position:_____   Date completed:_____

Instructions: Please indicate which of the following behaviors this inmate exhibits. If the behavior describes the inmate, circle the "1." If it does not, circle the "O." *Please complete every item.*

0	1	1. Worried, anxious
0	1	2. Tries, but cannot seem to follow directions
0	1	3. Tense, unable to relax
0	1	4. Socially withdrawn
0	1	5. Continually asks for help from staff
0	1	6. Gets along with the hoods
0	1	7. Seems to take no pleasure in anything
0	1	8. Jittery, jumpy; seems afraid
0	1	9. Uses leisure time to cause trouble
0	1	10. Continually uses profane language; curses and swears
0	1	11. Easily upset
0	1	12. Sluggish and drowsy
0	1	13. Cannot be trusted at all
0	1	14. Moody, brooding
0	1	15. Needs constant supervision
0	1	16. Victimizes weaker inmates
0	1	17. Seems dull and unintelligent
0	1	18. Is an agitator about race
0	1	19. Continually tries to con staff
0	1	20. Impulsive; unpredictable
0	1	21. Afraid of other inmates
0	1	22. Seems to seek excitement
0	1	23. Never seems happy
0	1	24. Doesn't trust staff
0	1	25. Passive; easily led

CORRECTIONAL ADJUSTMENT CHECKLIST (continued) _____

0	1	26. Talks aggressively to other inmates
0	1	27. Accepts no blame for any of his troubles
0	1	28. Continually complains; accuses staff of unfairness
0	1	29. Daydreams; seems to be mentally off in space
0	1	30. Talks aggressively to staff
0	1	31. Has a quick temper
0	1	32. Obviously holds grudges; seeks to "get even"
0	1	33. Inattentive; seems preoccupied
0	1	34. Attempts to play staff against one another
0	1	35. Passively resistant; has to be forced to participate
0	1	36. Tries to form a clique
0	1	37. Openly defies regulations and rules
0	1	38. Often sad and depressed
0	1	39. Stirs up trouble among inmates
0	1	40. Aids or abets others in breaking the rules
0	1	41. Considers himself unjustly confined

Source: Herbert C. Quay, Ph.D.

RAW SCORE FORM: CORRECTIONAL ADJUSTMENT CHECKLIST (CACL) _____

Name and number of inmate:_____

Name of person completing this checklist:_____

Your position:_____ Date completed:_____

Instructions: For each "1" circled on the Correctional Adjustment Checklist, place a checkmark on the line corresponding to the item number. Add the checkmarks to obtain the Raw Score for each group.

Group

I	II	IV	V
			1. _____
		2. _____	3. _____
		4. _____	5. _____
6. _____		7. _____	8. _____
9. _____			
10. _____			11. _____
		12. _____	
13. _____		14. _____	
15. _____			
16. _____		17. _____	
18. _____	19. _____		
20. _____			21. _____
22. _____		23. _____	
	24. _____	25. _____	
26. _____			
27. _____	28. _____	29. _____	
30. _____			
31. _____			
32. _____		33. _____	
	34. _____	35. _____	
36. _____			
37. _____			38. _____
39. _____			
40. _____	41. _____		

Total (Raw Score): _____ _____ _____ _____

Source: Herbert C. Quay, Ph.D.

CHECKLIST FOR THE ANALYSIS OF
LIFE HISTORY RECORDS OF ADULT OFFENDERS (CALH) _____

Name and number of inmate:_____

Name of person completing this checklist:_____

Your position:_____ Date started: _____

Instructions: Circle each behavior trait that describes this inmate's life history.

1. Has few, if any, friends
2. Thrill-seeking
3. Preoccupied; "dreamy"
4. Uncontrollable as a child
5. Has expressed guilt over offense
6. Expresses need for self-improvement
7. Socially withdrawn
8. Weak, indecisive, easily led
9. Previous local, state, or federal incarceration
10. Tough, defiant
11. Irregular work history (if not a student)
12. Noted not to be responsive to counseling
13. Gives impression of ineptness, incompetence in managing everyday problems in living
14. Supported wife and children
15. Claims offense was motivated by family problems
16. Close ties with criminal elements
17. Depressed, morose
18. Physically aggressive (strongarm, assault, reckless homicide, attempted murder, mugging, etc.)
19. Apprehension likely due to "stupid" behavior on the part of the offender
20. Single marriage
21. Expresses feelings of inadequacy, worthlessness
22. Difficulties in the public schools
23. Suffered financial reverses prior to commission of offense for which incarcerated
24. Passive, submissive
25. Bravado, braggart
26. Guiltless; blames others
27. Expresses lack of concern for others

Source: Herbert C. Quay, Ph.D

RAW SCORE FORM: LIFE HISTORY CHECKLIST (CALH) _____

Name and number of inmate: _____

Name of person completing this checklist:_____

Your position: _____ Date completed: _____

Instructions: For each item circled on the Checklist for the Analysis of Life History Records of Adult Offenders, place a checkmark on the line corresponding to the item number. Add the checkmarks to obtain the Raw Score for each group.

	Group	
I	**III**	**IV**
		1. _____
2. _____		
		3. _____
4. _____		
	5. _____	
	6. _____	
		7. _____
		8. _____
9. _____		
10. _____		
11. _____		
12. _____		13. _____
	14. _____	
	15. _____	
16. _____		17. _____
18. _____		19. _____
	20. _____	
		21. _____
22. _____	23. _____	
		24. _____
25. _____		
26. _____		
27. _____		
Total (Raw Score):	_____	_____ _____

Source: Herbert C. Quay, Ph.D.

RAW SCORE TO NORMALIZED T-SCORE CONVERSIONS
FOR CORRECTIONAL ADJUSTMENT CHECKLIST (CACL)_____

Scale I		Scale II		Scale IV		Scale V	
Raw score	T-score	Raw score	T-score	Raw score	T-score	Raw score	T-score
0	41	0	44	0	40	0	39
1	49	1	54	1	47	1	46
2	53	2	59	2	51	2	50
3	56	3	62	3	54	3	54
4	58	4	65	4	56	4	57
5	59	5	70	5	59	5	61
6	60			6	61	6	65
7	61			7	63	7	71
8	62			8	65		
9	63			9	69		
10	64			10	73		
11	65			11	78		
12	66						
13	67						
14	68						
15	69						
16	71						
17	73						
18	76						

RAW SCORE TO NORMALIZED T-SCORE CONVERSIONS
FOR LIFE HISTORY CHECKLIST (CALH)

Scale I		Scale III		Scale IV	
Raw score	T-score	Raw score	T-score	Raw score	T-score
0	35	0	39	0	39
1	43	1	47	1	47
2	47	2	52	2	53
3	51	3	58	3	58
4	55	4	64	4	62
5	58	5	70	5	66
6	61	6	76	6	70
7	64			7	74
8	67			8	82
9	71			9	90
10	75				
11	82				

CLASSIFICATION PROFILE FOR ADULT OFFENDERS _____

Name and number of inmate: _____

Name of person completing this profile: _____

Your position: _____   Date: _____

	Scale	Raw Score	T-score
1. Correctional Adjustment Checklist (CACL)	I	_____	_____
	II	_____	_____
	IV	_____	_____
	V	_____	_____
Checklist for the Analysis of Life History Records (CALH)	I	_____	_____
	III	_____	_____
	IV	_____	_____

	Scale	CACL T-score		CALH T-score		Final T-score
2. Combined Scores	I	_____	+	_____	+ 2 =	_____
	II	_____			=	_____
	III			_____	=	_____
	IV	_____	+	_____	+ 2 =	_____
	V	_____			=	_____

3. Assignment   _____ Group I   _____ Group III   _____ Group IV
                       _____ Group II   _____ Group V

CLASSIFICATION PROFILE FOR ADULT OFFENDERS (continued) _____

Instructions:

1. Transfer Totals from Raw Score forms onto appropriate Raw Score lines.

   Using the appropriate conversion table, convert each Raw Score to a T-score.
   - If two CACLS are used per inmate, convert all Raw Scores to T-scores; then add the T-scores obtained for each scale and divide the sum by 2.

2. List the final CACL and CALH T-scores on the appropriate lines in the Combined Scores section.
   - For Scales I and IV, add the T-scores and divide by 2.

3. Use the highest Final T-score to make the final assignment.

   If the two scores are tied, use the following tie-breaker rules:
   - If Group I and Group II are tied for highest,
     —and there is one housing unit for *both* groups, assign to Heavy.
     —and there is one housing unit for *each* group, assign for the best balance or use of available housing.
   - If Group IV and Group V are tied for highest,
     —and there is one housing unit for both groups, assign to Light.
     —and there is one housing unit for each group, assign for the best balance or use of available housing.
   - If Group I *or* Group II are tied with any other group, assign to Heavy.
   - If Group IV *or* Group V are tied with Group III, assign to Light.

(Note: Before using any tie-breaker rules, recheck all scoring and calculations.)

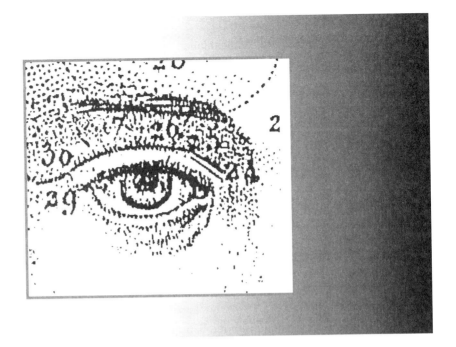

Index

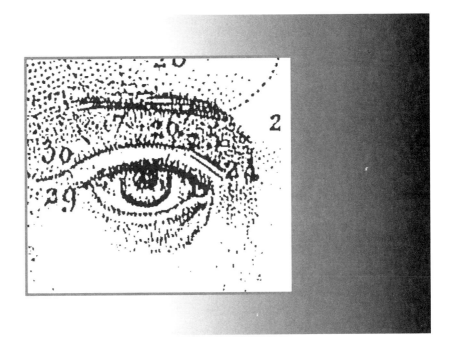

About the Authors

Anthony Walsh received his Ph.D. in criminology from Bowling Green University in Ohio in 1983. He has field experience in both law enforcement and corrections. He teaches criminology, law, and statistics at Boise State University, in Idaho. He is the author, co-author, editor, or co-editor of 27 books and more than 100 journal articles. His primary interest is in the integration of the biological and social sciences in the development of a truly scientific criminology. His latest books are *Law, Society, and Justice: A Sociolegal Introduction* (2008), *Criminology: A Text/Reader* (2009); and *Biology and Criminology: The Biosocial Synthesis* (2009). He is married to the sweetest and most drop-dead gorgeous woman on the planet.

Mary K. Stohr is a professor of criminal justice at Boise State University. She received her Ph.D. from Washington State University in 1990. She has had field experience working as a correctional officer and counselor. She has taught management, corrections and gender, and environmental crime. She is co-founder of the Correctional Section of the Academy of Criminal Justice Sciences (ACJS). She has published three books and numerous articles dealing with correctional and management issues in criminal justice.